Acclaim for V. S. Naipaul's

THE WRITER AND THE WORLD

V. S. Naipaul

THE WRITER
AND THE WORLD

V. S. Naipaul was born in Trinidad in 1932. He went to England
on a scholarship in 1950. After four years at Oxford he began to
write, and since then he has followed no other profession. He is
the author of more than twenty-five books of fiction and nonfiction and the recipient of numerous honors, including the
Nobel Prize in 2001, the Booker Prize in 1971, and a knighthood
for services to literature in 1990. He lives in Wiltshire, England.

ALSO BY V. S. NAIPAUL

NONFICTION
Literary Occasions
Between Father and Son: Family Letters
Beyond Belief: Islamic Excursions Among the Converted Peoples
India: A Million Mutinies Now
A Turn in the South
Finding the Center
Among the Believers
The Return of Eva Perón (with *The Killings in Trinidad*)
India: A Wounded Civilization
The Overcrowded Barracoon
The Loss of El Dorado
An Area of Darkness
The Middle Passage

FICTION
Half a Life
A Way in the World
The Enigma of Arrival
A Bend in the River
Guerrillas
In a Free State
*A Flag on the Island**
The Mimic Men
*Mr. Stone and the Knights Companion**
A House for Mr. Biswas
*The Suffrage of Elvira**
Miguel Street
The Mystic Masseur

*Published in an omnibus edition entitled
The Nightwatchman's Occurrence Book

THE WRITER
AND THE WORLD

Essays

V. S. Naipaul

Edited and with an Introduction by Pankaj Mishra

VINTAGE CANADA

Some of the essays in this work were originally published in the following
Alfred A. Knopf titles: *The Overcrowded Barracoon*, copyright © 1972 by V. S. Naipaul;
The Return of Eva Peron, copyright © 1980 by V. S. Naipaul;
Finding the Centre, copyright © 1984 by V. S. Naipaul.

The following essays were first published in the publications below: "The Air-
Conditioned Bubble" in *The New York Review of Books* (October 25, 1984); Section 6
of "Argentina and the Ghost of Eva Perón" was previously published as "Argentina:
Living with Cruelty" in *The New York Review of Books* (January 30, 1992); "A Handful
of Dust: Cheddi Jagan in Guyana," in *The New York Review of Books* (April 11, 1991);
"Heavy Manners in Grenada" in *Harper's Magazine* (March 1984).

"Our Universal Civilization" was a speech given at the Manhattan Institute.

National Library of Canada Cataloguing in Publication

Naipaul, V. S. (Vidiadhar Surajprasad), 1932–
The writer and the world / V.S. Naipaul.

ISBN 0-676-97520-8

I. Title.

PR9272.9.N32W75 2003   824'.914   C2003-902244-7

Book design by Virginia Tan

www.randomhouse.ca

Printed in the United States of America
10 9 8 7 6 5 4 3 2 1

Contents

AMERICAN OCCASIONS

Introduction

BETWEEN 1929 and 1935, the English novelist Evelyn Waugh published no less than four books about his journeys to Africa, South America and the Mediterranean. "I was simply a young man, typical of my age," Waugh later explained. The travel to such far-off exotic places as British Guyana and Belgian Congo was an "initiation to manhood," as much for Waugh as for his friends, Graham Greene, who went to Liberia, and Robert Byron, who travelled to Persia and Afghanistan.

When in 1945, Waugh made a selection from his four travel books, his mood was elegiac. The Second World War had just ended; the long day of the Empire, when the going was, in Waugh's own words, good, seemed about to wane. As Waugh saw it, "All that seeming-solid, patiently built, gorgeously ornamented structure of Western life" had melted, leaving "only a puddle of mud." The world that he had once felt to be "wide open before us" was now full of "displaced persons"; there was little room in it for travel books, or tourists.

There is something melodramatic you now sense about such pessimism, in which the clichés of the time—the decline of the West, the rise of barbarism—seem to have got mixed up with Waugh's own disdain for the vulgar present and a longing for the Georgian certainties of his hectic youth. It makes a poor guide to the history of the last half century. For while it is true that the European empires created in the nineteenth and early twentieth centuries have disappeared, the power and the wealth of the West that made the world seem wide open to Waugh and other English travellers has increased in a way few people could have imagined in the 1940s.

Indeed, the gap between Europe and the parts of the world it once directly ruled has widened even further. Modernity, an accomplished fact in the West, remains a fraught, repeatedly frustrated aspiration in other parts of the world. One consequence of this has been the arrival in the revitalized cities of Europe and North America of hundreds of thousands of immigrants: the once-picturesque natives of Africa, Asia and South America who have had to flee the chaos and diminishing possibilities of their half-modern societies.

Half a century later, these "displaced persons," who Evelyn Waugh feared would break into and upset the old world order, contribute, with increasing confidence, to the cosmopolitan life and culture of cities like London and New York. In England itself, there is an ever-growing literature that describes their varied lives: the experiences of colonial subjects who have had to remake themselves out of a bewilderingly diverse material for a new life in the old imperial centre. Much publicity and excitement currently attends this literature. Various academic categories—Commonwealth, Multicultural, Diasporic, Indo-Anglian, Caribbean, African, etc.—have proliferated around it, encouraging among individual writers a correct political passion that often compensates for the maturity and skill only a few of them have fitfully achieved.

But even this young literature, still only developing its own traditions, would have been hard to imagine in 1945, when the prospect for Britain as well as its new immigrants looked bleak. This is why it is astonishing to realize that less than five years after Waugh's grim vision of a post-war world, V. S. Naipaul travelled to England as a scholarship student from the tiny Caribbean island of Trinidad; and by 1957, decades before our glamorous multicultural times, had already begun, with scarcely an audience in sight, in what now looks like a dispiriting vacuum, one of the most brilliant—and by far the unlikeliest—literary careers of the last hundred years.

IN ENGLAND, Naipaul was doubly, or trebly, displaced. The dereliction of late-nineteenth-century North India had forced his Brahmin grandparents to make the long journey by sea to the plantation colony of Trinidad, where they worked as indentured labourers. In 1932, when Naipaul was born, his father, Seepersad, had barely begun to lift himself out of his family's near-destitute circumstances in the Trinidad countryside.

There was little place in Trinidad for people in Naipaul's position, to whom the larger, more complex societies elsewhere alone promised an escape from a life of squalor and deprivation. And then, as if life in a foreign land as a young man a long way from home wasn't arduous enough, the promise of escape, in Naipaul's case, had become tied to an absurdly high literary ambition.

As a badly paid journalist for the *Trinidad Guardian*, Seepersad had written some short stories about the village life of his childhood. His son inherited his quite miraculous—given the general background of peasant poverty—literary aspiration, and took it with him to England where it became confused, during a time of poverty and insecurity, with a longing for metropolitan glamour and serenity: with the desire to be a writer like Evelyn Waugh, "aloof everywhere, unsurprised, immensely knowing."

Six long years of struggle and futility followed before Naipaul discovered, in such books as *Miguel Street* (1959), *The Mystic Masseur* (1957), *The Suffrage of Elvira* (1958) and *A House for Mr. Biswas* (1961), his true subject. It was a discovery that was essentially of his own self: of the colonial who had grown up on a tiny, backward island in the Caribbean, amidst an insular Indian community, and then with the racially mixed population of Port of Spain: the man who had no clear past or affiliations, and who had to figure out the world he had been thrown into while attempting to perceive the many strands that made up his self.

WHEN IN 1960, WITH THREE books behind him, Naipaul travelled to the British, Dutch and French colonies of Jamaica, Trinidad, Guyana, Surinam and Martinique, he was only beginning to comprehend the great movements of history that had produced and marked him: the Muslim invasions of India, the rise of the European empires, the colonization of the Caribbean islands by Spain and Britain, the setting up of the sugar plantations, the transport of cheap slave labour from Africa and Asia, the unprecedented mixing of Indian, African and Chinese populations on a few small dependencies of the British empire.

In the book Naipaul wrote subsequently, *The Middle Passage* (1962), his first work of nonfiction, you can see his curiosity as well as knowledge shaped by what John Updike called a "pained partial identification" with his subjects. Some of the colonies Naipaul visited were then readying themselves, after the centuries of exploitation and misery, for self-rule. Naipaul found himself a "colonial among colonials": among a people isolated from, but also dependent upon, the outside world, eagerly embracing the "new slavery of tourism," or competing, as in the case of Indian and Black Trinidadians, for the favours of "an unacknowledged white audience."

An intense personal fear of "the void of non-achievement" seemed to lie behind Naipaul's acute analyses in *The Middle Passage* of the colonial habits of dependence and mimicry. A greater precision marks the essays Naipaul wrote after travelling in 1969 through British Honduras, St. Kitts, Anguilla and Trinidad. The Caribbean was then awash with the ideologies, imported from the United States, of Black Power and Pan-Africanism. With characteristic nuance, Naipaul admitted the political potential of black identity in the United States. But he saw it in the Caribbean as a "sentimental trap, obscuring the issues," which were related as much to "the smallness of the islands and the absence of resources" as to the past of "slavery and colonial neglect."

The problems in the Caribbean were of "manufactured societies, labour camps" that had been dependent for a very long time on empire for "law, language, institutions, culture, even officials." "How, without empire, do such societies govern themselves?" There were no easy answers. In Naipaul's bleakly realistic—but also deeply felt and prophetic—view, a "renewed or continuing exploitation" awaited the small islands which were "dangerous only to themselves" with their eruptions of frustration and rage. For—and this was to be proved true again and again over the next decades—"they will always be subject to an external police. United States helicopters will be there, to take away United States citizens, tourists; the British High Commissions will lay on airlifts for their citizens."

Four years later, Naipaul would write about Michael X and how the torment and despair concealed by the slogans of Black Power— something middle-class whites in "provincial, rich and secure" England co-opted into the fashionable causes of the sixties, and then abandoned just as quickly—had degenerated into lunacy and murder in Trinidad. In 1984, Naipaul would witness in Grenada the confused aftermath of another pseudo-revolution: a small island unable yet again to deal with its free state, and overrun by Americans, "serving their own cause."

But already, in 1969, he has a sharp, if melancholy, sense of the way real—as opposed to rhetorical—power works in the world. The same year Naipaul had published *The Loss of El Dorado*, a narrative about Trinidad that describes several crucial events between Walter Raleigh's raid on the island in the sixteenth century to its virtual abandonment by the British in the early nineteenth century. By 1969, Naipaul had also spent much time in India and some newly independent parts of Africa. The intense, ironic observer you meet in the essays is as alert to the self-deceptions being bred by new ruling elites in post-colonial societies as he was to the older cruelties and delusions of the Spanish and British empires in Trinidad.

OF NAIPAUL'S travels in the 1960s, the visits to India seem to have yielded the greatest number of intellectual and personal discoveries. India was the land of his ancestors, about which Naipaul had inherited a noble idea—an idea that long separation rather than first-hand experience had strengthened among the Indian community in Trinidad, and, supported by the prestigious names of Gandhi and Nehru, had formed part of Naipaul's identity in England.

But the India Naipaul travelled to, in the last days of Nehru, was a country made complacent and sanctimonious by the victories of the freedom movement; and while expecting to find a vibrant post-colonial country with many human possibilities, Naipaul came across wretchedness of the sort his ancestors had escaped from almost a century ago.

Instead of metropolitan confidence and generosity, he met "colonial self-distrust" and "a spirit of plunder." In Calcutta, once the capital of India's first modern culture, Naipaul found a decaying city, full of the freak products of a "violent" encounter between the East and the West: an Indian-built extravagantly European marble palace, Lord Curzon's "studiedly derivative" Victoria Memorial, golf-playing corporate executives with nicknames like Jimmy and Bunty. Elsewhere, Gandhi was being imitated, in a ritualistic way: a further disaster in a country that was still trapped in the quasi-religious self-righteous passivity that Gandhi had turned into a partially effective anti-colonial program. Naipaul's later visits to India—in 1967, against a background of serious political and economic crisis, and then in 1971, to cover a parliamentary election in Rajasthan—only confirmed his perception of a "profoundly dependent" country ruled by "slogans, gestures and potent names," still in thrall to its ancient decaying civilization, and far from the inevitable and many-sided reckoning with the modern world that Naipaul later described in *India: A Million Mutinies Now* (1990).

IN 1969, NAIPAUL also travelled to the United States; and although these essays covering Norman Mailer's mayoral campaign in New York City and John Steinbeck's Cannery Row in California describe a society much more organized and secure than the one found in the Caribbean and India, the writer's restless moral intelligence continues to insist on standards of clarity and rationality.

The Monterey peninsula in California, just a few miles away from the "endless lettuce level fields of Salinas, the bitter landscape of stoop-labour," has been turned into "fairyland": a fantasy in which Naipaul sees Steinbeck, despite his social concerns, as having played a part. The existentialist pose of Mailer and the "glamour and ambiguity" of his campaign are not very different from the "equivocations of Black Power" that offer "something to everybody": in both cases drama and style become a substitute for practical politics.

Later, in 1984, at a time of right-wing ascendancy in America, Naipaul would describe the "tribal-religious" nature of the Republican party convention in Dallas. If a great intellectual tension seems to have produced the short sentences, the swift paragraphs, and the briskly summarized arguments of Naipaul's early writings, the wit, intimacy and insight of the later essays are of a writer possessed of greater knowledge and experience. At Dallas, the celebrations of Americanism and Bible-Belt Christianity remind Naipaul of a Muslim missionary gathering in Pakistan: "I felt it would not have been surprising, in Dallas, to see busy, pious helpers going around giving out sweets or some kind of symbolic sacramental food."

In oil-rich Texas, Naipaul saw the "consciousness of power and money and rightness" as leading to an "intellectual vacancy." In Argentina, which Naipaul repeatedly visited in the 1970s and travelled to again in 1991, somewhat similar assumptions of wealth and grandeur had pushed its quasi-European population into gigantic national self-deceptions. The banality and avarice and ruthlessness of European discoverers and settlers in the New World—the theme of Naipaul's essay on Christopher Columbus—weren't things the Argentines were able to face up to in their not so distant past. Even the great Borges was vulnerable to the "ancestor worship" that had replaced history in Argentina—

the unillusioned comprehension of the greed and brutality with which settlers from Italy and Spain had exterminated the native Indian population, parcelled out the huge rich land among a few families, and then, while holding down the poor, tried to re-mould themselves, mostly through wholesale imports from the Old World, in the image of the civilized European.

"The politics of a country"—and this is one of Naipaul's key perceptions—"can only be an extension of its idea of human relationships." As he saw it, Peronism, as much as the aimless guerillas and the brutal military dictators of the 1970s, was inevitable in Argentina: far from being a program, it was an expression of rage and despair, an "insurrection" against a heartless materialist society, where the exploiter-exploited relationship had long offered the only model of human association, a revolt that itself fed off, and could only feed, other insurrections.

Travelling to Mobutu's Zaire in 1975, Naipaul encountered another kind of cynicism and blindness about the past. Mobutu had carefully preserved the various forms of Belgian despotism. But his rhetoric dealt in African "authenticity"; and he and his courtiers arbitrarily dismantled the apparatus of the colonial state—the life of the bush meanwhile going on as it always had—and replaced it with nothing other than his personal authority. It was totalitarianism sanctified by a bogus Africanism. Together, it had stifled the nascent intellectual life of Zaire: the growth, for instance, of the bright students at the university, who can talk of Stendhal and Fanon, whose enthusiasm "deserves a better-equipped country," but who, with only a government job in sight, already are "Mobutists to a man."

THESE unsettled men with peasant or tribal backgrounds are always there in Naipaul's essays. These are people swallowed up by a cruel history—like the extinct native Indians of the Caribbean and South America Naipaul often remembers—or thwarted by the ideologies of revolution and racial or cultural identity.

It is easier to examine the ideologies now: they are what newly educated and privileged men in post-colonial nations took from their former imperial masters even while turning away from them—the ill-adapted borrowings, which, once glossed over in the heady days of post-colonial nationalism and Third Worldism, now preoccupy a new generation of scholars and academics, long after they locked whole societies in a fruitless cycle of false expectations, disappointment, rage and despair.

The individuals these ideologies work upon are usually absent from academic and journalistic accounts of African and Asian countries. But in Naipaul's essays, they stand very clearly, in the midst of the chaos and pain of their underdeveloped societies, and "awakening to ideas, history, a knowledge of injustice and a sense of their own dignity." You can place them at the beginning or middle of the journey Naipaul himself has made: the slow climb from destitution; the makeover in the new world; the long glance back at one's ancestral societies; the illusion-free awakening to the larger world—all the self-discoveries of uprooted men that are the cumulative work of generations but in Naipaul's case have been telescoped, through the rigours of writing and travel, into just one lifetime.

Naipaul's own multi-layered experience—the many deprivations of Trinidad, the painful wretchedness of India, the "rawness of his nerves" as an outsider in England—is ever present in these essays. It pre-empts in them the abstractions of politics and economics; keeps away the fleeting shallow passions of the journalistic report or overview, accounts for their rare fusing of personal and social enquiries, and suffuses them, despite the occasional severity of tone and judgement, with a profound compassion.

They consistently uphold a belief in modern civilization, and all that it offers to peoples around the world: the dignity of individuality, of self-knowledge, so many different private and professional fulfilments. But this faith in the redemptive power of modernity is balanced by a sense of wonder about the past. Naipaul's regard for vanished or threatened ways of being—for the "completeness" of La Rioja, the remote Spanish-built half-Indian city in Argentina, for the mysteries of animist religion in the Ivory Coast, for the "logical life" of the African bush—gives a melancholy undertow to the vigorous humanism of his essays.

This is the melancholy that shadows Ralph Singh, the failed post-colonial politician and aspiring imperial historian in Naipaul's novel *The Mimic Men* (1968), as he surveys, from a suburban hotel in England, his life and times, and finds himself overwhelmed by the "great upheaval" he wishes to write about: by "the great explorations, the overthrow in three continents of established social organizations, the unnatural bringing together of peoples who could achieve fulfilment only within the security of their own societies and the landscapes hymned by their ancestors."

Ralph Singh wants to elaborate upon his vision of the history that has deracinated and then rendered him weightless and futile. But he finally sees himself as "too much of a victim of that restlessness which was to have been my subject." In a powerful sense, the great intellectual endeavour Singh hopes to begin one day is what his creator, Naipaul, though faced with much stronger odds, has completed over the last four decades, eloquently expressing, without being undermined by, the same world-wide turmoil and restlessness that, in 1945, Evelyn Waugh, secure until then within empire, had shrunk from.

It is hard to think of a writer more fundamentally exilic, carrying so many clashing fading worlds inside him. But what's more remarkable is that Naipaul's acute sense of lost glory and contentment, his anguished perception of deception and tragedy—things inseparable from his background and experience—co-exist with an attitude of acceptance and optimism, with a well-founded faith in human striving and perfectibility. These visions aren't usually compatible. But they work together in Naipaul, give his work its peculiar tension and richness, and make it the most sustained and wide-ranging meditation on our world.

Pankaj Mishra

·❦ **I N D I A** ❦·

In the Middle of the Journey

COMING from a small island—Trinidad is no bigger than Goa—I had always been fascinated by size. To see the wide river, the high mountain, to take the twenty-four-hour train journey: these were some of the delights the outside world offered. But now after six months in India my fascination with the big is tinged with disquiet. For here is a vastness beyond imagination, a sky so wide and deep that sunsets cannot be taken in at a glance but have to be studied section by section, a landscape made monotonous by its size and frightening by its very simplicity and its special quality of exhaustion: poor choked crops in small crooked fields, under-sized people, under-nourished animals, crumbling villages and towns which, even while they develop, have an air of decay. Dawn comes, night falls; railway stations, undistinguishable one from the other, their name-boards cunningly concealed, are arrived at and departed from, abrupt and puzzling interludes of populousness and noise; and still the journey goes on, until the vastness, ceasing to have a meaning, becomes insupportable, and from this endless repetition of exhaustion and decay one wishes to escape.

To state this is to state the obvious. But in India the obvious is overwhelming, and often during these past six months I have known moments of near-hysteria, when I have wished to forget India, when I have escaped to the first-class waiting-room or sleeper not so much for privacy and comfort as for protection, to shut out the sight of the thin bodies prostrate on railway platforms, the starved dogs licking the food-leaves clean, and to shut out the whine of the playfully assaulted dog. Such a moment I knew in Bombay, on the day of my arrival, when I felt India only as an assault on the senses. Such a moment I knew five months later, at Jammu, where the simple, frightening geography of the country becomes plain—to the north the hills, rising in range after ascending range; to the south, beyond the temple spires, the plains whose vastness, already experienced, excited only unease.

Yet between these recurring moments there have been so many others, when fear and impatience have been replaced by enthusiasm and
delight, when the town, explored beyond what one sees from the train,
reveals that the air of exhaustion is only apparent, that in India, more
than in any other country I have visited, things are happening. To hear
the sounds of hammer on metal in a small Punjab town, to visit a chemi-
cal plant in Hyderabad where much of the equipment is Indian-designed
and manufactured, is to realize that one is in the middle of an industrial
revolution, in which, perhaps because of faulty publicity, one had never
really seriously believed. To see the new housing colonies in towns all
over India was to realize that, separate from the talk of India's ancient
culture (which invariably has me reaching for my *lathi*), the Indian aesthetic sense has revived and is now capable of creating, out of materials
which are international, something which is essentially Indian. (India's
ancient culture, defiantly paraded, has made the Ashoka Hotel one of
New Delhi's most ridiculous buildings, outmatched in absurdity only by
the Pakistan High Commission, which defiantly asserts the Faith.)

I have been to unpublicized villages, semi-developed and undeveloped. And where before I would have sensed only despair, now I feel that
the despair lies more with the observer than the people. I have learned to
see beyond the dirt and the recumbent figures on string beds, and to look
for the signs of improvement and hope, however faint: the brick-topped
road, covered though it might be with filth; the rice planted in rows and
not scattered broadcast; the degree of ease with which the villager faces
the official or the visitor. For such small things I have learned to look:
over the months my eye has been adjusted.

Yet always the obvious is overwhelming. One is a traveller and as
soon as the dread of a particular district has been lessened by familiarity,
it is time to move on again, through vast tracts which will never become
familiar, which will sadden; and the urge to escape will return.

Yet in so many ways the size of the country is only a physical fact.
For, perhaps because of the very size, Indians appear to feel the need to
categorize minutely, delimit, to reduce to manageable proportions.

"Where do you come from?" It is the Indian question, and to people
who think in terms of the village, the district, the province, the community, the caste, my answer that I am a Trinidadian is only puzzling.

"But you look Indian."

"Well, I am Indian. But we have been living for several generations in Trinidad."

"But you look Indian."

Three or four times a day the dialogue occurs, and now I often abandon explanation. "I am a Mexican, really."

"Ah." Great satisfaction. Pause. "What do you do?"

"I write."

"Journalism or books?"

"Books."

"Westerns, crime, romance? How many books do you write a year? How much do you make?"

So now I invent: "I am a teacher."

"What are your qualifications?"

"I am a B.A."

"Only a B.A.? What do you teach?"

"Chemistry. And a little history."

"How interesting!" said the man on the Pathankot-Srinagar bus. "I am a teacher of chemistry too."

He was sitting across the aisle from me, and several hours remained of our journey.

In this vast land of India it is necessary to explain yourself, to define your function and status in the universe. It is very difficult.

If I thought in terms of race or community, this experience of India would surely have dispelled it. An Indian, I have never before been in streets where everyone is Indian, where I blend unremarkably into the crowd. This has been curiously deflating, for all my life I have expected some recognition of my difference; and it is only in India that I have recognized how necessary this stimulus is to me, how conditioned I have been by the multi-racial society of Trinidad and then by my life as an outsider in England. To be a member of a minority community has always seemed to me attractive. To be one of four hundred and thirty-nine million Indians is terrifying.

A colonial, in the double sense of one who had grown up in a Crown colony and one who had been cut off from the metropolis, be it either England or India, I came to India expecting to find metropolitan attitudes. I had imagined that in some ways the largeness of the land would be reflected in the attitudes of the people. I have found, as I have said, the psychology of the cell and the hive. And I have been surprised by similarities. In India, as in tiny Trinidad, I have found the feeling that the metropolis is elsewhere, in Europe or America. Where I had expected largeness, rootedness and confidence, I have found all the colonial attitudes of self-distrust.

"I am craze phor phoreign," the wife of a too-successful contractor said. And this craze extended from foreign food to German sanitary fittings to a possible European wife for her son, who sought to establish his claim further by announcing at the lunch table, "Oh, by the way, did I tell you we spend three thousand rupees a month?"

"You are a tourist, you don't know," the chemistry teacher on the Srinagar bus said. "But this is a terrible country. Give me a chance and I leave it tomorrow."

For among a certain class of Indians, usually more prosperous than their fellows, there is a passionate urge to explain to the visitor that they must not be considered part of poor, dirty India, that their values and standards are higher, and they live perpetually outraged by the country which gives them their livelihood. For them the second-rate foreign product, either people or manufactures, is preferable to the Indian. They suggest that for them, as much as for the European "technician," India is only a country to be temporarily exploited. How strange to find, in free India, this attitude of the conqueror, this attitude of plundering—a frenzied attitude, as though the opportunity might at any moment be withdrawn—in those very people to whom the developing society has given so many opportunities.

This attitude of plundering is that of the immigrant colonial society. It has bred, as in Trinidad, the pathetic philistinism of the *renonçant* (an excellent French word that describes the native who renounces his own culture and strives towards the French). And in India this philistinism, a blending of the vulgarity of East and West—those sad dance floors, those sad "Western" cabarets, those transistor radios tuned to Radio Ceylon, those Don Juans with leather jackets or check tweed jackets—is peculiarly frightening. A certain glamour attaches to this philistinism, as glamour attaches to those Indians who, after two or three years in a foreign country, proclaim that they are neither of the East nor of the West.

The observer, it must be confessed, seldom sees the difficulty. The contractor's wife, so anxious to demonstrate her Westernness, regularly consulted her astrologer and made daily trips to the temple to ensure the continuance of her good fortune. The schoolteacher, who complained with feeling about the indiscipline and crudity of Indians, proceeded, as soon as we got to the bus station at Srinagar, to change his clothes in public.

The Trinidadian, whatever his race, is a genuine colonial. The Indian, whatever his claim, is rooted in India. But while the Trinidadian, a colonial, strives towards the metropolitan, the Indian of whom I have been speaking, metropolitan by virtue of the uniqueness of his country, its achievements in the past and its manifold achievements in the last decade or so, is striving towards the colonial.

Where one had expected pride, then, one finds the spirit of plunder. Where one had expected the metropolitan one finds the colonial. Where one had expected largeness one finds narrowness. Goa, scarcely liberated, is the subject of an unseemly inter-State squabble. Fifteen years after Independence the politician as national leader appears to have been replaced by the politician as village headman (a type I had thought peculiar to the colonial Indian community of Trinidad, for whom politics was a game where little more than PWD contracts was at stake). To the village headman India is only a multiplicity of villages. So that the vision of India as a great country appears to be something imposed from without and the vastness of the country turns out to be oddly fraudulent.

Yet there remains a concept of India—as what? Something more than the urban middle class, the politicians, the industrialists, the separate villages. Neither this nor that, we are so often told, is the "real" India. And how well one begins to understand why this word is used! Perhaps India is only a word, a mystical idea that embraces all those vast plains and rivers through which the train moves, all those anonymous figures asleep on railway platforms and the footpaths of Bombay, all those poor fields and stunted animals, all this exhausted plundered land. Perhaps it is this, this vastness which no one can ever get to know: India as an ache, for which one has a great tenderness, but from which at length one always wishes to separate oneself.

1962

Jamshed into Jimmy

"YOU'VE come to Calcutta at the wrong time," the publisher said. "I very much fear that the dear old city is slipping into bourgeois respectability almost without a fight."

"Didn't they burn a tram the other day?" I asked.

"True. But that was the first tram for five years."

And really I had expected more from Calcutta, the "nightmare experience" of Mr. Nehru, the "pestilential behemoth" of a recent, near-hysterical American writer, a city which, designed for two million people, today accommodates more than six million on its pavements and in its *bastees,* in conditions which unmanned the World Bank Mission of 1960 and sent it away to write what the *Economic Weekly* of Bombay described as a "strikingly human document."

Like every newspaper-reader, I knew Calcutta as the city of tram-burners and students who regularly "clashed" with the police. A brief news item in *The Times* in 1954 had hinted memorably at its labour troubles: some disgruntled workers had tossed their manager into the furnace. And during my time in India I had been following the doings of its Congress-controlled Corporation, which, from the progressive national-ist citadel of the twenties, has decayed into what students of Indian affairs consider the most openly corrupt of India's multitudinous corrupt public bodies: half the Corporation's five hundred and fifty vehicles dis-abled, many of them stripped of saleable parts, repair mechanics ham-pered, accounts four years in arrears, every obstacle put in the way of "interference" by State Government, New Delhi and a despairing Ford Foundation.

At every level I found that Calcutta enjoyed a fabulous reputation. The Bengali was insufferably arrogant ("The *pan*-seller doesn't so much as look at you if you don't talk to him in Bengali"); the Bengali was lazy; the pavements were dyed red with betel-juice and the main park was littered with used sanitary towels ("very untidy people," had been the comment of the South Indian novelist). And even in Bombay, the seat of gastro-enteritis, they spoke of Calcutta's inadequate (thirteen out of twenty-two Corporation tubewells not working) and tainted water supply with terror.

I had therefore expected much. And Howrah station was promising. The railway officials were more than usually non-committal and lethargic; the cigarette-seller didn't look at me; and in the station restaurant a smiling waiter drew my attention to a partly depilated rat that was wandering languidly about the tiled floor. But nothing had prepared me for the red-brick city on the other bank of the river which, if one could ignore the crowds, the stalls, the rickshaw-pullers and the squatting pissers, suggested, not a tropical or Eastern city, but central Birmingham. Nothing had prepared me for the Maidan, tree-dotted, now in the early evening blurred with mist and suggesting Hyde Park, with Chowringhee as a brighter Oxford Street. And nothing had prepared me for the sight of General Cariappa in the Maidan, dark-suited, English-erect, addressing a small relaxed crowd on the Chinese invasion in Sandhurst-accented Hindustani, while the trams, battleship-grey, with wedge-shaped snouts, nosed through the traffic at a steady eight miles an hour, the celebrated Calcutta tram, ponderous and vulnerable, *bulging* at entrances and exits with white-clad office workers, the neon lights beyond the Maidan gay in the mist: the invitations to espresso bars, cabarets, air travel. Here, unexpectedly and for the first time in India, one was in the midst of the big city, the recognizable metropolis, with street names—Elgin, Allenby, Park, Lindsay—that seemed oddly at variance with the brisk crowds, incongruity that deepened as the mist thickened to smog and as, travelling out to the suburbs, one saw the factory chimneys smoking among the palm trees.

And where in that bright heart, forgetting the pissers, were the piles of filth and refuse I had been told about, and the sanitary towels? In fact, as the publisher said, I had come to Calcutta at the wrong time. The city had recently been subjected to a brief and frenzied clean-up by the "volunteers" of the new Chief Minister of Bengal; it had been hoped that this would fill the Corporation's professionals with "enthusiasm." An "Operation Bull" had sought to clear the main streets of bulls which the devout Hindu releases into central Calcutta to service the holy cow. The idea was that the cows would follow the bulls. As it turned out, the cows had stayed; the bulls were returning. And no inhabitant of Calcutta doubted that with the withdrawal of the volunteers, and with so many things in India suspended because of the Emergency—suspension and prohibition being the administration's current substitute for action—the filth too would return. But for the moment some of the unfamiliar gloss remained.

All the four main cities in India were developed by the British, but none has so British a stamp as Calcutta. Lutyens's New Delhi is a disaster, a mock-imperial joke, neither British nor Indian, a city built for parades rather than people, and today given a correctly grotesque scale by the noisy little scooter-rickshaws that scurry about its long avenues and endless roundabouts. Madras, though possessing in Fort St. George one of the finest complexes of eighteenth-century British architecture outside Britain, is elsewhere lazily colonial. Bombay owes much to its Parsi community, enterprising, civic-minded, culturally ambiguous; the hysterical American already quoted speaks of Bombay's "bandbox architecture," and indeed this city, the best-run in India, is cosmopolitan to the point of characterlessness. Calcutta alone appears to have been created in the image of England, the British here falling, unusually, into the imperialist practice of the French and the Portuguese. And what has resulted in Calcutta is a grandeur more rooted than that of New Delhi: "the city of palaces" they called Calcutta, the palaces, Indian or British, built in a style which might best be described as Calcutta Corinthian: Calcutta, for long the capital of British India, the second city of the British Empire.

In India the confrontation of East and West was nowhere more violent than in Calcutta, and two buildings, both now regarded as monuments, speak of this violence: the Mullick Palace and the Victoria Memorial. Decaying now, with servants cooking in the marble galleries, the Mullick Palace still looks like a film set. It is dominated by tall Corinthian columns; Italian fountains play in the grounds; its excessively chandeliered marble rooms are crowded out with the clutter of a hundred nineteenth-century European antique shops, this dusty plaster cast of a Greek nymph hiding that faded, unmemorable painting of red-coated soldiers repulsing some native attack. In the courtyard four marble figures represent the major continents; and on the lower floor the monumental statue of a youthful Queen Victoria makes a big room small. None of the dusty treasures of the Mullick Palace is Indian, save perhaps for a portrait of the collector: the original Bengali babu, anxious to prove to the supercilious European his appreciation of European culture. And on the Maidan stands the Victoria Memorial, Curzon's answer to the Taj Mahal, as studiedly derivative as the Mullick Palace, here recalling the Taj, there recalling the Salute. "Passing through the Queen's vestibule into the Queen's Hall under the dome," says Murray's *Handbook*, which characteristically gives twice as much space to this Raj Taj as to the Kailasa Temple at Ellora,

> one sees the dignified statue of Queen Victoria at the age when she ascended the throne (the work of Sir Thomas Brock RA); this gives the keynote to the whole edifice.

Yet out of this confrontation there emerged something new in India, an explosive mixture of East and West, a unique culture which, however despised by the non-Calcutta Bengali as jumped-up and camp-following, gave Indian nationalism many of its prophets and heroes. The Bengali will tell you that British officials were urged to treat the South Indian as a slave, the Punjabi as a friend, and the Bengali as an enemy. But when the Bengali tells you this he is speaking as of lost glories, for today, with Independence and the partition of Bengal (in Calcutta the words are synonymous), the heart has gone out of Calcutta. It is a city without a hinterland, a dying city. Even the Hooghly is silting up, and everyone agrees that Calcutta has ceased to grow economically, however much it might spread physically. Though there are endearing vestiges of the Mullick Palace mentality in, say, the literary criticism of Professor Sadhan Kumar Ghosh (compassionately dealt with in the *New Statesman* by Malcolm Muggeridge), Calcutta is exhausted, its people withdrawn. It has Satyajit Ray, the film director; it has in Sunil Janah a photographer of world stature; Bengali typography, nervously elegant, is perhaps the best in India. But the glory lies in the past, in Tagore, in Bankim Chandra Chatterji, in the terrorists, in Subhas Chandra Bose. (1962 was a good year for the Bose legend: one libel action brought by a member of the family against an Englishwoman, and another reported reappearance, this time as a sadhu in the Himalayas.)

Calcutta remains what it always has been through growth, creative disorder, quiescence. It is still, despite the strong challenge of Bombay, India's principal commercial city, and the element of Calcutta culture which might be said to be dominant is that represented by the business buildings of Dalhousie Square and the squat business houses of Imperial

Tobacco and Metal Box on Chowringhee. There in air-conditioned offices may be found the young Indian business executives, the box-wallahs, the new Indian élite. A generation ago such positions would not have been acceptable to any Indian of birth; and he almost certainly would not have been accepted. But the Indian genius for compromise is no less than that of the British. The box-wallah culture of Calcutta is of a peculiar richness, and if it has not yet been explored by Indian writers this is because they have been too busy plagiarizing, or writing harrowing stories about young girls drifting into prostitution to pay the family's medical bills and stories about young girls, poor or pretty, who inexplicably die. This culture, though of Calcutta, is not necessarily Bengali. Commerce is controlled by the British and increasingly since Independence by the Marwaris—it is almost with pride that the Bengali tells you there is no Bengali businessman worth the name. The Marwaris are Indian but are spoken of throughout India as a community even more alien than the British: the feeling against them in Calcutta is something you can cut with a knife. No one of standing wishes to be directly employed by the Marwaris. The conditions are not as good as those offered by the British who are reputable; in the public mind Marwari businessmen are associated with black-marketing and speculation. No one who works for the Marwaris can therefore properly be considered a box-wallah—your true box-wallah works only for the best British firms. ("Tell me," they were asked at Imperial Tobacco, "was that very large painting of the Queen put up especially for the Queen's visit?" "No," was the box-wallah reply. "It is *always* there.")

No one in Calcutta is sure of the origin of the word box-wallah. It has been suggested that it comes from the street pedlar's box; but in Calcutta the word has too grand and restricted a significance, and it seems to me more likely to have been derived from the Anglo-Indian office-box of which Kipling speaks so feelingly in *Something of Myself*. Perhaps the office-box, like the solar topee (still worn with mournful defiance by those ICS officers who despair of further promotion), was a symbol of authority; and though the symbols have changed, the authority has been transferred and persists.

The Calcutta box-wallah comes of a good family, ICS, Army or big business; he might even have princely connections. He has been educated at an Indian or English public school and at one of the two English universities, whose accent, through all the encircling hazards of Indian intonation, he rigidly maintains. When he joins his firm his first name is changed. The Indian name of Anand, for example, might become Andy; Dhandeva will become Danny, Firdaus Freddy, Jamshed Jimmy. Where the Indian name cannot be adapted, the box-wallah will most usually be known as Bunty. It is a condition of Bunty's employment that he play golf; and on every golf course he can be seen with an equally unhappy Andy, both enduring the London-prescribed mixture of business and pleasure.

Bunty will of course marry well, and he knows it will be counted in his favour if he contracts a mixed marriage; if, say, as a Punjabi Hindu he marries a Bengali Muslim or a Bombay Parsi. Bunty and his wife will live in one of the company's luxury flats; they will be called Daddy and Mummy by their two English-speaking children. Their furnishings will show a happy blend of East and West (Indian ceramics are just coming in). So too will their food (Indian lunch followed by Western-style dinner), their books, their records (difficult classical Indian, European chamber music) and their pictures (North Indian miniatures, Ganymed reproductions of Van Gogh).

Freed of one set of caste rules, Bunty and his wife will adopt another. If his office has soft furnishings he will know how to keep his distance from Andy, whose furnishings are hard; and to introduce Andy, who shares an air-conditioned office with Freddy, into the home of Bunty, who has an office to himself, is to commit a blunder. His new caste imposes new rituals on Bunty. Every Friday he will have lunch at Firpo's on Chowringhee, and the afternoon-long jollity will mark the end of the week's work. In the days of the British this Friday lunch at Firpo's celebrated the departure of the mail-boat for England. Such letters as Bunty sends to England go now by air, but Bunty is conscious of tradition.

It is impossible to write of Bunty without making him appear ridiculous. But Bunty is the first slanderer of his group; and enough has been said to show how admirable, in the Indian context, he is. Where physical effort is regarded as a degradation and thick layers of fat are still to many the marks of prosperity, Bunty plays golf and swims. Where elections are won on communal campaigns, Bunty marries out of his community. Bunty is intelligent and well-read; like most educated Indians, he talks well; though he has abandoned the social obligations of the Indian joint family, he is generous and hospitable; he supports the arts. Not least of his virtues is that he keeps a spotless lavatory. East and West blend easily

in him. For him, who has grown up in an independent India, Westerniza-
tion is not the issue it was to his grandfather and even his father. He carries no chip on his shoulder; he does not feel the need to talk to the visitor
about India's ancient culture.

Occasionally, very occasionally, the calm is disturbed. "These
damned English!" Bunty exclaims. "When are they going to learn that
1947 really happened?" The words are like an echo from the Mullick
Palace. But it is a passing mood. Soon Bunty will be out on the golf
course with Andy. And golf is a game they both now love.

1963

A Second Visit

Tragedy: *The Missing Sense*

THE RAJA RECLINES below a broken chandelier in a dark narrow room right at the back of the palace. The room is in the third courtyard, the only part of the palace that still works. The raja's armchair belongs to an extensive "sofa-set"—English suburban, 1930—distributed down the length of the room; the magenta upholstery is grimy. A rag-carpet completely covers the floor. It has been cut out from a more enormous piece, and is folded under where it doesn't fit. It is in a violent pattern of yellow and green that camouflages the million flies that buzz in and out of the rags. A photograph of the raja's father hangs forward from the wall; flat against the wall are a photograph of a family group, a hunting print in a rustic frame, and, at the top, in the yellowing colours of an unsuccessful reproduction process, a row of misty European landscapes.

Against this the raja sits, young, plump, cool in loose white cotton, and listens without expression to his last courtier, who sits at his feet on the rag-carpet and, holding a creased typewritten memorandum of many pages, outlines once again the complications of the inter-family litigation about the property that remains. The courtier is gaunt, his bony face finer than his master's; his clothes are dingier. He is a B.A.—the achievement is still fresh in his mind. He entered the service of the raja's family nearly fifty years ago, and now—his own son is dead—he has nowhere else to go.

Lunch is ordered for the visitors. The raja's younger brother, lean, elegant in movement—he is an attractive badminton player—offers to show the sights. The palace is in the nondescript Lucknow style, and not old. Most of what we see was built in the 1920s, at a cost of half a million pounds. The family's revenue then was £60,000. An oval-shaped garden in the forecourt, overgrown. Tall carved wooden doors from a provincial exhibition of 1911 (the Raj then in its glory, with at least two society magazines in Calcutta, the capital). The clock-tower courtyard, with crude roundels down the archway: an English couple between the Hindu and the Muslim: he in broad-lapelled jacket and sun-helmet, she in the loose lines of the 1920s. Beyond, the apartments, miniature palaces, of the former raja's wives: the source of the present litigation.

The raja's younger brother says there are six hundred rooms in all. The statement is disturbing. It is surely an exaggeration. Exaggeration does not belong to tragedy; it destroys the mood. And once, just twenty-five, thirty years ago, five hundred servants looked after the twenty-five members of the family. Round figures again, no doubt. But the palace had its own generating plant, stables for horses and elephants, its own zoo, its own reservoir. All this is shown from the clock-tower, the English machinery broken, the plaster broken. But the view from the clock-tower also shows no other building of consequence. It shows only the grass roofs of the bazaar settlement just outside the palace gates, and the flat scorched fields.

The eagerness of the raja's brother denies sadness. And there can be no sadness. Because there was no true grandeur. There was only excess and exaggeration, dying at the stroke of the legislator's pen that abolished large estates. The palace rose out of this dust; it expressed this dust, nothing more; it is returning to dust again; and the cycle had been unfruitful (the sofa-set, the landscape prints). Peasant, briefly prodigal, is turning to peasant again, as the kitchens of the third courtyard show. There is no vacuum; litigation totally engages the calm mind. There is no tragedy. There is, as perhaps there always has been, drabness. In this plain landscape wealth itself had been just another simplicity, an event, like decay.

THIS IS THE HOAX OF INDIA. We take the country too personally. We go with a sense of tragedy and urgency, with the habit of contemplating man as man, with ideas of action; and we find ourselves unsupported.

There was a famine in Bihar. It had taken some time to prepare; and in this time the wits of Delhi had called it the "shamine." Now it was real: thirty million people were starving, bodies wrecked beyond redemption. But famine was never the subject of conversation; there was more about it in foreign newspapers than in Indian newspapers, which continued to be occupied with the post-election manoeuvring and speeches of politicians. The Films Division made a film about the famine; in Bombay and Delhi it was discussed as a film, a documentary breakthrough. The famine was like something in a foreign country, like the war in Vietnam. It was something you went to; it tested the originality of artists.

The civil servant in Calcutta said: "Famine? Can that be news to us?" The editor in Delhi said: "Famine? Can I turn that into news every day?"

It was the pattern of Indian conversation. After the frenzy, the reasoned catalogue of disasters and threats—China, Pakistan, corruption, no leaders, devaluation, no money, no food—after this the frenzy burnt itself out, and the statement was made that it didn't really matter, that it wasn't news. The young poet I met in Delhi had made the statement in a long English poem on which he had been working for months. The poem was a dialogue between historical India and spiritual India; its subject was "the metaphysical timelessness" of India. The absurd words had a meaning. The poet was saying, with the civil servant and the editor, that there was no disaster, no news, that India was infinitely old and would go on. There was no goal and therefore no failure. There were only events. There was no tragedy.

It was what, in his own stylish way, the Maharishi Mahesh Yogi was telling the inaugural meeting of his Spiritual Regeneration Movement. The red-and-black cotton banner hung out on the Delhi Ring Road, next to the Indian Institute of Public Administration; and inside, in the shuttered gloom, the Maharishi, small, black-locked, bearded, in a cream silk gown, flowers and garlands about him, sat cross-legged before the microphone, backed on the platform by his American, Canadian and other white disciples on chairs, the men in dark suits, the women and girls in silk saris: India, it might be said, getting a dose of her own medicine from the West.

The Maharishi reproved his reverential middle-class Indian audience for running after "isms" and failing to keep in tune with the infinite which lay below flux. No wonder the country was in a mess. The reproof was rubbed in by the glamorous figures on the platform who went one by one to the microphone, now raised, and gave witness to the powers of Indian meditation, the key to the infinite. A youngish, grey-haired Canadian was described by the Maharishi as a man who had given up drilling for oil to drill for truth. He gave his witness; and then, apparently on behalf of the world, thanked India. So that at the end it was all right. Everybody had just been talking; there was no problem; everything was as before.

The infinite, metaphysical timelessness: it always came to this. From whatever point they started—the Maharishi had even mentioned Bihar and glancingly attacked the folly of giving land to ignorant peasants, as though that would solve the food problem—there always came a moment when Indians, administrator, journalist, poet, holy man, slipped away like eels into muddy abstraction. They abandoned intellect, observation, reason; and became "mysterious."

It is in that very area that separates India from comprehension that the Indian deficiency lies. To see mysteriousness is to excuse the intellectual failure or to ignore it. It is to fall into the Indian trap, to assume that the poverty of the Indian land must also extend to the Indian mind. It is to deal in *Bengal Lancer* romance or *Passage to India* quaintness. It is, really, to express a simple wonder.

Because it is the simplicity of India which disappoints and in the end fatigues. There is a hoax in that quaintness. The barbaric religious rites of Hinduism are barbaric; they belong to the ancient world. The holy cow is absurd; it is, as Nirad Chaudhuri suggests in *The Continent of Circe*, an ignorant corruption of an ancient Aryan reverence. The caste-marks and the turbans belong to a people who, incapable of contemplating man as man, know no other way of defining themselves. India lies all on the surface. Once certain basic lessons are learnt, it is possible to make everything up, to chart conversations, to gauge the limit of comprehension. It was even possible for me to anticipate much of what was said at the inaugural meeting of the Spiritual Regeneration Movement. Where there is no play of the intellect there is no surprise.

The beatniks of America, Australia and other countries have now recognized India as their territory. Their instinct is true. Five years ago Ginsberg left America to make an initial exploration. He found the local Indians friendly; they were flattered by the attention of someone with a name so bright and modern; it was another tribute to the East from the West. Now the beatniks are everywhere, withdrawn, not gay, and sometimes in moving little domestic groups: papa beatnik, mama beatnik, baby beatnik, the man protected by his beard and jeans, the thin young woman more exposed, the dirt showing on her sandalled feet and on the tanned but pale skin of her bony, finely wrinkled face. They are guests in temples (the Sikhs feed everybody); they thumb lifts on the highways and travel third on the railways; sometimes they compete with the beggars in cities; they attach themselves to the camps of holy men, like the one I heard about in Hyderabad, whose big trick was to pull a prick (I never found out whose) out of his mouth. In India they have rediscovered the wayfaring life of the Middle Ages.

There is a difference, of course. The maimed to the maimed, the West returning mysteriousness and negation to the East, while the humiliating deals are made in New Delhi and Washington for arms and food: it is like a cruel revenge joke played by the rich, many-featured West on the poor East that possesses only mystery. But India does not see the joke. In March the glossy *Indian Hotelkeeper and Traveller* introduced a "Seers of India" series:

> India's seers and sages have something to offer to the world outside. To some of the materially affluent but psychologically sick and spiritually rudderless foreigners from far-flung corners of the world, India's saints and sadhus provide irresistible magnets of attraction. India, steeped in spirituality, has a singularly unique facet to project to the world outside which at once commands attention and admiration.

The absurdity of India can be total. It appears to ridicule analysis. It takes the onlooker beyond anger and despair to neutrality.

WE WERE FAR FROM THE DROUGHT and famine area. But even here no rain had fallen for some time, and on the leafless trees in the administrator's compound the sharp spring sun had brought out the bougainvillaea like drops of blood. Twenty miles away hailstones destroyed a village's crops. The villagers, relishing the drama, the excuse for a journey, came in a body to report. We went to have a look. On the way we made surprise stops.

We stopped first at a primary school, a small three-room brick shelter beside a banyan tree. Two brahmins in spotless white cotton, each washed and oiled, each with his top-lock of caste, each "drawing" ninety rupees a month, were in charge. Twenty-five children sat on the broken brick floor with their writing boards, reed pens and little pots of liquid clay. The brahmins said there were 250 children at the school. The administrator said:

"But there are only twenty-five here."

"We have an attendance of a *hundred* and twenty-five."

"But there are only twenty-five here."

"What can you do, sahib?"

Beyond the road some of the children not at school rolled in the dusty fields. Even with twenty-five children the two rooms of the school were full. In the third room, protected from sun and theft, were the teachers' bicycles, as oiled and cared for as their masters.

At the next school, a few miles down the road, the teacher was asleep in the shade of a tree, a small man stretched out on his tiny teacher's table, his feet balanced on the back of the chair, so that he looked like a hypnotist's subject. His pupils sat in broken rows on strips of matting that had been soaked and pressed into the earth and was of its colour. The teacher was so soundly asleep that though our jeep stopped about eight feet away from his table he did not immediately awaken. When he did—the children beginning to chant their lessons in the Indian fashion as soon as they saw us—he said he was not well. His eyes were indeed red, with illness or sleep. But redness disappeared as he came to life. He said the school had 360 pupils; we saw only sixty.

"What is the function of a schoolteacher?"

"To teach."

"But why?"

"To create better citizens."

His pupils were in rags, unwashed except by snot, their hair, red from sun and malnutrition, made stiff and blond with dust.

Two or three and stop. The Hindi slogan on the walls of the family planning centre looked businesslike, but the centre itself was empty except for charts and more slogans and a desk and chair and calendar, and it was some time before the officer came out, a good-looking young man in white with a neat line moustache and a wrist-watch of Indian manufacture. He said he spent twelve days a month on family planning. He led discussions and "motivated" people to undergo vasectomy. The administrator asked:

"How many people did you motivate last month?"

"Three."

"Your target is one hundred."

"The people here, sahib, they laugh at me."

"How many discussions did you lead last month?"

"One."

"How many people were there?"

"Four."

"What were you doing when we came?"

"I was taking food and a little rest."

"What did you do this morning?"

"Nothing."

"Show me your diary."

Loose forms for travelling expenses fell out of his diary. The diary itself hadn't been filled for two months. The young man had been holding down the job for two years; every month he drew 180 rupees.

"Try to motivate me," the administrator said. "Come on. Tell me why I should go in for family planning."

"To raise the standard of living."

"How would family planning raise the standard of living?"

It was an unfair question, because concrete, and because it hadn't been put to him before. He didn't answer. He had only the abstraction about the standard of living.

Birth control here; and, not so far away, the artificial insemination centre. A peasant sat on the concrete culvert of an abandoned flower-bed, holding his white cow by a rope. In a stall at the other end of the garden was the black zebu bull. Contraception, insemination: whatever the aim, nature was taking her own way in this district. It was clear what was about to happen wasn't going to be artificial: the male villagers were gathering to watch. And the centre was well equipped. It had a refrigerator; it had all the obscene paraphernalia of artificial insemination. But the bull, the officer said, had lost its taste for artificial stimuli; which was not surprising. The bull itself was running down. Certain potent rations had been fixed for it by the authorities, but the rations hadn't been collected. Seventy natural inseminations had taken place in the last year. But no one could tell the percentage of success, in spite of the ledgers in filing cabinets and the multi-coloured charts on the walls. It hadn't occurred to the follow-up officer that he had to follow up.

"What is the purpose of artificial insemination?"

"It allows one bull to cover many cows."

This explained everything. The larger purpose—the gradual improvement of cattle in the district—had escaped him. Where the mind did not deal in abstractions, it dealt, out of its bewilderment, in the literal and the immediate.

To abstraction itself, then: to the district degree college, the humanities, and the Professor of Literature. He was a tiny man in a white shirt and flagrant yellow trousers belted without tightness over a gentle little paunch bespeaking total contentment. He looked very frightened now: the visit wasn't fair. His mouth was open over his projecting top teeth, which were short, fitted squarely one against the other, and made a perfect ivory arc. He said he taught the usual things. "We begin with Eshakespeare. And——" Then he went shy.

"The Romantics?" the head prompted, turning it into a supporting inquiry.

"Yes, yes, the Romantics. Eshelley."

"No moderns?" asked the administrator. "Ezra Pound, people like that."

The Professor grunted. Shoulder against the head's table, he leaned forward over his little paunch, his mouth collapsed, his eyes terrified. But he kept up with modern writing. "Yes, yes. I have been reading *so* much Esomerset Maugham."

"What do you think is the point of teaching literature in a country like ours, Professor?"

"Self-culture." He had been asked that before. "Even if there is dirt and filth, the cultured mind, as Aristotle says, gets this purge. And this catharsis, as they call it, helps the self-culture. Because it is the cultured mind that even from all this dirt and filth gets the education the lower sort of mind cannot get."

"Lady Chatterley?" the head interrupted. He had, mysteriously, understood.

The Professor cast him a swift look of gratitude and ended with relief, "This is the value of literature."

POOR PROFESSOR, poor India. Yet not poor—that was only the estimate of the onlooker. The Professor, and the other officers we had met, considered themselves successful. In the midst of insecurity, they drew their rupees. The rupees were few but regular; they set a man apart. All of India that was secure was organized on this tender basis of mutual protection; no one would apply to others the sanctions he feared might one day be applied to himself. Survival—the regularity of the rupees— was all that mattered. Standards, of wealth, nourishment, comfort, were low; and so, inevitably, were those of achievement. It took little to make a man happy and free him of endeavour. Duty was irrelevant; the last thing to ask in any situation of security was *why.* A colleague of the Professor's had said that the problems of teachers in the district were two: "Estatus and emolument." (But he liked alliteration; he described his pupils as "rustics or ruffians.")

So the abstractions and good intentions of New Delhi—the dangerous administrative capital, all words and buildings, where chatterers flourished and misinterpreted the interest of the world, where analysts who had never considered the vacuum in which they operated reduced the problems of India to the day-to-day scheming of politicians, and newspapers, which had never analyzed their function, reported these schemings at length and thought they had done their duty to a country of five hundred million—so the abstractions of New Delhi remained abstractions, growing progressively feebler, all the way down. Insecurity merged with the Indian intellectual failure and became part of the Indian drabness.

And the physical drabness itself, answering the drabness of mind: that also held the Indian deficiency. Poverty alone did not explain it. Poverty did not explain the worn carpets of the five-star Ashoka Hotel in New Delhi, the grimy armchairs in the serviceless lounge, the long-handled broom abandoned there by the menial in khaki who had been cleaning the ventilation grilles. Poverty did not explain the general badness of expensive, over-staffed hotels, the dirt of first-class railway carriages and the shantytown horror of their meals. Poverty did not explain the absence of trees: even the Himalayan foothills near the resort of Naini Tal stripped to brown, heat-reflecting desert. Poverty did not explain the open stinking sewers of the new middle-class Lake Gardens suburb in Calcutta. This was at the level of security, the rupees regularly drawn. It did not speak only of an ascetic denial of the senses or of the sands blowing in from the encroaching desert. It spoke of a more general collapse of sensibility, of a people grown barbarous, indifferent and self-wounding, who, out of a shallow perception of the world, have no sense of tragedy.

It is what appals about India. The palace crumbles into the dust of the countryside. But prince has always been peasant; there is no loss. The palace might rise again; but, without a revolution in the mind, that would not be renewal.

2

Magic and Dependence

A YEAR OR SO AGO AN INDIAN holy man announced that he had fulfilled an old ambition and was at last able to walk on water. The holy man was claimed by a progressive Bombay weekly of wide circulation. A show was arranged. Tickets were not cheap; they went to among the highest in the land. On the day there were film teams. The water tank was examined by distinguished or sceptical members of the audience. They found no hidden devices. At the appointed time the holy man stepped on the water, and sank.

There was more than embarrassment. There was loss. Magic is an Indian need. It simplifies the world and makes it safe. It complements a shallow perception of the world, the Indian intellectual failure, which is less a failure of the individual intellect than the deficiency of a closed civilization, ruled by ritual and myth.

In Madras State the Congress had been overthrown in the elections. The red-and-black flags of the Dravidian party were out everywhere, and it was at first like being in a colony celebrating independence. But this was a victory that could be fully understood only in Hindu terms. It was the revenge of South on North, Dravidian on Aryan, non-brahmin on brahmin. Accounts had been squared with the Hindu epics themselves, sacred texts of Aryan victory: no need now to rewrite them from the Dravidian side, as had been threatened.

The students of a college held a meeting to "felicitate"—the Indian English word—a minister-designate. "The evening is cool and mild winds are tickling us," a student said in his speech of welcome. He was heckled; the evening was hot. But we had moved away from reality already: the student was inviting the minister-designate to drown the audience "in the honey of his oration." The minister-designate responded with pieces of advice. A cunning man never smiled; at the same time it was wrong for anyone to keep on laughing all the time. Some people could never forget the loss of a small coin; others could lose six argosies on the ocean and be perfectly calm. Reality was now destroyed, and we were deep in the world of old fairytale: the folk-wisdom, the honey, that was the satisfying substitute, even among politically active students, for observation, analysed experience and inquiry.

The national newspaper that reported this reception also reported a religious discourse:

MEDITATION ON GOD ONLY WAY TO REDEMPTION
Madras, 9 March

Even an exceptionally intellectual and astute person is likely to falter and indulge in a forbidden act and perform a suicidal act under the influence of destiny. One has to suffer the consequences of his errors in previous life . . .

This, in South India, was still news. There had been an election, though, a process of the twentieth century. And here, on the main news page of another newspaper, were post-election headlines:

MASSES MUST BE EDUCATED TO MAKE DEMOCRACY A SUCCESS
—Prof. Ranga

PAST MISTAKES RESPONSIBLE FOR CURRENT PROBLEMS
—Ajoy Mukherjee

CONGRESS REVERSES ATTRIBUTED TO LACK OF FORESIGHT

A nation ceaselessly exchanging banalities with itself: it was the impression Indians most frequently gave when they attempted analysis. At one moment they were expressing the old world, of myth and magic, alone; at another they were interpreting the new in terms of the old.

. . .

THERE is an 1899 essay, *Modern India,* in which Swami Vivekananda, the Vedantist, takes us closer to the Indian bewilderment and simplicity. Vivekananda came from Bengal, the quickest province of India. He was pained by the subjection of his country and his own racial humiliation. He was also pained by the caste divisions of Hinduism, the holy contempt of the high for the low, the "walking carrion" of Aryan abuse. Vivekananda himself was of the Kayastha caste, whose status is still in dispute. In religion Vivekananda later found compensation enough: he exported the Vedas to the West itself, and found admirers. *Modern India* can be seen as a link between Vivekananda's political distress and its religious resolution. It is an interpretation of Indian history in apocalyptic Hindu terms which barely conceal ideas borrowed from the West.

Every country, Vivekananda states axiomatically, is ruled in succession by the four castes of priests, warriors, merchants and *shudras,* the plebs. India's top castes have decayed. They have failed in their religious duties, and they have also cut themselves off from the source of all power, the *shudras.* India is therefore in a state of "*shudra*-hood," which perfectly accommodates the rule of the *vaishya* or merchant power of Britain. *Shudra* rule, though, is about to come to the West; and there is the possibility, in India as well as in the West, of a "rising of the *shudra* class, *with their* shudra-*hood.*" The emphasis is Vivekananda's; and from his curious position he appears to welcome the prospect, while saying at the same time that *shudra*-hood can be rejected by India, just as "Europe, once the land of *shudras* enslaved by Rome, is now filled with *kshatriya* [warrior] valour."

So, out of mock-Western historical inquiry, out of borrowed ideas and personal pain, Vivekananda reduces the condition of his country to a subject for simple, though slightly distorted, Hindu religious contemplation. Failure was religious; redemption can come only through religion, through a rediscovery by each caste of its virtuous duty and—at the same time—through a discovery by India of the brotherhood of all Indians.

Modern India is part of the unread but steadily reprinted literature of Indian nationalism. It is not easy to read. It wanders, is frequently confused, and is full of the technicalities of Hindu metaphysics. It could never have been easily understood. But with Indian sages like Vivekananda, utterance is enough; the message is not important. A nation exchanging banalities with itself: it cannot be otherwise, when regeneration is believed to come, not through a receptiveness to thought, however imperfect, but through magic, through reverential contact with the powerful, holy or wise. The man himself is the magic.

There is a whole department of the Central Government at work on The Complete Works of Mahatma Gandhi; they have an entry, under that name, in the Delhi telephone directory. But *The Hindu* newspaper of Madras reported in March that 90 per cent of high-school students in one district knew nothing of Gandhi except that he was a good man who had fought for independence. In a southern city I met a twenty-year-old Dravidian student. He was a product of independence, privileged; and we met at, of all twentieth-century things, an air show. The uncertain native, of Jabalpur or Gerrard's Cross, seeks to establish his standing in the eyes of the visitor by a swift statement of his prejudices. And all this student's social attitudes were anti-Gandhian. This was news to him. He reverenced the name. It was the name alone, the incantatory magic, that had survived.

Mind will not be allowed to play on the problems of India. It is part of the Indian frustration.

But now Indians have a sense of wrongness. They have begun to feel, like the Spaniards, that they are an inadequate people; and, like the Spaniards, they feel they are inadequate only because they are uniquely gifted. "Intelligent" is the word Indians use most often to describe themselves, and the romantic view is gaining ground that they might be intelligent to the point of insanity. In India self-examination is abortive. It ends only in frenzy or in generalities about the Indian "character."

The humanities are borrowed disciplines that always turn discussions about famine or bankruptcy into university tutorials. There can be no effective writing. The ritual of Indian life smothers the imagination, for which it is a substitute, and the interpretation of India in the Indian novel, itself a borrowed form, is at a low, unchanging level. "I don't wait for another *novel*," Graham Greene says of the Indian writer he admires; he waits for an encounter with another stranger, "a door on to yet another human existence." The Delhi novelist R. Prawer Jhabvala has moved away from the purely Indian themes with which she started; she feels unsupported by the material.

In such a situation the novel is almost part of autobiography, and

there have been many Indian autobiographies. These—always with the
exception of the work of Nirad Chaudhuri—magnify the Indian deficiency. Gandhi drops not one descriptive word about London in the
1880s, and even Mr. Nehru cannot tell us what it was like to be at Harrow
before 1914. The world in these books is reduced to a succession of stimuli, and the reacting organism reports codified pleasure or pain: the
expression of an egoism so excluding that the world, so far from being
something to be explored, at times disappears, and the writers themselves
appear maimed and incomplete. All Indian autobiographies appear to be
written by the same incomplete person.

So the sense of wrongness remains unresolved. But it is possible now
for the visitor to raise the question and at times to tease out a little more,
especially from men under thirty-five. At a dinner party in Delhi I met a
young businessman who had studied in America and had felt himself at a
disadvantage. He said, "I felt that intellectually"—the Indian pride!—
"they were far below me. But at the same time I could see they had something which I didn't have. How shall I say it? I felt they had something
which had been *excised* out of me. A sort of motivational drive, you
might call it."

The jargon was blurring, but I felt that, for all his businessman's
adventurousness, he was like the peasants I had met some hundreds of
miles away. It was a late afternoon of dust and cane-trash, and golden
light through the mango trees. The peasants were boiling down sugar-
cane syrup into coarse brown sugar. The bullocks turned the mill; a black
cauldron simmered over a fire-pit. A bare-backed, well-built young man
scraped up sugar from the shallow brick trough level with the ground
and pressed it into balls. His father chewed *pan* and watched. He said, just
giving information, that his son had to write an examination in the morning. He would fail, of course; another son had written an examination
six months before and had failed. In his mind, and perhaps in his son's
mind, there was no link between failure and this labour in the fields. The
peasants were Kurmis, a caste who claim Rajput ancestry. The British-
compiled gazetteers of the last century are full of praise for the Kurmis as
diligent and adaptable cultivators; they are praised in exactly the same
way by Indian officials today. But they have remained Kurmis, demanding only to have their Rajput blood acknowledged.

What had been excised out of the Kurmis had been excised out of the businessman: "motivational drive," that profound apprehension of cause and effect, which is where magic ends and the new world begins.

CAUSATION: it was the theme of the Buddha 2,500 years ago in the distressed land of Bihar. It was the theme 150 years ago of Raja Rammohun Roy, the first British-inspired Indian reformer. It is the necessary theme today. It is depressing, this cycle of similar reform and similar relapse. Reform doesn't alter; it temporarily revives. Ritual and magic forever claim the world, however new its structure.

The process of relapse can be charted in our own time in the work of Vinoba Bhave, the Gandhian land-reformer of Bihar, who fifteen years ago made the cover of *Time* magazine. "I have come," *Time* reported him saying, "to loot you with love." His programme was simple: he would ask landowners to give away land to the landless. It was the spiritual way of India. "We are a people wedded to faith in God and do not give ourselves to the quibblings of reason. We believe in what our Rishis [sages] have taught us. I have the feeling that the present-day famines and other calamities are all due to our sins." It was not therefore his business to think in any practical way of the food problem or of creating economic units of land. "Fire merely burns; it does not worry whether anyone puts a pot on it, fills it with water and puts rice into it to make a meal. It burns and that is the limit of its duty. It is for others to do theirs."

With this there went ideas about education. "Human lives are like trees, which cannot live if they are cut off from the soil . . . Therefore, everyone must have the opportunity to tend the soil . . ." Agricultural work will also keep the population down, because it takes the mind off sex. Care has to be taken in choosing a craft for a school, though. Fishing, for example, wouldn't do, because "I have to show [the children] how to deceive the fish"; poultry-keeping is better. Literature should not be neglected. "It is a fault in the Western system of education that it lays so little stress on learning great lines by heart." But the best education is the one Krishna, the mythological-religious figure, received. "Shri Krishna grazed cattle, milked them, cleaned the cowshed, worked hard, hewed firewood . . . ; later, as Arjuna's charioteer, he not only drove his horses but also cared for them."

It isn't only that so much of this is absurd, or that Bhave was taken seriously until recently. It is that Bhave's sweetness adds up to a subtle but vital distortion of the Mahatma's teaching. The stoic call to action and duty becomes, with Bhave, an exercise in self-perfection, an act of self-indulgence and holy arrogance. He will not see his responsibility through to the end; it is the duty of fire only to burn. He separates, in a way the Mahatma never did, the private religious act from its social purpose. He misapplies the doctrine of bread-labour by which the Mahatma hoped to ennoble all labour, including that of the untouchables. Bhave says that the untouchables do work which is "not worthy of human dignity"; they must become tillers and landowners. He leaves them, in effect, where he finds them. And he does nothing to solve the food problem which, in India, is related to the ignorant use of land.

Bhave goes back again and again to the scriptures: their rediscovery becomes an end in itself. So, in the name of reform, the Mahatma and goodness, Bhave slips into reaction. The old world claims its own.

Indians are proud of their ancient, surviving civilization. They are, in fact, its victims.

REFORM this time will be more brutal. China presses; Pakistan threatens; non-alignment collapses and America drives hard bargains. The new world cannot be denied. Incapable of lasting reform, or of a correct interpretation of the new world, India is, profoundly, dependent. She depends on others now both for questions and answers; foreign journalists are more important in India than in any other country. And India is fragmented; it is part of her dependence. This is not the fragmentation of region, religion or caste. It is the fragmentation of a country held together by no intellectual current, no developing inner life of its own. It is the fragmentation of a country without even an idea of a graded but linked society.

There is no true Indian aristocracy, no element that preserves the graces of a country and in moments of defeat expresses its pride. There have been parasitic landowners, tax-farmers; there have been rulers. They represented a brute authority; they were an imposed element on a remote peasantry; in moments of stress they have—with exceptions—proclaimed only their distance. They are the aptly named "native princes"; and though here and there their brute authority, of money or influence, has been reasserted, they have disappeared and nothing marks their passing. In Hyderabad you wouldn't have known that the Nizam had just died, that a dynasty older than Plassey had expired. Every Indian, prince or peasant, is a villager. All are separate and, in the decay of sensibility, equal.

There are contractors and civil servants in Delhi, where a "society lady" is usually a contractor's wife. There are business executives in Calcutta, which still has an isolated, ageing set with British titles. There are the manufacturers and advertising men and film people of Bombay, where "suave," "sophisticated," and "prestigious" are words of especial approval. But these are trade guilds; they do not make a society. There is an absence of that element, to which all contribute and by which all are linked, where common standards are established and a changing sensibility appears to define itself. Each guild is separate. Even the politicians, with the state withering away for lack of ideas, are sterilized in their New Delhi reserve. And each trade—except the entertainment trade—is borrowed.

Every discipline, skill and proclaimed ideal of the modern Indian state is a copy of something which is known to exist in its true form somewhere else. The student of cabinet government looks to Westminster as to the answers at the back of the book. The journals of protest look, even for their typography, to the *New Statesman*. So Indians, the holy men included, have continually to look outside India for approval. Fragmentation and dependence are complete. Local judgment is valueless. It is even as if, without the foreign chit, Indians can have no confirmation of their own reality.

But India, though not a country, is unique. To its problems imported ideas no longer answer. The result is frenzy. The journals of revolt are regularly started; they are very private ventures, needing almost no readership and having responsibility to no one; within weeks they are exhausted and futile, part of the very thing they are revolting against. Manners deteriorate. Each Indian wishes to be the only one of his sort recognized abroad: like Mr. Nehru himself, who in the great days was described, most commonly, by visiting writers as the lonely Indian aristocrat—his own unexplained word—presiding over his deficient but devoted peasantry. Each Indian, looking into himself and discovering his own inadequacy, attributes inadequacy to every other Indian; and he is usually right. "Charlatan" is a favourite word of Indian abuse. The degree of this self-destructive malice startles and depresses the visitor.

"The mutual hatred of men of their own class—a trait common to *shu-dras*": the words are Vivekananda's; they describe a dependent people.

This dependent frenzy nowadays finds its expression in flight. Flight to England, Canada, anywhere that lets Indians in: more than a flight to money: a flight to the familiar security of second-class citizenship, with all its opportunities for complaint, which implies protection, the other man's responsibility, the other man's ideas.

IT WAS WRITTEN, of course. It was the price of the independence movement.

The movement, as it developed under Gandhi, became a reforming religious movement, and it was in the Indian tradition that stretched back to the Buddha. Gandhi merged the religious emphasis on self-perfection in the political assertion of pride. It was a remarkable intuitive achievement. But it was also damaging. It was not concerned with ideas. It committed India to a holy philistinism, which still endures.

At the beginning of the nineteenth century Raja Rammohun Roy had said that forty years of contact with the British would revivify Indian civilization. He spoke before the period of imperialist and racialist excess; the technological gap was not as wide as it later became; the West, to the forward-looking Indian, was then less the source of new techniques than the source of a New Learning. But the gap widened and the mood changed. The independence movement turned away, as it had to, from people like Roy. It looked back to the Indian past. It made no attempt to evaluate that past; it proclaimed only glory. At the same time the imaginative probing of the West was abandoned. It has never been resumed. The fact escapes notice. The West, so much more imitable today than in 1800, might be pillaged for its institutions and technology; its approval is valuable. But the political-religious-philistine rejection still stands. The West is "materially affluent but psychologically sick"; the West is a sham. No Indian can say why. But he doesn't need to; that battle has been won; independence is proof enough.

A scholar in Delhi reminded me that Macaulay had said that all the learning of India was not worth one shelf of a European library. We had been talking of aboriginal Africa, and Macaulay was brought in to point out the shortsightedness of a certain type of obvious comment. Later it occurred to me, for the first time, that Macaulay had not been disproved by the Indian revolution. He had only been ignored. His statement can be reaffirmed more brutally today. The gap between India and the West is not only the increasing gap in wealth, technology and knowledge. It is, more alarmingly, the increasing gap in sensibility and wisdom. The West is alert, many-featured and ever-changing; its writers and philosophers respond to complexity by continually seeking to alter and extend sensibility; no art or attitude stands still. India possesses only its unexamined past and its pathetic spirituality. The Indian philosopher specializes in exegesis; the holy man wishes to rediscover only what has been discovered; in 1967 as in 1962 the literary folk squabble like schoolmen, not about writing, but about the proprieties of translation from all their very ancient languages. India is simple; the West grows wiser.

Her revolution did not equip India for a twentieth-century independence. When that came, it existed within an assumption of a continuing dependence: an accommodating world, of magic, where Indian words had the power Indians attributed to them. The bluff had to be called; the disaster had to come.

ONE BY ONE INDIA has had to shed ideas about herself and the world. Pain and bewilderment can no longer be resolved by the magical intervention of a Vivekananda, a Gandhi, a Nehru, a Vinoba Bhave. Fifteen years ago Bhave said, more or less, that his aim was the withering away of the state. He called it "the decentralized technique of God," and even the pious dismissed him as a dreamer. The state has now withered away. Not through holiness; it is just that the politicians, homespun villagers in New Delhi, no longer have an idea between them. Magic can no longer simplify the world and make it safe. India responds now only to events; and since there can be no play of the mind each disagreeable event—the Chinese attack, the Pakistan war, devaluation, famine and the humiliating deals for food with the United States—comes as a punishing lesson in the ways of the real world. It is as if successive invasions, by the reaction they provoked, that special Indian psychology of dependence, preserved an old world which should have been allowed to decay centuries ago; and that now, with independence, the old world has at last begun to disintegrate.

The crisis of India is not political: this is only the view from Delhi. Dictatorship or rule by the army will change nothing. Nor is the crisis only economic. These are only aspects of the larger crisis, which is that of a decaying civilization, where the only hope lies in further swift decay. The present frenzy cannot be interpreted simply as a decline from stability. That was the stability of a country ruled by magic, by slogans, gestures and potent names. It was the stability of a deficient civilization that thought it had made its peace with the world and had to do no more. The present mood of rejection has dangers. But it alone holds the possibility of life. The rejection is not religious, even when its aims are avowedly the protection of a religion. It does not attempt reform through self-perfection. The *mode* is new, and of the new world.

It may be that I exaggerate; that I forget the holy man putting his thumb in his mouth and pulling out a prick, to applause; that I forget the pious who, in a time of famine, pour hundreds of gallons of milk over a monumental idol while an Air Force helicopter drops flowers. But magic endures only when it appears to work. And it has been proved that man, even in India, can no longer walk on water.

1967

The Election in Ajmer

WHOM TO VOTE FOR? the English-language poster in New Delhi asked. And when, in mid-February, a fortnight before the first polling day, I went south to Ajmer in Rajasthan, it seemed that the half a million voters of this Indian parliamentary constituency, part urban, part rural, part desert, had a problem. The Congress had won freedom for India, and for more than twenty years, through four election victories, it had ruled. Now the Congress had split. The split had led to this mid-term election. But both sides continued to use the name. *Kangrace ko wote do,* the posters of both sides said: Vote Congress. And the same saffron, white and green flag flew from rival campaign jeeps: the jeep the favoured campaign vehicle, authoritative and urgent in the dusty streets of Ajmer, among the two-wheeled tonga carriages, the battered buses, bicycles by the hundred, handcarts and bullockcarts.

Both sides would have liked to use the old election-winning Congress symbol of the pair of yoked bullocks. But the courts had decided that the yoked bullocks shouldn't be used at all; and both sides had devised complicated and naturalistic symbols of their own. A cow licking a sucking calf: that was the Congress that was with Mrs. Gandhi, the Prime Minister. A full-breasted woman at a spinning-wheel (the fullness of the breasts always noticeable, even in stencilled reproductions): that was the old or Organization Congress, that had gone into opposition. Both symbols, in India, were of equal weight. The spinning-wheel was Gandhian, the cow was sacred. Both symbols proclaimed a correct, Congress ancestry.

It was in some ways like a family quarrel, then. And, as it happened, for this Ajmer seat the candidates of the two Congresses were related. There were five candidates in all. Three were independents and of no great consequence. "They are only contesting by way of their hobby," a man from the Election Department said. "They will put down their security of five hundred rupees. They will get a few thousand votes and forfeit their deposit and sit quietly, that is all. It is only their hobby."

The main candidates were Mr. Mukut Bharvaga and Mr. Bishweshwar Bhargava. Mr. Mukut was standing for the old Congress and all its opposition associates. He was the uncle of Mr. Bishweshwar, who was defending his seat for the Indira Congress. And here—a local reflection of the national quarrel about legitimacy—was the first issue in Ajmer: who was morally in the wrong? The uncle, for fighting the nephew? Or the nephew, for fighting the uncle?

Mr. Mukut, the uncle, was sixty-eight years old, a lawyer, and blind. He was famous in Rajasthan for his prodigious memory and his skill in matters of land revenue. His fees were said to be as high as one thousand rupees a day, about £50; his earnings were put at two lakhs a year, about £10,000. But Mr. Mukut was also known for his free services to peasants, who still came to Ajmer to look for "the lawyer without eyes." Mr. Mukut was an old Congressman and freedom fighter and he had gone to jail in 1942. His political career since independence had been unspectacular, but steady and without blemish: he was perhaps best known for his campaign to have clarified butter easily distinguishable from its groundnut-based substitute. He had won the Ajmer seat for Congress in 1952, 1957 and 1962. In 1967, at the age of sixty-four, he had retired, handing over the Ajmer seat to his thirty-six-year-old nephew and protégé, Mr. Bishweshwar. Now, with the Congress split, Mr. Mukut wanted his seat back; and, to get it, he had allied himself with all his old political enemies. Was Mr. Mukut right? Was Mr. Bishweshwar wrong, for resisting?

The answer, overwhelmingly, was that Mr. Bishweshwar was wrong. He should have withdrawn; he should not have fought his uncle, to whom he owed so much. It was what Mr. Mukut's son, who was Mr. Mukut's election agent, said; and it was what Mr. Bishweshwar's agent said. Mr. Mukut himself always spoke of the contest with a sense of injury. "The State Congress chose the meanest weapon," he said, "setting my own nephew to fight me. They know I'm a man of strong family feeling and they were hoping *I* would withdraw." The Maharana of Udaipur, who was supporting Mr. Mukut, told an election meeting, "The Indira Congress is dividing the country, and not only ideologically. They are breaking up families." And the Rajput village headman, loyal to his Maharana, agreed. "A nephew who cannot love the members of his own family, how can he love the public?"

But wasn't the uncle also wrong to try to pull down his nephew? "I didn't want my father to fight this election," Mr. Mukut's son said. "I said, 'Bapuji you are old now, you are disabled.' But then I was overwhelmed by his answer. It brought tears to my eyes. He said, 'This is a time for sacrifice.' "

Sacrifice: it wasn't a claim Mr. Bishweshwar could make, and for much of the campaign he looked harassed and uncertain and sometimes hunted. Unlike his uncle, who always spoke freely, even elaborately, Mr. Bishweshwar had little to say; and his manner discouraged conversation. He stared blankly through his glasses, like a man alerted not to say anything that might be used against him. Once he said, "I cannot understand how my uncle can go against all those principles I imbibed from him." It was the only comment on his uncle I heard him make, and it was spoken very quickly, like a prepared line.

Mr. Bishweshwar wasn't a popular man. He suffered from all comparisons with his uncle. Mr. Mukut was small and lean and brown, an ascetic politician of the old school, with a jail-record. Mr. Bishweshwar was as tall and plump as a film star. He was a post-independence politician, an organization man. People in his own party said of him: "Politics is his profession." And: "If politics were taken away from him he would hardly be having two square meals a day." And: "His uncle massacred hundreds of party workers for him." But that wasn't held against the uncle; that was held against Mr. Bishweshwar.

"I'm not working for Bishweshwar," his campaigners said. "I'm working for Indira." And this was what they said even on polling day, waiting in the brightly coloured party tents for voters. "The people aren't voting for Bishweshwar. They're voting for Indira."

Which, as everybody said, was what the election was about: Indira, Mrs. Gandhi, that formidable lady in New Delhi, who had done a de Gaulle on the Congress and taken over, who had abolished the old consensus politics of the Congress. She had declared war on privilege; her appeal was to the poor, the untouchables, the minorities. She had nationalized the banks; she had "de-recognized" the princes; and, to deprive the princes of their privy purses, she intended to change the constitution.

Indiscipline, people like old Mr. Mukut said, grieving for all those old members of the party who had fallen. *Indira Hatao*, the opposition posters said: Remove Indira. And on the other side: *Garibi Hatao*, Remove Poverty. The rich, the poor: the wonder was that, in India, this basic division had taken such a long time to be politically formulated. The socialists and communists hadn't done that: they offered theologies. And this was the first election in Ajmer in which the parties had issued manifestoes.

RICH AND POOR. But there was a regional complication. Rajasthan is a land of princes. Ajmer itself, though in the centre of Rajasthan, hadn't been a princely state and had no maharaja. But the Ajmer constituency was vast: two hundred miles, mainly of desert, rock and jagged brown hills, between Ajmer and Char Bazaar: more than six hours in a jeep. Two of its districts belonged to the former state of Udaipur; and the Maharana of Udaipur, who had supported Mr. Bishweshwar at the last election, had declared for Mr. Mukut in this. The princes of Rajasthan, "de-recognized" by the government, their privy purses threatened, were in their different ways up in arms against the government. And they could take their case to the people and get a hearing, because they were princes.

For other people in the opposition, supporters of Mr. Mukut, it wasn't so easy. Mr. Kaul, an old Congressman of Mr. Mukut's age, was now a member of the Indian Upper House. Mr. Kaul ate only one meal a day and he said he had acquired the habit during his time in jail in 1932. But there was no jail-taint to him now; the post-independence years of power, honour and politicking had worn him smooth; and Mr. Kaul thought that personal canvassing should be banned.

"We issue our manifestoes. Why should we go to the people personally? By canvassing the way is found for bribing them. Our people are poor; they don't understand what we are fighting for. Their ignorance is being exploited. The Indira Congress is spending crores of rupees, spoiling them, the peasants, the villagers, the uneducated and the labour classes. Giving them slogans. All slogans. It's our national character."

I asked him about the national character.

"Our people don't think in terms of country first."

"What do they think of?"

"*Nothing.*" He laughed. "Haven't you noticed? They're indifferent."

·   ·   ·

AND ON THAT FIRST day in Ajmer the election seemed far away. The tongas carried advertisements for the Apollo Circus; walls everywhere were painted with family-planning slogans in Hindi. It was a Tuesday, the day of the weekly service at the Hanuman temple; and monkeys from the temple hopped from tree to tree on the nearby Circuit House hill. At the top of the hill there was a view of the clear lake beside which Ajmer is built, the water a surprise after the dust of the streets. On the black rocks at the lake-edge scores of washermen were beating the cotton clothes of the poor to death, swinging the twisted wet hanks with a steady circular motion and grunting competitively at every blow.

The sun rose higher. The brown mist lifted over the brown hills. The washermen spread out their lengths of cotton, white and coloured, and went away. Hawks hovered over the lake, at whose margin clouds of midges swirled and thinned like cigarette smoke in a wind, and then re-formed. From the flat-roofed white-and-ochre town below there came the sound of a loudspeaker: cinemas announcing their attractions. In the late afternoon there was music: a wedding procession.

The Ajmer calendar was full. On Saturday there was the eighty-ninth prize-giving of Mayo College, one of India's important English-style public schools, founded for the education of the sons of princes. Three days later came the Hindu festival of Shivratri and the opening of the Ajmer Flower Show. So, quickly, after the disorder of the main street—the mixed traffic, the cows, the rubble, the dust, the exposed food-stalls—Ajmer revealed itself as excessively ordered. There was the railway town with its great locomotive workshops and its severely graded housing. There was the medieval, narrow-laned town around the famous Muslim shrine, an object of pilgrimage. There were the newer residential areas; there was the bazaar, an extension of the disorder of the main street; and there were the ordered acres of Mayo College, where only the servants' quarters spoke of India.

Beyond the brown hills were the smaller towns and the thousand villages that made up the constituency, each village as fragmented and ordered as Ajmer itself: every man in his caste, his community, his clan: divisions not strictly racial and not strictly social: more as if, in an English village, where everyone more or less looked alike, spoke the same language and had the same religion, every man yet remembered that he was a Dane or Saxon or Jute and stuck to his kind. Cow-and-calf, spinning-wheel: poor and rich, left and right: how could these divisions apply?

In the evening I went to the Honeydew, one of the three recognizable cafés that Ajmer, with a population of 300,000, just about supports. It was air-conditioned and dim and the waiters were in white. A young man I fell in with told me that the Honeydew was for the young and "modern" of Ajmer. He spoke sardonically but he too wanted it known that he was modern. "My father was a semi-literate. He joined the Railways in 1920 and retired thirty-seven years later. Then he died. At the end of his life he was making three hundred rupees a month. For my father it was his luck, his *karma*. What he had sown in a past life he was reaping in this. I am not like that. I am only making four hundred. But let people look at my suit and tie and see me spending in the Honeydew and think I'm rich."

A cup of Honeydew coffee cost about three pennies. You could ask the waiter for a cigarette; he would place an open packet on your table and you paid only for those you took. Luxuries were small in India and little gestures were fundamental acts of defiance. To wear a tie, when money was immemorially scarce, to have a coffee in the Honeydew: that was more than extravagance. That was to deny one's *karma*, to challenge the basis of one's father's faith.

And it was of defiance that Mr. Desai, once Mrs. Gandhi's Deputy Prime Minister, now in the opposition and supporting Mr. Mukut, was speaking in Naya Bazaar that evening. In the bazaar lanes the narrow shops, raised on platforms, glittered with electric light, tempting custom. In the wide open area of Naya Bazaar itself, beyond the heads of the crowd, beyond the flags and bunting and posters strung across the street, and at the end of two little colonnades of fluorescent tubes, there was another platform, very clean and very bright, and there—with Mr. Mukut and Mr. Kaul and others no doubt sitting at his feet—Mr. Desai, not looking his seventy-four years, was talking about "the Indira psychosis," nationalization and the danger to the constitution.

At first it seemed, to use the Indian word, "sophisticated." But an election address, in that street, before that crowd, without an analysis of the distress that was so visible, without a promise for the future! An election address, about economic and legal matters, cast in terms of personal injury! And when Mr. Desai was talking of nationalization he was talking of more than an economic issue. He was talking of an act of defiance, a threat to order and *dharma*, an impious shaking of the world. In the place of that defiance he was offering himself: his Gandhi-cap, his white home-spun, his simple brown waistcoat, his well-known asceticism, his Gandhian habit of spinning: all his personal merit built up through many years of service. Religion, *dharma*, the Hindu "right way" given a political expression: the crowd was in tune with what was being said. They listened respectfully; there was even some slight applause.

Garibi Hatao, Remove Poverty: it was possible to understand why no one before Mrs. Gandhi had raised this simple political slogan. And it was also possible to understand why it was said in Ajmer that the issues of the election—Remove Poverty, Remove Indira—were too abstract and remote. There would have been more interest, people said, in elections for the State Assembly, when the politicians could play on the more immediate issues of caste and community and offer tangible rewards: a tarred road, a water-tank, electricity.

But that evening, less than twenty miles away, on the Jaipur road, the forty-six-year-old Maharaja of Kishangarh, politically active on the opposition side, a member of the State Assembly, was murdered.

KISHANGARH was part of the neighbouring constituency. It is one of the lesser names of princely Rajasthan—the state, as it existed in 1947, was just over 650 square miles—but the Maharaja was linked by blood to the great houses. He was well known in Ajmer. He played badminton at the Ajmer Club and tennis on the Mayo College courts.

That evening he and the Maharani were going to a wedding. They were about to leave when the telephone rang. Kishangarh took the call himself. Then he told the Maharani he had to go out for a little and would be back in ten minutes. When he left the palace, driving himself in a little Indian-made Fiat, he had a revolver and many rounds of ammunition; he also had about 1,500 rupees. A few miles from the palace, on a straight stretch of the Jaipur-Ajmer road, the car stopped or was made to stop; and Kishangarh was shot in the right ear. His revolver was taken; his money wasn't touched.

This was the story that broke the next morning. And it was strange, at eleven, in the bright desert light, neem trees and cactus beside the road, thorn trees scattered about the dug-out brown land, to see the little "champagne-green" Fiat, not princely or tragic, not a dent anywhere, not a window cracked, only a finger-wipe of blood on the driving door, at rest on the sandy verge with its front bumper against a tall clump of the *ker* shrub, by whose red flowers the strength of the monsoon can be foretold. The princely licence-plate, white on red, said: *Kishangarh No. 11.* A line of stones marked the course of the car as it had come off the road. On the other side of the road were the jeeps of the district police and a crowd of dhoti-clad, turbanned peasants.

Some local politicians were also there, among them Mr. Makrana, small and fat and grim, with dusty trousers, a worn green pullover and a very white muslin turban the size and shape of a scooter tyre. "I am a Marwari," he said, "and we Marwaris wear these turbans, white or khaki, at sad deaths, funerals." Mr. Makrana was a member of the State Assembly and the whip of the party to which the Maharaja had belonged. "The Maharaja was having a very nice influence for us. Some big person is behind this killing." Once Mr. Makrana had owned about 2,500 acres of land. "I lost my land when the *jagir* system went out." Under this system his tenants used to give him a third or a half of what they made. "With that percentage we used to manage our establishment. Now I am in the marble business. I couldn't survive if I had to depend on politics. I live from the marble. Politics is only my hobby." And, leaving me, he began again to walk up and down the road before the still peasants, his plump face set and petulant, his white turban on his head, very visibly mourning a member of his party.

The Ajmer District Magistrate, in a suit, and two senior police officers, in khaki, came in a black saloon which flew a blue police pennant. The peasants watched; Mr. Makrana himself stopped to watch. A smiling, green-bereted sub-inspector from the Jaipur Dog Squad arrived and reported. And then Mr. Kaul, the member of the Indian Upper House, turned up. He scrambled briskly out of his car—tight trousers stylishly creased, long brown coat—and hurried across the road to the officials, like a man used to being well received everywhere; and then gravely, as though looking at the corpse itself, he examined the Fiat.

Mr. Kaul wasn't a man for white turbans and country mourning. His manner was of New Delhi; and very soon he was to issue a statement, in English: ". . . dastardly murder . . . general atmosphere of lawlessness and violence . . . leaders of the Ruling Party from the Prime Minister downwards . . . using such derogatory epithets against the so-called capitalist, industrialist and feudal order . . . inciting the feelings and sentiments of the masses, particularly of the Youth of the lower rungs of Society . . ."

In Kishangarh the shops were shut, but the streets were full of people, stunted, thin-limbed peasants from the interior who, as soon as the news had broken that morning, had begun to make their way on foot or cycle to the palace. It was a ramshackle Indian country town, the new concrete buildings all balconies and balustrades at the top, slum at road-level, with rough additional lean-tos roofed with canvas or thatch. The asphalt road was like an irregular black path through dust and dung, unpaved sidewalks, heaps of rubble and old gravel. Then, unexpectedly, there was a lake, and in the centre of the lake an old stone building, possibly a summer pavilion; and at the end of the lakeside road the high walls of Kishangarh fort and the old town.

Inside, the procession had started to the cremation ground and the waiting pyre, prepared with sandalwood and other scents. The road and the city walls were packed, ablaze with the colours of peasant Rajasthan, red and orange and saffron. The open jeep with the body came out of the palace gate. The relations of the dead Maharaja were in white. White here the terrible colour of mourning.

In the middle of the afternoon the Fiat was still where it had been, against the *ker* bush. Some of the marker stones had been scattered. No one watched now. Some distance away two or three peasants sat in the shade of a thorn tree. The brown hills were pale in the glare. The private tragedy was over. Mr. Mukut and Mr. Kaul had already addressed a condolence meeting.

THE KISHANGARH affair had upset Mr. Bishweshwar's schedule, and when I went to his house only his wife was there. The house was in an open area at the end of a dirt lane where Mr. Mukut also had his law office. The ambiguous Congress flag hung limp in the little garden where flowers and shrubs grew out of bald earth.

I had been told that Mr. Bishweshwar lived simply. The trellis-enclosed veranda where I sat first of all had a dark, tarnished, homely air, with rough-and-ready furniture and a strip of dirty matting. The small terrace upstairs was even less formal, with a plain concrete floor, and local five-rupee basket-chairs brought out as required. A servant squatted on the floor in a small room near the steps and scoured dishes. A Hindu country interior: there was nothing, except perhaps the telephone, to suggest that this was one of the rising political households of Rajasthan and that Mrs. Bishweshwar's father had been in his time a famous politician, so fierce in faction fights against Mr. Kaul that Mr. Nehru had had to intervene.

Mrs. Bishweshwar was a pretty woman of thirty-three, pale and slightly pinched, with her head covered modestly with a dark-red sari. At first she spoke only in Hindi. She said she couldn't speak English well; but later she relented, and it turned out that she spoke English impeccably. She had been educated in a pastoral institution that her father had founded. There she had studied Indian classical music and had learned to spin. Later she took her B.A. in music and English and Hindi literature. She still spun. "I believe in Gandhiji's teachings." But she had let the literature go. "I don't like modern literature. I can't understand it. I don't like Hindi modern literature either. I like Shakespeare, Browning, Shelley."

She didn't like political life. "My husband is not a politician. He is a worker." It was the Gandhian word: a doer of good works. "I too am an ardent believer in improving the lot of the downtrodden. But I want to work silently. I don't want publicity for myself. But I would like a lot more for my husband. People should recognize his ability. If he is a sincere and hardworking man, people should know."

Mr. Bishweshwar arrived, tall and plump, in trousers and a brown sports shirt. He looked harassed and winded and had clearly been rattled by the Kishangarh affair. He had also missed a meeting at a village called Saradhna; and it was for Saradhna that we immediately started, accompanied—perhaps for luck on this unlucky day, perhaps for reasons of piety—by a small, energetic sadhu clad from top to toe in saffron. The sadhu seemed about to chatter with cold; it was the effect of his saffron head-dress, which was cunningly tied from one piece of cotton and looked like a cross between a mitre and a jester's cap, with flaps over the ears.

The Rajasthan village huddles together, a solid built-up mass where space is suddenly scarce. Saradhna was like this. We stopped near the two tea-shacks, their fires glowing in the dark. There was no one to receive us and we walked around to the other side of the village. Then, at a great pace, Mr. Bishweshwar began to walk through the village, kicking up dust, the rubber-sandalled sadhu running at his heels, ear-flaps sticking out. We raced past stripped trees, over piles of rubble, past broken court-yards, over runnels of filth. The narrow lane twisted and turned and opened abruptly into miniature squares. We passed a group of smokers sitting peaceably in the thick warm dust around a brass plate with their smoking things; and then we were out of the village and near the tea-shacks again.

Some men came to Mr. Bishweshwar then and whispered. *Unanimous, unanimous*: the English word was quite clear in all the Hindi. Not far away a man squatted in the dust, cooking some mess in a tiny black pot over an enormous straw blaze.

Mr. Bishweshwar said, "They held their own meeting. The whole vil-lage has decided to support me."

"*Unanimous,*" a black-capped villager said, shaking his head from side to side.

It was hard to push the matter any further; and our business was therefore, quite unexpectedly, over.

As we were driving back to Ajmer it occurred to me that Mr. Bish-weshwar's trousers and shirt were unusual for a campaigning Congress politician. I said, "So you don't wear homespun?"

He thought I was criticizing. He plucked at the sleeve of his brown sports shirt and said, "This is homespun. Sometimes I wear trousers for the convenience. But I often wear the dhoti. I like the dhoti."

So he was only out of uniform. He wasn't, as I had thought, the new-style politician, matching Mrs. Gandhi's new-style campaign. He was a Congressman, aspiring after the old style; he had, as he had said, imbibed his principles from his uncle. When the Congress had split, leaving Mrs. Gandhi at the head of a minority government, the leaders of the local State Congress had hesitated about which side to join; and Mr. Bishwesh-war, as he admitted, had hesitated with them. When they had declared for Mrs. Gandhi, he had gone along with them. The new-style politics was Mrs. Gandhi's, and Mrs. Gandhi's alone. In Rajasthan the Congress organization, the whole structure of Congress control, remained what it was. It was Mrs. Gandhi who had appeared to turn this party, ruling since independence, into the party of protest.

But for Mr. Bishweshwar it remained a gamble. In 1967 he had got 145,000 votes; his main opponent, from the party known as the Jan Sangh (The National Party) had got 108,000. But in 1967 Mr. Bishweshwar had

had the support of Mr. Mukut and the Maharana of Udaipur. Now Udaipur and the Jan Sangh were supporting Mr. Mukut. Udaipur could take away Rajput votes from Mr. Bishweshwar; the Kishangarh affair could have the same effect.

Mr. Bishweshwar was going that evening on a two-day country tour. In his campaign headquarters—the ground floor of a villa: a stripped central room with an empty fireplace, high blue walls with little oblong windows just below the ceiling, worn rugs on the cracked concrete floor, small side rooms enclosed by latticework and wire netting—among his workers, some paid (forty rupees a month, £2, for two hours a day), some minor politicians in their own right, whose rustic manner belied the revolutionary promises of the posters sent out from New Delhi, among the barefoot boys sitting on the floor and pasting *Vote Bishweshwar* posters on cardboard, he looked very harassed indeed.

BUT MR. MUKUT had his problems too. Officially he was the candidate of the opposition or Organization Congress. But the Organization Congress had no organization in Ajmer. Mr. Mukut was depending on the organization of the Jan Sangh; and Mr. Mukut and the Jan Sangh had until recently been enemies. The central executives of the opposition parties had formed an alliance; they had agreed on a division of seats; and Ajmer had gone to the Organization Congress and Mr. Mukut.

The Jan Sangh in Ajmer had been planning to put up their own man. Now they had to support Mr. Mukut; and Mr. Sharda, the president of the local Jan Sangh, who had contested the seat in 1967, didn't like it. He said, "This is a Jan Sangh seat and some Jan Sangh man should have contested. I would have been a better candidate than the man they chose. Have you seen him? He's an old man of sixty-eight, blind, can't see. All the time our people come to me asking why Jan Sangh is not contesting, why I am helping this blind old man."

And it was an unusual alliance. The Jan Sangh, founded in 1951, had grown in strength, Mr. Sharda said, because the Congress was corrupt; but for most of this time Mr. Mukut was the ruler of the Congress in Ajmer. It wasn't only for its opposition to Congress corruption that the Jan Sangh was known, though. The Congress was non-sectarian; Mr. Mukut had a good record as a defender of Muslim rights. The Jan Sangh had come into prominence in North India as the militant Hindu party of the right, rallying Hindus against Muslims, and, within the Hindus, the Aryan, Hindi-speaking north against the Dravidian south. It spoke of the pampering of minorities; its slogan was "Indianization." Latterly, scenting parliamentary power, the Jan Sangh had softened its communal, Aryan line; it had decided that the enemy was Communism; but its communal reputation remained its strength.

"We don't want to take ideas from Russia and Kosygin," Mr. Sharda said. "We have a heritage, a culture. We have the Vedas, the first book of the human race. With the Vedas' light other people have developed their cultures. So when we have got such an old heritage we believe that our race is great, is noble. My grandfather, Harbilas Sharda, has written a book called *Hindu Superiority*. In the 1930s. He has given all the facts and figures to show how the Hindu race is superior to others."

Mr. Sharda was in his fifties, small, compactly built, in a striped brown suit. He wore tinted glasses; for all his aggrieved talk of the "blind old man" his own eyes were not too good. Eye trouble, in fact, had made him give up the practice of law and go into business as a commission agent dealing in cement and cloth. He lived in a new concrete bungalow at the bottom of the Circuit House hill, opposite a rock wall plastered with drying cow-dung cakes. He had a glass case of knick-knacks in his drawing-room; bits of vine grew out of whisky bottles, one brown, one green. On the white wall there was a portrait, like a tinted photograph, of Harbilas Sharda, the author of *Hindu Superiority*: a gentle old brahmin with a drooping moustache, in British days an elected member of the Central Legislative Assembly, given the title of Dewan Bahadur (one step below the knighthood), and famous in India as the author of the Child Marriage Restraint Act (still known as the Sharda Act), which in 1930 had banned child marriage.

"My family were the first to revolt against the social evils of the country," Mr. Sharda said. But his party was now committed to the protection of the sacred cow, as it was committed to the creation of an Indian nuclear armoury. There was no inconsistency. Like parties of the extreme right elsewhere, the Jan Sangh dealt in anger, simplified scholarship and, above all, sentimentality. It spoke of danger and distress—"Our civilization is in danger," Mr. Sharda said—and from present impotence it conjured up a future of power, as pure as the mythical Hindu past, before the British conquest, before the Muslim invasions.

"We want nuclear bomb for the safety of the country. But this is a

matter of our all-India policy. I don't talk too much about it to our villagers." The cow was different. "We feel that cow is a very important
animal in our country, being an agricultural country, and as such should
not be slaughtered. There is a candidate in Delhi, Mr. Ram Gopal Shal-
wala, is fighting only on that. Government should give protection and
give good bulls to have a better type of animal. Good arrangements of
fodder should also be made, because generally there is famine in this area
and thousands of animals die of famine."

He didn't think Muslims would object. "Muslims who live in villages
and are agriculturalists like to live as Hindus do. It is only the educated
fanatics who want to create this gulf of Hindus and Muslims for their
own selfish motives." But later, when we were talking about the way the
forty thousand Muslim votes would go, Mr. Sharda said in his direct,
unrancorous way, "They will be divided. But generally most of the Muslim votes do not go to Jan Sangh."

As I was leaving, a barefoot servant in a torn dhoti brought in the
up-country edition of *The Motherland,* the new English-language Jan
Sangh daily published in Delhi. The Kishangarh story, and the charge of
political murder, was still big on the front page.

THE MUSLIM votes wouldn't go to the Jan Sangh. But Mr. Mukut
thought they would go to him personally, for his past services. This was
on a day of exaltation when, after an evening of well-received speeches,
he seemed to think that by allying himself with his former enemies he
had left almost no votes for the other side.

We were driving in one of the campaign jeeps from Ajmer to the military town of Nasirabad, through country that had been stripped almost
to desert by eight successive years of drought. Between the driver and
myself Mr. Mukut sat or half-reclined, small, frail, easily tossed about, in
a dhoti and a black waistcoat, with his fine head thrown back, his sightless
eyes closed, his delicate hands occasionally clutching at air. Sometimes,
between sentences, his wide, expressive mouth opened and closed wordlessly, and he was then like a man gasping for breath. His gentle manner
and fragility imposed gentleness on all who came near him; and I occasionally felt, as I leaned close to catch his exalted words, that I was rush-
ing a garrulous invalid to hospital, and not racing with one of Rajasthan's
master-politicians to a hard day's campaigning.

A leaflet had appeared in Ajmer calling on Jan Sangh supporters to boycott Mr. Mukut. Mr. Mukut said this was another trick of Mr. Bishweshwar's party; he had, he said, been astonished by the loyalty of his Jan Sangh workers. Mr. Mukut spoke, not quite as one who had seen the error of his Congress ways, but as someone who was at last able to speak of the errors of the Congress. The Jan Sangh said that the Congress was corrupt. It was true, Mr. Mukut said. "The power corrupted us. Our politicians became Gandhian only in name." But he himself had been helpless; he had never been a minister. And now he saw no moral or political complication in his alliance with the Jan Sangh. His position was simple: it was as a Gandhian that he was fighting the Indira Congress, which was illegitimate, Communistic and Westernizing.

"Gandhiji's ideology was quite different from the ideology of Western politicians. The foundation of his political tactics is that means should be as fair as the end." He didn't think this could be said of Mrs. Gandhi. He was also concerned about nationalization. "It will ruin the country. All our state-owned enterprises are so badly run." His support of private enterprise brought him close to the hard anti-Communist line of the Jan Sangh. But Mr. Mukut didn't appear to be concerned either about efficiency or capitalism. His opposition to nationalization was embedded in an over-riding Gandhian doubt about the machine age. The machine had destroyed the West, as Mr. Mukut had heard; the machine would destroy India. "What I particularly admired about Gandhiji was that he went to Buckingham Palace in 1931 in a dhoti."

I asked why that was admirable.

"Because he put the picture of poor India before the world."

"Mr. Nehru said that the danger in a country as poor as India was that poverty might be deified."

"Did he say that?" Mr. Mukut paused. The idea was new, "Western" and perhaps intellectually unmanageable. "I never heard him say that." He opened and closed his mouth wordlessly; and again, head thrown back, eyes closed, he was like a gasping invalid.

We passed the new Shiva temple, still with its bamboo scaffolding, that the peasants had built to celebrate the end of the eight-year drought. It stood white in a desolation of young thorn bushes. Once there had been woodland here; but towards the end of the drought, at a time of famine, the trees had been cut down for charcoal. And then we were in the military area: barracks old and new in the stripped land, soldiers with

rifles on their shoulders running in groups of two or three on the asphalt
road.

The main street of Nasirabad was brilliant with stalls of fruit and
vegetables. Here we stopped. Many reverential hands helped Mr. Mukut
out of the jeep and led him, limp-shouldered, limp-armed, between the
vegetable-stalls and across the narrow pavement to a dark little office,
over the front door of which, on the outside, were dusty framed diplomas
from Lucknow University and, on the inside, brightly coloured Hindu
religious prints. It was a lawyer's office, with a whole glass-cased wall of
Indian law books covered in brown paper, the frame of the case painted
yellow, with each section roughly labelled in red.

Mr. Mukut said to me, "He's one of my disciples."

The lawyer, a middle-aged man in a chocolate-purple sports shirt,
said very loudly, as though addressing the street, "Everything I am I owe
to Mr. Mukut."

They made Mr. Mukut sit on a basket-chair. They brought him tea
and a large, fly-infested *cachoree*, a local fried delicacy.

The lawyer said, "Mr. Mukut made me what I am. He has served
many people here without payment. The people of Nasirabad remember
these things."

And Mr. Mukut, leaning back, his slender legs drawn up onto the seat,
his hands fumbling for the *cachoree* that had been broken for his convenience into little pieces, opened and closed his mouth, like a man about to
sigh.

But the lawyer had pointed out the weakness of Mr. Mukut's campaign. Some of the people in the office were linked to Mr. Mukut by interest. The others were Jan Sangh and they for the most part were small
shopkeepers. Even the forbidding, kohl-eyed young man in a cream-
coloured suit and pointed black shoes, even he, who was a teacher, came
from a shopkeeping family. The Jan Sangh was an urban party; it had no
organization in the villages. The only party with a village organization
was the Congress. It was that village organization that had to be captured; and Mr. Mukut's only weapon was his influence. Mr. Bishweshwar's strength was that he belonged to the ruling party; a ruling party had
its ways of exerting pressure.

"I will tell you how they won the last State Assembly by-election,"
the lawyer said. "At that time this area was affected by famine. Rural people were jobless. The government machinery opened famine works in a

number of places. And these famine-relief workers were given one slogan: 'If you vote for the other side, famine-relief work will be closed down.' " And now the ruling party was again up to their old tricks, this time with the untouchables or Harijans, whom they were bribing in all sorts of ways and especially with loans from the nationalized banks.

A prominent Christian in Ajmer had complained to me that as a result of all the political attention the Harijans were getting out of hand. They were being "brought up" too fast, before they had a proper "footing"; there had been strikes. "I am even afraid to speak harshly to some of them now," the Christian said. I thought that the lawyer might be trying to say something like this in an indirect, un-Christian way. So I asked him, "They're behaving badly then, these scheduled castes?"

"Badly?" The lawyer didn't understand my question. He was a Hindu; he didn't have the Christian social sense; he couldn't share the Christian's resentment. Caste was not class. No one, however successful, denied his caste, however low, or sought to move out of it; no one tried to "pass"; no one's caste-security was threatened by any other caste. So the lawyer floundered. "No," he said at last, "they are not *behaving* badly. It's just that they're being fooled."

But what did Mr. Mukut have to offer? How was he going to balance this powerful appeal of the other side? Was he campaigning, for instance, for cow-protection? Mr. Mukut was astonished that I should ask. Everyone in Ajmer knew his record. During his time in parliament he hadn't only campaigned for a ban on cow-slaughter and the punishment of cow-killers; he had also campaigned for free grazing for cows anywhere.

"We are too Western-oriented," Mr. Mukut said. He was sitting up now, small and neat and cross-legged in his basket-chair. "Go to the villages. Everybody in the village now wants to wear jacket and tie. Look at our own *ayurveda* medicine. It was only after a long fight that we managed to get it accepted, these remedies that are much cheaper than any modern drugs. And then there are the pipelines."

I said, "Pipelines, Mr. Mukut?"

"Even in the villages. The pipelines in the villages is going too far. It's all right in the cities. But in villages the healthy water from the well is good enough. But they are taking piped water now to many villages. For our womenfolk this going to the well and drawing water was one of the ways in which their health was maintained. They now have got no substitute exercise for the women. Similarly, we have our own indigenous *chakki* [a quern] for grinding grain on the floor. Now they have substituted these mills run by electric power or oil-fired machines. So now the whole village sends its grain to these mills, with the result that the women are missing this exercise as well. Previously even in cities this grinding with *chakki* was done by small families. But now everything is being Westernized. It is morally bad because it tells upon the health and habits of our womenfolk. And unless some alternative employment is found for them it naturally makes them sluggish."

In a famine area! From an election candidate! But Mr. Mukut could go into the villages to ask for votes because he was a Gandhian who knew that his own merit was high. He had achieved merit through service and sacrifice. Service for its own sake, sacrifice for its own sake. "Since Mr. Kaul and I left the Congress," Mr. Mukut said, "there is no one there with a record of service. Mr. Kaul was in jail; I was in jail." Democracy, the practice of the law, the concern with rights: one set of virtues had been absorbed into another, into a concept of *dharma*, the Hindu right way; and the distortion that resulted could sometimes be startling.

KISHANGARH was murdered on Tuesday evening. On Friday evening All-India Radio announced that the police had "worked out" the case and arrested a student. On Saturday the details of the arrested man's "confession" were all over Ajmer, and in the afternoon there were Hindi leaflets in the streets:

LOVE STORY: A POLITICAL OPERA

Bhim Jat, the killer of the Maharaja of Kishangarh, has confessed, and the whole affair is crystal clear. The Maharaja had a farm a few miles from Kishangarh. Bhim Jat and his beautiful sister worked for the Maharaja on this farm. The Maharaja took advantage of the girl's poverty and for a long time had illicit relations with her. Bhim Jat, a youth of nineteen, could not stand this looting of his sister's honour. He took the law into his own hands and with his country-made pistol shot the Maharaja dead.

But politics corrupts the truth and deals in lies. Some politicians immediately called a meeting to mourn the Maharaja's death and with a great show of sorrow tried to tell the voter to take his revenge by defeating the Indira Congress.

Would you vote for a party which plays with the honour of your daughter or sister? There should be rejoicing not tears at the death of these rajas-maharajas whose only princely habit is that they know how to take advantage of the poverty of young girls. Rise and utterly crush these debauched people so that never again will they come to you for votes with the name of Gandhi on their lips . . .

Has Mr. Mukut no shame, to be sitting in the lap of the Jan Sangh, who were once his bitter enemies? The election should be fought on policies. Mr. Mukut shouldn't be misleading the voters for his own selfish purposes. Mr. Mukut has used the Maharaja's funeral-pyre to cook himself a meal of votes.

Other versions of the story were no less sad. Bhim Jat's sister had left her husband to become Kishangarh's mistress; and Bhim Jat had been ostracized by his caste for the dishonour his complaisance had brought on them all. Kishangarh had given Bhim a house on the farm; he was paying for Bhim's education; he had promised Bhim the farm itself. But then a well on the farm gushed water. In the desert water was money; and Kishangarh, worried about his "de-recognition" and the possible loss of his privy purse, had sought to go back on his promise.

Kishangarh was the name of an eighteenth-century school of painting. Now it was linked with a peasant woman, a farm, a well: a peasant drama, far removed from the princely pageantry of the prize-giving at Mayo College that afternoon. Kishangarh was remembered there, in the obituary section of the headmaster's speech, as a distinguished and popular old boy, like the late Maharaja of Jaipur, "who died in the U.K., where he had gone to play polo, his favourite sport."

The boys were exquisite in tight white trousers, long black coats and pink long-tailed Rajput turbans. They sat on the steps of the Mogul-style Bikaner Pavilion, with a view of the cricket field, the blank score-board, the college grounds and, in the distance, the sunlit brown hills of Ajmer. The guest of honour was the Canadian High Commissioner. Prominent among the visitors on the lower steps of the pavilion were some of the princes of Rajasthan: the Maharaja of Kotah, a couple from the house of

Jodhpur, and the Maharana of Udaipur, whose ancestor had been the first to respond to an appeal of the Viceroy, Lord Mayo, for funds for a princely public school and had, a hundred years ago, almost to the day, given a lakh of rupees, then worth about £10,000.

In the open area at the foot of the pavilion were the parents, many of them box-wallahs, business executives, some from as far away as Calcutta. All week they had been gathering in Ajmer: India's modest middle class, products of the new industrial society, as yet with no common traditions or rooted strength, still only with the vulnerability of the middle classes of all very poor countries. In the poverty of India their ambition was great, but their expectations were small; they were really very easily pleased. India always threatened to overwhelm them—those servants at the edge of the cricket field—as the desert and the peasants and the new politics had overwhelmed Kishangarh and his ancient name.

BUT THE MAHARANA of Udaipur hadn't come to Ajmer only for the prize-giving. He had been campaigning hard against Mrs. Gandhi and her party in a princely freelance way, offering his services wherever they were needed; and he was in Ajmer to give Mr. Mukut a hand. He had come in an open dark-green 1936 Rolls-Royce with a chauffeur, an Election Secretary and two bodyguards. He proved his worth almost at once. That very evening, while the Mayo College boys were doing *A Midsummer Night's Dream*, Udaipur addressed a meeting in the bazaar area. His name was like magic. Fifteen thousand people came to hear him.

The next day, Sunday, was the big day. Udaipur was going with Mr. Mukut and Mr. Sharda on a tour of those districts of the constituency that had belonged to the former Udaipur State. The little convoy started from the red-brick King Edward VII Guest House on Highway 8, not far from the mock-Mogul Queen Victoria Golden Jubilee clock-tower.

It was such an unlikely alliance. There was Mr. Sharda, "Western" and businesslike in his suit, but with his pastoral Jan Sangh dream of an untouched Hindu world; he was in a jeep, packed at the back with bedding and other supplies. Mr. Mukut, the Gandhian and old-time Congressman, but now formally dressed in tight white trousers and a long cream-coloured coat, was in a grey saloon. Udaipur was in his open Rolls, a man in his forties, of medium height and build, with a black beret, dark glasses and dark-blue nylon windcheater. The thirty-six-year-old Election Secretary, very tall, with a paunch, a corrugated beard and glinting black locks, was all in loose white cotton and looked like a holy man. At the back of the Rolls the two khaki-uniformed, orange-turbanned bodyguards sat up high with their rifles: it was like a proclamation of the danger in which, in Rajasthan, princes now lived.

Udaipur was the star. That was accepted. And so briefly did Mr. Mukut speak at Nasirabad, our first stop, that by the time my own jeep, after a wrong turning, had got to the meeting-place, he had finished and was sitting cross-legged on the improvised platform, eyes closed, good and quiet and patient at Udaipur's suede-shod feet, like a man accepting his own irrelevance. But Udaipur remembered him. "People ask me, 'But isn't Mr. Mukut a blind man?' I say, 'He is blind on the outside, not on the inside. When you go to a temple, mosque or church you close your eyes to pray. You can't see, but you aren't blind on the inside.' "

Mr. Mukut sat as still as a man meditating in a temple. But a packed day lay ahead. Suddenly—no speech from Mr. Sharda—the meeting was over and the mood of meditation and repose vanished. So quickly did Udaipur and Mr. Mukut scramble off the platform, so quickly did they bolt for their vehicles, that I lost them almost at once and didn't catch up with them again until Beawar, thirty miles away.

After Beawar it was desert; and it was desert after Bhim. No irrigated green patches, no trees, no peasants on bicycles; just rock and sometimes cactus, and the empty road. Sometimes a camel, sometimes a peasant in rags with patched leather sandals and a home-made gun: bandit country. But regularly in this wilderness little Rajput groups ran out into the road to stop the convoy and to look for the Maharana they had never seen (a Maharana of Udaipur had last been here in 1938). When Udaipur stood up in the Rolls drums beat and sometimes, unexpectedly, a trumpet sounded.

They garlanded him and dabbed his forehead with sandalwood paste; they sprinkled him with red or purple water (he had dressed for this). Ceremoniously, as though he were a god in a temple (and his dark glasses gave him a suitable inscrutability), they circled his face with fire (a blazing lump of camphor in a brass plate). Once a woman fed him some substance with her hand. Here Udaipur was more than a prince. Here he was *Hinduon ka suraj*, the Hindu Sun, an ancient title of Rajput chivalry that had merged into religion. At one stop a man cried out, "You are our god!" And Udaipur was quick to reply, correctly, "The God that is, is the same for you and me."

Mr. Mukut wasn't forgotten. When the Rolls moved on, the Rajputs surrounded the grey saloon. Mr. Sharda always waved me on then in his impatient way and so I couldn't tell whether the men of the desert weren't exacting some tribute from Mr. Mukut for their devotion to their Maharana.

Early in the afternoon we reached the walled town of Deogarh. There was pandemonium at the main gate; in the middle of the crowd a white horse with a white sheet on its back was waiting for Udaipur. The loudspeaker-man in our convoy became frenzied. "Your Maharana has come. For fourteen hundred years you have known Maharanas. Now he has come, the Hindu Sun. You have longed for him as you have longed for clouds and rain. Now your Maharana has come." But already, as in some spectacular film, the walled town was emptying; and men and women in bright turbans and saris were hurrying across the desert to the temple of Karni Devi, goddess of the town, where Udaipur was to speak.

Mr. Sharda, who was, I thought, a little buttoned-up in the company of his two old political enemies, whispered to me, "Jan Sangh. All organized by Jan Sangh."

And soon to his desert audience—bright turbans and smiling faces against a background of sand, the walled city and fort, the jagged hills faint in the haze—Udaipur was talking about Mrs. Gandhi's threat to democracy and the constitution. Mr. Mukut sat cross-legged on the canopied platform. The bodyguards were dusting down the Rolls in the shade of a thorn tree.

Udaipur had changed his beret for a Rajput turban. One man, so many roles. But Udaipur was a good speaker because he accepted all his roles—god, Rajput, democrat—and made them fit together. "I am not a god. I am just a sort of representative. We are all worshippers of Lord Shiva, *Ek Ling Nath*." He was not a politician; he wanted no man's vote. "I am not a supporter of the Jan Sangh. I am a supporter of freedom." The Rajputs applauded that. "We have no policemen here and we need none. We are not like the Indira Congress. There is love between us, because we are one and the same." They laughed at the political hit and applauded the definition of the basis of their Rajput loyalty.

Afterwards, leaving Mr. Mukut to the electorate, we went to have lunch in the bare and run-down palace of Udaipur's vassal. Here the election was as if forgotten. The vassal and his infant son glittered in Rajput court costume. A red carpet lay across the dusty courtyard. Drums beat; a smiling doorkeeper took the swords of guests; in an inner room women sang. A bright-eyed old retainer came and recited ancient verses about the duties of kings. Other smiling people—everyone was smiling—came to make obeisance and offer token tributes of one rupee and five rupees.

"You see," Udaipur said in English, his face still stained red and purple, "how *unpopular* we are."

THE NEWSPAPERS were being gloomy about Mrs. Gandhi's chances, and the success of Udaipur's tour disheartened many people on Mr. Bishweshwar's side. They had no comparable glamour figure. The visit of Mr. Chavan, one of Mrs. Gandhi's most able ministers, had been a failure; Mrs. Gandhi herself wasn't coming. All that Mr. Bishweshwar's people could look forward to was the visit, on Tuesday, of Mr. Bishweshwar's political patron, the Rajasthan Chief Minister. He was hardly glamorous. He was very much the local party boss, and he was coming less to make speeches than to settle certain internal party disputes which had begun to threaten Mr. Bishweshwar's campaign.

The Ajmer Congress was famous for its faction fights. In 1954, when Mrs. Bishweshwar's father was politically active, the administration had virtually stalled; and Mr. Nehru had written a long and impatient "note" about the local party: ". . . giving us continuous headaches . . . The government cannot be considered to be an efficient government . . . The Community Project Scheme in Ajmer was one of the least successful. In fact, for a long time practically nothing was done there." That was the tradition. And after all its further years in power the local party was full of people who thought they had been badly treated and were taking advantage of the election to sulk. Mr. Bishweshwar, aiming at independence, and trying to free himself of old intrigues by "creating" new men of his own, had made matters worse. One aggrieved man said, "Mr. Bishweshwar is in the position of a man who has stopped believing in the loyalty of his honest wife and has begun to believe the protestations of loose girls."

So now I heard that Mrs. Gandhi hadn't come to Ajmer because she disapproved of Mr. Bishweshwar, that she remembered how he had hesitated at the time of the party split, and that she was now letting him sweat it out. Other people, with memories of Mrs. Bishweshwar's father, said that Mr. Bishweshwar's heart wasn't in the election and that he had only been pushed into it by his wife. Everybody agreed that Mr. Mukut's workers were more selfless and less mercenary and less given to sabotage. There was a lot of talk of sabotage. One man high in the party told me that of all Mr. Bishweshwar's workers, paid and unpaid, 30 per cent were saboteurs.

And it was only then that I heard about the Rawats. The Rawats were originally a caste of animal-skinners. They had been advancing for some time into agriculture, the army and the police. In Jodhpur the Maharaja had decreed twenty-five years before that they were to be considered a Rajput caste. But in Ajmer the Rawats were still low, almost untouchable. They should therefore have been solidly behind the Indira Congress and Mr. Bishweshwar. But there had been a crisis. Some weeks before a young Rawat wife in the Nasirabad area had been enticed away by a Rawat Christian convert. The community had been doubly dishonoured, by the adultery (in India an offence punishable with rigorous imprisonment), and by the fact that the enticer was a Christian. There had been complaints to the police, but nothing had been done; and some Rawats felt that Mr. Bishweshwar and some of his Christian supporters had connived at the inactivity of the police. A leaflet had been distributed in Rawat areas:

RAWATS, BROTHERS! THE INDIRA CONGRESS CANDIDATE
BISHWESHWAR NATH BHARGAVA TRIFLES WITH THE HONOUR OF
OUR WIVES AND DAUGHTERS. BEWARE OF HIM!

There were fifty thousand Rawat voters. Kishangarh, Udaipur, Rajputs, Rawats, and sabotage: Mr. Bishweshwar seemed to be in trouble all round that Monday. And this, very roughly, was the assessment of the Ajmer situation that appeared in the *Times of India*. A day or two later a large "human-interest" photograph of Mr. Mukut—a blind candidate— made the front page of the New Delhi *Hindustan Times*.

. . .

IT WAS FROM MR. KUDAL that I heard about the Rawats. Mr. Kudal was a Congressman of fifty and he had a modest ambition: he wanted to be Mr. Bishweshwar's Election Agent. The appointment was to be made on Tuesday, when the Chief Minister came; but when I saw Mr. Kudal, late on Monday evening, he had heard nothing at all and was in a state of some nerves. He said, "I very much fear that the intelligentsia is being cleverly weeded out all over India from political life."

Mr. Kudal was a lawyer. He lived in a lavatorial lane off Highway 8, in a large three-storeyed house built in the Rajasthani style with galleries around a central court-yard, and with an iron grille at the top to keep out intruders. Narrow enclosed concrete steps took you up past his law offices and his servants' rooms to the flat roof and his pink-and-red sitting-room. Upholstered chairs were pushed against three walls and there was a glass case with figures made from shells, plastic models of Hindu deities, and other knick-knacks. It was a little like a waiting-room, with all the chairs, but Mr. Kudal had many visitors. He kept in touch with the constituency; he had prepared himself for the job of Election Agent.

He was worried about the Rawats. He was less worried by Udaipur's tour. "These public meetings are just *tamashas,* excitements. Nothing." Elections were won with votes, and vote-getting required work. "By work I mean the direct approach to the voters. Taking them out of the houses and sending them to the booths. I will tell you as a zealous worker that all will depend on the work we put in in the last two or three days." And in that lay Mr. Kudal's promise and his threat.

He said, "I could swing the election in certain districts without leaving this room. It would take me a week. If I went out on the road it would take me two or three days."

I asked him how.

"I am a man of the masses." It was something he had worked at. He was a brahmin and a townsman and he said he had wasted a lot of time on bridge and chess before he had thought of service to the poor. He had gone out then "among the lowest sections of the community—the Harijans and the serpent-charmers." Not many people had done that; and it was well known in Ajmer that Mr. Kudal had a lot of influence in certain low quarters. "That is why people get worried when they hear that Kudal has joined the fray."

So on this last evening Mr. Kudal rehearsed his case, and his slightly desperate attitude was that, ready as he was to serve, he was also perfectly prepared to let Mr. Bishweshwar stew in his own juice, that if the Chief Minister and Mr. Bishweshwar wanted his services, if they cared at all about things like the snake-charmer vote, they would have to seek him out the next day. Mr. Kudal himself intended to do absolutely nothing the next day. It was the festival of Shivratri; he was a devotee of Shiva; for him it was to be a day of temple, prayer and meditation.

EARLY in the morning, too early, Mr. Bishweshwar came to the Circuit House to look for the Chief Minister. He looked even more harassed than I remembered. He was with a gang of rustics in dusty dhotis, brown waistcoats and Gandhi-caps. Pointlessly, like a swarm of midges, they bustled back and forth about the spacious lounge, following Mr. Bishweshwar's nervous lead. When Mr. Bishweshwar stood still, they all settled down on the carpet, the way the Circuit House servants did when they thought no one was about. After some fearful jabbering, four or five people speaking at once, the same things said again and again, they decided that the Chief Minister wasn't in the Circuit House and was probably somewhere else. And suddenly they all swarmed out again.

But the Chief Minister did come. And he must have had a hard day. He was still at the Circuit House at 7:30 that evening, when he should have been down in the city addressing a meeting at Kesarganj. It was just as well. Shivratri, the weekly service at the Hanuman temple, the Flower Show and the illuminations in Shah Jehan's lakeside gardens had drawn the holiday crowds; and there were only three or four hundred people— government officers, Muslims, people proving their loyalty—at Kesarganj. For an hour we were deafened by music, songs and election jingles. The crowd grew. And when at last the Chief Minister arrived, with all his party notables, I was glad to see that Mr. Kudal had been called out of his retreat and was with them.

After a day spent on personality squabbles the Chief Minister now dealt only in principles. *Garibi Hatao*: nothing about Rajputs and Rawats; not a word against Mr. Mukut; hardly anything about Mr. Bishweshwar. Mr. Bishweshwar didn't speak. Like the figure of the wife in some Egyptian sculpture, small at the feet of her lord, like Mr. Mukut at the feet of Udaipur, Mr. Bishweshwar sat still and modest at the feet of the Chief

Minister. He leaned back on his arms; his paunch showed to advantage; and I thought I had never seen him so relaxed.

"HE HAS EVERY reason to look relaxed," Mr. Kudal said, as we drove to Nasirabad with some of his workers the following afternoon. "Yesterday at 9:30 a.m., after he saw the Chief Minister he came and surrendered before me. He and his wife and his sister, his wife with tears in her eyes. I told him, 'But you, Bishweshwar, must know that I was always helping you, because I believe in the principles of Mrs. Gandhi, and not because of any affection I bear to you.' " So, indirectly, Mr. Kudal announced that he was the Election Agent. Then he added, "Now is the time for onslaught."

But first we stopped at the new Shiva temple, and Mr. Kudal, grateful devotee of Shiva, paid his respects to the lingam, which was set in the ground in the centre of a concrete lotus with a serrated rim. The yellow clothes of the images were damp with a sweet substance and black with sated, drugged flies.

"Here at Nasirabad," Mr. Kudal said, when we were on the road again, "I will introduce you to Mr. Mukut's and Mr. Bishweshwar's staunchest supporters. They are both my closest friends and they will both offer you a cup of tea. Sometimes I contest these elections like sports."

"Like a hobby," a worker in the back of the jeep said.

And at Nasirabad the news was as bad as Mr. Kudal could have wished. Mr. Jain, the plump little jeweller ("High Class Military Novelties and Gold Ornaments") who was also the Treasurer of the Ajmer Rural District Congress Committee, seated us against bolsters on his porch, in the cosy little space—at once his office and his day-bed—between the showcase and the front wall, gave us tea and *cachoree*, and told us that the way things were going Mr. Bishweshwar would be lucky to get 35 per cent of the town vote and 50 per cent of the village vote. "They are neglecting the old workers. The new workers they've brought in drink and go to hotels and abuse the opposition and they think they're winning votes."

The lawyer who was Mr. Mukut's Nasirabad man—his office was just across the road—gave the same figures. "Oh yes," the lawyer said in his booming voice. "Things are going right for Mr. Mukut. Because of somebody. You can say it is because of me. And the Jan Sangh. And Mr. Mukut—he's a great asset. And the poor personality of the opponent. All these things have combined."

We left Nasirabad and drove off into the desert.

"Depressed?" Mr. Kudal said. "I'm a warrior who knows no defeat."

A worker in the jeep said, "Mr. Kudal can turn the tables."

"I'm a man of the masses," Mr. Kudal said. "I will take you now to a village where very few people go. The Harijans there have built a Shiva temple and dedicated it to me. When I went to work among them they were an alcoholic community. I made them take the pledge. It wasn't easy. It took months."

Sunset in the desert: neem trees and Australian dogwood black against the ochre sky. And then, on an eminence, a walled village, a high gateway, a dusty road, a temple, and a crowd around the jeep shouting, "*Indira Gandhi ki jai!* Long live Indira Gandhi!" It was as Mr. Kudal had said: he was known here. Babies were shown to him, children re-introduced; boys read out the inscription on the temple gateway to show how well they could read now. And Mr. Kudal, tall, bald, one of his legs shorter than the other, walked among the Harijans with his awkward gait, blinking fast behind his glasses. Without any Gandhian trappings, he was a dedicated man; and it was moving.

We went on in the dark to a village where Mr. Kudal said he wanted to do "some CID work." I recognized the village as Saradhna. I had been there with Mr. Bishweshwar and I remembered that he had been promised "unanimous" support. But Mr. Kudal doubted whether Mr. Bishweshwar would get 40 per cent of the vote. Saradhna was a village of Jats; a Jat political party had recently emerged, hostile to Mrs. Gandhi; and the previous evening Mr. Mukut and some of the leaders of the Jat party had held a meeting at Saradhna.

"CID, CID," Mr. Kudal said to his workers when we stopped. They went to the tea-stalls and we sat silent in the jeep. Our presence couldn't have been all that secret, though. Cups of tea were brought out to us. A villager came and whispered that only 75 per cent of the village was for Mr. Bishweshwar. "He is only giving me butter," Mr. Kudal said in Hindi. But another villager came and whispered that Mr. Bishweshwar couldn't expect more than 90 per cent; and the workers, coming back from the tea-stalls, said 80 per cent.

So it seemed that the caste-appeal hadn't worked at Saradhna. And I began to wonder whether Mrs. Gandhi hadn't simplified Mr. Kudal's labours; whether she hadn't lifted this mid-term election high above the local politics Mr. Kudal understood and enjoyed; whether in Ajmer the choice wasn't between Mrs. Gandhi and the Jan Sangh in some areas, between Mrs. Gandhi and Udaipur in other areas, and between Mrs. Gandhi and poor old Mr. Mukut everywhere else.

No drama on the road, then, for Mr. Kudal. But when we got back to Ajmer we found that someone had been distributing leaflets accusing Mr. Kudal of sabotage.

MR. KUDAL had said that Friday was going to be a hard day. But by the time all our workers had come and we had ordered food from the bazaar it was half past eleven; and when we got to our first village it was time to eat. We sat in the rough little council-hall in the middle of a million furious flies. The workers ate off newspaper, Mr. Kudal and myself off dry peepul-leaves; and the kulaks, the local vote-catchers, who had been waiting for us, waited on us. Their manner was penitential, and Mr. Kudal hinted that he had come to rebuke them. They received their rebukes in private, after we had lunched.

The lunch had been heavy; the new famine road—part of the network built during the famine—was smooth. Mr. Kudal fell asleep. We passed a village. Mr. Kudal woke up and said he was sorry he had missed it, but he would send some of his workers there by bus that evening. We came to another village. A water-channel, freshly dug in the sand, barred our path; and Mr. Kudal decided to leave that village as well to his night workers.

"Well," he said later, "you're seeing the Nasirabad district. You've heard the assessments of both sides. So when the results come out you will know it is entirely the result of this"—he waved at the road and the boundless desert—"this movement. The result of this onslaught."

At the next village—more like a little town: a low-caste wedding procession in the dusty main street, a brass band in spectacularly tattered uniforms—we had cardamom tea in a cloth-seller's shop and Mr. Kudal talked to the Muslim village headman. Nothing more was needed, Mr. Kudal said; by evening everyone would know that Kudal was out campaigning for Indira and Mr. Bishweshwar. "They know that after the election they will still have to come to me." The statement worried him, and some time later he said, "I have helped these people. I have handled their cases for them without fee."

At the village after that we didn't leave the jeep. People saw us arrive, but the only man who came to us was a quarry-owner in a jacket and pullover. He said to Mr. Kudal in English, "The people need *guidance*."

"He is not for us," Mr. Kudal said afterwards. "He employs a lot of labour and he is going to spoil thirty per cent of the vote. But I don't argue with people three days before an election."

PUBLIC MEETINGS were to end in Ajmer at five on Saturday afternoon. But canvassing and private meetings could continue; and I heard from Mr. Mukut's son, who was also Mr. Mukut's election agent, that Mr. Mukut and Mr. Bishweshwar were to debate that evening before the Rotary Club of Beawar. A Rotary Club seemed an unlikely thing for a place like Beawar to have. But Beawar also had a Communist group. And it also, as I now learned, had one of India's most famous astrologers, Professor B. C. Mehta. Professor Mehta was a "commercial" astrologer: he specialized in market fluctuations. His cable address was MEHTA.

I heard all this from Professor Mehta's thirty-year-old lawyer son while we were waiting that afternoon for Mr. Mukut at his campaign headquarters. Professor Mehta, being only a commercial astrologer, hadn't issued any statement about the Ajmer election. But young Mr. Mehta was so confident of Mr. Mukut's victory and was so obviously welcome at campaign headquarters—"His father's an astrologer," Mr. Mukut's son said, introducing him—I felt there could have been no astrological discouragement. And Mr. Mukut, when he appeared in spotless white dhoti and koortah, with a black woollen waistcoat, was like a man touched with glory. The gentleness which he imposed on all who approached him now also held a little awe.

It was a long drive to Beawar. We got there at nightfall and found that nobody knew anything about a Rotary Club debate. Somebody said that Mr. Bishweshwar had got cold feet; but sabotage was sabotage, and all we could do was sit in the front room of the local hotel and drink coffee. I asked about Professor Mehta. The young hotel-owner said the Professor was not only his adviser but also a personal friend. He went out to telephone and came back with the news that the Professor was coming over as soon as he had finished his supper.

"From the beginning I've had faith in astrology," Mr. Mukut said. "Every year I have a reading on my birthday. On the 30th of January I entered my sixty-ninth year and I had a reading then."

He wouldn't say what he had been promised. And when I asked whether Professor Mehta was his astrologer he gave his crooked long-lipped smile and didn't reply.

He became reflective. "An election has three stages. There's the excitement of the campaign. Then there's the tension. Then the reaction, whatever the result."

"What are you prepared for?"

He opened his sightless eyes. *"Anything."*

But then he was restless; he wanted to leave; and he was led out to his car.

Professor Mehta was a small fat clean-shaven man of sixty in trousers and shirt. He had the distant manner of an overworked physician who has heard everything. He was unwilling to speak. As soon as he understood what I wanted he began to write, very fast, on a foolscap sheet: *Mrs. Indira will win her own election by more than 50,000 votes. But she won't be able to get full majority in Centre . . .*

I FEEL that after the busyness of the headquarters, and after the excitement of the drive, the mood of Mr. Mukut's men changed there, in the stuffy little room of the Beawar hotel, when Mr. Mukut's face clouded at the thought of the sabotaged evening.

On Sunday morning some of his supporters had premonitions of defeat. They came to me, as to an impartial witness, with stories that Mr. Bishweshwar's men were distributing liquor in two wards of the city, and with the warning that the next day there would be leaflets, purporting to come from Mr. Mukut, saying that he had withdrawn, that he had all along been for Mrs. Gandhi.

Premonitions of defeat. And in the morning the disaster was clear. Outside every polling booth on the road to Nasirabad there was a decorated Indira Congress tent, where young men sat with electoral rolls and waited to receive voters. At half past ten, the sun already blazing, some of

Mr. Mukut's tents were only just going up; and in some places there were no tents and sometimes not even tables. Mr. Mukut's son, defeat on his face, spoke of sabotage. Outside one booth two of Mr. Mukut's workers stood forlorn, separate from the crowd; one of them shrugged and said, "Harijan area."

In Nasirabad one young man was close to tears. The Congress had ruled in Rajasthan for as long as he could remember; it was rotten and corrupt and had at last seemed about to wither away; now Mrs. Gandhi had preserved it. "You've won, you've won," he said to Mr. Kudal; and Mr. Kudal, sympathetic to the young man's pain, blinked fast.

The Congress had not withered away. Its organization had remained intact and was behind Mrs. Gandhi and Mr. Bishweshwar. The Congress hadn't really split. There had only been defections, sufficient to provide acclamation and crowds (deceptive in a constituency with half a million voters) and what Mr. Kudal had called *tamashas*, excitements. In Ajmer the Opposition or Organization Congress, on whose behalf Mr. Mukut was standing, was a phantom party.

But Mr. Mukut also had the Jan Sangh. The Jan Sangh was strong in Ajmer City, and a bonus was that the poll there was usually high, 70 per cent as against 50 per cent in the rural areas. With a good majority in Ajmer City—dependent on a good poll—Mr. Mukut might still be in the fight. But it was in the Jan Sangh areas of the city that Mr. Mukut's disaster was most plain. In Naya Bazaar, the area of small traders, a Jan Sangh stronghold, the poll at one o'clock was under 40 per cent; and Mr. Mukut's election tent, without a table (and the formality that imposes), only with a long bench, was overrun by small children and already looked abandoned.

The Jan Sangh voters were abstaining. It was the possibility Mr. Mukut had always discounted. By allying itself with other parties, by supporting Mr. Mukut, its old enemy, by softening its racial-communal Hindu line, the Jan Sangh had compromised its right-wing purity. It had ceased to be a crusade; in the eyes of its supporters it had become as "political" and tricky as any other party. And later that afternoon, when the news everywhere was that Mr. Mukut was losing, some of those Jan Sangh abstainers were to go out and vote against him.

At half past four, half an hour before the booths closed, there were three people in Mr. Mukut's campaign headquarters: a wizened old secretary at a table with a telephone that was now idle, a thin black-capped accountant in a dhoti who sat with his legs drawn up on a straight-backed chair, and a boy. Someone came in with a bill. The black-capped accountant, without changing his posture, considered the bill and spiked it. I stretched out an inquisitive hand towards the spike. Wordlessly, the accountant spun the spike away from me to the boy, who put it in a corner of the paper-littered floor.

Mr. Bishweshwar, surrounded by his workers, sat in a basket-chair on the open concrete porch of his villa headquarters. He was in a state of great, laughing excitement and he was shouting into a telephone. Most of his workers were in trousers, shirts and pullovers. But Mr. Bishweshwar was in his politician's costume of homespun dhoti and koortah, the white panoply that spoke of Gandhian merit and, now, of its political rewards, all the things that went with being a member of parliament: the flat in New Delhi, the two free telephones, fifty-one rupees a day during parliamentary sittings, free first-class rail travel throughout India (with priority in reservations), and five hundred rupees a month.

It was some time before I saw that Mrs. Bishweshwar was also there, still and withdrawn, standing on the open porch as on a stage, draped in a dark-green sari, her head bowed and modestly covered in the presence of so many men: like a sorrowing classical figure, a symbol of downtrodden Indian womanhood.

TEN DAYS LATER, after the remoter districts had voted, the count took place. The weather had turned, the heat was beginning; and on Highway 8 there were handcarts with little conical heaps of green and red powder for the gaieties of the Festival of Spring on the following day. The counting was done in a marquee in the Collectorate yard. Neither Mr. Bishweshwar nor Mr. Mukut was there. "The commander-in-chief doesn't have to be at the front," a counter said.

And Mr. Mukut was spending this, the longest day of his political career, in his flat. It was going to be worse for him than we had expected. In Ajmer City—the counting was done district by district—he had only got nineteen thousand votes; Mr. Bishweshwar had forty-three thousand.

I said to Mr. Mukut's son, "So Professor Mehta advised you wrongly?"

"He didn't *advise* us wrongly. His calculations were wrong."

Mr. Bishweshwar was at his campaign headquarters. He was used now to his victory; he was at peace, but tired. The election had been a strain; he didn't share Mr. Kudal's delight in the "sports" side. He had suffered at that moment when important people had seemed about to defect. He had been badly frightened by the Rawats, and he hadn't forgiven that damaging leaflet. "I'm going to sue. Let them apologize and so on. There's a lakh or two there."

But he had suffered mostly because of Mr. Mukut, in whose shadow he had lived for so long. I asked whether he thought they might now have broken for good. He said, "I don't know. I went to see him yesterday. He didn't talk to me." And Mr. Bishweshwar was anxious to show that he too, though young, had a record of service and sacrifice. He hadn't been to jail, like Mr. Mukut; but because of his social work he hadn't found time to marry until he was thirty-two. "From the beginning I was interested in social service. I was scoutmaster in Government College. I don't know why, the poorer sections always attracted me. Since 1952 I have devoted myself to the peasantry."

He made it sound like a hobby. He had modelled himself on his uncle; he too was half Gandhian, half politician, and claimed the right to exercise political power because he had earned religious merit. And Mr. Bishweshwar might so easily have been on the other side, against Mrs. Gandhi. "It was a testing time for me," he said, speaking of the Congress split, "the choice between principle and personality." In the end he had managed to combine both: Gandhian principle and Mrs. Gandhi's personality.

All afternoon his lead lengthened. At last it reached sixty-six thousand. Mr. Mukut, in the days of his glory, had never had such a majority. The caste issues had nowhere mattered. The Kishangarh affair hadn't mattered; nor had the Rawat enticement. Only Udaipur's tour had had some effect. In that remote district, where he was a god, Udaipur had cut Mr. Bishweshwar's lead to just over three thousand. The electorate had everywhere voted for Mrs. Gandhi and *Garibi Hatao*; they had voted out of their common distress and need.

At about half past three Mr. Bishweshwar and his wife came to the Collectorate. They were both in homespun, he in white, she in blue. He was smiling quite helplessly; she was abashed and delicate. As they walked up the middle of the marquee all of us at the District Magistrate's table rose. Someone ran up with a garland of gold and silver tinsel: it was for Mr. Kudal, the triumphant election agent. The second garland, of marigold and white champa flowers, was for Mr. Bishweshwar.

Outside, the crowd grew. And when, just before the results were announced, Mr. and Mrs. Bishweshwar left, going out the way they had come, the counters, who hadn't saluted their arrival, stood up with palms joined in the gesture of greeting and respect. The brass band, waiting outside, struck up *Colonel Bogey*. There was a float with the cow and calf in white. Men in a packed jeep scattered coloured powder on the crowd: the Festival of Spring, occurring one day early. And copies were being distributed of a one-sheet "extra" of the Hindi *Rajasthan Patrika*:

BISHWESHWAR GETS HUGE MAJORITY
Nephew Crushes Uncle

I thought I would go to Mr. Mukut.

"I will come with you," Mr. Kudal said. And when we were in the car he said, "I must come with you. Terrible. A man who has controlled the destinies of this district for two decades, to be defeated now by his nephew, his own creature."

In the top floor flat the unlined curtains were drawn in the front room and Mr. Mukut sat cross-legged and still on his narrow bed. His eyes were closed and his head was held to one side. He was in clean white cotton, and the white was momentarily shocking, like the colour of death and grief. Half a dozen men, among them the black-capped accountant, were sitting silent on a spread on the terrazzo floor. Mr. Kudal didn't speak; he went and sat on the floor with the others.

Mr. Mukut's son came out and offered me a chair. He bent over his father, said, "Bapuji," and gave Mr. Kudal's name and mine. At first Mr. Mukut didn't move. Then, abruptly, he turned his head to face the room and, in a terrible gesture of grief, beat the back of his open hand hard on the bed.

No one spoke.

Mr. Mukut's son brought out tea. He pulled the curtain open a little way: the barred, wire-netted window, the sunlight on the white wall of the terrace, the brown hills. He hung a brown waistcoat on his father's shoulders and the effect of the white was softened.

"They were canvassing votes for Indira," Mr. Mukut said, "not for the candidate. Nowhere was the candidate in the picture." He hadn't yet accepted his defeat; he still dealt in the politics of personal merit. I asked whether he and Mr. Bishweshwar might be friends again. He said, "I don't know. He came here yesterday. But he didn't say a word to me." He turned on the transistor and the six o'clock English news from Delhi was of Mrs. Gandhi's landslide victory all over the country, of the defeat everywhere of old Congressmen who had miscalculated like Mr. Mukut.

"There are no morals now," Mr. Mukut said. "The Machiavellian politics of Europe have begun to touch our own politics and we will go down."

Mr. Kudal stood up.

"As election agent I have to make an appearance in the procession," Mr. Kudal said, when we were outside. "Otherwise my absence will be misinterpreted."

We caught up with the procession in the bazaar. Men in open lorries were pelting everybody with little balls of coloured powder. "Give me seven minutes," Mr. Kudal said, and disappeared into the crowd. When he came back his clothes and hair and face were satisfactorily stained with red. Red the colour of spring and triumph, and sacrifice.

1971

AFRICA
AND THE
DIASPORA

Papa and the Power Set

AFTER more than twenty years as a folk leader, one of the Negro shepherd-kings of the Caribbean, Robert Bradshaw of St. Kitts—"Papa" to his followers—is in trouble. Two years ago he became the first Premier of the three-island state of St. Kitts–Nevis–Anguilla. The state had a total area of 153 square miles and a population of 57,000. It has since become smaller. Anguilla has seceded and apparently gone for good, with its own islet dependencies of Scrub Island, Dog Island and Anguillita: a loss of 35 square miles and 6,000 people. There is discontent in Nevis, 50 square miles. In St. Kitts itself, Papa Bradshaw's base, there is a dangerous opposition.

The opposition union is called WAM, the opposition political party PAM. WAM and PAM: it is part of the deadly comic-strip humour of Negro politics. These are still only the politics of kingship, in which there are as yet no rules for succession. It is only when leaders like Papa Bradshaw are in trouble, when they are threatened and fight back, that they become known outside their islands; and it is an irony of their kingship that they are then presented as dangerous clowns. Once Papa Bradshaw's yellow Rolls-Royce was thought to be a suitable emblem of his kingship and courage, a token of Negro redemption. Few people outside knew about the Rolls-Royce; now it is famous and half a joke.

The folk leader who has been challenged cannot afford to lose. To lose is to be without a role, to be altogether ridiculous.

"Papa Bradsha' started something," a supporter says. "As long as he lives he will have to continue it."

Bradshaw prepares to continue. The opposition are not allowed to broadcast; their supporters say they do not find it easy to get jobs. Men are recruited from the other Caribbean islands for the police. The St. Kitts army, called the Defence Force, is said to have been increased to 120; Papa Bradshaw is the Colonel. There are reports of a helicopter ready to police the island's sixty-eight square miles.

It has been played out in other countries, this drama of the folk leader who rules where he once securely agitated and finds that power has brought insecurity. In St. Kitts the scale is small, and in the simplicity of the setting the situation appears staged.

THINK of a Caribbean island roughly oval in shape. Indent the coastline: beaches here, low cliffs there. Below the sharp and bare 4,000-foot peak of a central mountain chain there is a forest. Then the land slopes green and trimmed with sugar-cane, uncluttered with houses or peasant allotments, all the way down to the sea. A narrow coast road encircles the island; it is impossible to get lost. The plantation workers live beside this road, squeezed between sugar-cane and sea. Their timber houses are among the tiniest in the world.

All the history of St. Kitts is on this road. There, among those houses on low stilts, whose dirt yards run down through tangled greenery to the sea, Sir Thomas Warner landed in 1623, to found the first British colony in the West Indies. Here, in the barest opening in the sugar-cane, are two rocks crudely carved by the aboriginal Caribs, whom the English and French united to exterminate just there, at Bloody River, now a dip in the road. Sir Thomas Warner is buried in that churchyard. Not far away are the massive eighteenth-century fortifications of Brimstone Hill, once guarding the sugar-rich slave islands and the convoys that assembled in the calm water here for the run to England. The cannons still point; the site has been restored.

In the south-east the flat coastal strip broadens out into a little plain. Here, still set in the level green of sugar-cane, are the air-strip and the capital, Basseterre. There is one vertical in this plain: the tall white chimney of the island's single sugar factory.

The neatness and order is still like the order of the past. It speaks of Papa Bradshaw's failure. He hasn't changed much. His fame came early, as an organizer of the sugar workers; a thirteen-week strike in 1948 is part of the island's folk-lore. But Bradshaw's plantation victories mean less today to the young. They do not wish to work on the plantations. They look for "development"—and they mean tourism—on their own island. The air over nearby Antigua rocks with "Sunjets" and "Fiesta Jets." St. Kitts only has brochures and plans; the airfield can only take Viscounts. It is unspoiled; the tourists do not come. The feeling among the young is that Papa Bradshaw has sold out to the sugar interests and wants no change.

And Bradshaw's victories were only of St. Kitts. They meant little to the peasant farmers of Nevis, and nothing to the long-independent farmers and fishermen of Anguilla, seventy miles away. The Nevisians and Anguillans never voted for Bradshaw. Bradshaw didn't need their votes, but he was irritated. He said he would put pepper in the soup of the Nevisians and bones in their rice; he would turn Anguilla into a desert and make the Anguillans suck salt. That was eleven years ago.

"Gahd bless Papa Bradsha' for wa' he do." It is only the old and the devout among the plantation Negroes in St. Kitts who say that now. They remember the *ola* or trash houses, the cruel contract system, the barefoot children and the disease. Bradshaw himself worked as a young man in the Basseterre sugar factory; he carries a damaged hand as a mark of that service. Like many folk leaders, he never moved far beyond his first inspiration. It is also true that, like many folk leaders, he is responsible for the hope and the restlessness by which he is now, at the age of fifty-one, rejected.

THE WEATHERBEATEN little town of Basseterre also has a stage-set simplicity. There is a church at the end of the main street. PAM hangs its home-made board in the veranda of a rickety little house. Directly opposite is a building as rickety, but larger; this is labelled "Masses House" and is the headquarters of the Bradshaw union. At times of tension this section of the main street is known as the Gaza Strip.

Masses House has a printery which every day runs off 1,200 copies of a ragged miniature newspaper called *The Labour Spokesman*. Even with large headlines there isn't always enough news to fill the front page; sometimes a joke, headlined "Humour," has to be added. Sport is good for a page or two or three. A cricketer like Sobers can make the local sportswriter ambitious. "The shy boy of seventeen, not yet lost his Mother's features on his debut against England in the West Indies in 1954, has probably rose to the pinnacle of being the greatest cricketer both of our time and the medieval age. If W. G. Grace were to twitch in his grave at the comment he would only turn over on the other side to nod his approval."

A few doors away from Masses House is Government Headquarters, a modernistic building of three storeys. Grey air conditioners project from its façade; a pool in the patio is visible through the glass wall. The hotel is opposite, a converted old timber house. The manager is a gentle second-generation Lebanese whose nerves have been worn fine by the harassments of his large family, his staff, untrained or temperamental, the occasional assertive Negro group, and the political situation. "Have you seen our Premier, sir?" He supports Bradshaw but avoids controversy; he knows now he will never see Beirut.

A short side street leads to Pall Mall Square: the church, the timbered colonial-Georgian Public Library and Court, the St. Kitts Club, the private houses with lower floors of masonry, upper floors shingled, white and fragile, and steep four-sided roofs. The garden is unkempt, the wire fences around the central Victorian fountain trampled down, the lamp-standards empty and rusting; but the trees and flowers and the backdrop of mountains are still spectacular. Pall Mall Square is where PAM holds its public meetings. It is also, as all St. Kitts knows, the place where, among trees and flowers and buildings like these, "new" Negroes from Africa were put up for auction, after being rested and nourished in the importers' barracoons, which were there, on the beach, not far from today's oil-storage tanks.

The past crowds the tiny island like the sugar-cane itself. Deeper and deeper protest is always possible.

AT ABOUT ten every morning the guards change outside Government Headquarters. The green-bereted officer shouts, boots stamp; and the two relieved soldiers, looking quickly up and down the street, get into the back of the idling Land-Rover and are driven to Defence Force Headquarters, an exposed wooden hut on high ground near ZIZ, the one-studio radio station.

Against the soft green hills beyond Basseterre, the bright blue sea and the cloud-topped peak of Nevis, a Negro lounges in a washed-out para-trooper's uniform, thin and bandy-legged, zipped-up and tight, like a soft toy.

It seems to be drama for the sake of drama. But there are bullet marks on the inside of the hut. These are shown as evidence of the armed raid that was made on Basseterre by persons unknown in June 1967, at the beginning of the Anguillan crisis. The police station was also attacked.

Many shots were fired but no one was killed; the raiders disappeared. Bradshaw added to his legend by walking the next morning from Government Headquarters to Masses House in the uniform of a Colonel, with a rifle, bandolier, and binoculars.

The raid remains a mystery. Some people believe it was staged, but there are Anguillans who now say that they were responsible and that their aim was to protect the independence of their island by kidnapping Bradshaw and holding him as a hostage. The raid failed because it was badly organized—no one had thought about transport in Basseterre—and because Bradshaw had been tipped off by an Anguillan businessman.

Days after the raid leading members of PAM and WAM were arrested. They went on trial four months later. Defence lawyers were harassed; and Bradshaw's supporters demonstrated when all the accused men were acquitted. Ever since, the rule of law in St. Kitts has appeared to be in danger. The definition of power has become simple.

> *I see them*:
> *These bold men; these rare men—*
> *Above all other men that toil—*
> *That LIVE the truth; that suffer:*
> *These policemen. We love them!*

The poem is from *The Labour Spokesman*. There may no longer be a danger from Anguilla, but the police and the army have come to St. Kitts to stay.

I FIRST saw St. Kitts eight years ago, at night, from a broken-down immigrant ship in Basseterre harbour. We didn't land. The emigrants had been rocking for some time in the bay in large open boats. The ship's lights played on sweated shirts and dresses, red eyes in upturned oily faces, cardboard boxes and suitcases painted with names and careful addresses in England.

In the morning, on the open sea, the nightmare was over. The jackets and ties and the suitcases had gone. The emigrants, as I found out, moving among them, were politically educated. Copies of *The Labour Spokesman* were about. Many of the emigrants from Anguilla, which had been recently hit by a hurricane, were in constant touch with God.

The emigrants had a leader. He was a slender young mulatto, going to England to do law. He moved among the emigrants like a trusted agitator; he was protective. He was a man of some background and his political concern, in such circumstances, seemed unusual. He mistrusted my inquiries. He thought I was a British agent and told the emigrants not to talk to me. They became unfriendly; word spread that I had called one of them a nigger. I was rescued from the adventure by a young Baptist missionary.

I didn't get the name of the ship-board leader then. In St. Kitts and the Caribbean he is now famous. He did more than study law. He returned to St. Kitts to challenge Bradshaw. He founded PAM. He has been jailed, tried, and acquitted; he is only thirty-one. He is Dr. William Herbert. A good deal of his magic in St. Kitts, his power to challenge, comes from that title of Doctor—obtained for a legal thesis—which he was then travelling to London to get.

He came into the Basseterre hotel dining-room one morning. As soon as we were introduced he reminded me of our last meeting. The ship, he said, was Spanish and disorganized and he was young. He was as restless and swift and West Indian–handsome as I had remembered: his five months in jail have not marked him.

"I don't want to frighten you," he said, when he came to see me later that day. "But you should be careful. Writers can disappear. Two soldiers will be watching the hotel tonight."

We drove to a rusting seaside bar, deserted, a failed tourist amenity.

"Have you seen Bradshaw?"

I said that the feeling in Government Headquarters was that I might be a British agent. Mr. Bradshaw wouldn't give an interview, but he had come over to the hotel one morning to greet me.

"He's an interesting man. He knows a lot about African art and magic and so on. It perhaps explains his hold, you know."

We went to look at Frigate Bay, part of the uninhabited area of scrub and salt-ponds which is attached like a tail to the oval mass of St. Kitts. The government had recently announced a £29-million tourist development plan for Frigate Bay. Some in-transit cruise passengers had been taken to inspect the site a few days before; *The Labour Spokesman* had announced it as the start of the tourist season.

"Development!" Herbert said, waving at the desolation. "If you come here at night they shoot you, you know. It's a military area. They say we are trying to sabotage."

On the way back we detoured through some Basseterre slum streets. Herbert waved at women and children. *"How, how, man?"* Many waved back. He said it was his method, concentrating on the women and children; they drew the men in.

HERBERT is the first and only Ph.D. in St. Kitts. Beside him, Bradshaw is archaic, the leader of people lifted up from despair, the man of the people who in power achieves a personal style which all then feel they share. In St. Kitts and the West Indies Bradshaw is now a legend, for the gold swizzle-stick he is reputed to bring out at parties to stir his champagne, the gold brush for his moustache, the formal English dress, even the silk hose and buckle shoes on some ceremonial occasions, the vintage yellow Rolls-Royce. He has a local reputation for his knowledge of antiques and African art and for his book-reading. He is believed to be a member of several book clubs. He reads much Winston Churchill; his favourite book, his PRO told me, is *The Good Earth*; his favourite comic strip, *Li'l Abner*.

It is an attractive legend. But I found him subdued, in dress and speech. I was sorry he didn't want to talk more to me; he said he had suffered much from writers. I understood. I looked at his moustache and thought of the gold brush. He is well-built, a young fifty-one, one of those men made ordinary by their photographs. We talked standing up. His speech was precise, very British, with little of St. Kitts in his accent. He stood obliquely to me; he wore dark glasses. As we walked down the hotel steps to the Land-Rover with his party's slogan, "Labour Leads," he told me he was pessimistic about the future of small countries like St. Kitts. He worked, but he was full of despair. He had supported the West Indian Federation, but that had failed. And it is true that Bradshaw began to lose his grip on St. Kitts during his time as a minister in the West Indian Federal Government, whose headquarters was in Trinidad.

The Negro folk leader is a peasant leader. St. Kitts is like a black English parish, far from the source of beauty and fashion. The folk leader who emerges requires, by his exceptional gifts, to be absorbed into that higher society of which the parish is a shadow. For leaders like Bradshaw, though, there is no such society. They are linked forever to the primitives who were the source of their original power. They are doomed to smallness; they have to create their own style. Christophe, Emperor of Haiti, creator of a Negro aristocracy with laughable names, came from this very island of St. Kitts, where he was a slave and a tailor; the inspiration for the Citadel in Haiti came from those fortifications at Brimstone Hill beside the littoral road.

THE DIFFERENCE between Herbert and Bradshaw is the difference between Herbert's title of Doctor and Bradshaw's title of Papa. Each man's manner seems to contradict his title. Herbert has none of Bradshaw's applied style. His out-of-court dress is casual; his car is old; the house he is building outside Basseterre is the usual St. Kitts miniature. His speech is more colloquial than Bradshaw's, his accent more local. His manners are at once middle-class and popular, one mode containing the other. He never strains; he moves with the assurance of his class and his looks. To all this he adds the Ph.D.

"Tell me," Bradshaw's black PRO asked with some bitterness, "who do you think is the more educated man? Herbert or Bradshaw?"

It would have been too sophisticated a question to put to the young and newly educated who went to Herbert's early lectures on economics, law, and political theory in Pall Mall Square.

"Studyation is better than education," Bradshaw said, comforting his ageing illiterates from the canefields. It became one of his *mots*.

But Herbert grew as the leader of literate protest. Everything became his cause. New electricity rates were announced: large users were to pay less per unit. Standard practice in other countries, but Herbert and PAM said the new rates were unfair to the poor of St. Kitts. The poor agreed.

Bradshaw and one of his ministers became law students; Bradshaw was almost fifty. The faded notifications of their enrolment in a London Inn are still displayed in the portico of the Court in Pall Mall Square; both men were said to be eating dinners during their official trips to London. Then Anguilla seceded; PAM and WAM were as troublesome as their names; the world press was hostile. Herbert, jailed, tried, acquitted, became a Caribbean figure. Bradshaw was isolated. He appeared to be on the way out. But then he recruited a young St. Kitts lawyer-lecturer as his Public Relations Officer.

This man has saved Bradshaw, and in a few months he has given a new twist to St. Kitts politics. Bradshaw's tactics have changed. He is no longer the established leader on the defensive, attracting fresh agitation. He has become once again the leader of protest. It is in protest that he now competes with Herbert. The young PRO has provided the lectures and the intellectual backing. He is known to the irreverent as Bradshaw's Race Relations Officer. The cause is Black Power.

The avowed aim is the dismantling of that order which the geography of the island illustrates. The word the PRO sometimes uses is Revolution. The word has got to the white suburb of Fortlands and the Golf Club, where the little group of English expatriates is known as the Whisperers.

Someone put it like this: "What Bradshaw now wants to do is to make a fresh start, with the land and the people."

The politics of St. Kitts today, opaque to the visitor looking for principles and areas of difference, become clearer as soon as it is realized that both parties are parties of protest, in the vacuum of independence; and that for both parties the cause of protest is that past, of slavery. What is at stake is the kingship, and this has recently been simplified. The difficult message of Black Power—identity, economic involvement, solidarity, as the PRO defines it—has become mangled in transmission. It can now be heard that Bradshaw, for all the English aspirations of his past, is a full-blooded Ashanti. Herbert is visibly mulatto.

Herbert's father was Labour Relations Officer for the sugar industry at the time of Bradshaw's famous thirteen-week strike. It was a difficult time for the Herbert family. They were threatened and abused by the strikers; and the St. Kitts story is that Herbert, still a boy, met Bradshaw in the street one day and vowed to get even. Herbert says the meeting may have taken place, but he doesn't remember it.

I asked him now whether power in St. Kitts was worth the time, the energy, the dangers.

"A man is in the sea," Herbert said. "He must swim."

THERE is still a Government House in St. Kitts, a modest, wide-verandaed timber house on an airy hill. The butler wears white; a lithograph of a local scene, a gift of the Queen, hangs in the drawing-room; there is a signed photograph of the Duke of Edinburgh. The governor is a Negro knight from another island, a much respected lawyer and academic. He is without a role; he is isolated from the local politics of kingship, this fight between the lawyers, in which the rule of law may go. He has spent much of his time in Government House working on a study of recent West Indian constitution-making. It is called *The Way to Power*.

THE PRO on whom Bradshaw depends, the lawyer-lecturer to whom he has surrendered part of his power, is Lee Moore, a short, slight, bearded, country-born Negro of about thirty. Moore says that when he came back to St. Kitts from London he rejected the view that what was needed in St. Kitts was a Negro aristocracy. But the political usefulness of Black Power was only accidentally discovered, in the excitement that followed a lecture he gave on the subject.

Now, like Herbert, Lee Moore drives around the circular St. Kitts road, mixing law business with campaigning, waving, mixing gravity with heartiness. On his car there is a sticker, cut out from a petrol advertisement: *Join the Power Set*.

I made a tour with him late one afternoon. Shortly after nightfall we had a puncture. He was unwilling to use the jack; he said he didn't know where to put it. He crouched and peered; he was confused. Some cars went by without stopping. I began to fear for his clothes and dignity. Then two cyclists passed. They shouted and came back to help. "We thought it was one of those brutes," one of them said. A van stopped. The jack wasn't used. The car was lifted while the wheel was changed.

Moore was in a state of some excitement when we drove off again, and it was a little time before I understood that is was an important triumph.

"It's how I always change a wheel. Did you hear what those boys on the cycles shouted? *'It's Lee Moore's car.'*"

Power, the willing services of the simple and the protecting: another man of the people in the making, another Negro on the move.

After a while he said reflectively, "If it was Herbert he would still be there, I can tell you."

Herbert, though, might have used the jack.

1969

The Shipwrecked
Six Thousand

AMONG the green and hilly islands of the Caribbean Anguilla is like a mistake, a sport. It is seventeen miles long and two miles wide and so flat that when Anguillans give you directions they don't tell you to turn right or left; they say east or west. It is rocky and arid. There are no palm trees, no big trees. Mangrove is thick above the beaches, which look as they must have done when Columbus came. The forests that then existed have long been cut down; and the Anguillans, charcoal-burners and boat-builders, are the natural enemies of anything green that looks like growing big.

Sugar-cane used to grow in some places, but even in the days of slavery it was never an island of plantations. In 1825, nine years before the abolition of slavery in the British Empire, there were about three hundred white people and three hundred free coloureds, people of mixed race. Between them they kept about three thousand Negroes. The Negroes were a liability. On other Caribbean islands Negroes were let off on Saturdays to work on their own plots. In Anguilla they were turned loose for half the week to forage for themselves.

Today there are only about twelve thousand Anguillans. Half of them live or work overseas, in the nearby United States Virgin Islands, in Harlem, and in Slough in Buckinghamshire, known locally as Slough-bucks. But there are houses and plots for most of them to return to; the desolate island has long been parcelled out.

In mid-December last year, when I was there, the island was filling up for Christmas. The Viscount aircraft of LIAT, Leeward Islands Air Transport ("We fly where buccaneers sailed"), had stopped calling ever since Anguilla rebelled in 1967 and broke away from the newly independent three-island British Commonwealth state of St. Kitts–Nevis–Anguilla. But the Anguillans (after chasing away an American and his

DC-3) had set up three fiercely competitive little airlines of their own, Air Anguilla, Anguilla Airways, Valley Air Services, each with its own livery and its own five-passenger Piper Aztecs regularly doing the five-minute, five-dollar connecting hop from St. Martin.

More than any other Caribbean community, the Anguillans have the sense of home. The land has been theirs immemorially; no humiliation attaches to it. There are no Great Houses, as in St. Kitts; there are not even ruins.

FOR THE ANGUILLANS history begins with the myth of a shipwreck. This was how the white founders came, the ancestors of the now multi-coloured clans of Flemings, Hodges, Richardsons, Websters, Gumbs. About the arrival of the Negroes there is some confusion. Many know they were imported as slaves. But one young man was sure they were here before the shipwreck. Another felt they had come a year or two after. He didn't know how or why. "I forget that part." The past does not count. The Anguillans have lived for too long like a shipwrecked community.

They are not well educated. Instead, they have skills, like boatbuilding, and religion, which is a continual excitement. Few Anguillans act without divine guidance. The Anguillan exodus to Sloughbucks that began in 1960 had the sanction of God; and a similar certitude is behind the secession from St. Kitts and the boldness of many recent Anguillan actions.

So close to God, the Anguillans are not fanatical. They have the Negro openness to new faiths. Eight years ago Mr. Webster, the now deposed President, re-thought his position and, at the age of thirty-four, left the Anglicans for the Seventh Day Adventists. He would like to see more and varied missionary activity on the island. "If the Jehovah's Witnesses or any other denomination convert one or ten souls they are doing a good job and serving the community. Because our basic plan is to keep Anguillans as pious as possible. This keeps out partial and immoral thoughts."

The island has its own prophet, Judge Gumbs, Brother George Gumbs (Prophet), as he signs his messages to the new local weekly. He is not without honour; he is consulted by high and low. When the spirit moves him he cycles around with a fife and drum, "a short black man with a cap" (an Anguillan description), preaching and sometimes warning. He is said to get a frenzied feeling about a particular place, a field, a stretch of road; a few days later the disaster occurs. In December, three or four days after Mr. Webster said that Anguilla was going to leave the Commonwealth altogether, Judge Gumbs was out, preaching. I didn't see him, but I was told he had no news; he just asked the people to pray. No news from Judge Gumbs was good news.

Certain other reverences remain, to bind the community: certain families act or take decisions in times of crisis. The reverences follow the antique patterns, whose origins have been forgotten. Colour is accidental, and nothing angers the Anguillans more than the propaganda from St. Kitts, seventy miles away, that their rebellion is the rebellion of a slave island, with the blacks loyally following the whites and browns. The reverences are of Anguilla, and the Anguillans describe themselves as Negroes. Mr. Webster, who could be of any race between the Mediterranean and India, describes himself as a Negro. It is true: losing the historical sense, the Anguillans have also lost the racial sense. It isn't an easy thing to put across, especially to St. Kitts, which is now playing with its own concept of Black Power.

ANGUILLANS have never liked being administratively linked with St. Kitts, and they have hated Robert Bradshaw, the St. Kitts Premier, ever since, angered by their indifference, he said he would turn the island into a desert and make the Anguillans suck salt. They were frightened by the idea of an independent St. Kitts–Nevis–Anguilla under Bradshaw's rule; and there was a riot in February 1967, when, as part of the independence celebrations, St. Kitts sent over some beauty queens to give a show in the Anguilla High School. The police used tear gas, but inefficiently. They gassed the queens and the loyal audience, not the enraged Anguillans outside. Reinforcements from St. Kitts's one-hundred-man police force were flown in the next day. Houses were searched; the Anguillan leaders took to the bush.

It was the signal for a general revolt. The Warden's house was set on fire; the Warden fled. From time to time during the next three months shots were fired at the police station at night. The hotel where the acting Warden was staying was set on fire; he too left. The next day the bank manager was attacked. Two days later several hundred Anguillans rushed the police station. The seventeen policemen offered no fight; they were put on a plane and sent back to St. Kitts; and the Anguillans set up their own five-man police force.

Ten days later, fearing outside intervention (Jamaica nearly sent in troops), and guided now by that religious certitude, the Anguillans raided St. Kitts and shot up the police station and Defence Force Headquarters. The raid, by twelve men, was openly planned; people went down to the wharf in the afternoon to wave as the fifty-foot cutter left for St. Kitts. Five and a half hours later the cutter tied up, quite simply, at the main pier in St. Kitts. Then the Anguillans discovered they hadn't thought about motorcars. They had intended to kidnap Bradshaw; they had to be content with scaring him.

Some time later there was a report that thirty-five men from St. Kitts had invaded Anguilla. The man who was the Provisional President flew over the reported landing area in an Aztec, dropping leaflets asking the invaders to surrender. But there were no invaders. The fighting was over. All that followed were words; secession was a fact. Anguilla had become the world's smallest republic.

Its status was ambiguous. It still considered itself within the Commonwealth. It looked to London for a constitutional settlement, for some sanction of its separation from St. Kitts. London didn't know what to do. For more than two hundred years, in fact, no one had really wanted Anguilla or had known what to do with it. The place was a mistake.

IT HAD ITS FORMALITIES. When you got off the Piper Aztec you went through Anguillan Immigration and Customs; they were both in one room of the two-roomed airport building. The Immigration man had a khaki uniform, an Anguilla badge, and an Anguilla rubber-stamp. You needed an Anguillan driving licence; it cost a dollar; you paid at the Police Station in the long low Administration Building. The five-man police force was enough; there was little crime. Women quarrelled and used four-letter words; the police visited and "warned"; that, in the main, was the routine. There was a jail, and there was one prisoner. He had been there for a year, a St. Kitts man on a charge of murder. There was no magistrate to try him. Mr. Webster was hoping to deport the man as soon as the secession issue was settled.

In the Post Office you bought Anguillan stamps, designed and produced by an English firm and sold by them to overseas collectors for a

15 per cent commission. Incoming mails were regular; Anguilla had beaten the St. Kitts postal ban by having two box numbers on the half-French, half-Dutch island of St. Martin. In the Treasury, next door to the Post Office, there was a notice about the new 2 per cent income tax. Other taxes, on liquor and petrol, had been lowered, to increase consumption and revenue; and it had worked. People told me there were more cars in Anguilla than ever before.

The administration, spare and efficient, had been inherited with the Administration Building. An elected fifteen-man Council ruled. This structure of government was like sophistication in a community that had for long organized itself around its own reverences. The island ran itself; it worked. After half a day the visitor had to remind himself of size and quaintness. It was there, in the new flag, designed by some Americans: a circle of three orange dolphins on white, a lower stripe of turquoise. And in the fanciful anthem, composed by a local "group":

> . . . *An island where the golden corn is waving in the breeze!*
> *An island full of sunshine and where Nature e'er doth please.*

The visitor heard that the beaches were watched every night, in case St. Kitts invaded; that there were secret military exercises every fortnight; that the Anguillans had more than the four machine-guns, fifty-five rifles, fifteen shotguns, and two boxes of dynamite they had at the time of secession. There was talk of a repeat raid on St. Kitts; there was even a hint of a fighter being called in. St. Kitts was still claiming Anguilla and still advertising it in its tourist brochures ("Island of charm . . . for the holiday-seeker who wants to get away from it all"). But the Anguillans were secure. They knew that St. Kitts had its own political dissensions, that many people in St. Kitts were on their side, and that the 120-man St. Kitts army had enough to do at home. The Anguillans didn't talk much about Bradshaw and St. Kitts. They talked more of their own dissensions, their own politics.

Shipwrecked and isolated, the community had held together. With the quick semi-sophistication that had come with independence, the feeling that the island was quaint, famous, and tourist-precious, the old rules and reverences had begun to go. A few months before, on the quaint air-strip, the engine of a Piper Aztec had been smashed up at night with a hammer. Family rivalry was said to be the cause.

THERE is only one hotel with electricity in Anguilla, the Rendezvous. It is like a rough motel; and the lights go off at nine. It is owned by Jeremiah Gumbs, half-brother of Judge Gumbs, the prophet, and is run by Jeremiah's sister, who has spent many years in the United States and speaks with an American accent; the atmosphere of Negro America is strong.

I knew about Jeremiah Gumbs. He had been described to me as "the smart Anguillan," the only one who had made good in the United States. He was a considerable local benefactor; and he was Anguilla's link-man with the bigger world. He had given a number of interviews to American newspapers, had presented Anguilla's case at the United Nations, and had led an Anguillan delegation to the OAS building (they found it closed).

He was there, assessing and formidable (I had been told in St. Kitts never to laugh at Anguillans), while his sister showed me round.

"And here, young man, you can plug in your shaver. Which is more than you did this morning."

She was very large; she was called Lady B. I recognized her as a "character." Characters lie on my spirit like lead; and I resolved never to shave while I was at the Rendezvous.

At lunch Jeremiah, sucking fish, began to boom across the dining-room, at first as though to himself.

"They call it a rebellion." His accent too was American. "Most peaceful rebellion in the world. Rebellion? It's a rebellion against years of neglect, that's all. What's wrong with being small? Why shouldn't a small country have dignity? Why shouldn't a small country have pride? Why shouldn't—"

I tried to break into his harangue. "Gumbs. It's an old island name."

"One man," he said. "One man gave this island a library. One man set up the X-ray unit in the hospital. One man did all this. What did Bradshaw do? Police, plastic bombs, tear gas, things we never saw before. Now he says *I* am the big villain, the leader of the rebels."

I had heard no such thing.

"One man. Joe Louis. Marian Anderson. You get no more than one in a generation. It's because I care. I remember when I was a child we had four successive droughts in this island of Anguilla. I know what poverty is. I remember days in New York in the Depression when I didn't have the subway fare and had to walk one hundred blocks to school. Days when I didn't even eat an apple."

It hadn't marked him. He was an enormous man. Fifty-five, sharp-nosed, with a moustache and thin greying hair, he was like somebody out of those Negro Westerns of thirty years ago, *Two-Gun Man from Harlem*, *Harlem on the Prairie*. It was the way he ate, the way he walked and talked; it was the rock and the dust outside. He was the man opening up a territory.

"You come to write something, huh?"

I said, with acute shame, that I had.

"You go ahead and write. They come all the time. They sit on the beach and write all day long." His voice began to sing in the American way: "Just like Nature intended."

I resolved never to set foot on his beach.

We met that afternoon on the dusty road, he in his high jeep, a territory-opener, I in the low exposed mini-jeep I had rented from him.

"You making out all right?"

I was choking with dust and had already been lost twice (those Anguillan compass directions), but didn't tell him: he had sold me a map.

"You write and tell them. You tell them about this bunch of rebellious savages."

FOR A SHORT time after secession the Anguillans flew the flag of San Francisco, the gift of an editor who belonged to what is known in the island as the San Francisco Group. The Group took a whole-page advertisement in the *New York Times* in August 1967 for "The Anguilla White Paper," which they composed.

Anguillans, the White Paper said, were not backward simply because they didn't have telephones. "Do you know what one Anguillan does when he wants to telephone another Anguillan? He walks up the road and talks to him." But the absence of telephones was part of the case against St. Kitts; and it isn't easy to get about the island without a jeep. There are people in West End (where the people are mainly blackish, with occasional blond sports) who have never been to East End (where many of the fair people are).

Anguillans didn't "even want one Hiltonesque hotel"; it would turn them into "a nation of bus boys, waiters, and servants." They didn't want more than thirty "guests" at one time; it wouldn't be polite for a guest to go away without at least lunching with the President. They didn't want "tourists."

The White Paper—it offered honorary citizenship for $100—made $25,000 for Anguilla. Some Anguillans felt that they had been made ridiculous by the White Paper. But Mr. Webster, who signed it as Chief Executive, told me he stood by it. Jeremiah Gumbs, though, was extending his hotel; other people had put up establishments of their own of varying standards (the tourist future could still be one of rough bars and souvenir-stalls and ice-cream stands, very private enterprise); and Mr. Webster himself said that he would like to see Anguilla as a tourist resort.

It was part of the Anguillan confusion. Too many people had wanted to help, finding in Anguilla an easy cause, a little black comedy. The Anguillans, never seeing the joke, always listened and then grew frightened and self-willed.

One member of the San Francisco Group was Professor Leopold Kohr of the University of Puerto Rico, a sixty-year-old Austrian who went to live in America in 1938. Kohr has long promoted the theory of the happy small society; his book, *A Breakdown of Nations,* was published in London in 1957 (it is now out of print). In 1958 Kohr addressed the Welsh Nationalist Party that wants Wales to break away from England; he is now on a year's sabbatical at the University of Swansea. Kohr feels that small communities are "more viable economically than larger powers," and he thought Anguilla "the ideal testing ground." Immediately after secession the Anguillan leaders were beating up support in the nearby islands. They met Kohr and the San Francisco Group in Puerto Rico. "My team," Kohr says, "was accepted within twenty-four hours."

There appeared to be early proof of economic viability when it was rumoured that Aristotle Onassis had offered a million dollars a year for the right to use Anguilla as a flag base. The story is still current in the West Indies and Kohr still appears to believe in it. In St. Kitts and Anguilla, however, it was dismissed as one of Jeremiah Gumbs's stories. Mr. Webster, as Chief Executive, wrote twice to Onassis but got no reply. The commercial offers that did come from the United States were, in Kohr's words, from "interests of all shady shades."

A local man I met at the airport one Saturday—like market-day, then, with the cardboard boxes and baskets and parcels coming off the Aztecs, the women waiting for letters, messages, remittances from their men in the American Virgin Islands—a local man whispered to me about the Mafia and their agents among the local people. (From recent newspaper reports I feel he has been whispering to many other visitors.) I asked Mr. Webster about this. He said, puzzlingly, that this whispering about the Mafia was official Anguillan policy, to keep the Mafia away. He also asked me not to pay too much attention to white "stooges." At this stage I began to feel I was sinking in antique, inbred Anguillan intrigue.

There were people, though, who, while not wishing to go back to St. Kitts, had become less happy about the future than Mr. Webster or Professor Kohr. They had seen no "development" in a year of ambiguous independence and they feared what would happen if Anguilla officially declared itself outside the Commonwealth. Anguilla, like Rhodesia, would be outlawed. It would attract outlaws.

The new weekly, *The Beacon* (typewritten and offset, the equipment a gift from a Boston firm), had run an editorial warning against a unilateral declaration of independence. It had created some doubt in the island; it made independence appear a little more difficult.

"If we sell away our rights to American businessmen now," the young electrician-editor said to me in a bar, "we will be the laughing-stock of the Caribbean and the world. Don't get me wrong," he added, speaking slowly while I took down his words. "If Britain don't do nothing, then I feel we should go on our own."

"I go put his balls through the wringer," a young man said angrily to Mr. Webster at the air-strip, showing *The Beacon*. Such violence of language was once reserved for Bradshaw of St. Kitts. Mr. Webster, hiding his distress—it was Saturday, his sabbath—calmed the young man down.

The frightened, the bold, "stooges," "Mafia": this was the rough division at which the visitor arrived, feeling his way through intrigue that appeared to follow no race or colour line. Responsibility, acquired lusts and fears now balancing the old certitude, had brought dissensions, the breaking up of that sense of isolation and community which was the point of independence.

THERE was the Canadian with the idea for a radio station, for which for some reason he required stretches of beach. There was Jeremiah Gumbs's plan for a Bank of Anguilla (he actually started building), which frightened many people. There was Jeremiah Gumbs's plan for a "centre for physical medicine." "The trouble is, will I get my people to understand it? Or will they object to it like the American Medical Association?" I could never understand what he meant; I heard it said that he wanted to bring down an American who had a magic cure. I remembered Jeremiah's half-brother, Judge Gumbs.

The Anguillan faith in Jeremiah Gumbs as their guide to big American investment had been shaken by these projects and he had been dropped as an adviser to the Council. When I was in Anguilla I felt he was in disgrace, sulking at the Rendezvous. And his own attitude to Anguilla changed from meal to meal. Sometimes he was a patriot. "St. Kitts will be sorry if they attacked us. When we have finished with them, the British Government will have to feed them on crackers and molasses, I guess." Sometimes he was despairing about Anguillans. "They don't know they don't know." He could give this a gloss. "The trouble," he said during one gloomy meal, "is that colonialism has made the Anguillan a *shell*."

His changes of mood were linked with the arrival, examination, and dismissal of another American with an idea. This man was looking for a "franchise": a grant of land and, I believe, a twenty-five-year monopoly in the quarrying and block-making business. His examination by the Council and the Council's lawyer, who had flown in from Trinidad, lasted eight hours; and when he appeared at Jeremiah Gumbs's table at dinner, a young soft-bellied man in trousers of shocking Sherwood green, he looked bruised. I heard later that toward the end of his examination he was close to tears.

It was a subdued Jeremiah Gumbs who padded about the dining-room in his slippers, pouring water, offering bread, like a man still with a duty to his ranch-hands. Afterwards he led me through the wire-netting door to the open verandah. Sand-flies and mosquitoes pounced. He slapped and clapped his big hands, killing and calm.

"Who is this lawyer guy? Is he a constitutional lawyer, a company lawyer, a criminal lawyer? Does he know anything about economics? You tell Webster. He's got to have a development plan. Otherwise he's going to frighten off a lot of people. And they are not that many. They are not that many."

In the morning the sad American left, green check jacket matching his trousers.

Jeremiah Gumbs still suffered. "He was gonna invest plenty. He wasn't gonna make money for four years. *Then* you'll let someone *else* in? These people don't understand economics. If Webster could worry he'd be worried. He was gonna build that road, open up that whole area. Put value on people's property. Houses going up alongside the road. But these people don't understand. Look at me. *I* put this place up. *I* advertised Anguilla. Now other people have put down their little places. The tourist comes to the airport, the taxi-drivers rush him, take him this place, that place. *I* advertised." His voice began to sing. "It's not a way to live. I don't know. I feel there's another way to live."

I said I felt he had done enough for Anguilla.

He said he wouldn't rest until he had done a lot more. "I love this country. I love the people. I know what poverty is like. I know what drought is like. I care. I remember when I was a boy . . ."

On my bill there was a charge for an Anguillan flag. I told Lady B. I hadn't had one.

"You want one, young man?" She waved it at me when she gave it, and did a gigantic little mimicry of a drum-majorette. "Anguilla, here I come."

I put it in my pocket, the flag of the territory that Jeremiah Gumbs didn't look like opening up.

Independence, as a smooth administration: that worked. Independence as the preserver of an old community: that made sense. Independence as "development" and quick tourist money: that, as the San Francisco Group romantically sensed, defeats itself. Anguilla was going to disappoint more of its supporters. Independence had only just come; and Anguilla already required pacification.

PACIFICATION came, heavy-handed and absurd—but only to the outsider looking for comedy or a manageable cause. The Anguilla problem remains: the problem of a tiny colony set adrift, part of the jetsam of an empire, a near-primitive people suddenly returned to a free state, their renewed or continuing exploitation.

When I left Anguilla, Jeremiah Gumbs was giving instructions to the workmen (and a very slow, contemplative, sand-sifting workwoman) who were running up the barrack-like extension to the hotel. The other day, quite by chance, I saw him in a dark suit, his ring on the small finger of his large left hand, in the Delegates' Lounge of the United Nations. Four English journalists were taking down his grave words.

The British invasion was two days away. Jeremiah—an American citizen, his business in the United States the Gumbs Fuel and Oil Burner Service of Edison, New Jersey—was the petitioner that day for Anguilla, before the Committee on Colonialism. He spoke lucidly and without exaggeration; his tone was one of injury, familiar to me; but everything he said about the planned British invasion was true.

He was the official Anguillan spokesman again. He was back in favour in Anguilla. And it was not surprising to learn from newspaper reports that the American in green had returned to Anguilla. He had returned as a lawyer. He had no law degree, but he had "an extensive law library"; he was given a permit to practise. He did more. He advised on the new Anguillan constitution. (The previous one, very short, had been drafted by a Harvard professor, who had somehow ceased to be important in Anguilla.) The *National Observer* gave some of the provisions of the new constitution. Businesses, foreign or local, could not be expropriated by the Anguillan government; foreign governments could not bring tax suits against Anguilla-based businesses. A judge of the Anguillan Supreme Court didn't have to be an Anguillan or a lawyer; all he needed was a permit to practise law in Anguilla, and he had to be over thirty-five. The *National Observer* also gave some details of the franchise the American had asked for in December, for his basic building-materials plant: twenty-five years tax-free, the Anguillan government to get five hundred dollars a year in return.

After the British invasion the American was put on a Cessna and sent off the island.

"It may seem strange to people who have lost faith in the United Nations," Jeremiah Gumbs said to reporters a week later, "but on our little island the United Nations is still regarded, in spite of its imperfections, as the great hope of small nations and people of goodwill anywhere."

It was the *New York Times* Quotation of the Day. The *Times* also presented, as news, some lines from the two-year-old Anguillan anthem. Anguilla—as cause, as comedy—appeared set for a re-run.

1969

The Ultimate Colony

BRITISH HONDURAS is the last British territory on the American mainland, and the present Governor ought to be the last. But this is uncertain. After five years of internal self-government, with a Premier and ministers, complete independence is still difficult. The problem is one of succession. Guatemala says that British Honduras is hers and should be returned to her. American mediation has failed. In British Honduras itself the Opposition has grown strong on the charge that the government is preparing to sell out to Guatemala. The government says it isn't. But it cannot act. It requires independence to prove its point, and independence will come only when the point is proved.

The Governor who is there, withdrawn, waiting to hand over, is Sir John Paul. His service before this was in West Africa, in Sierra Leone and the Gambia. British Honduras is his last colonial posting. He is fifty-three; his own future is uncertain. He is no longer a pensionable officer and he has as yet no job in England to go back to. In British Honduras he has little to do. He assents to bills in the name of the Queen; he is head of the Civil Service; he handles external affairs. His only direct responsibility is defence—there is a small British garrison—and public order—he shares control of the police with the minister concerned.

"Security and stability. Very important, but rather boring. One doesn't really have a full-time job. One tends to be a little isolated and divorced. Quite rightly: the country runs itself. One doesn't want to impinge."

The Governor's tact is like sensibility, an expression of a natural cool melancholy. He is a tall man, heavy but still athletic. During office hours he wears a white shirt and a tie, no jacket: the dress expressing the ambiguous formality of his job.

"So long as it's a dependent territory the Governor can't be an anomaly. But he can have damned little to do. It's even worse when you're a Governor-General. There's even less to do. I had a year of that in the Gambia. I saw that the only way of getting out was to write a republican constitution. I did so. We put it to the electorate and they rejected it."

White water-skis and fishing rods lean against the wall of the Governor's office, airy and light. A half-open umbrella hangs from the grey steel safe. There is a wall-map: this all but empty British territory—nine thousand square miles, one hundred thousand people—incongruous in Latin America: Mexico the industrial giant to the north, Guatemala of the high mountains, the political assassinations, the temperate flowers and fruit, the Spanish and Mayan architectural antiquities, to the west and south. The wire-netted windows of the Governor's office show the sparse gardens of Government House, the two tall royal palms. Just beyond the garden wall is the Caribbean, not blue here, thick with catfish, restless scavengers of the waters of this city built on swampland.

THE EMPIRE here was never grand. It began as a seventeenth-century coastal intrusion on the Spanish American Empire. The territory doubled its size in the last century. But it was acknowledged as an intrusion and was never settled; it never became a land of plantations. The first interlopers came with their Negroes to cut logwood; their successors went further inland to cut mahogany. The mahogany forests have all been cut down. Bush remains, and scattered little bush communities: Maya Indians, who move among the mighty ruins of their civilization like any other degraded immigrant group; Black Caribs, transported from the West Indian island of St. Vincent, considered by Negroes to be very black and ugly, with a bad smell; Spanish and mestizo refugees from Yucatan; and, in the last ten years, some thousands of Mennonites, a Bible-reading German-American sect, who have transformed many square miles of tropical bush, bought at fifteen shillings an acre, into the landscape of pioneer America. The descendants of the Negro log-cutters, now two-thirds of the population, and confirmed lovers of city life, live in the overcrowded coastal capital, Belize City.

From the air Belize City is an arbitrary white huddle at the edge of a sodden land where forests occasionally reflect the sun as a pale white disc. The coastline is untidy with drowned islets, like darker cloud shadows; during the 1961 hurricane one "exclusive" American-owned islet, the cause of some local resentment, sank with its three cottages. Corrugated-iron latrines overhang the wide, slow canals of the city; in one night-club tourists are invited to feed the catfish.

In this city to be buried in "a good dry hole" is to be lucky. In the late afternoons Negroes in jackets and ties—famous throughout Central America for their immunity to disease—walk behind the hearses to the cemetery just outside the town, waving white handkerchiefs. Afterwards they stand relaxed and emblematic among the higher tombstones, chatting, waving in the dusk. It is like a ceremony of bewildered farewell at the limit of the world. But they are only keeping off the mosquitoes and sandflies.

IN BELIZE CITY the Union Jack is the flag of Negro protest against the Guatemalan claim. The Negroes of British Honduras were not plantation slaves. They were foresters. And though until recently some private houses in Belize City could still show their old slave punishment cells, with the original chains, the Negroes look back with pride to the days when, securely British, they fought shoulder to shoulder with their proprietors against the Spaniards.

"If you mention slavery here," the Negro leader of the Opposition says, "people would stare at you and wonder what you are talking about."

The Guatemalans say jokingly that Guatemala should take back British Honduras and Britain should take back her Negroes. The Mexicans have a joke like this too: Mexico will take British Honduras, Guatemala will take the *negritos*.

The Vice President of Guatemala, one of his country's leading intellectuals, doesn't find the joke funny. He doesn't want the Negroes, and he is frightened of Mexico. Mexico too has a claim, to a good half of British Honduras; but Mexico will act only if Guatemala does. The Guatemalan Vice President despairs. He is an Indian and a patriot; he thinks that Guatemala has lost British Honduras, her twenty-third department, that the land has been spitefully spoiled by the British, who packed it out with Negroes and now require neither the land nor the Negroes.

"We have no Negro problem. A Negro has only to square his shoulders, and ten of our Indians will run. We are a weak race. The British brought over those Negroes from the Congo, Angola, the Sudan. They can work well in the heat; our Indians can't. Negroes don't fall ill easily.

Malaria doesn't touch them. When the Negro mates with the Indian he produces the *sambo*. That is a race that quickly becomes degenerate."

But Vice Presidents change; the Guatemalan claim can at any time become a Guatemalan crusade. Nothing will happen, though, while British Honduras remains British; and the question of who will get the Negroes will remain academic so long as there is a Governor and the Union Jack flies over Government House, not as protest, but as a sign of a continuing order.

GOVERNMENT HOUSE is a white two-storeyed wooden building that looks like a large private house. It has only three—enormous—bedrooms. Its neutral style conceals its age. It was begun in 1815, and is not like the Government Houses of the later Empire. It has been neglected for periods and has been through many hurricanes. The tidal wave that followed the last, in 1961, covered the main floor and disfigured the central mahogany staircase, the building's only notable feature.

"It was all much grander in the Gambia. There had been East African governors before. They had, I think quite rightly, very strong views about how a Governor should be looked after. Most beautiful garden too. But of course this house suits the resources of the country."

Government House costs the Government of British Honduras £11,000 a year. That covers everything: the monogrammed china and silver, bought through the Crown Agents in London; the three stewards, Lloyd, Garnett and George; Leone, the cook, Adela, the laundress; the two secretaries in the Governor's outer office; and the Governor himself. The Governor's ADC is an adjutant in the local Volunteer Guard.

"He's part-time. There's very little formality about this job now. The flag is lowered at 6:30. The police sentries do it. In the Gambia it was done with ceremony, with sounding—what do they call it—the Retreat. We did it once here and I must say I thought it was jolly impressive. We had a presentation of insignia and we had 350 to 400 guests and the flag was lowered and they beat the Retreat. But it taxed our resources so much we haven't done it since.

"We have receptions every month or so. Generally. It's the one place where everybody can meet. It's not a criticism, but people here tend to mix with their own group. My wife does the whole thing herself. I have no housekeeper. So when I am on my own the entertaining is restricted.

"We had a fine new car. It's just been smashed up. Brand-new Austin Princess, possibly a write-off. Most infuriating. It's been sent to England for repairs. So we are reduced to a 1962 Rover."

The Governor has a Land-Rover for touring. His tours are official, but muted and almost private: the Premier of British Honduras has made it clear that he doesn't like official public "confrontations" with the Governor.

"He's very sensible. One can only talk piously."

The Governor has been to the Assembly only once. He has only once seen, and can no longer remember, the locally designed costume—black coat, white lace cuffs, white cravat, long red gown—which the mace-bearer, a former stevedore, complainingly wears. The Assembly has been adjourned and adjourned: the Governor has never made a Speech from the Throne.

"Not that this concerns me," the Governor says.

The Governor has taken up painting again. "It keeps me out of mischief." His Gambian watercolours—precise, meticulous, limpid—hang on the grey walls of Government House among old official photographs, a tarnished oil painting of the Berkshire downs and a view of the Thames.

"The Governor," the Premier says, "is like St. John the Baptist. He gets smaller every day. Government House isn't Government House. Government House is the Premier's Office and the Assembly."

NEXT TO GOVERNMENT HOUSE is the Premier's official residence. It is an inelegant wooden bungalow, white with blue facings—the colours of the Premier's party—and a red tin roof.

In the dining-room there is a larger-than-life portrait of the Premier, done by a local artist from a photograph. It shows a youthful, mischievous man of fifty in glasses and wearing an open-necked shirt. The mischief is in the eyes and the mouth; the lips are welted and look bruised and parched. The artist had trouble with the mouth, and managed to hit it off only while listening to the Premier's voice on the radio. The Premier is heard every morning on the programme called *Wake up and Work*. The Premier is a man of mixed race: Maya Indian, European, some seepage of African. He looks white; this painting makes him black.

The Premier, the Honourable George Price, does not live in his official residence. He lives in his old family house in the run-down centre of Belize City. The unpainted house, on tall stilts, had been weathered black. It is blank and shuttered behind a high fence; and it has no front steps.

The Premier goes home early. He is unmarried; a neighbour cooks for him. He receives few visitors at home and he seldom takes home official papers. He reads novels—Thomas Mann is a favourite—and theological works. He says his prayers before going to bed. He is up at five and goes to Mass at 5:30. He does not worry through to political decisions; they come to him after the night of prayer and rest; and he is in his office punctually at eight. He has no grey hairs.

When he was a young man George Price studied for the priesthood—the disturbing mouth is that of a self-willed priest—and even his enemies say that neither age nor power has changed him. He is not interested in money; he is known to give away money; his outer office is always full of suppliants. His official car is a Land-Rover; he ceaselessly tours the empty country, greeting, checking. Then, abruptly every day, the public life ends.

"Mr. Price is not like the rest of men," the leader of the Opposition says. "The rest of us have wives and families, recreations. Mr. Price has a one-track mind. He wants to get rid of the British but we believe he is quite willing to replace the British by the Guatemalans."

"This is a subtle thing," the Premier's second-in-command says. "The subtlety is that if Guatemala takes over, Mr. Price has less to lose. Mr. Price's complexion and racial make-up have given some credence to this belief."

"It usually is a good way," the Opposition second-in-command says, "to parade as a religious person. Who's Price trying to kid? Price has long dreamed of a glorious Latin-Catholic Central American Empire."

"Price doesn't look it," the Guatemalan Vice-President says, "but he is a Negro. If he was a Maya Indian and a patriot, as some people say, he wouldn't have got mixed up with all those Negroes over there."

Once, when he was only a nationalist agitator, the first in British Honduras, the Guatemalan claim was useful to George Price. Now, as Premier, he is trapped by the claim; it erodes his power.

"I DON'T THINK anybody felt the life was going to come so quickly to an end. After Ghana one could do nothing about it and one wanted to do nothing about it."

A visit to Trinidad in 1934–35 was the Governor's first glimpse of a colony. It made him think of a career in the Colonial Service.

"I liked the *ambience,* the friendliness of the people. Mark you, in those days there were far fewer opportunities for people like myself in the industrial or commercial world, for people who had—it tends to be a dirty word—a public school education." The Governor was at Weymouth in Dorset. "Long since defunct."

"I applied to join the Colonial Service before the war. I was at Cambridge, came down in June 1939. Thought I might as well have a regular commission and get properly involved instead of hanging around getting pushed around. I was a prisoner most of the war. I was in the Royal Tank Corps. Captured in Calais in 1940. After the war I was seconded as ADC to Sierra Leone. When I was released from the Army I joined the Colonial Service and became a District Commissioner. I had great difficulty getting rid of my regular commission. Not because they particularly wanted me—I'm sure of that—but on principle . . .

"The work of ADC was one of the most fascinating jobs you could ever have. You were virtually on your own in those days. You got very attached to the people. We all felt a sense of participation. One talks of colonialism now . . . People tend to look at Empire in the context of the last fifty or one hundred years. But I think it fair to say that without Empire over the centuries there wouldn't have been the spread of knowledge. Africa is the most contentious example, I suppose. I feel there must be something on the credit side. This is no criticism of the local people. They were prisoners of their own circumstances . . .

"It was the most rewarding part of my life. You were very clearly defined. One knew exactly, in one's modest way, what one was trying to do. You weren't humbugged too much by what we used to call the Secretariat. We were alone much of the time. Pretty early evenings, no electric lights. We had small children. That kept us pretty busy. We used to read a lot. One spent a lot of time on tour. Of course, in those days one walked, seeing what was going on."

ON THE STROKE of eight the Land-Rover sweeps up the short drive to the portico of Government House. The Premier, tall and slender, in an open-necked braided Yucatan-style shirt, bounces out after his aide.

"Morning, Excellency!"

The Premier likes to use titles and he always appears to put them between inverted commas.

It is the day of the Premier's weekly tour; the visiting writer will go with him. The Governor, in white shirt and tie, is there to greet the Premier. The formalities are brief and urgent. The aide runs to close the Land-Rover door, and soon we are on the road.

"Marnin', Miss Virginia."

When the Premier waves he abandons conversation and concentrates; he is like a man giving a benediction.

Nine men are standing around a small patch on the main road. The PWD lorries have broken down again. The Premier makes a note. Later we pass PWD mounds of earth.

"Jarge Price, clean the road!" someone shouts.

We stop often.

"Marnin', marnin'."

The Premier strides ahead in his flapping shirt, loose tan trousers and big black shoes. The aide runs, to protect the Premier against enraged dogs. The muscular young Negro driver stands beside his vehicle, chewing gum, tall, in boots, tight jeans and jersey, dark glasses.

"Marnin'. It's Jarge Price, the Premier. Lemme see your kitchen. Lemme see wa' you cook this marnin'."

He lifts lids, examines breakfast plates, gives his benediction. And we bolt for the Land-Rover.

WHEN GEORGE PRICE left the seminary, for financial reasons, he found a job with a local self-made timber millionaire. He stayed with him for fourteen years as secretary and travelling companion.

"We travelled everywhere. I remember one day at a hotel in Chicago putting a value on the people around the dining table. I made it three hundred million dollars. When you mix with people like that all the time you can't feel too much envy. I very early on had the feeling of *sic transit gloria mundi*. Turton had all this money. But he was a sick man . . .

"Whenever I went into a bank I used to feel: you are entering the temple of the capitalists. I suppose I used to say it sometimes. Turton didn't always like the things I said. I was quoting to him one day from the 1931 Encyclical—I think it was *Quadragesimo Anno*. About relations between employer and worker, the living wage and so on. He listened and I thought I was getting through. At the end he said, 'Jarge, the Pope doesn't know a shit about business.'

"It was Turton who made me go into politics. He said, 'You will go into politics.' He made me run for the Belize City Council in 1944. I lost. Now if a doctor said to me to give up politics, I wouldn't."

But politics do not stand still. The colonial politician who is the first leader and educator is also the man who most speedily makes himself out of date. Politics as the vocation of the failed priest, the empty land as the parish: it no longer answers. The Guatemalan claim has made the politics of British Honduras artificial and static. Development, like independence itself, recedes. The Premier has been to these villages too often before; he is no longer a man with news.

"They don't seem to be looking for a messiah," the Premier's second-in-command says. "They seem to want participation. Or collective leadership. I think Mr. Price senses this change in the country. He has recently enlarged his cabinet."

"I am getting old," the Premier says. "I am not a fighter as I used to be."

"ONE'S CAREER has changed quite completely from the way one envisaged it," the Governor says. "One of the ironies is that most of the time one's been working oneself out of a job. I've been extremely lucky. Very few left now, out of the old Colonial Service. Infinitesimal number really."

THE WORLD intrudes. The sons of people once content with the Premier's benediction go away to study and come back and curse both parties. They talk of Vietnam and Black Power. They undermine the Negro loyalty to the slave past.

"The whites are buying up the land. English colonialism tried to condition the black man against using the land. There was a concerted effort by the English colonialists to have their black slaves remain log-cutters. It became a sort of phallic symbol to the black to be a log-cutter."

The politics of British Honduras have always had a racial-religious undertone: the Negro-Protestant town, the Roman Catholic country. Now race threatens to make the old politics even more irrelevant. The

Premier, white below his carefully maintained tan, a political vanity, is especially vulnerable.

The Governor gets a report on the latest Black Power meeting.

"They pulled in 150 last night. I must say I couldn't make head or tail of what was said."

We are having drinks around the small new pool at the side of Government House. The sea breeze is moist.

"Do you think he'll have lunch with me?" the American Consul asks. He is concerned: the local spokesman for Black Power, who is just twenty-one, went to an American university on an American government scholarship. "I wish someone would give me twelve thousand dollars to send my son to college."

The Consul is friendly, intelligent. He has had some experience of British colonies in transition. He "watched" the affairs of British Guiana at a time when the Jagan government was being overthrown by Negro racist riots and an American-supported strike.

The United States has an interest: it is the true issue of imperial succession.

THE GOVERNOR, anxious to be active again, thinks of his own future.

"There is no obligation on the part of the government to find another job for me. I don't know what the future holds. But we've been lucky. The big concern was the education of one's daughters, and we are more or less at the end of that tunnel."

The Governor will leave the Colonial Service with an affection for the countries he worked in, but with no great nostalgia. He will remain concerned about the debasing effect of tourism on backward countries, and all that these countries have to do.

"Take the Gambia. You couldn't get people to go to school in some areas. Most awful waste of manpower. Those people, as of now, they've not a hope in hell, and they'll be living for, what, sixty, seventy years."

The Governor will also be taking back a memory of the midnight handover in the Gambia: the Union Jack coming down, the lights going off and coming on again, the new Gambian flag in place, the handshakes from the Gambians, delighted but also managing in that moment to express a personal concern for the Governor.

The flag that came down that midnight is in the Governor's Hampshire cottage. It was hung out of the window to celebrate his daughters' success in the A-level examinations.

THE PREMIER plans to build a retreat in the cool Mountain Pine Ridge region.

"Mr. Price knows how to survive," the Premier's second-in-command says. "He's a natural politician. I don't see the demise of Mr. Price."

But in the clerical mischievousness of the Premier, which can at times be like arrogance, and in his daily routine, there is already more than a hint of withdrawal. He will fight to the end. But he also tells his supporters, "My day will come. I will go."

He has never cared for the things of the world. But for most of his life he has been immersed in them, and he often reflects on the strangeness of his career.

"I have this recurring dream. I am in church. Someone is saying mass—Turton, my old employer, or Pinks, one of his managers—and I wonder why I, who would so much like to be up there, am not, and that old sinner is."

1969

The Overcrowded Barracoon

SIX CARPENTERS leave the Indian Ocean island of Mauritius to go to Swaziland in Southern Africa to work for a year, and it is front-page news in *L'Express*, the leading Mauritius newspaper. Six mouths less to feed; six families saved, at least for a year. Twenty-five nurses, men as well as women, are chosen for hospitals in England. England will swallow them up; but for the moment they are famous in their island, with their names at the top of the front page of the *Mauritius Times*. Perhaps ten thousand applied for those twenty-five vacancies. That is what is believed; those are the odds.

"Your Majesty," a young Mauritian writes to the Principal Nursing Officer of a Scottish hospital, "will you please find me a seat?" The newspaper correspondent who reports the joke back, himself a Mauritian, one of the lucky ones who got away, says that flattery like this will get young Mauritians nowhere. The correspondent is not unsympathetic; he says he knows that the young people of Mauritius are obsessed with the idea of escape and are "all the time morally and physically fatigued"; but the only ones who will succeed are those with "a fair knowledge of up-to-date things and a (really) good character and a love for nursing."

But so many are qualified. Since the only Mauritians acceptable abroad are nurses, in Mauritius they all love nursing. They are a nation of nurses. And they hang around the ministers' doors in Port Louis, the capital, waiting for the call to serve. The ministers are all-powerful in Mauritius; nothing can be done except through a minister. But what can the ministers do? Once manna fell from heaven—this is how the Foreign Minister put it—and the Germans asked for five hundred nurses. But manna doesn't fall every day; the hope that the French would take five thousand units a year remains a hope.

There is a Minister of State for Emigration, a plump, chuckling mulatto, a former motor mechanic. But he can give no figures for emigration. He says he doesn't carry these figures in his head; and, besides, he is preoccupied with a local election. "All our energies are devoted to this by-election at Curepipe. We think that Mauritius must have a good political climate to solve our problems."

The Minister can give no figures because there are not many figures to give. So the young men hang around, sometimes for years, waiting for their careers to begin. They meet in little clubhouses of concrete or corrugated iron, decorated with posters from the British Information Services or cut-outs from foreign magazines, and talk and talk. Some of them begin to suffer from spells of dizziness and have to stay at home. Many of them get headaches, those awful Mauritian headaches that can drive an unemployed labourer mad, interrupt the career of a civil servant, and turn educated young men into mindless invalids.

It was on Mauritius that the dodo forgot how to fly, because it had no enemies: the island, 720 square miles, was once uninhabited. Now, with more than a thousand people to the square mile, the island is overpopulated.

The Dutch attempted to settle Mauritius in the seventeenth century. They cut down the ebony forests and introduced sugar-cane. When the Dutch left—driven out, it is said, by rats—the French came. The French, mainly peasants from Brittany, stayed and continued to flourish after the British conquest in the early nineteenth century. They grew sugar-cane, depending for labour first on slaves from Madagascar and Africa, and then, when slavery was abolished, on indentured immigrants from India.

Throughout the nineteenth century labour was short, and immigration from India continued until 1917, so that today Indians make up two-thirds of the population. Even with this immigration the population held steady. In 1931 the population was more or less what it had been in 1901, just under 400,000. Then the disaster occurred. In 1949 malaria was finally eradicated. The population jumped. It is now about 820,000. Three Mauritians out of five are under twenty-one. No one knows how many unemployed or idle people there are—estimates vary from 50,000 to 80,000—and the population grows by about 12,000 every year.

The economy, and the social structure, is still that of an agricultural colony, a tiny part of an empire: the island has been independent for only three years. The large estates, the big commission agents and the sugar factories are white (though there are many Indian landowners and there is an Indian aristocracy of sorts); rural labour is Indian; mulattoes are civil servants; Negroes are artisans, dockworkers and fishermen; Chinese are in trade.

Sugar remains the main crop and virtually the sole export. Sugar-cane covers nearly half the island, so that from the air this island of disaster looks empty and green, dotted with half-pyramids of stone that are like the relics of a vanished civilization. The stone comes from the sugar-cane fields: "de-stoning"—and the boulders are enormous—is a recurring task. Once the de-stoning was done by hand; now it is done by bull-dozers. Sugar has always been an efficient industry, and in Mauritius the efficiency shows. Lushness has been abolished; order has been imposed on the tropical landscape. The visitor who keeps to the main highways sees an island as well-kept as a lawn, monotonous except for the jagged volcanic hills, miniature green Matterhorns.

An island roughly oval in shape, 720 square miles in the Indian Ocean, far from anywhere, colonized, like those West Indian islands on the other side of the world, only for sugar, part of the great human engineering of recent empires, the shifting about of leaderless groups of conquered peoples: to the travel writers, who have set to work on Mauritius, the island is "a lost paradise" which is "being developed into an idyllic spot." It is an island which the visitor leaves with "a feeling of peace." To the Mauritian who cannot leave it is a prison: sugar-cane and sugar-cane, ending in the sea, and the diseased coconut trees, blighted by the rhinoceros beetle.

Twenty thousand tourists came to Mauritius last year. The lost paradise already has a casino, and the casino company, in tune with the holiday tastes of these low latitudes, has also put in fruit machines in the island's leading hotels. The tourists prefer the fruit machines. In the Park Hotel in Curepipe the fat women and their fatter girls start playing the machines after breakfast; in the late afternoon, when the television also blares, conversation in the lounge of this allegedly eighteenth-century building becomes impossible.

The casino is patronized mainly by local Chinese, sitting as blank-faced here before the bright tables in the dark-red hall as they do behind their shop counters in the villages, having apparently only changed from khaki shorts and singlets into suits. The Chinese are a race apart in Mauritius, and impenetrable; it is a cause for awe that people can be so reckless with money which, in the Mauritian myth, they have made by such tedious treachery. In the myth, the Chinese shopkeeper spends a part of every working day extracting one or two matches from every box in his stock, so that out of, say, twenty boxes of matches he makes twenty-one and so picks up an extra quarter-penny of pure profit.

The casino picks up more than quarter-pennies, and many Mauritians are pleased with the success and modernity of the place. I couldn't find out what there was in the casino venture for the Mauritius Treasury or the tourist trade. To enquire was only to probe a kind of native innocence. But everyone knew that the casino employed a number of people and that the white and mulatto girls who operated the tables—their satiny old-fashioned evening-dress uniforms labelled with their first names—had until a few months before been idle and unemployed. Now, very quickly, they had acquired this difficult modern skill: in this "adaptability"—a recurring Mauritian word—lay the hope for the future. In Mauritius it always comes to this: jobs, employment, a use of the hands, something to do.

The tourists come from the nearby French island of Réunion (technically a department of France), from Madagascar, England, India, and South Africa. Relations with South Africa are close. South Africa buys, at more than a fair price, every kilo of the somewhat flavourless tea that Mauritius produces; and to see what "Made in South Africa" looks like in Afrikaans, all you have to do is to turn over the ash-tray in your hotel room. Mauritius is no place for the anti-apartheid campaigner. Many French Mauritians have family or business links with South Africa; and during the period of French "over-reaction" before independence ("We always over-react here")—when the French rallied their loyal Negroes (anti-apartheid people really should stay away from Mauritius) and there were rumours of a French–South African commando takeover—during this period of over-reaction a number of French people moved to South Africa.

As visitors the South Africans are popular. And not all the South Africans who come are white. BLACKS IN SOUTH AFRICA SHOULD NOT COMPLAIN: this is the front-page headline in the *Mauritius Times* over a question-and-answer interview with a visiting South African Indian, Mr. Ahmed Cajee Khan.

Q: Mr. Khan, how do Indians fare in South Africa?
A: Very well economically integrated with the government . . .
    Some of our people are multi-millionaires.

Q: How did this powerful position come about?

A: It's traditional among Indians . . .

Q: Would you say that a lot of what we hear against South Africa is incorrect?

A: . . . In Mauritius I was surprised when somebody told me there were separate toilet facilities on board South African Airways. This is false . . .

Q: But surely there are some inflexible situations?

A: All countries have their domestic problems.

Q: Mr. Khan, there is a school of thought which believes that the political battle in South Africa is lost. Do you subscribe to this view?

A: Not for a minute . . .

Q: Your happiness about this régime baffles me. Would I be right in saying that it's because you don't feel the pinch like the blacks?

A: No! Nobody feels the pinch. Everybody has a job . . . although we should make allowance for the eternal grumblers.

Earlier this year Black Power slogans in French and the local French patois appeared in many towns and villages: *C'est beau d'être noir, Noir ene jolie couleur, Noirs au pouvoir.* It was the idea of the Foreign Minister, Gaëtan Duval. Duval himself isn't black. He is a brown-skinned, straight-haired man of forty, as handsome as a pop star and with a pop star's taste in clothes. As part of his Black Power campaign he took to wearing black leather and making public appearances on a black horse called Black Beauty. For many years Duval was regarded as the leader of the island's blacks. But then two years ago, forgetting pre-independence disputes, he took his party into a coalition government; and since then, as the government's popularity has gone down, so has Duval's.

Black Power was Duval's way of fighting back. It was intended, so far as I could gather, to scare off political poachers. It certainly wasn't intended to frighten ordinary white people. Duval supports the idea of trade with South Africa, and he would like to see more South African tourists. He would like to see South Africans buying houses in special tourist developments. Statistics showed, he told me one day at lunch, that a hotel room provided employment for only two servants. A house provided employment for four.

THE GOVERNMENT recognizes a problem of unemployment. A White Paper says that 130,000 new jobs will have to be created by 1980. The government doesn't recognize a problem of over-population and discourages investigation of its effects. It disapproves of "crude" family planning programmes on TV. Mauritius is a conservative, wife-beating society and the government doesn't want to offend anybody.

There are also good political reasons. At a seminar on unemployment, which began the day after I arrived, a spokesman for the Labour Party, the major party in the ruling coalition, said: "We have rejected the all too facile and simple explanation that unemployment is a consequence of overpopulation and the lack of capital and investment possibilities . . . In fact it is clear that the holders of economic power, either for fear of inadequate protection of their interest or again out of a carefully elaborated political strategy, refused to be involved in the necessary political process . . . The Mauritian situation, therefore, presents a picture where the holders of political power are separated by a wide, almost unbridgeable gap from those holding economic power."

So, by stressing unemployment and by playing down over-population, the government defends itself and seeks to remain the instrument of protest, as in colonial days. Protest against the rich, so often white, whose talents and money are yet needed; protest against the sugar-cane, the slave crop, hateful yet indispensable.

But the government is unpopular. If there were an election tomorrow the government would be overthrown, not by its old enemies, most of whom it has anyway absorbed, but by the young, those people who have grown up during the years of the population explosion.

The Prime Minister, an Indian in an island with an Indian majority, is seventy. The political party of the young, whose sudden popularity has rocked the government, was founded in 1968 by a French Mauritian student, then aged twenty-three and fresh from the events of Paris. The Prime Minister has a background of rural Indian poverty. Education and self-education, the long years in London in the 1920s, first as a student, then as a doctor, trade union work on his return to Mauritius, politics: it has been a long haul, against an almost "settler" opposition, and his achievement has been remarkable. Over the last twelve years he has created a rudimentary welfare state in Mauritius. There are extensive social services; there is a system of "relief work" for the unemployed (four rupees, thirty pence, four days a week); there is a monthly allowance of ten rupees, about seventy-five pence, for families with three children below the age of fourteen.

This rudimentary welfare state has saved the society from collapse; and the people who have benefited are the young. They are better educated and better fed than their parents. An excellent television service keeps them sharp and well informed. Their expectations are higher; they are no longer an uncomplaining part of the old serf society. The flaw is that this welfare state has been created, perhaps at the expense of development, within a static colonial economy where sugar is still king. The higher skills are not required in Mauritius. Elsewhere, only those with really good characters and a love of nursing need apply.

"They blame the government. Once they have the certificate in hand they never think of anything else except securing a job with government. There are organized groups in agriculture, but the bulk would like to sit behind a desk and have papers to scratch all day." "The government has made the people of Mauritius beggars. The thing is we had an extended family system here we could have made better use of. What has happened is that all this government relief has weakened the family system." "Our people have no sense of adventure." "People are becoming accident-conscious. Malingering. My surgery is pestered with malingerers hoping to get compensation from the government for their 'accidents.' "

These are middle-class comments on the Mauritius welfare state, and they are supported to some extent by a White Paper. Too many people, the White Paper says, live at the "relief" level; too many people do "unproductive" relief jobs (sometimes relief workers are sent to clean the beaches); and as a result "the will to work among those employed, who see it is possible to live with less work or even without working, is being affected."

And it is easy for the visitor to be irritated. Those well-built, well-dressed young men idling away the afternoons in the choked village lanes: they are too well drilled, too ready to be an audience and sit in rows in their clubhouses. The complaints come easily. "If you want a job they put the Riot Unit against you. This happens three times in one month." "Every day you will see people knocking at the deputy's door asking for a job, because everyone believes, 'The deputy will give my son a job, daughter a job.' " "To see a minister you have to pay people money. We only see the pictures of the ministers."

So they sit and complain, and threaten. "Change the government. Replace it by the socialist party. The government tolerates capitalism." The socialist party is the party of the young. What will it do? How will it replace capitalism? There is no clear idea. But the government must be punished. The government is the government, and can do anything it really wants. "The government has failed not because they are foolish or wicked but because they are selfish."

Is this really all to their life, this hanging about in the village lane, these games of dominoes, these endless political discussions in the club-houses? Are there no other activities, no pleasures, no festivals? "No money, no pleasures, sir." Rum, at fifty-five Mauritian cents a nip, just under four pennies, is expensive, *bien, bien cher*; all they can afford is the local banana spirit, which sells at two and a half pennies a pint. The cinema is expensive, one rupee or seven and a half pennies in the third class, two rupees twenty-five in the first. "I haven't been to the cinema for ten years." "I haven't been for three years." "There is no pleasure for us even in Diwali [the Hindu festival of lights]. We can't buy presents for the children or give them new clothes."

But that fat, open-mouthed, jolly boy, who is on "relief," has just got married and is clearly the clown of the group. That handsome, stylishly dressed boy comes from a polygamous Muslim batch of seventeen. And that sullen man of thirty-five, with the pot-belly, has had six children in the six years he has been on relief.

But irritation is unfair. The sugar-cane, the cramped villages where the sugar workers and their families live, the little market towns: what the visitor sees is all that there is in Mauritius. There is little room for adventure, except at the top, for the French (who have always had large families), for the Chinese, for the well-to-do Indians. At the bottom, where life has been brutish, vision is more restricted, and there is only this communal sense of helplessness and self-disgust.

The relief worker, the father of six, knows he is doing a nonsense job; he doesn't attend; he goes only to sign and get his money. The weeding gangs on the sugar estate know that they are a substitute, and a less efficient and more expensive substitute, for herbicide. Everyone knows only that once the government was good and things appeared to be getting better; and that now, for reasons which both government and opposition say are political, things are getting worse.

The newspapers are so full of local politics that they have no space for foreign news. So in the village clubhouses they talk politics; politics absorbs all their frenzy. Speech and elections are free; real power is unobtainable; and politics is the opium of the people.

A RAINY Sunday afternoon, overcast yet full of glare, and sticky between the showers. In the gravelled back street of this new *cité*, an artisans' settlement of small concrete and corrugated-iron houses just outside the town of Curepipe, an election meeting warms up. It is only a municipal by-election, but in Mauritius an election is an election, and this one has been built up into a trial of strength between the party of Gaëtan Duval, the Foreign Minister, the Black Power man, and the party called the Mauritius Democratic Union, the UDM. Duval says the initials stand for Union des Mulâtres, the Union of Mulattoes. That is Duval's line of attack. There may be other issues; but the visitor, even after he has read all the newspapers, will not be able to detect them.

This is a UDM meeting. There is as yet no audience. Only a few Negro or mulatto boys, some in over-size jackets that belong to fathers or elder brothers; and little groups of unarmed policemen, many of them Indian, in peaked caps and slate-blue raincoats. A microphone on a lorry plays a *sega*, a Mauritian calypso in the local plantation patois.

> *Femme qui fume cigarettes*
> *Mo' pas 'oulé.*
> *Li a coule la mort tabac*
> *Dans 'ous la gue'le.*
> *(Woman who smoke cigarette I don't like.*
> *She leaking stale tobacco in your mouth.)*

More and more little boys come out. One thirteen-year-old boy in his brother's jacket (three brothers, seven sisters, father out of work, mother a cook) is against the UDM. Another boy of mixed race (four brothers, four sisters, no father, no mother) likes the UDM meetings, *parce qu'ils redressent le pays.* This is a version of the UDM slogan: elections here, like Christmas elsewhere, wouldn't be the same without the children. The road bristles with bony little legs; it is like a schoolyard at recess. ("When I go about now," Duval tells me later, "it's like Gulliver in Lilliput. Small children are trying to lift me up.") The UDM *sega* continues. A game of football starts in the sodden sunken field beside the road.

A motor-car rocks down a side road and pulls up next to the lorry. Stones fly. And all at once, to shouts and curses, enraged mulattoes and blacks are fighting around the car and the lorry. The football game breaks up; the children scatter, big jackets swinging above matchstick legs, and then stop to watch. The amplified *sega* continues. The gentle policemen intervene gently, leading away angry men in different directions, each man shouting over his shoulder.

The rain, the bush, the cheap houses, the poor clothes, the mixture of races, the umbrellaed groups who have come out to watch: the hysterical scene is yet so intimate: adults fighting in front of the children, the squalor of the overcrowded barracoon: the politics of the powerless.

The disturbance clears, the car drives off. The *sega* stops. The man on the lorry coughs into the microphone and the meeting begins.

"M. Duval le ₹our li Black Power, le soir li blanc." ("Mr. Duval is Black Power in the daytime. In the night he white.")

"Black Power?" the Negro girl in a pink blouse says. "For me it is a joke."

"M. Duval na pas content créole petit chevé. Mr. Duval don't like black people crinkly head. *'Quand mo' alle côte ₹'aut' donne-moi man₹e macaroni et boire rhum blanc. Moi content man₹e un pé c'est qui bon.'* Hear him: 'When I go by other people let them give me macaroni to eat and white rum to drink. I like eating a lil good food.' "

For the Negro girl the UDM is also a joke. "I don't care for politicians. I come here for *distraction*. There are many like me here. Seventy-five per cent of the girls and boys here don't work. The people are becoming poorer after independence. *Travaillent moins.*"

She is twenty-one, small and thin, narrow shoulders quite square, her eyes hollow. She left school at the fifth standard in 1960. "I have done nothing since 1960. I have my typing certificate, but no work." But, like every other young person in Mauritius, she has a story of a job which once she nearly got. "There was a job advertised for a clerk in a filling station. I and another Muslim girl went. The Muslim girl was selected. Why? I cannot say. I called before the Muslim girl." She is calm now, will condemn no one; but she was angry at the time. "I returned home and said to my mother, 'But look what's happened. I didn't get the job.' I had been registered for five years, the Muslim girl for five months. I think the man at the filling station was a Muslim man, but I don't know. I don't know." The memory is fresh; but this happened three years ago, when she was eighteen. Anger is useless; she will not be angry, she will criticize no one.

Her father is a painter; her mother doesn't work. She has four sisters and three brothers. "I am the eldest. I was hoping to be a teacher. I've been to see Gaëtan Duval many times, but he's just promised and promised." When her father is in work he earns between twenty and thirty rupees a week, between £1.50 and £2.25. The rent of their house in the *cité* is twenty-five and a half rupees a month; electricity costs another nine rupees. "We eat rice, curry, salt fish. Sometimes we eat rice, oil and fried onions. Salt fish is dear now, a little piece for five cents [about a third of a penny]. It is very difficult for eight children. I can stay without food, but the young ones cannot."

Amusements? The cinema? "For five years I haven't been to the cinema. *On n'connaît pas. Connaît pas. Je suis découragée.*" She stays at home and reads poems; she has a schoolbook, *A Book of Longer Poems*. "In Mauritius there are no boy friends." She means that there can be no casual encounters; she cannot go out unchaperoned to mixed gatherings. To go out with a boy, the boy will have to write to her parents for permission; but there can be no boys because her family are too poor to invite anyone to their house. "I have a rich friend from school days. Her father is a policeman. She invites me to parties, but I can't go. Because my mother will not let me go alone. One day perhaps I may get married. By chance."

For another girl a little way up the road the prospects are brighter. She has a job as a teacher in a junior school. She is of mixed race—part of what, in Mauritius, is oddly called the General Population—and she is quite striking, with attractive, well-formed lips and almost straight hair, her looks marred only by a slight pimpliness. Her green pullover is tight over her little breasts; she wears a plaid skirt and a short fawn raincoat, a proper lined raincoat (lined because Mauritius is just outside the temperate zone and has a winter). The spirited girl supports all this stylishness on her salary of fifty rupees a month, just under four pounds. Of course she goes to parties; of course some boy has "written in" for her, and has been rejected.

The sun breaks through. The election speeches continue. Whole households stand outside the small houses, all up the road; and it is a little like a fair. This group is eating peanuts (locally grown: a new and profitable crop, planted between the sugar-cane rows on the big estates, part of the attempt to "diversify"). There are ten people in this group, shelling peanuts, laughing at the speech, scattering peanut-hulls on the wet verge. Ten who live in the little house behind the little hedge. The tall man is out of work. Behind the hedge, at the end of the garden path, is the father, whom at first I couldn't believe in—couldn't believe what I had seen. A man sitting on the threshold, brought out for the afternoon's election entertainment, a man without arms, and with legs cut off just below the hips. Tetanus.

THE SYMPTOMS of depression: dizziness, a heaviness in the head, an inability to concentrate.

The mulatto civil servant who is no longer young and no longer sure of his racial status becomes nervous about his job and his future and the future of his children. He wants to get away, to leave. But the talents that support him in Mauritius cannot support him in Australia or Canada; he has little capital; he can escape, with security, only if he gets his government pension. He can resign with the pension only if he is medically unfit. Depression, then, quite genuinely incapacitates him. In time he appears before a medical board; he is "boarded out," out of the civil service, out of Mauritius.

The unemployed young Indian labourer or labourer's son, seeing his twenties waste away, turns to studies, making unlettered attempts at the Cambridge School Certificate—always big news in the press, the arrival of the papers from England, the arrival of the results— preparing himself for a job that doesn't exist. "I am twenty-nine. I am not married. I passed my School Certificate in 1965. I got a third grade. I applied for several posts. I never got it. Still now I am applying. I passed my School Certificate in 1968, when I was twenty-six. I got another third grade. I now work as a relief supervisor. It is not a promising job. According to my certificate it is not sufficient. I applied for Teachers' Training College six times. I like that very much." He is all right. But some break up. They yield to their headaches, give up the impossible goal of the Cambridge School Certificate and become horribly idle, at home or in the hospital.

The travel-writer, reporting on the happy-go-lucky island customs, will tell you that a bottle of rum will gain you admittance to a *sega* party. Local doctors will tell you that alcoholism is a serious and growing problem. Rum, at eight rupees a bottle, sixty pence, is expensive, almost a tourist luxury; the standard drink is the local banana spirit, which sells at nine pennies a bottle. A few years ago one out of ten patients sent to the mental hospital was an alcoholic; now it is one out of seven. These figures are unverifiable; the government, perhaps correctly, disapproves of such investigations.

It is no secret, however, that many cases of mental disorder are caused by malnutrition and severe anaemia. Just as it is obvious that this very thin young woman in the family planning clinic is starved and quite withdrawn. No amount of family planning will solve her problems now. This morning she had tea; yesterday, for dinner, she had a kind of soup: boiled rice soaked in tea. With lackluster eyes in a skeletal and already moronic face, she sits listless on the wooden bench. She wears a green sari; there is a small handkerchief in her bony hand, a trace of powder on her face. Mauritius is not India; there is no longer that knowledge of fate, *karma*, in which distress is absorbed. Everyone is responsible for himself, everyone is genteel.

Three years ago a woman of thirty-five decided to allow one of her children to starve to death, to save the others. She did so; then she fell into a depression.

For the past ten years and more economists have been visiting Mauritius and writing alarming reports, making "projections" of population and unemployment. Disaster has always appeared to lie in the future; it is assumed that at the moment people are somehow carrying on. A Mauritian journalist told me that the common people had their own little ways and could live on twenty-five cents a day, two pennies. It isn't true. But how can the journalist, or anyone else who has to live in Mauritius, be blamed for not seeing that the disaster has occurred?

THE MAURITIUS economy, a government white paper says, "is not technically backward." The sugar estates are as efficient as can be; they engage in continuous research and are far more efficient than the small farmers. Any plan for breaking up the estates into smaller units runs the risk of damaging efficiency, and it is uncertain whether it will actually create more jobs.

Such a fragmentation may be socially satisfying. The party of the young, the Mouvement Militant Mauricien (MMM), says in its New Leftish manifesto: *"On ne fait bien sûr pas d'omelette sans casser d'oeufs."* ("You can't make an omelette without breaking eggs.") That New Left omelette again; but the MMM's analysis is not all that different from the government's. They both recognize the efficiency of the economy, and its brutality. They both speak of the need to diversify agriculture and selectively to industrialize. They would both like to separate the sugar factories from the sugar estates, to separate, that is, management and money from the land. And they both seem to recognize that, at the end of the day, they will be left with what they started with: an agricultural colony, created by empire in an empty island and always meant to be part of something larger, now given a thing called independence and set adrift, an abandoned imperial barracoon, incapable of economic or cultural autonomy.

Both the MMM and the government speak, as they must speak, of a Mauritian nation. As though immigrant nations are created by words and exhortation and not by the possibilities of the land. No one has yet devised, or attempted to devise, a political philosophy for these independent island-barracoons; and it may be that their problems defy solution. The French, with their strange imperial-linguistic dreams, have made the nearby island of Réunion a department of France. Of what country can Mauritius be a department?

The MMM talks of "a global solution." Faced with the problems of Mauritius, even the New Left founders, and compromises. Tourism is degrading, the MMM manifesto says; and for two well-documented pages it catalogues the disasters that have befallen some Caribbean islands. But, the manifesto concludes, the situation in Mauritius is so desperate that tourism must be developed, though of course *"un tourisme visant non la classe très riche des pays étrangers, mais la classe moyenne de ces pays* [a tourism aimed not at the very rich class in foreign countries, but at the middle class]." The MMM would like to see 300,000 tourists a year, fifteen times the present number; this is also the stated target of the government.

In the circumstances, the concrete plans that are put forward often have a Robinson Crusoe, boy-scout quality. Set the unemployed to plant trees on riverbanks, create a National Youth Service (to do what? to be financed by what?): these were ideas put forward by the Labour Party at the seminar on unemployment.

Mr. Duval, the Black Power man, has his own *Projet Cochon,* Operation Pig. He distributes piglets to potential minders and hopes in this way to create a pig-rearing industry. A good idea, I was told, with export possibilities; and there have been some successes. But it happens that pork is the Negro's favourite food; and the Chinese of course dote on it. In an island of hungry Negroes and epicurean Chinese a piglet-distributing scheme runs certain risks. I could get no figures; but it seems that enough of the distributed piglets have been eaten for *Projet Cochon* to be known now to some people as the *cochon projet.*

THE TENEMENT stands on the site of a great house in Port Louis, the capital. The high concrete wall of the great house survives; within, the front of the yard is rubbled, with faded cigarette packets, dusty cellophane wrappers and dead leaves between the stones and crushed old masonry. In one corner, right against the wall, some boys and young men, seated on boxes, are playing cards, in the middle of this hot morning. Beyond the rubble, and below two old trees, the tenement sheds of corrugated iron and wood, much repaired and added-to, run down in two parallel lines, past the communal tap and many ancillary little sheds, to the communal lavatories. The ground is rocky here; the earth, where it shows, damp and black.

A red-tiled floor in the first room on the right, quite dark below the naked corrugated-iron roof. A bed, two tables, some boxes, a clothesline. A *Playboy* pin-up above the bed, a little bundle on the bed: a tiny red-brown baby, ten days old. The mother went out this morning to get some milk from the Child Welfare Centre, but was sent back because she hadn't taken the correct papers. Yet the "papers," frail with handling, are there, on the table, in a little plastic envelope. She will go again tomorrow. Her fourth child: now six sleep in that room.

Her husband, an electrician, has been out of work for ten months. Once he worked in the Fire Brigade; and his Fire Brigade belt hangs on the line, the only unnecessary object in that room. He is out on the wharf this morning, hoping to get fifty cents, three and a half pennies. Yesterday there wasn't even fifty cents; and this morning she borrowed twenty-five cents from a neighbour. She sent a girl to buy some food, but twenty-five cents couldn't buy enough for a meal. So the girl bought a loaf and some chutney for eleven cents—that loaf there—and brought back the change, fourteen cents, there, on the table, next to the tin of Nivea Creme, the broken comb, the worn powder puff, the half-full bottle of Cologne Impériale (a gift to the baby from the hospital nurse), the rubber dummy, and a pencil. Possessions.

She used to do family planning. But she quarrelled with her husband once and he threw away the pills, and she didn't go back to the clinic. Her husband gets angry when there is nothing to eat. He beats her then and she goes away. But then she thinks: what can the poor man do? So she stays outside for a little, cries for a bit and then goes back. She thinks now she'll put the children in a nursery and see if she can't get a job. According to her customs—she is a Tamil—she shouldn't go out for forty days after the birth of her child. But she has already broken that rule, and she needs money. So now she will go out. She will go from house to house, asking whether there are clothes to mend or dishes to wash. She'll probably make about three or four rupees a week, between twenty and thirty pennies.

The next room is larger, brighter, lighter: pale ochre walls, lino on the floor. No kitchen area at the front: the kitchen is in an adjoining room: this is an apartment. An Indian girl, a Bihari, pale and fine-featured, lives here, with a Negro girl, a friend perhaps, who has now cast herself in the role of maid. They are both very young, about eighteen, and both very small. The black girl looks shrunken and undersized. A transparent pinkish blouse shows her brassiere and the simplicity of her bony body. No sexual intent there; there is a curious guilelessness about the black girl. She is the maid; she lives through her young mistress. The Bihari girl is perfectly proportioned, even plump-thighed as she sits on the edge of the bed, occasionally nervously rocking her knees together in the Indian way. The mistress is obviously as anaemic as the maid, and perhaps even more unwell; she has the sunken, too-bright eyes of the hysteric.

A large photograph of a sailor hangs on the wall. The Bihari girl says he is Swedish.

"Is why she take *two* rooms," the black girl says in English. "She cook in other room. She stay here all day."

The Bihari girl says in patois, "My mother is at home in Petite Rivière. She lives alone since my father disappeared. My father went mad." It is said just like that. "Five years ago my father stopped working. He used to work as a cane-cutter. Then he began to get headaches and went to hospital. And then he disappeared. I was fourteen. My mother did a little cleaning and washing to get some money. In December of that year I came here to Port Louis. I told my mother I was coming to Port Louis. But it was my own idea. I go to see my mother sometimes; she doesn't come here. I have two brothers in school. One does a little work in a *magasin*. Here now I just sit and read and talk."

"She no tell you," the black girl says. "But she no work. All month this man"—the man on the wall—"give this girl money. Fifty, sixty rupees, I don't know. She have baby for this sailor. The baby die. Two years now."

There are other photographs of men stuck in the door of the glass cabinet. All the men are Europeans.

"*No Mauritius!*" the Bihari girl says in English, seeming to shriek as she switches language. "No have job here for man."

On the oilcloth-covered table, a Post Office savings book.

"*Fini,*" she says. "*Fini*. All fi-neshed."

She began to save in 1967. Twenty rupees after a year; fifteen rupees after eighteen months. Then the regular monthly deposits—ten, twenty, twenty-five, even thirty rupees—until the later months of her pregnancy and the miscarriage. For six months the account bleeds, and for a year after that it seems dead. In February 1971 a miraculous transfusion: six hundred rupees, £45, from an English boy, commemorated by that coloured snap in the glass cabinet: a family snap, clearly from England. Only forty rupees remain now. She has paid off her debts. She has bought a transistor, and she has bought medicines. She feels tired. She has bought Sanatogen, for her nerves, and *Sirop des Chiens*, for her blood. All there on the table, with the savings book. Above the door, a Sacred Heart, to protect this Hindu girl and her maid.

They are free now, and independent. But the pimps and gangs of Port Louis await, and the new Chinese-run brothels at Pointe aux Sables. It was at one of those places, some days later, that I saw the two girls: the maid, very demure, keeping an eye on her mistress.

A lawyer says, "I've seen many people going into prostitution just to give a chance in life to their eldest brother or youngest brother. The girls who go aboard the ships are from the best schools in the colony."

· · ·

THE GANGS started four or five years ago. They grew out of job-seeking and job-sharing street brotherhoods; they became pimping groups; they became gangs for hire. A recent gangster's job: throwing acid on the face of a manager who sacked a worker. The fee: sixty-five rupees, £5.

In this country court consider this gang, had up for damaging property: three black boys, brothers, and a badly mutilated young red-skinned mulatto. Consider the procession of shabby youths with bright faces had up for the pettiest of petty larceny. The scene is almost domestic. Much of Mauritian official architecture is on a domestic, plantation-house scale, and the little wooden court-house is as small as a drawing-room. The magistrate sits against the back wall; there is a window on either side of his chair; and there are fruit trees just outside the windows.

The law is the law, and in Mauritius a job is a job. But the police officer is depressed by his duties. He says, "This district is one of the poorest in the island. After the crop season they have nothing to do. They fish a little and they collect acacia seeds, for which they get twelve cents [one new penny] a pound. So life is hard. It takes a lot of acacia seeds to make one pound."

A Muslim lawyer says, "We were more serene in 1962. We hope this is a passing phase. But that is what everyone says: 'It cannot last, it cannot go on.' And now this new party, the MMM, adds to the desperation. People withdrawing their capital. Prices going up. Taxes going up. Probably once a month we say, 'It is only a passing phase.'"

A mulatto doctor says, "The boy who in a richer society might have gone into another, mixed social group, in the end here, through depression and frustration, collapses into his old society and resigns himself to it. It is what is saving Mauritius, this climate of acceptance of fate, of things as they are, which the Indians irradiate to the others. We are ruled by two myths. The government; and the sugar estates, the malignant white god. The white man has become a myth. If the white man didn't exist, in Mauritius we would have to invent someone like him."

A HUGE SWASTIKA is painted on the main road that runs through the little Indian town of Triolet. The swastika is the Indo-Aryan good-luck sign and part of the decoration of a Hindu house, but here it is used politically, the emblem of a new party called the Jan Sangh, which seeks to remind Indians of their racial loyalties. Both swastika and Mr. Duval's Black Power are responses to the inter-racial, New Left MMM. Fantasy responding to fantasy: it was in Triolet that the MMM won its first election victory, but in this clubhouse, just a few weeks after the election, nothing seems to remain of MMM doctrine.

There are the standard stories of Mauritian weariness, of School Certificate people who cannot get jobs and "just stay at home pursuing their studies. They are sick with life, tired with life." About thirty or forty have gone to England to do nursing. "But most of us don't get it. That depends on the minister. Sometimes he doesn't allow us to go. They give favours to their families." There is the story of the boy—that young man just passing in the road outside—who "drank away" the little land that was his patrimony and is now like everybody else. "Now he is in crisis."

And there is a version of the Mauritian legend of the missed job. This is the story of a boy who two years ago lost a government job through the trickery of a clerk: a job as a messenger, worth 5½ rupees a day, 40 pence. Everyone in the clubhouse knows this story and has his own version; and the failed messenger, when he appears, a handsome, energetic young man, is clearly a glamour figure. His neighbour got the job. "I am not angry with him. I leave the matter in the hands of God." In the meantime he wears a mauve MMM shirt, to express his defiance of the government.

Someone says, "People here help one another in cases of accident. But it's different when it comes to jobs. Then families are jealous. And the bad blood comes out when they're drinking."

They have such a developed sense of injustice. Have they no sense of danger? They have such confidence in their rights, their votes, the power of their opinions. They regard their independence as settled and permanent; they do not see its fragility. An internal coup, an armed takeover from outside: neither hard to imagine in this area: have they no thoughts of that?

The young men in the clubhouse say, "The government will look after that."

But as the afternoon fades and the traffic lessens and many radios are turned on to the Indian music programme, as the talk becomes slower and less aggressive, it becomes clear that these young men are beyond the sense of danger. They see themselves, profoundly, as victims; the enemy won a long time ago.

"Today in Mauritius there is the rhinoceros beetle which can damage a coconut tree. These beetles were introduced deliberately for the medicines to be sold. Our forefathers never knew these beetles. So they made money two ways. They destroyed our coconuts and they sold the medicines. We can't suppose that the Ministry of Agriculture did this. We can suppose that some strangers did that."

"They uprooted our orange trees, in order to get us to buy oranges from South Africa. We suppose it. They came and told us that our orange trees had a certain fungus."

"Day after day now we hear of our people being struck down by illnesses which we did not possess."

"Malaria."

It was the eradication of malaria that led to the population explosion.

"No. Malaria was common here."

"Cholera. For example, cholera was not common here. There are other illnesses now. I cannot say their names. But people do suffer from them. We suppose that certain things happen in Mauritius."

"Sysilis."

He is corrected. "Syphilis. That's on the increase, especially at Port Louis. The government is taking steps to legalize prostitution. They give the girls licenses nowadays."

It is the Japanese, whose trawlers use the harbour, who have introduced a system of licensing.

"On the one side the government is fighting prostitution. On the other side it is encouraging it."

"They are right to do so, become prostitutes. They are suffering from poverty. They should do it. As I myself know—"

"I will kill my daughter if she does that."

"But prostitution is good for them, if it gives them money. Many students have become prostitutes, especially at Port Louis."

"They are building a new hotel here. The government will give permits for girls to work there as prostitutes."

The talk is gentle, slow, without anger. Outside, on the road, the swastika, emblem of threat and power, and the walls scrawled and counter-scrawled with political slogans and the initials of parties.

BUT SOME ARE LUCKY. Some get away. Like this very small twenty-year-old boy, encountered not far from the Government Buildings in

Port Louis, still delicately holding his "papers," the duplicated foolscap sheet with the precious ministerial signature and ministry stamp. He is off to England; a hospital has accepted him. He is very small and pared-down, his frailty the result of an illness when he was six. He got his School Certificate in 1968, when he was seventeen, and for the last three years he has been doing nothing, just waiting for this. He is solemn and slightly defiant, as though afraid to express pleasure and ready to defend his success. He is clearly of good character. But does he have a real love for nursing? He says that he's wanted to do nothing else, ever since he was a boy; he even joined the St. John's Ambulance Brigade.

His father works in a sugar factory and earns 150 rupees a month, just over £11. He has four sisters and two brothers. Their usual breakfast is bread and butter and bananas. During his years of idleness he would help with the housework in the mornings; then he would go to the British Council library to read, returning home for a lunch of rice and vegetable curry. Sometimes he fell ill and couldn't eat. Sometimes he was just too miserable to eat. He went out walking then with his friends and they had "nice baths by the river." His headaches could come at any moment, especially when he was alone; and as he found it hard to sleep he would stay out on the road talking to his friends until midnight. He visited his friends a lot. They would tell one another that in a year's time they would be "safe," they would get a job; in this way they "inspired one another with confidence."

Certain problems remain: the raising of the £50 surety and the 1,640-rupee fare to London, the two sums equivalent to his father's wages for fifteen months. But the bank will help, and he will be able to repay from the eight or nine pounds a week he will be getting from the English hospital. He is absolutely unconcerned about racial problems in England; it will not matter to him what people say to him or about him; and he doesn't care if he never sees Mauritius again. He and his friends have given up local politics. Politics can't help anyone in Mauritius now. The government can't help anyone now. "The MMM is also the same. It is better to depend on yourself."

IN A BIGGER, richer country Gaëtan Duval, the Foreign Minister, might have been an actor or a pop star. He has the disquieting attractiveness (though, at forty, his looks have begun to go, and he is concerned about his softening waistline); he has the hair, the clothes; and he has the actor's needs. His enemies say politics provides him with a "periodic mob-bath"; he says, as an actor might say, that he is in politics for "the love." "You get people to love you and you feel love for them." And he was especially pleased, when I met him, with his "Black Is Beautiful" campaign. "In these few weeks I have created a psychological revolution in the mind of the black man in this country."

But he was also advocating trade with South Africa. How was that linked with Black Power?

"They're *not*! That is the point." And he roared with laughter, rocking back in his chair, his lace-trimmed black shirt open all down his milky-brown chest. He called, *"Madame Bell! Madame Bell!"* And when the middle-aged white receptionist-secretary came in from the outer office, he asked her for the text of the speech that had been made in his praise a fortnight before in Paris, when he had been presented with the Gold Star of Tourism by the Société des Gens de Lettres de France.

The speech was brought in, a foolscap sheet, and—though there was really no need: in the morning the text was to be in the newspapers— Duval began to read it out. *"Monsieur le Ministre, laissez-moi d'abord saluer le Ministre des Affaires Etrangères, l'Homme d'Etat, l'Ecrivain, le Penseur, l'Homme d'Action. Vous êtes le symbole de tout ce que nous aimons en l'Ile Maurice* [Minister, let me first of all salute you as Foreign Secretary, statesman, writer, thinker, man of action. You are the symbol of everything we love in Mauritius] . . . That's the sort of thing that makes our Franco-Mauritians mad. That a black man should be a symbol of French culture. And I am the sort of man who rubs it in."

Until recently, Duval said, the French believed that there were only ten thousand French-speaking people in Mauritius—the French Mauritians. Now they knew that one-third of the island, and that meant a lot of black people, spoke French. "The French are pouring money on me. They gave me four million rupees. Another million this week. And now we've sent fifty-three workers to France. I'm fighting this election on my *foreign* policy." But the South Africans were *slow*. "They're slower than the old Boers." He had asked them for a three-year supply of subsidized pig-food for his pig scheme, but so far they hadn't done anything.

Someone came into the office.

"Meet François," Duval said. "Factotum, friend." We were all going to lunch in Curepipe. As we were leaving the courtyard, Duval called out to someone, "Good news. Germany is taking thirty-six more. Lufthansa, in Frankfurt." Thirty-six workers.

"In addition to the hundred?"

"Yes. I will announce it at the meeting today." And as we drove along the scenic highway (its flowering roadside shrubs and roundabout gardens maintained by relief workers) he said, "I told the Germans when I was there that if they had anything to give me they had better give it to me before the election. Otherwise they would have to give it to somebody else . . . It doesn't matter at all whether we lose this municipal seat or not, because we have such a majority. But I create this atmosphere of tension. I can't live otherwise. I can do these things because everyone thinks I am a little mad and do not act altogether rationally . . . What do you think of these?" He passed me, from a full box, his new publicity photographs, taken especially for the election: sitting in his black leather suit on Black Beauty, sitting astride a motorcycle, and standing with crossed legs against the front of his sports car. "They are for the women. I appeared on French television in an Indian outfit and I am still getting letters. The English don't like me, even when they try. The French are different. Do you know what they said about me in the French papers? A handsome black god."

When we were in the restaurant in Curepipe I told him—after a glass or two of wine—that I found it hard to think of him as a politician. He said he could leave politics; he was a farmer. I said I'd heard that some of the piglets he had distributed had been eaten. He was instantly serious and offended; but then, almost at once, he said that perhaps some had been eaten, but that wasn't what he had heard.

François, factotum, friend, spoke in patois.

At the end Duval said, "I've just been hearing a sad story. The father of all the little pigs died. Black Power."

A waiter came and said, *"M. Duval, téléphone pour 'ous."*

"Qui sanne là-ça?"

"Consul africain."

"The South Africans," Duval said.

When he came back he said, "The consul has just had a telephone call from South Africa. They've offered a gift of fifty sows and two boars and free food for them for one year. I told him to tell Pretoria to send me a telegram." No doubt for the meeting.

I said, "I thought you asked for pig-food for three years."

"That was subsidized. This is free. They're scared."

There was a French consulate wedding party in a private room of the restaurant. A young Frenchwoman came out, became ecstatic at the sight of Duval and, ignoring the rest of us, embraced him and began to talk. Then a blue-suited man came out and said, *"Gaëtan, ils te demandent de venir les bénir."* ("Gaëtan, they want you to come and bless them.")

"Je n'ai pas mon collier de maire." ("I don't have my mayoral chain.")

But he got up and went. He came back many minutes later. His eyes were champagne-bright and he was smiling. "I've just heard something very funny. This girl who's got married, you see, is half-Belgian and half-Polish. Typically French. She was there with her brother. I said to them, 'If you are Polish, why aren't you more beautiful?' And the brother said, *'Parce que nous sommes habillés.'* " ("Because we have our clothes on.")

Later, in the crowded town hall, Duval had some of his supporters sing one of his campaign songs for me.

> *Black Beau-tee! Black Beau-tee!*
> *Black is beautiful!*
> *Beautiful, beautiful*
> *Is black.*

"This is going to be the uniform," Duval said, showing some bits of material. "Black and red. Black belts with red trousers. Black shirt. Wet look."

The following day, when I went to the Foreign Ministry to check my notes of our lunch, Duval introduced a little Negro boy in the outer office as the composer of his campaign *sega*. The boy beat time on Madame Bell's table and sang:

> *Mo' dire 'ous: la frapper.*
> *Laisse-mo' trappe-li,*
> *Laisse-mo' batte-li.*
> *Mo' alle condamné,*
> *Jamais mo' va laisser mulâtre*
> *Faire mari de mon endroit.*
> (*I tell you, hit them. Lemme catch them, lemme lash them.*
> *I rather go to jail than let a mulatto man boss me around.*)

"The level of political thought here is *fantastically* low," Paul Bérenger, the twenty-six-year-old French Mauritian founder of the MMM, said. He had been shot at a few days before from the town hall in Curepipe where Duval's men had sung the Black Beauty song for me. And now—in Port Louis, in this new air-conditioned basement restaurant, almost empty after lunch—Bérenger was with his bodyguard, a black giant called Muttur, running slightly to fat, but still famous locally as a boxer. Bérenger was in his own way as stylish as Duval, and in Mauritius as exotic. Small, slender, soft-spoken, with tinted rimless glasses, a thin handlebar moustache, and a black leather jacket hanging over his shoulders, he was like a European, of Europe. There was no trace of Mauritius in his speech or accent; and he looked what he was, a man from the Paris barricades of '68. "A good year, if I may say so."

He said, "Of course the government talks only of *unemployment*. That word tends to make it only an issue of economics, to take the human and political aspects out of it . . . Before 1968 in Mauritius people didn't have to think or offer serious economic or political programmes. They simply had to play the racial card. In the past the people at the top sought to take the pressure out of the situation by having the different races fight and kill each other, and they would start the same thing again if they could . . . The history of this country is the history of several different struggles succeeding one another and then fighting each other. That's the drama of this place. The first struggle was the struggle of the slaves. The head of a rebellious slave, a Malagasy chief, was kept in our museum here in Port Louis for many years. Then you have the rise of the coloureds [mulattoes]. In 1911 there were riots here in Port Louis between coloureds and whites. Then the Indians. The coloureds, following the white example, became anti-Indian. Then the creoles [blacks] also fell for that. And the main agent of that change was Duval. That is the importance, the malefic importance, of Duval: bringing over the blacks on the side of the whites. Duval is a myth. He is a creation. He is King Creole. Created by the newspapers. It's a myth that's dead. But he doesn't want to die."

Bérenger snapped his fingers. The black bodyguard brought out a paper-bag of what looked like sweets. Bérenger took one; the bodyguard took one. Bérenger said, "Hack's Cough Drops."

Bérenger comes from an old French Mauritian family. His father was a civil servant. Not a planter, not a landed man; and there are people in Mauritius who say that this is at the heart of Bérenger's own rebellion. In

1963, at the age of eighteen, before going to university (North Wales), he worked for a while as a sailor. "The MMM was started during a holiday in Mauritius in 1968. Though that makes it sound more casual than it was. The government made us a present. We planned to demonstrate peacefully against Princess Alexandra's visit. The government threw eighteen of us into jail. Why Alexandra? Well, Alex's husband is Ogilvy, Ogilvy is Lonrho, and Lonrho is extremely powerful here—hotels, sugar factories, import-export. Plus the waste involved in the reception. I've been in jail four times since then . . . The situation is bad. People feel it can blow up at any moment. I doubt whether we'll go past this year without the government crumbling or an uprising or general elections."

I told him I had found no trace of MMM doctrine in Triolet. The socialism his party had expounded seemed to have been absorbed into the paranoid myth of the enemy.

He didn't answer directly. He said, "There is always *something* behind the myth." And then, tentatively, like a man thinking aloud, he began to talk around the subject of myth-making. "Things can go fantastic distances in the minds of people here. I suppose the size of the island has something to do with it . . . There is a definite melodramatic tendency. In Port Louis, for example, I was said to have an *electric* baton. I don't know what they meant by that. In Curepipe it was a baton with a chain. And my black leather jacket is supposed to be bullet-proof. And I suppose that if as I walk past the municipality office in Curepipe I am shot at; and if there is a minister, supposedly the protector of the black, who wears black leather and sits on a black horse; then you are in a situation that can give rise to any kind of myth.

"You live with certain things; you don't put them together. There's one of our ministers—it's only now, as I am talking here, I see how extensive this myth-faculty is—this minister, on election day he wore his paratroop uniform. Ramgoolam [the Prime Minister] used to be a myth. The *chacha* or uncle of the Hindus. Very active and powerful, but somehow floating above it all. There is a biography of Ramgoolam by one of our local writers. It's a biography without a date. It's fantastic mythology and poetry and things . . . I believe the real depression comes when you go through our education system. There's the linguistic aspect. The language we all use is despised." (The MMM is romantic about the local patois, which it sees as an important part of a "national" culture.) "The Franco-Mauritians too have their myths. When I came back the story among them was that *I* had brought de Gaulle down. You can find it still. 'If Paul brought de Gaulle down, what chance does poor old Ramgoolam have?' They all deal in fantasies. And it's rooted in the colonial situation."

He made the two hours pass quickly. As he left with his bodyguard he smiled and said, "I've got to go now and get some 'tough guys' for the forum this afternoon."

But the tough guys were not needed. No one tried to break up the MMM meeting that afternoon, which was in the town of Rose Hill. The hall was packed with several hundred students. A racially mixed audience, a mixed platform, ideas being treated like news: it was the brightest gathering I had seen in Mauritius. And by its very existence it was—but perhaps only in the eye of the visitor—a tribute to the liberal administration that was being rejected.

"IT IS AN IMITATION," Sir Seewoosagur Ramgoolam, the Prime Minister, says. "They are trying to imitate Mao, Fidel Castro. Fantasy? They are not dealing in fantasy; they think their ideas will take root here. There *is* poverty. But we are trying to contain that by social services. We spend about thirty million rupees on assistance. People criticize us for that, for giving things like family allowances. My reply is: 'Children are born. I cannot allow them to grow up stunted. If they are well fed, well educated, they are not a burden on society. Otherwise they will become backward, mentally.' "

A different vocabulary, different concerns: a different life. The Prime Minister is nearly as old as the century; and that poetic biography Bérenger spoke about is an attempt to do justice to a subject which— though the scale is small, the setting restricted—is worthy of legend: the rise to power of a man born into a depressed and leaderless community, in an agricultural colony, in the darkest age of colonialism. Few colonial leaders have shown such courage and tenacity as Ramgoolam; few, having achieved power, have been so anxious to heal old enmities and rule humanely. But already the new state, as incomplete as it ever was, is threatened, and from more than one direction.

Bérenger says, "This hanging around ministers' offices, people looking for jobs, this is encouraged by the ministers. Each minister is trying to succeed Ramgoolam and each is trying to play his card."

The Prime Minister says, "Now we have the Public Service Commission. This waiting outside the doors of ministers is a mistake. It is a relic of colonial days."

The old enemy. And also the new: "Colonialism is a destructive institution. It creates parasites and hangers-on. And they are still with us—people of all races who profited from the stay in this country of a foreign power. I don't know whether they've completely reconciled themselves to the changes. I think this new movement, the MMM, is a devious approach by these same people to revive themselves. I think they want to have their own back on me especially and my party."

The Prime Minister has one bad eye, damaged by a cow's horn when he was a child. The drawing-room of his new house in Port Louis, built on the site of his old house, is full of the mementoes of his long political life: signed portraits, photographs of airport meetings, ponderous official gifts in a variety of national styles. Here, among his souvenirs, he constantly entertains. He likes informal dinner parties, conversation, chat. He would like to retire, to become his legend, to be "above it all."

But tranquillity recedes. The barracoon is overcrowded; the escape routes are closed. The people are disaffected and have no sense of danger.

1972

Power?

THE TRINIDAD CARNIVAL is famous. For the two days before Ash Wednesday the million or so islanders—blacks, whites, the later immigrant groups of Portuguese, Indians, and Chinese—parade the hot streets in costumed "bands" and dance to steel orchestras. This year there was a twist. After the Carnival there were Black Power disturbances. After the masquerade and the music, anger and terror.

In a way, it makes sense. Carnival and Black Power are not as opposed as they appear. The tourists who go for the Carnival don't really know what they are watching. The islanders themselves, who have spent so long forgetting the past, have forgotten the darker origins of their Carnival. The bands, flags and costumes have little to do with Lent, and much to do with slavery.

The slave in Trinidad worked by day and lived at night. Then the world of the white plantations fell away; and in its place was a securer, secret world of fantasy, of Negro "kingdoms," "regiments," bands. The people who were slaves by day saw themselves then as kings, queens, dauphins, princesses. There were pretty uniforms, flags and painted wooden swords. Everyone who joined a regiment got a title. At night the Negroes played at being people, mimicking the rites of the upper world. The kings visited and entertained. At gatherings a "secretary" might sit scribbling away.

Once, in December 1805, this fantasy of the night overflowed into the working day. There was serious talk then of cutting off the heads of some plantation owners, of drinking holy water afterwards and eating pork and dancing. The plot was found out; and swiftly, before Christmas, in the main Port of Spain square there were hangings, decapitations, brandings and whippings.

That was Trinidad's first and last slave "revolt." The Negro kingdoms of the night were broken up. But the fantasies remained. They had to, because without that touch of lunacy the Negro would have utterly despaired and might have killed himself slowly by eating dirt; many in Trinidad did. The Carnival the tourist goes to see is a version of the lunacy that kept the slave alive. It is the original dream of black power, style and prettiness; and it always feeds on a private vision of the real world.

During the war an admiration for Russia—really an admiration for "stylish" things like Stalin's moustache and the outlandish names of Russian generals, Timoshenko, Rokossovsky—was expressed in a "Red Army" band. At the same time an admiration for Humphrey Bogart created a rival "Casablanca" band. Make-believe, but taken seriously and transformed; not far below, perhaps even unacknowledged, there has always been a vision of the black millennium, as much a vision of revenge as of a black world made whole again.

SOMETHING of the Carnival lunacy touches all these islands where people, first as slaves and then as neglected colonials, have seen themselves as futile, on the other side of the real world. In St. Kitts, with a population of thirty-six thousand, Papa Bradshaw, the Premier, has tried to calm despair by resurrecting the memory of Christophe, Emperor of Haiti, builder of the Citadel, who was born a slave on the island. Until they were saved from themselves, the six thousand people of Anguilla seriously thought they could just have a constitution written by someone from Florida and set up in business as an independent country.

In Jamaica the Rastafarians believe they are Abyssinians and that the Emperor Haile Selassie is God. This is one of the unexpected results of Italian propaganda during the Abyssinian war. The Italians said then that there was a secret black society called Niya Binghi ("Death to the Whites") and that it was several million strong. The propaganda delighted some Jamaicans, who formed little Niya Binghi play-groups of their own. Recently the Emperor visited Jamaica. The Rastafarians were expecting a black lion of a man; they saw someone like a Hindu, mild-featured, brown and small. The disappointment was great; but somehow the sect survives.

These islanders are disturbed. They already have black government and black power, but they want more. They want something more than politics. Like the dispossessed peasantry of medieval Europe, they await crusades and messiahs. Now they have Black Power. It isn't the Black

Power of the United States. That is the protest of a disadvantaged minority which has at last begun to feel that some of the rich things of America are accessible, that only self-contempt and discrimination stand in the way. But in the islands the news gets distorted.

The media cannot make the disadvantages as real as the protest. Famous cities are seen to blaze; young men of the race come out of buildings with guns; the black-gloved hands of triumphant but bowed athletes are raised as in a religious gesture; the handsome spokesmen of protest make threats before the cameras which appear at last to have discovered black style. This is power. In the islands it is like a vision of the black millennium. It needs no political programme.

In the islands the intellectual equivocations of Black Power are part of its strength. After the sharp analysis of black degradation, the spokesmen for Black Power usually become mystical, vague, and threatening. In the United States this fits the cause of protest, and fits the white audience to whom this protest is directed. In the islands it fits the old, apocalyptic mood of the black masses. Anything more concrete, anything like a programme, might become simple local politics and be reduced to the black power that is already possessed.

Black Power as rage, drama and style, as revolutionary jargon, offers something to everybody: to the unemployed, the idealistic, the dropout, the Communist, the politically frustrated, the anarchist, the angry student returning home from humiliations abroad, the racialist, the old-fashioned black preacher who has for years said at street corners that after Israel it was to be the turn of Africa. Black Power means Cuba and China; it also means clearing the Chinese and the Jews and the tourists out of Jamaica. It is identity and it is also miscegenation. It is drinking holy water, eating pork and dancing; it is going back to Abyssinia. There has been no movement like it in the Caribbean since the French Revolution.

So in Jamaica, some eighteen months ago, students joined with Rastafarians to march in the name of Black Power against the black government. Campus idealism, campus protest; but the past is like quicksand here. There was a middle-class rumour, which was like a rumour from the days of slavery, that a white tourist was to be killed, but only sacrificially, without malice.

At the same time, in St. Kitts, after many years in authority, Papa Bradshaw was using Black Power, as words alone, to undermine the opposition. Round and round the tiny impoverished island, on the one circular road, went the conspiratorial printed message, cut out from a gasoline advertisement: *Join the Power Set.*

Far away, on the Central American mainland, in British Honduras, which is only half-black, Black Power had just appeared and was already undermining the multi-racial nature of both government and opposition. The carrier of the infection was a twenty-one-year-old student who had been to the United States on, needless to say, an American government scholarship.

He had brought back news about the dignity of the peasant and a revolution based on land. I thought the message came from another kind of country and somebody else's revolution, and wasn't suited to the local blacks, who were mainly city people with simple city ambitions. (It was front-page news, while I was there, that a local man had successfully completed an American correspondence course in jail management.)

But it didn't matter. A message had come. "The whites are buying up the land." "What the black man needs is bread." "It became a phallic symbol to the black to be a log-cutter." It was the jargon of the move-ment, at once scientific-sounding and millenarian. It transcended the bread-and-butter protests of local politics; it smothered all argument. Day by day the movement grew.

EXCITEMENT! And perhaps this excitement is the only liberation that is possible. Black Power in these black islands is protest. But there is no enemy. The enemy is the past, of slavery and colonial neglect and a soci-ety uneducated from top to bottom; the enemy is the smallness of the islands and the absence of resources. Opportunism or borrowed jargon may define phantom enemies: racial minorities, "elites," "white niggers." But at the end the problems will be the same, of dignity and identity.

In the United States Black Power may have its victories. But they will be American victories. The small islands of the Caribbean will remain islands, impoverished and unskilled, ringed as now by a *cordon sanitaire,* their people not needed anywhere. They may get less innocent or less corrupt politicians; they will not get less helpless ones. The island blacks will continue to be dependent on the books, films and goods of others; in this important way they will continue to be the half-made societies of a dependent people, the Third World's third world. They will forever consume; they will never create. They are without material sources; they will never develop the higher skills. Identity depends in the end on achievement; and achievement here cannot but be small. Again and again the protest leader will appear and the millennium will seem about to come.

FIFTY years ago, writing at a moment when Spain seemed about to disintegrate, Ortega y Gasset saw that fragmented peoples come together only in order "to do something tomorrow." In the islands this assurance about the future is missing. Millenarian excitement will not hold them together, even if they were all black; and some, like Trinidad and Guyana and British Honduras, are only half-black. The pursuit of black identity and the community of black distress is a dead end, frenzy for the sake of frenzy, the self-scourging of people who cannot see what they will have to do tomorrow.

In *We Wish to Be Looked Upon,* published last year by Teachers College Press, Vera Rubin and Marisa Zavalloni report on surveys of high-school students in Trinidad they conducted in 1957 and 1961, at a time of pre-independence, messianic optimism. (Eric Williams had come to power, suddenly and overwhelmingly, in 1956.) The students were asked to write at length about their "expectations, plans and hopes for the future."

Black: I would like to be a great man not only in music but also in sociology and economics. In the USA I would like to marry a beautiful actress with plenty of money. I would also like to be famed abroad as one of the world's foremost millionaires.

Black: In politics I hope to come up against men like Khrushchev and other enemies of freedom. I hope I will be able to overcome them with my words, and put them to shame.

Black: I expect to be a man of international fame, a man who by virtue of his political genius has acquired so much respect from his people that he will be fully capable of living in peace with his people.

Black: I want to be a West Indian diplomat. I would like to have a magnetic power over men and a stronger magnetic power over women. I must be very intelligent and quick-witted: I must be flu-ent in at least seven languages. I must be very resourceful and I must say the correct thing at the correct moment. With these qualities and a wonderful foresight and with other necessary abili-ties which I can't foresee, I would be able to do wonders for the world by doing wonders for my nation.

East Indian: I will write a book called the *Romance of Music and Literature*. I will make this book as great as any Shakespeare play; then I will return to India to endeavour to become a genius in the film industry.

East Indian: I want to develop an adventurous spirit. I will tour the earth by air, by sea, and by land. I shall become a peacemaker among hostile people.

East Indian: When I usually awake from my daydream, I think myself to be another person, the great scientific engineer, but soon I recollect my sense, and then I am myself again.

Coloured (mulatto): Toward the latter part of my life I would like to enter myself in politics, and to do some little bit for the improvement and uplift of this young Federation of ours.

Coloured: I am obsessed with the idea of becoming a statesman, a classical statesman, and not a mere rabble-rouser who acts impulsively and makes much ado about nothing.

White: I am going to apprentice myself to a Chartered Accountant's firm and then to learn the trade. When I want to, leave the firm and go to any other big business concern and work my way up to the top.

White: I want to live a moderate life, earning a moderate pay, slowly but surely working my way in the law firm, but I don't want to be chief justice of the Federation or anything like that . . . Look around. All the other boys must be writing about their ambitions to be famous. They all cannot be, for hope is an elusive thing.

White: By this time my father may be a shareholder in the com-pany, I will take over the business. I will expand it and try to live up to the traditions that my father has built up.

Without the calm of the white responses, the society might appear remote, fantastic and backward. But the white student doesn't inhabit a world which is all that separate. Trinidad is small, served by two newspapers and two radio stations and the same unsegregated schools. The intercourse between the races is easier than inquiring sociologists usually find; there is a substantial black and East Indian middle class that dominates the professions. When this is understood, the imprecision of black and East Indian fantasy—diplomacy, politics, peacemaking—can be seen to be more than innocence. It is part of the carnival lunacy of a lively, well-informed society which feels itself part of the great world, but understands at the same time that it is cut off from this world by reasons of geography, history, race.

THE SUB-TITLE of Rubin and Zavalloni's book is "A Study of the Aspirations of Youth in a Developing Society." But the euphemism is misleading. This society has to be more precisely defined. Brazil is developing, India is developing. Trinidad is neither undeveloped nor developing. It is fully part of the advanced consumer society of the West; it recognizes high material standards. But it is less than provincial: there is no metropolis to which the man from the village or small town can take his gifts. Trinidad is simply small; it is dependent; and the people born in it—black, East Indian, white—sense themselves condemned, not necessarily as individuals, but as a community, to an inferiority of skill and achievement. In colonial days racial deprivation could be said to be important, and this remains, obviously, an important drive. But now it is only part of the story.

In the islands, in fact, black identity is a sentimental trap, obscuring the issues. What is needed is access to a society, larger in every sense, where people will be allowed to grow. For some territories this larger society may be Latin American. Colonial rule in the Caribbean defied geography and created unnatural administrative units; this is part of the problem. Trinidad, for instance, was detached from Venezuela. This is a geographical absurdity; it might be looked at again.

1970

Michael X and the Black Power Killings in Trinidad: Peace and Power

I

A CORNER file is a three-sided file, triangular in section, and it is used in Trinidad for sharpening cutlasses. On December 31, 1971, in the country town of Arima, some eighteen miles from Port of Spain, Steve Yeates bought such a file, six inches long. Yeates, a thirty-three-year-old Negro, ex-RAF, was the bodyguard and companion of Michael de Freitas—also known as Michael X and Michael Abdul Malik. The file, bought from Cooblal's Hardware, cost a Trinidad dollar, 20p. It was charged to the account of "Mr. Abdhul Mallic, Arima," and Yeates signed the charge bill "Muhammed Akbar." This was Yeates's "Muslim" name. In the Malik setup in Arima—the "commune," the "organization"— Yeates was Supreme Captain of the Fruit of Islam, as well as Lieutenant Colonel (and perhaps the only member) of Malik's Black Liberation Army.

Malik's "commune" was a residential house in a suburban development called Christina Gardens. The house, which Malik had been renting for eleven months, ever since his return from England, was set in a one-and-a-half-acre plot. On this land, with its mature garden and mature fruit trees, Malik and his commune did "agriculture." Or so Malik reported to old associates in England and elsewhere.

Malik had spent fourteen years in England. He had gone there as Michael de Freitas, a Trinidad seaman, in 1957, when he was twenty-four. In Notting Hill, where he had settled, he had become a pimp, drug pusher and gambling-house operator; he had also worked as a strong-arm man for Rachman, the property racketeer, who specialized in slum properties, West Indian tenants and high rents. A religious-political "conversion" had followed, and Michael de Freitas had given himself the name

Michael X. He was an instant success with the press and the underground. He became Black Power "leader," underground black "poet," black "writer." In 1967, when he was at the peak of his newspaper fame, he was convicted under the Race Relations Act for an anti-white speech he had made at Reading, and sent to jail for a year. In 1969, with the help of a rich white patron, he had established his first commune, the Black House, an "urban village" in Islington. This had failed. At the same time there was more trouble with the law. And in January 1971 Michael X— now with the Black Muslim name of Michael Abdul Malik—had fled to Trinidad.

The agricultural commune in Christina Gardens was not Malik's only "project" in Trinidad. He was simultaneously working on a "People's Store." Letterheads had been printed, and copy prepared for a brochure: "Empty shelves Shows the lack of Genorosity [sic] of the haves to the have nots . . . The wall of honour bears the name of our heroes and those that give . . . All praise is due to Allah the faults are ours." The only thing that was missing was the store; but in a note on the scheme Malik had written: "Public Relations are the key-words to success." During his time in England Malik had learned a few things; he had, more particularly, acquired a way with words. In Trinidad he was not just a man who had run away from a criminal charge in England. He was a Black Muslim refugee from "Babylon": he was in revolt against "the industrialized complex." Trinidad was far enough away; and so, in a country town, in the mature garden of a rented suburban house, Malik could say that he did agriculture, with his new commune.

On January 1, 1972, the commune could be said to include two visitors, who were living in a rented house on the other side of the road. One was a Boston Negro in his late thirties who wore a gold earring and had given himself the Muslim name Hakim Jamal. The other was Gale Ann Benson, a twenty-seven-year-old middle-class English divorcée who had been living with Jamal for about a year.

Jamal was an American Black Power man. A few months before, when he was being taken around London by Gale Benson, he had described himself to the *Guardian* as "excruciatingly handsome, tantalizingly brown, fiercely articulate." That was his style. From Trinidad he wrote to a white associate in the United States: "Money is a white people thing—the thing they protect. The heaviest thing they have to carry."

And Jamal was anxious to lighten the load: he was full of schemes for black uplift that needed white money; one such scheme had brought him down to the West Indies. He was in some ways like Malik. But Malik did black agriculture and black communes, and Jamal did black schools and black publishing; and the two men did not clash. Malik claimed that he was the best-known black man in the world; and Jamal appeared to agree. Jamal's own claim was that he himself was God. And Gale Benson outdid them both: she believed that Jamal was God.

This was Benson's distinction in the commune, her private cult of Jamal. Not her whiteness; there were other white people around, since for people like Malik there was no point in being black and angry unless occasionally there were white people to witness. Benson wore African-style clothes and had renamed herself Halé Kimga. This wasn't a Muslim or an African name, but an anagram of Gale and Hakim; and it suggests that in her madness there was an element of middle-class play.

Some weeks later Malik's wife told a reporter of the Trinidad *Evening News* that Benson was "a very mysterious person." She must have used the word ironically, because she went on: "She was sort of a fake . . . She will give a fake name and maintain her fake position." A thirty-year-old black woman, a secondary-school teacher, said of Benson, "She was pretty. Different. Simple. Money oozing out of the clothes." White, secure, yet in her quiet middle-class way out-blacking them all: Benson could not have been indifferent to the effect she created. The absurd cult, the absurd name, the absurd clothes—everything that is remembered of Benson in Trinidad suggests the great uneducated vanity of the middle-class dropout.

But to be a fake among fakes: in the melodramatic atmosphere of the commune that was dangerous. She was alien, impenetrable. It was felt that she was an agent; there was talk of an especially secret branch of British Intelligence called M10. Her execution, on January 2, 1972, was sudden and swift. She was held by the neck and stabbed and stabbed. At that moment all the lunacy and play fell from her; she knew who she was then, and wanted to live. Perhaps the motive for the killing lay only in that: the surprise, a secure life ending in an extended moment of terror. She fought back; the cuts on her hands and arms would show how strongly she fought back. She had to be stabbed nine times. It was an especially deep wound at the base of the neck that stilled her; and then she was buried in her African-style clothes. She was not yet completely dead: dirt from her burial hole would work its way into her intestines.

IN TRINIDAD at this time there was a young Indian fortune-teller, Lalsingh Harribance, whose uncanny and daring public prophecies were making news. *The Bomb*, a popular local weekly, carried an article about Harribance; and Malik, who had written for *The Bomb*, found out from the editor where Harribance lived.

Harribance lived in the south of the island, in the oil-field town of Fyzabad, a winding two-hour drive from Port of Spain. Malik went down with some members of his commune in two cars. That was Malik's travelling style in Trinidad—the "retinue," the large American hired cars, the chauffeur. Rawle Maximin, a partner in the car-hire firm that Malik patronized, and a boyhood friend of Malik's, went with them. They got to Fyzabad late in the evening and were told that Harribance was at home but was seeing nobody. A seer's privilege. They decided to wait.

Rawle Maximin says they waited in the cars until morning. "And just when I was thinking 'You mean they not even sending out a little coffee or something?' Harribance sent out a woman with some coffee. And Michael got to see Harribance. And Harribance said to Michael, 'You will not stay in Trinidad. You will go to Jamaica. And then you will be the ruler of the Negroes in the United States.' But then he said to Michael as we were leaving, 'I want to see you again.' But Michael never saw Harribance again."

Harribance, as it happened, very shortly afterwards joined the brain drain to the United States. An American woman married him; and the story in Trinidad is that Harribance is now at an American university helping with ESP research.

Patrick Chokolingo, the editor of *The Bomb*, has something to add to Maximin's story of the visit to Harribance. "There was a pointed question to Harribance about hanging. I have this story from Harribance's cousin. Malik wanted to find out at all costs whether he would die by hanging. The answer was that he would *not* die by hanging."

Many stories come up after an event. But it is possible that this prophecy—the promise of immunity and of further great success—explains something of what was to follow.

In an inside page of the Trinidad *Guardian* of February 13, 1972, there was a small, odd item: DIVERS FAIL TO FIND BODY. Steve Yeates—Muhammed Akbar, Supreme Captain of the Fruit of Islam, Lieutenant Colonel of Malik's Black Liberation Army, the foreman of the Malik commune, Malik's bodyguard and familiar—had drowned.

He had drowned three days before at Sans Souci, which is known to all beach-going Trinidadians as one of the most dangerous bays on the rocky north-eastern coast. Around a small central shelf, which is reasonably calm, the current has gouged out deep holes in the sea floor; even a few feet from the shore, in waist-high water, it is not easy to keep one's footing; every breaking wave takes the bather out and to the west, to a litter of rocks, a long reef, and high, crashing waves. Bodies are seldom recovered from Sans Souci. Once they are swept beyond the reef, local fishermen say, they are eaten by the giant fish known as the grouper. There are safer bays before Sans Souci, at Balandra and at Mission; but it was at Sans Souci that the Malik party of eleven had stopped to bathe. Two of the girls had quickly got into trouble. Yeates had saved one, and had disappeared trying to save the other. A fishing boat had later gone out and rescued the second girl; but the body of Yeates hadn't been recovered.

What was odd about the item in the *Guardian* was that it was presented as a statement by Malik, two days after the event. Patrick Chokolingo, editor of *The Bomb*, didn't like the story. "I thought it was funny—the way it was presented—because to me anybody associated with Malik was news, and this drowning deserved bigger treatment. I rang a few people and the police, and a police officer did mention to me that they suspected Malik had drowned Yeates—but this was very much an off-the-cuff statement. You can imagine my surprise when the following day Malik turned up in my office and he said he wanted me to do a story on Steve Yeates, a hero, who tried to save an Indian girl—Malik again, trying to squeeze some race out of it. Off the cuff I blurted out, 'But, Michael, the police say you kill the man.' And he said, 'I don't care about what the police say.' "

This was on Tuesday, February 15. At 11:25 on Saturday night the Arima fire station heard that the Malik house in Arima was on fire. For a one-storey house with concrete floors and walls and a corrugated-iron roof, the fire was unexpectedly fierce. But the annexe at the back, separated from the main house by a concrete patio, wasn't touched; and everything that was stored in the annexe was intact: the African art objects that Malik had brought from England and on which he placed a value of £60,000 and the £400 piano, which was said to be a gift from John Lennon. A mysterious fire: no member of the commune was present, and Malik and all his family had flown out earlier in the day to Guyana.

That was a journey of some style. The travelling companion of the Malik family was a Guyanese Negro called McDavidson, fat and smooth-skinned, a sharp dresser, one of the ambitious nondescripts thrown up by the new politics of the region. McDavidson's wife was a minor minister in the Trinidad government, and his nephew was Junior Minister for Youth Affairs in the Guyana government. Malik had paid for McDavidson's ticket; McDavidson had spoken on the telephone to the office of the Guyana Prime Minister; and the Malik party, on their arrival in Guyana, was welcomed by the Junior Minister for Youth Affairs and driven away in two cars. Such a reception no doubt led to early press reports that Malik had gone to Guyana as a guest of the government to attend the second-anniversary celebrations of Guyana's "Cooperative Republic," and that on Saturday evening he was among the dinner guests of Mr. Burnham, the Guyana Prime Minister. These reports were quickly denied. What is true is that on Sunday Malik addressed some members of the Youth Socialist Movement, the "youth wing" of Mr. Burnham's political party.

In Arima the road that led to Malik's burned-out house had been barred off by light aluminium rails and patrolled by Negro and Indian policemen with automatic rifles (new to Trinidad, and called, because of the perforated barrel, "see-through guns"). The fire commissioner suspected arson; the police were concerned about hidden arms.

At three o'clock on Tuesday afternoon the Trinidad police, searching the grounds of the house in Arima where Malik and his commune did agriculture, discovered a six-foot grave below a recently planted bed of lettuce, in the feathery shade of a flamboyant tree and beside a hedge of peach-coloured hibiscus. The grave was estimated to be seven to ten days old, and the body in blue jeans and a green jersey found in a sprawling position at the bottom was horribly decomposed, its sex not immediately apparent to the policemen or the professional grave diggers who had been called in, the face distorted and half-melted away around bared teeth, one of which was capped in gold. The blue jeans were lowered: white underpants. Not a woman. A man, Negro or Negroid, five feet nine inches tall, whose head had been almost severed from his body.

But not Steve Yeates, whose death by drowning Malik had reported to the press just a week before. Steve's denture had no gold, his father said when he went with the police to the Port of Spain mortuary. Steve's hair was different; there was no need for his father to look for the large scar on the back, the relic of a fight Steve had had in England. Not Steve Yeates, an anonymous woman caller told *The Bomb* the next day: the body was that of another "brother" in the "organization." "The man died last week Monday night, and the whole thing was accidental. They did not go to kill him. Just beat him up . . . He died foolishly as he won't abide by the rules of the organization."

And that was not far wrong. The body was identified the day after as that of a twenty-five-year-old Port of Spain man, Joseph Skerritt, a man once charged with rape (like Steve Yeates himself) but otherwise quite undistinguished: the failure of his respectable lower-middle-class family, one of thousands of the city's half-educated young men, unemployed and superfluous, drifting through their twenties, idling in streets scrawled with empty slogans: BLACK IS IN, BASIC BLACK. Joe Skerritt had last been seen alive a fortnight before on February 7. On that day Malik, with his retinue, had called at the Skerritt house in Port of Spain and taken Joe away to Arima.

Malik's house was the only one on the western side of the approach lane. To the north of the house, beyond a boundary line of young coconut trees and the high wire-mesh fence, there was a piece of wasteland, ending after two hundred feet or so in a narrow tree-hung ravine, its water slow and shallow and not fresh. On the southern bank of this ravine, two days after the discovery of the body of Joe Skerritt, a second grave was found. This grave was shallower, about four feet, and the smell was soon high. A blue dress with a flowered pattern, red panties, a twisted, decomposing body: Gale Benson.

She had been stabbed to death on January 2. And here, on the ravine bank, she had lain for more than seven weeks. And no one had missed her, not even the two English people who were visiting the commune at the time. But they no doubt had other things on their minds. Simmonds, the woman, well-nourished, with big, widely spaced top teeth, told *The Bomb* that during her six weeks at the commune she had had "total involvement" with Steve Yeates: Muhammed Akbar, Supreme Captain of the Fruit of Islam, who on December 31 (before the public holiday on January 1) had gone to Cooblal's Hardware and bought a six-inch corner file.

And Jamal—Benson's master—what had Hakim Jamal done? Simmonds remembered that one morning in January, after they had all dined together the previous evening, Jamal had said that he and Benson had had a quarrel and Benson had gone away. And that was that. Eighteen days later Jamal left the Malik commune to return to the United States. He didn't leave alone. He left with the "co-worker" he had summoned down from the United States in mid-December, a man who had remained in the background, and of whom little was remembered: an American Negro known in the commune by the African-sounding name of Kidhogo or Kidogo.

In Trinidad now there were many rumours of fresh finds at the commune; one rumour was that a tinful of mixed penises had been found. But the ground had given up its dead. Six men were charged with the two murders. Five were Trinidadian; one was American. This wasn't Jamal, but his co-worker Kidogo. Kidogo was one of the five charged with the murder of Benson. Kidogo was in hiding in the United States. Jamal gave interviews, and now he was as sober and anxious to survive as everybody else. He spoke of "the atmosphere of violence" at the commune; he said he was lucky to be alive; he said he would like to see Malik and ask him a few questions about Benson.

So, in sobriety and self-absolution, the Malik commune ended. The ground had been dug up, the house burned out. All that remained were the two Malik dogs, bewildered, never barking or whining, restless, scampering about the grounds and the road, excited by the sound of every stopping car. But no car brought the people they were looking for.

IN GUYANA, Malik was on the run. McDavidson, who had travelled with the Malik family from Trinidad and had, as uncle of the Junior Minister for Youth Affairs, arranged their reception in Guyana, shaved off Malik's Black Power beard and trimmed his hair. Someone else went to get new clothes and a new pair of shoes; and Malik, in his new outfit, had booked in under another name—perhaps "Mr. T. Thompson"—at another hotel. Michael de Freitas, Michael X, Michael Abdul Malik, and now Mr. Thompson, Mr. Lindsay, Joseph George. So many names, so many personalities, so many ways of presenting himself to people: that was his great talent, but now, at the end, he was close to breakdown.

He stayed for three days in the hotel, the curtains always closed in his room. He told the Indian chambermaid that he had malaria and couldn't stand the sunlight. He ordered nothing from the bar or the kitchens. The chambermaid went out to buy him sandwiches and soft drinks, paper and two ballpoint pens. He had important messages for various people. He was only a "middleman," he had told McDavidson; the really important man, the man with the "massive plan," was coming down soon from the United States to meet him in Guyana. The chambermaid, taking in a flask of iced water, for which he had asked, saw him "writing letters." But he wasn't happy using the ballpoint pen; he would have preferred a tape recorder. In the darkened hotel room he became obsessed with the need for a tape recorder, and once he nearly telephoned his wife to bring him one. "I wanted," he said later, "to record on tape all the things that had happened to me. I wanted to get it on record." Words were important to him; he had lived by words. Words could give shape to an event, and words were never more important than they were now.

In England there were people who had told him that he was a writer, even a poet; and often, in a marijuana haze ("I am high I love it"), he had tried to be a writer, writing out the marijuana mood in a page or two and coming to a halt. In these writings fact and fiction sometimes flowed together. With words he remade his past; words also gave him a pattern for the future. And, bizarrely, he had once written of an adventure that was like the one he was having in Guyana.

The narrator, who may be Malik himself, is on the run. With only twenty pounds in his pocket, he is taken in by someone called Frank and told he can stay for six months. That night the narrator sleeps and has no nightmares. Then the door opens. "My Friend My saviour Frank, with a [indistinct] breakfast and a Newspaper, all smiles. You in the paper today he says, and I panic again, they found me. I think [indistinct] more. Let me see! I say there was I not too bad a picture and a short story. One of Trinidad's more famous sons returns home to finish writing his novel. In an Exclusive Interview at—and it goes on and on, I smile relieved the Journalists here have an Imagination like anywhere else—"Here the fragment ends.

But in Guyana the nightmare did not break. The reports in the Guyana newspapers, which he was reading in the hotel, were getting worse. And two days after the discovery of the body of Gale Benson he left the hotel, took a taxi south to the bauxite town of Mackenzie (now called Linden, after the first name of Mr. Burnham, the Guyana Prime

Minister), and then, in his new long-sleeved blue shirt and red-checked short trousers, with an airline bag containing some of his hotel writings (some he had left behind in the hotel room), some Guyana ten-dollar notes, biscuits, milk, sardines and other tinned food, and with a piece of cutlass, he headed for the interior, along the south-west trail.

Two hundred miles away, beyond the forest and the brown savanna land with the giant anthills, lay the Brazilian border. It seemed that he was making for this, but later he said: "I knew of a person in the interior who was a good and wise person to counsel with. I thought I would find this person . . . I have always been to counsel with people who can see things. You have a man here in Trinidad called Harribance. I go to him. I like these people. I thought I would go to this person and counsel with him and find out what is happening because it was not something I could reason out."

He was on the trail for three days. He was now barefooted: the new shoes that had been bought for him in the capital didn't fit or had become too painful. About four or five in the afternoon of the third day he saw two Land-Rovers. Government Land-Rovers: a survey team: a camp. He waited for two or three hours. About half-past seven he went to the men in the camp. He said, "Good night, gentlemen," and introduced himself as a journalist. They gave him a cup of coffee. He said—too vaguely— that he wanted to go "down the trail"; and after about half an hour he and a man called Caesar and another man left the camp in a Land-Rover.

Malik asked Caesar about the road to Brazil, and about his religion. Caesar, a handsome man, big and very black, said he belonged to a local Africanist group which was something like a Black Power group. Malik—the X again—said that police all over the world were looking for him. But then he must have had an intimation of betrayal. And his mind worked fast. He said there were two messages he wanted Caesar to take back to Georgetown, the capital. One was for Mrs. Malik: Caesar was to tell her that he, Malik, was safe. The other message was for Caesar's Black Power Leader: Caesar was to tell him that there was a police informer in the group.

After five or six miles Malik, who had become restless, was set down at a place called Bishop's Camp. Bishop was a small elderly Negro, a soli-tary in his bush "farm"; and his "camp" was two thatched shelters, one with no walls. He gave Malik some stew-and-rice and "sweet broom" herb tea. Thousands of police were after him, Malik said; and Bishop said (the real-life adventure, now in an unexpected forest setting, echoing that scrap of Malik's man-on-the-run fiction) that Malik could stay in the camp for the rest of the year.

Malik was tired, and during this last night of freedom his talk was disordered. He asked repeatedly about Brazil, and his safety in the camp; he said he had no faith in Caesar. He remembered the Trinidad commune, and that fantasy of "agriculture" became fact. He said he would teach Bishop "how to grow greens." He said he wanted a job: he could "plant." Bishop should plant mustard and celery in boxes and after three weeks plant them out eighteen inches apart. He asked Bishop if the river was far. Bishop said it wasn't far; but Malik said he would show Bishop how to get water from the river without walking to the river. He remembered England, and especially Rachman, the slum landlord for whom he had worked in the early days in London; and Bishop must have been puzzled. To Bishop it seemed that Malik was saying that he had owned a big boarding-house in London, with a big garden, that he had kept a big dog and a revolver, and that when tenants couldn't pay he had put them out, but that he had always been nice to Guyanese.

Bishop made up a low "cot" for Malik in the open shelter. Malik, lying down, seemed to groan. He said his feet were cold; Bishop gave him a sack for his feet. Malik presently fell asleep. But Bishop didn't sleep: he was frightened of Malik's "piece of cutlass." All night he watched Malik.

At about half-past five, when it was still dark, the camp dogs barked, and Bishop saw the police; Caesar was with them. They surrounded the shelter and waited. It quickly became light, and "the form of a fair-skin man lying on the lower or western cot" became distinct to the police superintendent. At five to six they began to close in. Bishop, still watchful, pointed to Malik's airline bag and cutlass. At six, daybreak, the superintendent tapped Malik and awakened him.

When he saw the police he was, as he said later, relieved. His feet were hurting; he doubted whether he could walk. He was taken to Georgetown; the next day he was declared an undesirable immigrant and flown back to Trinidad.

THE DISCOVERY of the body of Gale Benson had been the sensation; but the first inquiry was about the killing of Joseph Skerritt, who had been buried below the lettuce patch, and it was for the murder of Skerritt that Malik and three of his commune were tried four months later. When the grave was discovered, an anonymous woman caller had told *The Bomb* that the body, then not yet identified, was that of a "brother" who had failed to "abide by the rules of the organization." And Skerritt's killing was indeed in the nature of an execution.

Malik was uneducated, but people in England had told him that he was a writer; and he did his best to write. There were also people who had told him—ponce, con man—that he was a leader (though only of Negroes). So he had read books on leadership; and once, borrowing a good deal from what he had read, he had even written a paper on the subject. "I have no need to play an ego game," he wrote, explaining his position, "for I am the Best Known Black man in this entire [white western world *deleted*] country." Leaders were workers, doers, finders of tools, "be it money, hammers or saws": the "masses" came of their own accord to such leaders. But it was not always pleasant to be a leader. "Leaders are feared even by those closest to him . . . and others will envy him . . . here one needs an Iron Hand for one may be tempted to placate the doubter with a gift, and the only real gift one can give is silence." Borrowed words, almost certainly; but Malik was made by words. And Joe Skerritt was a doubter.

The previous year, when Skerritt had been charged with rape, he had gone to Malik for help, and Malik had talked the girl out of making trouble for Skerritt. But then Skerritt had become uneasy with Malik; he began to hide from him; and to Mrs. Skerritt it even seemed that her son was being ungrateful. At last, on February 7, Malik came with some of his commune to the Skerritt house in Port of Spain; and they took away Joe with them to Arima "for a few days."

Skerritt loafed about the garden that day, doing the odd jobs. In the evening he and three of the commune got into a hired car and went for a drive. When they were on the Arima-Port of Spain highway, Abbott, the driver, said they were going to raid a police station for arms. Skerritt said he wanted none of that; and Abbott immediately drove back to Christina Gardens. Malik said, "Joe, boy, you say you ready for work, and now that I've sent you to work, you refuse to go?" He looked at Skerritt and shook his head, and said to the man escorting Skerritt to his sleeping quarters that he should give Joe a Bible or something to read.

A sudden decision, it would seem; but—from the evidence given at the trial—what followed was well planned. In the morning Steve Yeates drove Mrs. Malik and her children to Port of Spain. That wasn't unusual. Malik announced that the commune was going to dig a "soakaway" that day. That wasn't unexpected. The ground flooded easily; a soakaway helped drainage, and Malik had taken advice from a qualified man about soakaways. A pit had to be dug down to where the soil changed; and then it was to be filled in with a bottom layer of stones and a top layer of earth.

So all morning—Malik from time to time interrupting his "writing" in the "study" to superintend—some men dug and two others brought jeeploads of stones to the house. Joe Skerritt, in his "old clothes," jeans and a green jersey, helped with a wheelbarrow, taking the stones from where the jeep dropped them to the far north-western corner of the garden. At about one o'clock the pit was deep enough. Malik told the two men in the jeep to go and "cool off " at a farm they all knew and then to bring a load of manure.

When they left, there remained in the garden Malik, three men, and Joe Skerritt. One of the three men walked away from the hole. Malik, with his revolver in a shoulder holster, and with a cutlass in his hand, went down into the pit and said to Abbott, "I am ready. Bring him." Abbot locked his arm around Skerritt's neck and jumped with him into the pit. Malik, using his left hand to hold Skerritt by his long Afro hair, chopped him on the neck and then, still with his left hand, threw him aside. The gesture, of "contempt," appalled Abbott. Skerritt cried out, "Oh, God! Oh, God!" and began stumbling about the pit. Malik, now out of the pit, lifted a large soakaway stone with both hands and brought it down on Skerritt's head, and Skerritt, close to death, cried out like a child, "I go tell! I go tell!" Malik hurled three or four more stones at Skerritt, and then Skerritt was quiet. Then the four men—the fourth man called back to help—began to fill in the pit, the stones below, the earth on top.

When the two men returned with the jeepload of manure from the farm, they saw that the stones had disappeared, the soakaway was half–filled in; they helped finish the filling in. And when presently the Malik family returned from Port of Spain, the commune was the commune again. As for Skerritt, "the strange young man" who had turned up the day before, he had just gone away again. The foolish boy had gone to Canada or the United States, but he was going to find things hard "outside": that was what Mrs. Skerritt was told. And that, at the trial, was Malik's story: that Joe Skerritt had just disappeared.

ABBOTT, who had jumped with Skerritt into the pit, was sentenced to twenty years. Malik was condemned to hang. Some people stood by him. One of them was Rawle Maximin, a boyhood friend, the garage owner whose cars Malik had often hired. Maximin visited Malik at the Royal Gaol in Port of Spain. One day, many months later, when he was waiting for the verdict on his appeal, Malik said to Maximin, "You were with me that day when I went to see Harribance. Can you remember what Harribance said?" "He hadn't forgotten," Maximin says. "He just wanted to hear me say it. So I said to him, 'Harribance told you that you would leave Trinidad and go to Jamaica, and then you will be the ruler of the Negroes in the United States.' And he said, 'Good, good.' And began to pace up and down that little cell."

To be the ruler of Negroes: so that, at the end, for Malik and his well-wishers abroad (mainly white, and they continued to send him money), Negroes existed only that Malik might be their leader. Malik saw himself as a man who had always risen: a semi-educated Port of Spain idler, one of thousands; then a seaman; then a Notting Hill pimp and gangster; then the X of London; then, at thirty-seven, "the Best Known Black man in this entire white western world." It was as a London success that he had come back to Trinidad in January 1971. "I'm not here to make my way," he told the Trinidad *Express*. "I've made that already." But he believed he could "help." "I'm not interested in elections and stuff like that. The only politics I ever understood is the politics of revolution—the politics of change, the politics of a completely new system."

Revolution, change, system: London words, London abstractions, capable of supporting any meaning Malik—already reassembling his gang, his "commune"—chose to give them. There were people in London who were expecting Malik, their very own and complete Negro, to establish a new government in Trinidad. There had been a meeting; someone had made a record. The new government was going to under-write the first International University of the Alternative, "the seat of the counter-culture of the Alternative." Words, and more words: "I cannot go into details," Malik had said. "But I can say this. The new university will be an experimental laboratory of a new and sane life-style." But—the eternal warning of the X, the eternal thrill and flattery—the white people who came to Malik's Trinidad (an airbus service was promised to all international capitals) had to remember that there was "a just hatred of the white man" in the heart of every black; and they had somehow to get over the fact that they "belonged to the race of the oppressors."

The leader, the unique spokesman of Negroes dangerous with a just hatred; but the crowds at his trial were good-humoured, even gay. No one jeered; he was a martyr to no cause. Only Simmonds, the white woman who had had "total involvement" with Steve Yeates during her six weeks at the commune, only Simmonds, flying down from England, gave the photographers a clenched-fist salute; but she had a return air ticket. To the Trinidad crowds Malik had become a "character," a Carnival figure, a dummy Judas to be beaten through the streets on Good Friday. Which was all that he had been in London, even in the great days of his newspaper fame as the X: the militant who was only an entertainer, the leader who had no followers, the Black Power man who was neither powerful nor black. He wasn't even black; he was "a fair-skin man," half-white. That, in the Trinidad phrase, was the sweetest part of the joke.

2

IT WAS IN LONDON that Malik became a Negro. And perhaps only someone who knew that he wasn't really a Negro—someone who knew that when the time came he could go off and play another game—could have worked so hard at the role, and so guyed it. He was shallow and unoriginal; but he sensed that in England, provincial, rich and very secure, race was, to Right and Left, a topic of entertainment. And he became an entertainer.

He was the X, the militant, the man threatening the fire next time; he was also the dope peddler, the pimp. He was everybody's Negro, and not too Negroid. He had two ideas of his own. One was that the West Indian High Commissions in London paid too little attention to their nationals. The other, more bizarre, was that the uniform of the Trinidad police should be changed; and this was less an idea than an obsession. Everything else was borrowed, every attitude, every statement: from the adoption of the X and the conversion to Islam, down to the criticism of white liberals ("destroying the black man") and the black bourgeois ("they don't know the man from the ghetto"). He was the total 1960s Negro, in a London setting; and his very absence of originality, his plasticity, his ability to give people the kind of Negro they wanted, made him acceptable to journalists.

"Michael X once told me," Richard Neville writes in *Playpower*, "that hippies were the only whites his people could talk to." And Malik was always willing to be instructed in his Negro role. Late in 1965, when he was working on his autobiography (subsequently ghosted by an Englishman, and published in 1968 under the title of *From Michael de Freitas to Michael X*), he sent the manuscript to an English adviser, and received a long memorandum in reply. ". . . At this juncture you may look at the negro's relationship with the whiteman throughout the world. Use South Africa, Rhodesia, England, Portugal and America to speak of the heartlessness of white society. Use slavery, use the recent massacre of the Jews at Auschwitz and Belsen . . . *Chapter 15* You ought to close powerfully, frighteningly perhaps, on 'This I Believe.' Your own true statement of one displaced black man in this particular context of history . . ."

So cliché led to cliché. And, inevitably, the racial clichés that Malik was led to, via the "counterculture," were sometimes pre-revolutionary. Once, aiming no doubt at the underground press, he wrote a kind of parable about an Anglo-Saxon called Harold, a Jew called Jack, and a Negro, who was himself. "All we have in common is two hands, two feet a head. I must admit mines are infinitely nicer to look at for their bodies are covered with a sickly pale whitish skin and even they can recognize it for what it is. Harold expressed a desire early in our talk to go somewhere in the sun and transform. I see his point for when he was saying this I followed his eyes caressing my beautiful golden brown skin my inheritance from my African [*insertion*: and Portuguese] forefathers."

It is a "difficult task for three people of as diverse Racial Charisterics as ourselves to truly communicate." But they are good friends, and agree to talk of their "most secret desires." Harold the Anglo-Saxon wants to search for truth. "Jacks not as simple as that": Jack the Jew wants to "make things for people, the people he's closest to are naturally his own people, Jews he will make whatever they need, money, Clothes, Factories." And Malik, the Negro, sees "the great divides that exist between us of different Races for my own search is one of happiness to create Joys for myself and others to hear Laughter, to give . . . But what a strange dilima this throws us into when I give to him the seeker after truth my humble present and he in his search looks into my little gesture for a deeper motivation or Jack when he makes a garment, and I say how lovely, could I have one and he tells me *x* Pounds."

Malik's ghosted autobiography was a publishing failure; one of his white patrons bought up most of the copies. The tone of the book is determinedly gay; there are lots of sex and parties—the ghost, easily turning oppressed blacks into abandoned spooks, seems in places to have excited himself with thoughts of a Michael X musical. But it is not an easy book to read.

It is not the story of a life or the development of a personality. The narrator, from his London eminence as the X, the reformed Negro ponce who is now the Negro leader, assumes that the events of his life are well known; and he is concerned only to present himself in all his Negro roles. Events accumulate confusedly around him; he is without a personality; he is only a haphazard succession of roles. On page 116—at the time of his meeting with an unidentified young property millionaire, who is interested in art—the narrator appears, without warning, as a painter ("my abstracts and surrealist portraits"); and he supports this role for exactly seventeen lines. Equally sudden, equally successful, and almost as brief, are his manifestations as Negro poet, writer, and even as a teacher of "basic English" at something called the London Free School.

The only other considerable figure in the autobiography is Malik's mother; and she is as puzzling as Malik. She appears first of all as a ferocious old-fashioned black woman, concerned about appearances and forever preaching the beauty of whiteness. She doesn't like her son to play with black children or to get his hands dirty; she is snobbish; when she goes to the Port of Spain market she refuses to speak French patois to the *marchandes* and insists that her son speak English; she sends her son to an "exclusive" school. This is overstated, but it has a certain logic. But then, just twenty pages later, the mother is suddenly a drunkard, hysterical, quarrelsome, wearing appalling Negro-woman's clothes. One day her son finds her sleeping in the fowl coop, which she says she has converted. Suddenly she is a "hustler"; suddenly, coming to London, she is transformed into a successful and jolly brothelkeeper.

The childhood of the leader, the rebel who learned to love black, no longer makes sense; the emphasis is wrong. Certain facts about his mother are too important to the narrator for him to leave out. But the facts have been scattered about the picaresque narrative: a pain greater than the one stated is being concealed. When the facts are put together, the childhood of the leader can be interpreted in quite another way.

Malik's father was a Portuguese shopkeeper who later left Trinidad to do business on the island of St. Kitts. His mother was an uneducated black woman from Barbados. In Trinidad, and especially in the tight lower-middle-class Negro community of Belmont in Port of Spain, she was a stranger, with different manners and a different accent. If she didn't speak the local French patois it was because she didn't know it. She was a stranger with a "red bastard," and she was never allowed to forget it by the black taxi driver with whom she lived. (He used to tell her that all she had got from the Portuguese man was a big cunt and a red bastard. This is not in the autobiography; it was part of Malik's statement at his trial.)

The mother was disgraced by the son; the son, growing up in Port of Spain, going to St. Mary's College (a major school, but not so "exclusive": the fees were just over three pounds a term), his home life known to all, was disgraced by the mother. She was uneducated, drunken, vicious; they tormented one another. He fled from her whenever he could, going off into the hills with his friends. Once he got all her clothes together and burned them. But she pursued him everywhere with her public scenes, even after he had been expelled from the college, even after he had grown up. He could escape only by leaving Trinidad, by becoming a seaman; at one time he thought of going to live in Guyana. In the end he went to England; but she followed him even there, getting off the boat train at Waterloo in a red bathrobe.

In 1965, when his London fame was beginning, and when in his own eyes he had made good, Malik began a letter to his mother.

London, April 1st, 1965

Dear Mamma,

My hand is shaking and my head hurts, I want to tell you a few things, for I am not afraid anymore. I am a negro, you told me I was different, its not true, I tried to be. I was ashamed not of being a negro but of you. I would like first to tell you what made me write this last year. I was at home and Steve rang me, he asked me if I knew what happened to you, Well you were arrested. At sixty odd years of age for running a Brothel, this I could of tried to understand, I would of blamed anybody for this, the white man, my father, myself, but when you gave your name as de Freitas because as you said you wanted to protect your own name, that was the end. Its *x* months since that day and I have only just recovered enough to say something about it. I don't hate you, that is impossible to do, I would like to think that was a thoughtless action but I said all the other horrible things you did were thoughtless too, you have humiliated me once too often, you usually give a lot of thought to things before you do them remember in Trinidad when you were still living with your husband and you threw boiling water on him in bed, you thought that one out didn't you, you must off . . .

She had got into bed with the man, and when he was asleep she had got out; she had heated the water beforehand. The incident doesn't appear in the autobiography. Everything else does; but in the padded-out, picaresque narrative, the passion and the pain vanish, simplified, and vitally altered, to give a smoother account of the boyhood of the leader.

This letter is the truest thing Malik ever wrote, and the most moving. It explains so much: the change of name from de Freitas to X, the assumption of so many personalities, the anxiety to please. A real torment was buried in the clowning of the racial entertainer. Black Power gave order and logic to the life; it provided Malik with a complete system. He couldn't write a book; but it was better for him to say, as he does in the preliminary note to his autobiography, that the book was ghosted because black English is different from white English.

A LONDON journalist who had some hand in the making of Malik says, "Michael took the press for a ride, and vice versa. And out of it grew a monster." The monster already existed; but there is something in the judgement. Malik was made in England. England gave him friends, a knowledge of elegance, a newspaper fame which was like regard, and money. England always gave him money; no one, for so many good black causes, needed money so badly. It occurred to him, for instance, late in 1966, when his wife was in arrears with her mortgage payments and receiving solicitor's letters, that West Indians needed adequate representation in the courts. He interested people in this cause. The London

O7 of February 1967 announced the West Indian legal need, and in heavy letters at the top of the page prescribed the remedy: " 'Defence' needs money. Send to Michael Abdul Malik, Leith Mansions, Grantully Road, W9."

England made many things easy for Malik. But England in the end undid him. Malik exaggerated the importance of his newspaper fame. He exaggerated the importance of the fringe groups which seemed to have made room for him. He was an entertainer, a play-actor; but he wasn't the only one. He failed to understand that section of the middle class that knows only that it is secure, has no views, only reflexes and scattered irritations, and sometimes indulges in play: the people who keep up with "revolution" as with the theatre, the revolutionaries who visit centres of revolution, but with return air tickets, the people for whom Malik's kind of Black Power was an exotic but safe brothel. Malik thought he shared the security of his supporters. One day, half doodling ("No Money"), half jotting down memoranda ("Letter from Lawyer"), he wrote: "My inheritance is London—all of it."

His fame didn't last long. It began in 1965, and came to an end in 1967, when he went to jail for an offence under the 1965 Race Relations Act. It was in July 1965 that Colin McGlashan, in a major article in the *Observer*, told of the existence in England of a militant black organization, the Racial Adjustment Action Society (RAAS), with a membership of more than forty-five thousand, that had been created "in near-secrecy" by Michael de Freitas. "Some immigrants," McGlashan reported, "already talk of Michael X." It was a good story: ". . . revolutionary fervour . . . near-national organization . . . formidable professionalism . . . underground technique . . . system of cells . . . financed from donations and Mr. de Freitas's own money . . . organizers, in the best revolutionary tradition, accept a pittance . . . a shy, gentle and highly intelligent man . . . the authentic voice of black bitterness . . . Says a friend: 'It is a crime against humanity that people like Michael happen . . .' "

It was a good story, and if it was a string of newspaper clichés it was only because what was being presented to McGlashan, as a good story, was a string of newspaper clichés. From his autobiography, published three years later, it seems that at the time of the McGlashan article Malik was perhaps more concerned with a beautiful white widow, whom he calls Carmen. Carmen was thirty, "with a lovely, supple body," and rich. Once she opened her handbag and gave Malik "a bundle of £10 notes";

another time she wrote him a cheque for £500. He took all that she gave—"I have no doubt that the ponce element produced in the black man by the ghetto was with me that night"—but it was all for the cause, the Racial Adjustment Action Society. Still, he suffered: "My speeches became more and more bitter." And there was Nancy, another white woman, who was his steady. Carmen had to go. "With the departure of Carmen, RAAS had no more income." And in four pages, which also cover the story of Carmen, the membership of RAAS drops from sixty-five thousand "on paper" to two thousand "hard core."

Malik loved his publicity. He cut out and filed every reference to himself in the British press, however slight, however critical (the *Daily Telegraph* must have been his favourite paper). He filed two copies of McGlashan's article; and when he brought out his RAAS brochure—which was really a brochure about Michael X, complete with press notices (no other name was mentioned)—he used two separate quotes from McGlashan, together with quotes from the *Daily Mirror*, the *Daily Telegraph*, the *Sunday Times*, *Peace News*, and the *New York Times* ("Students, intellectuals, moderates and radicals are all being wooed. Some have already been won over").

RAAS was of course a joke. The initials spell out an obscenity which is Jamaican (and not Trinidadian) and is nothing more than a corruption of "arse." A crude joke, and in the autobiography it is grotesquely extended. "In the first place RAAS is a West Indian word for a menstrual blood cloth. It has some symbolic significance in view of the way the black man has been drained of his life blood for so long. In the second place there is the similar African word *ras* (from the Arabic *ra's*—head) meaning Ruler or Leader." A "satirical" joke; but it could only have been made by a man who felt that he could, when the time came, withdraw from his Negro role.

Malik's Negro was, in fact, a grotesque: not American, not West Indian, but an American caricatured by a red man from Trinidad for a British audience. West Indians are not black Americans. American blacks are an excluded minority. West Indians come from countries with black majorities and black administrations; they have a kind of political tradition. Boscoe Holder, a black Trinidad dancer who was in London at the time, says, "When I heard about this X guy I thought, 'There goes one of our con men.' And I wished him well, because he was in England and because they told me he was Trinidadian." It was the West Indian attitude: the jester was recognized and accepted as a jester, but was otherwise kept at a distance. Occasionally Malik's publicity excited a student or a writer or a politician. In 1965, after the McGlashan article, the leader of the Trinidad opposition—mainly an Indian party—thought of asking Malik down to Trinidad to help with the elections.

But Malik never held these people. And in London he didn't really need them. A West Indian Malik had recently met—and who was eventually to act as his political deputy—was a young Trinidadian called Stanley Abbott, like Malik a college boy who had dropped out, and like Malik a red man with Spanish or Portuguese antecedents (Abbott sometimes called himself De Piva). Abbott had come to England at the age of nineteen in 1956, and was very quickly adrift in London, a lost soul adding and adding to a police record: wilful damage in 1956, breaking and entering in 1958, Borstal and supervision between 1958 and 1962, assault in 1964.

And already the West Indian closest to Malik was Steve Yeates, black but in other respects a man like Malik himself, a dropout from Malik's own Belmont district in Port of Spain: Steve Yeates, soon to be given the Black Muslim name of Muhammed Akbar, who had been expelled from St. Mary's College, Malik's old school, for getting a fourteen-year-old girl from a Carmelite reform school pregnant; Steve Yeates who, later, at the age of sixteen, while he was a student at another college, had been charged with nine others for the gang-rape of a girl in the Girl Guides hut in Belmont; who, acquitted but disgraced, had been sent by his family to England, where he had joined the RAF, but had then got into trouble of some sort and gone absent without leave; who had been badly wounded in the back during a fight and carried the scar.

The absence of responsible West Indian support ought to have told against Malik. But he turned it to his advantage; American Black Power had provided him with a complete system. If educated West Indians wanted nothing to do with Malik, it was only because the black bourgeoisie and intelligentsia, "a tiny minority within a minority," had cut themselves off from "the man in the ghetto." In Malik's system, the Negro who had not dropped out, who was educated, had a skill or a profession, was not quite a Negro; there was no need for anyone to come to terms with him. The real Negro was more elemental. He lived in a place called "the ghetto," which was awful but had its enviable gaieties; and in the ghetto the Negro lived close to crime. He was a ponce or a drug peddler; he begged and stole; he was that attractive Negro; and now this Negro was very angry. The real Negro, as it turned out, was someone like Malik; and only Malik could be his spokesman.

Malik's revolutionary Negro was in many ways the familiar crap-shooting spook. But it was a construct for a provincial market, and Malik's instinct about the kind of Negro the British newspapers wanted or would tolerate was sound. In the *Guardian* for August 9, 1971, Jill Tweedie made the limits of British tolerance plain.

Tweedie did two Negroes for her page that day. One was Annie P. Barden, a "school counsellor" at an all-black elementary school in Washington, D.C. Tweedie gave her a rough time. Annie Barden wanted to talk about her work; Tweedie wanted to hear about race and drugs and black militancy. They showed films about drugs, Annie Barden said; they "talked through" things like slavery and the position of blacks in the South; she hadn't sensed any militancy in her pupils (some of whom were four, and none older than thirteen). But what about Malcolm X and Martin Luther King? How had Annie Barden herself become aware of race prejudice? Had things really changed? How many Americans regarded the black as a human being? The majority? Half? Were there *any* jobs for her pupils? The professions mightn't be closed to blacks, but wasn't it more difficult for them? At the suggestion, now amounting to insistence, that she was a Negro and her teaching job therefore a waste of time, Annie Barden offered her interviewer tea. "She is evidently embarrassed," Tweedie noted, "by the whole question."

For her other Negro, a man, Tweedie had a lot more time, and space. He was an American Black Muslim and he was in England to "promote" his autobiography. It wasn't clear what he did for a living. He had started a Malcolm X Montessori school in California, but he didn't teach at the school because he hated white people——"No SS man could invest the word 'Jew' with any more contempt," Tweedie noted——and he didn't want his hate to rub off on two-year-olds. "If you're going to kill, it must mean something. You should kill people because they are evil, not because they are white . . . They call me a nigger but I've invented my own kind of nigger. My nigger is me, excruciatingly handsome, tantalizingly brown, fiercely articulate." Tweedie was taken: "This black man is a handsome man, a brigand with a gold ring in his ear . . . tall and spare and stoned on agro, sometimes overt, sometimes spread over with honeyed words about as sweet to receive as a punch in the kidneys. With a woman the agro comes masked, translated into sexual terms . . ."

"Personally," Tweedie concluded, "I find Miss Barden's passivity far more depressing than Hakim Jamal's anger, and far less hopeful for the future." Hakim Jamal—that was the name of the brigand with the gold earring. The autobiography he had come to England to sell was a conformist and very late addition to the Negro autobiographies of the 1960s: poverty and self-hate, drugs, Islam, reform, celebrities, sex, hate. His claim that he was God had won him an "odd spot" appearance on the *World at One* radio programme. But he apparently hadn't told Tweedie that he was God. And if he didn't teach at his Malcolm X school it was because it had lasted one year, with one teacher, had closed down fifteen months before, and existed now only in the brochures he carried around with him. As for Annie Barden, she no doubt went back to her elementary school in Washington, counseling a thousand pupils.

Malik's instinct, in the late 1960s (the Tweedie article appeared in 1971), about the kind of Negro that was wanted was sound. But the role was a consuming one. The black rebel, even if he wanted to, couldn't do a job; he couldn't appear to be declining into "passivity"; anything like repose could extinguish his reputation. No one expected him to act out his threats, but the poor black was required ceaselessly to perform.

In July 1967 Malik—filling in for the more internationally known Stokely Carmichael—went to Reading and spoke to a mixed group of about seventy. "If ever you see a white man laying a hand on your black woman, kill him immediately." It was quite harmless, just the usual cabaret. But Malik was charged under the Race Relations Act. At his trial he told the recorder to sit down and "cool it"; he had the Koran wiped with warm water before he swore on it; and he was allowed to perform Islamic "ablutions" before giving evidence. He was sent to jail for a year. All the newspaper reports of his trial were cut out and filed for him. But the carnival was abruptly over.

IN APRIL 1965, at the start of his great fame, he had written to his mother: "I am not afraid anymore." All the torment of his early life had been submerged in his role as the racial entertainer. Now his bluff had been called. His Black Power was no power in England, his newspaper fame offered no security. His ghosted autobiography, *From Michael de Freitas to Michael X,* came out while he was in jail and was poorly reviewed. The publicity declined. His release eight months later, though noted by television, was scarcely an event. A carnival element persisted: outside the prison gates there was a welcoming Negro who, refining on the X business, had given himself the name of Freddie Y. But Malik had changed.

He planned a second volume of autobiography. The title he first thought of was *My Years with RAAS*—the old Malik, the old joke. But as his mind darkened he changed that to *Requiem for an Illusion.* What was the illusion? England? His idea of his place in England? His career as the X?

From a long (at least fifty pages) and primitive novel he later began to write about himself, it is clear that he had begun to secrete a resentment, soon settling into hatred, not of white people or English people, but of the English middle class he had got to know: the people with money or connections who patronized him in both senses of the word, who were secure, who could fix anything, who held Negroes in contempt but were fascinated by him. In his novel, which is a childlike grafting of fantasy to fact (he is himself, with his own name), he has this middle-class English fascination turn to awe, perhaps even to love, and then, unexpectedly, to physical alarm. The setting isn't London, but Guyana. Malik has made himself a hero in that country, a great orator, and there are people in the streets who shout for him to be king.

It is hard, with Malik, to speak of a plan; he was a man who moved from event to event. But it seems that when he came out of jail his thoughts turned to real power. In 1968 he joined the Black Eagles, a Negro fantasy outfit intended as a Notting Hill version of the Black Panthers. Malcolm X, Michael X; Black Panthers, Black Eagles. The "prime minister" of the Eagles was a former Trinidad steelbandsman who had given himself the name of Darcus Awonsu. Malik became his "minister without portfolio" and got a trip to Canada in a chartered aeroplane, to attend a Black Writers Conference in Montreal. Minister, writer; and now he found he had a reputation with Chicago and Toronto blacks as the only man in England to have gone to jail under the Race Relations Act. "Travelling first found out I was Hero": this is from the notes for *Requiem for an Illusion,* and it also says something about his attitude to his earlier career as the ponce X. "Hero Image greater overseas." He had somehow made it: he began to think that he was "the Best Known Black man in [the] . . . world."

There was further proof the next year. Nigel Samuel, the son of a property millionaire, offered money for a "Black House" project in Islington. A number of shops and offices, acquired on a twenty-one-year lease, were to be converted into a black "urban village." It was a coup: the demonstration of the creative, "Panther"-like side of the black revolutionary. But Malik had no talents. To believe in the Black House was to believe in magic; it was to share Malik's half-belief (the con man's semi-lunacy, which makes him so convincing) that words and publicity made real the thing publicized. Within a year the Black House was failing; and like Hakim Jamal's Malcolm X school, like RAAS, like the Black Eagles, like the ventures of so many Negroes who act not out of a sense of vocation but trap themselves into performing, as Negroes, for an alien audience, the Black House existed only in its brochures and letterheads.

"Emergence of American Prototype like Panthers—with home base wanting carbon copy whereas the nation encourage self." This is from the notes for *Requiem*. It reads like an attempt to rationalize the failure of the Black House, to suggest that it was part of his plan. But Malik was trying many things that year; he had begun to look beyond England. He had travelled with Nigel Samuel to Timbuktu in a chartered aeroplane, and later they had gone to Guinea to see Stokely Carmichael. He had sent a not very literate emissary to the OAU in Addis Ababa. And he and Steve Yeates and, fleetingly, Nigel Samuel had gone to Trinidad. Kingship called for a black country. Everything was now pointing to an eventual return to Trinidad.

TRINIDAD in 1969 was moving towards a revolution. The black government of Eric Williams had been in power since 1956; and something like the racial enthusiasm that had taken him to power now seemed about to sweep him away. Political life in the newly independent island was stagnant; intellectuals felt shut out by the new men of the new politics; and American Black Power, drifting down to Trinidad, was giving a new twist to popular discontents. Black Power in the United States was the protest of an ill-equipped minority. In Trinidad, with its 55 per cent black population, with the Asian and other minorities already excluded from government, Black Power became something else, added something very old to rational protest: a mystical sense of race, a millenarian expectation of imminent redemption.

A revolution without a programme, without a head: it was something Malik might have exploited. But he didn't make much of a political start. He "marched" with some striking bus drivers, but he puzzled them when he spoke, not of their cause, but of one of his obsessions: the need to change the uniform of the Trinidad police.

There was also talk of a "commune." Randolph Rawlins, a left-wing Trinidad journalist and academic, a man wearied by the simplicities and cynicism of West Indian racial politics, went one Sunday to the beach house, the site of the planned commune, where Malik was staying. Malik played tapes of Stokely Carmichael's speeches. Steve Yeates was there, and a "retinue" of young men. "They were totally subservient," Rawlins says, "and would react immediately. Malik's daughter was sick. He said to one of the men: 'Go and get a doctor.' The chap said he didn't know where to find a doctor. Malik said: '*Go* and get the doctor.' I got tired of sitting down and seeing this man look ominous and talking rubbish. I adjourned to the sea."

Already, though, a "retinue" in Trinidad; and when Malik and his family followed Nigel Samuel back to England, Steve Yeates stayed behind. After thirteen years in England, Yeates had come home for good. Letters from Malik—busy in London with the Black House, busy with Nigel Samuel in Africa—were infrequent that year, 1969. In October Malik sent regards to "all of the Brothers" and promised a second visit by Samuel; in November he announced his imminent return, with a party of thirteen. Nothing happened, but Steve Yeates waited. One day his father, who ran a little bar in Belmont, asked him about his relationship with Malik, and he said: "It's a long story, pappy." A long story: Steve Yeates, black, fine-featured, with "soft hair, soft curly hair you felt you wanted to touch," but now with the English scar on his back, and now with the Black Muslim name of Muhammed Akbar, Supreme Captain of the Fruit of Islam, Lieutenant Colonel in Malik's Black Liberation Army.

A black woman who had known him in the old days, when "he was the love of all the little girls in Belmont," fell in with him again.

He said he would never go back to England. He never spoke much about his life in London or his time in the air force. He used to tell me that I wouldn't talk to him if I had known him in London.

Steve had lots of friends, but when he came back from London he was a loner. He didn't like parties or where there were too many people. He walked. Every night. As long as he was in Port of Spain he walked around the Savannah. Sometimes he would stop and have a coconut-water. Sometimes, if I was with him, he would sit on a bench and chat. He wasn't working, but he always had money. He had told me he was an aircraft mechanic. I asked him why he didn't get a job with one of the airlines. He said he didn't want to be tied down. He never told me what his views were, but he read a lot. Castro, Che Guevara. At one time he seemed to be in on this black scene. But then he would tell you he was living with this white woman and had two children with this woman, and you couldn't understand where he was going to and coming from. He was kinda bored. At times he would be waiting for a call, and this coded call would come. He was definitely waiting on Michael. We broke up in 1970. Just like that. The last time I saw him was Carnival night.

With the Carnival that year in Trinidad there came the Black Power revolution that had been maturing. There were daily anti-government marches in Port of Spain; revolutionary pamphlets appeared everywhere, even in schools; sections of the regiment declared for the marchers. Even the Asian countryside began to be infected. A spontaneous, anarchic outburst: a humane society divided in its wish for order and its various visions of redemption. But the police held firm; there was no need for Venezuelans or Americans to land. The outburst died down.

Steve Yeates took no part in these events. And Malik was later to say unkind things about the revolution. "I cannot understand people who are hell-bent on all kinds of political nonsense," the Trinidad *Express* reported him as saying. "They want power or the trappings of power, but that entails hard work."

This was now his line, and perhaps also his delusion: that his time in England had been a time of work, that he had become the best-known black man in the world through work, and that there were lots of bogus Negroes about who wanted to reap without sowing. It was his way of rebutting those who had begun to criticize his handling of Black House money. And it was also his way of saying that though he had missed the revolution in Trinidad, he was its true leader. Negroes existed now only that Malik might lead them: life hadn't caught up with art, but play had ceased to be play: through jest and fraud, disappointment and self-deception, Malik had reached the position that every racist power-seeker occupies. And it can be no coincidence that in March 1970, immediately after the Trinidad revolution, he started on his largest fund-raising exercise, to make the big killing before his return to Trinidad.

HE ANNOUNCED a Black House Building Programme Appeal. The Bishop of London was asked for his "learned advice" about the "spiritual needs" of "the many thousands who will be participating in the Black House." A more direct appeal was made to Charles Clore: ". . . a fantastic world-famous reality . . . unique project . . . let us show the world that Britain is not prepared to be a drop-out in the great race of culture and progress . . ."

At the same time Malik consulted Patricia East of Patrick East Associates (International Public Relations), who did the PR for Sammy Davis, Jr., in England; and East offered to handle the account "personally." The Black House, she said, should be registered at once as a charity. She thought they should aim at setting up a string of Black Houses throughout the country. And she outlined a campaign which would, among other things, "promote the name of Michael X as a household word for the good of the community at large." There was a further point. For her services East required £3,500 (exclusive of expenses) for the first year, payable quarterly and in advance. This wasn't perhaps what was expected; and East, as she now says, "lost touch" with Malik.

He went to work on his own. A standard begging letter on the theme of "Peace and Love" was devised: ". . . The difference in culture should not prevent men from living in peace. The men of culture are true apostles of equality." A more businesslike letter went to Canada Life Assurance; they said no. Charter Consolidated said no, twice. A reminder was sent to Charles Clore, who hadn't replied; and now Clore's secretary said no.

It must have occurred to Malik at this stage that there was something wrong with his "image." Canon Collins was invited by "Brother Francis (Director, Planning and Development)" to pay another visit to the Black House, "this time at least for lunch." And Malik drafted letters—"Dear Brother"—to the presidents of the university unions of Cambridge,

Oxford, Reading, Swansea, Cardiff, Edinburgh and Glasgow, and asked to be invited to speak on Black Power or the Alternative Society. He claimed to have spoken at most of those universities "about three years ago"; he referred jocularly to his jail sentence; he used words like "confab" and "relate with"; in his letter to Edinburgh he said he was mentioning the names of Alex Trocchi, Ronnie Laing and Jim Haynes "as friends because it is possible that the only one you know me by could be Michael X."

At the same time, as a Muslim, "a worker and producer," a builder of a mosque, a converter of the infidel and a trainer of the young ("we are able to train in excess of 500 directly and an unresearched multiple indirectly"), he was making an assault on the treasury of the Emir of Kuwait. He wrote to the Kuwait Student Union and asked to be invited to Kuwait: "As an articulator for our people I am invited to speak by all of our major universities in England." He sent an autographed copy of his ghosted autobiography to the Kuwait embassy and, no doubt for reasons of drama, asked for it to be packaged in the presence of an embassy official and sent by diplomatic carrier to the Emir, together with a letter. He wrote two letters to the Kuwait ambassador. One asked for an "audience even if it is only for five minutes," and drew attention to the second letter, which had been put in an envelope marked "X." X marked the spot: "As you know, the biggest property owners in this country are Jews. Our landlords are Jews. We must get them off our backs . . . We ask you to deal with this our request of direct financial aid as an urgent and top priority matter. In terms of money the figure of £100,000 (one hundred thousand pounds) is a very realistic and immediate need . . . Yours in Islam, Michael Abdul Malik."

It was as another kind of Muslim, Harlem and very devout, that he wrote to his Black Muslim contacts in the United States. He reported success ("an urban village . . . a beautiful place to live in"); he confessed his fears about the Jews. But he reversed the Kuwaiti approach. The hard request came first; the flannel followed. "We need most desperately, a large injection of capital . . . Sometimes I feel very much abandoned and alone when I preach the word of the Messanger [sic]. Sometimes, when our need is very great and there seems no way to turn a Brother who has never spoken to the Holy Aposle [sic] would say to me 'Why don't you bare your heart to him, surely he will help.' But somewhere in my head and maybe this is because I had the honour to sit with him and look in his eyes, I feel that it is my duty to go out and search for our needs in the wilderness of Babylon."

Later, in a statement at his trial, Malik summed up this period. "I returned to the United Kingdom and started winding up my business, liquidizing certain of the assets that my family had acquired for the many years we spent in Europe."

He encouraged some of the people around him to believe that he was successfully "liquidizing": money or the show of money would win him those "recruits" he was looking for. But he went too far. Like a man touched by the fantasies of his own begging letters, he began to speak of fantastic sums; and he trapped himself. He said he had got £250,000 from Nigel Samuel for the Black House; and there were people who believed him. (In the *Sunday Times* of March 12, 1972, the "Insight" reporters gave an outside figure of £15,000.) But the Black House had little to show for £250,000; in February 1970 a cheque for £237 to the London Electricity Board had bounced; and it began to occur to some people, during this fund-raising year, that Malik might be preparing to get away to Trinidad with the equivalent of a million Trinidad dollars.

". . . Within found out that threats become Real—like being shot at—Problems with Black and Whites on organization." The notes for *Requiem for an Illusion* are cryptic. But, as in the autobiography, Malik distorts one story by fragmenting it into many scattered stories; and the notes themselves later provide the key. "Relation with outside—myth of immense wealth—How did this come about." Malik was beginning to feel that in London he was close to danger. And even later, in Trinidad, he was never to lose the fear—perhaps some threat had been made—that his children might be kidnapped.

And there was trouble with the law again. Earlier in the year Malik and seven of his followers had been charged with demanding money with menaces from a London businessman—"a local Jewish businessman," Malik had written to a Black Muslim in the United States. It was a complicated story about an employment agency, a black American, a job, a ring pledged in lieu of a fee. The sum involved was small, five pounds. But the businessman had been led about the Black House in a dog collar, and the case had attracted attention. Malik, for some reason, had written to the New China News Agency asking them to take an interest in the case; but what had appeared "farcical" became less so when in November Malik and five of his men were committed for trial at the Old Bailey.

Flight to Trinidad was now urgent. But Black Power had provided Malik with a complete system; even at this stage he made it fit. He gave interviews; he went on television; and he spoke now like a Black Panther. He was giving up Black Power, he said; henceforth he was going to devote himself to constructive work. He handed over the management of the Black House to Stanley Abbott, a fellow Trinidadian to whom—in the absence of Steve Yeates in Trinidad—Malik had grown especially close during the past year: Abbott of the pale complexion and the dreamy, bruised eyes, five feet six, neat and powerful, with a straight back and immensely muscular arms. Abbott was now thirty-three, fifteen years away from home, with a life already in ruins, with fresh convictions during the two previous years for possessing marijuana, for theft and for assault. Abbott believed that Nigel Samuel had given £250,000; Abbott believed that Malik was rich, and Abbott was loyal.

All was now set for Malik's flight to Trinidad. Steve Yeates was there, waiting, a bodyguard. But then Malik, remembering the Black Power revolution that had failed in Trinidad, remembering the Stokely Carmichael tapes he had played and the strikers he had marched with, became anxious about how he might be received. One day, playing records to "mood" him, "for this city is full of— and viciousness and I want to feel clean and talk the truth," he began to write to Eric Williams, the Trinidad Prime Minister. The letter quickly became hysterical, marijuana-hazy, and spread through a long postscript to seventeen pages.

He wrote, as he had so often written, to explain himself. The bewilderment of his early life had turned, with success, to awe at himself; he could put so many patterns on his disordered experience. And now, once again, he spoke of the poverty of his boyhood; of his name of de Freitas ("there was so much dirt with him"); of his Notting Hill success ("I ran the most successful string of Gaming house and Whore houses that any Black person ever did in England"); of his great fame ("I know my name is a household word": the Patricia East PR proposals "to promote the name of Michael X as a household word" had clearly made an impression on him).

As he wrote, his awe at himself grew. He saw himself "living in danger on the real front line," and from this military metaphor he developed a fantasy about his life in England:

Up here we are walking a tightrope, at the moment its like a suicide mission, you cannot come to our aid Militarily but here we can aid you they cannot Bomb London, Birmingham Liverpool etc. to get us, it must be man to man, we are ready. There are 52,000 English troops in Germany the Reserves are low, the Irish conflict contained enough explosive Power to draw 9,000 out of Germany, and they were ill equipped. I don't know how much longer we can hold out, A few weeks ago they were talking of Gas Ovens in the English Parliament but our morale is high.

So many personalities during this last year in England, so many voices: the real man had long ago been lost. Yet, promoting himself as a Negro, he everywhere "passed."

The Black House, after three weeks under Stanley Abbott, ended in chaos, in a general looting. And with that, Malik's London career was over. Abbott saw Malik the night before Malik left. From a pile of five-pound notes Malik gave Abbott two hundred pounds. "Liquidized" assets: a glimpse of real money. When later, from Trinidad, Malik sent Abbott a letter with the one word "Come," Abbott would take the next plane out.

3

AFTER fourteen years his London career had ended in flight, and it might have been thought that he was finished. But Malik flourished in Trinidad as a free man for one year.

Trinidad in 1971 was his perfect setting. Trinidad, with its oil economy, was rich, with a standard of living equalled in South America only by Venezuela and Argentina. Every consumer comfort was at hand, and Malik was soon pleasantly settled in the country town of Arima, in a newish house with a large garden. But Trinidad was far away. In London, Chicago and Toronto, fund-raising centres, Trinidad could pass as an impoverished island where a black leader, fleeing persecution, and also reacting against "the industrialized complex," might settle down, in a "commune," to constructive work with despairing blacks, who needed only this leadership, and little gifts of money, to get started in black agriculture, black fruit-growing. And, later, even a little black fish-ing: a trawler (obtainable through "contractural relationships with . . . Schichting-Werft shipyard, Travemuende") would cost £18,000, but "initial feasibility studies indicate that the profits . . . would exceed £30,000 a month." Remote Trinidad held this kind of possibility for its enthralled blacks; all that was needed was the leadership.

And in Trinidad Malik presented himself as a London success. Shortly after he came he sought out Raoul Pantin of the Trinidad *Express*. "He wanted me to do this interview. I was to prepare both the questions and the answers, and I was to make it sound good. He was hir-ing a skill. His comment when I resisted this was: 'How do you think I became famous if I couldn't find people in England to do this for me?' " Some people were also shown a letter purporting to come from an English lawyer, in which the writer said that Malik couldn't expect a fair trial in England. Malik was also a friend of the famous. The names weren't always known in Trinidad and could be mangled—Feliks Topol-ski becoming Saponski or Topalowski, painter of the Queen, Alex Troc-chi becoming Trotsky—and there were people who thought that Malik might only be a name-dropper. But the well-publicized visit in April 1971 of John Lennon as Malik's house-guest stilled all doubts.

He was successful; he had money; he had style. Rawle Maximin was a partner in the car-hire firm Malik now patronized. Maximin is a big, handsome man, half-Indian, half-Venezuelan, with no racial anxieties and no interest in the subject. But his business success, perhaps greater than he expected, now makes Maximin wish he were better educated; and he remembers Malik as someone who never made him feel less than a man.

Michael impress me a lot when he come back. He always move in a big way. If they are selling orange juice in that bar there for a dollar a glass and they are selling the same orange juice in that other bar for two dollars, he want the two-dollars one. If you go to the supermarket with him he fulling up two trolleys, one with meat only. You only hearing these slabs of meat dropping in the basket like iron—you know how they freeze and hard. He don't want all he buy and you know some of it will go rotten. But he want people around to see. Another thing. He never argue your price. And as friendly as we were he would never say, "Lend me that car." He would say, "How much for that car?" He had his own car but he would hire mine, for the show. He want this crowd around him. "I am the leader." I liked him very much. He never made me feel less than a man. And he always give. I still have a pair of black socks of his.

Style, and money, were also noted by a black woman, a teacher, who went up to the Malik house in Arima at a time when there was some talk that she might teach the Malik children, who, because of the fear of kidnapping, couldn't be sent to school.

If you ran out of cigarettes you weren't offered a pack. You were offered a carton. Soft drinks by the case. Michael talked about the prices he had paid for this and that, and talked about the dogs he was bringing down from London. I was impressed by the décor of the house. You could see money oozing out of everything. You walked into a room, you saw taste. The house was very clean, everything well chosen and put away.

The local Belmont boy, with the common black mother who wore washerwoman's clothes, had made good. And with his success there had come a change in his manner. Patrick Chokolingo, editor of *The Bomb*, had met Malik in London in 1965, at the beginning of his fame. "He told me that the white man was a devil. I said to him, 'But you are living in a white man's country and you are part white.' He said, 'That may be so. But my heart is black. They made it black.' He did capture me; he did excite me." Shortly after Malik's return to Trinidad in January 1971, Chokolingo went to see him at the Chagacabana Hotel.

He was occupying one of the cabanas, and with him was Steve Yeates. I found he was trying to impress me—which I didn't think that time in London. He was selling me Michael, and his entire demeanour had changed. In the Marble Arch flat in London he had looked a little bit wild, a little bit fanatical, excitable, moving about in fits and jerks. In Trinidad he sat cross-legged in a reclining chair and his voice had changed. It had become very soft and persuasive. This was the first thing that struck me—that I was talking to a completely different person.

The new light voice, the relaxed manner: other people noticed the change as well. Malik was made by words, his and other people's. He needed a model always, and a clue to his new manner may be provided by the ghosted autobiography of 1968. Malik doesn't say much about Rachman, the London property racketeer for whom he worked as a strong-arm man. But what he says is oddly admiring. Rachman, in his book, is cool and stylish, almost a Hollywood character, "a good-looking man with a strong face." He is introduced, Hollywood-fashion, sitting at a desk, surrounded by his Alsatians, and with two bodyguards, one just sitting, one reading a newspaper. "He was very well dressed and groomed and spoke in a quiet voice which I never heard him raise. In short, he exuded quiet charm." Rachman, in Notting Hill, was in his "manor." It might be that Malik, in Trinidad, fancied that he was in his.

Chokolingo asked Malik to write for *The Bomb,* and found that he was "pushing at an open door." Malik began a series on brothels. "He would not be satisfied, he said, until he had wiped brothels off the face of Trinidad. He did not see how Chinese men could come here and destroy the little girls of Trinidad. He was particularly aiming his barbs at the Korean Chinese who were running brothels in Port of Spain. Two were prosecuted. One hanged himself in his cell." But then the police came to Chokolingo and told him it was a shakedown: Malik had raised ten thousand Trinidad dollars, £2,000, from two brothel operators. Rich Trinidad, demoralized by years of racial politics, and tense after the Black Power upheaval of 1970, offered this kind of possibility. Later, when he had settled in, Malik thought of a £50,000 "foundation," to be named after his wife; and he prepared a list of local people who might be asked to contribute.

And he didn't neglect the "agricultural" side. Chokolingo says:

Sometime in '71 he went up to Toronto and Chicago, and one day I got a call from Michael in Toronto. He said, "Do you remember that worm that was destroying the cabbages of the dirt-farmers on the Highway?" Worm? Cabbages? And then I realized that he had an audience at the other end, and I said, "Oh yes. Yes." And he said, "Well, I've got the people at the University of "—I can't remember—"who are prepared to investigate this, and I would like you to put some of those worms in a bottle and mail it to me at this address." The next time it was from Chicago. That time I was a little wiser. "That project we were discussing about those farmers and their arid lands on the east coast—I've got some people who are prepared to move the silt from Orinoco basin and deposit it in this area. So you can pass the message on to the farmers." Shortly after he came back he started to splurge. He bought a Humber Super Snipe and a jeep.

And in Trinidad the "commune" grew. No agricultural commune grew so fast; on no kibbutz did fruit trees mature so swiftly. Within months, from his suburban garden, Malik was reporting to a correspondent in the United States on the expanding commune's need for "more moving equipment—another tractor, a bulldozer," claiming at the same time "a [*sic*] impressive surplus of coconuts, limes, oranges, grapefruit, mangoes, milk, Anthorium [*sic*] lilies, cow and horse manure."

He had an option to buy the Arima house at the end of the year—the £1,000 he had paid was in effect a year's rent—but people believed the house was his. One day he told a visitor—the black woman teacher—that he had also bought the large French-style house at the back and was going to have it redecorated. Ringo Starr was the next Beatle coming down, and that was where he would stay. He looked over a £4,000 piece of land in Guanapo, in the hills to the north; he didn't buy, but he later "incorporated" it into his commune as "extra land acquisition . . . able to absorb from the U.S. initially sixty young men and women on a construction redevelopment programme."

In Carenage, a seaside slum settlement west of Port of Spain, he rented a £35-a-month house from Oswald Chesterfield McDavidson, the black Guyanese entrepreneur involved with things like beauty competitions who was the husband of a Trinidad government minister. This house was "The People's Store." Its "trustees" were Steve Yeates and Stanley Abbott and it handled the "produce" of the commune. Letterheads had been printed and copy prepared for a brochure. According to this, the profits of the store were to be handed over each month to a different black cause.

In Arima itself there was a racing stud farm, owned by a Portuguese who was another Belmont boyhood friend, and with whom Malik now struck up a relationship. That was also "incorporated" into the commune: it was the source of the milk and the manure that formed part of the commune's "impressive surplus."

Everything in Malik's commune existed; nothing belonged to him. It was like a return, in maturity, to that time of his childhood in Belmont when he had stolen a bicycle and had been arrested. He hadn't stolen an ordinary bicycle. He had stolen a distinctive racing cycle that belonged to a well-known racing cyclist, St. Louis; and then, claiming the cycle as his own, a gift from his uncle, he had cycled about Belmont, where St. Louis lived.

Trinidad was Malik's manor. Trinidad has a population of just over a million. Much of this population lives in the north-west of the island between the Northern Range and the flat sugar belt, in an urban or a semi-urban sprawl, seemingly unplanned and grabbing, that begins five miles west of Port of Spain and ends about sixteen miles east of the city. Agricultural land is steadily invaded; the hillsides are scratched higher and higher with houses and squatters' shacks and show more brown every year; open spaces, both within the city and outside it, are filled in. The built-up areas choke; the highways are clogged with motorcars; the railway system has been abandoned. Black carrion corbeaux guard the entrance to Port of Spain; and over much of the eastern end of the city, where green hills have been quarried by illegal immigrants from the other islands into dusty red shanty towns, there now hangs the reek of the city's new rubbish dump, burning in the mangrove that once sheltered the scarlet ibis.

It is a "consumer" squalor. It is not supported by agriculture, which declines, or by industry, which, where it exists, is rudimentary, protected and inflationary. It is supported by what the visitor seldom sees: oil, drilled for in the sea to the north and the south-east, and inland in the south, in forest reserves that are like a country within a country.

Trinidad's urban north-west is a great parasitic suburb, through which money is yet magically cycled. Much of the population is superfluous, and they know it. Unemployment is high but labour is perennially short. The physical squalor, the sense of a land being pillaged rather than built up, generates great tensions; cynicism is like a disease. Race is an irrelevance; but the situation is well suited to the hysteria and evasions of racial politics. And racial politics—preaching oppression and easy redemption, offering only the theory of the enemy, white, brown, yellow, black—have brought the society close to collapse.

Malik, an operator acting always in the racial cause, found in Trinidad his perfect camouflage. He created nothing; but he converted race into money (it didn't matter whose) and success; and that was what many hoped to do. A young "Black Panther"—connected with a heavily subsidized ninety-acre agricultural cooperative, unproductive because unworked—said admiringly of Malik, even after Malik had fallen: "He was prime minister of himself and his little group. He was like a little country by himself." In his year in Trinidad Malik penetrated the society at many points. It was known what he was, but among the cynical and parasitic new men of Trinidad that was like respectability.

He might have risen higher. But then, towards the end of the year, his life took a new twist. Hakim Jamal and Gale Benson arrived from Guyana: Benson, the twenty-seven-year-old English divorcée, in her self-created role as white-woman slave to Jamal's black master, Jamal himself more or less living off a German and anxious about money and his hustling projects. Jamal's line was black schools for the very young and black publishing. He had abandoned his family in California; and he and Benson had been together for about a year, an itinerant hustling team, travelling about the United States in a Volkswagen minibus. They had just been to England to promote Jamal's autobiography; and there they had arranged to come down to Guyana to do a little black business in publishing. Jamal had hoped to take the Guyana government into partnership. But after a month in Guyana he was asked to leave.

Jamal, true American, travelled with his hustler's paraphernalia: life-size printed photographs of himself, brochures of his non-existent Malcolm X Montessori school, and copies of his autobiography. He used the book to introduce himself at Rawle Maximin's garage. He gave Maximin a copy and Maximin told him that Michael X was in Trinidad. "And it was as though I had told him there was a million dollars under that chair there." Later Maximin drove Jamal from the Port of Spain Hilton to Arima. "He asked how far I had got in the book. I said not very far. He took the book and as we were driving he started reading it out. And when he started reading, like he don't want to stop. He spent that night by Michael. In the morning I went to the Hilton and moved down Gale to Arima."

THE RELATIONSHIP among these three during November and December 1971 cannot now be known. Jamal used to claim, especially with those white people whom he knew the claim would excite, that he was God; and as God he was Benson's master. But in the Malik commune at Arima, Jamal recognized a more successful outfit and saw its great potential; and Jamal almost immediately decided that Malik was *his* master. He settled in right away, in the house obliquely opposite, which he rented; and soon he was writing a hectoring half-farewell note to a white friend in California, saying that he was through with white people and was for the first time among friends.

Money was short—at the end of November Jamal deposited five hundred Trinidad dollars, £104, in a Canadian bank in Port of Spain, and a month later was down to ninety-four dollars, £19—but ideas came thick and fast. Jamal's black schools and black publishing merged with Malik's black agriculture into a stupendous black cause. On 10th December Malik wrote to a correspondent in the United States: "We are now producing reams of literature." Much of this—copy for the commune—was knocked off by Jamal on the typewriter. Malik was no writer; to Jamal, an American, salesman's prose came naturally. Jamal needed a harbour; Malik depended on other men's ideas. Their talents and roles were complementary; they did not clash.

And it is possible that Gale Benson now became more of an outsider than she had been. She wore African-style clothes that were extravagant even in Trinidad; she had given herself the name of Halé Kimga, an anagram of Gale and Hakim; she went on begging errands for her master. But her cult was of Jamal alone. She didn't appear to be serving the general cause; and she had a way of putting people off. Rawle Maximin found her "very serious." When he offered to show her local nightclub dances, she said, "I haven't come here for that." When she met Lourenço, the Portuguese owner of the stud farm Malik had "incorporated" into his commune, she spoke to him in Spanish; and Lourenço didn't care for that.

At the same time there was some displeasure in the United States. Jamal, serving Malik and the commune, had been neglecting some of his old associates; and Benson was blamed. It was felt that she possessed him too completely. In December, three weeks before Benson was stabbed to death, an American, writing critically of Benson to some friends in Guyana (and the letter got to Jamal in Trinidad), drew a distinction between Halé Kimga, the devotee, and "Gailann the secretary." And that points to something else: Benson's Englishness in spite of her African clothes, and the middle-class manner that seemed at variance with her slave role. "She was sort of a fake": this was what Malik's wife said later.

Jamal served Malik. But it is possible that he also took him over and gave him a new idea of his role in Trinidad. Jamal dealt in the vehement racial passions of the United States and was obsessed with white people. He didn't understand a place like Trinidad; he didn't understand Malik's position in black and independent Trinidad as "prime minister of himself and his little group." He saw it in American terms, as the triumph of a "nigger." And so he celebrated it in an eight-page article about Malik (part of the commune literature) which was intended for younger readers—Jamal's first love was black Montessori schools.

> He is always giving. You feel bad that there are people who misunderstand him. He teaches, not just by talking, he shows you, for example; he grows orchards [*sic*]. In his front yard, hanging from his trees there are orchards, dainty flowers that need intense care, but they [yield and *deleted*] blossom. He grows vegetables for his table and also feeds those passersby who need food . . . His chicken farm that feeds thousands of Trinidadians meat. His cows that give milk for babies and for our own health. Then too, there is the stable of horses, thoroughbreds. As he shows them to you, he lectures, but the lecture is real because as he talks about a certain horse, there is the horse. When he speaks of milking cows, you are at the farm, seeing the cows being milked . . . You are almost worthy of hearing this man, seeing this man, talking with this man. A man, that England would try to destroy, because they know that somehow this slave, this captured African, had the power of UNDERSTANDING—and what's worse—he understands the slave—he loves the slave—and Brother Michael Abdul Malik, has the nerve, the gall—to be black. Even in a time when he could be anything he wants to be, rich, famous, fashionable, safe—it seems Brother Malik is already too busy being happy as a NIGGER.

A caricature of a caricature; but Jamal, turning Malik into an American, infecting Malik, in the security of Trinidad, with the American-type racial vehemence Malik had so far only parodied, was creating a monster. "Nigger," success as a kind of racial revenge: these are among the themes of the novel Malik was writing about himself in a cheap lined quarto writing pad, solid unparagraphed pages in pencil or ballpoint, the writing small, very little crossed out, the number of words noted at the top of each page. At least fifty pages were written; and some of them survived the events they seem so curiously to foreshadow.

The setting is Guyana. A well-appointed house, Malik's, is being described: modern furniture imported from England, fitted carpets, radio phonograph, records, "a gigantic bookshelf Shakespeare [*sic*] Shaw Marx Lenin Trotsky Confucius Hugo." The narrator takes up "Salammbo that masterpiece of Flaubert's" and finds it dust-free. "I discover that he not only have the books but actually reads and understands them I was absolutely bowld, litteraly. I took a seat, and gazed upon this marvel, Mike."

The narrator is a thirty-year-old Englishwoman, Lena Boyd-Richardson. She has been four years in Guyana, doing a bogus job created for her in the firm of Clarkson's by Sir Harold, a friend of her father's; and she is "really of the opinion these natives are all shiftless good for Nothings." Her house is not far from Michael Malik's, and she often sees "Mike leaning against the Coconut tree like some statue on a Pedestal, some god, and his little subjects, his little people, Paying Homage to him." He is in the habit of greeting her in pidgin: "Like it gwine rain today, mam"; but they do not meet until, for some reason (the early pages are lost), she visits the house. And then "to top it all he was even talking with a slight Cockney accent to stupify me the more." He plays some jazz for her on the phonograph, and the "Thihikosky 1812"; and then the time comes for her to bid "goodbye to this Amazing man with the Promise to call again." So the first chapter ends.

Chapter Two is titled "Run in with Fate." Lena doesn't call again; but she drives past Mike's house every day and begins to note "his eyes sometimes Mocking and laughing." She notes his light complexion and wonders about his idling, his shabby clothes, his "weird double Life." "And then again I find myself closing up my doors at night . . . the truth I am [afraid *deleted*] scared I am mortally afraid of this man of this Mike the grinning ape, and I can't help liking him, something about him drawing you to him. I wonder how he would look without that Big Beard."

The run-in with fate follows. Lena, driving through the town one day, nearly runs over a young girl. The girl is Jenny, Mike's eldest daughter, and Lena offers to take her home. Jenny is uneasy, "scared of what daddy will do if he finds out"; but allows herself to be driven home. "And there was Mike leaning against the tree as usual with his little ret-

inue around him." Terror. "Mike's voice boomed, 'Jenny come here.' "
Jenny screams and doesn't move; she is "shaking too much to say any-
thing sensible." "Was it fear?" Lena wonders. "And if so Fear of what?"
Mike's wife, pregnant, runs up "at a fantastic speed despite her large
Stomach." Mike himself doesn't leave the coconut tree; but "His Retinue
Pulled slightly away from where they were but still out of earshot."
Jenny is led by her younger sister to Mike. Lena—curiously choosing
this moment to observe "what a great Bond there was" between Jenny
and her father—explains that nothing has happened. Mike kisses Jenny,
who sobs and says, "They didn't touch me, daddy." He walks off
towards the house, but the girl still sobs.

"It took me Just one minute to see why the child kept insisting 'They
didn't touch me,' Just a minute to see why she was so scared, and what of.
For her father came walking out of the front door as Calm as Ever with a
shot gun Under his Arm and Box of shells stuffing some down in his
Pocket." Mike's wife is about to faint, but Lena catches her; and when
Mike comes to her, "she then made a most amazing Transformation,
recaptured her poise and said to her husband, 'Be Careful darling, and
think first All the time.' For someone who did not know the happenings
before they could never imagine what this man was going to do. There
was that look of finality about him." Jenny pleads; Lena—"I too was like
if I was dumb"—is silent; the wife faints. And Mike walks down the road
to the corner.

This is how Lena becomes involved with the family. After some missing pages we find Lena and Mike's wife exchanging memories of
England, and Lena hears of Mike's courtship. Nothing, apparently, has
happened; tension has been created for its own sake, to prove a point
about Mike. Not the least illogical aspect of the scene—with a child
screaming, a wife fainting—is the stress on Mike as a family man; but
Jamal, in his article about Malik for younger readers, had laid that on
with a heavy American hand. A few more pages are missing here; but it is
fairly clear that some kind of relationship has developed between Lena
and Mike.

And then something extraordinary happens. There is a stumble in the
narrative: the writer, without knowing it, suddenly loses his narrator,
Lena. In a few connected lines the writer moves from the first-person
narrative to third person and then back to first. But now it is Sir Harold,
Lena's father's friend, appearing in Guyana, who is the narrator.

Sir Harold comes upon Mike addressing a street-corner meeting in pidgin. Mike's speech is given at length; it is quite incoherent. People must work; but there is nothing wrong with being lazy; Mike himself is lazy and can be seen any day standing in the shade of his tree; he doesn't like to work; but he has worked hard since he was fourteen, and he has worked in England; in England no one pays for the doctor and everything is free, but the taxes are high. The crowd, mixed African and Asian, receives this speech ecstatically. Then Mike, switching from pidgin, says to Sir Harold: "You come late Sir Harold, I am never at my best when I have my wife waiting."

Lena, lost for some pages, now reappears. " 'What do you think about him,' she asked. I met him once before in England, I said, now I don't know for he seems somehow different. We noticed a movement in the bushes to the side of the house 'Don't Pay any attention to that' she said 'that Probably some of his Retinue, wherever he is you can be sure there will be some of them hanging around.' I felt a Cold wind Pass through me, and decided to go inside." Mike and his wife prepare to leave. "Jenny will not sleep if I am not at home," Mike says. And Sir Harold continues: "I stood at the door and watched them walk down the Path about thirty seconds after I saw six dark figures slowly follow them 'England was never like this' I said to myself and turned inside."

The pages are now disconnected: "We could not tear ourselves away from the Presence of this man"—"the fantastic following he had in the country"—Mike ill with malaria, contracted in Africa when he was young ("never less than two score People standing around the house with a look of anxiety about them": which reads like a borrowed sentence)— Sir Harold offering a job with Clarkson's—shouts in the street: "We go crown him king."

An autobiography can distort; facts can be realigned. But fiction never lies: it reveals the writer totally. And Malik's primitive novel is like a pattern book, a guide to later events. That scene of causeless tension at the house with the daughter, the wife, the retinue: just such a scene was witnessed at Arima by a black woman visitor on the Sunday before Joe Skerritt was murdered. "I can't describe it. I spent just ten minutes in that house that day. Michael was in the street flying kites. Jennifer wanted some Coke. Her mother said she had to ask her father." That "look of finality" that made Lena Boyd-Richardson "like if I was dumb": it was with "a satanic look," according to Stanley Abbott, that Malik, cutlass in hand and about to murder Skerritt, ordered Abbott: "I am ready. Bring him." The political speech in Guyana: even that was to take place, twelve days after the murder of Skerritt. The malaria: that was the excuse Malik gave when, on the run in Guyana, he stayed for three days in his hotel room without drawing the curtains. There remains the mystery of Lena Boyd-Richardson, repelled, fascinated, involved, and then abruptly disappearing as narrator.

So, during November and December 1971, Hakim Jamal and Michael Abdul Malik, in the security of the commune, produced their literature: Jamal, on the typewriter, offering the vision of a triumphant "nigger," Malik dourly writing his novel in ballpoint and soft pencil, counting each word, awakening old disturbances, arriving at some new definition of himself.

The uneducated Belmont boy had become a man of culture. The London X had become a political hero at home. The man with the silent retinue was the man who in 1965 had told Colin McGlashan of the *Observer,* "It may sound melodramatic, but there are people who would die for me." Such a success required witness, English witness; and people like Lena Boyd-Richardson and Sir Harold felt a cold wind of terror. "England was never like this": Malik, as he wrote, filling the cheap pad, was discovering that he, like his bodyguard and familiar, Steve Yeates, carried the wound of England.

In December, Gale Benson was sent to Guyana to beg for money. To Stanley Abbott, in England, Malik sent a letter with one word: "Come." "Peace and love": that was how the "brothers" usually signed off in their letters. But the cable from Stanley Abbott that was telephoned to Malik at half-past four on December 10 read like this:

ARRIVING 1055 PM SATURDAY 11TH STOP FLIGHT 537 FROM NEW YORK MUCH LOVE TO ALL PEACE AND POWER STANLEY.

From Jamal there went a summons to the United States, to the Negro known as Kidogo, one of his "co-workers." Four months before, in London, Jamal had told Jill Tweedie of the *Guardian*: "If you're going to kill, it must mean something. You should kill people because they are evil, not because they are white." "He [Jamal] told me he wanted to send for one of his co-workers," Malik said in his statement afterwards. "And just about the same time I noticed through the correspondence I was having from Abbott that he too was coming down to Trinidad."

So, in December 1971, they began to gather in the two houses of the Arima commune. Simmonds, a white woman who said she had known Malik for ten years, came down from England; and—as she told *The Bomb* afterwards—had "total involvement" with Steve Yeates, "an excellent lover ... compassionate ... understanding ... a sense of humour ... a wonderful man." Kidogo arrived; he didn't stay with Jamal, who knew him, but with Malik, who said he wanted to talk to him about America. Abbott stayed across the road with Jamal. In the third week of December Benson returned from Guyana. She had failed in her begging mission.

On December 31 Steve Yeates, using his Black Muslim name of Muhammed Akbar, went to Cooblal's Hardware and bought a six-inch corner file, charging it to the account of "Mr. Abdhul Mallic, Arima." Such a file is used in Trinidad for sharpening cutlasses. There was a party at the commune that evening: it was Simmonds's thirtieth birthday. She remembered the food. "We had bought a calf," she told *The Bomb*, "and we had a nice birthday party. A big feed." Jamal had other memories. He remembered the "atmosphere of violence" at the commune, and he especially remembered the slaughter of a cow on a neighbouring farm around Christmas time. He told the Boston correspondent of the *Daily Mail* he believed Malik had drunk some of the blood. "They handed me the cup but I ain't no blood drinker."

On January 2, 1972, Gale Benson was stabbed nine times, one stab going right through the base of her neck. She was buried while still alive in a four-foot hole on the bank of the ravine some two hundred feet north of Malik's house. And she was not missed. Simmonds stayed at the commune until mid-January. Jamal and Kidogo left for the United States on January 20. Benson's body was not discovered until February 24. Five men were charged with her murder: an Indian boy called Parmassar, who had attached himself to Malik; a well-to-do Indian of good family called Chadee, who had become mixed up with the commune in December; Malik; Stanley Abbott; and the man called Kidogo, who has still not been found.

· · ·

NINETEEN SEVENTY-TWO was a year of rain and floods in Trinidad. Everything was green; bush grew fast. Nineteen seventy-three opened with drought. Every day the hills smoked with scores of separate fires; bamboo clumps ignited; fire, almost colourless in the sunlight, crackled on the roadside verges. The year before the grave of Gale Benson was fresh, hidden from the road by low bush; this year the ravine bank was brown and bare, and the grave was only a shallow hole, dry, crumbling, cleansed by light and heat. During the great days of the commune, Jamal, "looking out of the glass doors and seeing green, blue and cloud covered mountains," had written to a white correspondent in the United States: "It is very hot here in the tropics, but it is peaceful, and that is what I both want and need." Sixteen months after the murder of Benson, Jamal was himself put down, shot on May 2, 1973, by a four-man black gang in Boston.

The commune had ended swiftly. Jamal survived it by more than a year. On February 7, 1972, five weeks after the death of Benson, Joseph Skerritt, a renegade recruit, was brought down to the commune from his mother's house in Belmont. A hole was prepared for him the next morning, and just after midday he was chopped on the neck and buried in the position in which he fell, sprawling, legs apart and slightly raised.

Two days later the commune went on an excursion to Sans Souci bay in the north-east, and Steve Yeates was drowned. A length of bamboo attached to a rope was thrown out to him but he didn't grasp at it. Did he give a grimace of pain before he went under? Or did he grin? Stanley Abbott said: "Steve gave his life." So it ended for him, after the thirteen years in England, after the two years of waiting in Trinidad, after the solitary night walks around the Queen's Park Savannah in Port of Spain and the coded messages from the leader in London. After the commune had lasted exactly a year and a day, after the two killings, Muhammed Akbar, Supreme Captain of the Fruit of Islam, Lieutenant Colonel of the Black Liberation Army, was swept out to sea. Nine days later, on February 19, Malik and his family flew to Guyana. That evening the empty commune house burned down.

The lease had expired on February 9. Malik, unwilling or unable to exercise his option to buy, had, after a long wrangle with his landlords, received notice to quit. He had gone wild when he had heard, Stanley Abbott said. And to Abbott himself, after the two killings and the drowning of Steve Yeates, the news that Malik didn't own the house, owned nothing, came as a surprise. He felt "ashamed" and "deeply hurt." He had given Malik a book on leadership; and when he saw Malik reading this book, after they had discussed the notice to quit, and after they had discussed their "needs," Abbott felt like "going outside for the cutlass" and killing Malik. But then he thought of Malik's children and Malik's pregnant wife.

Abbott told Malik he was tired and needed a rest. Malik gave him a hundred dollars, twenty pounds; and, two days before Malik and his family went to Guyana, Abbott went to Tobago. He stayed with relatives and didn't try to hide. He spent four sleepless nights after he heard that the house had burned down. On February 24—the body of Gale Benson being disinterred, Malik hiding in a darkened hotel room in Guyana—Abbott flew back to Trinidad. From the airport he took a taxi to Port of Spain. He told the driver to drive slowly. He and the driver talked. He told the driver about the commune. The taxi stopped a little way from police headquarters, and the driver shook Abbott by the hand. Abbott walked to the main entrance of the Victorian Gothic building, spoke to the police sentry at the top of the steps and passed inside. It was a few minutes before midnight.

A YEAR LATER the Malik house was as the fire had left it. The garden was overgrown, the grass straggly and brown. But the drought had drawn out bright colour from every flowering plant, and bougainvillaea was purple and pink-red on the wire-mesh fence. Beside the peach-coloured hibiscus hedge in the north-west, the hole of Joe Skerritt was dry and cleaned out and shallow, as without drama as that other hole, on the ravine bank. The cover of the septic tank had been dislodged: a dead frog floated. A moraine of litter flowed out from the back door of the house onto the concrete patio between the blackened main house and the untouched servants' quarters. Solidified litter—many burned copies of Malik's autobiography, newspapers and magazines burned and sodden and dried into solid charred cakes. The kitchen was black; the fire was fiercest here. The ceilings everywhere had been burned off and showed the naked corrugated-iron roof, a sheet of which hung down perpendicularly in the living room. All the woodwork was charred. But already a green wild vine, a single long green vine, had run from the over-grown garden onto the gritty terrazzo of the living room.

A murderer can become celebrated and his survival can become a cause. A murdered person can be forgotten. Joe Skerritt was not important, and he is remembered, as a person, only in his mother's house in Belmont. A large unframed pencil portrait is pinned to the wall of the small living room. There are framed photographs of his more successful brother, Anthony (in sea scout uniform), who is in Canada, and of his sister, who was for many years a nurse in England; on a glass cabinet there are the sporting cups won by Michael, another brother. The house is shabby; Mrs. Skerritt does lunches for some schoolchildren, but money is short. She looks after her mother, who is senile and shrunken, skin and bones, with thin grey hair tied up tight and sitting on the skull like a coarse knotted handkerchief. Mrs. Skerritt ceaselessly relives that morning when Malik came for her son. He called her "Tantie" and she looked up and saw "that red man."

The streets of Belmont are still full of Joe Skerritts. The walls are still scrawled with the easy threats and easy promises of Black Power. The streets are still full of "hustlers" and "scrunters," words that glamourize and seem to give dispensation to those who beg and steal. Another Malik is possible. At every stage of his career he was supported by some kind of jargon and could refer his actions to some kind of revolutionary ideal.

Malik's career proves how much of Black Power—away from its United States source—is jargon, how much a sentimental hoax. In a place like Trinidad, racial redemption is as irrelevant for the Negro as for everybody else. It obscures the problems of a small independent country with a lopsided economy, the problems of a fully "consumer" society that is yet technologically untrained and without the intellectual means to comprehend the deficiency. It perpetuates the negative, colonial politics of protest. It is, in the end, a deep corruption: a wish to be granted a dispensation from the pains of development, an almost religious conviction that oppression can be turned into an asset, race into money. While the dream of redemption lasts, Negroes will continue to exist only that someone might be their leader. Redemption requires a redeemer; and a redeemer, in these circumstances, cannot but end like the Emperor Jones: contemptuous of the people he leads, and no less a victim, seeking an illusory personal emancipation. In Trinidad, as in every black West Indian island, the too easily awakened sense of oppression and the theory of the enemy point to the desert of Haiti.

Malik, Jamal, Skerritt, Steve Yeates, Stanley Abbott, Benson: they seem purely contemporary, but they played out an old tragedy. If the tragedy of Joe Skerritt and Steve Yeates and Stanley Abbott is contained in O'Neill's 1920 drama of the false redeemer, the tragedy of Gale Benson is contained in an African story of 1897 by Conrad, which curiously complements it: "An Outpost of Progress," a story of the congruent corruptions of colonizer and colonized, which can also be read as a parable about simple people who think they can separate themselves from the crowd. Benson was as shallow and vain and parasitic as many middle-class dropouts of her time; she became as corrupt as her master; she was part of the corruption by which she was destroyed. And Malik's wife was right. Benson was, more profoundly than Malik or Jamal, a fake. She took, on her journey away from home, the assumptions, however little acknowledged, not only of her class and race and the rich countries to which she belonged, but also of her ultimate security.

Some words from the Conrad story can serve as her epitaph; and as a comment on all those who helped to make Malik, and on those who continue to simplify the world and reduce other men—not only the Negro—to a cause, the people who substitute doctrine for knowledge and irritation for concern, the revolutionaries who visit centres of revolution with return air tickets, the hippies, the people who wish themselves on societies more fragile than their own, all those people who in the end do no more than celebrate their own security.

> They were [Conrad wrote] two perfectly insignificant and incapable individuals, whose existence is only rendered possible through the high organization of civilized crowds. Few men realize that their life, the very essence of their character, their capabilities and audacities, are only the expression of their belief in the safety of their surroundings. The courage, the composure, the confidence; the emotions and principles; every great and every insignificant thought belongs not to the individual but to the crowd: to the crowd that believes blindly in the irresistible force of its institutions and of its morals, in the power of its police and of its opinion.

One of the last letters Benson received was from her father, Captain Leonard Plugge, who lived in California but continued to use writing paper headed with his Belgravia address. With this letter Captain Plugge sent a translation he had done—typed out on the Belgravia paper and photocopied—of some lines by Lamartine:

> *On these white pages, where my verses unfold,*
> *May oft a souvenir, perchance your heart recall.*
> *Your life also only pure white pages behold,*
> *With one word, happiness, I would cover them all.*
> *But the book of life is a volume all sublime,*
> *That we cannot open, or close just at our time,*
> *On the page where one loves, one would wish to linger,*
> *Yet the page where one dies, hides beneath the finger.*

March–July 1973

4

Postscript

ABBOTT was given twenty years for the murder of Joe Skerritt. Malik was sentenced to death by hanging. Both Malik and Abbott appealed against their sentences. And it was only after their appeals had been dismissed—and after the above account had been written—that the trial for the Gale Benson murder took place.

Five men were accused of the murder. But only two were actually tried: Abbott again, and an Indian motorcar salesman named Chadee, who had been hoping to sell twelve cars to Malik and had then become mixed up with the Malik group. Three of the accused couldn't be tried. Steve Yeates was dead, drowned at Sans Souci, his body never recovered; Kidogo, Jamal's American "co-worker," was in the United States and couldn't be found; Malik was already under sentence of death. So Malik was never tried for the murder of Benson. It was Abbott who had to go through the calvary of two murder trials.

The murder of Benson was decided on by both Malik and Jamal. It was at the time when the two men were working on one another and exciting one another and producing "reams of literature." Jamal was writing his exalted, off-the-mark "nigger" nonsense about Malik; and Malik, in his novel, with this Jamal-given idea of his power (and no longer a man on the run, as in his previous fiction), was settling scores with the English middle class, turning the fascination of "Sir Harold" and "Lena Boyd-Richardson" into terror.

This was a literary murder, if ever there was one. Writing led both men there: for both of them, uneducated but clever, hustlers with the black cause always to hand, operating always among the converted or half-converted, writing had for too long been a public relations exercise, a form of applauded lie, fantasy. And in Arima it was a fantasy of power that led both men to contemplate, from their different standpoints, the act of murder. Jamal, when he understood that Trinidad wasn't the United States, began to feel that in an island where the majority of the popula-tion was black he didn't "look good" with a white woman at his side. And Benson, English and middle class, was just the victim Malik needed: his novel began to come to life.

Malik summoned Abbott from London. He sent a one-word letter: "Come." And Abbott took the first flight out, travelling first to New York and then down to Trinidad. Malik and Steve Yeates met him at the airport and drove him the few miles to the Malik house in Christina Gar-dens in Arima. Malik's wife was there; the Malik children were asleep. And there Abbott met Jamal for the first time. Later Abbott was taken across the road to the other house, the one Jamal and Benson were rent-ing; it was where he was to stay. Abbott didn't see Benson there; she had gone to Guyana to try to raise money for Jamal, but was going to be back in a few days. (Benson's movements at this time are not absolutely clear. Her papers were destroyed the day she was killed.)

The four men—Abbott, Malik, Steve Yeates and Jamal—talked through the night. At one stage Abbott asked about The People's Store. This was Malik's first Black Power "commune" project in Trinidad; and Abbott had earlier in the year worked on it for a month, helping with the painting and the polishing. Abbott said he wanted to see what the place looked like, and the four men drove the twenty miles or so to Carenage, where the store was.

While they drove—in the Sunday-morning darkness—Malik said they now had the best working group in the universe, that they were going places, and were the chosen ones. Abbott thought that Malik was talking to impress Jamal. "With Jamal," Abbott said, "he kept on with this mind-destroying talk." And Abbott was disappointed by what he saw of the Carenage house, on which he and Yeates and others had worked so hard just a few months before. "I saw the house and saw three men—Negroes—living there. I said the house was dirty and it appeared the men were neglected. It looked as though Michael had just placed these men there and neglected them." They drove back to Arima and Christina Gardens. It was now light; and as though to make up for the Carenage disappointment, Malik showed Abbott the improvements he had made in the Arima house and yard.

The men at Carenage had looked neglected. And that was how Abbott soon began to feel. After the drama of the urgent summons to Trinidad, it seemed that there was nothing important for him to do. He was made to do various yard jobs. He cut bamboo grass for the goats Malik kept and made long journeys to get the hibiscus Malik said the goats needed; he mowed the lawn; he washed the car and the jeep; and he was sent out by Malik to work without payment on the farm that supplied a gallon of milk a day to the Malik family and commune. Abbott said he wanted to be released, to go and live at his mother's. Malik refused.

It was Malik's custom to wake Abbott up at seven in the morning. One morning—two days before Christmas, and less than a fortnight after he had arrived—Abbott saw blood on Malik's mouth and beard. "I told him his mouth was bleeding. What had happened? He said they had killed a calf on the Lourenço farm that morning, and he was drinking blood. I felt scared and sick." And there was soon another reason for fear. "I heard him speak to Hakim Jamal before the Christmas. He told him to send for somebody in the United States whom he, Jamal, could trust. At that point I walked off, because they were not talking to me. A couple days later this American man, Kidogo, arrived. I again beseeched Michael to allow me to go home, now that he had someone else around to help him. He told me Kidogo was not there for manual work. He told me Kidogo was a hired killer. He elaborated that Kidogo had killed police and all sorts in Boston in the United States, and for me to shut up from now on."

Kidogo, as an American, didn't need a visa. And in Christina Gardens he swanned around, a Bostonian among the natives, taking a lot of photographs with an Instamatic camera, helping with none of the household or menial chores, apparently saving himself for his special job. He bought a cutlass and fooled around with it in the yard; in his idleness he carved the letter K on the wooden haft.

If Abbott was afraid of Kidogo because he thought of Kidogo as a professional, there were people in the commune who were just as afraid of Abbott. One day, when Abbott was washing the jeep, Malik said to Chadee, the motorcar salesman, "That man is a psychopath." Chadee never trusted Abbott after that. This was how, in the commune, Malik orchestrated fear and kept everyone in his retinue up to mark.

Benson returned from Guyana, and it was full house at the commune on Christmas Day. Abbott would have liked to visit his mother that day, but he wasn't allowed to go. He stayed with the others; and in his statement afterwards he spoke of the Christmas gathering at Christina Gardens with an odd formality, an odd deference to the women of the two houses. "We all spent Christmas together, including Mrs. Michael, her children, and Jamal's lady, Halé, who was an Englishwoman whom I met at Michael's house." There were two other English people: a man called Granger, and the woman called Simmonds, then in "total involvement" with Steve Yeates.

On December 31, Yeates, Simmonds's "excellent lover," found time to buy a six-inch file. And it must have been that file Abbott saw Kidogo using—that very day, or the day after—on the cutlass on whose haft he had carved the letter K. Kidogo's cutlass was a "gilpin." The blade of the gilpin widens at the end and curves backward to a sharp point, like a scimitar. Abbott saw Kidogo filing off "the gilpin part" of the cutlass and asked him why. Kidogo—a professional, but clearly inexperienced with cutlasses—said it didn't "balance properly."

In the evening there was a party: Old Year's Night, and it was also Simmonds's thirtieth birthday. They ate the calf that had been killed eight days before; and Simmonds enjoyed the "big feed."

Malik had invited Chadee, the motorcar salesman, to the Old Year's Night party. Chadee, a man of thirty, of a goodish Indian family but of no great personal attainments (he was also a part-time debt collector), thought that Malik was very rich. At their first meeting, a few months before, Malik had said he wanted to buy twelve new cars, and Chadee was hoping to do big business with Malik. Malik saw Chadee as a man with many interesting contacts, a possible commune recruit, and he had begun to involve Chadee in the commune's social occasions. Two or three weeks before the calf feast, Chadee had been taken by Malik on a moonlight beach picnic.

And now, just after midday on New Year's Day, Chadee came again to Christina Gardens. He called first on Jamal and Benson. Chadee had been introduced to them a month or so before by Malik; and Malik had told Chadee at the time that Jamal didn't really like Benson, that Jamal didn't think he looked "good" with a white woman in Trinidad. Chadee now wished Benson and Jamal a happy new year; and Benson, who apparently didn't have too much to say to Chadee, then left the two men together. They sat out in the veranda. Jamal, still besotted by his own writing, read out passages from his autobiography to Chadee, in all the heat of the early tropical afternoon, and spoke of the book he was writing about Malik.

Later Chadee went across the road to Malik's and wished Malik a happy new year. He saw Abbott. Abbott had been given permission to visit his mother that day, and Abbott asked Chadee to drive him there (Malik never lent his vehicles). Chadee agreed; and he and Abbott decided to take along Parmassar, an Indian boy who was glamoured by Malik and was a member of Malik's group. They drove to Montrose Village, to Abbott's mother's house. Abbott's mother was a retired schoolteacher, seventy-one years old. Abbott was proud of her and Chadee found her "a pleasant, charming person; she was articulate and expressed herself well." The three men were given cake and ginger ale. They left at seven, and it was about half-past seven when they got back to Malik's house in Christina Gardens. Malik asked Chadee to drive his car into the yard. When Chadee did so, the gate was closed. Malik then asked Chadee to hang around with the boys for a while, and Chadee hung around.

At a quarter to nine—and at this stage everything appears to follow a timetable—Malik told the men present that he wanted to talk to them privately in the servants' quarters at the back of his house. One of Malik's daughters was there, listening to records with a black girl who did occasional secretarial work for Malik. Malik told the two girls to go elsewhere. There were cushions on the floor; Malik asked the men to sit. Malik himself sat on a chair. Steve Yeates sat on a cushion on Malik's right, Kidogo on a cushion on Malik's left. Facing them, and sitting on cushions, were the boy Parmassar, Chadee and Abbott. Jamal was not there.

Malik said that Jamal was suffering from mental strain, that Benson was the cause of the strain, and that she had to be got rid of. Abbott said Malik could give her a plane ticket and let her go back where she came from. At this, Yeates—the man with the wound of England on his back—jumped up and said he wanted "something definite." "Michael just sat stroking his beard," Abbott said, "and said he wanted blood." Blood was the only thing that could keep them together.

Kidogo said nothing. He just looked at Abbott and Abbott saw murder in Kidogo's eyes, and Yeates's, and Malik's. Abbott didn't look at
Parmassar or at Chadee. And Chadee was sick with fear. Malik had told
him that Abbott was a psychopath, and Chadee felt now that it was true.
He didn't believe what Abbott had said about giving Benson a plane
ticket. He thought it was said to trap him into making a statement that
would turn them all against him. So Chadee said nothing, and Malik outlined his plan.

In the morning they would dig a hole for Benson, by the manure
heap at the dead end of the road. Steve Yeates would take Benson to the
farm to get milk and keep her looking at the cows while the hole was
being dug; Malik would take Jamal to some other place, take him out
for an early-morning drive. The hole would have to be dug fast, in forty-
five minutes. That was all that was said then by Malik: a hole was to be
dug in a certain place, within a certain time, for a certain purpose. Steve
Yeates was to bring Benson to the hole; but nothing was said about how
Benson was to be killed, or who was to kill her. And nobody asked. As for
Chadee, he wasn't to go home. He and the other Indian, the boy Parmassar, were to sleep in that room, on the cushions. And, Malik said, everybody should go to sleep early and get up before the sun. At ten o'clock
the meeting was over.

Abbott left to go across the road to Jamal's house, where he had his
room. Malik reminded Abbott to lock the gate as he left the yard; and
Chadee saw in that instruction about the gate a direct threat to himself, a
further order to stay where he was. Malik, after this, got up and went to
the main house. Chadee didn't see what he could do. The boy Parmassar
was with him; Steve Yeates was in the second bedroom of the servants'
quarters; Kidogo had the back bedroom in the main house, just across the
patio from the servants' quarters. Chadee lay down on the cushions next
to Parmassar. His mind was "in a mess"; he had never heard "such a conversation" before. He prayed to God and hoped that in the morning the
plan would be forgotten. Then his mind went blank and he fell asleep.

Across the road, in the house with Jamal and Benson, Abbott didn't
sleep. He was lying down in his clothes, thinking. He thought about his
mother and what Malik might do to her. He remembered the looks Malik,
Kidogo and Steve Yeates had given him earlier in the evening.

At six in the morning Malik woke Parmassar. Parmassar woke
Chadee, sleeping beside him on the cushions. And then Malik sent Par-

massar across the road to get Abbott, to tell him that the time had come to start digging the hole for Benson. Parmassar didn't have to wake Abbott: Abbott hadn't slept, and was still in his clothes.

They were all up now. Chadee saw Steve Yeates and Kidogo come out of Kidogo's room. Yeates called Chadee out into the yard, and Chadee sat outside against the kitchen of the main house. Kidogo and Parmassar (reappearing) went "to the back" and began to collect tools: a spade, a fork, two shovels, a cutlass and a file. They asked Chadee to help. He took the two shovels. Parmassar had the fork and the spade; Kidogo had the cutlass and the file. Abbott was waiting outside the gate. They passed the tools to him, climbed over the gate and walked down the road to the dead end, two hundred feet away from the house, on waste ground above the ravine.

Not long afterwards Malik reversed his Humber car to where the four men were—Abbott, Kidogo, Parmassar and Chadee—and showed them where the hole was to be dug. It was beside a manure heap; Chadee saw "a lot of bamboo poles around the manure." Malik asked Kidogo for the time. Kidogo said it was six-twenty, and Malik said again that they had forty-five minutes to dig the hole. Malik himself wasn't going to be present while anything happened. As he had said the previous evening, he was going to take Jamal out for a drive, to keep Jamal out of the way. And it was only now—sitting in his car—that he gave his final orders. Not to all of them, but only to Abbott. He called Abbott over to the car.

Abbott went and said, "Oh, God, Michael, you don't have to do this. Spare the woman." Malik said he didn't want to hear any more of "that old talk from last night." "He sat behind the wheel pulling his beard and watching me. He told me that Steve Yeates would drive up in the jeep; he will bring the woman Halé out. I was to tell her when she saw the hole, if she got suspicious, that it was for stuff to be decomposed, or words to that effect. He told me I was to grab that woman and take her into the hole. When I had her I was to tell her what the hole was for: to tell her it was for Jamal." As for the killing itself, that was to be done by Kidogo. "He told me Kidogo had his orders. He said that if I did anything to endanger the safety of the men around that hole, or his family or himself, by not obeying, I would die. What he was telling me was I would die that morning with the knowledge that my mother would be dead also, because that was where he was heading with Jamal." Abbott prepared to obey.

"He also told me, as I was walking off, to remind Kidogo that the heart is on the left side. He wants the heart."

Malik drove away, and Abbott passed on his instructions: Kidogo was to do the killing, and Kidogo had to remember that the heart was below the left breast. The four men began to dig furiously. Kidogo was in charge, and he told them to burn themselves up, one man digging at a time, as hard and as fast as he could, until he could dig no more. Chadee, the salesman, suffered; Abbott helped him. It was Abbott, in fact, in his particular frenzy, who did most of the digging. When they had been digging for some time, Steve Yeates came with the jeep. He was about to take Benson to the farm, and he wanted a watch. Chadee lent him his; and Kidogo and Steve Yeates synchronized the watches before Steve Yeates left.

When the hole, which was about four feet square, was four feet deep, Kidogo said they had dug enough. Kidogo rested. He gave his cutlass to the boy Parmassar and asked Parmassar to sharpen it. Parmassar sharpened the cutlass and gave it back to Kidogo.

At seven-fifteen the jeep came reversing down the road. Steve Yeates was driving, and Benson was with him. The jeep stopped; Yeates got out and told Benson to come out, too, and see how hard the boys had been working. She got out of the jeep. She was in a light African-style gown; the boy Parmassar remembered that it had short sleeves. She said, "Good morning," and the men around the hole said, "Good morning."

Abbott said, "Come and see what we are doing." She walked nearer the hole. She said, "What is it for?" Abbott said, "It is to put fresh matter to be decomposed. Come and look. Do you like it?" She said, "Yes. But why?" Abbott didn't say, "It is for Jamal." He forgot that. He said, "It is for you." He held his right hand over her mouth, twisted her left hand behind her with his left hand, and jumped with her into the shallow hole. Kidogo jumped in at once with his sharpened cutlass and began to use it on her, cutting through the African gown, aiming at the heart. She fought back hard; she kicked. She called out to Steve Yeates, "Steve, Steve, what have I done to deserve this?" He remained leaning against the jeep, watching.

And Kidogo, after all, didn't know how to use a cutlass to kill. He just slashed and stabbed, inflicting superficial cuts; and Benson was asking him why, speaking "intimately" to him, as it sounded to Abbott, who was struggling to hold the frantic woman. Abbott's own thoughts were far away. He was thinking of his mother: she would ask Malik and Jamal in, when they got to the house in Montrose Village, and they just had to tell her that he, Abbott, was ill, and she would get into Malik's car and be brought to Arima. Kidogo was still using the cutlass on Benson. He was like a madman, and with the three of them in that small hole Abbott began to fear that he might himself be killed. In his panic and confusion he called out, stupidly, *"Somebody help! Somebody do something!"* And when Chadee looked he saw a great cut on the left elbow Benson had raised to protect herself against Kidogo's cutlass. It was her first serious wound.

Steve Yeates, still beside the jeep, looked at Chadee and at Parmassar. Then he went to the hole and took away the cutlass from Kidogo. There were now four of them in the hole. But Yeates didn't need much room. With his left hand he placed the sharpened point of the cutlass at the base of Benson's throat; with his right hand he hit the haft hard. It was a simple, lucid action, the most lucid since Abbott had taken Benson into the hole; but of all the men there Yeates was the one with the purest hate. The broad blade went in six inches, and Benson made a gurgling noise. She fell and began to "beat about" in the hole. Yeates and Kidogo and Abbott got out of the hole. It would have been about seven-thirty.

Kidogo called, "Cover!" Benson's feet were still beating about. Chadee began to pull manure from the manure heap into the hole. Yeates, lucid as ever, stopped Chadee. It would look strange if the manure heap was disturbed, he said. Better to go to the farm and get a fresh load. He and Yeates went in the jeep. When they came back they found Benson already buried in her hole, and they dumped the manure to one side.

They all went back then to the Malik house. Chadee went to the kitchen and drank a glass of water. Yeates parked the jeep. Kidogo cleaned his cutlass. Parmassar and Abbott sat side by side on the kitchen steps.

The telephone in the kitchen rang. It didn't awaken Malik's wife or children. Chadee answered the phone. It was Malik, telephoning from Abbott's mother's house. Was everything all right? Malik asked. Chadee said yes. When Yeates, coming in just then, asked about the telephone, and Chadee told him, Yeates "blew"—he gave, that is, a sigh of relief. It was eight o'clock.

At half-past eight Malik came back with Jamal. Malik said, "Is the tree planted?" Agriculture, the commune, the life of labour: Malik always had his own coded way with language. Abbott wasn't sure if anyone answered. Malik asked how deep the hole was, and everyone gave a different depth. He said they should put on a couple of loads of manure.

Agricultural conversation: that was all that Jamal could say he had heard, after his morning's drive to Abbott's mother's house, and his cup of coffee with the old lady. Because it had apparently been decided that Jamal should be involved in no way. Jamal had to see nothing and hear nothing; and had to be able to say that Benson had just gone away, taking her things. That remained to be done: getting rid of Benson's things. And Jamal was not to see; and the two English visitors at the commune were not to see or suspect; and Malik's wife and two daughters, and Malik's secretarial assistant, who was coming in that morning. Everyone had to see only another busy commune day.

It had been planned in detail. There were seven men in all (leaving out the English visitor), and their movements that morning and afternoon had been plotted in advance. Malik, after that agricultural conversation, announced a commune building job. They were going to Parmassar's mother's house, to help the poor lady rebuild her kitchen. It wasn't far away. Abbott, Kidogo, Chadee, Yeates and Parmassar himself were sent ahead in the jeep. Malik and Jamal came later. They broke down the old kitchen and sketched out a plan for the new one. But they didn't have cement and sand. Malik sent Chadee and Kidogo in the jeep back to Christina Gardens, to get sand and a bag of cement from his yard—it was a day of movement like this, movement and camouflage.

When they got to Malik's yard, Kidogo disappeared, leaving Chadee to load the cement and sand by himself. Chadee loaded up, and looked for Kidogo. He couldn't find him. It was one of Malik's daughters who told Chadee that Kidogo was in Jamal's house across the road. Chadee went to the house—where less than twenty-four hours before he had wished Benson a happy new year—and found Kidogo in Jamal's and Benson's bedroom.

Kidogo—doing his job—was packing Benson's clothes and papers. He had already packed one bag and wrapped it in cloth; he was packing a second. He told Chadee to bring the jeep round. When Chadee went to Malik's yard to get the jeep, he had a little fright. Malik's secretarial assistant asked for a lift to the Arima taxi stand. Chadee explained about the sand and cement and said he would send Steve Yeates to give her a lift; and the girl didn't insist. He took the jeep round to Jamal's and Kidogo threw in the bags with Benson's things.

Malik was waiting for them at Parmassar's mother's house. Chadee reversed the jeep right into the yard, and Malik and Kidogo took the bags and put them in the boot of Malik's car. The sand and cement were unloaded, and concrete was mixed for the new kitchen. Parmassar's mother and sisters had prepared lunch for the working party. But Chadee didn't eat; he just had some fruit juice. When he came out of the house after the lunch he saw that somebody had put some dry wood in the jeep. And then Malik and Yeates took the bags with Benson's things from the boot of Malik's car and put them back in the jeep.

Chadee, Abbott and Kidogo were told to go in the jeep with Yeates. As they drove off, Yeates said they were going "up the river" to burn Benson's clothes. They stopped at a filling station in Arima and bought some kerosene, and they drove eight miles to Guanapo Heights, beside the Guanapo River. Yeates left the three men there, with the wood and kerosene and the bags. And he gave them a message from Malik: they were to keep the fire burning, because in an hour's time Malik and his children were coming to the river to bathe.

Chadee stood guard while Abbott and Kidogo got a fire going on the riverbank with the wood and the kerosene. They burned Benson's clothes and papers piece by piece. Certain things couldn't be burned. Chadee buried these a short distance away, digging a hole two feet deep. There was less of a rush now than in the morning, and the digging came more easily to him. Kidogo and Abbott left Chadee for a while; and Chadee, doing as he had been told, looked for more wood and kept the fire going. When Kidogo and Abbott came back they were carrying fruit in one of the bags into which Benson's things had been stuffed earlier: it was an extra precautionary touch.

Shortly afterwards, keeping strict time, Steve Yeates drove up with the jeep, and he had brought a whole party: Malik, Malik's two daughters, Jamal, and the young Englishman who was a guest in the commune. They all bathed in the river, and then they warmed themselves at the fire. No one asked about the fire. Malik didn't ask Abbott or Kidogo or Chadee any questions.

Blood in the morning, fire in the afternoon. But to an observer who wasn't looking for special clues, to someone on the outside seeing only the busyness with car and jeep and sand and cement, it would only have been a good commune day: constructive work in the morning, and then a bathing party in a tropical wood.

That bathing party, with the fire on the riverbank: it was the crowning conception of an intricate day. Like an episode in a dense novel, it served many purposes and had many meanings. And it had been devised by a man who was writing a novel about himself, settling accounts with the world, filling pages of the cheap writing pad and counting the precious words as he wrote, anxious for world fame (including literary fame): a man led to lunacy by all the ideas he had been given of who he was, and now, in the exile of Arima, under the influence of Jamal, with an illusion of achieved power. Malik had no skills as a novelist, not even an elementary gift of language. He was too self-absorbed to process experience in any rational way or even to construct a connected narrative. But when he transferred his fantasy to real life, he went to work like the kind of novelist he would have liked to be.

Such plotting, such symbolism! The blood of the calf at Christmas time, the blood of Gale Benson in the new year. And then, at the end of the sacrificial day, the cleansing in the river, with Benson's surrogate pyre on the bank. So many other details: so many things had had to be worked out. Neither Chadee nor Abbott (with their special anxieties) had been left alone for any length of time during the day; both men had always been under the eye of Kidogo or Steve Yeates. And Jamal had always been sheltered. He had been at Abbott's mother's house while Benson was being killed and buried; and he had been at Parmassar's mother's house, helping with the kitchen, when Kidogo was clearing away Benson's clothes and papers from the bedroom that had been hers and Jamal's.

It had been thought out over many weeks. And it worked. Benson had always been withdrawn, and now she was not missed. For a fortnight or more everybody in the two houses at Christina Gardens stayed together. The two English visitors remained, the woman Simmonds continuing in her "total involvement" with Steve Yeates; towards the end there was even some talk of a restaurant that she and Yeates might run together.

Chadee didn't go home. On the evening of the murder Malik told him that he and Parmassar, the two Indians in the group, had become "members for life"; and that night, after he had gone with Steve Yeates to fetch his clothes, Chadee slept again in the bedroom of the servants' quarters in Malik's house. Later he was given a room in Jamal's house, and he began to mow the lawn and do other yard jobs.

But then the commune Christmas party began to break up. The two English visitors went away. And—eighteen days after the murder—Jamal and Kidogo went away, back to Boston. Jamal acknowledged

Malik as the master, and Malik thought of himself as the master. But Malik had grown to need Jamal more than he knew. Without Jamal's own lunacy, his exaltation, his way with words, his vision of the master, Malik's fantasies of power grew wilder and unfocused, without art, the rages of a gangster. He thought of kidnapping the wife of a bank manager; he ordered Abbott to plan the "liquidation" of a family. And then, for no reason except that of blood, and because he was now used to the idea of killing with a cutlass, he killed Joseph Skerritt.

It was the murder of Skerrit that finally unhinged Steve Yeates, "Muhammed Akbar," Supreme Captain of the Fruit of Islam. Yeates dealt in racial hate; he was pure in his hate; and he couldn't understand why Skerritt had been killed. Every time he looked through his window he saw Skerritt's grave; and the fast that Malik ordered after the killing of Skerritt didn't help. They were all weakened and perhaps made a little light-headed by four days of fasting when they went on the excursion to the dangerous bay of Sans Souci; and Yeates, when he got into trouble with the strong currents, seemed at a certain moment to have decided not to listen to the shouts of people anxious to save him, not to struggle, to surrender. Abbott thought that Yeates drowned himself; and Abbott thought that before he went down Yeates gave a final wave with his left hand.

That was the beginning of the end of the commune. Blood didn't keep them together for long. Abbott helped Chadee and Parmassar to escape; Abbott himself went to Tobago; Malik went to Guyana, and the house in Christina Gardens burned down.

Fifty-five days after the killing of Benson, Chadee took a police inspector to Guanapo Heights and showed where he had buried those things of Benson's that couldn't be burned. This was the police inventory, which Chadee certified:

One brown leather sleeveless jacket; one brown leather hippy bag; one pair of lady's pink mod boots; one pair of brown shoes; one pair of brown slippers; three silver bracelets; one empty small bottle; one tube Avon Rose-mint cream; one tube of Tangee cream; one small circular face mirror; a quantity of black wool; two hippy pendants; one tin containing Flapyl tablets; one small scissors; one plastic rule; one triangular key holder; one empty Limacol bottle; one brown small tablespoon; one Liberation of

Jerusalem medallion with 7.6.1967 stamped thereon; one brown belt with a buckle made in the form of a heart; one damaged grey suitcase; one large scissors; one blue ballpoint pen; one damaged brown suitcase; one silver ring with the Star of David; and one gold ring with two stones.

Malik appealed many times against the death sentence. And it was only when legal arguments were exhausted, and the appeal was on the grounds of cruelty—on the grounds that, after the long delay, the carrying out of the death sentence would be an act of cruelty—it was only then that the point was made that Malik was mad. The point, if it had been made at the beginning, might have saved Malik's life. But, for too many people in London and elsewhere, Malik had embodied, at one and the same time, the vicious black man and the good black cause. A plea of insanity would have made nonsense of a whole school of theatre; and among the people abroad who supported Malik there were those who continued to see his conviction for murder as an act of racial and political persecution. So Malik played out to the end the role that had been given him.

He was hanged in the Royal Gaol in central Port of Spain in May 1975, three years and four months after the killing of Benson. His wife sat in a square nearby. There was a small silent crowd with her in the square, waiting for the sound of the trapdoor at eight, hanging time. The body of the hanged man was taken in a coffin to the Golden Grove Prison, not far from Arima; and there barebacked prisoners in shorts carried the coffin to its grave in the prison grounds.

Chadee was sentenced to death, but this was later commuted to life imprisonment. Abbott, after his twenty years for the murder of Skerritt, was sentenced to death for his part in the murder of Benson. His was the true agony: he rotted for nearly six years in a death cell, and was hanged only in April 1979. He never became known outside Trinidad, this small, muscular man with the straight back, the soldierly demeanour, the very pale skin, and the underslept tormented eyes. He was not the X; he became nobody's cause; and by the time he was hanged that caravan had gone by.

1979

A New King for the Congo: Mobutu and the Nihilism of Africa

THE CONGO, which used to be a Belgian colony, is now an African kingdom and is called Zaire. It appears to be a nonsense name, a sixteenth-century Portuguese corruption, some Zairois will tell you, of a local word for "river." So it is as if Taiwan, reasserting its Chinese identity, were again to give itself the Portuguese name Formosa. The Congo River is now called the Zaire, as is the local currency, which is almost worthless.

The man who has made himself king of this land of the three Zs— *pays, fleuve, monnaie*—used to be called Joseph Mobutu. His father was a cook. But Joseph Mobutu was educated; he was at some time, in the Belgian days, a journalist. In 1960, when the country became independent, Mobutu was thirty, a sergeant in the local Force Publique. The Force Publique became the Congolese National Army. Mobutu became the colonel and commander, and through the mutinies, rebellions and secessions of the years after independence he retained the loyalty of one paratroop brigade. In 1965, as General Mobutu, he seized power; and as he has imposed order on the army and the country so his style has changed, and become more African. He has abandoned the name of Joseph and is now known as Mobutu Sese Seko Kuku Ngbendu Wa Za Banga.

As General Mobutu he used to be photographed in army uniform. Now, as Mobutu Sese Seko, he wears what he has made, by his example, the Zairois court costume. It is a stylish version of the standard two-piece suit. The jacket has high, wide lapels and is buttoned all the way down; the sleeves can be long or short. A boldly patterned cravat replaces the tie, which has more or less been outlawed; and a breast-pocket handkerchief matches the cravat. On less formal occasions—when he goes among the people—Mobutu wears flowered shirts. Always, in public, he wears a leopard-skin cap and carries an elaborately carved stick.

These—the cap and the stick—are the emblems of his African chieftaincy. Only the chief can kill the leopard. The stick is carved with symbolic figures: two birds, what looks like a snake, a human figure with a distended belly. No Zairois I met could explain the symbolism. One teacher pretended not to know what was carved, and said, "We would all like to have sticks like that." In some local carving, though, the belly of the human figure is distended because it contains the fetish. The stick is accepted by Zairois as the stick of the chief. While the chief holds the stick off the ground the people around him can speak; when the chief sets his stick on the ground the people fall silent and the chief gives his decision.

Explaining the constitution and the president's almost unlimited powers, *Profils du Zaire*, the new official handbook (of variable price: four zaires, eight dollars, the pavement seller's "first" price, two zaires his "last" price), *Profils du Zaire* quotes Montesquieu on the functions of the state. *Elima*, the official daily, has another, African view of government. "In Zaire we have inherited from our ancestors a profound respect for the liberties of others. This is why our ancestors were so given to conciliation, people accustomed to the palaver [*la palabre*], accustomed, that is, to discussions that established each man in his rights."

So Montesquieu and the ancestors are made to meet. And ancestral ways turn out to be advanced. It is only a matter of finding the right words. The palaver is, after all, a "dialogue"; chief's rule is government by dialogue. But when the chief speaks, when the chief sets his carved stick on the ground, the modern dialogue stops; and Africa of the ancestors takes over. The chief's words, as *Elima* (having it all ways) has sometimes to remind "anti-revolutionary" elements, cannot be questioned.

It is said that the last five words of Mobutu's African name are a reference to the sexual virility which the African chief must possess: he is the cock that leaves no hen alone. But the words may only be symbolic. Because, as chief, Mobutu is "married" to his people—"The Marriage of Sese [Mobutu]" is a "revolutionary" song—and, as in the good old days of the ancestors, *comme au bon vieux temps de nos ancêtres*, the chief always holds fast to his people. This marriage of the chief can be explained in another, more legalistic way: the chief has a "contract" with his people. He fulfils his contract through the apparatus of a modern state, but the ministers and commissioners are only the chief's "collaborators," "the umbilical cord between the power and the people."

The chief, the lord wedded to his people, *le pouvoir*: the attributes begin to multiply. Mobutu is also the Guide of the Authentic Zairois Revolution, the Father of the Nation, the President-Founder of the Mouvement Populaire de la Révolution, the country's only political party. So that, in nomenclature as in the stylish national dress he has devised, he combines old Africa with what is progressive and new. Just as a Guy Dormeuil suit (160 zaires in the Kinshasa shops, 320 dollars) can, with cravat and matching handkerchief, become an authentic Zairois national costume, so a number of imported glamorous ideas bolster Mobutu's African chieftaincy.

He is citizen, chief, king, revolutionary; he is an African freedom fighter; he is supported by the spirits of the ancestors; like Mao, he has published a book of thoughts (Mobutu's book is green). He has occupied every ideological position and the basis of his kingship cannot be questioned. He rules; he is grand; and, like a medieval king, he is at once loved and feared. He controls the armed forces; they are his creation; in Kinshasa he still sleeps in an army camp. Like Leopold II of the Belgians, in the time of the Congo Free State—much of whose despotic legislation (ownership of the mines in 1888, all vacant lands in 1890, the fruits of the earth in 1891) has passed down through the Belgian colonial administration to the present regime, and is now presented as a kind of ancestral African socialism—like Leopold II, Mobutu owns Zaire.

MUHAMMAD ALI fought George Foreman in Kinshasa last November. Ali won; but the victor, in Zaire, was Mobutu. A big hoarding outside the stadium still says, in English below the French: "A fight between two Blacks [*deux noirs*], in a Black Nation [*un pays de Nègres*] organized by blacks and seen by the whole [world] that is a victory of Mobutism." And whatever pleasure people had taken in that event, and the publicity, had been dissipated by mid-January, when I arrived. I had chosen a bad time. Mobutu, chieflike, had sprung another of his surprises. A fortnight before, after a two-day palaver with his collaborators, Mobutu had decided on a "radicalization of the revolution." And everybody was nervous.

In November 1973 Mobutu had nationalized all businesses and planta-tions belonging to foreigners—mainly Greeks, Portuguese and Indians—and had given them to Zairois. Now, a year later, he had decided to take back these enterprises, many of them pillaged and bankrupt, and entrust them to the state. What, or who, was the state? No one quite knew. New people, more loyal people? Mobutu, speaking the pure language of revo-lution, seemed to threaten everybody. The three hundred Belgian fami-lies who had ruled the Congo, he said, had been replaced by three hundred Zairois families; the country had imported more Mercedes-Benz motorcars than tractors; one third of the country's foreign earnings went to import food that could be produced at home.

Against this new Zairois bourgeoisie—which he had himself created—the chief now declared war. "I offer them a clear choice: those among them who love the people should give everything to the state and follow me." In his new mood the chief threatened other measures. He threat-ened to close down the cinemas and the night-clubs; he threatened to ban drinking in public places before six.

Through the Belgian-designed *cité indigène* of Kinshasa, in the wide, unpaved streets, full of pits and corrugations between mounds of rubbish sometimes as high as the little houses in Mediterranean colours, in the green shade of flamboyant, mango and frangipani, schoolchildren marched in support of their chief. Every day *Elima* carried reports of *marches de soutien* in other places. And the alarm was great, among the foreigners who had been plundered of their businesses and had remained behind, hoping for some compensation or waiting for Canadian visas, and among the gold-decked Zairois in national costume. Stern men, these Zairois, nervous of the visitor, easily affronted, anxious only to make it known that they were loyal, and outdone by no one in their "authen-ticity," their authentic Africanness.

But it is in the nature of a powerful chief that he should be unpre-dictable. The chief threatens; the people are cowed; the chief relents; the people praise his magnanimity. The days passed; daytime and even morning drinking didn't stop; many Africans continued to spend their days in that red-eyed vacancy that at first so mystifies the visitor. The night-clubs and cinemas didn't close; the prostitutes continued to be busy around the Memling Hotel. So that it seemed that in this matter of public morals, at least, the chief had relented. The ordinary people had been spared.

But the nervousness higher up was justified. Within days the axe fell on many of the chief's "collaborators." There was a shake-up; the circle of power around the chief was made smaller; and Zairois who had ruled in Kinshasa were abruptly dismissed, packed off to unfamiliar parts of the bush to spread the word of the revolution. *Elima* sped them on their way.

The political commissioner will no longer be what he was before the system was modified. That is to say, a citizen floating above the day-to-day realities of the people, driving about the streets and avenues of Kinshasa in a Mercedes and knowing nothing of the life of the peasant of Dumi. The political commissioners will live with the people. They will be in the fields, not as masters but as peasants. They will work with the workers, they will share their joys and sorrows. They will in this way better understand the aspirations of the people and will truly become again children of the people.

Words of terror. Because this was the great fear of so many of the men who had come by riches so easily, by simple official plunder, the new men of the new state who, in the name of Africanization and the dignity of Africa, were so often doing jobs for which they were not qualified and often were drawing salaries for jobs they were not doing at all. This, for all their talk of authenticity and the ways of the ancestors, was their fear: to be returned from the sweet corruptions of Kinshasa to the older corruption of the bush, to be returned to Africa.

And the bush is close. It begins just outside the city and goes on forever. The aeroplane that goes from Kinshasa to Kisangani flies over eight hundred miles of what still looks like virgin forest.

CONSIDER the recent journey of the subregional commissioner of the Equator Region to the settlement of Bomongo. Bomongo lies on the Giri River and is just about one hundred miles north of the big town of Mbandaka, formerly Coquilhatville, the old "Equator station," set down more or less on the line of the Equator, halfway on the Congo or Zaire River between Kinshasa and the Stanley Falls. From Mbandaka a steamer took the commissioner's party up the main river to Lubengo; and there they transferred to a dugout for the twenty-mile passage through the Lubengo "canal" to the Giri River. But the canal for much of its length was only six feet wide, full of snags, and sometimes only twelve inches deep. The outboard motor had to be taken up; paddles had to be used. And there were the mosquitoes.

At the very entrance to the canal [according to the official report in *Elima*], thousands of mosquitoes cover you from head to ankles, compelling you to move about all the time ... After a whole night of insomnia on the Lubengo canal, or rather the "calvary" of Lubengo, where we had very often to get out in the water and make a superhuman effort to help the paddlers free the pirogue from mud or wood snags, we got to the end of the canal at nine in the morning (we had entered it at 9:30 the previous evening), and so at last we arrived at Bomongo at 12:30, in a state that would have softened the hardest hearts. If we have spoken at some length about the Lubengo canal, it isn't because we want to discourage people from visiting Bomongo by the canal route, but rather to stress one of the main reasons why this place is isolated and seldom visited.

Ignoring his fatigue, *bravant sa fatigue*, the commissioner set to work. He spoke to various groups about the integration of the party and the administration, the need for punctuality, professional thoroughness and revolutionary fervour. The next morning he visited an oil factory in Ebeka district that had been abandoned in 1971 and was now being set going again with the help of a foreign adviser. In the afternoon he spoke out against alcoholism and urged people to produce more. The next day he visited a coffee plantation that had been nationalized in 1973 (the plantations in Zaire were run mainly by Greeks) and given to a Zairois. This particular *attribution* hadn't worked well: the labourers hadn't been paid for the last five months. The labourers complained and the commissioner listened; but what the commissioner did or said wasn't recorded. Everywhere the commissioner went he urged the people, for the sake of their own liberty and well-being, to follow the principles of Mobutism to the letter; everywhere he urged vigilance. Then, leaving Lubengo, Bomongo and Ebeka to the mosquitoes, the commissioner returned to his headquarters. And *Elima* considered the fifteen-day journey heroic enough to give it half a page.

YET BOMONGO, so cut off, is only twenty miles away from the main Congo or Zaire. The roads of the country have decayed; the domestic services of Air Zaire are unreliable; the river remains, in 1975, the great highway of the country. And for nearly a hundred years the river has known steamer traffic. Joseph Conrad, not yet a novelist, going up the river in the wood-burning *Roi des Belges* in 1890, doing eight miles in three hours, halting every night for the cannibal woodcutters to sleep on the riverbank, might have thought he was penetrating to the untouched heart of darkness. But Norman Sherry, the Conrad scholar, has gone among the records and in *Conrad's Western World* has shown that even at the time of Conrad's journey there would have been eleven steamers on the upper river.

The steamers have continued, the Belgian *Otraco* being succeeded by the Zairois *Onatra*. The waterway has been charted: white marker signs are nailed to trees on the banks, the river is regularly cleared of snags. The upstream journey that took one month in Conrad's time now takes seven days; the downstream journey that took a fortnight is now done in five days. The stations have become towns, but they remain what they were: trading outposts. And, in 1975, the journey—one thousand miles between green, flat, almost unchanging country—is still like a journey through nothingness. So little has the vast country been touched: so complete, simple and repetitive still appears the African life through which the traveller swiftly passes.

When the steamer was Belgian, Africans needed a *carte de mérite civique* to travel first class, and third-class African passengers were towed on barges some way behind the steamer. Now the two-tiered third-class barges, rusting, battered, needing paint, full of a busy backyard life, tethered goats and crated chickens packed tight among the passengers, are lashed to the bow of the steamer; and first-class passengers sleep and eat outside their cabin doors in a high, warm smell of smoked fish and smoked monkey.

The *cabine de luxe,* twice as expensive as first class, is used by the sweating *garçon* as a storeroom for his brooms and buckets and rags and as a hiding place for the food, *foo-foo,* he is always on the lookout for: securing half a pound of sugar, for instance, by pouring it into a pot of river-brewed tea, and secreting the tea in the wardrobe until nightfall, when he scratches and bangs and scratches at the door until he is admitted.

The curtains of the *cabine* hang ringless and collapsed. *"C'est pas bon,"* the *garçon* says. Many light bulbs are missing; they will now never be replaced; but the empty light brackets on the walls can be used to hang things on. In the bathroom the diseased river water looks unfiltered; the stained and leaking wash basin has been pulled out from the wall; the chrome-plated towel rails are forever empty, their function forgotten; and the holes in the floor are mended, like the holes in a dugout, with what looks like mud. The lavatory cistern ceaselessly flushes. *"C'est pas bon,"* the *garçon* says, as of an irremediable fact of life; and he will not say even this when, on an over-cast afternoon, in a temperature of a hundred degrees, the windows of the *cabine de luxe* sealed, the air-conditioning unit fails.

The bar is naked except for three bottles of spirits. Beer is *terminé,* always, though the steamer is full of dazed Africans and the man known as the maître d'hôtel is drunk from early morning. There is beer, of course; but every little service requires a "sweetener." The steamer is an African steamer and is run on African lines. It has been adapted to African needs. It carries passengers, too many passengers for the two lifeboats displayed on the first-class deck; but it is more than a passenger steamer. It is a travelling market; it is, still, all that many of the people who live along the river know of the outside world.

The steamer, travelling downstream from Kisangani, formerly Stanleyville, to Kinshasa, stops only at Bumbe, Lisala and Mbandaka. But it serves the bush all the way down. The bush begins just outside Kisangani. The town ends—the decayed Hôtel des Chutes, the customs shed, the three or four rusting iron barges moored together, the Roman Catholic cathedral, then a large ruin, a few riverside villas—and the green begins: bamboo, thick grass spilling over the riverbanks, the earth showing red, green and red reflected in the smooth water, the sky, as so often here, dark with storm, lit up and trembling as with distant gunfire, the light silver. The wind and rain come; the green bank fades; the water wrinkles, the reflections go, the water shows muddy. Jungle seems to be promised. But the bush never grows high, never becomes forest.

Soon the settlements appear: the low thatched huts in scraped brown yards, thatch and walls the colour of the earth, the earth scraped bare for fear of snakes and soldier ants. Boys swim out to the steamer, their twice-weekly excitement; and regularly, to shouts, the trading dugouts come, are skilfully poled in alongside the moving steamer, moored, and taken miles downstream while the goods are unloaded, products of the bush: wicker chairs, mortars carved out of tree trunks, great enamel basins of pineapples. Because of the wars, or for some other reason, there are few men here, and the paddlers and traders are all women, or young girls.

When the traders have sold, they buy. In the forward part of the steamer, beyond the second-class w.c.s, water always running off their steel floors, and in the narrow walk beside the cabins, among the defecating babies, the cooking and the washing and the vacant girls being intently deloused, in a damp smell of salted fish and excrement and oil and rust, and to the sound of gramophone records, there are stalls: razor blades, batteries, pills and capsules, soap, hypodermic syringes, cigarettes, pencils, copybooks, lengths of cloth. These are the products of the outside world that are needed; these are the goods for which such exertions are made. Their business over, the dugouts cast off, to paddle lightless upstream miles in the dark.

There can be accidents (a passenger dugout joining the moving steamer was to be overturned on this journey, and some students returning from the bush to Kinshasa were to be lost); and at night the steamer's searchlights constantly sweep the banks. Moths show white in the light; and on the water the Congo hyacinth shows white: a water plant that appeared on the upper Congo in 1956 and has since spread all the way down, treacherously beautiful, with thick lilylike green leaves and a pale-lilac flower like a wilder hyacinth. It seeds itself rapidly; it can form floating islands that attract other vegetation; it can foul the propellers of the steamer. If the steamers do not fail, if there are no more wars, it is the Congo hyacinth that may yet imprison the river people in the immemorial ways of the bush.

In the morning there are new dugouts, fresh merchandise: basins of slugs in moist black earth, fresh fish, and monkeys, monkeys ready-smoked, *boucané*, charred little hulks, or freshly killed, grey or red monkeys, the tips of their tails slit, the slit skin of the tail tied round the neck, the monkeys bundled up and lifted in this way from the dugouts, by the tails, holdalls, portmanteaux, of dead monkeys. The excitement is great.

Monkey is an African delicacy, and a monkey that fetches six zaires, twelve dollars, in Kinshasa can be bought on the river for three zaires.

On the throbbing steel deck the monkeys can appear to be alive and breathing. The wind ruffles their fur; the faces of the red monkeys, falling this way and that, suggest deep contented sleep; their forepaws are loosely closed, sometimes stretched out before them. At the stern of the steamer, on the lower deck, a wood fire is lit and the cooking starts: the dead monkey held face down over the fire, the fur burned off. In the bow, among the goats and hens, there is a wet baby monkey, tightly tethered, somebody's pet or somebody's supper (and in the lifeboat there will appear the next day, as a kind of African joke, a monkey's skull, picked clean and white).

So day after day, through the halts at Bumbe, Lisala and Mbandaka— the two-storeyed Belgian colonial buildings, the ochre concrete walls, the white arches, the green or red corrugated-iron roofs—the steamer market goes on. On the riverbanks bamboo gives way to palms, their lower brown fronds brushing the yellow water. But there is no true forest. The tall trees are dead, and their trunks and bare branches stick out white above the low green bush. The lower vegetation is at times tattered, and sometimes opens out into grassy savanna land, blasted-looking and ghostly in the afternoon heat mist.

The river widens; islands appear; but there is no solitude in this heart of Africa. Always there are the little brown settlements in scraped brown yards, the little plantings of maize or banana or sugar-cane about huts, the trading dugouts arriving beside the steamer to shouts. In the heat mist the sun, an hour before sunset, can appear round and orange, reflected in an orange band in the water muddy with laterite, the orange reflection broken only by the ripples from the bows of the steamer and the barges. Sometimes at sunset the water will turn violet below a violet sky.

But it is a peopled wilderness. The land of this river basin is land used in the African way. It is burned, cultivated, abandoned. It looks desolate, but its riches and fruits are known; it is a wilderness, but one of monkeys. Bush and blasted trees disappear only towards Kinshasa. It is only after nine hundred miles that earth and laterite give way to igneous rocks, and the land, becoming hilly, with sharp indentations, grows smooth and bare, dark with vegetation only in its hollows.

Plant today, reap tomorrow: this is what they say in Kisangani. But this vast green land, which can feed the continent, barely feeds itself. In

Kinshasa the meat and even the vegetables have to be imported from other countries. Eggs and orange juice come from South Africa, in spite of hot official words; and powdered milk and bottled milk come from Europe. The bush is a way of life; and where the bush is so overwhelming, organized agriculture is an illogicality.

The Belgians, in the last twenty years of their rule, tried to develop African agriculture, and failed. A girl on the steamer, a teacher, remembered the irrational attempt, and the floggings. Agriculture had to be "industrialized," a writer said one day in *Elima*, but not in the way "the old colonialists and their disciples have preached." The Belgians failed because they were too theoretical, too removed from the peasants, whom they considered "ignorant" and "irrational." In Zaire, as in China, according to this writer, a sound agriculture could only be based on traditional methods. Machines were not necessary. They were not always suited to the soil; tractors, for instance, often made the soil infertile.

Two days later there was another article in *Elima*. It was no secret, the writer said, that the agriculturists of the country cultivated only small areas and that their production was "minimal." Modern machines had to be used: North Korean experts were coming to show the people how. And there was a large photograph of a tractor, a promise of the future.

About agriculture, as about so many things, as about the principles of government itself, there is confusion. Everyone feels the great bush at his back. And the bush remains the bush, with its own logical life. Away from the mining areas and the decaying towns the land is as the Belgians found it and as they have left it.

APERIRE TERRAM GENTIBUS: "To Open the Land to the Nations": this is the motto, in raised granite, that survives over the defaced monument at Kinshasa railway station. The railway from the Atlantic, the steamer beyond the rapids at Kinshasa: this was how the Congo was opened up, and the monument was erected in 1948 to mark the first fifty years of the railway.

But now the railway is used mainly for goods. Few visitors arrive at the little suburban-style station, still marked "Kinshasa Est," and step out into the imperial glory of the two-lane boulevard that runs south of the river, just behind the docks. In the roundabout outside the station, the statue of King Albert I, uniformed, with sun helmet and sword (according to old postcards, which continue to be sold), has been taken down; the bronze plaques beside the plinth have been broken away, except for an upper fringe of what looks like banana leaves; the floodlamps have been smashed, the wiring apparatus pulled out and rusted; and all that remains of the monument are two tall brick pillars, like the pillars at the end of some abandoned Congolese Appian Way.

In the station hall the timetable frames swivel empty and glassless on the metal pole. But in the station yard, past the open, unguarded doors, there is a true relic: an 1893 locomotive, the first used on the Congo rail- way. It stands on a bed of fresh gravel, amid croton plants and beside two traveller's-trees. It is small, built for a narrow gauge, and looks quaint, with its low, slender boiler, tall funnel and its open cab; but it still appears whole. It is stamped *No. 1* and in an oval cartouche carries one of the great names of the Belgian nineteenth-century industrial expansion: *Société Anonyme John Cockerill—Seraing.*

Not many people in Kinshasa know about this locomotive; and per- haps it has survived because, like so many things of the Belgian past, it is now junk. Like the half-collapsed fork-lift truck on the platform of one of the goods sheds; like the other fork-lift truck in the yard, more thor- oughly pillaged, and seemingly decomposed about its rusted forks, which lie in the dust like metal tusks. Like the one-wheel lawn mower in the park outside, which is now a piece of wasteland, overgrown where it has not been scuffed to dust. The lawn mower is in the possession of a little boy, and he, noticing the stranger's interest, rights his machine and skil- fully runs it on its one wheel through the dust, making the rusted blades whirr.

The visitor nowadays arrives at the airport of Ndjili, some miles to the east of the city. Zaire is not yet a land for the casual traveller—the harassments, official and unofficial, are too many—and the visitor is usu- ally either a businessman or, if he is black, a delegate (in national cos- tume) to one of the many conferences that Zaire now hosts. From the airport one road leads to the city and the Intercontinental Hotel, past great green-and-yellow boards with Mobutu's sayings in French and English, past the river (the slums of the *cité indigène* well to the south), past the Belgian-built villas in green gardens. A quiet six-lane highway runs twenty or thirty miles in the other direction, to the "presidential domain" of Nsele.

Here, in what looks like a resort development, flashy but with hints of perishability, distinguished visitors stay or confer, and good members of the party are admitted to a taste of luxury. Muhammad Ali trained here last year; in January this year some North Korean acrobats and United Nations people were staying. There are air-conditioned bungalows, vast meeting halls, extravagant lounges, a swimming pool. There is also a model farm run by the Chinese. Nsele is in the style of the new presidency: one of the many grandiloquent official buildings, chief's compounds, that have been set up in the derelict capital in recent years, at once an assertion of the power of the chief and of the primacy of Africa. In the new palace for visiting heads of state the baths are gold-plated: my informant was someone from another African country, who had stayed there.

So the Belgian past recedes and is made to look as shabby as its defaced monuments. *Elima* gives half a page to the fifteen-day journey of the Equator subcommissioner to Bomongo; but Stanley, who pioneered the Congo route, who built the road from the port of Matadi to Kinshasa, has been dethroned. In the museum a great iron wheel from one of the wagons used on that road is preserved by the Belgian curator (and what labour that wheel speaks of); but Mount Stanley is now Mont Ngaliema, a presidential park; and the statue of Stanley that overlooked the rapids has been replaced by the statue of a tall anonymous tribesman with a spear. At the Hôtel des Chutes in Kisangani the town's old name of Stanleyville survives on some pieces of crockery. The broken coffee cups are now used for sugar and powdered milk; when they go the name will have vanished.

The Belgian past is being scrubbed out as the Arab past has been scrubbed out. The Arabs were the Belgians' rivals in the eastern Congo; an Arab was once governor of the Stanley Falls station. But who now associates the Congo with a nineteenth-century Arab empire? A Batetela boy remembered that his ancestors were slave-catchers for the Arabs; they changed sides when the Belgians came and offered them places in their army. But that was long ago. The boy is now a student of psychology, on the lookout, like so many young Zairois, for some foreign scholarship; and the boy's girl friend, of another tribe, people in the past considered enslavable, laughed at this story of slave trading.

The bush grows fast over what were once great events or great disturbances. Bush has buried the towns the Arabs planned, the orchards they planted, as recently, during the post-independence troubles, bush buried the fashionable eastern suburbs of Stanleyville, near the Tshopo falls. The Belgian villas were abandoned; the Africans came first to squat and then to pillage, picking the villas clean of metal, wire, timber, bath-tubs and lavatory bowls (both useful for soaking manioc in), leaving only ground-floor shells of brick and masonry. In 1975 some of the ruins still stand, and they look very old, like a tropical, overgrown Pompeii, cleared of its artifacts, with only the ruins of the Château de Venise night-club giving a clue to the cultural life of the vanished settlement.

And it is surprising how, already, so little of Belgium remains in the minds of people. A man of forty—he had spent some years in the United States—told me that his father, who was born in 1900, remembered the Belgian rubber levy and the cutting off of hands. A woman said that her grandfather had brought white priests to the village to protect the vil-lagers against harsh officials. But, ironically, the people who told these stories both might have been described as *évolués*. Most people under thirty, breaking out of the bush into teaching jobs and administrative jobs in Kinshasa, said they had heard nothing about the Belgians from their parents or grandparents.

One man, a university teacher, said, "The Belgians gave us a state. Before the Belgians came we had no state." Another man said he had heard from his grandfather only about the origins of the Bantu people: they wandered south from Lake Chad, crossed the river into an "empty" country, inhabited only by pygmies, "a primitive people," whom they drove away into the deep forest. For most the past is a blank; and history begins with their own memories. Most record a village childhood, a school, and then—the shock of independence. To a man from Ban-dundu, the son of a "farmer," and the first of his village to be educated, the new world came suddenly in 1960 with the arrival in his village of soldiers of the disintegrating Congolese army. "I saw soldiers for the first time then, and I was very frightened. They had no officers. They treated the women badly and killed some men. The soldiers were looking for white people."

In the colonial days, a headmaster told me, the school histories of the Congo began with the late-fifteenth-century Portuguese navigators, and then jumped to the nineteenth century, to the missionaries and the Arabs and the Belgians. African history, as it is now written, restores Africans to Africa, but it is no less opaque: a roll call of tribes, a mention of great kingdoms. So it is in *Introduction à l'Histoire de l'Afrique Noire*, published in Zaire last year. So it is in the official *Profils du Zaire*, which—ignoring Portuguese, missionaries and Arabs—jumps from the brief mention of mostly undated African kingdoms to the establishment of the Congo Free State. The tone is cool and legalistic. King Leopold II's absolute powers are spoken of in just the same way as the powers of older African kings. Passion enters the story only with the events of independence.

The past has vanished. Facts in a book cannot by themselves give people a sense of history. Where so little has changed, where bush and river are so overwhelming, another past is accessible, better answering African bewilderment and African religious beliefs: the past as *le bon vieux temps de nos ancêtres.*

IN THE PRESIDENTIAL park at Mont Ngaliema, formerly Mount Stanley, where the guards wear decorative uniforms, and the gates are decorated with bronze plaques—the bad art of modern Africa: art that no longer serves a religious or magical purpose, attempts an alien representationalism and becomes mannered and meaningless, suggesting a double mimicry: African art imitating itself, imitating African-inspired Western art—on Mont Ngaliema there are some colonial graves of the 1890s.

They have been gathered together in neat terraces and are screened by cypress and flamboyant. There, above the rapids—the brown river breaking white on the rocks but oddly static in appearance, the white crests never moving: an eternal level sound of water—the pioneers grandly lie. The simple professions recur: *commis, agent commercial, chaudronnier* [boilermaker], *capitaine de steamboat, prêtre, s/officier de la Force Publique.* Only Madame Bernard is *sans profession.* Not all were Belgians; some were Norwegians; one missionary was English.

In one kind of imperialist writing these people are heroic. Joseph Conrad, in his passage through the Congo in 1890, just before those burials began on Mont Ngaliema, saw otherwise. He saw people who were too simple for an outpost of progress, people who were part of the crowd at home, and dependent on that crowd, their strength in Africa, like the strength of the Romans in Britain, "an accident arising from the weakness of others," their "conquest of the earth" unredeemed by an idea, "not a sentimental pretence but an idea; and an unselfish belief in the idea."

"In a hundred years," Conrad makes one of these simple people say in "An Outpost of Progress" (1897), "there will perhaps be a town here. Quays, and warehouses, and barracks, and—and—billiard-rooms. Civilization, my boy, and virtue—and all." That civilization, so accurately defined, came; and then, like the villas at Stanleyville and the Château de Venise night-club, vanished. "Acquisitions, clothes, pretty rags—rags that would fly off at the first good shake": this is from the narrator of *Heart of Darkness* (1902). "No; you want a deliberate belief."

The people who come now—after the general flight—are like the people who came then. They offer goods, deals, technical skills, the same perishable civilization; they bring nothing else. They are not pioneers; they know they cannot stay. They fill the night-clubs (now with African names); they keep the prostitutes (now in African dress; foreign dress is outlawed for African women) busy around the Memling Hotel. So, encircled by Africa, now dangerous again, with threats of expulsion and confiscation, outpost civilization continues: at dinnertime in the Café de la Paix the two old men parade the young prostitutes they have picked up, girls of fourteen or fifteen. Old men: their last chance to feed on such young blood: Kinshasa may close down tomorrow.

"Everyone is here only for the money." The cynicism has never been secret; it is now reinforced by anxiety. With this cynicism, in independent Zaire, the African can appear to be in complicity. He, too, wants "acquisitions, clothes, pretty rags": the Mercedes, the fatter prostitutes, the sharp suit with matching handkerchief and cravat, the gold-rimmed glasses, the gold pen-and-pencil set, the big gold wristwatch on one hand and the gold bracelet on the other, the big belly that in a land of puny men speaks of wealth. But with this complicity and imitation there is something else: a resentment of the people imitated, the people now known as *nostalgiques*.

Simon's company, a big one, has been nationalized, and Simon is now the manager. (Expatriates continue to do the work, but this is only practical, and Simon doesn't mind.) Why then does Simon, who has a background of bush, who is so young and successful, remember his former manager as a *nostalgique*? Well, one day the manager was looking through the pay sheets and he said, "Simon isn't paying enough tax."

People like Simon (he has an official African name) are not easy to know—even Belgians who speak African languages say that. Simon only answers questions; he is incapable of generating anything like a conversation; because of his dignity, his new sense of the self, the world has closed up for him again; and he appears to be hiding. But his resentment of the former manager must have a deeper cause than the one he has given. And gradually it becomes apparent, from other replies he gives, from his belief in "authenticity," from his dislike of foreign attitudes to African art (to him a living thing: he considers the Kinshasa museum an absurdity), from the secretive African arrangements of his domestic life (to which he returns in his motorcar), it gradually becomes apparent that Simon is adrift and nervous in this unreal world of imitation.

It is with people like Simon, educated, moneymaking, that the visitor feels himself in the presence of vulnerability, dumbness, danger. Because their resentments, which appear to contradict their ambitions, and which they can never satisfactorily explain, can at any time be converted into a wish to wipe out and undo, an African nihilism, the rage of primitive men coming to themselves and finding that they have been fooled and affronted.

A rebellion like this occurred after independence. It was led by Pierre Mulele, a former minister of education, who, after a long march through the country, camped at Stanleyville and established a reign of terror. Everyone who could read and write had been taken out to the little park and shot; everyone who wore a tie had been shot. These were the stories about Mulele that were circulating in neighbouring Uganda in 1966, nearly two years after the rebellion had been put down (Uganda itself about to crumble, its nihilistic leader already apparent: Amin, the commander of the petty army that had destroyed the Kabaka's power). Nine thousand people are said to have died in Mulele's rebellion. What did Mulele want? What was the purpose of the killings? The forty-year-old African who had spent some time in the United States laughed and said, "Nobody knows. He was against *everything*. He wanted to start again from the beginning." There is only one, noncommittal line in *Profils du Zaire* about the Mulelist rebellion. But (unlike Lumumba) he gets a photograph, and it is a big one. It shows a smiling, gap-toothed African—in jacket and tie.

To Joseph Conrad, Stanleyville—in 1890 the Stanley Falls station—was the heart of darkness. It was there, in Conrad's story, that Kurtz reigned, the ivory agent degraded from idealism to savagery, taken back to the earliest ages of man, by wilderness, solitude and power, his house surrounded by impaled human heads. Seventy years later, at this bend in the river, something like Conrad's fantasy came to pass. But the man with "the inconceivable mystery of a soul that knew no restraint, no faith, and no fear" was black, and not white; and he had been maddened not by contact with wilderness and primitivism, but with the civilization established by those pioneers who now lie on Mont Ngaliema, above the Kinshasa rapids.

MOBUTU embodies these African contradictions and, by the grandeur of his kingship, appears to ennoble them. He is, for all his stylishness, the great African nihilist, though his way is not the way of blood. He is the man "young but palpitating with wisdom and dynamism"—this is from a University of Zaire publication—who, during the dark days of secessions and rebellions, "thought through to the heart of the problem" and arrived at his especial illumination: the need for "authenticity," "I no longer have a borrowed conscience. I no longer have a borrowed soul. I no longer speak a borrowed language." He will bring back ancestral ways and reverences; he will re-create that pure, logical world.

"Our religion is based on a belief in God the creator and the worship of our ancestors." This is what a minister told teachers the other day. "Our dead parents are living; it is they who protect us and intercede for us." No need now for the Christian saints, or Christianity. Christ was the prophet of the Jews and he is dead. Mobutu is the prophet of the Africans. "This prophet rouses us from our torpor, and has delivered us from our mental alienation. He teaches us to love one another." In public places the crucifix should be replaced by the image of the messiah, just as in China the portrait of Mao is honoured everywhere. And Mobutu's glorious mother, Mama Yemo, should also be honoured, as the Holy Virgin was honoured.

So Mobutism becomes the African way out. The dances and songs of Africa, so many of them religious in origin, are now officially known as *séances d'animation* and are made to serve the new cult; the dancers wear cloths stamped with Mobutu's image. Old rituals, absorbed into the new, their setting now not the village but the television studio, the palace, the conference hall, appear to have been given fresh dignity. Africa awakes! And, in all things, Mobutu offers himself as the African substitute. At the end of January Mobutu told the Afro-American conference at Kinshasa (sponsored by the Ford and Carnegie foundations): "Karl Marx is a great thinker whom I respect." But Marx wasn't always right; he was wrong, for instance, about the beneficial effects of colonialism. "The teachings of Karl Marx were addressed to his society. The teachings of Mobutu are addressed to the people of Zaire."

In Africa such comparisons, when they are made, have to be unabashed: African needs are great. And Mobutism is so wrapped up in the glory of Mobutu's kingship—the new palaces (the maharaja-style palace at Kisangani confiscated from Mr. Nasser, an old Indian settler), the presidential park at Mont Ngaliema (where Africans walk with foreigners on Sundays and pretend to be amused by the monkeys), the presidential domain at Nsele (open to faithful members of the party: and passengers on the steamer and the barges rush to look), the state visits abroad, intensively photographed, the miracle of the peace Mobutu has brought to the country, the near-absence of policemen in the towns—so glorious are the manifestations of Mobutu's kingship, so good are the words of the king, who proclaims himself a friend of the poor and, as a cook's son, one of the *petit peuple,* that all the contradictions of Africa appear to have been resolved and to have been turned into a kind of power.

But the contradictions remain, and are now sometimes heightened. The newspapers carry articles about science and medicine. But a doctor, who now feels he can say that he cures "when God and the ancestors wish," tells a newspaper that sterility is either hereditary or caused by a curse; and another newspaper gives publicity to a healer, a man made confident by the revolution, who has an infallible cure for piles, an "exclusive" secret given him by the ancestors. Agriculture must be modernized, the people must be fed better; but, in the name of authenticity, a doctor warns that babies should on no account be fed on imported foods; traditional foods, like caterpillars and green leaves, are best. The industrialized West is decadent and collapsing; Zaire must rid herself of the plagues of the consumer society, the egoism and individualism exported by industrial civilization. But in the year 2000, according to a university writer in *Elima,* Zaire might herself be booming, with great cities, a population of "probably" 71,933,851, and a prodigious manufacturing capacity. Western Europe will be in its "post-industrial" decadence; Russia, Eastern Europe and the Indian subcontinent will form one bloc;

Arab oil will be exhausted; and Zaire (and Africa) should have her day, attracting investment from developed countries (obviously those not in decadence), importing factories whole.

So the borrowed ideas—about colonialism and alienation, the consumer society and the decline of the West—are made to serve the African cult of authenticity; and the dream of an ancestral past restored is allied to a dream of a future of magical power. The confusion is not new, and is not peculiar to Zaire. Fantasies like this animated some slave revolts in the West Indies; and today, in Jamaica, at the university, there are people who feel that Negro redemption and Negro power can only come about through a return to African ways. The dead Duvalier of Haiti is admired for his Africanness; a writer speaks with unconscious irony of the Negro's need for a "purifying" period of poverty (unwittingly echoing Duvalier's "It is the destiny of the people of Haiti to suffer"); and there are people who, sufficiently far away from the slaughter ground of Uganda, find in Amin's African nihilism a proof of African power.

It is lunacy, despair. In the February 7th issue of *Jeune Afrique*—miraculously on sale in Kinshasa—a French African writer, Seydou Lamine, examines the contradictions of African fantasy and speaks of "the alibi of the past." Mightn't this talk of Africanness, he asks, be a "myth" which the "princes" of Africa now use to strengthen their own position? "For many, authenticity and Negroness [*la négrité*] are only words that stand for the despair and powerlessness of the man of Africa faced with the discouraging immensity of his underdevelopment."

And even *Elima*, considering the general corruption, the jobs not done, the breakdown of municipal administration in Kinshasa, the uncleared garbage, the canals not disinfected (though the taxis are, regularly, for the one-zaire fee), the vandalized public television sets and telephone booths, even *Elima* finds it hard on some days to blame the colonial past for these signs of egoism. "We are wrong to consider the word 'underdevelopment' only in its economic aspects. We have to understand that there is a type of underdevelopment that issues out of the habits of a people and their attitudes to life and society."

Mobutism, *Elima* suggests, will combat this "mental plague." But it is no secret that, in spite of its talk of "man," in spite of its lilting national anthem called the *Zairoise ("Paix, justice et travail")*, Mobutism honours only one man: the chief, the king. He alone has to be feared and loved. How—away from this worship—does a new attitude to life and society begin? Recently in Kinshasa a number of people were arrested for some reason and taken to Makala jail: lavatoryless concrete blocks behind a whitewashed wall, marked near the gateway DISCIPLINE AVANT TOUT. The people arrested couldn't fit easily into the cell, and a Land-Rover was used to close the door. In the morning many were found crushed or suffocated.

Not cruelty, just thoughtlessness: the visitor has to learn to accommodate himself to Zaire. The presidential domain at Nsele (where Muhammad Ali trained) is such a waste, at once extravagant and shoddy, with its over-furnished air-conditioned bungalows, its vast meeting halls, its VIP lounges (carpets, a fussiness of fringed Dralon, African art debased to furniture decoration). But Nsele can be looked at in another way. It speaks of the African need for African style and luxury; it speaks of the great African wound. The wound explains the harassment of foreign settlers, the nationalizations. But the nationalizations are petty and bogus; they have often turned out to be a form of pillage and are part of no creative plan; they are as short-sighted, self-wounding and nihilistic as they appear, a dismantling of what remains of the Belgian-created state. So the visitor swings from mood to mood, and one reaction cancels out another.

Where, in Kinshasa, where so many people "shadow" jobs, and so many jobs are artificial and political, part of an artificial administration, where does the sense of responsibility, society, the state, begin? A city of two million, with almost no transport, with no industries (save for those assembly plants, sited, as in so many "developing" countries, on the road from the airport to the capital), a city detached from the rest of the country, existing only because the Belgians built it and today almost without a point. It doesn't have to work; it can be allowed to look after itself. Already at night, a more enduring kind of bush life seems to return to central Kinshasa, when the watchmen (who also shadow their jobs: they will protect nothing) bar off their territory, using whatever industrial junk there is to hand, light fires on the broken pavements, cook their little messes and go to sleep. When it is hot the gutters smell; in the rain the streets are flooded. And the unregulated city spreads: meandering black rivulets of filth in unpaved alleys, middens beside the highways, children, discarded motorcar tyres, a multitude of little stalls, and everywhere, in free spaces, plantings of sugar-cane and maize: subsistence agriculture in the town, a remnant of bush life.

But at the end of one highway there is the university. It is said to have gone down. But the students are bright and friendly. They have come from the bush, but already they can talk of Stendhal and Fanon; they have the enthusiasm of people to whom everything is new; and they feel, too, that with the economic collapse of the West (of which the newspapers talk every day) the tide is running Africa's way. The enthusiasm deserves a better-equipped country. It seems possible that many of these students, awakening to ideas, history, a knowledge of injustice and a sense of their own dignity, will find themselves unsupported by their society, and can only awaken to pain. But no. For most there will be jobs in the government; and already they are Mobutists to a man. Already the African way ahead is known; already inquiry is restricted; and Mobutu himself has warned that the most alienated people in Zaire are the intellectuals.

So Mobutism simplifies the world, the concept of responsibility and the state, and simplifies people. Zaire's accession to power and glory has been made to appear so easy; the plundering of the inherited Belgian state has been so easy, the confiscations and nationalizations, the distribution of big shadow jobs. Creativity itself now begins to appear as something that might be looted, brought into being by decree.

Zaire has her music and dance. To complete her glory, Zaire needs a literature; other African countries have literatures. The trouble, *Elima* says in a full-page Sunday article, is that far too many people who haven't written a line and sometimes can't even speak correctly have been going here and there and passing themselves off as Zairois writers, shaming the country. That will now stop; the bogus literary "circles" will be replaced by official literary "salons"; and they must set to work right away. In two months the president will be going to Paris. The whole world will be watching, and it is important that in these two months a work of Zairois literature be written and published. Other works should be produced for the Lagos Festival of Negro Arts at the end of the year. And it seems likely, from the tone of the *Elima* article, that it is Mobutu who has spoken.

. . .

MOBUTU speaks all the time. He no longer speaks in French but in Lingala, the local lingua franca, and transistors take his words to the deep bush. He speaks as the chief, and the people listen. They laugh constantly, and they applaud. It has been Mobutu's brilliant idea to give the people of Zaire what they have not had and what they have long needed: an African king. The king expresses all the dignity of his people; to possess a king is to share the king's dignity. The individual's responsibility— a possible source of despair, in the abjectness of Africa—is lessened. All that is required is obedience, and obedience is easy.

Mobutu proclaims his simple origins. He is a *citoyen* like everyone else. And Mama Mobutu, Mobutu's wife, loves the poor. She runs a centre for deprived girls, and they devote themselves to agriculture and to making medallions of the king, which the loyal will wear: there can never be too many images of Mobutu in Zaire. The king's little magnanimities are cherished by a people little used to magnanimity. Many Zairois will tell you that a hospital steamer now serves the river villages. But it is where Mobutu appears to be most extravagant that he satisfies his people most. The king's mother is to be honoured; and she was a simple woman of Africa. Pilgrimages are announced to places connected with the king's life; and the disregarded bush of Africa becomes sacred again.

The newspapers, diluting the language of Fanon and Mao, speak every day of the revolution and the radicalization of the revolution. But this is what the revolution is about: the kingship. In Zaire Mobutu is the news: his speeches, his receptions, the *marches de soutien*, the new appointments: court news. Actual events are small. The nationalization of a gaudy furniture shop in Kinshasa is big news, as is the revelation that there is no African on the board of a brewery. Anti-revolutionary activity, discovered by the "vigilance" of the people, has to do with crooked vendors in the market, an official using a government vehicle as a night taxi, someone else building a house where he shouldn't, some drunken members of the youth wing of the party wrecking the party Volkswagen at Kisangani. There is no news in Zaire because there is little new activity. Copper continues to be mined; the big dam at Inga continues to be built. Airports are being extended or constructed everywhere, but this doesn't mean that Air Zaire is booming: it is for the better policing of the country.

What looked obvious on the first day, but was then blurred by the reasonable-sounding words, turns out to be true. The kingship of Mobutu has become its own end. The inherited modern state is being dismantled, but it isn't important that the state should work. The bush works; the bush has always been self-sufficient. The administration, now the court, is something imposed, something unconnected with the true life of the country. The ideas of responsibility, the state and creativity are ideas brought by the visitor; they do not correspond, for all the mimicry of language, to African aspirations.

Mobutu's peace and his kingship are great achievements. But the kingship is sterile. The cult of the king already swamps the intellectual advance of a people who have barely emerged. The intellectual confusions of authenticity, that now give such an illusion of power, close up the world again and point to a future greater despair. Mobutu's power will inevitably be extinguished; but there can now be no going back on the principles of Mobutism. Mobutu has established the pattern for his successors; and they will find that African dependence is not less than it is now, nor the need for nihilistic assertion.

To arrive at this sense of a country trapped and static, eternally vulnerable, is to begin to have something of the African sense of the void. It is to begin to fall, in the African way, into a dream of a past—the vacancy of river and forest, the hut in the brown yard, the dugout—when the dead ancestors watched and protected, and the enemies were only men.

1975

The Crocodiles of Yamoussoukro

I

YAMOUSSOUKRO, a place deep in the wet forests of the Ivory Coast, is one of the wonders of black Africa. It used to be a village, and perhaps then it was like some other West African bush villages, where grass huts perish after two years. But Yamoussoukro was also the seat of a regional tribal chief; and during the half a century or so of direct French rule in the interior, the authority of the chieftaincy—moral, or spiritual, or magical authority—was not forgotten.

The very old man who is still chief received a French education. He became what the French called a "colonial" doctor—not the finished French product, but a doctor nonetheless. Later he became a politician, a protest leader. With independence in 1960—the bush returned with alterations to its people—he began to rule the Ivory Coast. And he has ruled ever since.

He has ruled well. He has used the French as technicians, advisers, administrators; and, with no ready-made mineral wealth, with the resources only of tropical forests and fields, he has made his country rich. So rich, that the Ivory Coast imports labour from its more depressed or chaotic African neighbours. Labour immigration, as much as natural increase, has raised the population from three million in 1960 to nine million today. Abidjan, the capital, begun unpromisingly on the black mud of a fetid lagoon, has become one of the biggest ports in West Africa. And 150 miles inland, at the end of an auto-route that would not disgrace France itself, the president's ancestral village of Yamoussoukro, has been transformed.

The ancestral village has in fact vanished from public sight. The entire village—huts (if they still survive), common ground, the semi-sacred palaver tree—has been incorporated into the grounds of a new presidential palace. And all is hidden by a high palace wall that must be many miles long.

Down one side of the palace there is an artificial lake, and in this lake turtles and man-eating crocodiles have been introduced. These are totemic, emblematic creatures, and they belong to the president. There were no crocodiles in Yamoussoukro before. No one knows precisely what they mean. But to all Africans they speak at once of danger and of the president's, the chief's, magically granted knowledge of his power as something more than human, something emanating from the earth itself.

The power and wisdom of the chief have caused the forest around Yamoussoukro to disappear. Where once were African fields, unused common land, and wild trees there are now ordered, mechanized plantations. For square mile upon square mile mangoes, avocadoes or pineapples grow in straight lines, the straight lines that are beautiful to people to whom Nature is usually formless, unfriendly bush. Land in this part of Africa, it is said, belongs to the user; there can be no title in bush. And until they were given to the state some years ago, these plantations around Yamoussoukro were the president's personal estates.

The president's ideas have always been big, and his plans for Yamoussoukro are very big. He would like it to be one of the great cities of Africa and the world. The land has been levelled, and avenues as wide as runways outline the metropolis that is to be. Extravagant and sometimes brilliant modern buildings have been set down in the stripped wilderness and await full use.

To attract visitors, there is a great golf course, beautifully landscaped and so far steadfastly maintained against the fast-growing bush. It is the president's idea, though he doesn't play golf himself. The golf idea came to him when he was old, and now in his benign, guiding way he would like all his people, all the sixty or so tribes of the Ivory Coast, to take up golf. To house the visitors, there is a twelve-storey Hotel President, one of the French Sofitel hotel chain. The hotel brochure is printed in France; its silvery grey cover looks princely. "Find the traces of the native village of President Houphouët-Boigny," the brochure says, "and discover the ultra-modern prefiguration of the Africa of tomorrow."

The two ideas go together. The ultra-modern dream also serves old Africa. It is pharaonic: it has a touch of the antique world. Away from the stupendous modern frivolities of the golf course and the golf club and the swimming pool of the Hotel President there is the presidential palace with its artificial lake. Outside the blank walls that hide the president's ancestral village and the palaver tree from the common view, the president's totemic crocodiles are fed with fresh meat every day. People can go and watch. But distances in Yamoussoukro are so great, and the scarred, empty spaces so forbidding, that only people with cars can easily go; and they tend to be visitors, tourists.

The feeding ritual takes place in the afternoon, in bright light. There are the cars, the tourists in bright clothes, the cameras. But the crocodiles are sacred. A live offering—a chicken—has to be made to them; it is part of the ritual. This element of sacrifice, this protracted display of power and cruelty, is as unsettling as it is meant to be, and it seems to bring night and the forest close again to the dream of Yamoussoukro.

To the man from outside, whatever his political or religious faith, Africa can often seem to be in a state of becoming. It is always on the point of being made something else. So it arouses hope, ambition, frustration, irritation. And even the success of the Ivory Coast induces a kind of anxiety. Will it last? Will the Africans be able to take over from the French and the Israelis and the others who have built it all for them and still effectively run it?

And then at a place like Yamoussoukro, where the anxiety becomes most acute, it also begins to feel unreal. You get a glimpse of an African Africa, an Africa which—whatever the accidents of history, whatever the current manifestations of earthly glory—has always been in its own eyes complete, achieved, bursting with its own powers.

THIS IDEA OF AFRICAN completeness should not have surprised me. Something like this, a similar religious feeling, was, fleetingly, at the back of many of the slave revolts in the Caribbean. The idea of African completeness endures in various Caribbean religious cults; and touches the politics of the region. Many of the recent political movements in the black Caribbean have had a millenarian, ecstatic, purely African side.

West Africa peopled the slave plantations of the New World. But that wasn't the idea I took to the Ivory Coast. I went for simpler reasons. The world is too various; it can exist only in compartments in our minds. I wanted to be in West Africa, where I had never been; I wanted to be in a former French territory in Africa; and I wanted to be in an African country which, in the mess of black Africa, was generally held to be a political and economic success. African success, France in Africa—those were the glamorous ideas that took me out.

France in Africa was a private fantasy. It was based on my own love of the French language, a special schoolboy love, given me at Queen's Royal College in colonial Trinidad by teachers, many of them black or partly black, who were themselves in love with the French language and an idea (hinted at, never stated) of an accepting, assimilating France. France in Africa: I imagined the language in the mouths of elegant Africans; I thought of tall, turbanned women, like those of Mali and the Congo; I thought of wine and tropical boulevards.

But in the humidity of the Ivory Coast, the wine (stupefying at lunchtime) was mainly rosé and Moroccan; West African French was as broken and sourly accented as West African English; and there was nothing like a boulevard in the hard little commercial centre of Abidjan, where, here and there in the shadows of tall new buildings, Lebanese shops still spoke of a recent, duller colonial township. Instead of boulevards there was the African hubbub of "popular" African areas. Away from that there was—as in many other former colonial territories—the ready-made, enclosed glamour of new international hotels.

Around the swimming pool of the Forum Golf Hotel the small-breasted wives of French businessmen and technicians sunbathed topless, among the black-and-orange lizards. Africa came on at night, as the cabaret: not the Africa of the night-clubs in the African areas, but the Africa of officially approved "culture": the semi-religious or magical dances of the forest, done now in a landscaped garden, electric light playing on the big, bare breasts of dancing, chanting women.

I hadn't really thought I would find France in Africa—it was a fantasy. But I hadn't expected that in the Ivory Coast France and Africa would still be like separate ideas. It made more puzzling the success that was to be seen in the great capital city of Abidjan: in the urban highways, with direction boards that suggested France; the skyscrapers of the city centre; the university campus and the golf course; the spreading workers' areas, disordered but not poor; the many mixed—African and European—middle-class residential areas; the blocks of government-built flats; the big port and industrial zone; the tainted tropical lagoon reflecting at dusk the lights of the rush-hour traffic on the "corniche."

"Isn't it wonderful," an American from the embassy said to me one evening, looking at that view, "that they have done this with just a little bit of coffee and a little bit of cocoa?"

Out of apparently little, wealth had been created. And this wealth had been shared and used. The Ivory Coast boom had now abated. Coffee prices had dropped by a third and cocoa by a half, and the oil exploration people were leaving the Ivory Coast for other French African countries. There was some discontent now; protests had begun to be heard about the number of French people in the country. But something extraordinary had been achieved; in this corner of Africa even the continuing order of the state was like a miracle.

All around was chaos or nullity. Liberia, illiterate, impoverished, was ruled by its army after members of the previous government had been unceremoniously shot on the beach. (What pictures those news reports gave to the mind: the holiday setting, the bewildered men in suits or pyjamas, the uniformed men with guns, the sound of the sea.) Guinea, once like the Ivory Coast a French colony, and potentially richer than the Ivory Coast, was now bankrupt, a murderous tyranny, famous for the "black diet" of its condemned cells, where people were given neither food nor water and simply left to waste away. Ghana, at the time of its independence in 1957 far richer and better educated than the Ivory Coast, with institutions, was now after repeated coups in a state of anarchy, a source of migrant labour.

Yet, tribally speaking, the people of Ghana and Guinea were like some of the people of the Ivory Coast. The tribes, the *ethnies*, were not contained within national borders. And though the Ivory Coast was said to be liberal, it was also an African state, a one-party state, with its own cult of the leader: the man who had become president at independence had never stopped being president. What had been done in the Ivory Coast hadn't been done suddenly; it had been sustained over more than twenty years. Clearly, then, to explain this African success, there had been—over and above the personality of the president—some principle of organization that suited the people, something easily grasped and repeatable.

The explanations given to the visitor were simple, short, polished: they had been given to many other visitors before. The nationalist movement in a country like Ghana had been a movement of clerks and lawyers, ideologues seeking at once to ennoble and Africanize Africa by foreign ideas. The nationalist movement in the Ivory Coast had been simpler, a movement of farmers, *planteurs*, village people.

This was added to by an ambassador I saw not long after I arrived. The news he had just received was of the putting down of yet another coup in Ghana. The two countries were different at independence, the ambassador said. They shared only the climate and the vegetation. In Ghana after independence the nationalists concentrated on "administrative structures." In the Ivory Coast they concentrated on creating wealth, wealth from peasant farming. They were less concerned with Africanization. They built roads, to bring the villages closer to the market place. They gave the villages services and security—and security was important. They tried to keep people on the land by ending the isolation of the villages; and they had succeeded. There were now roads and hotels all over the Ivory Coast. The president's village of Yamoussoukro in the centre of the country was now just a three-hour drive from Abidjan.

THAT WAS HOW I FIRST heard of Yamoussoukro. It was the president's village, and it might have been no more than one of the farming villages opened up by a government concerned with agriculture.

Ambassadors have to choose their words. They do a specialized job and it is necessary for them to live ceremonial lives. As officials, their vision of a country shouldn't run too far beyond that of the local people with whom they have to deal. So, with ambassadors as with other expatriates in black Africa, there appears at a first meeting a kind of ambivalence. To say what they feel they have to say they appear to be denying or ignoring part of what they know. Expatriates may know African Africa, but this is not the Africa they put forward to a visitor at a first meeting. They are men with jobs, skills; their job is part of their self-esteem; and the Africa they present to the visitor is the Africa connected with their jobs. The ambivalence is natural; it is not disingenuous. The doing of certain kinds of work in Africa, the practise of certain disciplines or skills from another civilization, can be like a disinterested exercise of virtue. Many expatriates—those who last in freed black Africa—become genuinely good people; and not a few are oddly solitary.

It was from Philip, an expatriate, that I next heard of Yamoussoukro. Philip was English. He was in his late thirties, and much of his working life had been spent in Africa. He now worked for an inter-state African organization. His wife was a black Guyanese girl of great beauty, from a family settled in England. It was odd, Philip said, that he should be the African side of their marriage, and Janet the English, "from Huddersfield."

Her birthday fell that weekend. And, to celebrate, they were going on the expatriate Sunday excursion to Grand-Bassam on the beach. I went with their party: out of Abidjan, past the shack settlements of migrant labourers, past the coconut estates with coconut trees planted in rows and offering long vistas down the cleared spaces between the trees, past the lines of thatched huts selling African curios and artefacts, to the ruined old colonial capital of Grand-Bassam, abandoned after a yellow fever epidemic in 1899, concrete and corrugated iron and streets of thick dust, and at last the thatched Sunday restaurants on the sea: the excursion that, as I was to discover at the end of my second week, was part of the routine and tedium and constriction of expatriate life.

On the edge of Abidjan the highway became very wide, without any median divider. It was like that, Philip said, for parades.

"It's like Yamoussoukro," Philip said. "You should try to get there. Try to get there at night. You'll see the double row of lights. You'll wonder where you are. And in the morning you'll see that you are nowhere."

We passed low army barracks. They seemed to go on for a long time. They were the barracks of a French Foreign Legion regiment. They kept a low profile, Philip said. They were in the Ivory Coast only to train.

I said to him, "Does it depress you, being in all these African countries with their separate personality cults?"

It was too strong a question to put to him at this stage of our relationship.

He said, "There is the cult of personality everywhere. Looking at the Falklands business from the outside, I would say there was a great cult of the personality there. Mrs. Thatcher raised herself up."

I asked whether he really thought that the situations were the same.

He said with unexpected directness, "No." And a little while later he returned to the subject, as though to explain both himself and what he had said. "You must understand that Africans like the cult of personality better. It is what they understand. A multiplicity of parties and personalities confuses them. I've seen this happen."

AND AFRICAN attitudes to authority was one of the subjects that came up at an embassy lunch the next day. The president, I heard, had become aware of the growing discontent in the Ivory Coast. In his benignity, and out of his wish to do the right thing, he had tried to "democratize." There was only one party in the Ivory Coast, and normally at elections there was only one list of candidates; people in any particular constituency simply voted for or against the party's candidate. At the last election there had been an experiment. It was decreed that anyone in the party could contest any seat. For the 140 or so seats in the assembly there had been more than 600 candidates; and 80 per cent of the old deputies, some of whom had held their seats for twenty years, had been voted out.

Democracy of a kind had been served, but there had been a more than political consternation. The old deputies had built up followings; they had become elders; and in the African tradition an elder remained an elder till he died. A man stripped of authority couldn't simply go back to being an ordinary villager; he had been personally degraded. So the democratic experiment had damaged the cohesiveness of village life. Ever since the election there had been any number of programmes on the television about the need for "reconciliation." "Democracy," people's rule, was the imported idea; reconciliation was the African idea—in certain villages, among certain tribes, there actually was an annual ceremony of reconciliation, presided over by the local chief.

And—though the link wasn't made at the lunch—just as it was hard for an elder or deputy to stop being what he was, so it was hard for the president to stop being president, though he was now very old, eighty or more—no one really knew his age. An added reason for the president's holding on was the great enterprise of Yamoussoukro. The work there was far from completed, would not be completed in the president's lifetime. And that was why, democrat and anti-tribalist though he was, the president would have to choose as his successor someone from his own dominant Baoulé tribe. That was the only way he had of ensuring, or trying to ensure, that the work on Yamoussoukro would go on after his death.

So, as I heard about it, Yamoussoukro grew: from being an agricultural village in the interior, provided now with roads and services; to a place with very wide, brilliantly lit avenues that led nowhere; to a monumental city meant to make an African ruler immortal. And even as I understood the pharaonic scale of the project, I feared for it. I thought of the monuments of ancient Egypt where the cartouches of one pharaoh could be defaced by his successors; where the carved and polished stones of the monument of one sacred pharaoh could be broken up and used unceremoniously, as building blocks alone, in the monument of another.

And this African dream of Yamoussoukro was being created by people of another civilization: French and Israelis and others, whose skills might easily vanish from the continent.

So the first impressions of modern African success began to be qualified. Success became an expression of the nonideological personality of the ruler, the man of an established ruling family; this rested on an African idea of authority. And at the bottom of it all was magic.

This last idea, of magic, didn't come to me by any secret means. I came upon it openly, in the newspapers.

There was one daily newspaper in the Ivory Coast; at least, only one came my way. It was called *Fraternité Matin*. Every day on its front page, in the top left-hand corner, it carried a "thought" of the president's. The thoughts were mainly about development and the economy; and so were the big front-page stories. There were sports pages. But they didn't make the paper any less austere. There was no gossip, almost nothing from the police. *Fraternité Matin* suggested a nation at work and at school—even night school. But then, at the end of my first week, there was something like a real news story. It was spread over two inside pages of the weekend issue and was clearly about a well-known local sensation.

Seventeen kilometres out of Abidjan, in a village on the great auto-route to Yamoussoukro, there was a schoolteacher's house which from time to time blazed with mysterious fires. A reader had written to the paper that weekend with the suggestion that there was probably some escape of natural gas in the neighbourhood. But this letter, headed "A Scientific Solution," was placed at the bottom of the right-hand page. The main story, the *reportage*, was that the mystery of the fires at Kilometre 17 had been solved.

It had been solved by a preacher of the Celestial Christian sect. Even before they had been called in on the case—and while the teacher was spending a fortune on fetish-makers and Muslim magicians—the Celestial Christians had "discovered" through some divine communication that the Evil Spirit was at the bottom of the business. In investigations of this kind, according to the Celestial Christians, there were two levels that had to be considered, the mystical and the human. At the mystical level there was the Evil Spirit. At the human level, there was the person who had been possessed by the Evil Spirit and turned into a fire-raiser.

The Celestial Christians, with their special gifts, had found out who this person was. And the Evil Spirit, discovered in this way, was immediately at a disadvantage. The Spirit had gone to the Celestial Christians and pleaded with them to be left in peace, to get on with its wicked work in the Ivory Coast in secret. It had offered bribes. The Celestial Christians refused. However, they engaged the Evil Spirit in dialogue. They asked the Evil Spirit why it wanted to start fires in the schoolteacher's house. The Spirit didn't answer directly. It only said, "in a mystical way," that it was the owner of the house. This was apparently a frightening reply, and the Celestial Christians didn't wait to hear any more. They at once ordered the Evil Spirit not only to leave the house but also to get out of the Ivory Coast altogether. And the Spirit meekly went.

Now a protective cross was planted outside the schoolteacher's front door, and peace had returned to the tormented man. The Celestial Christians, making the most of their success, regretted only that the schoolteacher had spent so much money on fetishes and Muslim *marabout* magic. They, the Christians, had done what they had done only with their faith in Jesus Christ and a few candles.

So the story of Kilometre 17 had had a happy ending. It was a moral story; and like so much else in *Fraternité Matin*, it seemed to have an element of benign instruction and reassurance. The Evil Spirit had been defeated by a stronger force. More than the peace of mind of a village schoolteacher had been secured: the Ivory Coast itself had been cleansed.

The report in *Fraternité Matin* didn't say who the possessed person was. This might have been due to legal caution or more probably to some taboo about the Evil Spirit. The reporter only dropped hints: the possessed person was in and out of the house, was well known to the schoolteacher's family, did many things for the schoolteacher. The Sunday magazine, *Ivoire Dimanche*, in a two-page photographic feature on the case, showed photographs of the teacher and his two wives. Was the possessed person one of the wives? Both women looked equally enervated, as enervated as the teacher himself, though they were thin and he was plump. The presence of sorcery and the Evil Spirit seemed to have given them all a glimpse of hell. Sorcery was no joke; and the cover story of *Ivoire Dimanche* was, in fact, about the war of true religion and good magic against sorcery and bad magic.

The visitor saw the highways and skyscrapers of Abidjan, and he thought of development and African success. But Abidjan was in Africa, and in the minds of the people the world was to be made safe in another way as well. The reassuring message in the government-controlled press was that there was light at either end of the African tunnel.

2

I TRAVEL to discover other states of mind. And if for this intellectual adventure I go to places where people live restricted lives, it is because my curiosity is still dictated in part by my colonial Trinidad background. I go to places which, however alien, connect in some way with what I already know. When my curiosity has been satisfied, when there are no more surprises, the intellectual adventure is over and I become anxious to leave.

It is a writer's curiosity rather than an ethnographer's or journalist's. So while, when I travel, I can move only according to what I find, I also live, as it were, in a novel of my own making, moving from not knowing to knowing, with person interweaving with person and incident opening out into incident. The intellectual adventure is also a human one: I can move only according to my sympathy. I don't force anything; there is no spokesman I have to see, no one I absolutely must interview. The kind of understanding I am looking for comes best through people I get to like. And in the Ivory Coast I moved in the main among expatriates, white and black. I saw the country through them and through their varied experience.

One of these expatriates was Terry Shroeder, the public affairs officer of the American embassy. He was in his late forties, and a bachelor, a slender, handsome man with the kind of melancholy that attracts and resists women. He was going to retire early from the foreign service. The Ivory Coast was his last posting but one, and he was at the very end of his time there. It was Terry who had given me the phrase about "a little bit of coffee and a little bit of cocoa." He admired the economic achievements of the Ivory Coast. But he also had a feeling for its African side.

It was Terry who at our first meeting told me that there was in the Ivory Coast a famous and very old African sage who was the president's spiritual counsellor. The sage was open to other consultation as well, and Terry would have liked me to see him. But the sage was unfortunately "hospitalized," and remained so during my time in the Ivory Coast. The name of the sage was Amadou Hampaté Bâ. He had been in his time an

ambassador, and a member of an important Unesco body; but his fame in
the Ivory Coast was spiritual, and rested on his mastery of arithmology
and other esoteric studies. Terry knew him well enough to visit him in
hospital, and he always referred to him as Mr. Hampaté Bâ ("Hampaté
not far off in sound from "Humpty"). Hampaté Bâ was a Muslim from
Mali, to the north; but he had a large place in his heart for African religion. "Islam is my father, but Africa is my mother"—this, according to
Terry, was one of Hampaté Bâ's well-known sayings. Another saying
was: "Whenever an old man dies in Africa, a library has burned down."

At our first meeting Terry also told me about someone who was doing
research among the village witch-doctors or medicine men. Some of
these men did possess knowledge of a sort. They could deal in an African
way with African neuroses; they also knew about herbs and poisons.
They were secretive about the poisons. Their knowledge of poisons
made them feared and was one of the sources of their power.

This talk of poison made me think of the Caribbean islands on the
other side of the ocean. In the old days, on the slave plantations there,
constantly replenished with "new Negroes" (as they were called) from
places like the Ivory Coast, poison had been one of the special terrors of
slaves and slave-owners. Some poisoner was always about; in the slave
underground or underworld, the hidden Africa of the plantations, someone could usually be found with a stock of poison; and a vengeful slave
could do terrible things. In Trinidad in 1794 a hundred Negroes were
poisoned on the Coblenz estate in Port of Spain, and the estate had to be
abandoned. In 1801, when the estate was bought by the emigré Baron de
Montalembert, a poisoner went to work again, and in the first month of
his proprietorship the baron lost 120 of the 140 "seasoned" Negroes he
had put in.

As much as poison, the plantation owners in the Caribbean feared
African magic. Slavery depended on obedience, on the acceptance by the
slave of the logic of his position. A persuasive magician, awakening
African instincts, could give his fellows a sense of the unreality of the
workaday world, and could incite normally docile and even loyal slaves
to rebellion. Magicians, once they were identified, were treated with
great severity. In Trinidad and Martinique they could be burned alive.

Magic and poison—in the old documents of the islands, they had
seemed like the weapons of despair; and they probably had been. Here in
the Ivory Coast they were part of a world that was still whole. The

African culture that was officially promoted, and could at times seem to be only a source of tourist motifs, was an expression of African religion. Even in the masks in the souvenir shops, even in the dances beside the swimming pool of the Forum Golf Hotel, there was a feeling of awe, a radiation of accepted magical practices. Men here knew another reality; they lived easily in a world of spirit and spirits.

And it was Terry Shroeder who introduced me to Arlette. Arlette was a black woman from Martinique. Her French, beautifully enunciated, revived all my schoolboy love of the language. She was in her late thirties or early forties, a big woman, full of friendship, generous with her time and knowledge; she was to make me understand many things about the country. She had married an Ivorian, whom she had met in Paris, and she had lived for twenty years in the Ivory Coast. She was divorced now; her former husband had gone to Gabon, the newest French African land of oil and money. Arlette worked in an arts department of the university in Abidjan. She lived by herself; she had many friends in the foreign community; I felt she feared solitude. She was an expatriate—expatriates in the Ivory Coast were black as well as white.

Martinique, France, French-speaking Africa: the chain was obvious, and at one time—when I was at school in cramped Trinidad, learning French from black men who had a high idea of a welcoming, liberating French culture—Arlette's life journey would have seemed to me romantic. But when I had thought of going to the Ivory Coast, I hadn't thought of French West Indians making the roundabout journey back. So, in addition to the connections I could make for myself, other connections were offered to me. And the Ivory Coast became different from the country I had imagined.

We met Arlette at a piano recital sponsored by the Goethe Institute, the cultural wing of the West German embassy. Terry was going partly to give support to a fellow diplomat: these cultural evenings arranged by foreign embassies could be poorly attended. The Ivorians—rich, successful, served by foreign labour—were blasé about foreigners in general; it wasn't easy to entice them, Terry said. At his own cultural evenings Terry offered dinner beforehand, and hoped that people would stay on. It didn't always work. Foreign culture was too foreign. The biggest American event in the Ivory Coast had been the recent visit of the U.S.S. *Portland*, when the Americans, using marvellous landing craft, had staged a demonstration assault on an island off the coast.

Terry said, with melancholy pride, "That impressed the Ivorian military."

Arlette lived in a government flat, in a compound full of blocks of government flats. We couldn't find her when we went to pick her up. We went on to the Goethe Institute. She was there, waiting in the garden, a big, dark-brown woman in a shiny white dress, looking a little forlorn in the lamplight and tree shadows. She was chewing; she was always nervously chewing, or sucking on a sweet, or eating something. They had cut off the water to her flat, she said. She had objected to the bill, refused to pay; and they had cut the water off. Now she was using the bathrooms of various friends. (She fought that water battle for some days; but then she paid the bill.)

The audience for the piano recital was white. The pianist that the Goethe Institute was offering to French-speaking Africa was an Alsatian with a French name. He had done the French African circuit before for the Institute, and had a local reputation. He was a tall, thin, half-smiling man in chunky black shoes, and with strong, big, white hands. When applause came, he bowed, picked his way down two shaky, detachable steps from the platform, walked briskly to the end of the hall as though he was leaving us forever, but then he waited in the shadows, walked back to the platform, up the shaky steps, and bowed again. At the end he walked back twice and played two encores.

Arlette said in French, "I had a bet with Terry that there would be only ten black faces here. I was wrong. There are only three." Africans didn't like cultural music, Arlette said. They liked only African night-club music. Even in Paris that was what African students looked for. But still, Arlette said, shaking her head to the rhythm of her French speech, and acknowledging her own restlessness during the recital, the pianist had chosen some difficult pieces, *des morceaux difficiles.*

The pianist and the German cultural counsellor stood at the door to say goodbye. The pianist was neat and silent, black-suited. The counsellor was artistically casual, with big round glasses and a full round head of long red hair. He was pleased with the success of his evening. It was expensive, he said to Terry, putting on music of that quality. The Goethe Institute in Abidjan could do this kind of thing only once a year. The pianist should have been going on to Accra in Ghana, but—and the counsellor gave a diplomatic shrug, as though we all knew about events in Ghana, and it wasn't for him to comment.

We went afterwards, Arlette and I, to Terry's house. It was a bachelor's house. The sitting room was large and formal; many of Terry's cultural evenings took place there. There were mementoes of the East, where Terry had served, and there were African masks and objects. Terry offered wine, and went to the kitchen to make scrambled eggs.

Arlette told me about the French. She loved the culture of France, she said. But she detested the manners, *les moeurs*. She meant that the French were socially rigid and petty, extraordinarily fussy about having the correct glasses, the correct cutlery, the right wines. For the *petits français*—and especially in a place like Abidjan—these things were like moral issues. And there was the French obsession with food. It was part of the French myth, but Arlette didn't admire it. How could you admire people who, when you got back from a foreign country, could only think of asking: *"Mange-t-on bien là?"* ("Is the food good there?")

Arlette said that in the Ivory Coast the French West Indians, *les antillais*, behaved like French people. They looked down on the Africans and—because they thought of themselves as civilized and French—they expected the Africans to look up to them. *"Mais ils sont déçus."* The West Indians made an error; Africans looked up to nobody; and life was as a result full of stress for some West Indians in the Ivory Coast.

So, in spite of what she had said about Africans and night-club music, Arlette separated herself both from French people and from a certain kind of French West Indian. And it was also clear that, in spite of her failed African marriage and her present solitude, there was in her some deep feeling for the Africa that followed its own ways.

At our supper of eggs and brown bread and wine, the talk turned to Amadou Hampaté Bâ, the sage who was the president's spiritual counsellor.

Arlette said, with glittering eyes, "He's a great man. One of the great men of Africa."

Terry had a spare copy of Hampaté Bâ's booklet, *Jésus Vu par un Musulman*, "Christ Seen by a Muslim." The book had been presented nineteen months before by the sage to Flora Lewis of the *New York Times* and inscribed to her in a shaky hand.

It was in this copy that, later that night, I read of the arithmological calculations which, applied to invocations and other religious formulae, proved the essential oneness of Islam and Christianity.

Hampaté Bâ described himself as "a man of dialogue," and the last chapter of his little book was about the president of the Ivory Coast. He said that he and the president often had long spiritual discussions when the president's state duties permitted. He had asked the president one day for some story, some legend acquired perhaps from an African elder, that might serve as a parable of brotherly love. And the president had told Hampaté Bâ this story.

"There was a captive at the royal court of Yamoussoukro who looked after the education of the children. He liked me a great deal, and he gave me a lot of advice, advice necessary to someone like myself, who was being trained to be a chief. But I should say, before going any further, that among the Baoulé people 'captivity' was more a word than a fact. The fact that a man was a slave didn't take away from him his value as a human being."

It was from this slave or captive that the president, as a boy, got a story he never forgot. This was the story. Once upon a time there was a peasant. One year he had a good harvest and he took his crop to market. He sold well, and afterwards he wandered about the market. On a merchant's stall there was a beautiful knife. The peasant fell in love with it and bought it. The peasant cherished his knife. He made a sheath for it, and encrusted the sheath with pearls and shells. One day, when he was pruning a tree, he cut his finger with the knife. In his pain he threw the knife to the ground and cursed it. But then he picked the knife up, wiped off the blood, and put the knife back in the sheath that hung at his side. That was all the story. Why didn't the peasant throw away the ungrateful and wicked knife? It was because of love. The peasant loved his knife. That was the moral.

This was the story the captive at the royal court of Yamoussoukro told the boy who was to be chief. This was the story the president passed on to Hampaté Bâ, the sage, and Hampaté Bâ printed in his book.

Slavery, "captivity"—so it was an African institution. And, like poison, like sorcery, it continued. But what was the point of the abrupt little story? How could love for a knife translate into brotherly love? The story was in fact a parable—from an old president, an old chief—about power and reconciliation. Power was the prerogative of the chief; but the good chief, who followed the old ways, also sought reconciliation. Wicked men had been cast aside; but they had once been good and useful and loved; the chief would remember that, and he would forgive.

The benevolent ruler, the ruler seeking the sympathy of the ruled:

presented in this way, as an African ideal, the chief became attractive, affecting. I began to enter a little into the African world Arlette saw.

3

TERRY'S assistant was going to arrange my trip to Yamoussoukro. Arlette was going to put me in touch with an Ivorian at the Institute of Ethno-sociology at the university who had inaugurated a controversial course in "Drummologie," the science of talking drums. And I had been asking around for a guide to Kilometre 17, where the Evil Spirit had recently been at work, causing a schoolteacher's house to blaze mysteriously from time to time.

These projects began to mature and come together. My days became full and varied. After the random impressions and semi-official meetings and courtesies of the first days, I began to discover themes and people. I began to live my little novel.

Philip—the English expatriate who, with his Guyanese wife, had taken me on the expatriate Sunday excursion to the beach at Grand-Bassam—left a note at my hotel one day. He had found a young Ivorian who would be willing to take me to Kilometre 17 and generally introduce me to African magic. The young man had done some guiding of this sort before, helping a colleague of Philip's with Muslim *marabout* magicians. He was now unemployed—jobs were getting hard to find in the Ivory Coast, even for an Ivorian.

The next morning we all three—Philip leaving his office to act as go-between—met in a grubby little café in the centre of Abidjan.

The young man was well-made, strong, slender and firm at the waist. He had a finely modelled African face, every feature definite, and his skin was very black, a uniform colour, without blotch or tone. He was carefully dressed; his shirt was ironed and clean. I saw him only in this physical way. I couldn't tell whether in his intense eyes there was intelligence, vapidity, a wish to please, or a latent viciousness. His name was Djédjé. He was of the Bété tribe, the second tribe in the Ivory Coast after the Baoulé, to which the president belonged.

Much of our time was spent talking about money, assessing all the expenses that might come up during a visit to the house at Kilometre 17. There would be the taxi—Djédjé was going to arrange that: he knew somebody who would be cheaper than a hotel taxi. There would have to be something for the village chief; something for tips; and there would be Djédjé's fee—he was talking of going to the village beforehand to prepare people.

Djédjé's manner, as he leaned over the coffee cups on the plastic-topped table, was conspiratorial. But it was hard to get him to give a precise figure for anything, even his own fee. An absentness, a troubled lethargy, seemed to come over him when an item was being costed. Philip pressed him gently, never allowing a silence to last too long. It was necessary to fix a limit now, Philip said to me in English. Otherwise, when the time came to pay, Djédjé might grow "wild" and ask for any amount. It seemed to be settled at the end that the overall price would be between twenty and thirty thousand local francs, thirty-five and fifty pounds. Djédjé was going to telephone me the next day with the final figure, after he had talked with the chief and the taxi-driver.

Djédjé said he was a believer. He meant he believed in the spirits and in the power of magicians; and he said he had agreed to be my guide because he wanted me to be a believer too.

I asked whether there would be any trouble because I was a foreigner. He said no; then he said yes. I was a Hindu, wasn't I? Hindus had a great reputation as magicians, and a *féticheur* might see me as a rival and try to hide things from me. It would be easier for a European, easier for someone like Philip, though Philip and I were the same colour.

This last was an extraordinary thing to say; it was far from being true. But it was true for Djédjé. He still had the tribal eye: people who were not Africans were simply people of another colour.

I asked him to write out his full name for me, and he wrote his family name first, his French Christian name last. When I remarked on the French name, he frowned and made a small, brushing-away gesture with his writing hand. It wasn't important, he said; it was a name he used only in documents.

He telephoned in a message to the hotel desk the next day. *"Le rendez-vous du km 17 est OK."* And when he came to the hotel he told me that the taxi-driver had fixed the fare at eighteen thousand francs. I also understood him to say—but his language here was vague, difficult—that a further two thousand would be needed as tips. The taxi-driver was the brother of the village chief, he said. And the chief would need a bottle of whisky: alcohol had "a special value" for Africans.

He seemed to have kept the price within the limit we had agreed, and I took him to the bar to seal our bargain.

In the dark, "intimate" hotel bar—rosewood, metal-framed furniture, and buttoned black PVC upholstery—he was as much at ease, or as indifferent to his surroundings, as he had been in the café in the town. Sipping his beer, with the leisure and pauses with which he had drunk coffee in the café, he became conspiratorial again, leaning forward, talking softly, holding me with his intense eyes.

The development of the country had taken a wrong turn, he said. It had begun from the top. What did he mean by that? Not answering my question, but going on to his own concerns, he said that the university was "saturated"; and there was only one university; and there were stringent rules for entry. And now there was a lot of unemployment. People came to Abidjan and picked up Western ways and for them that was a misfortune. This was another idea. But why was it a misfortune? He lowered his voice, bent closer to me, and said—as though he expected me to understand the full import of what he was saying—that he himself had forgotten how to dance, to do the dances of his tribe, his *ethnie*. In his village he had danced, but in Abidjan he couldn't do the dances.

I asked about his family. He said he had nine sisters and eight brothers. His father was a *planteur*, one of the peasant farmers who had created the wealth of the Ivory Coast, and he had two or three wives. All the children were now in Abidjan. Djédjé himself lived in the house of an uncle, his father's brother. The uncle, a mechanic, had two wives and thirteen children.

I would have liked to hear more of Djédjé's family life, but he wanted to talk about magic. There were Ivorians in Abidjan, he said, who dressed in the modern way and spoke correct French with a French accent. They had lost touch with their *ethnies*, and they said they no longer believed in the African gods. But these people didn't want to go back to the villages because they were afraid of the sorcerers. In their hearts these French Africans believed.

I didn't feel I was understanding all that Djédjé said, and it wasn't a matter of language alone. Perhaps, forgetting his innocence, and misled by his opening statement that the country had taken a wrong turn, I had been looking in his conversation for something that wasn't there: an attitude, a thought-out position. Perhaps—uneducated, unemployed, a villager in Abidjan—he was genuinely confused by the development of the country "from the top." Equally, he might only have been trying to get me more interested in the magic to which he had been appointed my guide.

4

ONE OF THE NAMES I had been given before coming out to the Ivory Coast was that of Georges Niangoran-Bouah. The note on him said: "Anthropologist. Contactable at the Institut d'Ethnosociologie at the university. He's around fifty-five, world specialist on 'Drummologie,' form of communication of tribal drums. Knows African art well, has a fantastic collection of Ashanti weights."

He sounded quite a figure. And, as often happens when, as a traveller, I am given the names of important local people, I was shy of getting in touch. But I mentioned his name to various people, and I found out fairly soon that Mr. Niangoran-Bouah was academically controversial, that if he was a world expert on Drummologie it was because he had started the subject and had in fact invented the word. Drummologie was apparently as controversial a university course as the one on African philosophy. Some people doubted whether either Drummologie or African philosophy existed.

Arlette, who worked at the university, knew both Niangoran-Bouah and his secretary. The secretary was a fellow *antillaise*, a French West Indian. This lady telephoned me one morning. She had a pecking, fluting voice, and her French—unlike Arlette's—was not easy for me to follow, especially on the telephone. Her name was Andrée, and I understood her to say that her *patron*, Mr. Niangoran-Bouah, was still lecturing in the United States, but that I should come to the university to get Mr. Niangoran-Bouah's Drummologie book, fresh copies of which had arrived at the office that morning.

The campus was big. Some workmen sitting on the ground below a tree—the crab-grassed ground scuffed down to the roots of the young tree—pointed out the unexpectedly modest, and rather weathered, brick building which was the Institute of Ethnosociology. And it was quite exciting to see, inside, in a corridor hung with name-boards, the little board with the name BOUAH; to enter the little office, and to see the big posters for the course on Drummologie, and another poster with photographs of Ashanti gold-weights.

Andrée, the West Indian secretary, Arlette's friend, was a brown woman of more than forty. She was welcoming, but she wasn't like Arlette. She didn't have the vivacity, the size or the softness. Andrée was thinnish, with glasses over strained, big eyes. Her frizzy hair was pulled back tight and done in a bun. She wore a bright blue cardigan and a heavy plaid skirt: the office was air-conditioned. Her style of dress—respectable French, respectable West Indian—proclaimed her as not African. So did the knitting in her bag. She might have knitted the blue cardigan herself. She said—and she clearly had nothing to do in the office that morning—that she liked to keep her hands busy.

Her French was harder for me now than it had been on the telephone. Face to face, she talked faster, in a higher voice, making little rills of sound. I missed half of what she said, and my own poor French, with nothing in the other person's speech to lean on, became worse.

Her desk, with the knitting, was next to the window. She pointed to the big desk of the absent *patron*, next to the corridor wall, and the broad plastic-backed swivel chair behind the desk, and she made me feel the great vacancy in the little room.

But she had the *patron*'s books. She undid a brown paper parcel and gave me a copy of a large-format paperback, *Introduction à la Drummologie*. On the cover there was a photograph of Mr. Niangoran-Bouah seated at an open-air drumming and singing ceremony of some sort (with microphones). He was a big man, chieftain-like, draped in African cotton, and he was listening with half-closed eyes to the drums. He acquired a reality for me. He became more than his name and his oddly named subject; his desk became more personal. The little bronze pieces on his desk were indeed things of beauty, as were the gold-weights in the poster on the wall.

A recurring design in those weights—an ideogram or a unit of measure—was the swastika, or something close to it. I asked Andrée whether the weights might have had an Indian origin. I didn't make myself clear. She said only that the weights were very, very old. And that was what the poster said: these objects were old, African, proof of African civilization. To offer proof of African civilization: that, I began to feel, was the cause of the man whose secretary Andrée was.

Andrée, her morning's work done, put her knitting in her bag and locked up the office. She said she would walk with me to where I could get a taxi. As we walked among the students she said, à propos of nothing, that I should take a Nivaquine tablet every day. It was the best protection against malaria. This was something I had thought about doing but not done. She said she would come with me in the taxi to a pharmacy she knew. We went to the pharmacy at the edge of the campus; and it was to Andrée rather than to me that the European or Lebanese pharmacist gave instructions about the Nivaquine.

It was now nearly noon, lunch time. I had taken Andrée far from her office. But she didn't mind. She wanted the company; and I was Arlette's friend. She said she knew a restaurant in the centre.

As we passed the blocks of flats and came out into the main corniche road, Andrée pointed vaguely and said, "My mother lives there. She reads cards."

I pretended not to hear.

"My mother's a widow," Andrée said. "She reads cards. You should understand. You are a Hindu."

"Hindus read horoscopes."

She said, and her speech, clear and precise for the first time, sounded like something from a language lesson: *"Ma . . . mère . . . lit . . . les . . . cartes."* ("My mother reads cards.")

I said, allowing the taxi to take us further away from where Andrée's mother read cards, "It's a good gift. A good profession."

Andrée said sharply, "My mother's a trained nurse."

I wondered how Andrée and her mother, both from the island of Guadeloupe in the far-off West Indies, had found themselves in the Ivory Coast. I said, "Do you live with your mother?" Her voice went high and fluting. She said no. That was how Africans lived, all together. French people, and she meant people like herself, lived independently. I asked how she had come to the Ivory Coast. She said she had met an Ivorian in Paris, and they had married. The marriage had broken up when they came to live in the Ivory Coast.

The restaurant she directed the taxi to in the centre of the town was a big, barn-like building. The doors were open and there were painted menu-boards outside. "It's clean," Andrée said, and when we went in— there was as yet no crowd—she said again, "Isn't it clean?" And it was all right, and there was even a Lebanese in a tie eating fast at one of the tables, head down, jacket on the back of his chair, like a man with a business appointment to keep. But the smell of braised meat and other foods was so high, the air so smoked and oily, even with the doors open, I didn't want to stay. Andrée was disappointed.

We took a taxi to a hotel. It was the only place I knew. It was in a more humid part of town, in a commercial street lined with round-leaved tropical almond trees. There were Lebanese cloth shops, shoe-shine boys, and ragged Africans, most likely foreigners, sitting or lounging on the broken pavement in a smell of sweat. One African, white-capped and in a Muslim gown, was doing his midday prayer, kneeling and bending forward in a private stupor.

The hotel, one of a chain, was of the second rank, a considered blend of flash and shoddiness. But it excited Andrée. She said, "Expensive," and her manner improved to match her idea of the place. She gave the taxi-driver a tip on her own account, a fifty-franc piece. And as soon as we were seated in the dining room—next to the glass wall, with a view of the highway below, the black creek, the ships at the far side—she became exacting and French with the uniformed Ivorian waiter, asking precise questions about the menu, taking her time.

The waiter didn't like it. He was used to dealing with European couples, businessmen (there were a few Japanese), solitaries, people grateful for small mercies in unlikely places. Andrée ignored the waiter's exaggerated frowns. She chose; she gave her order. I asked for an omelette. Andrée was abashed. She said what she had chosen was too expensive, and she insisted—the waiter standing by—on changing. She settled for the *jambon* with *frites*.

She was now in a jumpy state, and as soon as the waiter went away she began to talk very fast. She said that life was hard for her. She was trapped in the Ivory Coast, and had no means of returning home—and she meant France, Guadeloupe in the West Indies, left behind many years before, now too far away in every sense. She earned ninety thousand francs a month at the university, £150; and she had been lucky, six years before, to get the job. Before that, she had taught at an infants' school. "Not nice," she said.

Her marriage to the Ivorian she had met in Paris ended four years after she had come to the Ivory Coast. Her husband's family had broken the marriage up, she said. *Françaises*, Frenchwomen like herself, who married Ivorians should stay in France, she said. In the Ivory Coast the Ivorian families broke the marriages up.

The boy brought the food. He looked pleased with himself. He was carrying six dishes on both arms, as though demonstrating French restaurant style to Andrée, who had been so French with him. She didn't return his smile. She was looking hard and doubtfully at what he was doing. And then—as though doomed by Andrée's stare to fulfil *petit français* ideas about African clumsiness—he dropped one of the six plates. It wasn't one of ours. When, defeated and downcast, he came back to clean up the mess on the carpet, Andrée was eating the *jambon* and *frites* daintily. She left one piece of *jambon* on one side of her plate while she dealt with the other, and it seemed as though she wasn't going to touch the piece of *jambon* she had put to one side. But at the end it had all gone—*frites, jambon,* jelly.

She talked again about her life in the Ivory Coast. She didn't take taxis often, she said; they were too expensive. So altogether I was giving her a treat, and I decided to make it as good a treat as the restaurant allowed.

I asked whether she would like cheese. Camembert, gruyère, she asked? I said yes. She said she loved camembert. Didn't she like *chèvre*? Yes, but camembert was the delicacy; and it was something else that was expensive.

She called the boy over, and in her firm way—showing him no compassion after his accident, ignoring and thereby killing the half-surliness with which he tried to fight back—she asked whether they had a variety of cheeses, a choice, a *plateau*. The boy said yes. He began to explain. She cut him short; she ordered him to bring the cheese board. He was recognizing her authority now; and when he brought the board she became very demure, as if rewarding his deference. She took just two little pieces of camembert, though for her *plateau* she could have had four times the quantity.

She said the camembert was good. It wasn't, really. I pressed her to have some dessert. She yielded; she called the boy and asked him to bring the tray with the desserts. She hadn't been abroad, she said, going neatly, without hurry, at the pallid slice of apple tart she had chosen. She hadn't even been to the neighbouring countries, Ghana, Liberia, Guinea. She didn't have the money to travel.

When the bill came she made a delicate attempt at paying, taking out her purse and opening it as though it contained a secret. I made her put the purse away. And then—French graces, West Indian mulatto graces, coming to her after the hotel parody of a French bourgeois lunch—she said she would like to visit me one day in my own country.

We took a taxi back. Andrée said she wanted to get off at the church. But the church, on this occasion at least, was only a marker. Andrée's widowed mother, who read cards, lived near the church, and lived alone, as a Frenchwoman should.

Such solitude, in this bright African light, so like the light of Caribbean afternoons. But how far away home must have seemed to Andrée, who, after Guadeloupe and Paris, now had only the Ivory Coast!

The highway curved on beside the lagoon, through a semi-diplomatic development zone, to the Forum Golf Hotel, opposite the half-developed golf course, where a few old, thick-trunked baobabs had been allowed to remain, reminders of tropical forest. In the garden of the hotel, around the swimming pool, with its artificial rocks, its hollow, plastic elephants, and its water chute, children played and the topless, breastless women sunbathed. African guards in brown uniforms sat at various security points. The white sand of what looked like a beach had been artificially mounded up: the sand rested on a concrete base, which showed two or three feet high at the water's edge. It was against this concrete that the tainted lagoon rocked. On this tainted water there grew a small, green, cabbage-like plant, with a root like a thin beard; and these water plants came together in sheltered places, in the lee of boats, or against sections of the concrete wall, to form little rocking carpets of living green.

I found, in *Introduction à la Drummologie*, that Andrée was given a special mention by Mr. Niangoran-Bouah: she was the conscientious *collaboratrice* of a difficult and obstinate *patron*. That made him sound attractive. And reading beyond the acknowledgements, I discovered that Mr. Niangoran-Bouah had indeed made up the word "drummologie." Other words had been thought of—*tamtamologie, tamtalogie, tambourinologie, tambourologie, tambologie, attangbanologie*. But these words had been rejected because they seemed to stress the art of drum-beating rather than the study of the "talking drum" as a record of tribal history and tradition. The talking drum mimicked, and preserved, the actual words of old chants: these chants were documents of the African past. As much as the Ashanti weights, with their elements of art and mathematics, true knowledge of the talking drum gave to Africa the old civilization which Europeans and colonialists said didn't exist. This was Mr. Niangoran-Bouah's cause. This was the cause Andrée, from Guadeloupe and France, served.

I TOLD ARLETTE, when we next met, that I had had great trouble with Andrée's French. Arlette said she had worried about that. Andrée's speech was difficult. Andrée was a little nervous, *un peu nerveuse*. But she was marvellous with her hands. She knitted and made tapestries. Her mother was a very good *voyante*. She read cards and always said interesting things.

Arlette said that Andrée had married again in the Ivory Coast, after the break-up of her first marriage. Her second husband had gone mad. That had had an effect on Andrée's health, and in fact Andrée's mother, a former nurse, had come out to the Ivory Coast to look after Andrée. They didn't live together. But they ate together: every day Andrée had lunch and supper with her mother.

And it was only an hour or so later—this information about Andrée followed by other talk—that Arlette told me that Andrée's second husband had gone mad when he was a political prisoner. He had been badly beaten.

We were walking—Terry Shroeder with us—in the Hotel Ivoire. The Ivoire was more than a hotel. With its bars, restaurants, shops, an area for pin-ball machines, a bowling alley, a skating rink (temporarily defrosted and rejigged into a football field), the Ivoire was the extravagant, air-conditioned fairground of Abidjan. It was a place that people came of an evening to look at and walk in, down the long corridors, and the air-conditioning was so good that many people came dressed against the cold.

Outside, in the warm, along the hotel drive, chasing cars as they arrived, there were prostitutes. So Arlette told me. (I had missed them; nobody had chased our car.) They were village girls, these prostitutes. More interesting—because it was practised as a sport, rather than out of real need—was student prostitution. Girls at the university didn't sleep with boys at the university. They slept with men in the government, men who had big jobs and could make gifts suitable to a girl who was at the university. It was left to the Abidjan schoolgirls, the *lycéennes*, to sleep with the poor *étudiants*; and since an *étudiant* had only his grant, a *lycéenne* might have an arrangement with two or three *étudiants* at a time, sleeping with each once or twice a week, and collecting her accumulated gratuities at the end of the month.

This kind of behaviour was acceptable because Africans believed in independence in relationships, Arlette said. They didn't look for or expect sexual fidelity. Infidelity as a cause for divorce would be considered frivolous. In a marriage the most important relationship was the relationship between the families. And that was why West Indian women—like Andrée, and like Arlette herself—who married Ivorian men found themselves in trouble when they got to the Ivory Coast. The men simply said goodbye.

Antillaises could be deceived in Paris. They could be dazzled by a man who said he came of a chief's family and had so many slaves and servants—*tant d'esclaves, tant de domestiques*—at home. West Indian women, with their own idea of love, could find in an African's declaration of love and even his offer of marriage things the man never intended. A West Indian woman in the Ivory Coast was without tribe or family; her African husband could, without guilt, say goodbye. If an Ivorian brought home a foreign wife his family chose an African wife for him and sent her to the house. If the African wife wasn't accepted, the man's family laid a curse on the man. And the man was so terrified of the curse (so terrified, too, of poison) that he usually obeyed.

This was Arlette's story. To live in Africa, she said, was to have all one's ideas and values questioned. And it was good, she added, for that to happen. So, as I had noticed before with Arlette, what seemed like criticism of Africa turned out not to be criticism at all. Arlette, in her own mind, had been re-educated and remade by Africa. Her solitude, as an expatriate, was different from Andrée's.

5

GIL SHERMAN, Terry Shroeder's assistant, was arranging my trip to Yamoussoukro; and Gil wrote one day that he had found just the man to take me there. The man was Ibrahim Keita. He was the son of a political associate of the president's in colonial times, and he was close to the president. The president wanted to see people playing golf in the Ivory Coast: Ibrahim Keita devoted himself to that cause. He was a keen player and was head of the Golf Federation. He was in charge of the famous golf course at Yamoussoukro. It was also said that he had been entrusted by the president with the general development of Yamoussoukro. He was just the man to show me round. He regularly drove up to Yamoussoukro in his very big and fast Mercedes.

But when I met Ibrahim Keita at Gil Sherman's, he didn't seem to know that he was to take me to Yamoussoukro. He said nothing about it and in fact hardly spoke. French, rather than English, was his international language. He was a big, handsome man of perhaps forty, athletic (and that evening rather tired) from the golf; in colour and features he was a little like Sidney Poitier. His wife, Eileen, was equally reserved that evening. Ibrahim Keita was Muslim; and it is possible that Eileen's reserve was a form of Muslim-African modesty. She was not African, in the strict sense of the word. She had been born in Ghana, but was of West Indian origin, with the family name of Busby: mulatto, middle-class, English-speaking, from the island of Barbados.

Her brother was with her. He too had been born in Ghana, but now he lived in London. He was interested in journalism and African publishing, and was in the Ivory Coast on a short business trip. He was an attractive, bearded brown man, in his thirties. His manner was London and middle-class West Indian; he was bright and good-humoured and open. And it was with him that I talked for much of the evening.

His family story was moving. It was in 1929 that his Barbadian father, after qualifying as a doctor in England, had decided to go and work in Africa. He would have been one of the earliest black professional men from the British West Indies. To someone like that in the 1920s every personal step ahead would have made sharper the feeling of racial deprivation. Slavery had been abolished in the British Empire in 1834; but in the British colonies of the West Indies—neglected, no longer of value—the racial attitudes of both black and white had hardly changed since then. A black professional man in the 1920s would have felt alone, even in his own community.

Dr. Busby did what a number of black men like himself talked about but few actually did: he decided to go back to Africa, to serve Africa, though Africa itself was a colony. He went to the Gold Coast—British-ruled, next door to the French-ruled Ivory Coast—and he worked there until he died.

The Gold Coast became independent Ghana in 1957. Nkrumah ruled, and fell. Now, twenty-five years after its independence, the state of Ghana was in ruins. And Dr. Busby's children lived out of the country.

I asked the young man, the doctor's son, what he thought of events in Ghana. He gave an answer that wasn't an answer. He said it was something the country had to go through. But in 1957—when the Ivory Coast had very little—Ghana was rich, with educated people, and institutions. How had that been squandered? Was it because of Nkrumah—the racialist-socialist ideology, the megalomania, the waste?

The illogicality of the reply surprised me. Nkrumah was a man ahead of his time, young Busby said. *Ahead?* Busby said, "Have you read Nkrumah's books? You should read his books." So it was in the words rather than the deeds that the greatness of the man was to be found? Nkrumah, Busby said, had a continental African vision. He was infinitely more than a tribal leader. That continental vision came out in his books, which continued to be revolutionary; and that was why he had built so extravagantly after independence, bankrupting the country. And Nkrumah had done more than anyone for the dignity of black men all over the world. "Ask any black American," Busby said.

Gil Sherman was a black American. But he, perhaps diplomatically, didn't hear (he was talking to Ibrahim Keita), and I didn't ask him.

The dignity of the black man—I wanted to pursue that with Busby. Wasn't that an antiquated idea now? Africa was independent, the black islands of the Caribbean were independent. Weren't there other things for black men to work for?

Busby said, "Old ideas might turn out to be the best ideas."

He was a man of faith. He had only the consistency of his racial passion. He was loyal to his father's cause; and after fifty years—though the world had changed—this cause had become like religion. Whatever were the disasters now, black Africa would win through. The world, he said, would still turn to Africa. Illiteracy was soon going to be a problem in England and other Western countries: the world would yet find virtue in African ways. He told an African story, which was like a fable, about a farming community and a boating community who despised one another but, through some ritualized arrangement that preserved the pride of both, yet managed to live together. This was the kind of solution Africa could offer the world.

He lived in England. As a journalist and publisher, he needed England as a base. But this fact, large as it was, played no part in his view of things. I asked him what he wanted for Africa. He said he wanted development. But not the development of the Ivory Coast: he looked for a development which permitted Africans to keep their own soul. He couldn't be more precise. Probably some political objection to capitalism prevented him from seeing how separate French and African ideas were in the Ivory Coast; probably he didn't know how whole the world of Africa still was. Probably, too, the family cause had with him turned to an impossible, religious idea of a pure African way.

He talked to Ibrahim Keita. It was about my trip to Yamoussoukro. And—through my own conversation with somebody else—I heard Keita say (now quite dazed with his golf fatigue) that when you were used to flying a 707 you couldn't take a passenger in a Cessna. It was the first indication I had had that Keita knew about our projected trip to Yamoussoukro. And the message that was coming over was that Keita couldn't take me. There was a problem about the tyres of the Mercedes, and there was apparently no question of a ride with him in the equivalent of a Cessna.

It was a pity about the tyres, Busby said, indirectly giving me the bad news. Ibrahim was a terrific driver; in the Mercedes he could do the 150 miles in two hours. But the replacement tyres Ibrahim had got from Nigeria were not good. Special tyres were needed for a Mercedes of that class, and Ibrahim had had to send to Germany for them.

They left—Ibrahim Keita, Eileen, and her brother. Gil Sherman said he would drive me himself to Yamoussoukro. And during what remained of the evening I heard more about the Mercedes and what nice people the Keitas were.

Andrée, Arlette, young Busby—Africa had called them all, and each had his own Africa. Busby's inherited cause was racial redemption. He needed his mystical faith in Africa. But it was a private cause, from another continent, another past, another way of looking and feeling. A man like Djédjé—my guide to the mysterious blazing house at Kilometre 17—still knew only about the gods and the tribes. Racially, Djédjé was an innocent.

6

THE SEVENTEENTH kilometre was on the auto-route to Yamoussoukro. It lay in the soft, ragged countryside beyond the "popular" African area of Adjamé, beyond the industrial zone. The taxi-driver was, according to Djédjé, the brother of the village chief we were going to see. And, in the half-country beyond the town proper, we stopped at a liquor shop to buy the bottle of whisky which, according to Djédjé, we would have to give the chief.

The shop was a single, rough room. It was basic, even chaste: a few shelves, a few bottles of a particular brand (like samples) on each shelf, a price-tag pinned to each shelf. The shopkeeper, a young man, sat indifferent and cool at a table that was bare except for a shallow, neat pile of old sheets of *Fraternité Matin*. We didn't buy whisky. Djédjé chose a bottle of gin for 3,100 francs, between five and six pounds. The shopkeeper wrapped the bottle in a sheet of *Fraternité Matin*, and Djédjé took the bottle, very carefully.

The land was soft, and the earth seemed stoneless. Trees were tall and scattered, and skeletal—coconuts and palms and the thick-trunked, stubby-branched baobabs. They didn't make a low line of vegetation on the horizon; the eye found only these separate, skeletal, vertical forms.

We turned off the auto-route into a red, unpaved lane, with green bush on either side. It looked as though we had at last got to pure countryside, but orange-coloured Abidjan taxis were bumping along the lane. And soon we passed metal sheds where bananas were stored. Kilometre 17 was not strictly a village; it was a settlement on the edge of Abidjan. There were no huts; there were only concrete houses. The road, now apparently following an old track, narrowed and twisted between mounds of garbage. But always there were the taxis.

We drove through a banana plantation: the trees in rows, deep drainage canals between the plots of black earth, a protective blue plastic sack over each bunch of growing fruit, the blue a violent, unnatural colour. On other plots, where the trees had borne their fruit and had been cut down to brown stumps, new suckers were growing out of the soft banana trash: a glimpse of the careful agriculture which had made the Ivory Coast rich.

The village we at last came out into had a wide, unpaved main street. The houses, one-storeyed, were of concrete, in bleached and dusty Mediterranean colours. There were many children about, kicking up dust. We stopped in the main street. We got out of the car, entered a narrow passageway between two concrete houses—a sudden sense, after the half-bush, of a town slum—and went into a room from the back. We were in the house of the chief, in his reception room.

Near the window overlooking the street was a set of bulky, plastic-covered, upholstered armchairs. The pea-green walls, grimed and shiny from leaning and touching, were hung, apparently at random, with photographs in passe-partout frames. There was a tall bookcase with open shelves: Christian books. The chief was a religious man, not a *pasteur*, but an *évangéliste*.

He came in from another room, tall, middle-aged, with gold-rimmed glasses, a big gold digital wristwatch, rubber sandals, and a big white surgical dressing on a damaged ankle. He wore a patterned chocolate-brown cloth that killed his colour, just as his colour made the cloth look drab and dirty: it was the African taste in fabrics.

Djédjé, grave, his face closed, was carrying the bottle of gin wrapped in the newspaper. The chief's eyes settled on it for a moment and then he didn't look at it; and when we sat on the chairs near the window Djédjé put the bottle behind him on his chair.

People in the street were shouting in through the open window, which was hinged at the top. From time to time, while he talked to us, the chief broke off and shouted to the children, chattering inquisitive faces pushed up between hinged window and window sill, to get away.

People, adults, men, came in through the back door and stood about, near a table strewn with newspapers and various things. Some of the men who came in gave the chief money and he, appearing to pay no attention, held the notes vertically in the closed palm of his left hand. He gestured with this moneyed hand while he talked. From time to time, when he opened his legs, to pat his cloth down between his legs, he showed his dark-blue shorts.

He was clearly pleased with the fame that had come to the village with the affair of the blazing house. But he said that he himself wasn't a believer. He meant he didn't believe in the power of sorcery, being a Christian and an evangelist. (On the wall above his chair there was a photograph of him in a suit receiving a diploma or certificate when he had been made an evangelist.) There had never been any trouble in the village, he said, no spiritual or magical manifestation, no sign of the Evil Spirit. But then this thing had begun to happen in the compound of the school. The house of one of the teachers, Mr. Ariko, had begun to catch fire. And that was an undoubted manifestation.

Of course the matter had been brought to his attention and he, as village chief, had made investigations. He discovered that Mr. Ariko had two wives. Mr. Ariko had not long before given money to both wives—forty thousand francs to each, about £70. But the second wife thought she had been given less than the first wife. That was what the chief had found out, and the case at that stage had seemed perfectly straightforward: the second wife, or the Evil Spirit within her, had "provoked" the fires. It was a simple enough matter, and there were ways of dealing with it.

There was a prophet in Bingerville, the old French colonial settlement not far from Abidjan. The prophet was quite well known and had a little sect of his own. He was consulted, and he prepared a white powder, which he gave to the chief. The powder was to be placed on the feet of the second, disaffected wife; it was guaranteed to destroy whatever magical powers she had been invested with by the Evil Spirit.

This was done. The second wife became ordinary again. But the fires continued in Mr. Ariko's house. The problem was extraordinary. It began to drive everyone to distraction. Muslim *marabouts* and other magicians were brought in to try their hand. The tormented Mr. Ariko was spending a lot of money. Sacrifices were made. But nothing happened. Then an evangelist of the Celestial Christian sect offered his services. The Celestial Christians were a new group, from Ghana; they had been in the Ivory Coast for only three years and were anxious to make their mark. The chief decided to let the Celestial Christian evangelist try.

The evangelist—who had a pretty shrewd idea of what was going on—watched the house. He saw that during the night a young girl, physically invisible, was moving freely in and out of the house. It was that girl, and no one else, who was doing the mischief. In the morning the Celestial Christian evangelist assembled all the young girls from the school compound. He went straight to the young girl who had made herself invisible during the night: she was the daughter of the second, disaffected wife. She confessed, and her story could scarcely be believed: the gift of sorcery had been passed on to her by her mother, before her mother's own powers had been destroyed by the prophet's white powder.

The Evil Spirit had been especially devious at Kilometre 17. It was that passing on of the sorcerer's gift that had baffled everybody. And that was why the case had caught the public imagination.

Powder had been put on the girl's feet, and she and her mother had been packed off to the mother's village. The other wife, out of simple prudence, had also been sent back to her village. Since then, the chief said, there had been no trouble at all.

The chief said reflectively, clutching the banknotes: "I tell you that there had been no trouble in the village before this business. But I think I should tell you that in this area we do in fact have some well known *génies*." Djinns, spirits. "Did you notice that very sharp bend in the road? Near the banana plantation. There are some *génies* at that corner. Very small hens." He made a little gesture with both hands. "Not chickens, but very small hens. If a driver sees them he is bound to have an accident."

I wondered about the wife and the daughter who had been sent back to the village. Would they remain sorcerers? It was possible, the chief said. And Djédjé, always more grave than the chief, said that in the village—far from good prophets and Celestial Christians—the power of the white powder could be annulled, *annulé*. How did people become sorcerers? The terrible gift could be passed on to them when they were children. It could be passed on to anyone; there was no question of personal wickedness.

Djédjé said, "Without civilization, everyone would be a sorcerer."

It was his vision of chaos, a world without reason or rules. I thought I understood that. But then I wasn't sure I knew what Djédjé meant by civilization. When we had last met he had spoken against "development from the top." He pined for village ways, the dances of his *ethnie*; he believed in fetishes. Was civilization the sum of those old, true things: an organized society, worshipping correctly, having access to the magic that protected it from arbitrary evil? Or was Djédjé saying something simpler? Was he, in the presence of the chief, a government official, repeating the government's case for "development"?

It was time for the chief to get his bottle of gin. He took the newspaper-wrapped bottle and, casually, half unwrapped it to check the label. His sour, care-burdened face momentarily looked fulfilled; and then, making purely social conversation, as if offering us a little extra in return for our gift, he grumbled for a bit about the difficulties of getting labour for his fields. People preferred to work for white men, foreigners from the big companies, who of course could afford to pay more.

On the table at the other end of the room was the copy of *Fraternité Matin* with the story about the burning house. Djédjé asked for the newspaper; the chief graciously gave it. And as we drove on in the taxi to the house itself—the chief had cleared our visit, and one of the young men who had come to the room was keeping us company—Djédjé read the newspaper story, ceaselessly fingering the paper, as though the type was raised.

He shook his head. He gave a short, wise laugh. He said, "The Celestial Christians are certainly making publicity with their success."

The schoolteacher's house was one of a cluster of little low concrete houses, all ochre-coloured and flat to the ground. The settlement—so ordinary, though so famous—was still a living place. But in the middle of its midday life there was mystery. The door of the schoolmaster's house was open; the front room was apparently empty. Outside the open door, and set firmly in the earth, was a wooden cross, about three feet high, with the metal crucifix of the Celestial Christians.

Each house in the settlement had its own open cooking shed at the back. The soft red earth between the sheds and houses had been swept and showed rake marks. Wood fires between stones burned below aluminum pots. One girl was sweeping up wet, nasty-looking rubbish with a broom made from the ribs of long coconut leaves. A few feet away a woman was using a pestle to grind aubergines in a little bowl set on the ground; and there was a neat child's turd near by.

There were little children everywhere. Some were rolling about playfully on a purple-patterned grass mat. Djédjé, translating what our official guide said, told me they were the children of the teacher. But the guide was wrong, or Djédjé had misunderstood him. The teacher's child was a melancholy little fellow, sitting alone and still, like a little old man, beside a cooking fire. Tears had stained his dusty face; he had fresh tears in his eyes. Sorcery was no joke; it had come here as a family disaster. The boy was being looked after by the sister of the teacher, now that the teacher's wives had been sent back to their villages. The sister, squatting beside her fire, was in a green African dress. It was only when she stood up I saw that she herself was very young.

The land rose up sharply at the back of the cooking sheds. It was planted with banana trees and other trees. Scattered there, like rubbish, were some of the partly burnt things from the teacher's house, scorched clothes, scorched furniture. Disappointing to me—I had expected evidence of bigger blazes. But these scorched small objects, though discarded as malignant things, were still on display. The mystery was still fresh, its relics (already legendary) still accessible.

In a cooking shed at the end of the row a group of women and girls—

to get a little of the visitors' attention—was encouraging a small child to dance. They chanted, clapped and laughed, and they looked from the child to us. And the toddler did for a few moments break into a slow, sweet, stamping dance: his feet alive, his legs alive, his child's face mournful and blank. The women and girls laughed. The child did another little dance. It was done for us, but there was no answering wave from the women to our wave of farewell.

We drove around the area. The bush, or what had looked like bush, had surprises. All around the settlement with the teacher's house (and the cross) were the buildings of a research institute of some sort. Many Europeans were about. I expressed surprise. The man with us as our official guide (he was the son of a former chief) resented my surprise. He spoke sharply to me, as to a foreigner and a fool; and he never returned to good humour. We set him down at the main road, the Yamoussoukro auto-route. His dark African cloth quickly turning him all black, he crossed with a stamping swagger to the township on the other side and was at once lost in the crowd.

7

THE DJÉDJÉ business ended badly. The fault was mine. I gave him too much money. He had said that he wanted two thousand francs for tips. I hadn't understood that this—less than £4—was his own modest fee. I gave him that; and added six thousand francs, £10, as his fee. His eyes popped. With the first violent or inelegant gesture I had seen him make he grabbed the notes I offered. And then, slightly stooped, as though arrested in the grabbing gesture, he trembled for a second or two with excitement.

He telephoned early the next morning. He said he was going to come in the afternoon to take me to a famous *féticheur* in Bingerville.

He came. When I went down to meet him in the hotel lobby he said he had forgotten to tell me in the morning that the *féticheur*'s fee for an *expérience* would be fifteen thousand francs. I said I didn't want an *expérience*; I just wanted to talk to the *féticheur*. Djédjé said it was a big *expérience*. The *féticheur* would cut his hand with a knife and make the wound close up again.

Djédjé said, "For fifteen thousand francs he will give you three *expériences*."

"How much for one?"

"Perhaps five thousand will be enough."

We went out to the hotel forecourt. He hadn't arranged a taxi this time; I thought he had. He asked me to sit in one of the hotel taxis. He stood outside with the driver and they began a palaver. It went on for a while. Djédjé's manner changed. He ceased to be grave. His body became looser; he propped himself in varying postures against the taxi and laughed and chattered like a street-corner lounger. I looked out of the window, to hurry things up. Djédjé, laughing and casual, as though he knew me very well, asked me to wait.

At last he and the driver got into the taxi, and we started. The driver didn't put the meter on. I took this to mean that the fare to Bingerville had been settled. But it hadn't, because after a mile or two the driver raised the subject. He said to me, "You will have no trouble getting a taxi back from Bingerville." I asked Djédjé what they had arranged about the fare. Djédjé said the taxi-driver had asked for ten thousand francs, and he had offered the driver a thousand. I took this to mean that some mid-way price was expected.

I said, "Would we be able to get a taxi back?"

Djédjé said, "Taxis are hard to get at Bingerville."

He began to talk about the powers of *féticheurs*. There was an even more famous one than the one we were going to see, but he had asked an astronomical price. That particular *féticheur* could make himself invisible and go through a closed door. It would have been a good *expérience* for me, but it wasn't worth the money.

The taxi-driver interrupted and spoke for some time in an African language.

I asked, "What's he saying?"

Djédjé said, "He wants fifteen thousand francs."

"But that's absurd."

"That's what I told him. I offered him five thousand for the trip out and five thousand for the trip back."

"So you've settled for the original ten thousand?"

"Yes."

It was very high, but there was no question of getting out of the taxi.

It was mid-afternoon, very hot, and so far on the road out of Abidjan I hadn't seen another taxi. I said, "Tell him that is to include an hour's waiting."

It seemed settled, at last.

The highway to Bingerville cut through soft slopes of bush: a wide view, the lower sky hazy in the heat.

Djédjé talked about fetishes. They could be very expensive, he said. Europeans often wanted fetishes. I remembered that in Djédjé's eyes I was like a European. I said I didn't want a fetish; I only wanted to talk to the *féticheur*.

"Yes, yes," Djédjé said, not believing a word. "Some Europeans, some Africans too, can pay up to one hundred thousand francs for a fetish."

The taxi-driver said, "Listen. About my fare—"

I said, "That's settled."

And Djédjé with an open palm made a silencing gesture at the driver.

Bingerville appeared, a scatter of ochre-coloured concrete buildings on low hills: like Grand-Bassam, another early French settlement in the Ivory Coast: degraded colonial architecture, concrete and corrugated iron, at the limit of empire.

Djédjé had said he had made arrangements with the *féticheur*. It turned out now that he didn't know where the *féticheur* lived.

We turned off into a dirt road. It soon became a track. We asked directions of a plump young man who was wearing an orange-coloured tee shirt printed *Bingerville*. He was all good nature. He was perfectly ready to direct strangers to the local *féticheur*.

We got back on to the highway. And Djédjé, to cover up his mistake, told of a particularly powerful fetish that had been prepared by the *féticheur* for a deputy of the national assembly at the last elections. The fetish converted votes given for the deputy's opponent into votes for the deputy. The deputy won by a big margin, and the deputy's opponent went mad wondering what had happened to all the votes that had been promised him.

We got lost for the second time. And again, this time stopping near a group of schoolchildren in uniform, we had to ask—or Djédjé had to ask, calling out of the window—where the house of the *féticheur* was. And again no one seemed put out or surprised by our inquiry. One man—stopped as he was walking busily by—not only told us where the house was, but also offered (as though he hadn't really been going anywhere) to be our guide. He got into the seat beside the driver and at once became very cheerful, relishing the idea of even a short ride.

The turning we wanted was unmarked. It was a track across waste ground, and it led past a ragged screen of trees and bushes to a village: abrupt life in what, from the road, had looked only like bush. There seemed to be no road at all in the village. We drove straight at houses, and the car turned between houses. Dusty yards opened into dusty, littered yards, one man's backyard somebody else's front yard: cooking fires, wood piles, cooking utensils on black, trampled earth, children, men and women in a variety of costumes: the relaxed afternoon life of the village.

We were just a minute or two from the splendid highway, with its logic of straight lines and easy curves. But already we were in an older and more tangled world, a version of a forest settlement. We continued to drive between houses. It continued to seem that we wouldn't be able to get round the corners, that we would have to stop. But we didn't stop.

Djédjé, getting more tense as we drove deeper into the village, said suddenly, "You changed money? Give me some thousand-franc notes. It would be better, the thousand-franc notes."

My money was in a side pocket of my trousers. I was sitting, and couldn't pull out the notes one by one. I pulled out what the bank at the hotel had given me: a set of ten new thousand-franc notes.

Djédjé said, "That's ten thousand, isn't it? Give me ten thousand."

But he had told me that five thousand would be enough for the *féticheur*, for one *expérience*.

I was uneasy at getting deeper in the village, which seemed to go on and on. And I was so uncertain now of Djédjé and the taxi-driver, who had changed their minds about every agreement, that I decided to give up the journey.

I said to the driver, "Go back to Abidjan. Go back to the hotel."

He had enjoyed the drama of taking his car between the houses. Now, stylishly, making a lot of dust, he turned in somebody's yard, and we twisted back through the village to the waste ground and the asphalt road. We bumped down into the road.

Just at that moment Djédjé shouted, "Stop!"

The driver stamped on the brake. Djédjé bent forward once, twice.

He said, "I have a bad conscience about this." He began to rock backward and forward in his seat. He said again, "I have a bad conscience about this."

The driver looked from Djédjé to me. The village and the *féticheur*, or Abidjan and the hotel?

I said, "The hotel."

We dropped our passenger—glad to get out of the car now—and went on to the highway. We drove for a mile or so: the bush, the black highway, the hot afternoon glow.

Djédjé said with passion, "Everything the *féticheur* does will be at my expense. At my expense."

Nothing was said to the driver. But he pulled in at the side of the highway.

Djédjé said, "You are making me feel bad. You are making me feel bad." His eyes went red; sweat broke out on his forehead. He was rocking himself again. I thought he was going to have a fit.

He said, "You see how I am sweating. You believe I was deceiving you. You make me feel bad. Everything I did, I did for you. I asked you for the money only to protect you. If the *féticheur* had seen a European pull out all those notes he would have asked for a lot of money. That was why I asked you for the ten thousand francs in thousand-franc notes."

The taxi-driver, always cool, said to Djédjé, "None of this alters my fare, you understand. He will have to settle my bill."

I said, "The hotel."

We drove back in silence, until Djédjé said, "Tomorrow. Come to town tomorrow. I will take you to a *féticheur* in town. He wouldn't do anything for you especially. He will be giving a display. You will see it free."

And that was what he said again when he followed me into the hotel lobby.

I felt foolish, drained, sad. I felt Africa as a great melancholy—that expensive highway, with its straight lines and curves; that village, with its antique, forest squalor and its *féticheur*; Djédjé's belief, his exaggerated emotions, his changes of personality.

Without civilization, Djédjé had said the day before, everybody would be a sorcerer.

8

To be black was not to be African or to find community with Africans. Many West Indian women who had married Africans had discovered that. So Janet told me. West Indian women, whatever their background, were house-proud; they found Africans dirty. And then there was the problem with the African families. Janet had heard versions of the story Arlette had told: the African family choosing an African wife for the man and sending this wife to the house, with the threat of a curse if she was rejected.

It was easier for a white woman to marry an African, Janet thought. The white woman would know she was marrying exotically; that would be part of the attraction. The West Indian woman, with her own racial ideas, would be looking in Africa for a double security.

Janet herself was black. She had grown up in England, where her Guyanese family had settled. She was blessed with great beauty (tall, slender, long-necked), and she had the security of her beauty. She had no anxieties about "belonging." Happily removed from the political nastiness of independent Guyana, she spoke of herself as someone "from England." She had come out to the Ivory Coast with her English husband Philip. Philip had spent most of his working life in Africa, and it was one of his sayings that in their mixed marriage Janet was the English partner; he was the African.

At dinner in a rough but well-known beach restaurant (Philip and Janet were great restaurant-goers), and later over coffee in their flat in the centre of Abidjan (the black lacquer furniture in the big sitting room from London, from Habitat), Philip told me how he had come out to Africa.

Just after he had left school, in Scotland, he "discovered" the motorcar. Motorcars became his obsession; he wanted to be a racing driver. Soon enough it came to him that he wasn't making any money from driving. So he enrolled as a trainee teacher in a programme run by a British government department concerned with overseas development. The trainees were sent out to East Africa, and East Africa was attractive to Philip, not only because of the sun and the easy life, but also because it was the territory of the great motor rally, the East African Safari.

There were forty trainees in Philip's year. They could be divided into four groups. There were those, about ten or twelve, who wanted to go out to Africa to convert the Africans to Christianity. There were a few, from very rich families, who were moved by the idea of charity. There were those who went to Africa to get away from personal distress, emotional entanglements. The fourth, and largest, group went out for the sun and the easy life. Philip belonged to this group. And it was people from this group who lasted; most of the others cracked within the first year and gave up Africa.

But the Uganda that Philip went out to soon became another place. Idi Amin, the former army sergeant, took over. Philip was having lunch one day in a little English-run restaurant in Kampala when Amin came in, just like that, without ceremony. This caused a stir; and Amin added to the excitement by paying the lunch bills of everybody who was then in the restaurant. Philip said, "So I can say Amin bought me lunch." On another occasion Amin appeared, again without warning, at a rugby match in which a representative Uganda team was playing. He stood in the back of his Land-Rover and watched, shouting, "Come on, Uganda!" Later he bought beer for all the players. This was how he was in the early days, the army man, grand of gesture, immensely popular with the expatriates, and quite different from the tribal politicians he had displaced. Then he had become more tribal than any, and he had drenched Uganda in blood.

I had spent some months in Uganda in 1966, at the time of an earlier coup. Philip, answering an inquiry of mine, said, "Many of the young people you knew would have been killed."

This was the Africa Philip had worked in. Events had carried him along. He had moved from contract to contract, country to country. He spoke calmly about Uganda; he had trained himself to that calm. He was still trying to arrive at a larger attitude. And now, I felt, he was touched by Janet's own detachment from Africa.

African countries, whatever their political horrors, genuinely valued education, Philip said. That gave meaning to whatever he had done. In England, he said, education had ceased to be valued. Once, when he was in London between contracts, he had taught at a comprehensive school. He had been shocked by the illiteracy and indifference of the students; one boy, dazzled by his contract with a football club, left the school absolutely without any training. Still, Philip liked England. It remained a good place, if not to work in, then to work from. He and Janet were negotiating to buy a house in London: he had photographs to show.

He had become an expatriate, a man out of his country, a man moving between two continents: one place always made bearable by the prospect of departure for the other.

About Djédjé—to whom he had introduced me—Philip wasn't surprised. He had from the beginning feared that Djédjé would grow "wild." And it was Philip's job at that moment—in the inter-state African organization for which he worked—to deal with high African officials who were going "wild," but on an astronomical scale, and were coming hotfoot to Abidjan to ask for millions. There was a way of dealing with this wildness without causing offence, Philip said. You asked questions, and more questions; you became technical. The official finally couldn't answer, and calmed down.

The flat where we were was high up in a high block. Tropical Ivory Coast rain had found a gap between the concrete and the metal frame of the sitting-room window and discoloured the wall. That nagged Janet. She said, "There is no maintenance." And I thought I saw in the discoloured wall the origin of something Philip had said when he had first driven me round the splendours of Abidjan. He had said, "Africa seeps through." I didn't know him then. I had seen him as a man with an African cause, and I had thought the comment was one of approval: Africa humanizing and softening the brutalism of industrial civilization. But he meant only what Janet said: there was no maintenance.

There was another side to that. In Africa, Philip said, distress came to those who cared more about Africa than Africans did, or cared differently. In the Ivory Coast, was there really virtue in maintaining what had been given? Was there a finality about the model?

He had come to Africa for the sun and the good life. Now Africa had become the starting point for speculation. He had become more thoughtful than he might have done if he had stayed in England; he had become more knowledgeable and more tolerant. And simply by being in Africa, he—like other expatriates I met—now took a special conscientiousness to his job. He had become a good man.

Yet men, especially in Africa, had to know why they did things. And—as I had felt after my talk with Busby—in Africa this issue could still only be left in the air.

9

IN THE MORNING I was telephoned from the hotel lobby by a man called Ebony. He said he had heard from Busby that a writer was in Abidjan, and he had come to meet this writer. He, Ebony, was himself a poet.

I went down to see him. He was a cheerful young man of regal appearance, with the face of a Benin bronze, and he was regally attired, with a brightly patterned skull-cap and a rich African tunic. He said the skull-cap and tunic were from Volta. His family employed labourers from Volta and he had always, even as a child, liked their clothes.

He had been a journalist, he said, but he had given it up, because in the Ivory Coast journalism was like smoking: it could damage your health. He liked the joke; he made it twice. But he was vague about the journalism he had done. He said he was now a government servant, in the department of the environment. He had written a paper on things that might be done environmentally in the Ivory Coast. But after twelve months he had heard nothing about his paper. So now he just went to the office and from time to time he wrote poetry.

He said, "I have a theory about African administrations. But it is difficult and will take too long to tell you."

He had come to see me—and the hotel was a good way out of the town—because he was sociable; because he wanted to practise his English; and because, as a poet and intellectual, he wanted to try out his ideas.

I offered coffee. He offered me a cola nut, the African token of friendship. I nibbled at my grubby, purple-skinned nut: bitter. He chewed his zestfully, giving little dry spits of chewed husk to his left and right, and then at the end of his chew taking out the remainder of the husk with his fingers and placing it on the ash-tray.

He asked why I had come to the Ivory Coast. I said because it was successful and French.

He said, "Charlemagne wasn't my ancestor."

I felt it had been said before, and not only by Ebony. He ran on to another idea. "The French run countries like pigsties. They believe that the sole purpose of men is to eat, to go to the toilet and to sleep." So the French colonialists created bourgeois people. Bourgeois? "The bourgeois want peace, order. The bourgeois can fit into any political system, once they have peace. On the other hand, the British colonialists created entrepreneurs." Entrepreneurs? "Entrepreneurs want to change things." Entrepreneurs were revolutionaries.

Antithesis, balance: the beauty rather than the validity of a thought: I thought I could detect his French training. I began to examine his ideas of the bourgeois and the entrepreneur, but he didn't encourage me. He said, playfully, it was only an idea.

Starting on another cola nut—he had a handful in his tunic pocket— he said, "Africans live at peace with nature. Europeans want to conquer or dominate nature."

That was familiar to me. I had heard similar words from young Muslim fundamentalists in Malaysia: ecological, Western romance bouncing back like a corroborating radio signal from remote, inactive worlds. But that again was an idea Ebony didn't want to stay with.

Ebony said, "I saw white men for the first time when I was fourteen or fifteen, when I went to school. That was the first time I discovered the idea of racial superiority. African children are trained not to look elders in the eye. It is disrespectful. At school the French teachers took this to be a sign of African hypocrisy."

What was the point of this story?

Ebony said, "So I thought my French teachers inferior."

I felt this racial story, with its triumphant twist, had previously had a sympathetic foreign listener. And it turned out that there was a Scandinavian woman journalist who had made a great hit with Ebony. She was now in Spain and Ebony earnestly asked me—two or three times—to look her up and pass on his regards.

Ebony said, "When my father sent me to the school, do you know what he said? He said, 'Remember. I am not sending you to the school to be a white man or a Frenchman. I am sending you to enter the new world, that's all.' "

I felt that in his own eyes Ebony had done that. He had made the crossing more easily than Djédjé. Ebony said he had no money, no car. The salary he got from the government was less than the rent he paid. He had come to the hotel on his bicycle. But I thought he was relaxed, a whole man. He knew where he was, how he had got there, and he liked the novelty of what he saw. There was no true anxiety behind his scattered ideas. At any rate he was less anxious than a romantic or concerned outsider might have wished him to be. Ideas about Africa, words, poetry, meeting foreigners—all this was part of his relishing of life, part of his French-inspired role as intellectual, part of the new world he had happily entered.

He went away on his bicycle, and I took a taxi later to a beach restaurant at the end of the city, beyond the industrial and port area. The lunch there, and the French style of the place, was usually worth the fare and the journey in the mid-day heat through the traffic and the crowds. But today it wasn't so.

It was more than a matter of an off-day. The waiters, impeccable the day before, were casual, vacant. There were long delays, mistakes; some of the portions were absurdly small; the bill, when it came, was wrong. Someone was missing, perhaps the French or European manager. And with him more than good service had gone: the whole restaurant-idea had vanished. An elaborate organization had collapsed. The waiters—Ivorian: these jobs were lucrative—seemed to have forgotten, from one day to the next, why they were doing what they did. And their faces seemed to have altered as well. They were not waiters now, in spite of their flowered tunics. Their faces and manners radiated various degrees of tribal authority. I saw them as men of weight in the village: witch-doctors, herbalists, men who perhaps put on masks and did the sacred dances. The true life was there, in the mysteries of the village. The restaurant, with its false, arbitrary ritual, was the charade: I half began to see it so.

Ebony had been told by his father: "I am not sending you to the school to become a white man. I am sending you to enter the new world."

The new world existed in the minds of other men. Remove those men; and their ideas—which after all had no finality—would disappear. Skills could be taught. What was fragile—to men whose complete, real life lay in another realm of the spirit—was faith in the new world.

It was in this unsettled mood that at last, on the public holiday that marked the independence of the Ivory Coast, I went with Gil Sherman to the president's ancestral village of Yamoussoukro.

1 O

THE AUTO-ROUTE went through a soft green land, and then through forests where grew the irreplaceable hardwoods that had given the economy a start. (Mighty trunks, just two or three or four at a time, chained on to heavy lorries on the road: mighty log piles on the timber docks—with a bustling dockers' settlement—in an oily black creek in Abidjan: the logs then chained again, and swung one or two at a time into the holds or on to the stripped decks of vessels with foreign, far-off names.) The country was organized; it was a country at work; and the money had spread down. Money had come to the people of bush and forest, and their villages were now built in concrete. In one small town where we stopped for a while there was even a parody of a modern hotel.

After 150 miles—regularly marked off in kilometres—we came to Yamoussoukro. The road rose. At the top, quite suddenly, it was like an airport runway in a cleared wilderness. Lamp standards lined the broad avenue on either side. In the distance was the twelve-tiered tower of the Hotel President, lifting above itself, to one side, two octagonal slabs of concrete (with the tower restaurant between the slabs), like a giant sandwich with the corners cut away. Towards that we drove: landscaped grounds, gardens, a white marble entrance, a lobby in red and chocolate marble, mirrors set in the chamfered angles of the marble pillars. The upholstered chairs were in virulent blue and green, not restful.

The room I was given was opulent. The bathroom fittings staggered. It was very cold: the air-conditioning was fierce. I turned the system off, but the room never lost its chill while I was there. The great window, of very thick glass, was sealed. It gave a view of the enormous swimming pool, around which, on a wide paved area, lounge chairs were set in a large circle.

Beyond that, and beyond the buildings of the older Hotel President (Yamoussoukro had never ceased to grow), was parkland: parkland created out of the African bush. It was the famous golf course, landscaped, with planting: a foreign eye had drawn out the picturesque possibilities of what to an African would have been only bush. The mist in the distance looked—to me—like the heat mist on the banks of the Congo river. But Yamoussoukro was cooler than the coast, and this was the mist of the harmattan, the cool, sand-charged wind that blew all the way down from the Sahara at this season.

It was a great creation, the golf course, perfection in a way. It represented prodigious labour. Yet it was only a view: one look took it all in. And soon it wasn't enough. Splendour on this scale, in this setting, and after a 150-mile drive, only created an appetite for more: the visitor began to enter the ambition and fantasy of the creator. There was a main street, very wide; there was a market; there were workers' settlements. Something like a real town was attaching itself to the presidential creation. But the visitor, always quickly taking for granted what had been created, continued to be distracted by the gaps, the scarred earth, the dusty vacancies. And, if you didn't want to play golf, there was nothing to do.

There were the president's crocodiles. They were to be fed at five. The presidential palace was some distance away, down one of the great avenues. Gil Sherman's car was necessary. In the levelled land, in the glare and emptiness of the afternoon, the scale of everything seemed magnified. The palace wall went on and on. Beside it was a lake. In the middle, an iron-railed causeway lined with young coconut trees led to a palace gate, guarded by soldiers of the presidential guard in maroon-coloured tunics. The cars of visitors—mainly white—were parked on the causeway.

In the lake on either side were the crocodiles. We saw the first just as we left the car: barely noticeable in the muddy water, a mere protuberance of eyes, until its thorny back became clear. We exclaimed. An African, possibly an official (from his lounging, casual stance), said, "Il est petit." A small one. Then we saw eyes and thorny backs everywhere on the surface of the water—the thorns like the thorns on the bark of the baobab tree.

On one side of the causeway there was a stone-paved embankment sloping down to the water. On this embankment were a number of crocodiles, small ones, absolutely still, eyes bright and apparently unseeing, jaws open, the lower jaw of each crocodile showing only as a great hollow, oddly simple in shape, oddly clean and dry-looking, yellow-pink and pale. Flies moved in and out of those open jaws. On the other side of the causeway there was no paved embankment, only a sandy bank, marked by the tails of crocodiles. White feathers, as of a chicken, were scattered about in the sand. There were crocodiles on the bank. They were like the colour of the sand and from a distance were not noticeable.

The feeder was already in attendance. He had come in a grey Land-Rover; it was parked on the causeway. He was clearly a special man. He was very tall, very thin. He wore a skull-cap and a flowered gown. He had an official with him, a man of more ordinary size in a grey, short-sleeved safari suit. In one hand the feeder had a thin, long knife; in his other hand he had a tin or bucket with pieces of meat. Heart or lungs, Gil Sherman told me: pale pink, with bits of animal "piping."

The feeder made a rattling sound on the iron rails. Then he threw the meat. The crocodiles on the paved embankment were awkward, slow. They had to tilt their long snouts against the flat paving stones—showing the pale-yellow underside of their bodies—to pick up the meat. They couldn't get the meat that had fallen on their own backs or into the crevices between the paving stones. They didn't seem always to know where the meat had fallen.

While the feeder threw the meat, the grey-suited official with him clucked and called softly to the crocodiles, speaking to them as to children. *"Avalez, avalez."* ("Swallow, swallow.")

Later, on the other side of the causeway, there was another ritual. The older, bigger crocodiles were there, yellow, with twisted snouts, heavy bellies, and teeth which, when closed together, suggested a long, jagged, irregularly stitched wound.

The tall feeder was now holding a black chicken by the wings. He swung the chicken slowly up and down. The squawks of alarm from the chicken died down. The chicken lost control of its neck, which hung limp. Two old crocodiles, as though used to the ritual, waited close together on the sand. More meat was thrown and gobbled up, except where it had fallen on the backs of the crocodiles. Turtles, appearing in the water, swam ashore for their meat. One young crocodile, having got his meat, swam away fast to a little sand-bank on the lake to eat or ingest his meat without disturbance. Then the chicken was thrown at the two old crocodiles. The open jaws snapped shut. The crowd gasped. But the feeder hadn't thrown straight; and the crocodiles hadn't moved. The stunned chicken fluttered its wings; it partly recovered from its stupor; it ran along to the end of the sandy bank, near the causeway.

The tall feeder in the flowered gown didn't allow the chicken to get away. He jumped over the rail to the bank and—his long thin knife his only means of defence—walked unhurriedly past the crocodiles to where the chicken was. The chicken didn't run. The feeder seized it, climbed back over the rail to the road. And again the ritual swinging of the bird by the wings was accompanied by clucking calls to the two waiting crocodiles from the grey-suited official. Again the bird was thrown. Again the jaws snapped; again the bird escaped. But now the clucking calls had brought from the water on to the sand a crocodile even bigger and older than the other two. His snout was battered at the tip. His teeth looked stained and old and worn. The chicken's limp neck was placed on the iron rail; the feeder began to bring down his knife. I didn't look.

A shout from the crowd told me that the chicken had been thrown. And when I turned I saw the bird turned to a feathery debris in the seemingly grinning maw of one crocodile, not the oldest, round unseeing eyes apparently alight with pleasure, black feathers sticking out on either side of the jaw. A moment's ingestion, and all was gone, except for a mash in the lower jaw. The ceremony was over. The feeder, skull-capped, prettily gowned, took his tin and walked back, unsmiling, to the Land-Rover.

A public ceremony of kingship outside the big blank wall of the presidential palace. Behind that wall there were trees, and somewhere among those trees was the president's ancestral village with the old palaver tree. That site, which felt sacred now, the scene perhaps of more private rituals, was not open to the public. Ibrahim Keita, the golfer, the president's protégé, the man said to be charged by the president with the development of Yamoussoukro, Ibrahim had seen the village behind the palace wall. But Ibrahim's West Indian wife hadn't.

Ibrahim was to have guided me around Yamoussoukro. But he hadn't been able to do that. He had, however, done a gracious and unexpected thing: he had deputed his elder brother to show Gil Sherman and me around. The brother came in the morning to the Hotel President. The brother was a doctor, smaller than Ibrahim, softer, grey-haired, with glasses, and with the confident manner of some black West Indian professional men of established family.

The Keita family was from the neighbouring state of Guinea; in the Ivory Coast they were refugees of a sort. And the doctor's story that morning, in the marble lobby of the Hotel President, was of his escape from Guinea in 1964. A quiet hint from someone, a false message to an official, an early-morning drive across the border: Dr. Keita still marvelled at his escape, was still shocked by the terrors of Guinea, where in 1964 people like himself, professional men, educated men, men of the *cheferie*, were being picked up and killed "like cattle," locked in cells and left to die, without food or water: the famous "black diet" of Guinea.

Just across the border, in a climate like this, among people like those one saw, there was that kind of African kingship. It gave an added wonder to Yamoussoukro, to the chieftaincy or kingship symbolized by the crocodiles. And driving around with Dr. Keita that morning, I found it hard not to be moved by the ambition of the president, his wish to build and create to the highest standards he knew.

In his magnificence there was religion. Just as in some societies the peasant reserves his very best for his god, so here this striving after material splendour served the divinity that protected the kingship. Yamoussoukro was like the Pyramids or Angkor Wat. But these monuments, looking to the rulers' afterlife, had no purpose beyond themselves. Yamoussoukro was to be a living metropolis. It was to be the ruler's ennobling benefaction to his people, people of the West African forest, and—like the crocodile ritual—it was proof both of his right to rule and the justness of his rule.

Far down a wide, empty avenue we came upon a university or a centre of higher education. It had a freestanding, purely decorative arcade all around, as high as the building itself. The arcade was faced with brown mosaic. Great walkways linked the four quarters of the main building. There was an Olympic-standard swimming pool (showing, already, some signs of neglect). There were dormitories for students, houses for faculty staff. And just a little way down the avenue was another, complementary educational complex.

How many students attended the university? Someone said six hundred; somebody else said sixty.

The metropolis of Yamoussoukro awaited full use. But it had been created by foreigners. It was something that had been imported and paid for; and modern buildings like the university were not simply physical monuments that would last; they were like pieces of machinery, liable to decay. The new world existed in the minds of others. The skills could be learned, but faith in the new world was fragile. When the president went, and the foreigners went away (as some people wanted them to), would the faith survive? Or would Africans be claimed by another idea of reality?

In the slave plantations of the Caribbean Africans existed in two worlds. There was the world of the day; that was the white world. There was the world of the night; that was the African world, of spirits and magic and the true gods. And in that world ragged men, humiliated by day, were transformed—in their own eyes, and the eyes of their fellows—into kings, sorcerers, herbalists, men in touch with the true forces of the earth and possessed of complete power. A king of the night, a slave by day, might be required at night never to exert himself; he would be taken about by his fellows in a litter. (That particular fact, about a slave king, came out at an inquiry into a slave "revolt" in Trinidad in 1805.) To the outsider, to the slave-owner, the African night world might appear a mimic world, a child's world, a carnival. But to the African— however much, in daylight, he appeared himself to mock it—it was the true world: it turned white men to phantoms and plantation life to an illusion.

Something of this twin reality existed at Yamoussoukro. The metropolis, the ruler's benefaction to his people, belonged to the world of the day, the world of doing and development. The crocodile ritual— speaking of a power issuing to the president from the earth itself—was part of the night, ceaselessly undoing the reality of the day. One idea worked against the other. So, in spite of the expense, the labour, the ambition, there was a contradiction in the modern pharaonic dream.

The crocodiles—I hadn't heard about them until I had got to the Ivory Coast. And now that I had seen them I kept on hearing about them. Everything I heard added to the religious mystery. I heard about one of the palace watchmen who had been killed on the sandy bank beside the causeway. A crocodile had laid its eggs in the sand. The watch-man didn't know. He walked past the spot. The crocodile rushed at him and seized him and dragged him into the water. There was another story about a man, a villager, who had fallen over the iron rail into the lake and had been mangled by a crocodile, as the black chicken had been mangled. Was that an accident? Or had the man been pushed, a forced sacrifice? That was one view. The other was that the man was a voluntary sacrifice, that he had been persuaded (perhaps by some threat) to do what he had done in order to save his village from some evil.

So the crocodiles—seen in daylight, by a crowd with cameras— became more than a tourist sight. They became touched with the magic and power they were intended to have, though the setting was so staged:

the broad avenue lined with lamp standards, the artificial lake (no doubt dug with modern excavators), the iron rails, the presidential guard with guns. The long-gowned feeder and the grey-suited official with him, when I called them back to mind, were especially unsettling. The official had smiled and clucked at the crocodiles, as though he knew them well, as though they were on his side.

And the symbolism remained elusive, worrying. Did the feeding ritual hold a remnant of ancient Egyptian earth-worship, coming down and across to black Africa through the Sudan? In a famous papyrus scroll from ancient Egypt, a woman in a plain white smock, hair undone, is shown bowed down before the crocodile, both on the horizontal line representing the earth, the horizontal line resting on the chevrons that in Egyptian art depict water. Or was the symbolism simpler? A crocodile was the strongest creature in water; it was universally feared; it lived long; it slept with its eyes open. And what was the significance of the hen? Was it an enemy? Or did it stand for reincarnation, as some people said: new life daily given to the crocodile, emblem of the ruler's power? Perhaps the concepts were not really translatable.

Outside the town, we came upon another kind of order, another kind of power: the president's agricultural estates. They went on for miles and miles: the disorder of dark tropical forest replaced by levelled, sun-struck fields, where mangoes, avocadoes and pineapples grew in rows. How had the president come by all this land? Had he converted unused, unclaimed forest into private land? Or did he as chief own all the land of his tribe? No one that morning seemed to understand my question; and the answer was no longer important. Two years before, the president had given his estates to the state. Like Yamoussoukro itself, it was a benefaction, a model for the future, and part of the ruler's religious sacrifice.

Doubly religious was the great mosque of Yamoussoukro. It was at once a gesture to the Muslims among the population, and the ruler's offering to another aspect of divinity. The mosque was square-towered, not fine in its detail, and I was told it was in the North African style, North Africa being the source of what was Islamic in this part of Africa. North Africa, France: the African ruler, aiming at material splendour, had to look outside black Africa. It was part of the pathos of Yamoussoukro. The mosque, off a wide, unfilled avenue, was in a big, bare yard, open to sun and the harmattan. Like many other buildings in

Yamoussoukro, it appeared—perhaps wrongly—to await full use. It felt like a shell; it was possible, in the barrenness of its unwelcoming yard, to see it as a ruin. But it was big, and it was one of the sights.

We had a late lunch at the golf club. Ibrahim Keita and an Ivorian banker were our hosts. Ibrahim, after his day on the course, was fatigued and said little. The architecture was in the luxurious and playful international style. The menu was French, too ambitious for its own good; the waiters were uniformed. Yamoussoukro might have been only a playground, a tourist spot. But we who were there were living out the president's ambitions for his ancestral village. We were, whether we liked it or not, in his religious embrace. In another part of the metropolis, in an hour or so, the crocodiles were to be fed again.

There were many cars on the road back to Abidjan: people returning to the other world from villages that were as sacred to them as Yamoussoukro was to the president. It was the end of the public holiday, the twenty-second anniversary of independence, celebrated by white, green and saffron flags everywhere, and coloured portraits of the very small, benign man who had ruled for all that time.

I I

IN ABIDJAN I met a middle-aged European who had worked all his life in Africa and had lived for many years in the Ivory Coast. He worked in the interior. His job was rough, unintellectual. He had little social life; and unlike the other expatriates I had met, he spoke about Africa without any obliqueness. He said, "All that you see here in Abidjan is make-believe. If the Europeans were to go away it would all vanish."

Africans, he said, were still ruled by magic. In the interior, when a chief or an important local man died, the man's servants and his wives were buried with him. If the servants had run away at the time of the death, then heads were bought. That explained the regular disappearance of children, as reported in the necrology page of the newspaper. On that page there was a coded way of referring to certain kinds of death. A death by poisoning was said to have occurred "after a short illness," *après une courte maladie*. A child reported as having disappeared was presumed to have been sacrificed. In the interior, for these funeral or other sacrifices, a head could currently be bought for ten thousand francs, less than

£20. Not long before, in the area where this European worked, an important local man died. Heads were needed—the man was very important; and the panic was so general that for three weeks no worker turned up for the night shift at the factory the European managed. At certain ceremonies of welcome a chief or an important man had to have his feet washed in blood. Usually it was the blood of a chicken or an animal. But to do a chief the highest honour, his feet should be washed in human blood, the blood of a sacrificed person, a child. And the child could be eaten afterwards.

I believed what this man said. He liked living in Africa; he had worked nowhere else; he could work nowhere else. His directness came from his acceptance of African ways. He was not concerned to score points off Africa. But his acceptance went with a correct distancing of himself from the continent and its people. And for him that perhaps was the charm of the expatriate life: the heightened sense of the self that Africa gave.

It was of that kind of expatriate that I heard not long afterwards from a young American lawyer. He worked for an international law firm and was posted in the Ivory Coast. Business sometimes took him to Zaire, the former Belgian Congo. The Zaire boom of 1971 and 1972 was long past, the lawyer said; but there were now more expatriates than ever in the country—Indians, Greeks, Lebanese. They were people hooked on the way of life. They liked living on the edge of Africa, as it were, at the extremity of their own civilizations. They knew how to manage in the country; they liked that too, that idea of knowing how to manage. Some did well; some ended badly; most just carried on.

Recently the lawyer had been to Zaire to make an inventory of the effects of an elderly American who had died. The American had gone to the old Belgian Congo in the 1930s, and he had stayed there through everything, colonial rule, the Second World War, Congolese independence, the civil wars. He had spent his last years in a one-bedroomed flat in Kinshasa. He was worth about a million dollars, but the personal possessions he had left behind were few: two suits, four pairs of trousers, a couple of pairs of shoes. He had done nothing big or adventurous. His business dealings had been simple, small, mainly in property. He had never used the money he had made. It lay idle in banks, in stocks. He had stayed in the Congo because he had been hooked on the life.

The young American lawyer didn't try to define the glamour of the life. But I thought it would be something like this: being in Africa, being a non-African among Africans. Discomfort and danger would add to the sense of the self, the daily sense of personal drama, which a man living safely at home might never know. Africa called to people for different reasons. Everyone who went and stayed had his own Africa.

And then—after Yamoussoukro and the crocodiles, and what I had heard (and believed) about the heads—I had a bad night. I dreamed I was on a roof or bridge. The material, of glass or transparent plastic, had begun to perish: seemingly melted at the edges. I asked whether the bridge would be mended. The answer was no. What had been built had been built; the roof or bridge I was on would crumble away. Was it safe, though? Could I cross? The answer was yes. The bridge was safe; I could cross. And in the dream that was the most important thing, because I wasn't going to pass that way again.

The buildings of Abidjan, seen in the morning mist of the lagoon, seemed sinister: proof of a ruler's power, a creation of magic, for all the solidity of the concrete and the steel: dangerous and perishable like the bridge in my dream.

I 2

ANDRÉE, Arlette's friend and fellow West Indian, telephoned from the university. Andrée's message was that her *patron*, Georges Niangoran-Bouah, the Drummologie expert, had returned from the United States. He sometimes went there, to universities that offered courses in "black studies."

When I went to the little office in the Institute of Ethnosociology I found a big and very black man, filling the big swivel chair behind the big desk. Without him, when Andrée was there alone, with her knitting, the office had seemed widowed. He had the physique of a chief, heavy flesh on his chest, folds of fat on his stomach; and the light-grey, short-sleeved sports shirt did not hide his size. His French, though accented, was clear and precise. His manner, a lecturing manner, was that of the French academic. He had been publishing sociological papers for twenty years. The note I had had about him said he was fifty-five; but he looked ten years younger.

He was pressed for time—he should have been with a class. But he outlined the ideas behind his Drummologie studies. The earliest European travellers in West Africa didn't know African languages. So, though they observed a lot, they also missed a lot. They were wrong about the talking drums. The drums didn't invite people to special feasts or beat out messages through the bush: "A white man is coming." Drums were far more important than that in West Africa. To Africans it wasn't the word that existed in the beginning; it was the drum. Africans said, "In the beginning was the drum." Drumming, and the chanting that went with it, were special skills, handed down through the generations. The drum mimicked human speech; a trained singer could re-discover, in a particular passage of drumming, a poem, an incantation, a piece of tribal history, a story of victory or defeat.

Drums were sacred objects, symbols of the king, the tribe, the state. And Mr. Niangoran-Bouah opened his book and showed photographs of famous tribal drums to prove his point. One drum was hung with jawbones, another hung with *cervelles,* the brains of enemies, wrapped up in skins. That was how important drums were to the tribe. Another photograph showed the great royal drum of the Baoulé people, the Kwakla drum, matted with the blood of many sacrifices. Some drums were so sacred they weren't allowed to rest in the ground. There was a recent photograph—taken by someone from the Institute of Ethnosociology— of a drumming-and-singing ceremony in which the great drum rested on the head of a slave—or so Mr. Niangoran-Bouah said.

The man said to be a slave was a muscular, shifty-looking fellow. He looked shifty perhaps because of the camera, at which he was glancing out of the corner of his eye; perhaps because of the weight of the drum and the din of the drumbeat just above his head (a small, bright-eyed old man, standing behind the drum-bearer, was pounding away with sticks on the drum); and perhaps because while the other men, elders and performers, wore their African cloths off the left shoulder, he, the drum-bearer, had to bare his chest and—in addition to supporting the drum with his left hand—had to keep up his cloth just above his waist with his right hand.

Mr. Niangoran-Bouah found the photograph full of interest. He clearly relished these ceremonies, coming down from the African past. Pressed for time as he was, he examined the photograph in detail with me, and said, "If the slave drops the drum he will be killed."

I said, "Killed?"

"But yes." Then he qualified what he had said. "In the old days. Today they would probably sacrifice an ox or an animal."

"Are there still slaves in the villages?"

Mr. Niangoran-Bouah said in his lecturer's manner, "Slavery is of two sorts. In matrilinear societies slaves are taken into the tribe. They father children for the tribe. In patrilinear societies slaves are—slaves. Today of course there are no slaves. But"—and Mr. Niangoran-Bouah smiled and threw back his chest and something of the chief's grand good humour came to him—"a man in a village cannot conceal his ancestry. Everybody knows that this one or that one is the son or grandson of a slave."

Somebody, a colleague or a student, came into the office and said that the class was waiting, had been waiting for half an hour. Mr. Niangoran-Bouah stood up, gave me an appointment for a few days ahead—he wanted to play me a few recordings of drums—and went off to his lecture on some aspect of African civilization.

I HAD DINNER at the Brasserie Abidjanaise. The French proprietress was soft and large and lacy, dreamy-eyed but commanding. She made me feel I had to be careful. The uniformed waiters, deferential to her and her ideas, were stern about the ritual of the house. The big balloon glasses were for wine, and wine was to be drunk only out of those glasses: I hadn't, after all, been careful enough. Later, at the Forum Golf Hotel, it was the Soirée Africaine: seven topless, big-breasted girls dancing to the sound of drums in La Cascade, the garden restaurant beside the swimming pool. Always, in Abidjan, these two holiday Africas, the French and the African. And the African was more real and rooted than might be supposed.

ANDRÉE sat at her desk by the window and did her knitting. With Mr. Niangoran-Bouah in his swivel chair, the scene was almost domestic. (The influence of literature, the influence of the French language! I saw Andrée as French; and fleetingly, though knowing it to be absurd in the setting, I saw her as a Balzac character.)

Mr. Niangoran-Bouah was in the same grey sports shirt. He had a big tape-recorder on his desk; he was ready to play his recordings. But I had heard a fair amount about the drums, and I wanted him to talk instead about burial customs. I thought the subject might be a touchy one, but Mr. Niangoran-Bouah was only too willing to talk about burial customs. He was fascinated by all aspects of traditional African life, and his attitude was purely descriptive. He didn't seem to think that these African things had to be either judged or defended.

When a big local planter died, his foreign labourers panicked and ran away. Mr. Niangoran-Bouah told this as a funny story. *"Ils se sauvent."* ("They scamper.") And he slipped one open palm off the other to suggest people running away fast.

African burial customs, he said, were like those of ancient Egypt. People believed that after death they continued the life they had lived on earth. So a man needed his wives and servants to go with him when he died. Some wives and servants understood this and accepted their fate. For those who didn't want to be buried with their master there were sanctuary villages. Mr. Niangoran-Bouah drew a rough diagram on the back of an envelope. This showed that for every village there were, at different points of the compass, and within easy reach, four established sanctuary villages. But wives and servants looking for sanctuary had to be sharp. They had to get out of the way before their husband or master died. Once they had made it to a sanctuary village and claimed the protection of the chief there they were safe. Still, not everybody could be trusted these days, and there could be accidents. That was why the government had decreed that the burial of chiefs and other important men should take place publicly. That was why there was so much about funerals on television and in the newspaper.

It was a poor life in the spirit world, Mr. Niangoran-Bouah said. He spoke with feeling; I was surprised. He forgot his good humour, his lecturer's manner. The dead needed money from the living. The dead had no clothes, had no money to buy clothes, and they were cold—and Mr. Niangoran-Bouah plucked at his own grey shirt. The dead had no food and were hungry—and the big man made a gesture with his fingers of taking food to his mouth. Because life in the spirit world was so wretched, Africans couldn't really believe in the Christian after-life. For Africans the good life was here and now, on earth. The end of that life was the end of everything good.

"So African Christianity is an African religion?"

Mr. Niangoran-Bouah said, "I am a Christian. The first in my family. But I am attached, profoundly attached, to African animist belief."

Djédjé, an altogether simpler person, had said much the same thing.

Arlette came into the office. She was chewing an aromatic gum, and she sat and talked quietly with Andrée, out of whose silent, busy knitting needles, and subdued "nervousness," there was emerging a fantastically coloured little garment.

With a quarter of my mind, while Mr. Niangoran-Bouah talked, I wondered—so far, after Yamoussoukro and the crocodiles, and the heads, and my own dream about the decaying bridge and general dissolution, had I been drawn into Mr. Niangoran-Bouah's spirit world—I wondered how Arlette had, as if in a novel or a play, and at another level of reality, walked into the office at that moment. And then I remembered. Arlette and Andrée were not only compatriots and friends; Arlette had also arranged my meetings both with Andrée and Mr. Niangoran-Bouah; Arlette worked in the university.

But if the here and now was all that mattered to Africans, as Mr. Niangoran-Bouah said, how did magic and the gods and the spirits fit in? Was it my own fantasy, that idea I had had of the two worlds in which Africans lived? Or was that double or twin reality something associated only with the lost slaves on the other side of the Atlantic?

I tried to find a suitable question.

I said, "Is it real for Africans, the European world? This city they have built here in Abidjan—do Africans consider it real?"

And I was so taken by what Mr. Niangoran-Bouah said that I asked for a sheet of paper to write down his words. Gently, like someone performing a welcome domestic duty, Andrée put down her knitting and gave me three sheets of thick new paper.

I wrote: "The world of white men is real. *But, but*. We black Africans, we have all that they have"—and Mr. Niangoran-Bouah meant aeroplanes, cars, rockets, lasers, satellites—"we have all of that in the world of the night, the world of darkness." (*"Le monde des blancs est réel. Mais—mais—nous avons, nous autres africains noirs, nous avons tout cela dans le monde de la nuit, le monde des ténèbres."*)

So that at night Africans today—like the slaves across the Atlantic two hundred years ago—lived in a different world.

Arlette, still chewing—but gripped now by our conversation, since

Andrée had broken off to give me the paper—Arlette, eyes bright, said, *"Ils pratiquent la nuit."* ("They do it all at night.")

And in some ways Africans had exceeded Europeans, Mr. Niangoran-Bouah said. Europeans could achieve only limited speeds, even with their rockets. Africans existed who could convert themselves into pure energy. Such an African might say, "Let me be for a while." And when after a second or so of concentration he came to again, he might give you news of Paris. Because in that time he had been to Paris and come back; and he had talked to people in Paris. So, without leaving Africa, a man might see his son in Paris and talk to him. But there could be no touching during those meetings. The man in Africa wouldn't be able to touch his son in Paris, because a man could maintain his physical footing in only one place.

"They have doubles," Arlette said. "They send their doubles. That is why they cannot touch."

"There are people in the villages today," Mr. Niangoran-Bouah said, "who can give you news every night of Paris and Russia. And they are certainly not getting it on the radio."

Arlette, explaining this African gift, spoke of the Dogon people in the north. They had a great knowledge of astronomy, especially about the star Sirius, and they were said to be in touch with extra-terrestrial spirits.

So the world absolutely changed at night for Africans?

I understood Mr. Niangoran-Bouah to say that it did. "We say that a woman is stronger at night than a man." (*"La femme la nuit est plus redoutable que l'homme."*) "The sick beggar you see begging alms all day on the pavement is really in the world of the night a great dignitary." (*"L'infirme ou le malade mendiant que nous voyons tout le jour sur le trottoir en train de demander de quoi vivre est en réalité par le monde de la nuit un grand dignitaire."*)

The electric light in the office went out.

Mr. Niangoran-Bouah, jovial, made a French exclamation. *"Catastrophe!"*

Andrée was reminded by the power failure that she had to make a telephone call. But now, she said, because the electricity had gone it wasn't possible. Mr. Niangoran-Bouah said the telephone worked on a different line. So Andrée put down her knitting and dialled. But the telephone, though working on a different line, gave trouble.

Mr. Touré, the head of the Ethnosociology Institute, not a big man, slightly military-looking in his near-khaki safari suit, came in with some banknotes in his hand. He gave the notes without ceremony to Mr. Niangoran-Bouah and Mr. Niangoran-Bouah—rather like the village chief at Kilometre 17—held the notes in his hand while he talked.

I asked, "When does the world of the night begin?"

Mr. Niangoran-Bouah said slowly and seriously, "As soon as the sun goes down."

Arlette said that in some parts of Abidjan electric light was altering the hours of the night, and interfering with the powers that came into play. There was a friendly altercation between Arlette and Mr. Niangoran-Bouah about this. I got the impression that Mr. Niangoran-Bouah was saying that electricity made no difference to the night world.

He went on to tell a story about men who could make themselves all energy. The darkest time of the colonial period, he said, was during the Second World War. And, as though the personal wound was still with him, he said it again, stressing the words: it was the darkest time. Arlette supported him. It was a time of forced labour; people were seized, as in the slave-catching days, and taken off to work on French plantations.

One old man was seized. He was bewildered; he didn't know what his captors wanted. They began to whip him. He said, "Why are you whipping me?" They told him: "We want you to carry this load to that place in the interior." The old man said, "Is that all you want? Is it for that alone that you are whipping me? To get this load to that spot? Well, if that is all you want, you go ahead." They said, "What do you mean?" He said, "I mean what I say. You leave me here. You will get your load." In the end they left the old man, thinking him mad, and when they got to where they were going—

"They found that he had got there before them," Arlette said, finishing Mr. Niangoran-Bouah's story for him, fixing me with her bright eyes, and nodding to the rhythm of her own words.

The old man had sent his double with the load. He had converted himself into pure energy.

It was a story that might have come from a Caribbean slave plantation two hundred years before. White men, creatures of the day, were phantoms, with absurd, illusory goals. Power, earth-magic, was African and enduring; triumph was African. But only Africans knew.

I asked Mr. Niangoran-Bouah about the crocodiles of Yamoussoukro and the sacrifice of the live chicken.

I had seen him academic, good-humoured, tender, passionate, always open. For the first time now I saw him momentarily at a loss. The crocodile ritual was not something he was willing to talk about. He said, "The crocodiles belong to the president." He added, "He feeds them." Then he said, "The emperor of Abyssinia also had certain animals that he fed."

Arlette, eyes twinkling, said the emperor of Abyssinia always kept a little animal with him. That little animal was his fetish.

Mr. Niangoran-Bouah didn't comment on that. He reassumed his academic manner. He said, "There are three symbols of kingship in Africa. On the savanna, the panther. In the forest, the elephant. In water, the crocodile. The crocodile is the strongest creature in the water. With one blow of that tail it can kill a man. Or"—and Mr. Niangoran-Bouah brought his palm down sideways on his desk—"it can break this desk."

The crocodile was wicked, *méchant*. It especially hated the dog. It was suicide to try to cross a crocodile lake or river in a pirogue if you had a dog with you; the crocodiles would certainly attack the pirogue and overturn it. Crocodile-hunters used the carcase of a dog as bait. The crocodile couldn't live in salt water. There used to be crocodiles in the lagoon of Abidjan until a cutting was made to the sea and salt water was let in. Now there were no crocodiles in Abidjan, though recently there had been reports of sightings.

The crocodiles of the Ivory Coast: the more one heard about them, the more they held the imagination. And it became easier to accept, looking at Mr. Niangoran-Bouah's photographs, that the swastika design on some Ashanti gold weights might have evolved from a simplified rendering of the crocodile: a creature all legs and snout and tail, murderous snout twisting or curving into murderous tail.

African art, African civilization, the density of African response: after his colonial wounding, that was Mr. Niangoran-Bouah's cause. In the Ashanti weights there was the beginning of writing and mathematics. In the chants that went with the ritualized drumming there were the beginnings of history and philosophy.

On the desk there was the big tape-recorder. At last he played some of his precious recordings: first the tribal song or ballad, then the drums that mimicked the beat of the words. It was impressive. I began to understand the richness of the material he had made his subject, and his passion to present this material adequately to Africans and the world.

He was going off that weekend with thirty of his students to a village.

The chief had invited them for the yam festival, *la fête des ignames,* an occasion so important that in some villages the sacred drums were brought out and played. In the village he was going to that weekend there were to be sacrifices of cattle, perhaps five or six. He was excited by the prospect of his weekend in the country. These old African rituals were as meat and drink to him. They were part of his past, his religion, his soul. He was also a writer and an academic, and these mysteries were among the many African things that awaited his pen and camera and tape-recorder.

But—thirty students in a village? Where were they going to stay? What arrangements would be made for them?

Mr. Niangoran-Bouah said, "Oh, there's a hotel."

I said jokingly, "So you are out in the field much of the time?"

He gave his chief's laugh. "*All* the time, *all* the time." (*"Toujours, toujours."*)

I left with Arlette. She admired Mr. Niangoran-Bouah and was pleased that the introduction she had brought about had worked so well.

I asked her about the crocodiles. "What does it mean, Arlette?"

She said, "Nobody knows. Only the president knows."

From other people, Africans and Europeans, I heard more. I heard that before the president had dug his palace lake and put in his crocodiles, there had been no crocodiles at Yamoussoukro. I heard that the keeper of the president's crocodiles was the president's sister and that she was unmarried. I heard that crocodiles were more dangerous on land than in water; then I heard the opposite. I heard that the crocodiles of Yamoussoukro, by a particular movement of their heads, warned the president of danger to the state. And at the end I felt that it was as Arlette had said: the crocodiles, so feared, were meant to be mysterious, to be felt as a mystery, and only the president knew what they, and the ritual of their feeding, stood for.

13

ON SATURDAY, while Mr. Niangoran-Bouah was at his yam festival, Arlette went to Grand-Bassam, the old, abandoned (and in parts still derelict) colonial capital. In Grand-Bassam there was a vernissage—local painters, both white and black, and Haitian painters—in a restored,

French-owned house of the colonial period. All cultural Abidjan was there—mainly expatriates, black and white; and in that cultural expatriate world Arlette was a figure. On Sunday Arlette went to Bassam again, in another party, for the expatriate Sunday treat of a swim in the ocean and a sea-food lunch in a beach restaurant.

She came back refreshed from that to take me in the evening to the house of Joachim Bony, *ancien ministre,* a former minister in the government, for an apéritif.

As a minister of education, Mr. Bony had for some time been Arlette's *patron,* and she still held him in awe. She was unusually abashed in his presence, and very concerned for the dignity of the occasion. And it was only two days afterwards that I learned from her that, for allegedly plotting against the president, Mr. Bony had been a political prisoner for five years before being pardoned by the president.

Mr. Bony lived in one of the richer residential areas of Abidjan: green streets, big houses, big plots. A gate, a drive, a modern concrete house, many vehicles. He came out to greet us, a gracious brown-skinned man in his late fifties. He walked with a limp; one foot was twisted. He took us up some steps that led directly from the garden to his sitting room. The furniture was modern, glass and steel, everything matching. He closed the aluminum-framed glass door and turned on the silent air-conditioning.

The other guests were an Ivorian doctor and his French wife, people in their fifties. Both Mr. Bony and his Ivorian friend, the doctor, had gone to France in the same year, 1946. The friend had stayed in France for twenty-one years, in Toulouse. His wife was from Toulouse. He was black to Mr. Bony's brown, and he was a physically bigger man. His wife said that when he had come back to the Ivory Coast from Toulouse he had spent more time in France than in Africa. But he had "re-integrated" himself into his family. He went to his ancestral village every weekend.

How did he spend the time there? He said he looked after his family land. On weekends, he said, he became a *planteur.* He added jokingly in English, "Gentle-man far-mer." Wasn't he a little detached now from African village ways and the religion that went with those ways? He said he wasn't a believer (he meant in African religion), but in moments of crisis—he spoke with some amusement—he found himself willing to turn again to old beliefs.

I asked Mr. Bony about the president's crocodiles. (I didn't at that time know the story of Mr. Bony's political fortunes.) He said—without awe, without hesitation—that the crocodile was the totemic animal of the president's family. His own family totem was the panther. He explained: the panther was prudent and—Mr. Bony made a gesture with the fingers of his right hand—when he leapt he was sure.

Could a hen be a totem? Yes, the doctor said. Could a family change its totem? No, the doctor said. No, Mr. Bony said; a totem was something inherited, something that came from way back.

Mr. Bony's manner was like that: direct, gentle, matter-of-fact, unawed. And just as he was the first person I had met to give a straight-forward explanation of the crocodiles, so he was the first to understand my question about the president's estates at Yamoussoukro. Some of the land would have been state land, Mr. Bony said; some would have been family land. The president's family were much more than village chiefs. They were *sous-chefs* of a great African kingdom; they might be described as local viceroys. In the colonial time their power had been reduced. But they had retained their authority in the eyes of the people.

It was of religion that we spoke after the doctor and his wife left. Religion was fundamental in Africa, Mr. Bony said. There were two worlds, the world of workaday reality and the world of the spirit. These two worlds ceaselessly looked for one another. *"Ces deux mondes se cherchent."* Mr. Bony didn't speak of the world of the day and the world of the night. But soon in his conversation the world of the spirit became the world of the supernatural. The supernatural couldn't be ignored, he said. He himself had had premonitory dreams of the deaths of his parents.

Europeans were inventive, creative people. That had to be allowed them. But because they stressed or developed only one side of man's nature they seemed to Africans like children, and sometimes because of their talents they seemed like *enfants terribles*. It had been especially dismal for him, when he had travelled in the communist countries of eastern Europe, to see men reduced to units, treated as economic beings alone. That was why, though dependent on Europeans for so many things, Africans thought of themselves as "older" than Europeans.

Apéritif time was technically over; and Mr. Bony—as gracious as Arlette would have liked him to be—sent us away in one of his cars, through his watchman-guarded gates.

Two days later I heard about his political fortunes. It cast an extra, retrospective dignity on the man. And this dignity made more curious his interest in the supernatural.

The supernatural Mr. Bony had talked about was not specifically African. But in Africa you slid so fast, so easily, into other realms. *Fraternité Matin,* continuing the government war against bad magic (and at the same time obliquely spreading the word that in the Ivory Coast sorcery was a thing of the past), was reporting on practices among the Bété people. No one in Africa—according to *Fraternité Matin*—was thought to die naturally. A sorcerer was always thought to be responsible, and suspected people could be put to terrible trials to prove their innocence. They were made to wear the dead person's clothes; they were made to eat "the mutton of death," mutton soaked in the juices of a putrefying corpse. Generally, among the Bété people, truth was obtained from suspected persons by dropping the sap of the "gôpô" tree in their eyes: it was believed that the eyes of the innocent would not be damaged by the gôpô.

And there had come my way a story which I didn't know how to treat. A defective refrigerated container on the Abidjan docks—part of a cargo from the Ivory Coast to Nigeria—had begun to give off an offensive smell. The container had been opened; it was found to contain severed heads. Sacrificial heads, for export; technology at the service of old worship. Was the story true, or was it an expatriate-African joke? (The humour of both Africans and expatriates could have coincided in a story like this.) I couldn't find out. All I could find out was that stories of this nature—and all the stories about poisoning, burials, the disappearance of children—were possessed by most expatriates. They lived with this knowledge of African Africa. But the Africa they kept in their hearts, the Africa they presented to the visitor, was the Africa of their respective skills.

1 4

THERE were expatriates and expatriates. The latest group, of women, had come from Harlem in New York. Not all were native-born Americans. Some, by their accents, had gone to the United States from the smaller islands of the English-speaking Caribbean. Another roundabout return to Africa: and they had come to spread their own kind of Christian worship. They had also come to Africa as to the motherland. They were ill-favoured, many of them unusually fat, their grossness like a form of self-abuse, some hideously bewigged, some dumpling-legged in short, wide, flowered skirts. They were like women brought together by a common physical despair.

Perhaps at the back of their minds was the idea that, being black, in Africa they could at last pass. But Africa was cruel: the Harlem ladies were among people with a sharp eye for tribe and status and physical carriage. Perhaps, with an opposite impulse, they had seen themselves as Americans, more advanced than the people left behind in the dark continent. But here too they were deceived: the Ivorians, when not blasé, deep in their own world, had a curious racial innocence. Whatever their motives, the Harlem ladies, having come to the Ivory Coast, had become shy. They seemed never to leave the hotel. Sometimes they preached to waiters, when they could catch a waiter alone; but generally they sat together in the lobby, and left their little tracts on the tables there.

The ladies were in the lobby—worn out from sitting, silent from doing nothing, and yet of overwhelming presence—when Arlette came for a farewell drink. We didn't stay in the lobby. We went to the bar.

Arlette's Africa was so different from the Africa to which the Harlem ladies had come. Shortly after we had met, she had said, when she was speaking of the failure of marriages between Ivorians and foreign women like herself, that to live in Africa and to understand its ways was to have all your old ideas unsettled. And that, Arlette had added, was a good thing. It was of her African learning that she chose to speak on this last visit, at first in the bar, and later, in the lagoon dusk, on the bar terrace.

She spoke of the two worlds, the world of the day and the world of the night, the two ideas of reality that made Africans so apparently indifferent to their material circumstances. She had seen it in the Ivory Coast, she said. Men of wealth and position could return easily to their villages at the weekend, could easily resume the hut life, could welcome that life. She had asked people from Ghana, now in chaos: "You were rich the other day. Now you are poor and your country is in a mess. Doesn't this worry you?" And they had said, "Yesterday we were all right. Today we are poor. That's the way it is. Tomorrow we may be all right again. Or we may not. That's the way it is." That was the way it was in the upper world. The inner world, the other world, continued whole. And that was what mattered.

I said, "So it wouldn't matter to you if by some accident this city of Abidjan fell into ruins?"

Arlette said, "No. It wouldn't matter. Men would continue to live in their own way."

Some Frenchmen had come out from the bar on to the terrace, not warm now, the light a dusty ochre. They sat at the next table. They were businessmen. They took out papers and folders from briefcases and began discussions. One of the men became interested in Arlette. Exaggerating his attentions, he considered her legs, her big, full figure. She had her back to him and she didn't notice. She was talking, and eating nuts and crisps as she talked.

In one of the conference rooms of the hotel there was a business conference of some sort, with many white men sitting at tables, listening to a man lecturing before a board: phantoms, preparing plans for things that were one day bound to perish. The sun was sinking in the haze of dust: the harmattan arrived at last on the coast. The lagoon was hazy; the far bank, lost in haze, was like a view from the temperate zone. To one side of the hotel works were going on in the grounds of new houses being built in this fast-rising area.

I said, "Arlette, you make me feel that the world is unstable. You make me feel that everything we live by is built on sand."

She said, "But the world is sand. Life is sand."

I felt she was saying what Hindus say as a doctrinal point, and feel as a truth in times of crisis: that life is illusion. But that was wrong: ideas have their cultural identity. And Arlette had arrived at her knowledge, her sense of the two worlds, by her interest in "esoteric studies" and African magic. This knowledge had come from her admiration of African tribal life: the chief's gift of pardon, the annual ceremony of reconciliation, the initiation ceremonies in the sacred wood, when for three months seven-year-old boys were subjected to tests that gave them a new idea of the world and their place in it. The Hindu's idea of illusion comes from the contemplation of nothingness. Arlette's idea of sand came from her understanding and admiration of a beautifully organized society.

She spoke with passion; she spoke poetically. She nibbled all the time, and all the time the Frenchman at the other table was looking at her legs.

She had a high regard for the African wise man, the man venerated as the sage. There was such a sage at this moment in Abidjan, in the African district of Treichville. He was very famous; the president himself would have liked to show him honour. But the sage preferred to live where he lived, in the courtyard of a simple house in Treichville. He said that if he moved to the middle-class area of Cocody the people who needed his help wouldn't be able to come to him. They would have to walk, not having money for taxis. And the watchdogs of Cocody would bite them.

Arlette said, "Some time ago I went back to Martinique to see my parents. It was horrible for me. The people of the Antilles are sick people. Their life is a dream. I will tell you this story. The plane back—it was a special plane—was delayed for two days. And that made me distraught. My mother was hurt that I should be so anxious to get away from her. I love my parents, but my anxiety to get away from Martinique exceeded my love for my parents. They are small-minded people over there, broken down by their history. Life is so big. The world is so big, but over there if a man gets a little job in a government department he feels he has done enough with his life. They think they are superior to Africans. But their life is a dream."

I asked her about Yamoussoukro. Why build that great city, if the world was sand?

She said, "It is the president's attempt to integrate Africa into the modern world."

And I thought she meant that to build a city like Yamoussoukro was not to accept what it stood for as the only reality. Ebony, the poet and civil servant, had hinted at something like that. Ebony's father had said to him, "I am not sending you to the school to be a white man or a Frenchman. I am sending you to enter the new world, that's all."

As we walked out we passed the Harlem ladies in the lobby.

Arlette said, "We get so many people like them from the United States. Black people who come here to convert the Africans. They are like everybody else who comes to do that. They bring their own psychic sickness to Africa. They should instead come to be converted by Africa. They are mad." (*"Ils sont fous."*)

November 1982–July 1983

·◖ A M E R I C A N ◗·
O C C A S I O N S

Columbus and Crusoe

THE ADVENTURE of Columbus is like *Robinson Crusoe*. No one can imaginatively possess the whole; everything beyond the legend is tedious and complicating. It is so even in Björn Landström's book, *Columbus*, which makes the difficult adventure as accessible as it can be made. The text itself is a retelling from the usual sources. The maps and illustrations are more important. The maps make medieval ideas of geography clear. The illustrations, a true labour of love, are numerous and exact: ships, the islands, the people, the weather, the vegetation, and even the Flemish hawk's bell which delighted the natives until it became a measure of the gold dust the discoverer required them to collect.

In the legend Columbus is persecuted by many enemies; he goes back to Spain white-haired, in chains, and he dies in poverty and disgrace. It is Columbus's own picture: he had a feeling for theatre. His concern for gold exceeded his sovereign's: he expected to get a tenth of all that was found. The chains were not necessary; he was begged to take them off. He wore them for effect, just as, after the previous disaster, he had returned in the Franciscan habit. That disaster had its profitable side. He had sent back slaves, as he had always intended. He claimed, or his son claimed for him, that he had got rid of two-thirds of the natives of Hispaniola in two years; the remainder had been set to gathering gold dust. (This was an exaggeration: he had got rid of only a third.) Even after his disgrace he fussed about his coat-of-arms, appropriating a red field for the castle of Castile, as on the royal coat-of-arms. He complained to the end about his poverty, but one of his personal gold shipments, again after his disgrace, amounted to 405 pounds. His father was a weaver; his sister married a cheesemonger; his son married a lady of royal blood. And at his death Spain hadn't gained very much. Mexico was thirteen years away; and the Indies, the source of his gold, where he thought he had discovered the Terrestrial Paradise, had become, largely through his example, *anus mundi*.

It is a story of extended horror. But it isn't only the horror that numbs response. Nor is it that the discoverer deteriorates so steadily after the discovery. It is the banality of the man. He was looking less for America or Asia than for gold; and the banality of expectation matches a continuing banality of perception. At the heart of the seamanship, the toughness, the avarice, the vindictiveness and the brutality, there is only this:

> 16 September. Here the Admiral says that on that day and all succeeding days they met with very mild breezes, and the mornings were very sweet, with naught lacking save the song of the nightingale. He adds: "And the weather was like April in Andalusia."
>
> 29 September. The air was very sweet and refreshing, so that the only thing lacking was the song of the nightingale; the sea was as calm as a river.

This is from *The Book of the First Voyage*, when he was at his most alert. The concrete details are deceptive. The sea and its life are observed, but mainly for signs of the nearness of land; just as, at the moment of discovery, the natives are studied, but only by a man "vigilant"—his own word—for gold. "Their hair is not curly . . . they are not at all black." Not an anthropological interest, not the response of wonder—disappointment rather: Columbus believed that where Negroes were, there was gold. Beyond this vigilance the words and the perceptions fail. The nightingale, April in Andalusia: the props of a banal poetry are used again and again until they are without meaning. They are at an even lower level than the recent astronaut's "Wow"—there is nothing like this pure cry of delight in Columbus. After the discovery, his gold-seeking seaman's banalities become repetitive, destroying romance and making the great adventure trivial. A book about Columbus needs to have pictures, and this is why Mr. Landström's book is so valuable.

The medieval mind? But Queen Isabella wrote during the second voyage to find out what the climate was like. April in Andalusia wasn't enough: she wanted pictures, and the romance. Marco Polo, whom Columbus had read, dealt in romance; and Amerigo Vespucci, after whom the continent is not unfairly named. Vespucci thought it worth mentioning that the natives of the islands and the Main pissed casually into the hot sand during conversation, without turning aside; that the women were wanton and used a certain animal poison, sometimes last-ingly fatal to virility, to increase the size of the male member. Perhaps he made this up; but though he too was vigilant and his own voyage ended in profitable slave-trading, he sought in the tradition of travel-romance to awaken wonder at the fact of the New World.

The facts about Columbus have always been known. In his own writ-ings and in all his actions his egoism is like an exposed deformity; he con-demns himself. But the heroic gloss, which is not even his own, has come down through the centuries. When the flagship ran aground at Haiti on the first voyage, the Indians were more than helpful: they wept to show their sympathy. Columbus was vigilant: he noted that it would be easy to subdue this "cowardly" unarmed race. This is what he presently did. Mr. Landström suggests that it was unfortunate and not really meant: it is the traditional gloss. On the third voyage Columbus thought he had discov-ered the Terrestrial Paradise. Mr. Landström, again following the gloss, says that Columbus wasn't very well at the time. But it was just this sort of geography that had made him attempt the Ocean Sea.

In this adventure, as in today's adventures in space, the romance is something we ourselves have to supply. The discovery needs a hero; the contempt settles on the country that, in the legend, betrays the hero. The discovery—and it would have come without Columbus—could not but be horrible. Primitive people, once exposed, have to be subdued and utilized or somehow put down, in the Indies, Australasia, the United States, Southern Africa; even India has its aboriginal problems. Four hundred years after the great Spanish debate, convened by the Emperor, on the treatment of primitive people, Rhodesia is an imperial issue. The parallel is there; only the contemporary debate, conducted before a mass-electorate on one side and a dispossessed but indifferent primitive people on the other, is necessarily more debased.

There is no Australian or American black legend; there is at the most a romantic, self-flattering guilt. But the black legend of Spain will persist, as will the heroic legend of Columbus. The dream of the untouched, complete world, the thing for ourselves alone, the dream of Shangri-la, is an enduring human fantasy. It fell to the Spaniards to have the unique experience. Generosity and romance, then, to the discoverer; but the Spaniards will never be forgiven. And even in the violated New World the Spaniards themselves remained subject to the fantasy. The quest for El Dorado became like a recapitulation of the whole New World adventure, a wish to have it all over again; more men and money were expended on this in twenty expeditions than on the conquest of Mexico, Peru and New Granada.

Robinson Crusoe, in its essential myth-making middle part, is an aspect of the same fantasy. It is a monologue; it is all in the mind. It is the dream of being the first man in the world, of watching the first crop grow. Not only a dream of innocence: it is the dream of being suddenly, just as one is, in unquestionable control of the physical world, of possessing "the first gun that had been fired there since the creation of the world." It is the dream of total power. "First, I made him know his name should be Friday, which was the day I saved his life. I called him so for the memory of the time. I likewise taught him to say master, and then let him know that was to be my name." Friday is awkward about religion; Crusoe cannot answer. Power brings problems. Crusoe sees some cannibals about to kill and eat a man. He runs to liberate. But then he stops. What is his right to interfere? Is it just the gun? Some Spaniards are to be rescued. How will his freedom and power continue? How will they obey? Where do sanctions start in the empty world? They must sign a contract. But there is no pen, no paper: a difficulty as particular and irrational as in a nightmare. It is from more than a desert island that he is rescued. The issues can never be resolved.

Later Crusoe makes good, in that very New World, but in the settled, beaten-down slave society of Brazil. The horror of the discovery, of being the first totally powerful man in the world: that happened a long time before.

1967

Jacques Soustelle and the
Decline of the West

FROM A DISTANCE Jacques Soustelle appears to be two men. There is the exiled politician whose cause, *Algérie française,* Algeria is France, has been destroyed. And there is the ethnologist and scholar, the imaginative interpreter of ancient Aztec life, whose first book, published when he was twenty-three, was *Mexique, Terre Indienne*: Mexico is Indian, you might say. Both careers have been remarkable and both are likely to continue. In the serenity of the last two or three years of exile, Soustelle has become a prolific scholar again. *Arts of Ancient Mexico,* published in England a few months ago, has been recognized as a major work. And he is still only fifty-five: he will not be a political exile forever.

Serenity is Soustelle's own word. It is one of the unlikely things that has come to him in his exile which, when it began in 1962, was "dreary and dangerous." He was then on the run, a figure of newspaper melodrama, alleged to be plotting in Italy, Portugal, Vienna.

Early in his exile he was denounced to the Italian police by a newspaper reporter who spotted him in a Brescia hotel. The name Soustelle used then was Jean Albert Sénèque. It "amused" him. (The Stoic philosopher Seneca, when he was very old, was accused of conspiring against the Emperor Nero, and was required to commit suicide.) But exile presently became less amusing. Soustelle was expelled from Italy, banned for a time by Switzerland and West Germany. After someone tried to kill de Gaulle in August 1962, French government agents became active all over Europe. During a carnival dance at a Munich hotel in February 1963, ex-Colonel Argoud, another exile, was kidnapped; he was found in Paris the next morning, badly beaten up, in a van near Notre Dame. After this Soustelle dropped out of the news. When, a year later, he was arrested in a Lausanne hotel and expelled from Switzerland, he was using a more commonplace name: Jacques Lemaire.

"Two attempts were made to kill or kidnap me. The first time I didn't know. The second time I knew. A clumsy attempt had been made to bribe someone with $100,000. We played hide-and-seek for a few days. Then I shook him off."

Now the pressure has lessened. France is still closed to him but he can move about freely outside. General de Gaulle is reported to have asked recently after Monsieur and Madame Soustelle and to have sent his good wishes to M. Soustelle through a common acquaintance. Mme. Soustelle still lives and works in Paris. She, too, is an Aztec scholar. She and Jacques Soustelle were married in 1932, when he was nineteen; they have no children. They keep in touch; Soustelle confirms the Paris story that the language of the Aztecs is their secret language, which they use, or used, on the telephone.

Last March, Soustelle was a candidate in the French elections in his old constituency of Lyon. Election would have given him immunity. But he would have been arrested if he had entered France to campaign; in that month a traveller saw his name prominent among the list of proscribed people at Orly airport. Soustelle sent over a tape-recorded speech. He came in second with eight thousand votes. Some people think that Soustelle should have gone to France then, that his arrest would have been a one-night affair. But Soustelle is cautious. Though he is open now to interviews and no longer feels he has to sit facing the main door of hotels, he still requires meetings to be arranged through his lawyer. And the lawyer sits in on all conversations. It is a remnant of the theatre that has surrounded Soustelle since his flight from Paris to Algiers in May 1958, when his aim was to use *Algérie française* to bring de Gaulle back to power. He was reported then to have escaped from Paris—where he was being watched—in the boot of a car.

He says it isn't true; and all that high adventure now seems so unlikely as, among the flowers and carpets of a grand hotel in the slack season, Soustelle breaks off to consider the wine list or to ask a solicitous waiter for a packet of Players *médium*. The pronunciation is for the waiter's benefit. Soustelle's own English is brisk, complex, colloquial. The occasional French words he uses—*éveilleur, acharné*—are those for which there is no ready English equivalent.

Photographs emphasize Soustelle's heaviness, his double chin, the firm set of the wide mouth, the rimless glasses and the dark pouches under the assessing eyes. But the face is mobile; eyes and lips are easily touched with humour. He knows about wine and will talk about it, but precisely: "I know the vineyard," "I know the owner." He draws your attention to the cigarettes he smokes. They are Players; they hold a story. In Lyon in 1927 Soustelle won an English essay competition. The prize was a fortnight in London. He stayed in a house near Clapham Common. He travelled a lot on the Underground, and it was from a machine in an Underground station that he bought his first packet of cigarettes. They were Players; he has smoked them ever since.

His manner is like that of a university lecturer who knows his own reputation and will not be drawn beyond his own subject. "If you have nothing to say to him," his lawyer says, "he has nothing to say to you." Soustelle is not interested in ideas for their own sake. He always appears to speak from a well-prepared position; and this is more than an attribute of exile. He gives the impression that he came to terms with himself a long time ago, perhaps even in his precocious adolescence, and that his areas of interest have been defined by his experience: his scholarship, Mexico, the war, Algeria. He still seems able to survey his experience with wonder; he seems continually to process and refine this experience as it expands within its defined limits. It is the method neither of the scholar nor of the politician, but of both together; and it comes close to the method of the novelist, making art of egotism, creating a private impenetrable whole out of fragments which from a distance might appear unrelated.

Consider the Players cigarettes. Soustelle is conscious of them as a link with his adolescence, his early academic brilliance, his first trip to London—and the Elgin Marbles. In that fortnight he spent much time among them in the British Museum. They made him want to go to Athens; and it was only last spring, in the serenity of exile, that he was able to go. He was overwhelmed; he had expected Greek monuments to be on a smaller scale. And there was another surprise. He had always liked Roman monuments; he found he didn't like them as much in Athens: they seemed so crude. The visit helped him to clarify his ideas about the United States and the "provincialization" of Europe. And these ideas have come directly from his experience as a scholar and politician.

Europe has been provincialized because she has withdrawn from the "wide spaces" of Africa. Civilizations are limited in space as well as in time; and this withdrawal, like the Roman withdrawal from Dacia and Britain, is "the first sign, the first wrinkles, of old age." Rome incorporated Gaul; France ought to have incorporated Africa. Instead, France yielded to the "idol" of decolonization and the pressures of mercantile capitalism and converted the low cultures of black Africa into a *poussière* of petty dictatorships.

"They will use what France left there to the last tractor, to the last bolt, to the last little teaspoon. After that, as in Tripolitania, they will let the goats graze where wheat formerly grew."

True decolonization would have come from incorporation, with equal rights and an equal advance for all. But this was rejected; it was too difficult.

France has failed and has retreated across the Mediterranean into her own "hexagonal" territory not through defeat—militarily Algeria was a French victory—but through decadence, through bourgeois selfishness, *les week-ends et les vacances d'été et d'hiver,* and through racialism: the unwillingness of the French to accept that Africans, Arabs, Berbers, and the Maltese, Spanish and Greek *colons* of Algeria might also have been made Frenchmen.

All civilizations have perished; even their ruins will go one day; there is no pattern and no goal. But it is Hegelian nonsense to say that the world's history is the world's justice; the stoic must always fight. Ideas which do not lead to action are just dreams; action without an "ideological orientation" is only nihilistic opportunism.

So, until the serenity and release of exile, Soustelle the scholar-politician has been trapped in his dual role. The politician is only a part of Soustelle; and his political views, when separated from his experience, can be simplified and used by people to whom they give comfort. Like de Gaulle himself in 1958, Soustelle can be all things to all men.

ALL SOUSTELLES must originally have come from the area around Soustelle, a hamlet in the Cevennes which today has a population of about one hundred, many of whom are named Soustelle. Jacques Soustelle was born in Montpellier and grew up in a semi-rural suburb of Lyon. He never knew his father; his mother remarried when he was ten; his stepfather, "a very good man," was a motor mechanic and worked at his trade until recently. The family was Protestant. Jacques Soustelle was an only child in a house which at one time held a grandfather and three aunts, one of whom managed the household. During the first war his mother worked in a post office; later she worked in an office. "We were not lumpen-proletariat. But we were proletariat."

It was his class teacher, "a very good man," who suggested to Mme. Soustelle that her son should look beyond the *certificat d'études* and go to a *lycée*. He was the first of those teachers, those very good men, as Soustelle today remembers them all, who helped and guided and arranged the scholarship examinations which led to Paris and the Ecole Normale Supérieure when he was seventeen, the *agrégation* and the diploma in ethnology three years later. "By the time I was twenty I had sat twelve competitive examinations. I wasn't very good in mathematics, but I came first in everything else." In Paris he had also ghosted a Fourier anthology and some detective stories, to supplement his scholarship money; and he gave lessons.

He had always read a lot, and his interests had set early. He read natural history and history; even as a boy he liked reading about the Roman Empire in its third-century decline, "that majestic and terrible spectacle"; and a taste for Jules Verne had led on to books of travel and books about exotic peoples. In Paris his thoughts turned naturally to ethnology after he met three scholars who were outstanding in the subject. Paul Rivet was one of these. Rivet was director of the Musée de l'Homme, then the Musée d'Ethnographie. Soustelle worked in the Musée de l'Homme for half the day, among the artefacts of the people he studied. To him these artefacts were works of art and not quaint; and through them he felt linked to the makers. He had developed the almost religious feeling that the finest and most comprehensive study was Man. About this time some dancers from New Caledonia came to Paris, and Soustelle was able to spend an evening with them. He remembers it as a privilege, part of his luck.

The peoples of Oceania—visited for the first time in 1945, when he was de Gaulle's Minister for the Colonies—were then his special interest. But Paul Rivet had visited Mexico in 1930 and had come back enthusiastic about the Otomí tribe, about whom little work had been done. Rivet said he would send Soustelle out to Mexico, where there was a French cultural mission, if Soustelle became *agrégé*. Soustelle shifted his interest to Mexico. And Rivet was as good as his word. The *agrégation* results came out in August 1932; in October Soustelle and his wife—they had not long been married—sailed for Mexico.

The Soustelles worked among the Otomí in Central Mexico. They also worked among the very small tribe called the Lacandones in the south-east. In the rainy season the Soustelles went to Mexico City. There they fell among Mexican intellectuals; they became friendly with the painter Rivera. "There was still something of the post-revolutionary fervour, a general awareness of the Mexican past. I remember that someone even organized a *velada*, a vigil, in honour of the old Aztec god Quetzalcoatl. On the other side there were people, sometimes of Indian ancestry, who thought that the Indian past was bloody and barbaric and should be forgotten. Of course I took the Indian side. But Mexico can be neither Indian nor Spanish. It is what it is: Indian and Spanish."

The Aztec universe, as Soustelle has described it, was fragile and unstable. The world had been destroyed more than once before and was going to be destroyed again. Destruction could be stayed only by a continual offering of human blood. "I never thought of human sacrifice as a barrier to my understanding of the Aztecs. I was imbued very early with the idea of the relativity of human morals." In Soustelle's writings this sacrifice becomes the tragic, ennobling, wearying act of men determined to keep their world going. But destruction came. Between 1519 and 1521 the Spaniards smashed the head and heart of the developing civilization. If the Aztecs had been left alone, Soustelle thinks, they would have taken Mexico into the equivalent of the Meiji era in Japan. And, strangely, in his writings there is little anger at the destruction, and little regret for what might have developed. "The Spaniards couldn't have acted otherwise. And we mustn't forget the efforts some Spaniards made to record and defend; or that they made possible the society in which Indian life was to reawaken."

It was this Mexican experience—so large, so complete: grandeur, destruction, decadence, incorporation, new life—that Soustelle sought twenty years later to apply to Algeria: the equation of Mexican Indians, who had only Mexico, with Arab guerrillas, who could look to a vast Muslim world, which had once just failed to overrun Europe itself.

SOUSTELLE was in Mexico, vice-president of a conference of Americanists, when the war broke out. He took a Dutch ship to Ramsgate and made his way to France to join the regiment in which he had done his military service in 1936. He had nothing to do for some months. Then he was recruited into the Ministry of Information which the Daladier government was establishing. He was sent back to Mexico and was there when France fell. He was prepared then to be an exile forever. He thought he would go to Canada and serve in a French Canadian regiment. But a friend in the British Consulate told him that there was a French general in London who was setting up an organization. Soustelle sent a cable to London; after three days he got a reply from one of de Gaulle's aides.

He was asked to stay on in Mexico for a little to organize support for the Free French from the local French community. Then, in a ship full of New Zealanders and Australians, future pilots, he went to England. "At Liverpool, where we docked, I had a lot of trouble to prove that I wasn't a dubious character. But it was all right at Carlton Gardens. By some chance de Gaulle's ADC was an old schoolfellow of mine from Lyon. I met de Gaulle that very day. Two or three days later I was invited to dinner." Then, as always later, de Gaulle's manner was one of icy formality. De Gaulle was fifty, Soustelle twenty-eight; it was the beginning of an association that lasted eighteen years. "The great qualities in him which attracted me can still be seen today, but only in caricature."

Soustelle was put in the "foreign service" section and sent back to Latin America once again. Later, in London, he was National Commissioner for Information with the Liberation Committee. When the Allies landed in North Africa he became Secretary-General for Action in France. His job was to pool the resources of the Free French Intelligence with those of the Vichy Deuxième Bureau, which had fled to North Africa after the German occupation of Southern France; and to supply the French underground. "We ran short of French banknotes, and in the end we were dropping little pieces of paper signed by Mendès-France promising to pay after the liberation. The winter of 1943–4 was horrible. So many people one knew disappeared, were killed or committed suicide. Such a waste of life. I don't think the underground in France would have lasted another year."

The liberation came, and disillusionment. "Everything just went back to what it was before. We overestimated the importance of the Resistance. You know, it was just point something per cent of the population that took part. I suppose the First World War was the beginning of the end for France. Fewer people were killed in the Second War. But France was occupied and we became hopelessly divided. We fought against one another in Syria and Dakar. And we didn't show sufficient restraint after the liberation. It would have been difficult, I know."

General de Gaulle presently withdrew from politics. But Soustelle stayed on. His academic career continued. In 1955, the year he published his master-work, *The Daily Life of the Aztecs,* he became— with de Gaulle's blessing—Governor-General of Algeria, where on the first of November 1954, the insurrection had broken out, with seventy separate incidents.

In time the insurrection tied down 500,000 French troops. When it was over in 1962, the French had lost 14,000 men, the insurgents 140,000; 3,000 European civilians had been killed, 30,000 Arabs.

In the legend, which has lasted, Soustelle underwent a conversion in Algeria. The sight of a massacre, it was said, unhinged him; overnight the reforming pro-Arab liberal became a supporter of *Algérie française;* and his head was finally turned, so the legend goes, by the adulation of the *colons* among the crowd of a hundred thousand who gathered to cheer him off at the end of his two-year term. The massacre story is in Soustelle's favour, but it is the part of the legend he most vehemently rejects. His aim in Algeria had always been integration, on the Mexican pattern. To hand the country over to a terrorist faction would have been irresponsible, illiberal and stupid. Integration would not have been easy. It would have taken time and money, but he was prepared to use the newly discovered resources of the Sahara to create this new Algeria. In 1958 integration was more than a possibility. But de Gaulle wasn't impressed. And to Soustelle all that has followed has been betrayal and destruction. "Destruction is not a style: it is the negation of all styles." The million *colons* have left; one Algerian dictatorship has been replaced by another. Arab Algeria sinks; an idea of France has been destroyed.

SOUSTELLE'S political career so far has been contained within two periods of exile. The scholar whose nationalism was aroused before the war by the German threat has known only political defeat. The defeats grew bigger even as his political authority grew. The fall of France has been followed by the fall of the French Empire. The vision of the Paris-Algiers-Brazzaville axis shrank to the vision of France stretching from

Dunkirk to Tamanrasset, the Touareg town in the Sahara. Now there is only France. But if Algeria went yesterday, Corsica and Brittany might go tomorrow: it is the logic of bourgeois indifference and decline. The Third World that France now seeks to lead is a chimera; de Gaulle's personal rule has taken France away from her friends. France, Soustelle feels, has been politically neutered. A fresh disaster is being prepared.

Dealing with defeat, the scholar, so exact in his own discipline, turns to the generalizations of emotion. He sees technical progress coinciding with moral and aesthetic decay. "Our civilization has had no style for a century." "A civilization which is exhausted no longer attracts." And his imprecise fears have now gone beyond the ruined idea of France to Western civilization itself. No capable enemy, no overwhelming external proletariat is yet visible. But that proves nothing.

These propositions are all debatable. Perhaps what is missing is a definition of the civilization that is threatened: perhaps such a definition will show that at the heart of the despair lies a patriotism that has been both nourished and wounded by defeat, as by a drug. Soustelle's main concern now is to return to his country. Inaction need not be ignoble. "I might abstain from political life. But I can't admit being ostracized after twenty-seven years in the service of my country." This is part of the serenity of exile and it may go when exile ends. The certainty of total defeat, the defeat that leaves no more battles to be fought, is its own dangerous solace. It can commit a man to hopeless duty and quixotic action and release him from the fear of failure.

This playing with the idea of defeat appears also to come from the Soustelle who makes art out of his experience and who now, in exile, has discovered all the consonances of this experience. The politician has known defeat; the ethnologist has studied a defeated people (a recent letter has told him that the Lacandones are in danger of extinction); the study of ethnology itself derives from a civilization that is on the defensive. The pattern, too neat, belongs to art. It is art, though, that comes close to self-indulgence. Even the stoicism is like romance: one of Soustelle's favourite historical tableaux is the second-century philosopher-emperor Marcus Aurelius holding the Germans on the Danube.

This romance, which holds the fear of the sudden unknown destroyer, can be taken beyond the scholar's discovery of the nervous

Aztec world, awaiting Cortés. When he was a boy in Villeurbanne in Lyon, Soustelle liked to read the Roman histories of Ammianus Marcellinus. In a footnote in his last book, *Les Quatre Soleils*, Soustelle re-tells a story from this historian. On a day in AD 241, Soustelle says, the citizens of Antioch were at the theatre. Suddenly one of the actors broke off and said: "Am I dreaming? Or are those Persians?" The audience turned. The archers of King Sapor stood on the topmost terrace; their bows were drawn.

1967

New York with Norman Mailer

NORMAN MAILER always campaigned in a correct dark-blue suit. Towards the end he cut his hair short. A week or so before election day the Mailer campaign staff lost some hair as well. The hefty thirty-year-old campaign manager shaved off his little beard, and the sideburns of others were abbreviated. Angry young necks showed fresh and clean; plain dark ties closed up open shirts. The first order, the one that had got rid of the manager's beard, had come from Mailer himself; it had worked its way down; and for three or four days in this last week the candidate and his staff were partially estranged.

"There's been some degree of role-confusion," one shorn young man said.

They were still loyal at headquarters, but they said they were loyal to the campaign, the cause, the ideas. They spoke less of "Norman"; they spoke of "the candidate" and they made the election sound like a day of sacrifice. Where someone had pinned up *Get Ready for the Norman Conquest* someone now chalked an anti-Mailer obscenity in red, but shyly, not using the name, only the initials.

Campaign headquarters (Senator Eugene McCarthy's last year) was a large grimy room on the second floor of a decaying building on Columbus Circle, above a couple of cafés and a sauna establishment. The lift didn't always work; it was safer to go around the corner to the staircase, where rubbish was sometimes left out on the landings in plastic sacks; New York in places is like Calcutta, with money. The headquarters room was divided into offices by low flimsy partitions, which for various reasons were knocked down one by one as the campaign progressed. The furniture was sparse, trestle tables, old folding chairs, duplicating machines; there was printed paper everywhere, on walls, floor, tables.

The helpers moved in little cliques within the larger club. Sometimes, when girls brought their babies strapped to their backs in aluminum frames, it was like a hippy encampment with its familial privacies and self-satisfied dedication. During the days of the estrangement privacies vanished; and, like amateurs miming dejection in a low-budget film, the helpers huddled round a table behind the last partition and tried with the help of some beer-cans to give the impression to correspondents—at first ignored, but then welcomed—that they were drinking heavily.

It had been an ambiguous campaign—professional-amateur, political and anti-political. *The other guys are the joke*, a Mailer campaign button said. But now it was possible to feel that the estrangement was also a cover-up for doubt, perhaps panic. A fortnight before, a New York writer, no friend of Mailer, had told me that Mailer's campaign would be as self-defeating as Goldwater's had been in 1964. Mailer, like Goldwater, was a licenced figure. The media would cheer him on, but only in this role. After a time Mailer would begin to suffer from a lack of serious attention; it would get worse as the campaign went on; and at the end Mailer's ideas, however good, would be discredited and Mailer himself would be running for cover.

It didn't work out like that. But this was the gamble Mailer was taking, at the peak of his reputation. Mailer never stopped complaining about poor press coverage; but he got a lot, and it became more and more serious. On election day forty-one thousand registered Democrats voted for him. A good sale for any writer; and for Mailer the seven-week politician, a triumph. The blue suit, the walking tours, the handshaking: Mailer's instincts had been right. The display of energy and campaigning orthodoxy—the politician's simple self-satire—had helped to establish Mailer's seriousness.

At the same time the campaign had never ceased to be an intellectual entertainment. Through all the repetitions and simplifications Mailer always rang true. He never lost his gift of the phrase, that made so many of his comments sound like epigrams. "Anonymity creates boredom." "Crime will be on the increase as long as it's the most interesting activity." "You will need more and more police to keep more and more bad government in power." To the end he was good in the direct interview. His replies then—after what looked like a flick of the tongue against the top teeth, as though a piece of chewing gum was being hidden away—were abrupt, swift and pithy. The writer's imagination, ceaselessly processing and ordering experience ("You are always writing that novel about yourself," he told me later), could at any moment pass inspection.

"If you win the Democratic nomination, which Republican would you like to run against?"

"Marchi. He says he's a conservative. I call myself a left conservative. We could have an extraordinary discussion about the meaning of conservative principles. Many people who call themselves conservatives are right-wing reactionaries. Which is a different thing altogether." Next question. And this was at the last press conference, when Mailer was tired with words.

He was least effective in the later, non-controversial TV tournaments, where each candidate did a one-minute joust in turn. The politicians won then. Though using words, they appeared to be dismissing words, even their own; they made it plain that they genuinely wanted power and knew what that power was. Mailer's words were part of Mailer. As a writer and politician he carried a double burden; and the ridiculous part of his gamble—so private, so public—was that irresponsibility in either role would have led to the disaster that many had seen coming.

The ideas were big—New York a dying city, alienation its major problem, a complete political reorganization the only hope, with New York as the fifty-first state, more directly controlling its own funds, and the more or less autonomous city districts developing their own lifestyles. There were attractive elements of fantasy: no cars in Manhattan (the city-state ringed by a monorail), free public bicycles, and a monthly sabbath, a Sweet Sunday, trafficless, when "nothing would fly but the birds."

The platform was like an anguished intellectual statement, and the publicity in the beginning had been a writer's publicity: rallying approval from the *New York Times* in a ponderous, punning editorial; the prizes for *Miami and the Siege of Chicago* and *The Armies of the Night*; a reported million-dollar contract for the new book about the Apollo moon shot.

The first meeting of the campaign, in Greenwich Village, was an intellectual-social occasion. It was rowdy. From press reports it appeared that Mailer was attempting a re-make of *Armies*. A false start—this was admitted later—but a writer's false start: the new book often begins like a repeat of the one just finished. Then the campaign changed. It found—what it had lacked—a political issue. It became political; it acquired substance.

The City College of New York, CCNY, which had been having its racial troubles, formulated a dual-admission policy: half of its places would be reserved for students from disadvantaged communities. There was an uproar. The disadvantaged would be black and Puerto Rican; Jewish students would suffer; standards would be lowered. Every mayoral candidate, Democratic and Republican, spoke out against the plan. Only Mailer and his "running mate" were for it. The campaign that had begun as an entertainment now seemed dangerous to some. "The Jews here regard Mailer as a sinner": this was the message from a Mailer worker in the Bronx. A poll showed opinion eight to one against dual-admission; and for the next few days, for five or six or more times a day, Mailer worked hard to show that what looked irresponsible had logic and was socially necessary. After a week there was a compromise; CCNY said they would take only 400 disadvantaged students, not 1,500; the issue faded. But the campaign had proved itself.

In the early days Mailer could say of a rival: "If I didn't make a vow to use no obscene language, I would say that Wagner was full of an unmarketable commodity." This was the Village Mailer. At the end he said of Wagner: "He's the lead hobby horse in a wooden field." This was funnier; it also made more political sense. On election night, the fight lost and won, the cheering crowd followed Mailer from headquarters across Eighth Avenue to his car. They were also cheering Mailer's wife and Mailer's mother, both of whom had taken part in the campaign. The politician as family man: to this extent the campaign had become orthodox.

Three weeks before, Mailer had told a television reporter that running a campaign was like writing a novel. The same confidence was required; there were analogous problems of creation. "Your brains are working all the time. The writer works on a world, brings it to a resolution; and that world changes him. When a writer finishes a novel he is a changed man."

IF MAILER had a political base, it was his glamour as a writer. But glamour also stood in his way.

At the annual dinner of the Village Independent Democrats the two speakers were to be men who had worked with Senator Eugene McCarthy and the late Senator Robert Kennedy. McCarthy, Kennedy: these were the magic names not only of the left, the protesting, the liberal, but also of those asserting an intellectual separateness and therefore content to lose. "I know a man who supported fourteen losing candidates," a visitor from the Lexington Avenue Democrats said. Mailer was going to lose, but the Lexington visitor wasn't prepared to admit Mailer as one of his losers. The ideas were good, but Mailer belonged to another area of American glamour.

Benign now, still powerfully built rather than "unwillingly fat" (his own words), a little tired after a day spent on a campaign paper, blue eyes twinkling in a harassed, mobile face, Mailer was undeniably a presence among the Village Independent Democrats at their pre-dinner cocktails.

"I've talked to Mr. Mailer," a forty-year-old woman said. (Over severe, separating foundations, her neckline plunged and plunged.) "And he says I can follow him around in the press car and I want to go everywhere he goes." Her escort, led by the hand, smiled neutrally.

Banning, the campaign manager, listed the evening's engagements. They were to end about midnight.

The woman hesitated, then chose the dinner.

Schwartzman, the nineteen-year-old student on the Mailer advance staff, said, "She probably said she was a freelance and writing a feature. You do get types like that. Now the agency girl, that's more my type of writer. A little tall, but still."

The agency girl, blonde, tanned, cool in a flaming red sweater, had just joined the campaign. She too was writing a feature. In the car afterwards she got out her notebook.

"Why haven't you gone to Vietnam, Mr. Mailer?"

"I don't want to get killed."

"I was there for two years. I wasn't killed."

"That is a horrible and obscene war. I would have done something. I would have got killed."

Banning leaned over the front seat to talk of campaign plans. Mailer sat forward, and the two men discussed walking tours and the wisdom of campaigning in certain East Side bars. Mailer didn't want to campaign in bars. It would mean either doing a lot of drinking in one place or getting in the way of a voter who wanted a drink.

The agency girl said, "Do you think you have enough of a political record, Mr. Mailer?"

Mailer turned to her and smiled. "As a man who's been married four times—take this down—I say to politicians never run on your past record."

While her pen worked, Banning talked about an article on the campaign in *Life*. "On Wednesday it was four pages. On Thursday it was two. On Friday it was one and a half."

Mailer said it was hard on the writer. "That's why *Life*'s going broke."

"People say," Banning said, "*Life*'s going broke because of what they're paying you for your moon shot article."

Mailer smiled at the agency girl. "Perhaps they're trying to rebuke me."

"Perhaps," the girl said, "I should get you angry. Mr. Mailer, why do you talk so much?"

It was the sort of newspaper feature the campaign was attracting.

We were in the Lower East Side. A "surviving" area, Mailer called it affectionately: decaying red-brick houses, narrow shops with dirty windows, an occasional empty lot.

"If you are Lithuanian," a man said on the steps of the East Midtown Reform Democratic Club, "how come your name is Mailer?"

"Lithuanian Jew," Mailer insisted. "On both sides."

It was a small hall, panelled down one side and decorated with KLM posters, bunting and the Stars and Stripes. There were about forty people on folding metal chairs.

"By the look of you," Mailer said, "I can see you are not a soft Democratic Club. Let's have the questions. I can see that the person who asks the first question is going to be in as much trouble as me."

The question was about the fifty-first state. "You think the Governor of New York would let you or anybody else get away from them?"

"We all know what breaks up an unhappy marriage. It's a smart Jewish lawyer. I submit that I am the smartest Jewish attorney in town."

The mood didn't last. A woman asked about CCNY. She sat next to a tweed-jacketed man who might have been her husband; they both looked like teachers. "Why don't you send them all to Harvard and give them all a really *good* education?" This was the Jewish backlash; she was speaking of the blacks and Puerto Ricans.

"You know you are just giving expression to your prejudice. Harvard's my old college—"

"That's why I said it."

"Let's assume that Harvard's going down the drain—"

"You're putting words in her mouth!" the man shouted.

"Our universities are to education what *The New Yorker* is to literature. A minor organ with a major function." Laughter cleared the air. "Pardon this digression. No one should trust a speaker who strays from the point." He addressed the man: "You recognize the unhappiness with which you speak?" It was a direct, gentle inquiry.

"I do," the man said. His response was like a reflex; his tone was confessional.

A moment of stillness: the man and woman, for all their passion, and the respectable jauntiness of their "budget" clothes, were older than they had first appeared.

It wasn't a perfect solution, Mailer said, exploiting the moment. But it was better that the colleges should make some adjustments rather than be destroyed altogether. If the blacks hadn't been betrayed so often, if opportunities had been given them, "you would have had blacks as mean and as ugly as any——" His mischievousness was like the other face of anger; he was deliberately destroying the mood.

"You are asking the kids to pay for it!" the woman shouted.

"Let him talk!"

"The kids will have," Mailer said, above the voices calling for order, "the exhilarating existential experience of going to school with black people."

That was the end. And, unexpectedly, there was applause, Mailer walking smartly down, arms held out wide, palms open, like a wrestler about to charge.

The next halt, a fund-raising one, was at a place called the Electric Circus in the Village. It was a good name. In the stairways and corridors blue, red and mauve neon strips reflected on walls that might have been papered with aluminum foil; and at the end of this neon fantasy was a wide white hall, packed with the young. It was a paid-up Mailer crowd. But Mailer, solitary before the microphone, appeared irritated. "You are here to see me work, is that it?" The questions were too sympathetic. "When we win, which would give all of us great concern——" But there was little of that. It was as though, out of his security here, Mailer had committed himself to frowns and silences and was waiting to be provoked. "Now, listen. I'm much more conservative than most of you people here. I'll work for and support your neighbourhood, but I don't think I'll approve of it."

After that, ten minutes at the League of Women Voters in the public library opposite the Museum of Modern Art. An anti-Rockefeller art-student demo going on outside that: a swift exchange of literature, campaign with campaign. And then a confusion of causes: Badillo, one of Mailer's rivals, coming out of the library with his staff, Mailer going in with his, everybody with leaflets for everybody else.

"Everywhere I go I see Badillo buttons. I feel Badillo's staked you guys."

"Norman, Norman," the Badillo supporter said. "That's not a nice thing to say."

A meeting with the East Side Democrats was on the schedule. But only the wife of the campaign photographer was there, in a belted pink mackintosh. She had been waiting on the pavement a long time; the club room was locked. The busy campaign, unexpectedly isolated, reassembled; and then Banning told us to hurry over to the West Side Democrats; we were already very late for them.

"Advance did a fine job," someone in the second car said.

"I've been talking to taxi-drivers," a foreign reporter said (he had joined us at the Electric Circus). "They may know about *The Naked*. But they don't always know who the author is."

"I was talking to an old Jew in Brooklyn yesterday. I told him about Mailer. He said, 'Isn't he the guy stabbed his wife?' Nine years, and he's talking about it like he'd read it in the paper that morning."

"He probably gets his papers late."

They talked about the agency girl.

"You think she's for real, a writer?"

"With looks like that she could be anything. But she's a groupie. She's only going for the big man."

We weren't late for the West Side Democrats. A dingy first-floor hall overlooking Broadway, photographs of Robert Kennedy, old Eugene McCarthy stickers, the Stars and Stripes. A mixed crowd of about fifty, some Puerto Ricans, a couple of blacks. One of Mailer's rivals was still talking.

". . . I tell you one thing we can do real fast to get better crime control . . ." This was Congressman Scheuer, spending half a million dollars to come last in the primary, below Mailer.

Mailer entered, his hair frizzing out now. The TV lights blazed on him. Heads turned; hands were shaken.

". . . get police out of all station-house and routine jobs . . . all non—crime control functions . . ."

The applause wasn't for the Congressman. It was for Mailer, withdrawing after his false entry. Presently, through the mêlée, the Congressman walked out, smiling, a private figure.

But they were a dull audience, and because they were dull, Mailer tried. Irony, to begin with. CCNY was being taken over, he said, by the same Communist plot Mayor Wagner had talked about some years ago. The audience remained vacant. "That was a joke." He told an Irish joke in an Irish accent. Silence. "Now that I've lost this club"—The laugh came; the audience relaxed. Mailer talked for twenty minutes; it was the best speech of the evening.

IN THE MORNING there was a story in the *New York Times*.

"CAMPAIGN" BY MAILER UPSTAGES THE ONCE FESTIVAL IN "VILLAGE"

. . . First, however, the audience at the last in the current Electric Ear series of multimedia affairs at the East Village rock hall witnessed a psychodrama of another variety, "The Campaign," starring Norman Mailer . . . While TV cameras captured the bizarre scene, Mr. Mailer urged statehood . . .

And at the Overseas Press Club they were gloomy. Neither the *Times* nor the *Post* nor the *News* had sent a man to the press conference that morning, when Mailer and his running mate—Jimmy Breslin, a popular columnist, a heavy, dark-haired Irishman of menacing and explosive appearance—were to present a paper on housing. Banning had brought a boxful of copies; he found only about fifteen takers, radio and TV people, who always served the campaign well, some foreign reporters, and the agency girl, now in green. The TV cameras and the lights played on her for a little. She remained cool. Out of a cross face Mailer smiled.

A reporter asked for a statement on the "integrity" of the New York press.

"The simple statement," Breslin said, "is that no one's here. They'll begin to listen when they hear shotguns on Park Avenue."

"Electric Circus," Mailer said afterwards, looking at the *Times,* which Banning had folded over to show the story. "I didn't like the name. I didn't like the building."

"It was a horrible building," Banning said.

"How much did we get out of it?"

"A couple of hundred bucks."

"Not worth it."

"I was talking to an AP man," Banning said, explaining the poor attendance at the conference. "They had a list up in the office. 'These stories we will cover this morning.' And another list. 'These stories we will not cover this morning.' We'll call *another* press conference tomorrow at the *same* time. *That's* the way to test them."

I was beginning to recognize Banning's style in drama. It might have been his diplomatic training; he had served for some time in the American Foreign Service. Or it might have been his later work in broadcasting. ("I couldn't tell you even today," he said after the campaign, "whether politics or show business is my first love.")

About thirty reporters came the next day. The agency girl wore cream. The *Times* sent a man; so did the *Post.* There had been a lot on the TV networks the previous evening—the interviews, so casual, given an extra, separate reality when slotted into the news programmes on the small screen—but Mailer was still complaining.

"We have to bludgeon our way into a newspaper office to get a small piece. They are trying to make our campaign ridiculous and up to a point they have succeeded. We have made mistakes on the way; we have played into their hands."

Tempers were shorter; there were fewer jokes. Mailer looked tired and aggressive; it was his face that suggested defeat. But he might have been acting: his face was so mobile, his moods so quick.

Two hours later, at his Wall Street rally, standing below the statue of Washington on the steps of the Old Treasury Building, he was a different man. Hands now in trouser-pockets below the buttoned jacket, now in jacket pockets, he appeared to strut, like a boxer in the new respectability of a suit, confident of his public spread out in rows on the wide steps, filling the famous narrow street below. The sound system was bad. All the words were lost, including Breslin's threat about the shotguns on Park Avenue. But the scene was dramatically right.

A stranger coming on Wall Street at that moment with a knowledge of America gained only from films would have found in the scene a familiar glamour. He would have seen the man up there as every type of American myth-figure: boxer, sheriff, bad man, mobster, even politician. It was the setting: the famous street in the famous city, the buildings, the flags, the rhetoric and history in the Washington statue. And it was also Mailer: his sense of the city, perhaps, his sense of occasion.

But when I talked to Mailer a week after the election I found that his own memories of the Wall Street rally were vague; the details of the campaign, of particular scenes and particular words, had blurred.

"You don't operate as a writer. You don't see what people are wearing. You are aware of people only as eyes, a type of response. It's more like being an actor."

THE DAY AFTER the Wall Street rally, after many more meetings, speeches, ceremonies, questions and answers and statements, Mailer said, "I've become duller. Steady, serious, duller. I've become a politician."

He was in shirtsleeves in headquarters. The grimy windows were pushed open; the afternoon was thundery. He had just given a twenty-minute "in depth" TV interview; and it was part of the wastefulness of campaigning: that excellent interview, and the events of the week, would make about five minutes on the network's Saturday news.

He had discovered, he said, that politics was hard work. Sleep was the thing he dreamt about and he understood now how sleep could be the politician's sex. "Someone should do a Freudian analysis of this thing, being a politician. It's all a matter of orality. It's the most oral people who get along. My tongue feels like a hippopotamus's. It's all a matter of tongue and lips. It's so strange for me, so different from my practice as a writer. I used to feel that if I talked about something I had lost it. I would go out to do an article. When I came back and my wife asked me what I thought about it, I wouldn't talk. That's why I feel I couldn't do a book about this."

"What do you think about him?" Schwartzman asked me afterwards. It was a question Mailer sometimes asked his staff after a meeting; it was a question the staff often asked reporters they had got to know. It was the burden of glamour: Mailer's staff required him never to fail, even in a short exchange with a reporter.

"FRIDAY'S a fun day," Banning said. "He's going to the races at Aqueduct."

"Fun?" I said. "You mean no campaigning?"

"There are going to be seventy thousand people there."

The special express trains funnelled them in from Manhattan and Brooklyn; and from the platform, level with the floor of the coaches, they poured down the covered ramp to the stand, spoiling the symmetry of the arrangement only when they broke out into the sunlight—the wide car-parks glinting like the open sea—to get to the two-dollar gates. First on the covered ramp (leading to the five-dollar gates) and then in the sunlight, Mailer and his party stood, facing the rush: Breslin, the columnist, more popular than Mailer here, Mailer in light check trousers and a blazer, smiling shyly, Mailer's wife, small, an actress, in a sober olive outfit, now part of the campaign.

The crowd swirled past them. But, like pebbles on a smooth beach, the campaign party was a disturbance, and disturbance built up around them: swift handshakes, an exchange, a little crowd, enough for the cameras, and even a little sound off-camera. "I've been thinking about this guy. I wanted to see him. He's in favour of dual-admission." "You haven't got a ghost of a chance, ya bum!" Then the party, going through the five-dollar gates, were taken up the escalators to the concourse, where they were soon untraceable.

I fell in with a young man, equally lost, from Liberation News Service. He was hairy and hippyish and aggrieved. He had had to fight his way into the campaign car that morning and he hadn't even had an interview with Mailer. He showed me a transcript he had made of his conversation with Banning.

"BANNING: Look, we need coverage from you New Left nuts like a hole in the head . . . You got to get votes from a lot of strange places to win in this town . . . He needs support from the left like he needs a shit haemorrhage."

"Mailer isn't offering an alternative to American politics," the man from Liberation News said, as we walked through the crowd, looking for the campaign. "He's offering only a distorted version of the old style."

The bright green centre of the track was patterned with flowers; in the distance the jets rose one after the other from the permanent kerosene haze over Kennedy Airport.

"The trouble is that Mailer sees himself as an existential hero. In America, where action is frowned on among intellectuals, the existential hero would say, 'The worst thing in the world is boredom. We must create drama by our own actions.' Mailer creates this excitement, without giving an analysis of why that world is boring and dull. He says, 'It is boring and dull, but it will be interesting if I inject myself into it.' "

Existential: it was a Mailer word I was beginning to learn; it explained much of what I had felt about the campaign, its glamour and ambiguity. He was only nineteen, the Liberation News man, but the fluency of the American young no longer surprised me.

"What is most important is that when Mailer is defeated it won't be said that he's been defeated by the unworkable and corrupt New York City system. It will be said that it was his individual failure. As a critical man he will have lost a marvellous opportunity of exposing the undemocratic nature of American politics."

It was easy to see why Banning didn't want him around. Just then, though, the Liberation News man very badly wanted to see Banning: he had forgotten a roll of exposed film in the campaign car.

We ran into one of the TV cameramen. I asked him how he assessed the day's campaigning.

"Oh, we'll make it look bigger."

"Is that official policy?" the man from Liberation News asked.

"We make everything bigger."

Outside the restaurant—Mailer having a slow lunch inside—we saw Banning, brisk and businesslike. His beard barely lifted; he ignored us.

"He *hates* me," the man from Liberation News said, and looked down at his soft suede boots.

I wanted company back to Manhattan. I gave the man from Liberation News some of my notes and persuaded him to forget his exposed film. The train was full of boys and girls, red from the beach. Everyone in the Mailer campaign spoke of the sickness of the society. But to the visitor no city appeared richer in pleasure, and more organized for it. And

Mailer's trip to the races made a three-column spread, with a photograph, in the *New York Times*: that was the reality of our afternoon excursion.

"THE THING about this campaign," the girl in headquarters said, "is that it's fantastically seductive." She was twenty-four, thin, with a sharp little nose. "These boys here on the campaign are all like Norman. They have the same tremendous ego and this makes them fantastic to be with. They're so fantastically alive every minute. Hardly anybody else is." She herself came from New Jersey. "I had to leave because I was like a freak there. I am like"—she sighed, and her eyes widened behind her tinted granny glasses—"well, a socialist." After the campaign she was going to do some summer work for GI Resistance. "It'll be idealistic to say it's because I have a brother in Vietnam. It's more like, well, being addicted."

"I don't know how the whole concept of doing your own thing became so sacred," Banning said when the campaign was over. "I don't know whether it's American or just youthful. I know how vicious the establishment is. I am twenty thousand dollars in debt—well, say fifteen thousand. But maybe I'm not as disillusioned as everybody else. Maybe everybody is uptight. Notice the difference between the Kennedy kids we had and the McCarthy kids. The Kennedy people want to win. The McCarthy-oriented types are addicted not just to lost causes but to a concept of lost causes. They just want to make a statement and stand around being right. 'I know what is wrong, I'm noble.' This I don't buy."

McCarthy types, Kennedy types, the New Left, the addicted, the Mailer-glamoured, the election-glamoured (bullhorns, loudspeaker cars, sticky labels): even with the heroic pattern-figure of Mailer, the wonder was that the campaign held together and looked professional, that the strains didn't show more.

The reporters came and went. The press became better and better. Dustin, who was in charge of Advance, told me that the article by the agency girl had come out. "They must have cut a lot," he said. There were occasional muted reports of internal trouble: a public outburst because of some carelessly displayed posters; an amateur art show not opened, Mailer's wife going instead to speak the nice words Mailer couldn't bring himself to speak. Then Banning lost his beard.

· · ·

THE GLOOMIEST day in headquarters was the Friday before the election. A Harlem rally had been planned for that day. But Clarence 27x Smith, a Black Muslim of some local renown, was shot dead in a lift in the morning (New York was always organized for drama, as it was for pleasure), and Mailer cancelled the rally. In headquarters they felt that Mailer had let them down; the show ought to have gone on. The cast and band of *Hair*, I was told, had been recruited and were game; black bodyguards could have been hired for a hundred dollars.

"Don't ask Banning too many questions," I was told. "He'll hit you like Norman."

Banning, tie-less, jacketless, with a beer-can, was dejected and acting tough. He said there was "an atmosphere of political death" over the campaign. I asked for the schedule. He mimicked my pronunciation. "Stick around," he said. "You'll hear." It struck me for the first time that he would have a good microphone voice.

"It isn't all Norman," the girl from New Jersey said. "Half of this is that it's all going to end on Tuesday and everybody on the campaign's got to go back to not having power. Everything else is going to go on. This stops on June 17, this closeness and intimacy with people who have become your whole life. And these boys, they fight with Norman, but they go to the meetings. And when Norman gets up there and tells it like it is, they all dissolve and you can tell it in their eyes. It's why they come the next day."

Banning wasn't in the office the next day. But Dustin and his wife and some others were, and after lunch we drove through the rain to Macy's department store, where—but no one was sure—Mailer was campaigning among the shoppers. All we saw from the car were some very young volunteers offering damp leaflets; they didn't know where Mailer was.

He and Mrs. Mailer were inside the store, as it turned out, until the guard asked them to campaign outside.

When we walked round the block we found them. Girl volunteers were asking people, "Have you met Mr. Mailer?" And the Mailers were shaking hands. Mailer looked worn, preoccupied, working only with his eyes; his hair, cut shorter, looked greyer. Mrs. Mailer was as composed as always. "I am an actress," she said later. "This is the biggest audience I've played to." A blind man stood beside Mailer, rattling his coins in a green cup and tapping his stick; his eyelids were sealed over hollow sockets so that his face, without expression, was like a dummy's.

It was an extraordinary, smiling scene. The Mailers smiled; the people whose hands had been shaken smiled, and they waited, smiling, to see others have their turn. The girl volunteers smiled; we were all smiling.

"It's *good*," Dustin said, his gloom vanished. "We could win." Dustin had been a Kennedy man.

Mailer, getting into the car, called Dustin over. A girl volunteer turned on me with big eyes. "I'm *crazy*!" A minute ago she had been demure. "I *love* him! I've read *all* his books. This is the first time I've *seen* him! I *love* him!" She sat down hard on the table with the campaign buttons. "I'm *crazy*!"

Dustin came back, exultant. "He wants a motorcade." Dustin liked motorcades.

Later, at the Sullivan Street fair—old brick houses with fire-escapes, the street muddy and littered, remote Italian women sitting with bandaged ankles and legs beside food-stalls and toystalls, sausages grilling over charcoal—Dustin and Mailer talked again.

"Look at them," Dustin's wife said. "Don't you think they look a little alike, with the hair?"

ON MONDAY, at the last press conference, Mailer bounced back to form after a tired, constricted TV appearance the previous day. Banning was there, friendly again, in a suit, stage-managing again. The four motorcade cars were waiting outside. A German producer said, "The film in Germany is finished. It was shown Saturday night." A girl with a foreign accent was told that press seats were reserved for the New York City press. Mailer, Mrs. Mailer and Breslin sat in the third car. Banning was in the loudspeaker car at the front; he was to do the talking.

"Mailer-Breslin and the fifty-first state. You've had the rest. Choose the best."

It was the motorcade slogan. The story was that it had been suggested to Mailer by a Negro. Banning didn't like it, but he was speaking it with conviction. On Broadway there were some waves and shouts. But Harlem, with its sullen privacies, where garishness and dereliction appeared one and indivisible, was silent. In the South Bronx the advertisements were in Spanish; and Banning—a new talent revealed—spoke in Spanish: *". . . dos coches atrás, en el carro abierto . . ."* His accent was good. But there was no response from the pavements. The motorcade slowed down in the traffic, merged into it.

Mailer signalled from the open car. Banning ran to confer, then came to us. "OK, we'll meet up at 50th Street and Sixth Avenue, in front of the Time-Life Building. We're just going to shake hands and cut the horse-shit with the motorcade." Banning hadn't liked the idea of the motor-cade. The motorcade broke up; and in silence, without loudspeakers, the cars raced separately back to Manhattan.

The reception outside the Time-Life building was very good. Mailer, with his vision of New York as two cities, spoke passionately for the disadvantaged. But his best audience was always the middle-class, the educated, the bohemian, the people who held him in awe.

THEY HAD LAID IN THE BEER IN HEADQUARTERS. The TV cameras and monitors had been installed. The last partition had gone, and at the end of the room they had built a platform, against a wall deco-rated with the campaign posters (already souvenirs, already being taken away by collectors). The mood was good. It was a victory mood, and victory meant not coming last.

"It's been important to me," Banning said, summing up the cam-paign. "Mailer's obviously going to be important to American history. He'll either be a force for enormous destruction or he'll be one of the great builders. He clearly is going to do something more than write *The Armies of the Night.*"

In the evening the hall began filling up: the media people (the TV reporters grave, aware of the envy of the young), the volunteers from the boroughs, a number of strays. There was a girl in half-Mexican, half-Hindu hippy costume sitting on the floor before a red candle. She had missed the point; she had also underestimated the crowd. The girl from New Jersey turned up with a Negro. Banning, dashing and unexpected in a pale-blue silk neckscarf, stood on the platform, like an actor in the lights, and repeatedly called for order. The results began to come in. They were as expected. Mailer was running above Congressman Scheuer, with 5 to 6 per cent of the votes; Breslin was doing even better in his contest for the Presidency of the Council: he was getting 10 per cent. There was applause and stamping.

Banning said that the building would collapse. "If you have the death wish, don't wish it on other people."

They were rebels, and the moment was high. But they were also Americans, careful of the self in every way, never reckless. They began to go.

At about midnight Mailer, Mrs. Mailer and Breslin came, cameras and lights preceding them. Through handshakes they walked to the platform. "We can hardly claim victory," Mailer said. It was their joke; victory was what they were celebrating. "Listen. You've been terrific. We've run further on less. We've spent one-tenth of what Wagner spent. I've got 5 per cent of the vote; he's got 30. So we've done twice as well as he." He was mischievous, the hero restored to his followers. Banning stood beside me, dissolving; it was as the girl from New Jersey had said.

The TV lights heightened colour, deepening the beauty of Mrs. Mailer. Mailer's eyes showed as the clearest blue. The posters on the wall glowed. It was a narrow hall, the platform central, and on the monitor screens the scene was like something out of a well-organized film. So that this last moment of glamour linked to that other, on the steps of the Old Treasury Building in Wall Street.

One notice hadn't been forgotten. *Anyone interested in GI Resistance work this summer please sign name* . . . There had been four signatures in the afternoon; now the sheet was full.

I HAD LUNCH with Mailer a week later. He had spent a few days in Cape Cod; he had been to the Frazier-Quarry fight the evening before; he was editing a film that day; he would soon have to start working on his moon shot articles. "That's going to be a strange assignment. The astronauts won't talk to me. They're writing their own book." His writer's life was catching up with him again.

Politics seemed far away. But he was sensitive to the charge that he had split the liberal vote and helped the cause of the backlash. He thought that many of the people who had voted for him wouldn't have otherwise voted. He didn't think he had done well enough; he had lost some votes in the last week; not enough people had been reached. It astonished him that people who had shaken his hand and had been friendly hadn't voted for him.

He said again that, becoming a politician, he had become duller.

But he understood now that politicians were serious when they spoke of "service." A politician had to serve, had always to give himself, to his supporters, to the public. It was his weakness, for instance, that he couldn't answer when people asked him whether he would clear their streets of garbage. He remained loyal to his ideas—the fifty-first state, power to the neighbourhoods—but he thought that perhaps another candidate, even someone very dull, might have done better politically with them.

Dull: it was the recurring word. It was as though, during the campaign, Mailer had redefined his writer's role by negatives. He couldn't assess the value of the campaign. "If you don't win, you change very little." Perhaps some of the ideas would survive: time alone would show. "Or it might just be a curiosity. Perhaps four years from now, at the next election, someone might say, 'Remember when that writer ran for Mayor?'"

1969

Steinbeck in Monterey

A WRITER is in the end not his books, but his myth. And that myth is in the keeping of others.

Cannery Row in Monterey, the one John Steinbeck wrote about, disfigures a mile of pretty Californian coastline. The canneries used to can sardines; but the sardines began to disappear from Monterey Bay not long after Steinbeck published his book in 1945; and today all but one of the canneries have closed down. The cannery buildings remain, where they have not been destroyed by fire: white corrugated-iron buildings, as squat and plain as warehouses, backing out into the sea over a low cliff, braced by timber and tons of concrete which now only blasting can remove. Some are abandoned and show broken windows; some are warehouses; some have been converted into restaurants, boutiques, gift-shops.

The old Row has gone: the stink of fish and fish-fertilizer, the cutters and packers who could work up to sixteen hours a day when a catch was in, the winos, the derelicts who slept in pipes in empty lots, the whores. It was what Steinbeck wrote about but transmuted. What remains is like a folk-memory of community, wine, sex and talk. The tourists come for the memory. The name, Cannery Row, was made official in 1958, long after the sardine went away; before that it was Ocean View Avenue. And today, in Ring's Café next door to the Steinbeck Theatre in Steinbeck Circle—the whole complex on the site of a former cannery—the new shop-keepers and business people of the Row are meeting to talk about what they might do to get the tourists in in 1970.

Nineteen seventy is the bicentennial of the founding of Monterey by the Spaniards. Some people in Ring's remember the centennial of 1947; that was the centennial of the American seizure. The main street of Monterey (today a wasteland, awaiting renewal) was painted gold and there was dancing in the streets. History in the Monterey Peninsula is this sort of fun. Steinbeck wrote angrily of Indian servitude and American land-grabbing; but there is a mixed-up myth here of a gay and gracious Mexican past, of heroic Spanish missionary endeavour, and numerous Indian slaves, all converts, happily accepting the whip for religious misdemeanours. In the dereliction of Monterey every adobe from Mexican times is preserved and labelled; there is even a movement to have the first Spanish missionary, "the first Californian," canonized. The American seizure is celebrated on the Fourth of July with a costume pageant devised by the Navy League and the Monterey History and Art Association: old-time señoritas and Yankees listening companionably to the proclamation of annexation.

Ring's Café has been in Monterey for some time, but on the Row for just over a year. Like many new places on the Row, Ring's honours the fishing past with a fishing net in its windows and wooden fish caught in the net. The proprietor is an old advertising man; from his café he publishes *The Monterey Foghorn,* a four-page satirical sheet whose cause is Cannery Row, gaiety and youth. Ring's offers "beer, skittles and vittles"; it says it is "under no management" and has "the world's cuisiest cuisine." There are paintings; the Peninsula is full of artists. At the top of the inner wall a *trompe-l'œil* painting continues the braced timber ceiling of the cannery. And above the bar, among other posters, is one advertising "Doc's Birthday."

This was an event that Ring's staged last year, to bring to life and perhaps to perpetuate something in the book. "Doc" was the marine biologist in *Cannery Row,* the educated man around whom the others idled. Mack and the boys gave a party for Doc's birthday, and the party went predictably wild. Doc was a real person on the Row, Doc Ricketts; *Cannery Row* is dedicated to him. Steinbeck lent him money to buy the low unpainted wooden lab which is squashed between two cannery buildings and will now, as a men's club, be preserved. In 1948 a Southern Pacific locomotive ran into Doc's motorcar one evening on the level-crossing just above the Row, and Doc was killed. On the bar of Ring's, below glass, is a large photograph of the accident: Doc on a stretcher in the grass, the wrecked Ford, the locomotive, the crowd.

Fact, fiction, folk-lore, death, gaiety, homage: it is unsettling. But it is how myth is made. Doc as the tallest "character" on the Row: it is as unquestioned now as the myth of gaiety. No one in Ring's can say why Doc was such a character. He was nice to everybody, they say; he drank a lot; he liked the girls. It is the book, of course, and Steinbeck. But the book itself recedes.

There are about thirty people in Ring's. Solid bald men; younger men in dark glasses; middle-aged ladies in suits; an intense young woman in a check suit and matching deerstalker cap; a mother of two, with the yawning two; a Chinese lady. The solemn young man with steel-rimmed glasses, drooping moustache, leather waistcoat and patched jeans is one of the Peninsula's artists; he and his wife run an ambitious boutique called Pin Jabs. He used to cycle up to the Row from Monterey in the old days. But most of the people here are new. Many have read *Cannery Row* and say they adore it; but some have not read any more Steinbeck.

The chairman, a gentle, slow-speaking sculptor of sixty-four, is one of the few people now on the Row who knew Steinbeck. He is a long-time Californian and knew Steinbeck in the 1930s, in the days of failure and poverty, when "if you didn't know about his background you wouldn't have known he was a writer." Steinbeck never spoke about his work; he was, outwardly, like the people he mixed with and wrote about. But the sculptor remembers the writing of the last page of *The Grapes of Wrath*. The novel ends in a black night of flood, when, the world a void, her own baby born dead, her family scattered, Rose of Sharon offers her breast to a lost and starving old man.

"I happened to be in his house that night. A little house he had then in Los Gatos. It was about three o'clock. I'd gone to bed and I heard him call out, 'I've got it! I've got it!' I got up, everybody else got up, and he read out this last piece. The only piece I ever heard him read out."

The sculptor is willing to forget Steinbeck's later books; for the early, Californian books, "when he was like in his own place," he feels the deepest affection; and his attitude to Steinbeck comes close to piety.

He rises now, calls the meeting to order, and asks for ideas for Cannery Row pageants or "projects" that might get financial support from the Monterey Bicentennial Committee and so get the tourists in next year.

"The only project we have so far is getting perhaps one of the old tanks and making a little house of it and having explanatory material there about the family that lived there." The Malloys of *Cannery Row* set up house in an old locomotive boiler, crawling in through the fire-door; they rented out subsidiary pipes to lodgers; but then Mrs. Malloy began to cry for curtains and nagged her husband away. "Only thing we have so far. We need projects. I sure need your help."

"I've just finished *Cannery Row*," a young woman says. After such a flourish, what? She suggests "a little kind of walking tour. With a map. Have the different spots, like Doc's place, what was there then, what's there now . . ."

"I suppose some kind of designation on the buildings."

"We don't want to get too historical."

The girl in the deerstalker suggests a tour of the surviving cannery.

"You mean the sequence of the machinery. Where the fish came in, where they went out . . ."

"What we want is a brochure like the Hearst Castle—"

"This isn't a Hearst Castle. This is spread out a little."

"—simultaneously bringing out the historical aspect."

Speech is slow, lingering. The ideas come slowly, linger, fade. A Steinbeck film festival. Steinbeck plays. The hiring of a "colourful character" to wander about the Row. Each shop featuring one Steinbeck book.

"If there could be a trade fair," the girl from Pin Jabs says.

"We have a lot of vacant lots. A lot of the action of the book took place in vacant lots, and—"

"Things happen in the vacant lot, and we get no activity at the other end. We want something that will give *complete* activity from A to Z."

"Something more like Doc's Birthday. Let Cannery Row be Cannery Row, and downtown be downtown."

"You're talking about something that's got to have some life going in it for three, four months."

". . . dancing in the streets."

"For three, four months?"

". . . in the empty lots. Every two hours have a different band."

"Trouble is, we talk about sunny California. But it gets pretty cold at nights."

"They could have like a pass to Cannery Row. It could cost five dollars and they could get a drink in the different places. A pass. The Gold Key of Cannery Row."

"You don't want to scare off the elderly."

The mother of the two rises with the two, now quite stupefied. She says she has to go. But she wants to say one thing. She is a mother of two, plump and pretty and perfectly serious; she gets respectful attention. They've got to raise money for the advertising, she says; and she has a couple of suggestions. "Like have a carnival down here or something.

Whole day." She loses her audience. She suggests auctions. "The restaurant people could auction a meal." The restaurant people don't twitch. "The other people could auction—"

There is a decent pause after she and the two leave.

"We're talking about auctions and things. We're talking about nickels and dimes."

They are not tycoons, these people who have invested in the Cannery Row name; they are a little like people infected by the atmosphere which they are promoting. They call themselves "the little people." The big people are offstage: the owners of the cannery buildings, investors in real estate, to whom the rents and a percentage of the profits go. Older, nontourist businesses might go on. Like the Natural Science Establishment, which for more than a decade has been offering embalmed cats, among other things. "We can make immediate shipment of any quantity. All our embalmed cats are shipped in waterproof plastic bags." But for the last six or seven years the little people have been coming and going with their boutiques and batiks. Where is yesterday's "Den of Antiquity"? Can "Anti-macassar Factory and Psychedelic Tea Cozies" depend on its sense of fun? Not all ventures on the Row last; at least one sculptor has hanged himself.

In fifteen years, when the leases begin to run out, the high-rise hotels will go up on this reclaimed bit of pretty Californian coastline. But by that time the Cannery Row myth, which the busy little people have created, will have grown hard.

MYTHS grow fast here. California, of the sun and the fruit and the cool Pacific shore, is where Americans go when they have been weakened by America. And the twenty-five or thirty square miles of the Monterey Peninsula are special. "It seems," says Wesley Dodge, one of the new "big people" of the Row (he's made eighty times his investment in cannery buildings and machinery), "it seems like there's always been a group or something here that's anti to what the mass is interested in." There have been beatniks and hippies. ("Hippies have money," the girl from Pin Jabs says, with respect and hope.) In the old days it was the bums with their "bindles," riding the freight cars to the Peninsula from all parts of the country.

And not only bums and beatniks. Many years ago a visiting Hindu yogi reported that the vibrations at Pacific Grove, to the west of Monterey—it begins where Cannery Row ends—were as good as anything he had found in the Himalayas. The leading bookshop in Monterey, among the restaurants and gift-shops on Fisherman's Wharf, is mystically inclined. And something of mystic exhilaration remains in the ordered pinewoods and timber lodges of Asilomar, a noted conference centre, where even on this Fourth of July weekend they are gathering for a Philosophical Roundtable.

Bang! Boom! With AURAS *flashing, sparkling and colorful as Fourth of July skyrockets, here we are* CELEBRATING *our latest Conference series get-together.* WELCOME EACH AND EVERYONE!! *We think we've a joyous and full-filled* PROGRAM, *so once again please write down those* DREAMS, VISIONS, IMPRESSIONS *and share them with all of us along with that* SPECIAL PAST LIFE COSTUME *for our* BIG PARTY NIGHT JUBILEE.

The Roundtable's cause is reincarnation. But the thin young girl from San Diego, whose sister was in it first, says that the aim is "to bring back like the people to God." Her eyelids are coloured green; her painted eyebrows slant upwards in a waving line. The weekend costs forty-five dollars.

Pacific Grove also has a famous festival in honour of the Monarch butterfly; a legend has been worked out which involves a lost princess and her sorrowing Indian subjects. Just to the south of the vibrations and the butterflies is an area of golf courses and country clubs dedicated to *Treasure Island*. Stevenson came to Monterey as a young man and used the topography of part of the Peninsula in that book; everything is appropriately named. And then there is Carmel-by-the-Sea.

If Monterey, just two miles away, is Mexican, then Carmel is English. Everything in Carmel is small. The houses are small, the signs are small, the shops are small and their windows display the littlest things. The smallness goes on and on; it becomes tininess, it becomes grand; it is tininess on the American scale. On a main street a cluster of rustic doll's houses with geraniums outside the tiny windows turns out to be an expensive motel. There are crooked little roofs, crooked little gates. A shop is called Hansel and Gretel, a house The Wooden Shoe.

Steinbeck called them "the Pixie people of Carmel." There was a vogue here in the 1920s for doll's houses for real people. There are no street lights in Carmel, no postal deliveries; the houses have no numbers; and there is a fiercely protective city council. The whole elfin English thing has become confused with an ideal not so much of literature and art as of the literary and artistic life, of culture flourishing in a certain "atmosphere" and expressing itself in a separateness from commercial America. The place is a raging commercial success. Four million tourists come every year; people come back again and again. There are 150 shops and boutiques. Every block of the rustic shopping centre is cross-hatched, sometimes on more than one level, with arcades, each with its directory of linked wooden slabs hanging from a wrought-iron standard.

Carmel deals, above all, in art. In galleries that look like those in Bond Street, in glass-fronted studios that are like film-sets, answering every concept of the glamour of the artistic life, waves break on rocks in sunlight and moonlight, at sunrise and sunset; Monterey cypresses bend before the wind in every twentieth-century idiom. "Verdult Art Gallery presents a showing of Dutch Master Paintings by William Verdult." "The immediate acceptance of her work by the public brought her to the decision that the painting profession was to be hers and her speciality in the art field was to be the ever present challenge of an ever changing sea." "While in high school, Garcia worked . . . for Ed Ricketts, the noted marine biologist and true-life model for 'Doc' in John Steinbeck's novel, *Cannery Row* . . . Although primarily an impressionist, Garcia's style has ranged from realism to abstraction."

In the setting, it is the quantity of this art, the confidence of it all, and again the quantity, that unsettle the visitor. It is as though, at its geographical limits, a culture is parodying itself: rich middle America, middle in everything, paying its holiday tribute to art, the idea of artists and freedom, and buying prettiness.

At Seaside the blacks are starting a boycott of something. At Fort Ord, just a couple of miles away, soldiers in green fatigues are training for Vietnam. Beyond that, the endless level lettuce-fields of Salinas, the bitter landscape of stoop-labour. But America ends where the Monterey Peninsula begins. On the Peninsula all is fairyland.

To be received into fairyland: it is a strange fate for Steinbeck, the novelist of social conscience, the angry man of the 1930s, the propagandist for the unions, the man who always scoffed at the myth-making capacity of his Peninsula. Probe among the shopkeepers and you find that Steinbeck didn't care, after Doc's death, what happened to Doc's lab. Look up the files of the *Monterey Peninsula Herald* and you find that in

1957, when there was some talk of preservation, Steinbeck, writing from Manhattan, where he had moved, was for pulling the whole Row down.

Or perhaps, he wrote, the canneries "should be kept as a monument to American know-how. For it was this forward-looking intelligence which killed all the fish, cut all the timber, thereby lowering the rainfall. It is not dead either. The same know-how is lowering the water-table with deep wells so that within our lifetime California will be the desert we all look forward to."

This is the sort of anger Monterey forgives and forgets. It is true that during the war the annual sardine catch suddenly doubled, to nearly a quarter of a million tons. But it is better for legend that the fish of Monterey should be as mysterious as the butterflies of Pacific Grove. It is better to say, as the lady from Carmel said, that "the sardines just *flipped* their tails and went away."

Steinbeck himself bears some responsibility. His sentimentality, when prompted by anger and conscience, was part of his strength as a writer. Without anger or the cause for anger he writes fairytales. He has the limitations of his Peninsula. He yielded to the success of *Cannery Row*; he wrote a sequel, *Sweet Thursday*. He parodied his charm; he turned the Row into fairyland.

DON WESTLAKE'S mother worked in a cannery from 1936 until 1950. Westlake himself began to work part-time in the cannery cafeteria when he was twelve. He graduated from the local high school in 1952; he is now in his early thirties. Westlake's mother and stepfather, Californian for five generations, left Monterey for Oregon last year. Westlake himself now lives in San Francisco and is a public relations man for a pharmaceutical firm.

He is tall and lean, easy of manner, the image of the healthy, educated Californian; and his Cannery Row background comes as a surprise. But it is Cannery Row that has driven him, as, he says, it has driven many of the sons of those "Okies" who worked in the Row.

"They weren't all Italians and Poles. Many people don't know that. Okie: that was the worst insult in the world. It was to be just next to an animal. But you have to be careful nowadays. The sons of those people are the leaders of California. You use the word in distinguished company and you notice strange looks." Not all broke away. "Some of the boys I knew fell into their parents' way of life. Some have been to jail. As far as I'm concerned they could burn the whole Row down. It's all right for the tourists. But they and Steinbeck are romanticizing something that wasn't there. Living in pipes and boilers. That wasn't funny. Those people were human derelicts. They had nowhere else to live."

Westlake talks less with anger than with distress. He talks like a man who will never exorcize a personal hurt.

"And the place used to *stink*. Not only the fish. The heads and tails they cut off and turned into fertilizer. Every cannery had its fertilizer plant. The fish came in in the morning. There were no sonic devices in those days. You could tell where the sardines were only by the phosphorescence at night. Every cannery had a special whistle, and when the catch came in the cannery would blow one whistle for their cutters and a later one for their packers. When you heard your whistle you would get up and drive down to the Row. We lived at Seaside; it was always the lower-class, working area.

"The girls would stand at a long trough, in front of what looked like a tractor-tread. They would drop one sardine in each tread. You would start at three in the morning and go on for twelve, fourteen, sixteen hours, until the packing was finished. In the thirties the girls were paid by the can. Sometimes they got no more than twenty-five dollars a week. During the war, when the unions came in, they were paid by the hour.

"Something you don't hear much about now is the fish poisoning. The pilchard sardine has a toxin to which some people are allergic. The hands then become red and raw and pitted and scaled like a fish. Blood poisoning can make the hands red right up the arm. Some people lost fingers through the gangrene. In those days the only cure for this fish poisoning was to soak your hands in epsom salts. My mother never had it badly. But you would see these frightened people soaking their hands in epsom salts. They were frightened because if their hands went bad they wouldn't get any more work for the rest of the season. And when the season was over there was no work for anyone. It was a boon to Monterey when the canneries were forced to close down and the people who were being exploited were forced to leave. Though most of those refugees from Monterey are still in packing. Fruit packing, in the valleys."

The only place Westlake remembers with affection is the Bear Flag, the brothel Steinbeck wrote about, one of six on the Row at its wartime peak.

"It was my favourite hang-out when I was five. Some nights my step-father and I would drive up to meet my mother and we would have to wait until the packing was finished. The girls would take me in then from the car. I can't remember what they looked like. All I remember is they were big motherly types. I was always warm and comfortable when I was there."

"SENTIMENTAL?" says Wesley Dodge, the post-cannery million-aire on the Row. "You going to be sentimental about whores? They're talking about things I didn't participate in. I didn't participate in the whores."

Dodge is a fat, pink man with glasses. He is sixty-four and says he is too old to be happy; but he smiles easily. His office, in a converted can-nery, is where the women's lavatories used to be. "Twenty on that side, twenty on this side." The purchase of this particular cannery was one of his coups. "Flause was asking two hundred forty thousand dollars. I said, 'Mr. Flause, I don't want to give you a price. We are too far away. Mr. Flause, all I will give you is seventy thousand dollars.' I called on the man every day for two years. I never mentioned price again. I would go around the cannery with him, inspecting the machinery. And he would turn the motors on, just to keep everything in order. One day he put his foot on a pump and it fell over and he said, 'Dodge, you've just bought yourself a cannery.' I paid a deposit, and as I sold the machinery, I paid him."

If the idle canneries had come up for sale all at once, Dodge and his associates mightn't have been able to buy the 70 per cent of Cannery Row they did buy. But the cannery owners held on, hoping that the sar-dine might come back. For a time some canned anchovies, labelling them "sardine-type." "The canneries dropped over nine years. One by one."

It was as a dealer in second-hand machinery that Wesley Dodge came to the dying Row. A Fresno man, one-eighth Cherokee, self-educated, used from youth to working "from can till can't," he had already made and lost two fortunes, in fruit in the 1930s, in a private airline in the 1940s. His knowledge of the second-hand machinery business came from his own love of machines and from "watching other nationalities," mainly Jews. "I am one of the few Gentiles in second-hand machinery." The secret is to buy well. "Everybody in America is a salesman. I learned to be a buyer. If you buy right, selling's no problem." He sold Cannery

Row machinery all over the world. "Apple-canning, fish-reduction, tallow plants which take chicken waste. I didn't necessarily sell back to the fish business." They sometimes got more from the machinery than they paid for the cannery.

And there was Dodge's interest in ocean property. "All my life I wanted to own ocean property. There's no ocean in Nebraska. Does that mean anything to you? No ocean in Oklahoma. There's an Atlantic Ocean, there's a Pacific Ocean. In between there's no ocean. In my commercial life anyone that's owned ocean property had it made."

There was a stripped cannery to be seen, the last. We drove there in his Cadillac.

"It's air-conditioned," he said, as I fumbled with the car window.

It was almost dark in the cannery building; the corrugated-iron roof looked higher inside. Small motors with fresh grey paint on their casings covered half the concrete floor. On the other side, no longer in sequence, under polythene, were the big, complicated machines. Moving lightly, he undraped, touched, felt, explained. Here, still looking new after twenty idle years, were the "tractor-treads" into which the girls—now scattered, and always women—dropped the sardines one by one, for hours; here was the sardine gut-sucker; here were metal arms so finely balanced that only full cans would depress them to that track which led to the capping machine.

"There's about eighty thousand dollars here," Dodge said. "I live this machinery. Machinery isn't difficult if you *live* it."

It was time for a drink. Dodge himself, after many years of whisky, eighteen to twenty shots a day, now drinks only orange juice and Seven-Up. We went to the Outrigger. It was on the sea side of a converted cannery, past gift-shops whose walls dripped pink bougainvillaea. Three gas jets on tall metal poles flared at the entrance. A spotlight picked out rocks in the sea. We entered a carpeted green grotto, of Polynesian atmosphere, with a waterfall, and stepped out into openness: the old cannery pier, carpeted, re-timbered and glassed-in. We were on water, in the middle of the bay, the lights of Seaside and Monterey curving far to the right. After the desolation of the Row, the beauty of rock and water was abrupt. It was the future.

"The square-foot value of the property will be many times greater than when Steinbeck was here," Dodge said. He pointed to where a basket-like metal frame rose out of the sea. "The old hopper. That's where they unloaded the fish. They were pumped in through a pipe into the cannery."

From the high-rise, resort future of Cannery Row Dodge has withdrawn. For two million dollars, paid in cash, he and his associates have sold out to a San Francisco millionaire. "He is seventy-five, but he has a different idea of his life than I have of mine." Dodge feels he has had a full business life; even while on the Row he went back into fruit, where he had failed thirty years before, and "made a lot there, a lot." Dodge, who has no children of his own, is interested now in educating the children of his relatives and friends. He would like to support a hospital or some kind of research; but he is concerned to make his money work. "You don't get the true value of your dollar with a foundation. You are just paying the salaries of the top men."

Later, driving down the Row back to the centre of Monterey, he slowed down beside an empty, fenced-in lot. "Frank Raiter's place. A real Cannery Row character. Over eighty, worth several millions. His cannery burned down two years ago. But every morning he comes here and sits in his—not a Cadillac, the one next to a Cadillac, I forget—and reads the *Wall Street Journal* for a couple of hours."

The Row bent and straightened again. It was just here that Doc Ricketts died in 1948—the scene under glass in Ring's café. Dodge talked about Steinbeck. He never met him; he spoke to him once, on the transatlantic telephone, to get permission to use his name for the Steinbeck Theatre.

"He hurt California terribly. I like *Tortilla Flat*, I like *Cannery Row*. I know those paisanos without knowing them, if you know what I mean. But he wrote *The Grapes of Wrath*. I've no background of being able to say this book's better than that one, but it hurt me to read *The Grapes*. It wasn't factual enough. You know what an Okie is? They moved here in *hordes*. Thousands. Thousands a *day*. I was making five to six dollars an hour, packing fruit. When they came they worked for fifteen cents, twenty cents. Fifty cents a day. Any amount a day. And I was out of a job. We had problems in 1932. They came and compounded our problems. But Steinbeck wrote *The Grapes*. It's something that people look at us as, as Californians. And he sold a lot of books. You can't assess the damage."

Argentina and the Ghost of Eva Perón, 1972–1991

I THE CORPSE AT THE IRON GATE

Buenos Aires, April–June 1972

OUTLINE it like a story by Borges.

The dictator is overthrown and more than half the people rejoice. The dictator had filled the jails and emptied the treasury. Like many dictators, he hadn't begun badly. He had wanted to make his country great. But he wasn't himself a great man; and perhaps the country couldn't be made great. Seventeen years pass. The country is still without great men; the treasury is still empty; and the people are on the verge of despair. They begin to remember that the dictator had a vision of the country's greatness, and that he was a strong man; they begin to remember that he had given much to the poor. The dictator is in exile. The people begin to agitate for his return. The dictator is now very old. But the people also remember the dictator's wife. She loved the poor and hated the rich, and she was young and beautiful. So she has remained, because she died young, in the middle of the dictatorship. And, miraculously, her body has not decomposed.

"That," Borges said, "is a story I could *never* write."

But at seventy-six, and after seventeen years of proscription and exile, Juan Perón, from the Madrid suburb known as the Iron Gate, dictates peace terms to the military regime of Argentina. In 1943, as an army colonel preaching a fierce nationalism, Perón became a power in Argentina; and from 1946 to 1955, through two election victories, he ruled as dictator. His wife Eva held no official position, but she ruled with Perón until 1952. In that year she died. She was expensively embalmed, and now her corpse is with Perón at the Iron Gate.

In 1956, just one year after his overthrow by the army, Perón wrote from Panama, "My anxiety was that some clever man would have taken over." Now, after eight presidents, six of them military men, Argentina is in a state of crisis that no Argentine can fully explain. The mighty country, as big as India and with a population of twenty-three million, rich in cattle and grain, Patagonian oil, and all the mineral wealth of the Andes, inexplicably drifts. Everyone is disaffected. And suddenly nearly everyone is Peronist. Not only the workers, on whom in the early days Perón showered largesse, but Marxists and even the middle-class young, whose parents remember Perón as a tyrant, torturer and thief.

The peso has gone to hell: from 5 to the dollar in 1947, to 16 in 1949, 250 in 1966, 400 in 1970, 420 in June last year, 960 in April this year, 1,100 in May. Inflation, which has been running at a steady 25 per cent since the Perón days, has now jumped to 60 per cent. The banks are offering 24 per cent interest. Inflation, when it reaches this stage of takeoff, is good only for the fire insurance business. Premiums rise and claims fall. When prices gallop away week by week, fires somehow do not often get started.

For everyone else it is a nightmare. It is almost impossible to put together capital; and even then, if you are thinking of buying a flat, a delay of a week can cost you two or three hundred U.S. dollars (many business people prefer to deal in dollars). Salaries, prices, the exchange rate: everyone talks money, everyone who can afford it buys dollars on the black market. And soon even the visitor is touched by the hysteria. In two months a hotel room rises from 7,000 pesos to 9,000, a tin of tobacco from 630 to 820. Money has to be changed in small amounts; the market has to be watched. The peso drops one day to 1,250 to the dollar. Is this a freak, or the beginning of a new decline? To hesitate that day was to lose: the peso bounced back to 1,100. "You begin to feel," says Norman Thomas di Giovanni, the translator of Borges, who has come to the end of his three-year stint in Buenos Aires, "that you are spending the best years of your life at the money changer's. I go there some afternoons the way other people go shopping. Just to see what's being offered."

The blanket wage raises that the government decrees from time to time—15 per cent in May, and another 15 per cent promised soon—cannot keep pace with prices. "We've got to the stage," the ambassador's wife says, "when we can calculate the time between the increase in wages and the increase in prices." People take a second job and sometimes a third. Everyone is obsessed with the need to make more money and at the same time to spend quickly. People gamble. Even in the conservative Andean town of Mendoza the casino is full; the patrons are mainly workpeople, whose average monthly wage is the equivalent of fifty dollars. The queues that form all over Buenos Aires on a Thursday are of people waiting to hand in their football-pool coupons. The announcement of the pool results is a weekly national event.

A spectacular win of some 330 million pesos by a Paraguayan labourer dissipated a political crisis in mid-April. There had been riots in Mendoza, and the army had been put to flight. Then, in the following week, a guerrilla group in Buenos Aires killed the Fiat manager whom they had kidnapped ten days earlier. On the same day, in the nearby industrial town of Rosario, guerrillas ambushed and killed General Sánchez, commander of the Second Army Corps, who had some reputation as a torturer. Blood called for blood: there were elements in the armed forces that wanted then to break off the negotiations with Perón and scotch the elections promised next year. But the Paraguayan's fortune lightened all conversation, revived optimism and calmed nerves. The little crisis passed.

The guerrillas still raid and rob and blow up; they still occasionally kidnap and occasionally kill. The guerrillas are young and middle class. Some are Peronist, some are communist. After all the bank raids the various organizations are rich. In Córdoba last year, according to my information, a student who joined the Peronist Montoneros was paid the equivalent of 70 dollars a month; lawyers were retained at 350 dollars. "You could detect the young Montoneros by their motorcars, their aggressiveness, their flashiness. James Dean types. Very glamorous." Another independent witness says of the guerrillas he has met in Buenos Aires: "They're anti-American. But one of them held a high job in an American company. They have split personalities; some of them really don't know who they are. They see themselves as a kind of comic-book hero. Clark Kent in the office by day, Superman at night, with a gun."

Once you make a decision [the thirty-year-old woman says] you feel better. Most of my friends are for the revolution and they feel much better. But sometimes they are like children who can't see too much of the future. The other day I went with my friend to the cinema. He is about thirty-three. We went to see *Sacco and Vanzetti*. At the end he said, "I feel ashamed not being a *guerrillero*. I feel I am an accomplice of this government, this way of life." I said, "But you lack the violence. A *guerrillero* must be *despejado*—

he mustn't have too much imagination or sensibility. You have to do as you are told. If not, nothing comes out well. It is like a religion, a dogma." And again he said, "Don't you feel *ashamed?*"

The film-maker says:

I think that after Marx people are very conscious of history. The decay of colonialism, the emergence of the Third World— they see themselves acting out some role in this process. This is as dangerous as having no view of history at all. It makes people very vain. They live in a kind of intellectual cocoon. Take away the jargon and the idea of revolution, and most of them would have nothing.

The guerrillas look for their inspiration to the north. From Paris of 1968 there is the dream of students and workers uniting to defeat the enemies of "the people." The guerrillas have simplified the problems of Argentina. Like the campus and salon revolutionaries of the north, they have identified the enemy: the police. And so the social-intellectual diversions of the north are transformed, in the less intellectually stable south, into horrible reality. Dozens of policemen have been killed. And the police reply to terror with terror. They, too, kidnap and kill; they torture, concentrating on the genitals. A prisoner of the police jumps out of a window: *La Prensa* gives it a couple of inches. People are arrested and then, officially, "released"; sometimes they reappear, sometimes they don't. A burned-out van is discovered in a street one morning. Inside there are two charred corpses: men who had been hustled out of their homes two days before. "In what kind of country are we living?" one of the widows asks. But the next day she is calmer; she retracts the accusation against the police. Someone has "visited" her.

"Friends of friends bring me these stories of atrocities," Norman di Giovanni says, "and it makes you sick. Yet no one here seems to be amazed by what's going on." "My wife's cousin was a *guerrillero*," the provincial businessman says at lunch. "He killed a policeman in Rosario. Then eight months ago, he disappeared. *Está muerto.* He's dead." He has no more to say about it; and we talk of other matters.

On some evenings the jackbooted soldiers in black leather jackets patrol the pedestrian shopping street called Florida with their Alsatians:

the dogs' tails close to their legs, their shoulders hunched, their ears thrown back. The police Chevrolets prowl the neon-lit streets unceasingly. There are policemen with machine guns everywhere. And there are the mounted police in slate grey; and the blue-helmeted anti-guerrilla motorcycle brigade; and those young men in well-cut suits who appear suddenly, plainclothesmen, jumping out of unmarked cars. Add the army's AMX tanks and Alouette helicopters. It is an impressive apparatus, and it works.

It is as if the energy of the state now goes into holding the state together. Law and order has become an end in itself: it is part of the Argentine sterility and waste. People are brave; they torture and are tortured; they die. But these are private events, scattered, muffled by a free but inadequate press that seems incapable of detecting a pattern in the events it reports. And perhaps the press is right. Perhaps very little of what happens in Argentina is really news, because there is no movement forward; nothing is being resolved. The nation appears to be playing a game with itself; and Argentine political life is like the life of an ant community or an African forest tribe: full of events, full of crisis and deaths, but life is only cyclical, and the year always ends as it begins. Even General Sánchez didn't, by his death, provoke a crisis. He tortured in vain, he died in vain. He simply lived for fifty-three years and, high as he was, has left no trace. Events are bigger than men. Only one man seems able to impose himself, to alter history now as he altered it in the past. And he waits at the Iron Gate.

> Passion blinded our enemies [Perón wrote in 1956] and destroyed them . . . The revolution [that overthrew me] is without a cause, because it is only a reaction . . . The military people rule, but no one really obeys. Political chaos draws near. The economy, left to the management of clerks, gets worse day by day and . . . anarchy threatens the social order . . . These dictators who don't know too much and don't even know where they are going, who move from crisis to crisis, will end by losing their way on a road that leads nowhere.

The return of Perón, or the triumph of Peronism, is anticipated. It has been estimated that already between six and eight thousand million dollars have been shipped out of the country by Argentines. "People are not involved," the ambassador's wife says. "And you must remember that anybody who has money is not an Argentine. Only people who don't have money are Argentines."

But even at the level of wealth and security, even when escape plans have been drawn up, even, for instance, at this elegant dinner party in the Barrio Norte, passion breaks in. "I'm *dying,*" the lady says abruptly, clenching her fists. "I'm dying—I'm dying—I'm dying. It isn't a life any longer. Everybody clinging on by their fingertips. This place is *dead.* Sometimes I just go to bed after lunch and stay there." The elderly butler wears white gloves; all the panelling in the room was imported from France at the turn of the century. (How easy and quick this Argentine aristocracy, how brief its settled life.) "The streets are dug up, the lights are dim, the telephones don't answer." The marijuana (forty-five dollars for the last half-kilo) passes; the mood does not alter. "This used to be a great city and a great port. Twenty years ago. Now it's fucked up, baby."

For intellectuals and artists as well, the better ones, who are not afraid of the outside world, there is this great anxiety of being imprisoned in Argentina and not being able to get out, of having one's creative years wasted by a revolution in which one can have no stake, or by a bloody-minded dictatorship, or just by chaos. Inflation and the crash of the peso have already trapped many. Menchi Sábat, the country's most brilliant cartoonist, says, "It is easier for us to be on the moon by TV. But we don't know Bolivia or Chile or even Uruguay. The reason? Money. What we are seeing now is a kind of collective frenzy. Because before it was always easy here to get money. Now we are isolated. It isn't easy for people outside to understand what this means."

The winter season still begins in May with the opera at the Colón Theatre; and orchestra seats at twenty-one dollars are quickly sold out. But the land has been despoiled of its most precious myth, the myth of wealth, wealth once so great, Argentines tell you, that you killed a cow and ate only the tongue, and the traveller on the pampa was free to kill and eat any cow, providing only that he left the skin for the landowner. Is it eight feet of topsoil that the humid pampa has? Or is it twelve? So rich, Argentina; such luck, with the land.

In 1850 there were fewer than a million Argentines; and Indian territory began one hundred miles west and south of Buenos Aires. Then, less than a hundred years ago, in a six-year carnage, the Indians were sought out and destroyed; and the pampa began to yield its treasure. Vast *estancias* on the stolen, bloody land: a sudden and jealous colonial aristocracy. Add immigrants, a labour force: in 1914 there were eight million Argentines. The immigrants, mainly from northern Spain and southern Italy, came not to be small holders or pioneers but to service the *estancias* and the port, Buenos Aires, that served the *estancias*. A vast and flourishing colonial economy, based on cattle and wheat, and attached to the British Empire; an urban proletariat as sudden as the *estancia* aristocracy; a whole and sudden artificial society imposed on the flat, desolate land.

BORGES, in his 1929 poem "The Mythical Founding of Buenos Aires," remembers the proletarian spread of the city:

> *Una cigarreria sahumó como una rosa*
> *el desierto. La tarde se había ahondado en ayeres,*
> *los hombres compartieron un pasado ilusorio.*
> *Sólo faltó una cosa: la vereda de enfrente.*

Which in Alastair Reid's translation becomes:

> *A cigar store perfumed the desert like a rose.*
> *The afternoon had established its yesterdays,*
> *And men took on together an illusory past.*
> *Only one thing was missing—the street had no other side.*

> *A mi se me hace cuento que empezó Buenos Aires:*
> *La juzgo tan eterna como el agua y el aire.*

> *Hard to believe Buenos Aires had any beginning.*
> *I feel it to be as eternal as air and water.*

The half-made city is within Borges's memory. Now, already, there is decay. The British Empire has withdrawn *ordenadamente,* in good order; and the colonial agricultural economy, attempting haphazardly to industrialize, to become balanced and autonomous, is in ruins. The artificiality of the society shows: that absence of links between men and men, between immigrant and immigrant, aristocrat and artisan, city dweller and *cabecita negra,* the "blackhead," the man from the interior; that absence of a link between men and the meaningless flat land. And the poor, who are Argentines, the sons and grandsons of those recent immigrants, will now have to stay.

They have always had their *curanderos* and *brujas,* thaumaturges and witches; they know how to protect themselves against the ghosts and poltergeists with which they have peopled the alien land. But now a larger faith is needed, some knowledge of a sheltering divinity. Without faith these abandoned Spaniards and Italians will go mad.

At the end of May a Buenos Aires church advertised a special mass against the evil eye, *el mal de ojo.* "If you've been damaged, or if you think you are being damaged, don't fail to come." Five thousand city people turned up, many in motorcars. There were half a dozen stalls selling holy or beneficent objects; there were cubicles for religious-medical consultations, from thirty cents to a dollar a time. It was a little like a Saturday-morning market. The officiating priest said, "Every individual is an individual source of power and is subject to imperceptible mental waves which can bring about ill-health or distress. This is the visible sign of the evil spirit."

"I can never believe we are in 1972," the publisher-bookseller says. "It seems to me we are still in the year zero." He isn't complaining; he himself trades in the occult and mystical, and his business is booming. Argentine middle-class mimicry of Europe and the United States, perhaps. But at a lower level the country is being swept by the new enthusiastic cult of *espiritismo,* a purely native affair of mediums and mass trances and miraculous cures, which claims the patronage of Jesus Christ and Mahatma Gandhi. The *espiritistas* don't talk of mental waves; their mediums heal by passing on intangible beneficent "fluids." The *espiritistas* say they have given up politics, and they revere Gandhi for his nonviolence. They believe in reincarnation and the perfectibility of the spirit. They say that purgatory and hell exist now, on earth, and that man's only hope is to be born on a more evolved planet. Their goal is that life, in a "definitive" disembodied world, where only superior spirits congregate.

Despair: a rejection of the land, a dream of nullity. But someone holds out hope; someone seeks to resanctify the land. With Perón at the Iron Gate is José López Rega, who has been his companion and private secretary through all the years of exile. Rega is known to have mystical leanings and to be interested in astrology and *espiritismo*; and he is said to be a man of great power now. An interview with him fills ten pages of a recent issue of *Las Bases*, the new Peronist fortnightly. Argentines are of many races, Rega says; but they all have native ancestors. The Argentine racial mixture has been "enriched by Indian blood" and "Mother Earth has purified it all . . . I fight for liberty," Rega goes on, "because that's how I am made and because I feel stirring within me the blood of the Indian, whose land this is." Now, for all its vagueness and unconscious irony, this is an astonishing statement, because, until this crisis, it was the Argentine's pride that his country was not "niggered up" like Brazil or mestizo like Bolivia, but European; and it was his special anxiety that outsiders might think of Argentines as Indians. Now the Indian ghost is invoked, and a mystical, purifying claim is made on the blighted land.

Other people offer, as they have always offered, political and economic programmes. Perón and Peronism offer faith.

AND THEY HAVE A SAINT: Eva Perón. "I remember I was very sad for many days," she wrote in 1952 in *La Razón de Mi Vida (My Life's Cause)*, "when I discovered that in the world there were poor people and rich people; and the strange thing is that the existence of the poor didn't cause me as much pain as the knowledge that at the same time there were people who were rich." It was the basis of her political action. She preached a simple hate and a simple love. Hate for the rich: "Shall we burn down the Barrio Norte?" she would say to the crowds. "Shall I give you fire?" And love for "the common people," *el pueblo*: she used that word again and again and made it part of the Peronist vocabulary. She levied tribute from everyone for her Eva Perón Foundation; and she sat until three or four or five in the morning in the Ministry of Labour, giving away foundation money to suppliants, dispensing a personal justice. This was her "work": a child's vision of power, justice and revenge.

She died in 1952, when she was thirty-three. And now in Argentina, after the proscribed years, the attempt to extirpate her name, she is a presence again. Her pictures are everywhere, touched up, seldom sharp, and often they seem deliberately garish, like religious pictures meant for the poor: a young woman of great beauty, with blonde hair, a very white skin and the very red lips of the 1940s.

She was of the people and of the land. She was born in 1919 in Los Toldos, the dreariest of pampa small towns, built on the site of an Indian encampment, 150 flat miles west of Buenos Aires. The town gives an impression of flatness, of total exposure below the high sky. The dusty brick houses, red or white, are low, flat-fronted and flat-roofed, with an occasional balustrade; the paraíso trees have whitewashed trunks and are severely pollarded; the wide streets, away from the centre, are still of dirt.

She was illegitimate; she was poor; and she lived for the first ten years of her life in a one-room house, which still stands. When she was fifteen she went to Buenos Aires to become an actress. Her speech was bad; she had a country girl's taste in clothes; her breasts were very small, her calves were heavy, and her ankles thickish. But within three months she had got her first job. And thereafter she charmed her way up. When she was twenty-five she met Perón; the following year they married.

Her commonness, her beauty, her success: they contribute to her sainthood. And her sexiness. *"Todos me acosan sexualmente,"* she once said with irritation, in her actress days. "Everybody makes a pass at me." She was the macho's ideal victim-woman—don't those red lips still speak to the Argentine macho of her reputed skill in fellatio? But very soon she was beyond sex, and pure again. At twenty-nine she was dying from cancer of the uterus, and haemorrhaging through the vagina; and her plumpish body began to waste away. Towards the end she weighed eighty pounds. One day she looked at some old official photographs of herself and began to cry. Another day she saw herself in a long mirror and said, "When I think of the trouble I went to to keep my legs slim! *Ahora que me veo estas piernitas me asusto.* Now it frightens me to look at these matchsticks."

But politically she never weakened. The Peronist revolution was going bad. Argentina's accumulated wartime wealth was running low; the colonial economy, unregenerated, plundered, mismanaged, was beginning to founder; the peso was falling; the workers, to whom so much had been given, were not always loyal. But she still cherished her especial pain that "there were people who were rich." Close to death, she told a gathering of provincial governors, "We mustn't pay too much attention to people who talk to us of prudence. We must be fanatical." The army was growing restive. She was willing to take them on. She wanted to arm the trade unions; and she did buy, through Prince Bernhard of the Netherlands, 5,000 automatic pistols and 1,500 machine guns, which, when they arrived, Perón, more prudent, gave to the police.

And all the time her private tragedy was being turned into the public passion play of the dictatorship. For her, who had turned Peronism into a religion, sainthood had long been decreed; and there is a story that for fifteen days before her death the man who was to embalm her was with her, to ensure that nothing was done that might damage the body. As soon as she died the embalming contract was signed. Was it for $100,000 or $300,000? The reports are confused. Dr. Ara, the Spanish embalmer—"a master," Perón called him—had first to make the body ready for a fifteen-day lying in state. The actual embalming took six months. The process remains secret. Dr. Ara, according to a Buenos Aires newspaper, has devoted two chapters of his memoirs (which are to be published only after his death) to the embalming of Eva Perón; colour pictures of the corpse are also promised. Reports suggest that the blood was first replaced by alcohol, and then by heated glycerin (Perón himself says "paraffin and other special matter"), which was pumped in through the heel and an ear.

"I went three times to look at Evita," Perón wrote in 1956, after his overthrow, and when the embalmed body had disappeared. "The doors . . . were like the gates of eternity." He had the impression that she was only sleeping. The first time he went he wanted to touch her, but he feared that at the touch of his warm hand the body would turn to dust. Ara said, "Don't worry. She's as whole [*intacta*] now as when she was alive."

And now, twenty years later, her embalmed wasted body, once lost, now found, and no bigger, they say, than that of a twelve-year-old girl, only the blond hair as rich as in the time of health, waits with Perón at the Iron Gate.

It came as a surprise, this *villa miseria* or shantytown just beside the brown river in the Palermo district, not far from the great park, Buenos Aires's equivalent of the Bois de Boulogne, where people go riding. A shantytown, with unpaved streets and black runnels of filth, but the buildings were of brick, with sometimes an upper storey: a settled place, more than fifteen years old, with shops and signs. Seventy thousand people lived there, nearly all Indians, blank and slightly imbecilic in appearance, from the north and from Bolivia and Paraguay; so that suddenly you were reminded that you were not in Paris or Europe but in

South America. The priest in charge was one of the "Priests for the Third World." He wore a black leather jacket and his little concrete shed of a church, over-simple, rocked with some amplified Argentine song. It had been whispered to me that the priest came of a very good family; and perhaps the change of company had made him vain. He was of course a Peronist, and he said that all his Indians were Peronist. "Only an Argentine can understand Peronism. I can talk to you for five years about Peronism, but you will never understand."

But couldn't we try? He said Peronism wasn't concerned with economic growth; they rejected the consumer society. But hadn't he just been complaining about the unemployment in the interior, the result of government folly, that was sending two Indians into his shantytown for every one that left? He said he wasn't going to waste his time talking to a *norteamericano*; some people were concerned only with GNP. And, leaving us, he bore down, all smiles, on some approaching Indians. The river wind was damp, the concrete shed unheated, and I wanted to leave. But the man with me was uneasy. He said we should at least wait and tell the father I wasn't an American. We did so. And the father, abashed, explained that Peronism was really concerned with the development of the human spirit. Such a development had taken place in Cuba and China; in those countries they had turned their backs on the industrial society.*

THESE lawyers had been represented to me as a group working for "civil rights." They were young, stylishly dressed, and they were meeting that morning to draft a petition against torture. The top-floor flat was scruffy and bare; visitors were scrutinized through the peephole; everybody whispered; and there was a lot of cigarette smoke. Intrigue, danger. But one of the lawyers was diverted by my invitation to lunch, and at lunch—he was a hearty and expensive eater—he made it clear that the torture they were protesting against wasn't to be confused with the torture in Perón's time.

He said, "When justice is the justice of the people, men sometimes commit excesses. But in the final analysis, the important thing is that justice should be done in the name of the people." Who were the enemies of

---

*The priest was killed two years later, in 1974, by unknown gunmen, and for a few days had poster fame as a Peronist martyr.

the people? His response was tabulated and swift. "American imperialism. And its native allies. The oligarchy, the dependent bourgeoisie, Zionism, and the 'sepoy' left. By sepoys we mean the Communist Party and socialism in general." It seemed a comprehensive list. Who were the Peronists? "Peronism is a revolutionary national movement. There is a great difference between a movement and a party. We are not Stalinists, and a Peronist is anyone who calls himself a Peronist and acts like a Peronist."

The lawyer, for all his anti-Jewish feeling, was a Jew; and he came of an anti-Peronist middle-class family. In 1970 he had met Perón in Madrid, and he had been dazzled; his voice shook when he quoted Perón's words. He had said to Perón, "General, why don't you declare war on the regime and then put yourself at the head of all the true Peronists?" Perón replied, "I am the conductor of a national movement. I have to conduct the whole movement, in its totality."

" THERE are no internal enemies," the trade union leader said, with a smile. But at the same time he thought that torture would continue in Argentina. "A world without torture is an ideal world." And there was torture and torture. "*Depende de quien sea torturado.* It depends on who is tortured. An evildoer, that's all right. But a man who's trying to save the country—that's something else. Torture isn't only the electric prod, you know. Poverty is torture, frustration is torture." He was urbane; I had been told he was the most intellectual of the Peronist trade union leaders. He had been punctual; his office was uncluttered and neat; on his desk, below glass, there was a large photograph of the young Perón.

The first Peronist revolution was based on the myth of wealth, of a land waiting to be plundered. Now the wealth has gone. And Peronism is like part of the poverty. It is protest, despair, faith, machismo, magic, *espiritismo,* revenge. It is everything and nothing. Remove Perón, and hysteria will be uncontrollable. Remove the armed forces, sterile guardians of law and order, and Peronism, triumphant, will disintegrate into a hundred scattered fights, every man identifying his own enemy.

"Violence, in the hands of the people, isn't violence: it is justice." This statement of Perón's was printed on the front page of a recent issue of *Fe,* a Peronist paper. So, in sinister mimicry, the south twists the revolutionary jargon of the north. Where jargon turns living issues into abstractions ("Torture will disappear in Argentina," the Trotskyist said,

"only with a workers' government and the downfall of the bourgeoisie"), and where jargon ends by competing with jargon, people don't
have causes. They only have enemies; only the enemies are real. It has
been the South American nightmare since the break-up of the Spanish
Empire.

WAS EVA PERÓN blonde or brunette? Was she born in 1919 or 1922?
Was she born in the little town of Los Toldos, or in Junín, forty kilometres away? Well, she was a brunette who dyed her hair blond; she was
born in 1919 but said 1922 (and had her birth record destroyed in 1945);
she spent the first ten years of her life in Los Toldos but ever afterwards
disclaimed the town. No one will know why. Don't go to her autobiography, *La Razón de Mi Vida,* which used to be prescribed reading in Argentine schools. That doesn't contain a fact or a date; and it was written by a
Spaniard, who later complained that the book he wrote had been much
altered by the Peronist authorities.

So the truth begins to disappear; it is not relevant to the legend.
Masses are held in Eva Perón's memory, and students now turn up in
numbers; but her life is not the subject of inquiry. Unmarked, seldom visited (though a woman remembers that once some television people
came), the one-room house in brown brick in Los Toldos crumbles. The
elderly garage owner next door (two vehicles in his garage, one an
engineless Model T), to whom the house now belongs, uses it as a storeroom. Grass sprouts from the flat roof, and the corrugated-iron roof collapses over the patio at the back.

Only one biography of Eva Perón has been attempted in Argentina.
It was to be in two volumes, but the publisher went bankrupt and the second volume hasn't appeared. Had she lived, Eva Perón would now be
only fifty-three. There are hundreds of people alive who knew her. But
in two months I found it hard to get beyond what was well known.
Memories have been edited; people deal in panegyric or hate, and the
people who hate refuse to talk about her. The anguish of those early
years at Los Toldos has been successfully suppressed. The Eva Perón
story has been lost; there is now only the legend.

One evening, after his classes at the Catholic University, and while
the police sirens screamed outside, Borges told me: "We had a sense that
the whole thing should have been forgotten. Had the newspapers been

silent, there would have been no Peronism today—the Peronistas were at first ashamed of themselves. If I were facing a public audience I would never use his name. I would say *el prófugo*, the fugitive, *el dictador*. The way in poetry one avoids certain words—if I used his name in a poem the whole thing would fall to pieces."

It is the Argentine attitude: suppress, ignore. Many of the records of the Peronist era have been destroyed. If today the middle-class young are Peronists, and students sing the old song of the dictatorship—

> *Perón, Perón, qué grande sos!*
> *Mi general, cuánto valés!*
>
> *Perón, Perón, how great you are!*
> *How good and strong, my general!*

—if the dictatorship, even in its excesses, is respectable again, it isn't because the past has been investigated and the record modified. It is only that many people have revised their attitudes towards the established legend. They have changed their minds.

There is no history in Argentina. There are no archives; there are only graffiti and polemics and school lessons. Schoolchildren in white dustcoats are regularly taken round the Cabildo building in the Plaza de Mayo in Buenos Aires to see the relics of the War of Independence. The event is glorious; it stands in isolation; it is not related, in the text books or in the popular mind, to what immediately followed: the loss of law, the seeking out of the enemy, endless civil wars, gangster rule.

Borges said on another evening: "The history of Argentina is the history of its separateness from Spain." How did Perón fit into that? "Perón represented the scum of the earth." But he surely also stood for something that was Argentine? "Unfortunately, I have to admit that he's an Argentine—an Argentine of today." Borges is a *criollo*, someone whose ancestors came to Argentina before the great immigrant rush, before the country became what it is; and for the contemplation of his country's history Borges substitutes ancestor worship. Like many Argentines, he has an idea of Argentina; anything that doesn't fit into this is to be rejected. And Borges is Argentina's greatest man.

An attitude to history, an attitude to the land. Magic is important in

Argentina; the country is full of witches and magicians and thaumaturges and mediums. But the visitor must ignore this side of Argentine life because, he is told, it isn't real. The country is full of *estancias*; but the visitor mustn't go to that particular *estancia* because it isn't typical. But it exists, it works. Yes, but it isn't real. Nor is that real, nor that, nor that. So the whole country is talked away; and the visitor finds himself directed to the equivalent of a gaucho curio shop. It isn't the Argentina that anyone inhabits, least of all one's guides; but *that* is real, *that* is Argentina. "Basically we all love the country," an Anglo-Argentine said. "But we would like it to be in our own image. And many of us are now suffering for our fantasies." A collective refusal to see, to come to terms with the land: an artificial, fragmented colonial society, made deficient and bogus by its myths.

To be Argentine was not to be South American. It was to be European; and many Argentines became European, of Europe. The land that was the source of their wealth became no more than their base. For these Argentine-Europeans, Buenos Aires and Mar del Plata became resort towns, with a seasonal life. Between the wars there was a stable Argentine community of one hundred thousand in Paris; the peso was the peso then.

"Many people think," Borges said, "that quite the best thing that could have happened here would have been an English victory [in 1806–7, when the British twice raided Buenos Aires]. At the same time I wonder whether being a colony does any good—so provincial and dull."

But to be European in Argentina was to be colonial in the most damaging way. It was to be parasitic. It was to claim—as the white communities of the Caribbean colonies claimed—the achievements and authority of Europe as one's own. It was to ask less of oneself (in Trinidad, when I was a child, it was thought that the white and the rich needed no education). It was to accept, out of a false security, a second-rateness for one's own society.

And there was the wealth of Argentina: the British railways taking the wheat and the meat from all the corners of the pampa to the port of Buenos Aires, for shipment to England. There was no pioneer or nation-making myth of hard work and reward. The land was empty and very flat and very rich; it was inexhaustible; and it was infinitely forgiving. *Dios arregla de noche la macana que los Argentinos hacen de día*: God puts right at night the mess the Argentines make by day.

To be Argentine was to inhabit a magical, debilitating world. Wealth and Europeanness concealed the colonial realities of an agricultural society which had needed little talent and had produced little, which had needed no great men and had produced none. "Nothing *happened* here," Norman di Giovanni said with irritation one day. And everyone, from Borges down, says, "Buenos Aires is a small town." Eight million people: a monstrous plebeian sprawl, mean, repetitive and meaningless: but only a small town, eaten up by colonial doubt and malice. When the real world is felt to be outside, everyone at home is inadequate and fraudulent. A waiter in Mendoza said, "Argentines don't work. We can't do anything big. Everything we do is small and petty." An artist said, "There are very few *professionals* here. By that I mean people who know what to do with themselves. No one knows why he is doing any particular job. For that reason, if you are doing what I do, then you are my enemy."

Camelero, chanta: these are everyday Argentine words. A *camelero* is a line-shooter, a man who really has nothing to sell. The man who promised to take me to an *estancia*, and in his private airplane, was only doing *camelo*. The *chanta* is the man who will sell everything, the man without principles, the hollow man. Almost everybody, from the president down, is dismissed by somebody as a *chanta*.

The other word that recurs is *mediocre*. Argentines detest the mediocre and fear to be thought mediocre. It was one of Eva Perón's words of abuse. For her the Argentine aristocracy was always mediocre. And she was right. In a few years she shattered the myth of Argentina as an aristocratic colonial land. And no other myth, no other idea of the land, has been found to take its place.

2   BORGES AND THE BOGUS PAST

BORGES, speaking of the fame of writers, said: "The important thing is the image you create of yourself in other people's minds. Many people think of Burns as a mediocre poet. But he stands for many things, and people like him. That image—as with Byron—may in the end be more important than the work."

Borges is a great writer, a sweet and melancholy poet; and people who know Spanish well revere him as a writer of a direct, unrhetorical prose. But his Anglo-American reputation as a blind and elderly Argentine, the writer of a very few, very short, and very mysterious stories, is so inflated and bogus that it obscures his greatness. It has possibly cost him the Nobel Prize; and it may well happen that when the bogus reputation declines, as it must, the good work may also disappear.

The irony is that Borges, at his best, is neither mysterious nor difficult. His poetry is accessible; much of it is even romantic. His themes have remained constant for the last fifty years: his military ancestors, their deaths in battle, death itself, time, and old Buenos Aires. And there are about a dozen successful stories. Two or three are straightforward, even old-fashioned, detective stories (one was published in *Ellery Queen's Mystery Magazine*). Some deal, quite cinematically, with Buenos Aires low life at the turn of the century. Gangsters are given epic stature; they rise, they are challenged, and sometimes they run away.

The other stories—the ones that have driven the critics crazy—are in the nature of intellectual jokes. Borges takes a word like "immortal" and plays with it. Suppose, he says, men were really immortal. Not just men who had grown old and wouldn't die, but indestructible vigorous men, surviving for eternity. What would be the result? His answer—which is his story—is that every conceivable experience would at some time befall every man, that every man would at some time assume every conceivable character, and that Homer (the disguised hero of this particular story) might in the eighteenth century even forget he had written the *Odyssey*. Or take the word "unforgettable." Suppose something were truly unforgettable, and couldn't be forgotten for a single second; suppose this thing came, like a coin, into your possession. Extend that idea. Suppose there were a man—but no, he has to be a boy—who could forget nothing, whose memory therefore ballooned and ballooned with all the unforgettable details of every minute of his life.

These are some of Borges's intellectual games. And perhaps his most successful piece of prose writing, which is also his shortest, is a pure joke. It is called "Of Exactitude in Science" and is meant to be an extract from a seventeenth-century book of travel:

> In that Empire, the craft of Cartography attained such Perfection that the Map of a Single province covered the space of an

entire City, and the Map of the Empire itself an entire Province. In the course of Time, these Extensive maps were found somehow wanting, and so the College of Cartographers evolved a Map of the Empire that was of the same Scale as the Empire and coincided with it point for point. Less attentive to the Study of Cartography, succeeding Generations came to judge a map of such Magnitude cumbersome and, not without Irreverence, abandoned it to the Rigours of sun and Rain. In the western Deserts, tattered Fragments of the Map are still to be found, Sheltering an occasional Beast or beggar; in the whole Nation no other relic is left of the Discipline of Geography.

This is absurd and perfect: the accurate parody, the grotesque idea. Borges's puzzle and jokes can be addictive. But they have to be recognized for what they are; they cannot always support the metaphysical interpretations they receive. There is, though, much to attract the academic critic. Some of Borges's hoaxes require—and sometimes disappear below—an extravagant display of curious learning. And there is the occasional baroque language of the early stories.

"The Circular Ruins"—an elaborate, almost science fiction story about a dreamer discovering that he himself exists only in somebody else's dream—begins: *"Nadie lo vió desembarcar en la unánime noche."* Literally, "Nobody saw him disembark in the unanimous night." Norman Thomas di Giovanni, who has been translating Borges full-time for the last four years, and has done more than anyone else to push Borges's work in the English-speaking world, says:

> You can imagine how much has been written about that "unanimous." I went to Borges with two translations, "surrounding" and "encompassing." And I said, "Borges, what did you really mean by the unanimous night? That doesn't mean anything. If the unanimous night, why not the tea-drinking night, or the card-playing night?" And I was astonished by his answer. He said, "Di Giovanni, that's just one example of the irresponsible way I used to write." We used "encompassing" in the translation. But a lot of the professors didn't like losing their unanimous night . . .

There was this woman. She wrote an essay on Borges for a book. She didn't know any Spanish and was basing her essay on two rather mediocre English translations. A long essay, about forty pages. And one of the *crucial* points was that Borges wrote a very Latinate prose. I had to point out to her that Borges could not help but write a Latinate prose, because he wrote in Spanish, and Spanish is a dialect of Latin. She didn't consult anybody when she was laying the foundation. At the end she calls out "Help!" and you run up and see this enormous skyscraper sinking in quicksand.

Di Giovanni went with Borges on a lecture tour of the United States in 1969:

Borges is a gentleman. When people come up and tell him what his stories really mean—after all, he only wrote them—he has the most wonderful line you've ever heard. "Ah, thank you! You've enriched my story. You've made me a great gift. I've come all the way from Buenos Aires to X—say Lubbock, Texas—to find out this truth about myself and my story."

Borges has for years enjoyed a considerable reputation in the Spanish-speaking world. But in "An Autobiographical Essay," which was published as a "Profile" in *The New Yorker* in 1970, he says that until he won the Formentor Prize in 1961—he was sixty-two then—he was "practically invisible—not only abroad but at home in Buenos Aires." This is the kind of exaggeration that dismays some of his early Argentine supporters; and there are those who would say that his "irresponsibility" has grown with his fame. But Borges has always been irresponsible. Buenos Aires is a small town; and what perhaps was inoffensive when Borges belonged only to this small town becomes less so when foreigners queue up for interviews. Once, no doubt, Borges's celebration of his military ancestors and their deaths in battle flattered the whole society, giving it a sense of the past and of completeness. Now it appears to exclude, to proclaim a private grandeur; and to many it is only egotistical and presumptuous. It is not easy to be famous in a small town.

Borges gives many interviews. And every interview seems to be like every other interview. He seems to make questions irrelevant; he plays, as one Argentine lady said, his *discos,* his records; he performs. He says that the Spanish language is his "doom." He criticizes Spain and the Spaniards: he still fights that colonial war, in which, however, the old issues have become confused with a simpler Argentine prejudice against the poor and backward immigrants from northern Spain. He makes his tasteless, and expected, jokes about the pampa Indians. Tasteless because just twenty years before he was born these Indians were systematically exterminated; and yet expected, because slaughter on this scale becomes acceptable only if the victims are made ridiculous. He talks about Chesterton, Stevenson and Kipling. He talks about Old English with all the enthusiasm of a man who has picked up an academic subject by himself. He talks about his English ancestors.

It is a curiously colonial performance. His Argentine past is part of his distinction; he offers it as such; and he is after all a patriot. He honours the flag, an example of which flies from the balcony of his office in the National Library (he is the director). And he is moved by the country's anthem. But at the same time he seems anxious to proclaim his separateness from Argentina. The performance might seem aimed at Borges's new Anglo-American campus audience, whom in so many ways it flatters. But the attitudes are old.

In Buenos Aires it is still remembered that in 1955, just a few days after Perón was overthrown and that nine-year dictatorship was over, Borges gave a lecture on—of all subjects—Coleridge to the ladies of the Association for English Culture. Some of Coleridge's lines, Borges said, were among the best in English poetry, *"es decir la poesía* [that is to say poetry]*"*. And those four words, at a time of national rejoicing, were like a gratuitous assault on the Argentine soul.

Norman di Giovanni tells a balancing story.

In December 1969, we were at Georgetown University in Washington, D.C. The man doing the introduction was an Argentine from Tucumán and he took advantage of the occasion to point out to the audience that the military repression had closed the university in Tucumán. Borges was totally oblivious of what the man had said until we were on our way to the airport. Then someone began to talk about it and Borges was suddenly very angry. "Did you hear what that man said? That they'd closed the university in Tucumán." I questioned him about his rage, and he said, "That man was attacking my country. They can't talk that way about my country." I said, "Borges, what do you mean, 'that man'? That

man is an Argentine. And he comes from Tucumán. And what he
says is true. The military *have* closed the university."

Borges is of medium height. His nearly sightless eyes and his stick
add to the distinction of his appearance. He dresses carefully. He says he
is a middle-class writer; and a middle-class writer shouldn't be either a
dandy or too affectedly casual. He is courtly: he thinks, with Sir Thomas
Browne, that a gentleman is someone who tries to give the least amount
of trouble. "But you should look that up in *Religio Medici*." It might
seem then that in his accessibility, his willingness to give lengthy interviews which repeat the other interviews he has given, Borges combines
the middle-class ideal of self-effacement and the gentleman's manners
with the writer's privacy, the writer's need to save himself for his work.

There are hints of this privacy (in accessibility) in the way he likes to
be addressed. Perhaps no more than half a dozen people have the privilege of calling him by his first name, Jorge, which they turn into
"Georgie." To everyone else he likes to be just "Borges" without the
Señor, which he considers Spanish and pompous. "Borges" is, of course,
distancing.

And even the fifty-page "Autobiographical Essay" doesn't violate his
privacy. It is like another interview. It says little that is new. His birth in
Buenos Aires in 1899, the son of a lawyer; his military ancestors; the
family's seven-year sojourn in Europe from 1914 to 1921 (when the peso
was valuable, and Europe was cheaper than Buenos Aires): all this is told
again in outline, as in an interview. And the essay quickly becomes no
more than a writer's account of his writing life, of the books he read and
the books he wrote, the literary groups he joined and the magazines he
founded. The life is missing. There is the barest sketch of the crisis
he must have gone through in his late thirties and early forties, when—
the family money lost—he was doing all kinds of journalism; when his
father died, and he himself fell seriously ill and "feared for [his] mental
integrity"; when he worked as an assistant in a municipal library, well
known as a writer outside the library, unknown inside it. "I remember a
fellow employee's once noting in an encyclopaedia the name of a certain
Jorge Luis Borges—a fact that set him wondering at the coincidence of
our identical names and birth dates."

"Nine years of solid unhappiness," he says; but he gives the period only four pages. The privacy of Borges begins to appear a forbidding thing.

> *Un dios me ha concedido*
> *Lo que es dado saber a los mortales.*
> *Por todo el continente anda mi nombre;*
> *No he vivido. Quisiera ser otro hombre.*

Mark Strand translates:

> *I have been allowed*
> *That which is given mortal man to know.*
> *The whole continent knows my name.*
> *I have not lived. I want to be someone else.*

This is Borges on Emerson; but it might be Borges on Borges. Life, in the "Autobiographical Essay," is indeed missing. So that all that is important in the man has to be found in the work, which with Borges is essentially the poetry. And all the themes he has explored over a long life are contained, as he himself says, in his very first book of poems, published in 1923, a book printed in five days, three hundred copies, given away free.

Here is the military ancestor dying in battle. Here, already, at the age of twenty-four, the contemplation of glory turns into the meditation on death and time and the "glass jewels" of the individual life:

> *. . . cuando tú mismo eres la continuación realizada*
> *de quienes no alcanzaron tu tiempo*
> *y otros serán (y son) tu inmortalidad en la tierra.*

In W. S. Merwin's translation:

> *. . . when you yourself are the embodied continuance*
> *of those who did not live into your time*
> *and others will be (and are) your immortality on earth.*

Somewhere around that time life stopped; and all that has been followed has been literature: a concern with words, an unending attempt to stay with, and not to betray, the emotions of that so particular past.

I am myself and I am him today,
The man who died, the man whose blood and name
Are mine.

This is Norman di Giovanni's translation of a poem written forty-three years after that first book:

Soy, pero soy también el otro, el muerto,
El otro de mi sangre y de mi nombre.

Since the writing of that first book nothing, except perhaps his discovery of Old English poetry, has provided Borges with matter for such intense meditation. Not even the bitter Perón years, when he was " 'promoted' out of the library to the inspectorship of poultry and rabbits in the public markets," and resigned. Nor his brief, unhappy marriage late in life, once the subject of magazine articles, and still a subject of gossip in Buenos Aires. Nor his continuing companionship with his mother, now aged ninety-six.

"In 1910, the centenary of the Argentine Republic, we thought of Argentina as an honourable country and we had no doubt that the nations would come flocking in. Now the country is in a bad way. We are being threatened by the return of the horrible man." This is how Borges speaks of Perón: he prefers not to use the name.

I get any number of personal threats. Even my mother. They rang her up in the small hours—two or three in the morning— and somebody said to her in a very gruff kind of voice, the voice you associate with a *Peronista,* "I've got to kill you and your son." My mother said, "Why?" "Because I am a *Peronista.*" My mother said, "As far as my son is concerned, he is over seventy and practically blind. But in my case I should advise you to waste no time because I am ninety-five and may die on your hands before you can kill me." Next morning I told my mother I thought I had heard the telephone ringing in the night. "Did I dream that?" She said, "Just some fool." She's not only witty. But courageous . . . I don't see what I can do about it—the political situation. But I think I should do what I can, having military men in my family.

Borges's first book of poems was called *Fervour of Buenos Aires*. In it, he said in his preface, he was attempting to celebrate the new and expanding city in a special way. "Akin to the Romans, who would murmur the words *'numen inest'* on passing through a wood, 'Here dwells a god,' my verses declare, stating the wonder of the streets . . . Everyday places become, little by little, holy."

But Borges has not hallowed Buenos Aires. The city the visitor sees is not the city of the poems, the way Simla (as new and artificial as Buenos Aires) remains, after all these years, the city of Kipling's stories. Kipling looked hard at a real town. Borges's Buenos Aires is private, a city of the imagination. And now the city itself is in decay. In Borges's own South-side some old buildings survive, with their mighty front doors and their receding patios, each patio differently tiled. But more often the inner patios have been blocked up; and many of the old buildings have been pulled down. Elegance, if in this plebeian immigrant city elegance really ever existed outside the vision of expatriate architects, has vanished; there is now only disorder.

The white and pale blue Argentine flag that hangs out into Mexico Street from the balcony of Borges's office in the National Library is dingy with dirt and fumes. And consider this building, perhaps the finest in the area, which was used as a hospital and a jail in the time of the gangster-dictator Rosas more than 120 years ago. There is beauty still in the spiked wall, the tall iron gates, the huge wooden doors. But inside, the walls peel; the windows in the central patio are broken; farther in, court-yard opening into courtyard, washing hangs in a corridor, steps are broken, and a metal spiral staircase is blocked with junk. This is a gov-ernment office, a department of the Ministry of Labour: it speaks of an administration that has seized up, a city that is dying, a country that hasn't really worked.

Walls everywhere are scrawled with violent slogans; guerrillas oper-ate in the streets; the peso falls; the city is full of hate. The bloody-minded slogan repeats: *Rosas vuelve*, Rosas is coming back. The country awaits a new terror.

Numen inest, here dwells a god: the poet's incantation hasn't worked. The military ancestors died in battle, but those petty battles and wasteful deaths have led to nothing. Only in Borges's poetry do those heroes inhabit "an epic universe, sitting tall in the saddle": *"alto . . . en su épico universo."* And this is his great creation: Argentina as a simple mythical land, a complete epic world, of "republics, cavalry and mornings [*las repúblicas, los caballos y las mañanas*]," of battles fought, the fatherland established, the great city created and the "streets with names recurring from the past in my blood."

That is the vision of art. And yet, out of this mythical Argentina of his creation, Borges reaches out, through his English grandmother, to his English ancestors and, through them, to their language "at its dawn." "People tell me I look English now. When I was younger I didn't look English. I was darker. I didn't feel English. Not at all. Maybe feeling English came to me through reading." And though Borges doesn't acknowledge it, a recurring theme in the later stories is of Nordics growing degenerate in a desolate Argentine landscape. Scottish Guthries become mestizo Gutres and no longer even know the Bible; an English girl becomes an Indian savage; men called Nilsen forget their origins and live like animals with the bestial sex code of the macho whoremonger.

Borges said at our first meeting, "I don't write about degenerates." But another time he said, "The country was enriched by men thinking essentially of Europe and the United States. Only the civilized people. The gauchos were very simple-minded. Barbarians." When we talked of Argentine history he said, "There is a pattern. Not an obvious pattern. I myself can't see the wood for the trees." And later he added, "Those civil wars are now meaningless."

Perhaps, then, parallel with the vision of art, there has developed, in Borges, a subsidiary vision, however unacknowledged, of reality. And now, at any rate, the real world can no longer be denied.

In the middle of May Borges went for a few days to Montevideo in Uruguay. Montevideo was one of the cities of his childhood, a city of "long, lazy holidays." But now Uruguay, the most educated country in South America, was, in the words of an Argentine, "a caricature of a country," bankrupt, like Argentina, after wartime wealth, and tearing itself to pieces. Montevideo was a city at war; guerrillas and soldiers fought in the streets. One day, while Borges was there, four soldiers were shot and killed.

I saw Borges when he came back. A pretty girl helped him down the steps at the Catholic University. He looked more frail; his hands shook more easily. He had shed his sprightly interview manner. He was full of the disaster of Montevideo; he was distressed. Montevideo was something else he had lost. In one poem "mornings in Montevideo" are among the things for which he thanks "the divine labyrinth of causes and effects." Now Montevideo, like Buenos Aires, like Argentina, was gracious only in his memory, and in his art.

3   KAMIKAZE IN MONTEVIDEO
October–November 1973

INTEREST rates went down in Uruguay this year. Last year, at the height of the Tupamaro crisis, you could borrow money at 60 per cent. The interest, payable in advance, was immediately deducted from the loan; so that, having borrowed a million pesos, you left the bank with 400,000. And that was good business, with the peso losing half its value against the dollar during the year, and with inflation running at 92 per cent.

Now it is a little less frenzied. The Tupamaros—there were about five thousand of them, mainly townspeople from impoverished middle-class families—have been destroyed. The army—essentially rural, lower middle-class—is in control and rules by decree. Interest rates have dropped to around 42 per cent, with the taxes; and inflation this year has been kept down to 60 per cent. "Prices here don't just rise every day," the businessman said. "They also rise every night."

Yet until the other day, they tell you in Uruguay, roadworkers could be seen grilling their lunchtime steaks in the open air; and the Uruguay peso was known as the *peso oro*, the gold peso. In 1953 there were three pesos to the U.S. dollar; today there are nine hundred.

"My father bought a house in 1953 with a 6 per cent loan from the Mortgage Bank. At the end, in 1968, he was still paying thirty pesos a month on his mortgage." Thirty pesos: twelve cents, ten pence. "That may be funny to you. For us it is a tragedy. Our Parliament refused to revalue mortgage repayments—the politicians didn't want to lose votes. So everybody had his house as a gift. But they condemned the future generations."

The law has now been changed. Interest rates, like salaries, are tied to the cost-of-living index; and the Mortgage Bank these days offers depositors 56 per cent—7 per cent true interest, 49 per cent the inflationary "adjustment."

Mr. Palatnik, the advertising man who handles the Mortgage Bank campaign, has also been engaged by the military government to help calm the country down. And, to the disgust and alarm of Left and extreme Right, Mr. Palatnik doesn't appear to be failing. He hasn't so far made himself or the government absurd. Again and again on television, in the commercial breaks in the Argentine soap operas, after the talk of government plans, hope comes in the form of a challenge: *"Tenga confianza en el país, y póngale el hombro al Uruguay."* Literally: "Have faith in the country, and put your shoulder to Uruguay."

But in Uruguay these days it is hard not to offend. *New Dawn*, the weekly newspaper of a new right-wing youth group ("Family, Tradition, Property"), published a strong attack on Mr. Palatnik, with a distinctly anti-Semitic cartoon. Mr. Palatnik, who is middle-aged, challenged the editor to a duel. He sent his *padrinos* to the *New Dawn* office, but the challenge wasn't accepted. The *New Dawn* group isn't important; but, like many businessmen in Montevideo, Mr. Palatnik now carries a gun.

The precaution is excessive. The army at the moment is in control and on the offensive; it continues to arrest and interrogate; the days of guerrilla kidnap in Montevideo are over. Montevideo, so dangerous last year, is now safer than Buenos Aires; and some of the more ransomable American business executives in Argentina have moved across the Río de la Plata to Montevideo, to the red-brick tower of the Victoria Plaza Hotel in the main square, with the equestrian statue of Artigas, the founder of the Uruguayan state, in the centre.

Government House is on one side of the square. There are sentries in nineteenth-century uniform, but also real soldiers with real guns. On another side of the square the Palace of Justice, begun six years ago, stands unfinished in the immense crater of its foundations. Grass, level and lush as if sown, grows from the concrete beams, and the concrete columns are stained with rust from the reinforcing steel rods.

Montevideo is safe. But the money has run out in a country whose official buildings, in the days of wealth, were of marble, granite and bronze. All the extravagant woodwork in the Legislative Palace, all the marquetry that rises from floor to ceiling in the library, was made in Italy and shipped out, they say, in mahogany crates. And that was just fifty years ago. Now the palace is without a function, and soldiers, making small gestures with their guns, urge passers-by to keep their distance.

Fifty years ago, before people built on the sea, the fashionable area was the Prado: great houses, some gothic follies, great gardens. The Prado park is now tended only in parts; the once-famous rose garden runs wild. Beyond the bridge with the tarnished *Belle Époque* sphinxes, a long drive, shaded by eucalyptus, plane and fir, leads to the Prado Hotel, still apparently whole, with its green walks and balustraded terraces and a fountain that still plays. But the asphalt forecourt is cracked; the lamp standards and urns are empty; the great yellow building—*Jules Knab arq 1911* incised halfway up—has been abandoned.

Montevideo is in parts a ghost city, its *nouveau riche* splendour still new. It is a city full of statues—copies of the *David*, the Colleoni statue in Venice, elaborate historical tableaux in bronze. But letters have dropped off inscriptions and have not been replaced; and the public clocks on street corners have everywhere stopped. The plane trees in the centre are not old; tall carved doors still open on to marble halls with fine ceilings that still look new. But the shops have little to offer; the pavements are broken; the streets are too full of people selling chocolate and sweets and other little things. The three or four fair restaurants that survive—in a city of more than a million—do not always have meat; and the bread is made partly of sorghum.

Even without the slogans on the walls—STOP TORTURING SASSANO, THE MILITARY ARE TORTURING SERENY, DEATH TO THE DICTATOR-SHIP, TUPAMAROS RENEGADES THIEVES SWINE, PUTAMAROS [*puta*, a whore]—the visitor would know that he is in a city where, as in a fairy story, a hidden calamity has occurred. A fabulous city, created all at once, and struck down almost as soon as it had been created.

"The country has grown sad," the artist said. He survives by living to himself, doing his work, and pretending that Uruguay is somewhere else. He doesn't listen to the radio or watch television or read the newspapers. What—apart from the football—had he missed in that morning's *El País*? A plane hijacked to Bolivia; five hundred secondary-school students suspended; five "extremists," three of them university students, indicted by the military court for "conspiring against the Constitution."

When Uruguay was rich, politics were a matter of personalities and the army hardly existed. Now the money has run out, and the little country—almost as big as Britain, but with less than three million people—tears itself apart.

"The army came for me at four in the morning. In the jail—they play pop music in the torture cells—I was made to stand with my feet together for ten hours. Then I was given the 'submarine.' I was winded by a heavy blow in the stomach and my head was held underwater. They're expert now. But they've had accidents. Then I was made to stand again. When I collapsed I was prodded between the legs with a bayonet." The "submarine" is "soft" torture. People who have been burned by the electric prod don't talk about their experiences.

E V E R Y O N E in Uruguay, whether on the Right or Left, knows now—sixty years too late—where the trouble started. It started with the president called Batlle (pronounced *Bajhay*); it started with the welfare state Batlle, after a visit to Switzerland, began to impose on Uruguay just before the First World War.

Uruguay had the money. Her exports of meat and wool made her rich; the peso was on a par with the dollar. "In those days," the banker says, "out of every dollar we earned abroad, eighty cents was pure surplus. A surplus provided by the land—the rain, the climate, the earth." The land might be said to be Indian land, but the Indians had been exterminated in the nineteenth century. A monument in the Prado park commemorates Uruguay's last four Charrua Indians, who were sent as exhibits to the Musée de l'Homme in Paris, where they died.

Pensions, every kind of worker's benefit, women's rights: month after month Batlle handed down the liberal laws to an astonished pastoral people. And suddenly Uruguay was modern, the best-educated country in South America, with the most liberal laws; and Montevideo was a metropolis, full of statues.

Sábat, the cartoonist, who left Uruguay eight years ago and now works in Buenos Aires, says: "Uruguay is a big *estancia*. Only a megalomaniac like Batlle could think that it was a country. It remains a big *estancia* with a city, Montevideo, that is crystallized on the 1930s. Creativity stopped then. The country was developing intellectually. After Batlle everything was *crystallized*."

The socialist teacher, more romantic, grieves for the gaucho past. "Batlle should not have been born in a bucolic country. He went to Europe and got all those lovely ideas and then looked around for a country where he could apply them. And as the country didn't exist he invented it. He invented the industrial worker, bringing in people from the country to the town. People used to drinking maté, watching sheep, sitting under the ombú tree—which wasn't bad, you know: it was beautiful: the twentieth century doesn't want us to live like that. He invented the workers and then he invented the social laws and then the bureaucracy—which was terrible. I am not certain why this should have led to corruption and venality, but it did."

The businessman: "Utopia is the worst thing for a man. He is old at thirty. That happened to us."

The banker: "All the productive infrastructure was built between 1850 and 1930 and was based on existing British investments. Very little was done afterwards. A power plant was finished after 1945; that was the most important addition. No new roads, no new bridges. The country was living like a retired person on a pension."

And with the new state, a new glory. Football, introduced by British railway workers, became the Uruguayan obsession. Sábat: "Our provincialism was backed up by our football—a proof of greatness that had no relation with reality. In 1924 in Paris and in 1928 in Amsterdam we were the Olympic champions. We were the world champions in Montevideo in 1930 and in Rio in 1950. And we thought: If we are world champions in football, then we must be world champions in everything."

In the park named after Batlle, the great football stadium, built in 1930 (together with the Legislative Palace) for the centenary of Uruguay's independence, and named after Batlle, still draws the crowds. The newspapers still devote half their news space to football. But football has decayed with the economy; and now, like the cattle, the better footballers have to be sold off to richer countries as soon as they are reared.

THERE are many jokes in Uruguay about the bureaucracy; and they all are true. Out of a workforce of just over a million, 250,000 are employed by the state. PLUNA, the Uruguayan airline, used to have one thousand employees and one functioning airplane. The people at ANCAP, the state oil company, tried to get to the office before it opened: there were more employees than chairs.

In 1958 the Ministry of Public Health recruited fifteen hundred new staff. In 1959 in Public Works there was one messenger for every six civil servants. In Telephones and Electricity there are forty-five grades of civil servants. Nothing is done by post; everything requires a personal visit. The service is slow; but the public, scattered among the messengers and the sleeping police dogs in the foyer, is uncomplaining: many of them are civil servants from other departments, with time on their hands.

It is a kind of ideal: government offices that are like clubs for public and staff, a whole country living the life of a commune, work and leisure flowering together, everyone, active and inactive, a pensioner of the state. But Uruguay still lives off meat and wool; and Montevideo, which contains more than a third of the country's population, is an artificial metropolis. The padding of the civil service, which began thirty years ago, in the time of wealth, disguises unemployment and urban purposelessness. Everyone knows this, but too many people benefit: the whole state has been led into this conspiracy against itself. "Everyone is pension-minded," the businessman says. And even the left-wing slogans of protest against the military government can be cautious and practical: *Paz Salario Libertad* [Peace Wages Liberty].

The girls in blue nylon coats in Telephones and Electricity earn about 120 dollars a month. In summer, from December to March, they work from seven to one. They go off then to a second job. Or they go to the beach. Montevideo is built along a beach; all roads south end in white sand and a bay.

And this is where Uruguayans regularly lose all sense of crisis, and the will to action is weakened: on the too accessible beach, in the resort developments just a few minutes outside Montevideo where many modest people have summer houses amid pines and dunes, and in Punta del Este, one of Uruguay's economic disasters, built mainly in the 1950s with loans from the Mortgage Bank, the satellite resort town of the artificial metropolis.

Everyone rejects Batllismo, but after sixty years everyone in Uruguay has been made by it. The resort life is all they know; its crumbling away leaves them confused. "Spiritually," the journalist said, "we feel we have gone back." Spiritually? "I don't like to be stressed permanently." He was a two-house man; but he had to do two jobs, one with the government; and his wife was doing two jobs. And cars were expensive, because of the 300 per cent tax. A new Volkswagen cost 8,000 dollars; even a 1955 Rover cost 3,500 dollars. "We won't progress. What's progress, though. America? That's consuming and stressing, keeping up with the Joneses. We don't have that kind of shit here, if you pardon the expression."

But there was the high price of cars.

"I'll tell you about Uruguay in one sentence," the architect said to me on my first evening in Montevideo. "The last Jaguar was imported in 1955."

These are withdrawal symptoms and they add up to a kind of spiritual distress: Montevideo, spreading along its beach, needs the motorcar. Without the motorcar, tracts of the city will have to be abandoned, as the Prado park has been abandoned. All that resort life, all that modernity of which the Uruguayans were until recently so proud, depends on consumer goods which Uruguay bought from more "stressed" countries and—wasting the talent of two generations in a padded civil service—never learned to make.

The antique cars of Montevideo—pre-1955, Citroëns, baby Morrises and Austins, Fords and Chevrolets of the 1930s, and other names now abandoned or superseded: Hupmobile, Willys-Overland Whippet, Dodge Brothers, Hudson—are not as gay as they first appear, part of the resort life. The country is under siege. The simplest things are smuggled in by lorry from Argentina; the supplies of modern civilization are running out.

Uruguayans say that they are a European nation, that they have always had their back to the rest of South America. It was their great error, and is part of their failure. Their habits of wealth made them, profoundly a colonial people, educated but intellectually null, consumers, parasitic on the culture and technology of others.

THE TUPAMAROS were destroyers. They had no programme; they were like people provoking a reaction, challenging the hidden enemy to declare himself. In the end they picked on the armed forces and were speedily destroyed. "The Tupamaros were not the beginning of a revolution," Sábat says. "They were the last whisper of Batllismo. They were parricides, engaged in a kind of kamikaze. In Uruguay now, everybody, whatever slogans he shouts, is either a parricide or a reactionary."

There is no middle way. Political attitudes have grown simpler and harder; and it is impossible not to take sides. On the last Saturday in October a student in the engineering faculty of the university blew himself up while making a bomb. The army closed the university—independent until that day—and arrested everybody. Parricide or reactionary, left-wing or right-wing, each side now finds in the other the enemy he needs. Each side now assigns a destructive role to the other; and, as in Chile, people grow into their roles.

Those who can, get out. They queue for passports at the rear entrance of the pink-walled Foreign Ministry, formerly the Santos Palace (built in 1880, the basin of the fountain in the hall carved from a single block of Carrara marble). In October there were reports of people queueing all night. At Carrasco Airport the other day someone chalked on a wall: *"El último que salga que apague la luz."* ("The last person to leave must put out the light.")

4 THE BROTHELS BEHIND THE GRAVEYARD

May–July 1974

THE PROPHECY—according to some old Argentine book of prophecies, which I often heard about but never saw—was that Perón would be hanged by his followers in the Plaza de Mayo, the main square in downtown Buenos Aires. But Perón died with his legend intact. "MURIO": "He is dead." The headline filled half the front page of *Crónica*, a popular Buenos Aires newspaper; and there was no need to give the name.

He was in his seventy-ninth year and in the ninth month of his third presidential term; and his legend had lasted for nearly thirty years. He was the army man who had moved out of the code of his caste and shaken up the old colonial agricultural society of Argentina; he had identified the enemies of the poor; he had created the trade unions. He had given a brutal face to the brutish land of *estancias* and polo and brothels and very cheap servants. And his legend, as the unique revolutionary, survived the incompetence and plunder of his early rule; it survived his overthrow in 1955 and the seventeen years of exile that followed; it survived the mob killings that attended his triumphant return last year; and it survived the failure of his last months in office.

The failure was obvious. Perón could not control the Argentina he had called into being twenty years before. He had identified the cruelties of the society, and yet he had made that necessary task seem irresponsible: he had not been able to reorganize the society he had undermined. And perhaps that task of reorganization was beyond the capacities of any leader, however creative. Politics reflect a society and a land. Argentina is a land of plunder, a new land, virtually peopled in this century. It remains a land to be plundered; and its politics can be nothing but the politics of plunder.

Everyone in Argentina understands and accepts this, and in the end Perón could only offer himself as a guarantee of his government's purpose, could only offer his words. In the end he had become his name alone, a presence, above it all, above the people who acted in his name, above the inflation and the shortages and the further steep decline of the peso, the faction fights, the daily kidnappings and guerrilla shoot-outs, the strong rumours of plunder in high places: above the Argentina whose brutality and frenzies he had divined and exploited, the Argentina he had returned to save, and which he now leaves behind him.

He was very old, and perhaps his cause had become more personal than he knew: to return to his homeland and to be rehabilitated. He made his peace with the armed forces, who had previously stripped him of his rank. He made his peace with the Church, against whom, in his second term, he had warred: he was to die holding the rosary given him by Pope Paul. He came back from exile a softened man, even philosophical, with ideas about ecology and the environment and the unity of Latin America ("By 2000 we shall be united or dominated"). But these ideas were remote from the anxieties of his followers and the power conflicts of the country. And towards the end he seemed to have recognized that the country was beyond his control.

Two years ago, when the military still ruled, everyone was Peronist, even Maoist priests and Trotskyist guerrillas. Perón, or his name, united all who wanted to see an end to military rule. But, inevitably, when Perón began to rule, it became necessary to distinguish the true Peronists from the "infiltrators." And the man who had returned as a national leader, as the "conductor" of all the warring elements of the movement that carried his name, began once again, like the old Perón, to detect enemies. There were enemies on the Left, among the guerrilla groups who had helped to bring him back to power. There were enemies on the Right. So many people were seen, as the months passed, "sabotaging the current political process." Week by week the semi-official *El Caudillo* identified new enemies. So many enemies: towards the end it was possible to detect in Perón's words the helpless, aggrieved tone of his writings after his overthrow in 1955.

On June 10, Perón's wife, the Vice President, in a speech printed the next day in full-page advertisements in the newspapers, spoke of the speculators and hoarders and other "executioners of the nation" who were responsible for the shortages and the high prices. Perón couldn't do it all, she said; and she wondered whether the country wasn't failing Perón. On June 11, Perón's former secretary, companion and soothsayer, López Rega, now Minister for Social Welfare, spoke more clearly. He told a group of provincial governors: "If General Perón leaves the country before his mission is accomplished, he won't be going alone. His wife will go with him, and your humble servant [*este servidor*]."

Perón, Rega said, couldn't do it all, and he shouldn't be expected to. "The philosophy of Justicialism isn't only a matter of shouting *Viva Perón*. It means taking to heart the meaning of this philosophy, which is simply that we should all, without question, comply with the objectives of greatness and fulfillment so that we might have a happy nation." Meaningless words—the translation is the best I can do; but after the identification of enemies, it was perhaps the only way Peronism could be defined.

The wife had spoken, the secretary had spoken. The next day Perón himself spoke. Abruptly, at a meeting where he had been expected to talk of other things, he announced that he was fed up and disheartened, and that if he didn't get more cooperation he was willing to hand over the government to people who thought they could do better.

The trade unions responded immediately. They asked their members to stop work. In the Córdoba Hills, where I was, the bus drivers didn't even know what it was all about or where the action was; they only knew, strike-hardened union men, that the buses weren't going to run after midday. The action, as it turned out, was confined to Buenos Aires, where in the Plaza de Mayo a great union rally was swiftly conjured up. Perón addressed the rally and received their applause; he pronounced himself satisfied, and it was assumed that he wasn't after all going to leave the country to stew in its own juice. The whole cabinet resigned that evening; one or two ministers gave grave interviews. It seemed at least that some treachery was going to be exposed and that some heads were going to roll. But no heads rolled; the whole cabinet was reappointed.

It was a curious event: so well prepared, so dramatic in its effect, and then entirely without sequel. The newspapers, full of crisis one day, reporting the entire republic in a state of tension, the next day quietly forgot about it. Newspapers are like that in Argentina. It was Perón's last demagogic act, his last political flourish. And no one will know what, if anything, lay behind it, whether illness and death put an end to some new development, something that was going to make clear the purpose and plans of the new government. It was what people were waiting for. No one knew what was happening in Argentina; and some people were beginning to feel that there might be nothing to know.

The mystery isn't the mystery of Perón alone, but of Argentina, where the political realities, of plunder and the animosities engendered by plunder, have for so long been clouded by rhetoric. The rhetoric fools no one. But in a country where government has never been open and intellectual resources are scant, the rhetoric of a regime is usually all that survives to explain it. Argentina has the apparatus of an educated, open society. There are newspapers and magazines and universities and publishing houses; there is even a film industry. But the country has as yet no idea of itself. Streets and avenues are named after presidents and generals, but there is no art of historical analysis; there is no art of biography. There is legend and antiquarian romance, but no real history. There are only annals, lists of rulers, chronicles of events.

THE SHARPEST political commentator in Argentina is Mariano Grondona. He appears on television, and is said to be of a good Argentine family. At the end of May, *Gente,* a popular illustrated weekly, interviewed Grondona and asked him to analyze the events of the past year: the year of the disintegration of Peronism as a national movement, the year of the detection and casting out of enemies. *Gente* considered Grondona's views important enough to be spread over five pages.

To understand Argentine history, Grondona said, it was necessary to break it up into epochs, *épocas.* Since independence in 1810 there had been seven epochs. Seven republics, almost: Argentina had to be seen as having a French-style history, a Latin history. The Latin mentality worked from principles; it exhausted one set of principles and moved through upheaval to a new set. Anglo-Saxons, more pragmatic, didn't define their principles. They were therefore spared periods of chaos; but at the same time they didn't enjoy "those magnificent moments in which everything is remade [*esos instantes magníficos en que todo recomienza*]."

The fifth epoch of Argentine history, from 1945 to 1955, was the epoch of Peronism. The sixth epoch, from 1955 to 1973, was the military epoch, the epoch of the exclusion of Peronism. The seventh epoch, beginning in 1973, was the epoch of revived institutions, the epoch of the return of Peronism. This last epoch, though only a year old, had been confusing; but it would be less so if it were divided into *etapas,* stages. Perón, like Mao, lived "in stages." Peronism had first to pass through a "smiling" stage, when it was looking for power, then an embattled stage, when it was fighting for power, and then an apparently established stage, when it had achieved power. A number of Peronists had remained stuck at the second, embattled stage; that was why they had to be got rid of.

There is no question, in Grondona's analysis, of people either acting badly or being badly treated. The people who had come to grief during the Peronist year simply hadn't understood this Argentine business of *épocas* and *etapas.* Some of them had got their *etapas* badly mixed up— like the dentist who had become President as Perón's nominee, but had then been deemed a traitor and dismissed.

Other difficult events of the year became clearer once it was understood that an *etapa* itself consisted of great days, *jornadas*; and there were *jornadas,* apparently chaotic, that could be broken up into phases, *fases.* "We are accustomed to this pattern of *épocas* and *jornadas* . . . There will be other epochs and other great days. I am convinced of that. All that we can ask of this one is that it should fulfil its historical duty."

This is how Grondona ends, fitting a sentence of Argentine rhetoric to an account of a year's murderous power struggle. To the outsider, Grondona, with his nimbleness and zest, is curiously detached: he might be speaking of a country far away. It is hard to imagine, from his account, that people are still being killed and kidnapped in the streets, or that in June the army was fighting guerrillas in Tucumán, or that newspapers, under the general heading *"Guerrillerismo,"* carry reports of the previous day's guerrilla happenings. There is detachment and an unconscious cynicism in Grondona's chronicle. The political life of the country is seen as little more than a struggle for political power. There seems to be no higher good. And—what is more alarming, more revealing of Argentina—the chronicle is offered to the readers of *Gente* as to people who know no higher good.

So Perón and his legend pass into the annals. The legend is admired now; in time it will almost certainly be reviled. But the legend itself will not alter: it will be all that people will have to go by. It is how history is written in Argentina. And perhaps a people who had learned to read their history in another way, who had ceased to accept the politics of plunder, might have spared themselves the futility of the last year of Perón.

But the history, as it is written, is of a piece with the politics. And the politics reflect the people and the land. There are Argentines who feel that their country deserved better than Perón. They feel that their country was ridiculed and diminished by the Peronist court rule of the last year: Perón the derelict macho, Isabelita his consort and Vice President, López Rega the powerful secretary-soothsayer—sultan, sultana and grand vizier.

But Perón was what he was because he touched Argentina so closely. He intuited the needs of his followers: where he appeared to violate, there he usually triumphed. He went too far when he made war on the Church in his second presidential term; but that was his only error as a people's leader. He brought out and made strident the immigrant proletarian reality of a country where, in the women's magazines, the myth still reigns of "old" families and polo and romance down at the *estancia*. He showed the country its unacknowledged half-Indian face. And by imposing his women on Argentina, first Evita and then Isabelita, one an actress, the other a cabaret dancer, both provincials, by turning women branded as the macho's easy victims into the macho's rulers, he did the roughest kind of justice on a society still ruled by a degenerate machismo, which decrees that a woman's place is essentially in the brothel.

Still, it remains odd about Perón: he spoke so much about the greatness of the country, but in himself, and in his movement, he expressed so many of his country's weaknesses and revealed them as irremediable.

THE AEROPLANE, coming down to land at Ezeiza Airport outside Buenos Aires, flies over the green land of Uruguay, once so rich and now, like Argentina, a land of disorder and sorrow; and then over the wide, chocolate-coloured estuary of the Río de la Plata. Quite abruptly on the tawny flat land south of the estuary the white and grey buildings of Buenos Aires are seen to arise: a city of inexplicable size that seems arbitrarily sited at the very edge of an empty continent, along that expanse of muddy water. The aeroplane shows it all: the great estuary, the sudden city of eight million, the outer rim of the vast, flat, empty hinterland— the simple geography of a remote southern land with a simple history of

Indian genocide and European take-over. Not resettlement: resettlement would have created a smaller city, might have peopled and humanized the Indian hinterland.

There is as yet in Argentina no myth of the noble Indian. The memory of the genocide is too close; it is still something to be dismissed in a line or two in the annals. In Argentina the detestation of the vanished pampa Indian is instinctive and total: the Argentine terror is that people in other countries might think of Argentina as an Indian country. Borges, who is very old, has often told his foreign interviewers that the Indians of Argentina couldn't count. And to a forty-year-old artist of my acquaintance, the pampa Indians were "like grass."

From the great town, highways push out in all directions through the once-Indian hinterland. The town dies hard; low, boxlike brick houses straggle beside the highways for miles. At last the land is clear; and very quickly, then, the flatness of the pampa, the height of sky, the distances and the emptiness numb response. No trees grew here. But in the unused rich soil trees grow fast now, and occasionally tall eucalyptus trees screen a park and a big house. The land is full of military names, the names of generals who took the land away from the Indians and, with a rapacity that still outrages the imagination, awarded themselves great portions of the earth's surface, estates, *estancias,* as large as counties.

It was the time of the great imperialist push in many continents. While President Roca was systematically exterminating the Indians, the Belgians were opening up their brand-new Congo. Joseph Conrad saw the Belgians at work, and in *Heart of Darkness* he catches their frenzy. "Their talk was the talk of sordid buccaneers; it was reckless without hardihood, greedy without audacity, and cruel without courage; there was not an atom of foresight or of serious intention in the whole batch of them, and they did not seem aware these things are wanted for the work of the world." The words fit the Argentine frenzy; they contain the mood and the moral nullity of that Argentine enterprise which have worked down through the generations to the failure of today.

The great private domains have split, but the *estancias* are still very big. The scale is still superhuman. The *estancias* are mechanized and require little labour; the landscape remains empty and unhumanized. There are little towns, sitting fragilely on the pampa, but they provide only the bare necessities: the stupefying night-club, which enables people who have said everything already to be together for hours without saying anything; the brothel, which simplifies the world even further; the garage. Away from the highways there is a sense of desolation. The dirt roads are wide and straight; trees are few; and the flat land stretches uninterrupted to the horizon. The sense of distance is distorted: things miles away seem close—an *estancia* workman on horseback, a clump of trees, a junction of dirt roads. The desolation would be complete without the birds; and they, numerous, unusually big, and gaudily coloured, emphasize the alienness of the land and the fewness of men. Every morning on the pampa highways there are dead brown owls.

The land here is something to be worked. It is not a thing of beauty; it has not been hallowed by the cinema, literature or art, or by the life of rooted communities. Land in Argentina, as I heard a South American banker from another country say, is still only a commodity. It is an investment, a hedge against inflation. It can be alienated without heartache. Argentina's wealth is in the land; this land explains the great city on the estuary. But the land has become no one's home. Home is elsewhere: Buenos Aires, England, Italy, Spain. You can live in Argentina, many Argentines say, only if you can leave.

The Argentina created by the railways and President Roca's Remingtons still has the structure and purpose of a colony. And, oddly, in the manner of its founding and in its implied articles of association, it is like a sixteenth-century colony of the Spanish Empire, with the same greed and internal weaknesses, the same potential for dissension, the cynicism and sterility. *Obedezco pero no cumplo,* I obey but I don't comply: it was the attitude of the sixteenth-century conquistador or official, who had a contract with the King of Spain alone, and not with the King's other subjects. In Argentina the contract is not with other Argentines, but with the rich land, the precious commodity. This is how it was in the beginning and how, inevitably, it continues to be.

There is no king (though Perón was that, a man in whose name everyone acted). But there is a flag (the colours, blue and white, honour a saint, but Argentines are taught that they are the colours of their sky). And people who feel that the land has failed them wave the flag: the workers in the cities, the young men in new suits, immigrants' sons who have become doctors or lawyers. But this patriotism is less than it appears. In Argentina, unmade, flawed from its conception, without a history, still only with annals, there can be no feeling for a past, for a heritage, for shared ideals, for a community of all Argentines. Every Argentine wants to ratify his own contract with the God-given land, miraculously cleansed of Indians and still empty.

THERE are many Argentinas, and they all exist within that idea of the richness of the land. In the north-west there is an older Argentina, settled by Spaniards spreading down south from Peru. At the foot of the Cordilleras is the city of La Rioja, founded nearly four hundred years ago by a Spaniard looking for gold. It is distinctive; its people are of the land, and half Indian. It has a completeness not found in the cities of the newer Argentina, from which it is separated by the waterless flat wilderness of the *llanos*, bisected to the very horizon, as it seems to the passenger in a bus, by the straight black road, whose edges are blurred by drifting sand.

But at the end of that road, and among the Córdoba Hills, where imported cypress and willow create irregular little Mediterranean patches on the barren hillsides, there is an English-style boarding school, recently founded. It is successful and well equipped; the headmaster, when I saw him, had just stocked the library with an expensive uniform set of the world's best books.

The school might seem an anachronism, the headmaster says; but the aim isn't to create English gentlemen; it is to create gentlemen for Argentina. There is rugger on Sunday morning. A school from Córdoba is visiting, and the school servants are grilling thick thongs of red meat over an enormous barbecue pit. "Just like Anglo-Saxons to make up a game like rugger," says the young teacher, fresh from the constrictions of London, and flourishing in the atmosphere of freedom and fantasy which the emptiness of Argentina can so agreeably suggest to people who have just arrived.

At the local church the elderly British residents, retired people, had that morning prayed for both Perón and the Queen. The previous evening they had gathered at a hotel to see the film of Princess Anne's wedding.

Half an hour away by bus there is an Italo-Spanish peasant town: low houses, cracked plaster, exposed red bricks, pollarded trees, dust, Mediterranean colours, women in black, girls and children in door-ways. Water is scarce. There is a big dam, but it was breached two years ago. The people grow cotton and olives and consider their town rich.

The ten-hour bus drive from the industrial town of Córdoba, where they make motorcars, to the city of La Rioja is like a drive through many countries, many eras, many fading ancestral cultures. The ancestral culture fades, and Argentina offers no substitute. It offers only the land, the cheap food and the cheap wine. To all those people on the road from Córdoba to La Rioja it offers accommodation, and what had once seemed a glorious freedom. To none does it offer a country. They are, by an unlikely irony, among the last victims of imperialism, and not just in the way Perón said.

ARGENTINA is a simple materialist society, a simple colonial society created in the most rapacious and decadent phase of imperialism. It has diminished and stultified the men whom it attracted by the promise of ease and to whom it offered no other ideals and no new idea of human association. New Zealand, equally colonial, also with a past of native dispossession, but founded at an earlier imperial period and on different principles, has had a different history. It has made some contribution to the world; more gifted men and women have come from its population of three million than from the twenty-three millions of Argentines.

Two years ago, when I was new to Argentina, an academic said to me, during the Buenos Aires rush hour: "You would think you were in a developed country." It wasn't easy then to understand his irony and bitterness. Buenos Aires is such an overwhelming metropolis that it takes time to understand that it is new and has been imported almost whole; that its metropolitan life is an illusion, a colonial mimicry; that it feeds on other countries and is itself sterile. The great city was intended as the servant of its hinterland and it was set down, complete, on the edge of the continent. Its size was not dictated by its own needs nor did it reflect its own excellence. Buenos Aires, from the nature of its creation, has never required excellence: that has always been one of its attractions. Within the imported metropolis there is the structure of a developed society. But men can often appear to be mimicking their functions. So many words have acquired lesser meanings in Argentina: *general, artist, journalist, historian, professor, university, director, executive, industrialist, aristocrat, library, museum, zoo*; so many words need inverted commas. To write realistically about this society has peculiar difficulties; to render it accurately in fiction might be impossible.

For men so diminished there remains only machismo. There is the machismo of the football field or the racing track. And there is machismo as simple stylishness: the police motorcyclist, for instance, goggled and gloved, weaving about at speed, siren going, clearing a path for the official car. But machismo is really about the conquest and humiliation of women. In the sterile society it is the victimization, by the simple, of the simpler. Women in Argentina are uneducated and have few rights; they are reared either for early marriage or for domestic service. Very few have money or the means of earning money. They are meant to be victims; and they accept their victim role.

Machismo makes no man stand out, because every man is assumed to be a macho. Sexual conquest is a duty. It has little to do with passion or even attraction; and conquests are not achieved through virility or any special skills. In a society so ruled by the idea of plunder, the macho's attractions, from the top to the bottom of the money scale, are essentially economic. Clothes, reflecting the macho's wealth or "class," are an important sexual signal. So is the wallet. And the macho's keys, symbols of property, have to be displayed. The symbolism is crude; but the society isn't subtle. The bus driver, a small-time macho, hangs his two keys from his belt over his right hip; the right hip of the "executive" can be positively encased in metal, with the keys hanging from the belt by heavy metal loops. Money makes the macho. Machismo requires, and imposes, a widespread amateur prostitution; it is a society spewing on itself.

The thing has been institutionalized; and the institution is served by a gigantic brothel industry. There are brothels everywhere, open night and day. Enormous new buildings, their function proclaimed by neon signs and a general garishness, are strung along the Pan American Highway. In the heart of the city, behind the Recoleta Cemetery, where the illustrious are buried, there is an avenue of tall brothels. The brothels charge by the hour. In the dim lobby of such a place a red spotlight might play on a crude bronze-coloured woman's bust: the bad art of Argentina. Every schoolgirl knows the brothels; from an early age she understands that she might have to go there one day to find love, among the coloured lights and mirrors.

The act of straight sex, easily bought, is of no great moment to the macho. His conquest of a woman is complete only when he has buggered her. This is what the woman has it in her power to deny; this is what the brothel game is about, the passionless Latin adventure that begins with talk of *amor*. *La tuve en el culo*, I've had her in the arse: this is how the macho reports victory to his circle, or dismisses a desertion. Contemporary sexologists give a general dispensation to buggery. But the buggering of women is of special significance in Argentina and other Latin American countries. The Church considers it a heavy sin, and prostitutes hold it in horror. By imposing on her what prostitutes reject, and what he knows to be a kind of sexual black mass, the Argentine macho, in the main of Spanish or Italian peasant ancestry, consciously dishonours his victim. So diminished men, turning to machismo, diminish themselves further, replacing even sex by a parody.

The cartoonist Sábat, in some of his Grosz-like drawings, has hinted at the diseased, half-castrated nature of machismo. In Buenos Aires the other day a new film opened and was a great success: *Boquitas Pintadas—Little Painted Mouths*—made by Argentina's most famous director and based on a novel by an Argentine writer, Manuel Puig. The film—clumsy and overacted and without polish—is the story of the life and death of a tubercular small-town macho. An aimless film, it seemed, a real-life chronicle on which no pattern had been imposed. But the Argentine audience wept: for them the tragedy lay in the foreseeable death of the macho, the poor boy of humble family who made his conquests the hard way, by his beauty.

To the outsider the tragedy lay elsewhere, in the apparent motivelessness of so much of the action. No relationship was hinted at, and no comment seemed to be offered by writer or director: it was as though, in the society of machismo, the very knowledge of the possibility of deeper relationships had been lost. After the macho's death one of his women had a dream: in bleached colour, and in very slow motion, the macho rose from his grave, in his pretty macho clothes, lifted her in his arms, flew with her through a bedroom window and placed her on a bed. On this necrophiliac fantasy the film ended. And the audience was in tears.

To go outside after this, to walk past the long queue for the film, to see the lights of packed cafés and bars, the young people in flared jeans, was to have the sharpest sense of the mimicry and alienness of the great city. It was to have a sense of the incompleteness and degeneracy of these transplanted people who seemed so whole, to begin to understand and fear their violence, their peasant cruelty, their belief in magic, and their fascination with death, celebrated every day in the newspapers with pictures of murdered people, often guerrilla victims, lying in their coffins.

AFTER the genocide, a great part of our earth is being turned into a wasteland. The failure of Argentina, so rich, so underpopulated, twenty-three million people in a million square miles, is one of the mysteries of our time. Commentators like Mariano Grondona, unravelling chaos, tying themselves up in *etapas,* will try to make sense of irrational acts and inconsequential events by talking of Argentina's French-style history. Others will offer political explanations and suggest political remedies. But politics have to do with the nature of human association, the contract of men with men. The politics of a country can only be an extension of its idea of human relationships.

Perón, in himself, as folk leader, expressed many of his country's weaknesses. And it is necessary to look where he, the greatest macho of them all (childless and reportedly impotent), pointed: to the centre of Buenos Aires and to those tall brothels, obscenely shuttered, that stand, suitably, behind the graveyard.

5   THE TERROR

March 1977

IN ARGENTINA the killer cars—the cars in which the official gunmen go about their business—are Ford Falcons. The Falcon, which is made in Argentina, is a sturdy small car of unremarkable appearance, and there are thousands on the roads. But the killer Falcons are easily recognizable. They have no number plates. The cars—and the plainclothesmen they carry—require to be noticed; and people can sometimes stand and watch.

As they stood and watched some weeks ago, in the main square of the northern city of Tucumán: the Falcons parked in the semi-circular drive of Government Headquarters, an ornate stone building like a nineteenth-century European country house, but with Indian soldiers with machine guns on the balcony and in the well-kept subtropical gardens: a glimpse, eventually, of uniforms, handshakes, salutes, until the men in plain clothes, like actors impersonating an aristocratic shooting party, but with machine guns under their Burberrys or imitation Burberrys, came down the wide steps, got into the small cars and drove off without speed or sirens.

The authorities have grown to understand the dramatic effect of silence. It is part of the terror that is meant to be felt as terror.

Style is important in Argentina; and in the long-running guerrilla war—in spite of the real blood, the real torture—there has always been an element of machismo and public theatre. In the old days policemen stood a little way from busy intersections with machine guns at the ready; at night the shopping streets of central Buenos Aires were patrolled by jackbooted and helmeted soldiers with Alsatian dogs; from time to time, as a dramatic extravaganza, there appeared the men of the anti-guerrilla motorcycle brigade. The war in those days was in the main a private war, between the guerrillas on one side and the army and police on the other. Now the war touches everybody; public theatre has turned to public terror.

Style has been taken away from all but the men in the Falcons. The guerrillas still operate, but the newspapers are not allowed to print anything about them. They can print only the repetitive official communiqués, the body counts, and these usually appear as small items on the inside pages, seemingly unrelated to the rest of the news: in such a place, on such a date, in these circumstances, so many subversives or *delincuentes* were killed, so many men, so many women. The communiqués are thought to represent only a fraction of the truth: too many people are disappearing.

In the beginning—after the chaos and near-anarchy of the Peronist restoration—the killings were thought to be good for the economy. War was war, it was said; the guerrillas—now like private armies, with no recognizable aims—had to be rooted out; the trade unions and their leaders had to be disciplined after the licence and corruption of the Peronist years. (No more free trips to Europe on Aerolíneas Argentinas for those union men, flashy provincial machos requiring attention from the crew, each man, after supper, settling down with his pile of comic books and photo-novels, light reading for the long night flights, the tips of ringed fingers wetted on the tongue before the pages were turned.) Another, more becoming, Argentina was to be created; the country (as though the country were an economic abstraction, something that could be separated from the bulk of the population) was to be got going again.

And while wages were kept down like sin, the banker-saints of

Argentina worked their own inflationary miracles. They offered 8 per cent a month or 144 per cent a year for the peso, and momentarily gave back faith to many good Argentines who had for years been praying only for the water of their pesos to be turned into the wine of dollars. During the early months of the terror the stock market boomed; fortunes were made out of nothing; Argentina seemed to be itself again. But now—even with that 144 per cent—the terror is too close.

No pattern can any longer be discerned in the terror. It isn't only the guerrillas and the union men and the country's few intellectuals who are threatened. Anyone can be picked up. Torture is routine. Even workmen unlucky enough to be in a flat at the time of a raid have been taken away, held for a few hours and tortured with everybody else, so automatic is the process: the tight blindfold, the eyes depressed in the sockets, the hooding, the beating, the electric shocks that leave burn marks for eighteen days, and then the mysterious journey in the boot of the Falcon and the sadism of release: "We are taking you to the cemetery . . . Now, count a hundred before you take off your blindfold."

Almost everyone in Argentina now knows someone who has disappeared or been arrested or tortured. Even military men have, by the intervention of military friends, been called to receive the corpses of their children, corpses which might otherwise have been destroyed or thrown away, sometimes to roll ashore, mutilated and decomposing, at Montevideo, on the other side of the Río de la Plata. One woman was sent the hands of her daughter in a shoe box.

There is still, for the distinguished, or well-known, legal arrest on specific charges. But below that there is no law. People are taken away and no one is responsible. The army refers inquirers to the police, and the police refer them back to the army. A special language has developed: an anxious father might be told that his son's case is "closed." No one really knows who does what or why; it is said that anyone can now be made to disappear, for a price.

Buenos Aires is full of shocked and damaged people who can think now only of flight, who find it no longer possible to take sides, who can see no cause in Argentina and can acknowledge at last the barbarism by which they have for long been surrounded, the barbarism they had previously been content to balance against the knowledge of their own security and the old Argentine lure of the spacious rich land, easy money and abundant meat, the lure expressed in the words that so often in Argentina close a discussion: *"Todavía aquí se vive mejor."* "Still, you live better here."

Barbarism, in a city which has thought of itself as European, in a land which, because of that city, has prided itself on its civilization. Barbarism because of that very idea: civilization felt as something far away, magically kept going by others: the civilization of Europe divorced from any idea of an intellectual life and equated with the goods and fashions of Europe: civilization felt as something purchasable, something always there, across the ocean, for the man or woman with enough money: an attitude not far removed from that of the politician of a new country who, while fouling his own nest, feathers another abroad, in a land of law.

The official history of Argentina is a history of glory: of a war of independence, with heroes, of European expansion, wealth, civilization. This is the past of which Borges sometimes sings; but a recurring theme of some of his later stories is of cultural degeneracy.

TORTURE is not new in Argentina. And though Argentines abroad, when they are campaigning against a particular regime, talk as if torture has just been started by that regime, in Argentina itself torture is spoken of—and accepted—by all groups as an Argentine institution.

In 1972, at an elegant provincial hotel, an upper-class lady of Spanish descent (still obsessed with the purity of race, still fighting the old Spanish wars) told me that torture had started in Argentina in 1810, when the country became independent of Spain; and—middle-aged and delicate at the dinner table, drinking the yellow champagne of Argentina, and speaking English with the accent of the finishing school—she said that torture remained necessary because the penal code was so benign. "You have to kill a man in the most horrible way to go to jail. 'My client was excited,' the lawyer says. 'Oh?' the judge says. 'He was excited?' And no jail."

A young Trotskyist lawyer didn't see the law quite like that. He thought only that torture had been used by "most of the governments" and had become "a pretty important feature of Argentine life." Its abolition seemed at first to form no part of his socialist programme; but then, noticing my concern, he promised, speaking very quickly, as to a child to whom anything could be promised, that torture would disappear "with the downfall of the bourgeoisie."

However, the high Peronist trade union man I later went to see—this was in mid-1972, and the union man was close to power, waiting for Perón to come back—couldn't promise anything. He said—and he might have been speaking of rain—that torture would always exist. It was this man, soft-voiced, reasonable, at that time still the representative of the oppressed, who told me—the map of the Paris metro and a photograph of the young Perón below glass on his desk—that there was good torture and bad torture. It was "all right" to torture an "evildoer"; it was another thing to torture "a man who's trying to serve the country."

And that was the very point made four years later by Admiral Guzzetti, one of the leaders of the present regime, when, defending the terror, he spoke to the United Nations in August 1976. The Admiral (who has since been wounded in a guerrilla attack) said: "My idea of subversion is that of the left-wing terrorist organizations. Subversion or terrorism of the right is not the same thing. When the social body of the country has been contaminated by a disease that corrodes its entrails, it forms antibodies. These antibodies cannot be considered in the same way as the microbes."

Yesterday's antibodies, today's microbes; yesterday's servants of the country, today's evildoers; yesterday's torturers, today's tortured. Argentine ideologies, in spite of the labels of Right or Left that they give themselves, are really quite simple. What harms the other man is right; what harms me is wrong. Perón was never more Argentine—in his complaints and his moral outrage—than when, in 1956, the year after he had been overthrown by the military, he published his own lachrymose account of the affair. He called his book *La Fuerza Es el Derecho de las Bestias*. The words mean, literally, "Force is the right of animals," and the title might be rendered in English as *The Law of the Jungle*.

In that book Perón wrote: "The revolution is without a cause because it is only a reaction. It seeks only to undo what has been done, to extirpate Peronism, to take away from the workers the benefits they have won." And Perón, if he were alive today, might use the same words about the present regime. So little has Argentina changed in the political seesawing of the last twenty years; so without point have been all the manoeuvrings and murders.

THE KILLER cars are not new. They began to operate in Perón's time, when Perón turned against the guerrillas who had brought him back to power. And the cars became more murderous in the time of Isabel, Perón's widow and successor, when the enemies became more personal, less politically definable. Then one day Isabel ceased to rule, and the Peronist cycle was over.

It happened simply. Late one evening the military, who had held off for a long time, had the presidential helicopter hijacked; and Isabel— flying back in style from Government House in downtown Buenos Aires—was told that the presidential house in the suburb of Olivos, where she thought she was going, was no longer her home. In the official story, she burst into tears, the former cabaret girl who had become the first woman president of Argentina. She was taken first to a city airfield; later she was taken under guard to the presidential house to pack her clothes. There she tried to get the household staff on her side. She thought that they were hers, loyal to her. But they, used to Argentine presidents coming and suddenly going, simply helped her pack.

That was how it ended for her, the poor girl born in the poor northern province of La Rioja. She was in a cabaret in far-off Panama when she met the exiled Perón in 1956, one year after his overthrow, four years after the death of Eva Perón. Isabel was never promoted as a replacement for Eva Perón; and Perón was never reproached by his followers for his association with her. To macho Argentina, infinitely comprehending of a man's needs, Isabel was only the new woman at the leader's side. And when she came back to Argentina with Perón in 1973, she came only as an "ambassador of peace," the "verticalizer," the woman who was to bind Argentina with her love, while Perón handled the hate.

"Perón conduce, Isabel verticaliza." ("Perón conducts, Isabel verticalizes.") The words are as difficult in Spanish as they are in English; but this was one of the slogans of the last days of Perón's rule, in 1974, when Peronism had already shown itself to be nothing but words, and the rule of Perón and his court was like a continuation of the hysteria that had brought them back; when official printed posters supplemented aerosol graffiti, and the walls of Buenos Aires were like tattered billboards. So many posters, quickly outdated: always some new martyr to be mourned (and forgotten within a week: nothing as dead, in Peronist Argentina, as last week's political poster), so many killings to be avenged: the leader seeking always to buoy himself up on a collective expression of anger, complaint and hate.

Now there is silence. Isabel is still in detention somewhere in the south, the subject of fading gossip; a private snapshot, released by the authorities, shows that she grew fat during her time in office. Many of the people who ruled with her have scattered. The astrologer López Rega—he was Isabel's manager when she was a cabaret girl in Panama, and he later became Perón's secretary—is out of the country; he has been accused by the present government of embezzling large sums during his time as welfare minister.

The political scandals connected with Perón's return to power, and the financial scandals of his rule and the rule of Isabel, continue. It was the guerrillas who made it possible for Perón to come back; they were the strong right arm of the Peronist movement in 1972 and 1973. But were they all guerrillas? The kidnappings and the bank raids—were they all for the cause? Or was some of the *guerrillerismo* mixed up with Argentine big business? Speculating this time not in land or the falling peso, but in idealism and passion, real blood and torture.

THE MILITARY like clean walls; and the walls of Buenos Aires are now whitewashed and bare. But here and there the ghostly political graffiti of old times show through the whitewash: the *"Evita Vive"* ("Evita Lives") of 1972; the emblems of the Peronist youth movement; the Peronist election slogan of 1973: *"Cámpora a la Presidencia, Perón al Poder"* ("Cámpora to the Presidency, the Power to Perón"); the later, and Peronistically inevitable, proclamation of *"Cámpora traidor"* ("Cámpora is a traitor"): friend mysteriously turned to enemy, now an unimportant part of dead Argentine history, the ghost of a ghost: all that dead history faint below the military whitewash.

Perón himself is not much talked about now. He is dead; he finally failed everybody; he and the years he wasted can be skipped. History in Argentina is less an attempt to record and understand than a habit of reordering inconvenient facts; it is a process of forgetting. And the middle-class politicians and intellectuals who campaigned for Perón's return, the people who by their unlikely conversion to the Peronist cause made that cause so overwhelming in 1972 and 1973, now avoid the subject or do not come clean.

They say they were hoping to change the movement from within; or they say, more fantastically, that what they really wanted was Peronism without Perón. But it was Perón they invited back from exile to rule over them; and they invited him back—even with his astrologer—because they wanted what he offered.

In her ghosted autobiography, *La Razón de Mi Vida,* Eva Perón says she found out about poverty when she was eleven. "And the strange thing is that the existence of the poor did not cause me as much pain as the knowledge that at the same time there were people who were rich." That pain about the rich—that pain about other people—remained the basis of the popular appeal of Peronism. That was the simple passion—rather than "nationalism" or Perón's "third position"—that set Argentina alight.

Eva Perón devoted her short political life to mocking the rich, the four hundred families who among them owned most of what was valuable in the million square miles of Argentina. She mocked and wounded them as they had wounded her; and her later unofficial sainthood gave a touch of religion to her destructive cause.

Even when the money ran out, Peronism could offer hate as hope. And in the end that was why Argentina virtually united in calling Perón back, though the first period of his rule had ended in repression and disaster, and though he was very old and close to death. In his eighteen years of exile, while Argentina floundered from government to government, he had remained oddly consistent. He had become the quintessential Argentine: like Eva before him, like all Argentines, he was a victim, someone with enemies, someone with that pain about others. As the years passed, his enemies multiplied; his old words of Argentine complaint began to read like prophecies ("The revolution is without a cause"; "The military rule but no one obeys"); until finally he appeared to have become the enemy of everybody's enemy.

Peronism was never a programme. It was an insurrection. For more than thirty years Argentina has been in a state of insurrection. The parallel is not with any country in Europe, as Argentine writers sometimes say. The parallel is with Haiti, after the slave rebellion of Toussaint: a barbarous colonial society similarly made, similarly parasitic on a removed civilization, and incapable of regenerating itself because slavery provided the only pattern of human behaviour, and to be a man meant only to be able to assuage that pain about the other, to be like the master.

· · ·

EVA PERÓN lit the fire. But the idea of reform was beyond her. She was too wounded, too uneducated; she was too much of her society; and always she was a woman among machos. Christophe, emperor of Haiti, built the Citadelle, at immense cost in life as well as money: the model was the British fortifications of Brimstone Hill in the small island of St. Kitts, where Christophe was born a slave and trained as a tailor. So Eva Perón in power, obliterating records of her early childhood, yet never going beyond the ideas of childhood, sought only to compete with the rich in their cruelty and wealth and style, their imported goods. It was herself and her triumph that she offered to the people, the *pueblo* in whose name she acted.

Her enemies helped to sanctify her. After Perón's overthrow in 1955 they put on a public display of her clothes, even her intimate garments. She had been dead three years; but that display (especially of the underclothes) was an Argentine, macho form of violation; and the people, *el pueblo*, were meant in addition to be shocked by the extravagance and commonness of their great lady. It was disingenuous: the violators themselves had no higher ideals, and the display of fairy-tale wealth—wealth beyond imagination coming to someone who was of the poor—added to the Evita legend.

Twenty years after her death she found legitimacy. Her small embalmed body—she was five feet two, and at her death she was wasted—now rests at the Duarte family vault in the Recoleta Cemetery, the upper-class necropolis of Buenos Aires. The stone and marble avenues of the mimic town are full of the great names of Argentina, or names which, if the country had been better built, would have been great, but can be seen now only as part of a pretentious, failed past. This legitimacy, this dignity, was all that the girl from Los Toldos wanted; it has taken her an insurrection, an unravelling of the state, to achieve it.

In the early Peronist days she was promoted as a saint, and she is now above Peronism and politics. She is her own cult; she offers protection to those who believe in her. Where there are no reliable institutions or codes or law, no secular assurances, people need faith and magic. And Nature in Argentina is overwhelming: men can feel abandoned in that land of great mountains and big blank spaces. (What desert and scrub and mountains separate the northern province of La Rioja from the softer but still limitless land of the pampa: La Rioja, site of old, lost hope, the town founded in sub-Andean desolation late in the sixteenth century, after Mexico and

Peru, as another of the Spanish bases for the search for El Dorado.) Desolation always seems close in the Argentine vastness: how did men come here, how have they endured?

In that desolation cults grow, and they can have a feel of the ancient world. Like the cult of the woman known as *La Difunta Correa*, The Deceased Correa. At some undated time she was crossing the desert on foot. She was starving; there was no water in the desert; and she died. But her baby (or the baby she gave birth to before she died) was found alive, sucking at the breast of the dead woman. Now there are little roadside shrines to her memory, and in these shrines people leave bottles of water. The water evaporates: it has been drunk by the Difunta Correa. *La Difunta Correa tomó el agua*: the simple miracle is ceaselessly renewed.

Eva Perón is that kind of figure now, without dates or politics. And offerings are made at the Duarte vault in the Recoleta. The sarcophagus cannot be seen, but it is known to be there. On the morning I went, white lilies were tied with a white scarf to the black rails, and there was a single faded red rose, unspeakably moving. On the ground, unprotected, was a white mantilla in a plastic wrapper. A woman came with a gift of flowers. She was a woman of the people, with the chunky body of someone whose diet was too starchy. She had come from far, from Mendoza, at the other end of the pampa.

(Mendoza, the wine region at the foot of the Andes, where in the bright southern light and clear air the imported trees of Europe, the willow and the plane, grow gigantically; and the view on one side is always bounded by the grey-blue wall of the mountains. Not the true snow-capped Andes, though: these will appear one day, very far away, apparently unsupported, like a faint white overprinting in the middle sky, giving a new idea of size, awakening wonder not only at the sixteenth-century conquistadores who came this way, but also at the Incas, who, without the wheel, extended their rule so far south, and whose irrigation channels the cultivators of Mendoza still use.)

The lady from Mendoza had a sick daughter—a spastic or a polio sufferer: it wasn't clear. *"Hace quince años hice la promesa."* "I made a vow fifteen years ago.") In 1962, that is, when Eva Perón had been dead for ten years and Perón was still in exile, with no hope of return; when the embalmed body of Eva was presumed lost. Now the miracle had occurred. The body was there; the daughter was well enough again for the vow to be fulfilled.

She placed the flowers on the ground; she went still for a little while, contemplating the rails and the blank vault; and then she became herself again, brisk and ready to go. She said, "*Ya cumplí.* There, I've done it."

6 ARGENTINA AND THE IDEA OF BLOOD

IN ARGENTINA in March 1977, at the time of the military government's "dirty war" against the guerrillas, I found myself taken off a long-distance bus by the police one day, and held for some hours as a suspected guerrilla.

This was in the far north of the country—an older, more tropical Argentina, deep in the continent, and still with the feel of the Spanish empire: wide valleys beside the Andes, miles and miles of sugar-cane, an Indian population. While in Buenos Aires I was an obvious stranger, here in the north I could pass. (And sometimes more than pass. Once, in a small town in the Córdoba hills, during an earlier trip, a middle-aged, Spanish-looking man had called out with great seriousness to me across a café: "You! You look like a *pistolero.*" A gangster.)

I was staying this time in the old colonial town of Salta. One morning I took a bus for the town of Jujuy, in the province to the north, on the border with Bolivia. Just outside Salta the bus stopped, perhaps at the provincial boundary. Indian policemen in dark-blue uniforms came in and asked for identity papers. Argentines are trained from childhood to carry their papers. I had none; I had left my passport in the hotel in Salta. So—with my gangster's face momentarily of interest to the other passengers, mainly Indian, before the bus went on—I was taken off.

I went with the two policemen to the small white concrete shed or hut at the side of the road. This shed was plain outside and inside. A third policeman was there, standing behind a chest-high counter; and I could see, on a table on his side of the counter, and close to his hand, the black-and-grey metal of a machine gun lying flat. There was nothing else on that table.

I was with serious people. They listened, but without much interest, to what I had to say. They talked among themselves; then they held consultations with someone else on the telephone or on a radio system. After a while I was taken—in what vehicle or by what ways I cannot remember: I made no notes about the events of this day—to a small low building standing by itself in a sunstruck patch of bush somewhere. This, though it didn't look it, was a police post or sub-post.

The men who had brought me there went away—rather like the morning bus to Jujuy. Salta began to feel far away. My idea of time changed; I learned to wait. I gave my details once again. The policeman who wrote them down then began to telephone. This wasn't easy; the Argentine telephone service was very bad. Telephone lines, legitimate and illegitimate, hung over the streets and *Belle Époque* buildings of central Buenos Aires like gigantic cobwebs; the Indian policeman was trying to tap into the cobwebbed city, from a patch of bush a thousand miles away. He dialled and dialled, sometimes talking, sometimes not. His companion never took his eyes off me: smiling eyes, civil now, but biding their time.

I sat on a bench against a smooth plastered wall. I looked at the bush and the light outside. I smoked the pipe I had brought with me. After some time I wanted to use a lavatory. I was told there were no facilities in the little building. The policeman with the smiling eyes pointed to a spot in the bush some distance away: I was to go there. He said, "If you try to run away, I'll shoot you." With the smile, it sounded like a joke; but I knew that it wasn't.

And then—unexpectedly—a call came through on the telephone: no one of my description was on any guerrilla list. I could go. The senior policeman said, with something like friendliness, "It was your pipe that saved you. Did you know that? That pipe made me feel that you really were a foreigner."

It was an African pipe, a small black Tanganyika meerschaum I had bought in Uganda eleven years before: I had noticed that it had interested them. But all the time I had been trusting to my appearance, my broken Spanish, my Spanish accent. It was only now that I understood that to these Indian policemen of the far north Argentina would have been full of foreigners. So it was only at the moment of release, coming out of the slight shock, my disturbed sense of time, that I began to understand how serious my position had been. In the city of Tucumán, just a few days before, I had stood with a small group of townspeople watching policemen with machine guns below their raincoats getting into their unmarked cars. Like a kind of country-house shooting party; but in Tucumán the dirty war was especially dirty, and Tucumán was just to the south of Salta.

I was free, but I had no idea where I was. Some little feeling was with me that the policemen should take me back to where they had picked me up, but I didn't put it to them. They showed me where the road was. I was walking in that direction when it occurred to me that I still had no "papers," and could be picked up again. I went back to the little building and asked the senior policeman for a certificate of some sort. He understood at once; he was almost pleased to be asked. He sat down at his table, put a narrow sheet of headed paper in his heavy old typewriter and began to type, at a speed which surprised me, a *constancia policial*, a police "certification." The language was formal: bearer had been detained, but had "recovered his liberty," because his detention was "not of interest," *por no interesar su detención*. With this I went and waited on the road. A young Italian immigrant driving a white pick-up truck gave me a lift back to Salta.

I gave up the idea of further travel in the north. The next day I started back for Buenos Aires; within a few days I had left the country. Over the next two or three weeks I wrote the article I had gone out to Argentina to write. But I was unhappy with the shape of what I had written; and then for three or four weeks more, trying to put it right, I found myself writing the same article again and again in more or less the same way. I became fogged, and laid the article aside.

Two years later, when I looked again at what I had written, I found it fair enough, and wondered at my confusion. It was as though, at the time, some writer's instinct had wanted me to keep the emotion of that day to myself, and not to expose it even indirectly in an article. Later that year I began to write a long imaginative work set in a country in Central Africa. I transferred, when the time came, the emotion of Argentina, and even the isolated police building in the bush of Jujuy, to my Central African setting. When the book was finished, the unpleasantness at Jujuy dropped out of my consciousness; I forgot about it; though it had marked the end of a five-year period of intermittent travel in Argentina, and though I wasn't to go to Argentina again for fourteen years, the day in Jujuy formed no part of my Argentine memories.

But, just as sensation returns to a jaw when a local anaesthetic wears off, so, more than ten years later, when the African book had worked itself out of my system and I could no longer be sure of details of a narrative I once knew by heart, so the day at Jujuy began to come back. And—without the shock of the day itself, and the disturbed sense of time, which kept me quite calm right through—I can be sickened at the thought of how close I was then to the dirtiness of the dirty war. Thousands of men and women were disposed of at that time. Torture was routine: it was there in the smiling eyes of the junior policeman. Only my little African pipe raised a doubt in the mind of the senior policeman—and by the end of the year, when I was deep in my Central African book, I was to stop smoking, and lay aside that pipe and all the others.

AND I NEVER thought the Argentine guerrillas had a good enough cause. Some were people of the left; some were Peronists, campaigning for the return of the corrupt and old Perón; some wanted Peronism—a mixture of nationalism and socialism and anti-Americanism—without Perón. Some I thought had no cause at all; and some were simple gangsters. They were a mystery to me in 1972, when I first went to Argentina. They were educated, secure, middle-class people, perhaps the first full generation of secure and educated people after the great migrations from Europe earlier in the century, and after the depression of the 1930s. Yet, barely arrived at privilege, they were—as it seemed to me—trying to pull their world down. What had driven them to their cause? There would have been the element of mimicry, the wish not to be left out of the political current of the 1960s. "What the students say in America, they want to make concrete here"—I was told this in 1972 by a woman whose guerrilla nephew had been killed by the police: the young man had taken his revolution more seriously than the American students whose equal he wanted to be. Another, younger woman told me how a friend of hers had made his decision. They had gone to the cinema to see *Sacco and Vanzetti*; afterwards her friend had said, "I feel *ashamed* at not being a guerrilla."

There was also the old Argentine idea of revolution. This held much more than suggestions of upheaval and chaos. It was the idea that it was always possible to put an end to any particular political mess and make a fresh start. Sábat, the Buenos Aires cartoonist, put it like this: "Every time a president is deposed they raise the flag and sing the national anthem." Robert Cox, the editor of the English-language *Buenos Aires Herald*, said, "When there is a coup everyone is exhilarated and walks the next morning with a spring in his step."

For a film-maker of Italian origin this idea of revolution went back to the early nineteenth century and the bloody wars of independence. He didn't think it was funny; he thought it contained "the mystical Spanish idea of blood." I thought the words were too grand; but I felt after some time in the country that they went some way to explaining the Argentine obsession with torture.

Before I had gone to Argentina I had been sent gruesome documents about torture. But some of the people I went to see in Buenos Aires didn't seem as frantic as the messages they had sent out; some seemed rather surprised that I should be taking the matter so seriously. A young Trotskyist lawyer said in a matter-of-fact way, "Torture is pretty important here." When he saw that I thought his tone too casual, he said, with a little reflex of irritation, like a parent wearily encouraging a difficult child, "Torture will disappear only with a workers' government and the downfall of the bourgeoisie." A Peronist trade union leader, sitting in his well-appointed office, said in the soft and reasoned way for which he was known, "A world without torture is an ideal world." Torture was going to continue; but there was good torture and bad torture. Bad torture was what was done by the enemies of the people; good torture was what, when their turn came, the enemies of the people got from the protectors of the people.

This was in 1972, when almost everyone was Peronist, and people were shouting about bad military torture, and keeping quiet about the good torture they were looking forward to when Perón came back.

Robert Cox said, "You can be fooled. You can run a campaign about someone represented to you as an innocent victim of the police. And then, at his graveside, there are great tributes paid to all the acts of violence he took part in."

Even with the element of mimicry, the guerrilla idea in Argentina had little in common with the student theatre of Paris and the United States. If revolution in Argentina didn't absolutely contain the mystical idea of blood, it held the idea of physical punishment for people on the wrong side. High political principles ran into this simpler idea of personal outrage, the personal quarrel, the blood feud: the denial first of the other man's cause and then of his humanity.

IN 1880 THERE would have been open sewers and unpaved streets in central Buenos Aires. The population then was 300,000. By 1915, after "the Conquest of the Desert," the wiping out of the pampa Indians and the seizure of their immense territory, and after the great European migration, the population of the city was 1,500,000; and the great *Belle Époque* Parisian city had been built, with the names of architects and engineers carved in stone or set in metal letters to one side of tall doorways. The elegance barely lasted. Just thirty years later, in 1945, the Peronist revolution began; and twenty-five years after that, the guerrillas appeared.

By 1977 the guerrillas had been all but destroyed. Now, fourteen years on, in a city showing the signs of many years of neglect, I went to talk to Ricardo about the movement. Ricardo had been a sympathizer.

He lived in an apartment in a run-down pre-1914 block in a central area. The flat was of its period, with a separate servants' entrance and minute servant rooms; the front rooms were light, the back rooms were very dark. Ricardo kept no servant. He was like a man camping in the old apartment. Layers of paint had coarsened the detail of ceilings and architraves and skirting boards.

He was in his early forties, middle-class by education. He seemed still disturbed by his country's recent history and was as yet without a settled profession. He was of the generation of the guerrillas, and had in fact gone to the school where some of the more important guerrillas had been educated. He had known them from a distance: when he was fifteen, they were seventeen.

The school, the National College of Buenos Aires, was famous; it was, Ricardo said, the best school in the country. It had been started by the Jesuits in the eighteenth century, and run by them until they were expelled from the Spanish empire. "When modern Argentina started, the school was reshaped by a Frenchman according to the French encyclopedic education of the times." In 1966, at that school, Ricardo heard some of the senior boys singing "the fascist hymn, the Mussolini hymn," in the changing room after the swimming period. "They were pretty serious about it." This was at the time of another military take-over: the internal, back-and-forth Argentine conflict going on, after the populism and economic mess of the Perón revolution.

Ricardo began to understand that in Argentina he had a fight on his hands. Something else added to his political education. "In the late fifties and sixties there was in Argentina this movement called Catholic Action, *Acción Católica*. It was a militant organization within the church. Two priests from *Acción Católica* were counsellors at our school. They were just two blocks away from the school. The Montonero guerrillas, the Peronist guerrillas, started because of the influence of those two priests. One of them was called Father Mujica. He was killed by para-military forces some years later, in 1974."

I said, "I met Mujica in 1972. I didn't know he was so important. I thought he was a very vain man."

Ricardo said, "Vanity plays a big part in this story. There is a word in Spanish, *soberbia*. It doesn't strictly mean pride. 'Arrogance' is better. Mujica had this *soberbia*. He came from an old Argentine family. Everybody knew that, and he did live in a good area. But sometimes arrogance and shame are brothers. Or arrogance and guilt. Many people who participated in this movement we are talking about felt guilt about the part played by their families in the version of Argentine history that was fashionable at that time."

When he was twenty, Ricardo managed to travel out of Argentina for some months.

"I left the country working on a cargo ship, looking for adventure, looking for trouble, trying to shape a personality." He got to Paris in May 1970. The evening he arrived he went for a walk, and he found he had walked into a riot. "Those people were celebrating May 1968, and there were policemen on one side and rioters on the other. It was very surprising to me." It made him more aware of his rage and frustration and passivity in Argentina. A short time afterwards he read in the newspaper of the kidnapping (and subsequent murder) by Montonero guerrillas of former President Aramburu, the Argentine general who had deposed Perón and had ruled as president from 1955 to 1958.

He went back to Argentina a changed man. The military were still in power, and he was ready then to be on the side of the guerrillas.

What did the guerrillas want?

He said, as though surprised that I should ask, "To destroy the army. Peripheric countries like ours receive very clearly what is thought in the northern hemisphere. 'Liberation' was the word. Cuba was recent. Chile was going on, Allende's Chile. Vietnam was going on too."

But why, since they wished to destroy the army, did they complain so much abroad that the army wanted to destroy them?

After all these years, his passion was still the passion of the feud, in which the other side had no cause at all.

He said, "They were using guns acquired with taxpayers' money. And they were using torture illegally. They were delinquents, in fact, delinquents protected by the state."

"Delinquent"—the military used this word as well, to describe the guerrillas.

But then, in spite of what he felt about the Argentine army, Ricardo began to have doubts about the Montoneros. They wanted Perón, the revolutionary of the 1940s, to come back; but Perón was now very old and surrounded by crooks.

"Their idea of Perón was not precise. The second point that was hard for me to swallow was they said they represented the interests of the working class, with which it was evident they had very little contact." But he didn't give up the guerrillas right away. "They were not trying to fool you. I think they were honest people. They were people I trusted because I knew them. And at the same time they had success. They had succeeded in building an organization out of nothing, and they had defied the police and the army, and they were there. So they must have had something right: they had not failed. Faced with that success, all I had were my intellectual doubts, which seemed not very relevant."

And there was the excitement of action itself, of secret meetings, of running away in a dozen different directions when the police appeared, and coming together again according to a pre-arranged plan somewhere else. Still, his doubts about the Montoneros grew.

"When we were in the crowds sometimes—in fact, every time—they showed pride in their own crimes." Kidnapping and murder, and bank robberies. The ideology wasn't always clear. The Montoneros said they were Peronist. Why, then, did they murder Rucci, the Peronist trade union leader? "That was one crime they had problems with. They could hardly tell people they had done it."

Paris in 1970 had given Ricardo, passive and frustrated, an idea of the possibility of action. But the conflicts of Argentina were not as formal and regulated as the celebratory riots of Paris, with the police on one side and the students on the other, and everybody going home afterwards. Argentina was full of hatreds that weren't all clear, couldn't always be reduced to principles. Argentina was much bloodier, full of real murder. Ricardo felt himself sinking into a moral and political mess. He had not yet undertaken any big action; he hadn't been compromised in that way; and it was possible for him to detach himself from the guerrillas.

He said, "Argentina made people dream too much. When the dreams fell apart the response was anger and looking for the guilty. Many of the guerrillas were grandchildren of immigrants. And the army men, too. There were many family links between the two sides, because it was basically a fight within a certain social segment of society. They were not big landowners; they were not working-class. They were people who expected a certain social development based on education, and they were beginning to feel that for various reasons the doors were closing."

There was a time, hard to imagine now, in the early part of the century, when Argentina, with all its rich, empty land, its conquered "desert," all its new pampa wealth, thought itself the equal of the United States; and it drew the same kind of European immigrant. But Argentina was a cheat; it was never a land for pioneers; it was a colonial agricultural economy on a vast scale, built around great *estancias* or estates. Argentina didn't require pioneers; it required only hands. In the United States in the late 1960s the grandchildren of immigrants, playing at revolution, were really only making their way in an open and rich and many-sided country. In Argentina the revolt of that same generation, of more or less similar antecedents, was more desperate.

The revolt had a religious side. I wanted to know more about that, and early one morning Ricardo took me to see a survivor of the 1970s. We met in the man's office in central Buenos Aires, before it opened for business. The lift didn't work; the turn-of-the century panelling was dim and tarnished. Like Ricardo's apartment, this business suite from a grander time seemed to be a place that was being camped in.

The man we had come to meet was biggish, in his forties, plump now. He was in a brown suit. Just as Ricardo gave off melancholy, so this man suggested heaviness and dullness. He did a dull job in his dim office; he had a white, expressionless face. It was hard to imagine him as a man with a gun.

His talk was abstract from the start.

He said, "The idea of bearing witness, of organizing a way of life [*un proyecto de vida*] around one's concern for others, that doesn't come only from a Catholic source. It also comes from the tradition of the Left."

The Catholicism was in his background. At his public school, where there were nationalist and fascist and leftist ideas, he found his Catholic instincts coinciding with the ideas of the Left. What ideas, especially? "The idea of the New Man, the idea of the revolutionary as an identity,

the revolutionary confronting injustice. If in the Judaeo-Christian culture it's one of the commandments to love your neighbour—which also
means that God is in the other man—then I cannot be indifferent to
the miseries of this man, and I mean not only his material miseries, but
also his cultural and spiritual miseries. That's part of the Gospel. It coincided at that moment with left-wing ideology—Che Guevara, the New
Man, the Cuban revolutionary tradition, the Marxist revolutionary
tradition. The New Man is a cultural attitude. It detects, opposes, and
denounces the prevailing culture"—the words came out like that: the
musical sounds of Spanish can beguile people into using more words
than they need, and more and more musical words—"when that culture
is seen as a mechanism of domination."

I wanted to know the stages by which his Catholic and New-Man
faith, so large and abstract, had narrowed down to guerrilla actions.
These actions were specific; they could sometimes appear—even to
someone like Ricardo—to be a matter of mysterious enmities.

He didn't give the kind of answer I was hoping for. He said, "It's like
a process of conversion, conversion in a political way. And it goes very
fast. You arrive at a vision that you can alter history, that history doesn't
follow its own fixed course. And I made my commitment. I gave up my
career, my family, my social life, and began doing what I had to do. You
also develop the clear sense of belonging to a group, a new group, different from the one you were given by your parents. Though my family
were tolerant and very supportive.

"The idea of commitment contained the idea of physical risk. It's
simple. If you are doing what is correct, you think that you are being correct, and you have a regard for what you do. At a certain level of action
you are trying to cope with your own anguish and solitude. But in my
case what was most important was not the action itself, but the self-
esteem that came to me from the action. The self-esteem came to me
from doing the correct thing."

I said, "This is a religious attitude. It's almost priestly."

The man in the brown suit said, "It was."

Ricardo said to me, "You find it strange? That's because you are not
a Christian. The psychological scenario had links with this cultural
tradition."

Footsteps sounded on the solid marble steps, and a woman came into
the outer office: a secretary, getting ready to start the working day.

The man in the brown suit said, "Our Catholic upbringing made us militant. That's where it started, in the idea of service and discipline." And then—someone else coming into the office, and Ricardo and I getting ready to leave—he stood up and said, "What resulted was sometimes a perversion." It was, at last, like an acknowledgement of the confusion, and the calamity, that had befallen his cause.

When we were in the street Ricardo said, "The guy"—Ricardo used the word neutrally—"was presenting himself to you as a defeated man, part of a defeated generation."

I wished, though, I could have got him to talk in a more concrete way. Perhaps, because his cause had failed so completely, he didn't want to talk of real people and real events. But it was also possible that his abstractions represented the way he thought. The principles by which he had tried to live were his own and were what he had to hold on to. The action (*protagonismo,* protagonism, was the word he used) into which those principles had led him had been worked out by others, to whom he had entrusted himself, and was incidental to his higher cause.

Ricardo and I had coffee in a students' café.

Ricardo said, "I am seduced by rigorous ideas when I can reach them. The lack of rigour is something we have paid heavily for."

The avenue we came out into was very wide: the turn-of-the century city had been planned for great things. Black smoke poured out of the exhausts of small and noisy Argentine-built buses, grating away between traffic lights. Above, the *Belle Époque* buildings were extravagantly cobwebbed—with the black telephone lines of a system that had been nationalized by Perón in 1945, at the start of his revolution, at great cost, a system that ever since then had been less of a public utility than a telephone workers' racket: the big black webs spun, as it were, out of the entrails of the city and hanging over it like an emblem of nearly half a century of revolutionary plunder and waste.

The guerrillas of the 1970s, educated men and women, grandchildren of immigrants, had carried on Perón's revolution. Twenty years on, they (with the repression they had provoked, and everything that had followed the repression) could be seen to have further impoverished and stultified the country.

Nearly everyone in that avenue would have been obsessed with money: not just with earning a living, but with maintaining the value of money. To ignore your money for a week was to lose it. The inflation that had started in Perón's time had raced away in the last twenty years. In 1972 I had been excited by bank advertisements offering 24 per cent a year; since then inflation had sometimes reached 100 percent a month; now, with the new stringency, it was, officially, about 4 per cent a month.

Ricardo said, speaking of the guerrillas of the 1970s, "Only a part of the intelligentsia was involved, but they were all massively attacked. Being an intellectual was risky at the time. The repression became massive." Just as in Argentina there was good torture and bad torture, depending on your side, so, still to Ricardo, there had been the good war, fought by the guerrillas, and the bad war, the "repression" by the army. "A good part of the intelligentsia had to flee, and this is something the country is paying for even now."

He began to project his own melancholy on to his vision of the future. There would be more guerrillas one day, he said. They would be without the "elegance" of the guerrillas of the seventies; they would be more like the Sendero Luminoso of Peru, animated by blood and rage.

"The guerrillas of the seventies tried to have some ethical attitude, some ethical advantage over their enemies. Sendero has given that up. They don't play the good guys anymore. That could happen here. You go out to the suburbs by train now, and you get into contact with people you wouldn't know how to reintegrate into the society of the future. They are not conceivable to us as human beings. They are mestizos." People of the old Indian north. "They are appearing like mushrooms in those suburbs."

What Ricardo said was true: in those suburbs the Parisian city seemed to be reverting to its South American earth.

"The feudal system of their origins, the system their parents came from, no longer wants them. It doesn't include them, or content them, anymore. And the capitalist system of the city has no place for them. So they are born outlaws. The Sendero-style guerrilla has some kind of appeal for that kind of person. So do some religious groups. That's an important new phenomenon, by the way: those American preachers on TV, they have begun to come here."

WHEN I MET FATHER MUJICA in 1972 I didn't know that he was one of the patrons of the guerrillas. I am sure now that Daniel, who took me to meet him, knew. Daniel very much wanted me to meet Mujica; but he told me only that Mujica was one of the "Priests for the Third World," and that Mujica was of the Argentine upper class. Daniel was a respectable middle-class businessman; and even at the time I thought his interest in what he had given as Mujica's cause a little strange. It showed to what extent in 1972, before Perón came back, and before things got really nasty, the guerrillas were operating from within the society and—in spite of the police dogs on the streets and the policemen with machine guns at street corners—were really protected people.

Mujica was running a church in a *villa miseria*, an Indian shantytown, in the Palermo district. Palermo is to Buenos Aires what Kensington Gardens are to London, or the Bois de Boulogne to Paris. Palermo has a great park. (And a fair amount of patriotic public statuary: too Paris-like for the local history: the park itself was laid out on the Buenos Aires estate of the rancher-warlord Rosas, who came to power some years after independence and then ran Argentina in his very rough way for nearly a quarter of a century, until 1852.)

The Palermo *villa miseria*, which was about fifteen years old, was hidden away. You could drive through on the wide, roaring avenues without seeing it. It was just next to the river, and it was unexpectedly large and solid and settled-looking. As soon as you came to it you felt you had left Palermo and Buenos Aires. The people were Indians from the far north, from Salta and Jujuy; Daniel said that some would have been even from Bolivia. The lanes were unpaved and muddy; the small buildings were low and cramped, but they were of brick, with here and there an upper storey. With its early-evening busyness and the softness of its electric lights, dim here as elsewhere in the city, it didn't look at all bad; in India this Argentine *villa miseria* might have passed as the well-off bazaar area of a small town.

Mujica's church was a big, unheated concrete shed. It had no overt religious emblems, or none that I remember; and there was nothing ecclesiastical in its divisions of space. It offered music: an amplified Argentine song—no hint of God or religion in that, either.

Mujica was there in his shed, and he seemed to be very much part of the same production. He was a big man, busy and serious and frowning. The black leather jacket he was wearing bulked out his arms and chest. He had a full head of hair and his eyes were angry. Daniel, who had met him before, at once fell into an attitude of deference, going quiet and still and keeping his eyes fixed on the great man. Mujica was pleased to be sought out; but I felt he was a bit of an actor and—to prove himself in front of Daniel—was going to make trouble.

Soon enough I gave him cause. I asked about the Priests for the Third World. He said, with some irony, that he also "happened to be" a Peronist; and then he added, irony quite overtaking him, touched at the end with a little rage, that as a Peronist he was *not* as concerned as some people were with economic growth.

I asked how many people there were in the *villa miseria*. He said, in his oblique way, that for every one who left, two came. I pressed him to give a figure. He said a few years ago there were only forty thousand; now there were seventy thousand. (Daniel had told me thirty thousand.) Because of the folly of the government there was no work in the interior, Mujica said; that was why the Indians kept coming down from the north.

I wondered how he could square this with his rejection, as a Peronist, of the idea of economic growth. I wasn't making a debating point. Argentina in 1972 was confusing for a visitor; and I didn't know what Peronism meant.

Mujica became enraged. He said he had better things to do, and he wasn't going to waste his time talking to a *norteamericano*, an American. He turned away from Daniel and me and, switching from rage to upper-class affability (as if to show us what we had missed), he walked towards a black-caped, frightened-looking Bolivian family group, no one more than five feet tall, who had just come into the concrete shed. He opened his arms as though he was about to crush them all to his leather-jacketed breast.

If I had known—what Daniel knew—that Mujica had guerrilla links, I might have approached him differently. As it was, I thought I had come to the end of this particular Priest for the Third World. It was, besides, cold and damp in the shed. It was late May, the Argentine winter; the evening mist from the River Plate was beginning to be noticeable in the dim electric light. And the Argentine song on Mujica's sound system was really very loud. I told Daniel we should leave. He looked unhappy. He was more on Mujica's side than mine. He said I should at least stay and tell the Father that I wasn't an American. I felt that if I didn't do as Daniel asked I would be damaging his credit with Mujica. So I waited. When Mujica was finished with the Bolivians, they went and sat meekly on a bench and looked down at the concrete floor, praying in the faint mist.

Daniel, overcoated, standing still, his eyes now fixed on Mujica's back, said to me, "Go and tell him."

I went and said to the leather-jacketed back, "Father, I am not an American."

He turned around; he was abashed. His eyes softened; but then, as we talked again, and I asked a little more about Peronism, his angry manner returned.

He said, "Only an Argentine can understand Peronism." Peronists weren't only the middle-class people I had been meeting: all the Indians in the Palermo *villa miseria* were Peronists. "I can talk to you for five years, and still you wouldn't understand Peronism."

As he explained it, Peronism contained both Castroism and Maoism. In Mao's China they had turned their backs on the industrial society and were more concerned with "the development of the human spirit." That was true of Castroism as well, and Peronism in Argentina had a similar goal. But there were enemies. He recited them (while his black-clad Bolivians prayed in his sanctuary): the oligarchy, the military, and American imperialism, expressed in Argentina through its economic control. These enemies were sucking the country dry.

From the abstraction of "the development of the human spirit" as a goal, which could forgive itself anything, Mujica had no trouble making a leap to the idea of the enemy, someone just there, and the very concrete idea of physical punishment. In this, Mujica was like the Jewish Peronist lawyer I had met who could categorize the enemies of the Argentine people in an almost Aristotelian way. "Fundamentally," the lawyer said, "the enemies are American imperialism and its native allies. These allies are: the oligarchy, the dependent bourgeoisie, international Zionism, the sepoy Left. By sepoys I mean the Communist Party and socialism in general."

Many people had little lists of enemies like this, and if you put a few of the lists together, then nearly everybody in Argentina turned out to be somebody's enemy.

A woman friend of Daniel's wife had a racial list. She said to me one evening at dinner, "If only we had more Nordic blood, more people from Europe—I don't mean Poles. If only we had more Germans, more English people, more Dutch, to renew and improve the race. In Buenos Aires and Rosario we have a good-looking race. But the people of the north, who are pure Indian, they are not good-looking. They are tiny. Horrible."

This woman's group was itself on the racial list of a man of remote Irish origins—an ancestor would have come out early in the nineteenth century as a shepherd or ditcher. He spoke only Spanish now, and worked in a provincial university. He was in no doubt about where the calamity of Argentina lay. Whispering one day in the library, he told me the story of former President Roca, the conqueror of the desert, visiting Buenos Aires towards the end of the nineteenth century and seeing a shipload of Italian immigrants. "My poor country," Roca said, "it will be a sad day for you when you are governed by the children of these people." And now, the unlikely Irishman said, in his penetrating Spanish whisper, that day had come.

"In Argentina," Sábat said in 1972, "there is a formal racial prejudice against everybody [*un perjuicio racial integral contra todos*]. What we are seeing here now is a kind of collective frenzy. Because it was always easy here before to get money. There is a saying here that the final revolution will come the day you can't get a beefsteak, the so-called *bife de chorizo*."

The immigrant society was being atomized, and Argentina was becoming as invertebrate as the Spain Ortega y Gasset had written about in the early 1920s. Disparate peoples, Ortega had written, come together not simply for the pleasure of living together, but in order to do something together tomorrow. That hope, necessary in the formation of an immigrant country, had gone, and in its place was a deepening cynicism and demoralization.

The young film-maker I had met defined this cynicism well. "I am an Italian myself, but many of the things I dislike here I relate to Italians—a kind of watching things happen, and taking advantage of the situation that results. It's a middle-class attitude, but I suppose you start being cynical when you take advantage of your own scepticism to make profit out of things."

To be without cynicism was to be without a kind of protection; it was to feel pain. The poet Jorge Luis Borges felt this pain. His ancestors went back to colonial Spanish times. Some had fought against Spain in the war of independence, and in the civil wars that had followed. Borges was born in 1899; he had memories, from his childhood, of the building of the great new city of Buenos Aires. His early poetry had been about his ancestors, and death, and the creation of a country. As a young man he had been an Argentine patriot, he said in 1972, much more of a patriot than his father. "We were taught to worship all things Argentine."

But then, when he was only in his early forties, the Peronist upheaval had occurred; and the country, hardly created, had begun to unravel. Borges had been humiliated in the Peronist period; he had been made to give up his modest job in the municipal library. Now, twenty years on, Peronist guerrillas were active in the city, armed policemen were in the streets; and Perón was about to return. The only way Borges had of coping with this new twist in Argentine history was to ignore it. The very name of Perón, he said, was too shabby to be used in public, "the way in poetry one avoids certain words." His work was his consolation. "We can look forward to a Trojan ending."

Some of his sadness came out in a short poem he addressed in this year, 1972, to the writer Manuel Mujica Lainez—a distant relation of Father Mujica's. Mujica Lainez (1910–1984) lived in English country-house style in a small town in the Córdoba Hills. His large, gloomy, well-furnished house in a damp little valley had something of the atmosphere of Stephen Tennant's Wilsford Manor in Wiltshire. The Conquest of the Desert, and the prodigious expansion of Argentina in the late nineteenth century, had brought wealth, education, and even a kind of old European style to a number of old colonial families, together with an idea of Argentina as something achieved, something correctly celebrated in the public statuary of Buenos Aires.

In 1934, in a poem in English, Borges had written about the public statues of his ancestors: "I offer you my ancestors, my dead men, the ghosts that living men have honoured in bronze." Now, in 1972, the poem Borges wrote to Mujica Lainez ended: "Manuel Mujica Lainez, we both once had a country—do you remember?—and we have both lost it."

> *Manuel Mujica Lainez, alguna vez tuvimos*
> *Una patria—recuerdas?—y los dos la perdimos.*

Two years later, in 1974, the other Mujica, the Third World Priest in the Palermo shantytown, expiating guilt and (as Ricardo said) the old idea of Argentine history, had been shot dead. He, too, had been on someone's list. Perón by this time had come back; he was very old and about to die. He had turned against the guerrillas who had helped to bring him back; so at the end the Peronism he—and his terrible court—had brought back was as plundering and murderous as it had been twenty years before. For a day or two, perhaps for a week, no more, posters gave the name of the killed Mujica. It was hardly honour. The walls of Buenos Aires were scrawled over with many different names and slogans. Those walls were the visual equivalent of a constant public din. There were too many martyrs now, too many enemies; the revolutionary causes had become indecipherable.

Two years later, the army was to take over again. They were to tear down all the posters and whitewash all the walls, and they were to start killing the guerrillas. Within a year they had destroyed the various movements; and the white walls of the city—old scrawls showing faintly through—were to speak of an eradicated generation, educated people who had, like their patron Mujica, converted high religious and political ideals into elemental Argentine-Spanish ideas of the enemy, and physical punishment, and blood.

AFTER fourteen years, I went again to Salta. I flew from Buenos Aires to La Rioja, and from there went on by bus, over two days, up and down the mountain passes and through the wide sugar-cane valleys.

In 1972 Borges, a man of Buenos Aires, had told me that when he was with Salta people he felt he was with foreigners. In the province of Buenos Aires, Borges said, a gaucho was a horseman of the flat pampas; in Salta a gaucho was a rider in the mountains. A different landscape, a different history: Buenos Aires lived by its Atlantic port, while Salta and all that northern part of Argentina had been colonized from Peru and the Pacific.

What distances—from Spain to the Caribbean, the portage to the Pacific, and from there to Peru and points south! Salta was at the end of an imperial route that Spain had protected and kept secure for more than two centuries. Spain felt unimaginably far away. Yet to be in the main square of Salta—laid out all at once, as the Spanish custom was, on a day in 1582—was to have a strong sense of Spain, the Spanish empire, the Spanish conquest. A government building was in the Paris style of Buenos Aires; the 1941 Hotel Salta, for holidaymakers, carefully "colonial," spoke of the last days of old Argentina, just before Perón. But nearly everything else in that square, the great church, the bell-towers, the arcaded pavements, the tall and rich green garden, spoke of Spain. The monument that marked the four-hundredth anniversary of the city was not—as it might have been in Buenos Aires in its more confident days—a tribute to Argentina, but a bust of the Duke of Lerma who, all that distance away in Spain, had sent out orders for the founding of a city at that spot. Whatever course history had taken elsewhere, whatever the present condition of Spain itself, Spain here continued paramount.

It was Easter. Loudspeakers attached to poles in the central garden amplified the singing in the church, but not too loudly—a woman's voice, alone, and pure, that seemed to add to the blessing of the green garden, a green so rich and deep it seemed to cast a cool green light all around. People sat on benches in that light, or walked, or sold or bought things. Some people stood on the steps of the church; some went and stood inside. The church, plain outside, glittered above the altar. You had to go quite far up, through the people standing, before you saw that the woman with the pure voice was a young Indian nun, short, her head covered, with the skirt of her modern habit falling not far below the knees of her bow legs. And with everything that one felt here about the wonder of Spain, and the Spanish civilities of Salta, from waiters and others, there came, at the sight of the young Indian nun, who had made peace with the world in her own way, a contrary judgement about the enduring cruelty of the Spanish conquest.

Of that cruelty of the sixteenth century, living on at the end of the twentieth, there was always an intimation in the north: in the sugar-cane fields, the Indian faces, the Indian houses. Gold and slaves, *encomiendas,* "grants" of Indians from the Spanish crown—that was what drove the first Spaniards down from Peru.

And there was cruelty in the other Argentinas that came after. Cruelty is really the theme of the gaucho folk epic, *Martín Fierro* (first part 1872), which is the nearest thing Argentina has to a national poem. In Buenos Aires buckskin-covered editions of this book are sold as keepsakes. In the Argentina imagination the poem—by José Hernández (1834–1886), known for nothing else—is a memorial of a better and purer time, when the gaucho, a free man, rode over the unfenced and limitless pampa, and the land was bright with possibility. But the Argentina of the poem, wild though it appears, is already corrupt, without justice. The gaucho hero is really a man on the run, caught between barbarisms, Indian and Argentine. He is in constant danger of being impressed—and robbed of his pay, and flogged for misdemeanours—to fight the Indians on the frontier, to win the land for others.

There is a similarity between *Martín Fierro* and a Russian novel of adventure, published just a few months later, Nikolai Leskov's *The Enchanted Wanderer* (1873). Leskov (1831–1894) is almost the coeval of José Hernández; his tale, coming at a time of Russian expansion, is of a simple Russian caught between Russian and Tartar barbarisms. Leskov is at his best when he has a strong story to tell; and his best stories are his most painful ones; his underlying subject, pointed up by his religious obsession, is Russian cruelty. Leskov's enchanted wanderer, when he becomes a prisoner of the Tartars, is like the gaucho Martín Fierro as a prisoner of the pampa Indians: they are both men in hell, and they both have little to run back to. The true Conquest of the Desert came immediately after the publication of the second part of *Martín Fierro* (1879). There was no valour in this conquest; with the help of the railways and the Remington rifle, President Roca, in six campaigns, wiped out the pampa Indians. A vast new territory, flat and fertile and tree-less, never used for cultivation, was shared out among a handful of people. It was as though, as with the first Spanish conquest, people who had been poor for generations, never knowing that human needs were assuageable, had, with opportunity, discovered in themselves only a boundless greed. Immigrants were brought over from Europe to service, but not to settle, this conquered Desert; and the new Parisian city of Buenos Aires was built. The "Paris" was not for everyone: in the dark and minute and shaming "maid's rooms" of the new apartment buildings may still be seen an important idea of the new Argentine wealth: other people had to be poor, nothing was to be shared. People who required nothing less than the sky and the horizon of the conquered Desert for themselves and their sheep and cattle, offered very little, offered nothing, to everybody else.

In 1972 the rage about this still flowed. A journalist who grew up in a small pampa town said, "I saw them cheating the workers who worked by the hour—they turned the clocks backward." That was hard to believe, but it was the kind of story people told. I heard that in the old days, before Perón, the maids who lived in those tiny rooms never had a day off; that some worked only for their keep. And there were stories that working people and Indians were not allowed to walk in the Barrio Norte, the upper-class area.

They sounded like stories, legends to keep the rage up. But then sometimes I wondered; when, for example, in an important provincial town, in an oily shed of a factory, where the floor was of earth, I saw this sign—in 1972, twenty years after the death of Eva Perón, and with the guerrillas campaigning for Perón's return—"If you work for a man, work for him. Speak well of him on every suitable occasion. Remember: an ounce of loyalty is worth a pound of intelligence." This statement was attributed to San Martín, honoured in Argentina as the Liberator, the winner of the country's independence from Spain.

The attitude, the simple obedience required (with very little offered in return), seemed to take one back very far, beyond the frontier cruelties of *Martín Fierro* to the tyrannies of the warlords like Rosas (Borges said he used to have executed people's heads spiked and displayed, "to give the others fair warning"); and even beyond that back to the Spanish conquest. In the tracing of Argentine attitudes, of rage and counter-rage, action and reaction, you go back always to the Spanish conquest, as to original sin.

It was Perón's gift or genius to tap all that rage, the rage not only of the European immigrants and their children, most of them workers, some of them educated people, a few of them entrepreneurs—not only that European rage, but the rage also of the dispossessed Indians in the north, the dispossessed in the regions that were not serviced by the new wealth: the *cabecitas negras,* the "blackheads" he brought into Buenos Aires to march and demonstrate. That rage he scratched into a national sore; and it still festers, though Perón and his court (with no other example in Argentina of wealth and style) were as plundering as any of the old oligarchy, and by nationalizations, gifts and rewards, made money and endeavour worthless.

I talked this year to a man of the Anglo-Argentine community whom I had talked to in 1972. He had then, in the midst of the movement for Perón's recall, said, "I'm beginning to feel completely at sea. Perón destroyed all my feeling that he stood for anything. Anything could be changed at any moment. And then here you really have no say in deciding who's going to rule. So in the end here you do become sheep. You lose confidence in politics, you lose confidence in the military, and there's nothing left." Now—when they were no longer a threat—this man spoke of the guerrillas with something like sympathy. He said, "Most normal people in this country have wanted to shoot the lot at the top. You see, nobody here gets punished; once you're at the top you're safe. It was very easy for the guerrillas to cash in on this frustration."

It was the trap of the situation, the Trojan ending Borges had prophe-

sied four years before the dirty war began: the educated guerrilla generation, grandchildren of immigrants, could hold on to the good abstract
ideas they had been educated into—the development of the human
spirit, the New Man confronting injustice—only by adding the old
Argentine-Spanish idea of blood, the enemy.

THERE are some stanzas in *Martín Fierro* where the gaucho overhears
the local judge scheming with another man to make money by pushing the Indian frontier back. Impressed soldiers will do the actual
fighting; and the gaucho's heart "grows small" as he listens to this talk of
"settlements and roads and raking in thousands," *proyetos/de colonias y
carriles/y tirar plata a miles.* If things go on like this, the gaucho thinks,
the pampas might soon become "a desert, with nothing but the whitening
bones of dead men."

This has a parallel in the Joseph Conrad story, *Heart of Darkness*
(1902), which is about Belgian empire-building on the other side of the
Atlantic, in the Congo, and refers to events which would have occurred
only some twenty years after the events of the Argentine poem. The
Conrad narrator, making his way inland to take charge of a river steamer,
finds himself in a rough station on the Congo River with sixteen or
twenty Belgians of the Eldorado Exploring Expedition. Unspeakable
things are happening all around; men are wasting away and dying. But
the Belgians don't notice.

"The only real feeling was a desire to get appointed to a trading-post
where ivory was to be had, so that they could earn percentages. They
intrigued and slandered and hated each other only on that account—but
as to effectually lifting a little finger—oh, no . . . Their talk . . . was reckless without hardihood, greedy without audacity, and cruel without
courage; there was not an atom of foresight or of serious intention in the
whole batch of them, and they did not seem aware that these things are
wanted for the work of the world."

The narrator is led to reflect on the idea of work. It is the missing
moral idea. "No, I don't like work. I had rather laze about and think of all
the fine things that can be done. I don't like work—no man does—but I
like what is in the work, the chance to find yourself. Your own reality—
for yourself, not for others—what no other man can ever know."

This is almost religious. It lies on the other side, as it were, of the colonial darkness. This high idea of human possibility can arise only in reasonably free and reasonably creative societies. It was the opposite of the idea behind the first Spanish conquest, the opposite of the idea behind the Conquest of the Desert. Such an idea might have driven some of the immigrants to Argentina, as it drove some to the United States; but Argentina would have frustrated the people it attracted.

In Argentina the missing moral idea has had other consequences. The great fortunes that came with the Conquest of the Desert haven't all lasted. Argentines will tell you that in Argentina there has been constant change at the top. A man of old family said in 1972, "In Peru you have the real aristocracy. They have a tradition of two to three hundred years. If you mention the names of the Argentine aristocrats between 1850 and 1900, today no one in Argentina knows them. Their descendants were weak, and the whole thing began to crumble." One of the few industrialists of old family put it like this, "Below the *Belle Époque* façade in Buenos Aires you must remember we had the tango man. Today the tango man has taken over."

I went this year to an *estancia* in the south of the province of Buenos Aires. Beyond the eucalyptus and other roadside trees, and the roadside puddles, the flat, brown-green grass went back to the horizon and seemed to swallow up the heads and legs of cattle, reducing them to the black or dark-brown dashes of their backs. This large piece of the Conquered Desert had long ago passed out of the hands of the family who had first been granted it; and twice since then it had gone derelict, once in the Depression, and later, after the wartime boom, in the time of Perón. The man who inherited it in 1960 found there wasn't even enough money for the upkeep of the homestead. He was an educated man; he decided to give his life to his estate, and he had brought it back. Not everyone was like him.

"We have next door an old Spanish family, friends. They are the biggest landowners in the district. They probably received the land way back, from Roca. They can't afford to go to Europe very often now. They haven't been able to adapt. They haven't changed the structure of their business. They still have their house and social life in town, in B.A., and they try to run things from there. They survive by selling off bits of capital. I know a big house, forty rooms, which now has only one hundred and thirty hectares to keep it up. It can't be done. But the old lady won't sell, though she has no hot water. Yet there are beautiful bathrooms, with lovely taps, designed in the art-deco style by an English architect in the 1920s. Cobwebs in most of the rooms, and leaks in the roof."

Susana came from a family like that, a family that had lost much of its money. She had married a professional, middle-class man, and still thought of herself as having done a bold thing. She still had the manners of her upbringing: the security, the pride, the curious innocence. She didn't know exactly how her family had lost their land. She didn't think Perón had anything to do with it; but her husband later told me that Susana's family, panicking about the new taxes when Perón came in, had taken bad advice and sold up.

Susana said, "What happened to my family didn't start with Perón. It goes back further. When Father was eighteen—this would have been in 1930 or thereabouts—he wanted to study. He wanted to be an architect. Father was charming, rather shy, extremely polite. A very weak character. He talked to his stepfather, and his stepfather advised him not to study, saying, 'Why study?' For his stepfather, if you had beautiful manners it was enough. Then a little bit later my father again felt he wanted to study. He wanted to study law this time, and again his stepfather said to him, 'Why study?' And so my father didn't study.

"For my father, too, you know, if you had beautiful manners, it was enough. Money was important—that went without saying: it was assumed that you had money. But there had to be the manners. If you went to my father's house and said hello beautifully, stood at the right moment, sat at the right moment, and said the right things, if you appreciated my father's furniture and silver, it was enough for him. I must tell you that I myself can still feel dazzled by beautiful manners. Our manners were very formal. As children we would be called into the sitting room sometimes, and we went in and said hello. But we didn't talk if weren't asked something directly. If we were sitting down we had to get up if someone came in. Sometimes we went to the dining room, to have dinner with father and mother and their guests, and I remember thinking on those occasions, 'What beautiful people, what beautiful manners.' But we weren't so beautiful. None of the daughters learned to do anything. Even now, you know, they talk of the old days. Days of having, of going to Europe, travelling, bringing back lovely things. But not days of doing."

This wasn't the only flaw in this Argentine aristocracy based on new land. Its language was Spanish; so were its attitudes and its deeper culture. That ideal of not working, of not talking about money—that was Spanish. (As Spanish as the inch-long nail on the little finger of the middle-aged gentleman I met in a café in La Rioja in 1974. We both had time on our hands, and he drove me about the countryside for half a day. His fingernail proclaimed him a man of leisure: it was a half-cylinder in shape, hard and horny-looking, striated, yellow, the colour of a very dirty tooth, oddly disagreeable to look at.) But Spain was known to be backward, the source of the poor immigrants known collectively in Argentina as *gallegos*.

Susana said, "Those beautiful manners of my father were an aspiration towards the idea of the *gentleman*. They were thought to be English manners. Father, all his education was looking to England. When my mother and father went to Europe they never went to Spain. Spain was—" and Susana made a gesture of disregard. The disregard for Spain contained a disregard for Spanish-speaking Argentina. "They had no pride in being Argentine. They thought they were English. They said *este país*, 'this country,' not *my* country. They would say, 'The people here are awful.' Not, '*We* are awful.' My husband says a lot of the problems here have to do with that *este país* attitude."

And perhaps, with a different idea of their aristocracy, the Argentine upper class might have sought to come terms with Perón, a man of their country; and the country would not have started unravelling with the revolution.

I wondered whether the formal manners of Susana's parents didn't also hold an element of stoicism or protecting ritual, enabling them to put up with the hard times that had come to them. I didn't make myself clear. Susana thought I was asking about the attitude of her family to the hardship of others. And she said, "No. When November, our summer, came, and we were very hot, my mother would point to the tenement behind our apartment and say, 'Think of them.' But I never thought she really cared."

When Susana understood the point about stoicism, she said, "Mother was very structured [*estructurada*]. They made her like that. I thought when I was young that Mama had the solution for everything. But when she had a grief in her family, Mother just collapsed. There was no substance in her."

. . .

THE INDIAN land, used prodigally, as though nothing had gone before and nothing was to come after, already has its ruins, of buildings and peoples. Like so many tracts of the New World, like the Guianas and the Caribbean islands, the Argentine pampa appears to have swallowed up its history; it is a place of disappearances. The pampa Indians have disappeared, and the gauchos. The Africans, descendants of slaves from the Spanish time, have disappeared. In *Martín Fierro* they are still very much there, in the Argentina of the 1860s, black and mulatto, men and women, stylish, not negligible, speaking the Spanish of the gauchos. And when Borges was a boy, in the first decade of the century, black people were still to be seen in Buenos Aires.

Borges said in 1972, "When I was a child if I saw a Negro I didn't report it at home. I don't know what happened to our black men. Our family wasn't wealthy. We only had six slaves." There is a reference in one poem to the slave quarters of the family house in the city. "They were quite unaware that their forefathers had come from Africa. They spoke a kind of singsong Spanish. They couldn't manage the R: they made it an L. But they were not regarded as different. In fact a Negro was as much of a *criollo*"—someone of old colonial Argentina, before the immigrant rush—"as everybody else. Here they were cooks, maids. You thought of a Negro as being a townsman. Many fine infantry regiments were made up of Negroes. One of my great uncles led a famous bayonet charge against the Spaniards in Montevideo—it would have been in 1815 or 1816—and all the soldiers were full-blooded Negroes from the south side of the town, near the National Library." That was where we were talking. Borges in 1972 was director; his salary had dwindled with inflation to the equivalent of $70 a month.

So Africans had fought for Argentine independence. If Borges hadn't told me I wouldn't have guessed: a hundred years later their descendants had vanished like magic into the new European population, and there was now no living memory of them.

In the shuffling about of peoples, the Spaniards of the old colonial north also suffered. They had been economically dependent on Peru. Now—after independence, and after the destructive civil wars, "the sword and danger and hard proscriptions" of a Borges poem, *la espada y el peligro, las duras proscripciones*—they had to look south. Once they had been at the end of a very long imperial route from Spain; now—at least until the railways came—they were at the end of a very long cart track from Buenos Aires. They had little to offer. The region ceased to have an economic point; the people had finally fallen off the rim of the world into wilderness.

They became pensioners of the government in the south. And so they have remained. It is said that the entire province of La Rioja (its chief town founded in 1591) now lives off the state. The money isn't simply offered to people as a dole: they have to take government jobs. Politicians looking for public favour invariably offer to create more public jobs. Mr. Luria, a lawyer and local historian, told me that between 1983—when military rule ended—and 1987 the number of government employees in La Rioja more than trebled, to 44,000. That number, quite high for a total provincial population of about 250,000, had since risen even higher, to 55,000.

These government jobs are not really jobs. There is nothing or very little to do, and it might seem that to get regular money for doing nothing is a kind of old Spanish dream come true, almost as good as the grant of Indians people once pined for. But this largesse comes with a touch of Spanish-Argentine cruelty. There is nothing to do, but people have to attend; they have to be present throughout the working day in the government office to which they are theoretically attached. At any moment a boss or head of department might order a spot check, might send out a *planilla volante*, a "flying roll-call," and then every man or woman on the pay list has to answer up.

Mr. Luria said, "This is a very serious matter. It results in La Rioja in what I call the culture of tedium." He was pleased with the words: *la cultura del tedio.* "Because these people are condemned to seven hours of desperation every day, pretending to do a job that doesn't exist." At the end of every day at the office these public employees, Mr. Luria said, are "tired, frustrated, fed up, enraged"; and then the families as well felt the effects of the accumulated tedium of the day. "I don't know what your own observations are, but this is a sad town, without heart, without initiative."

Mr. Luria spoke with feeling. He was a man of La Rioja through and through, partly of Indian ancestry. To him La Rioja was a land of the nineteenth-century warlords and hardy, valiant men. Government jobs, the culture of tedium, had broken the spirit of the people; they didn't even know their history now. Three attempts, Mr. Luria said, had been made to get the government employees into productive work in an industrial park; but the people who took those jobs invariably drifted back to the government offices, though the pay was lower. Mr. Luria said, "They prefer the illness."

Within the large cruelty of compulsory attendance, and the constant terror of the *planilla volante*, there were subtler forms of torment and control: the politicians who gave the jobs always wished to make their power felt. There were twenty-four grades of public employee. Most people started at Grade Six; only people put on the post office rolls started, for some reason, at a lower grade. Thereafter you worked your way up. But since no one did anything there was no way of measuring merit. It all depended on the politicians. They had to be kept sweet. You could keep them sweet by daubing their names on walls or—going far out of town—on rock-faces or tree trunks; you showed yourself energetic in their cause at election time, and generally grateful at other times. If you didn't, if you thought you had got your government job and that was that, then you had to take the consequences.

There was a woman who had been seventeen years in the government service. In that time she had moved only from Grade Six to Grade Nine, and that had happened only because one politician, on taking office, had—like a sovereign decreeing a general pardon to state prisoners— granted a rise of three grades to all government employees. This Grade Nine lady was famous in La Rioja. I was even taken to see her one morning in her office: short and plump, unmarried, but with a full and well-tended head of hair, and perfectly ready to tell her story all over again. As a Grade Nine she got $120 a month. The difference in pay between Grade Six and Grade Eighteen was only about $30. The difference, she said, became important only at Grade Twenty. But still.

There was a Grade Twenty-four lady present while the Grade Nine lady complained. She was thin and small and, though deprived-looking, not at all defensive about her Grade. She had a degree, she said, and in her second job (which perhaps she did in the afternoon) she was a professor. As a Grade Twenty-four she got about $400 a month; but then she looked after her family of sixteen brothers and sisters.

There was a smiling boy in a patterned shirt moving lightly in and out of the room while we talked. I asked about him. He was a special case. He had *entered* at Grade Twelve. How had he done that? Nobody could say; and the boy just smiled, going out of the room and then coming back again, while the others talked of money and politicians and inflation and prices and the Grade Nine lady said she hadn't been to a restaurant. They were not allowed to leave their offices; they were as people hemmed in by an invisible fence: confined and complaining, but timid, like a group of shades waiting for religious burial in a Virgilian netherworld.

At dusk, after the heat, the tedium of the day exploded: on unsilenced motorbikes the young men and their girls rode round and round in the streets off the main square in a blue-brown smoke haze, like people now accustomed to doing nothing.

ARGENTINA has consumed the people whom it has attracted; and the last twenty years have been particularly hard.

Jorge, an Anglo-Argentine, who worked as economic adviser to a large company, had said in 1972, "We could be on the verge of a real crisis." Inflation, running on an average at 25 per cent since the Perón years of the 1940s, had risen in that year to 60 per cent; and the colonial agricultural economy of the country hadn't really been altered. There was an industrial sector, but it ate up imports, which had to be paid for by agricultural exports.

Jorge said, "Perón precipitated this vicious circle. He didn't start basic industries. He had to be popular, so he did the light stuff, and distorted the economy further. Industrialization was an emotional response; there was no industrial policy." Argentine industrial goods were protected; they cost twice as much as equivalent goods abroad; and the average wage in 1972 was $50 a month. Perón had done much for the workers, but their wages could never keep up with the inflation that Perón's policies, and policies like Perón's, had produced.

The year before, Jorge had bought a flat. Prices were rising so fast that a week's indecision had cost him $200—his salary at that time was $400 a month. But already—less than a year later—his flat had appreciated 80 per cent. Nineteen years on, in 1991, that purchase seemed an even better bargain.

"I bought it with a twelve-year mortgage from the bank. A fixed price, the only variable thing being the interest payable on the balance. As from 1973, when John Sunday came back"—John Sunday: the Anglo-Argentine translation of Perón's given names, Juan Domingo—

"inflation rose even higher, and eroded the debt. So who paid? The rest of the community, the people who were not in debt. The terrible thing is that for the last forty-five years inflation has been growing steadily, month by month, with oscillations. Very few countries have been able to withstand this sort of inflation *over such a long time*. This is like the German experience of the twenties in slow motion.

"Things got really out of hand in 1974, after John Sunday's death, when his widow Isabelita and her astrologer–witch doctor took over. An ex-corporal in the police. There was a sudden burst of inflation. I remember this: I had paid down for a suit—say $200 in pesos—and the tailor had taken my measurement. Such was the convulsion at the time, the peso lost half its value in a month. I didn't feel I could hold the tailor to his price. And he preferred to forget about it. When we met we never talked about the suit. The stillborn suit: it was too embarrassing. He still owes me a suit—in today's currency it would be about ten cents.

"One of the curious things about Argentina's decline and fall—a decline without reaching the heights—is that much of the decline happened during the democratic period. The acceleration of the decline coincided with a return to democracy in 1983, after the Falklands. The irony is that both of the big parties, the Peronists, the Radicals, want to outdo one another in distributionism, and there is no longer John Bull or Uncle Sam to put in the pound sterling or the dollar.

"Things worked under the British, if you assume that we were informal members of the British empire. In 1917 our GNP was about three-quarters of the United States's. We had the markets, we had the productivity. We had the methods—the systems, the technology. Today we have none of these things.

"You must always remember in Argentina that you're only seeing the survivors. All the others are on Boot Hill or in mental homes. Inflation keeps you on your toes.

"Our company is in an industry where we can let you have only about four or five days' credit. Otherwise, with the kind of inflation we have, working capital gets murdered. In our company at any time we have out about twelve million dollars' working capital as credit to wholesalers. You want to keep that money turning over quick. If you can reduce the credit period by half a day, that's important. Companies that have a slower turnover, like consumer durables—they probably have to give sixty days' credit. If you're building a ship, you have to give a lot of credit, and you may sell only one ship a year. So you're really up shit creek, as the Americans say.

"Another negative aspect of inflation is that you cease to worry about productivity and even technology. Now, that is the secret of all progress: productivity. But you really can get no more than 3 or 4 per cent per annum improvement in productivity anywhere in the world. With inflation like ours you can get 10 per cent *in one day,* if you know when and where to invest. In our business we have on average to pay the government taxes every fifteen days. So in those fifteen days we have to invest that money as wisely as we can. It is much more important to protect your working capital than to think about long-term things like technology and productivity—though you try to do both.

"So capital investment in Argentina is not even covering capital wear and tear. In short, when the current plant reaches the end of its working life there won't be a provision built up to purchase new capital equipment. This is the inevitable result of inflation, which is the monetary disease. Your money is disintegrating. It's like a cancer. You live day by day. That's all you can do when you have inflation of more than 1 per cent a day. You cease to plan. You're just happy to make it to the weekend. And then I stay in my flat in Belgrano and read about ancient cricket matches.

"We are now 25 per cent poorer on a per capita basis than we were in 1975. The people who are really suffering are the people you won't see— the poor, the old, the young. These people get washed up at the big railway termini that curiously resemble Victoria and Paddington stations, because they were built by the British. The flotsam and jetsam of Argentine life—like spray from the sea, these people. I've never seen such signs of poverty in B.A."

WHAT JORGE said about industry and business was also true of agriculture: you had to remember you were seeing only the survivors. In Argentina they were either very big or very dedicated.

The Indian land had encouraged an immense greed in the four hundred families who came to possess it. And then, just sixty years after the Conquest of the Desert, Perón had appeared, driven by that same idea of the limitless wealth of the land, to plunder and to punish. At that time the big landowners were livestock farmers. Tenant farmers did the crop rotation, renting the land for short periods; in between, the land was put back to alfalfa, for grazing. Perón, when he came in, froze the rents of the farmers. This was when Susana's family, finding that their taxes were higher than their rents, panicked and sold. The people who held on endured some hard years. Foreign trade was nationalized; commodity prices were fixed by the state trade monopoly. The state looked for profit; it needed foreign exchange. So people had to sell at under world prices and sometimes under the cost of production. Agricultural production fell. In 1951 Argentina's exports, which were mainly agricultural, were less than they had been in 1901. Argentina's foreign reserves had been squandered on the nationalization of the railways and other utilities; and its imports now increased, to support such industrialization as had been got going. These imports could only be paid for by agriculture, in which people had ceased to invest. So the inflation began, ensuring that the land could never be worked by the small farmer.

Julio farmed three thousand acres. He was not of one of the old landowning families. He had turned late to agriculture, and was a dedicated man. In the 1960s he took over an estate which—from being prosperous and go-ahead during the war, and among the first in Argentina to use tractors—had fallen into ruin in the Perón time. Julio got a loan from a state bank. Of course, the manager made him wait, made him come back a few times, asked for plans, statements; and the clerks drank coffee and maté and looked straight through him and then invariably told him to go and see somebody else.

"We were lucky. We started all this on credit. We couldn't have done it otherwise. We got in at the very last stage when credit was subsidized: the interest rate was less than the inflation rate. The bank manager knew very well he was doing us a favour."

The inflation that worked for Julio at the start then became the tiger he had to ride.

"To survive, you have to do things that are unethical, strictly speaking. You have to be slow to pay your bills. Though now that all the bills are in dollars, you get no gain out of being late. You have to be diversified. And you have to be flexible. Under high inflation you start doing a lot of barter deals. You tend to leave the money economy. Say, I did a deal with wheat—getting fuel and fertilizer in return. You work out that you have to give four kilos of wheat for every kilo of fertilizer. We spend a lot of time now working on these things. It's a tricky business. You don't want to lose. It's important to be in a group with an adviser who would advise you on these barter deals.

"With reasonable inflation we get paid on time, and there's no problem. It's helped us a lot that our main product is milk. With milk we are reasonably protected. It's paid for like this: sixty per cent on a weekly basis, and forty per cent at the end of the following month. But once you get into hyper-inflation you're in real trouble. In 1989, near the end of the Alfonsín government, we had a hundred per cent inflation a month for four months, and we were being paid monthly for the milk—in short, we were getting practically nothing. Of course the same thing applied to the bills we had to pay, but the loss was still there. That's something you can't cope with. With milk you have to sell every day. If you are producing cattle or crops you can keep them in stock to sell on a cash basis.

"Alfonsín was doing nothing about hyper-inflation. He was just waiting for the new president, Menem, to take over. And Menem had been elected on a populist platform—which always means wage increases for everybody.

"At this time the company we were selling our milk to went into receivership. That meant that we weren't paid for the milk we had supplied for six weeks. From that stage on we asked to be paid on a weekly basis. And—even with the money we had lost—we did better than colleagues of ours who had always been paid, but on the old monthly basis. Because in hyper-inflation what matters is when you're paid.

"I was really worried that time. That was the only time. Once for ten days the banks were closed. Everyone wanted to take out his money to spend it."

WITH INFLATION like this everyone becomes a gambler, everyone lives on his nerves. And even people who win in some ways can feel exhausted and damaged, like Gui, now over sixty, who, starting with no capital, and acting at every stage out of desperation, managed over ten years to turn a $5,000 gratuity into a $140,000 apartment.

In the 1960s rents were rising; Gui and his family moved five times, each time moving down. He decided to buy. He found a little $15,000 house in a suburb which he thought he could afford. But the company he worked for didn't think so. They refused to give him a housing loan. Instead they offered him a gratuity if he left the firm. Gui was already committed to buying the house. So he left the company and took the gratuity—$5,000; borrowed a certain amount from his brother—$2,500; and with his brother's help got a four-year loan from a bank for $7,500.

"Normally, at that time, a loan like that had to be repaid in instalments over two years—which is no credit at all. Anyway. There we were. We had a house. It was a dreadful little house, and we were all ashamed of it. It was in one of those B.A. areas where literally in a space of a hundred yards you move from the nice area to the poor area, with people sitting out on the pavement in their pyjamas at night. We were in the poorer area.

"And then we had a bit of luck. The bank we had borrowed the money from failed. That's typical, in a way: a kind of Argentine windfall. So we didn't have to pay back the $7,500 we had borrowed from the bank—though my brother got stuck for $150,000.

"We decided to leave the horrible little house. We rented a flat in a good area, and rented the house out—badly, to a person who turned out to be poor and couldn't keep on paying the indexed rent. I should tell you also here that the district where the house was was famous for its bad administration. They would send you all the tax demands late, deliberately, so you had to pay a surcharge as well. That's also typical of the Argentine. And you would stand all day in a queue a block long to pay.

"That was why we decided to sell the house. And then we had an even bigger piece of luck. In 1978–79 in Argentina we had a period of 'sweet money,' *plata dulce,* easy money, when you could get thirty per cent a month on Argentine money, and the dollar became worth nothing. The factory car parks were full of workers' cars, and people were travelling to Miami and coming back with trolleys of electronic appliances. Land values skyrocketed, and we sold the little house for $65,000, more than four times what we had paid for it—and you must remember that half the original price we didn't even pay because of the bank crash.

"And then we thought we were caught. You couldn't get anything in B.A. for $100,000—at that price they were laughing in your face and you were looking at two-bedroom flats with a refrigerator hanging on a bedroom wall because there wasn't room in the kitchenette. My wife's family's house was on sale at $1,800,000.

"We had to invest our money. We invested it in Argentine money, to get the thirty per cent a month. You couldn't get a better rate anywhere in the world, and money was flooding in from abroad. The thing was to take your interest and get your money back into hard currency before the situation blew. I tell you, you were living on your nerves every minute. Every minute you were wondering whether you were doing the right thing—because at the first little whiff of insecurity or danger all that foreign money was going to leave. Within days the whole thing could blow, and you were running in to change money all the time.

"We timed it right. We got back into dollars ahead of the crash, which came in January or February 1981, when there was a ten per cent devaluation of Argentine money, followed a month later by a further twenty per cent. The whole thing just collapsed then. People who had borrowed to re-equip their factories lost fortunes.

"We invested our dollars and got a little more, and then we proceeded to lose a certain amount of what we had gained: our bank manager invested a third of our money in gold. We bought at $800, and got out at $680 an ounce. Still, at the end we had enough to buy this desirable flat in one of the best parts of the city. We bought in August 1982, when just for three weeks—because of the Malvinas war—prices were at their lowest for twenty years. At the end of those three weeks the prices rose again by more than sixty per cent. If we had delayed we wouldn't have been able to buy.

"In a place like Argentina you make money only by being lucky. There's always a crisis in one direction or other. What happens is that you have no sense of the future. You don't do anything for the future. The European idea of securing your future doesn't exist. I often wonder how I've adapted to this sort of thing. The other thing is the sensation you have all the time of being robbed, if you're an employee. If you don't have to go through that experience, and you can live in your own area of happiness, shall we say, it can be a delightful place to live in. And this, I suppose, is what lulls everybody."

IN 1972 BORGES said he never read the newspapers. "Those things sadden me. They are also trivial." Borges could say that—of the daily acts of guerrilla or police violence, and the manoeuvring of politicians, passing figures, who were far smaller than the moment—because for Borges Argentina was a country he had already lost.

What Borges said then others said now, in different ways. A woman I knew said, "We have become stupider." She had been Peronist in 1972, full of expectation. Perhaps then or a little later she had also been "Marxist," buoyant with her simplicities, ready to preach them. Now she had forgotten she had been either of those things, and—in the general enervation—was nothing; there were no political systems left to try. Women like her were turning now to "meditation"—every day the newspaper listed lectures and sessions.

Ricardo, who had known the guerrilla leaders at school and had felt some sympathy for the cause, grieved for that educated, destroyed generation. Those many thousands of New Men (and women), in whom religion and revolution had met, were the grandchildren of immigrants; they would now have been in their forties. As we were walking back after our meeting with the former guerrilla (who had presented himself as a defeated man), Ricardo said, with sadness, "Maybe we have to accept the idea that this country is not viable. The young people I meet take it for granted that Argentina will become a nation in the near future, and that might lead them to new adventures and false conclusions."

Ricardo was talking, like Borges, out of his own grief, out of his own need for philosophical systems, his now outdated ideas of revolution and right action. Those ideas had gone with the Trojan ending Borges had prophesied; and in their place, out of the very enervation and fatigue of that ending, new and simpler ways of thinking had come to Argentina.

A businessman I met listed these new ways of thinking. Argentina no longer believed in the foreign enemy; no longer believed it was a European country; and had lost the idea of the limitless wealth of the land.

The three ideas were linked: together, they added up to an intellectual revolution. That idea of wealth—it had been part of the folk wisdom of the country. My 1972 notebooks are full of it. "This country can never sink." "Still, you live better here." "God undoes at night the mess the Argentines create by day." That idea of wealth had come down from the Spanish time, and had been born again with the Conquest of the Desert. It had encouraged the great greed of the *estancieros,* who thought of the wealth of the country in the Spanish way, as something indivisible, which had to be denied to as many people as possible. This had in its turn encouraged the greed and plunder of Perón and his successors, and the claims of their supporters. It had destroyed the idea of the pioneer, the idea of self-fulfilment coming through work; it ennobled instead the idea of sharpness, *la viveza criolla.* It had encouraged the idea of blood and revolution, in unending sequence: just one more fresh start, the finding out and killing of just one more enemy, and the wealth of the country was going to cascade down.

All that had now gone. To continue, people would have to enter into a new contract with the land. This implied a new contract with other people, a new kind of political life. Argentina had made people dream too much, Ricardo had said; and now the country wasn't viable. But this kind of despair was as much of an abstraction as Father Mujica's revolutionary wish to undo the enemies of the people and develop the human spirit. In Argentina people needed simpler gestures, a simpler morality.

Together with news about the government's attempt to stabilize the currency, gossip about the new president's family life, and conjecture about why the embalmed body of Perón had had its hands cut off, there were reports about the weekly March of Silence, *la marcha del silencio*, in the northern town of Catamarca. Catamarca, warlord country in the early nineteenth century, and now very poor, was controlled by a single powerful family. A young woman had been murdered in Catamarca. Local people were outraged by the way in which the matter had been hushed up; and in that town, where there had been an authoritarian tradition since the Spanish time, and where now most people (of the twenty-four grades) depended for their livelihood on the patronage of their local rulers, there had started this weekly protest March of Silence, led by a nun. The number of the marchers had grown; the effect had been overwhelming; the federal government had had to intervene. The powerful governor had resigned; someone else had gone to jail. Then the marches had stopped; the nun had returned to her convent. Father Mujica and the guerrillas, in their own eyes New Men confronting injustice, had never done anything as brave, or made a profounder political and moral point. Perhaps no such gesture had been made here since the Spanish conquest.

Catamarca was a late-seventeenth-century foundation. It was on the site of an older Andean settlement which the Spaniards had attempted in the early 1550's, just twenty years after the conquest of Peru. This first town or settlement had been destroyed very soon afterwards by the local people, not yet abject. Its Spanish name—in honour of the marriage (1554–58) of Philip II of Spain to Mary Stuart—was Londres de la Nueva Inglaterra, London of New England.

The Air-Conditioned Bubble:
The Republicans in Dallas

EVERY session of the Republican Convention opened with an invocation (after the presentation of the flag and the singing of the anthem), and closed with a benediction. A different man of God was called upon on each occasion. The benediction at the very end, after the acceptance speech by Mr. Reagan, was spoken by Dr. W. A. Criswell.

Dr. Criswell is the pastor of the First Baptist Church of Dallas, and in Dallas he is famous, not only because he is a powerful preacher, but also because his church and church buildings, which are in a cluster in downtown Dallas, are now—with the boom—valued at $200 million. Money is revered everywhere but in Dallas it is holy; and something like grace—a reward for faith in God's land—attaches to real-estate success. Every day in Dallas (since journalists are obedient people, and also want to do what other journalists do) I read an article about, or an interview with, Trammell Crow, the local real-estate king, who has built many of the glass skyscrapers and hotels. Again and again I read that Trammell Crow was worth about a billion dollars. Dr. Criswell wasn't in that class, but—offering benediction to the Republicans where Trammell Crow could offer only welcome and money—he trailed his own double glory.

On the Sunday after the convention, when most of the delegates and press had gone away, and the congregation was nearly pure Dallas again, Dr. Criswell preached on "The White Throne Judgement." The title of his sermon was displayed in movable letters—like the title of a film or play—outside his redbrick auditorium. The auditorium—big, square, plain except for the coloured glass—was packed.

People like myself, arriving late, or without reserved places, stood at the back. The time came when we all had to kneel; and it was hard for me then, kneeling with the others, heads bowed in prayer all around me, to continue making notes on my own Sheraton-Dallas Hotel bed-side pad.

The choir wore dark red gowns. Dr. Criswell, like Mrs. Reagan at her first appearance in the convention hall, wore white or cream or a very pale colour. The colour contrast would have helped the television picture. There was a television camera in the aisle between the pews of Dr. Criswell's church. The service was being televised live, and a note in the program sheet (which also contained a "decision card") said that video cassettes of the service could be obtained from the "Communications Department" of the church.

DR. CRISWELL, working up to his Judgement theme, spoke of homosexuality. His language was direct. No euphemisms; no irony; no humor. He was earnest from beginning to end. He moved about on the platform and sometimes for a second or so he turned (in his white suit) to face his red-gowned choir.

"In our lifetime we are scoffing at the word of God . . . and opening up society and culture to the lesbian and sodomite and homosexual . . . and now we have this disastrous judgement . . . the disease and sin of AIDS . . ."

AIDS, on the first Sunday after the Republican Convention, and in that voice of thunder! But if you thought about it the topic wasn't so unsuitable. There was something oddly Biblical (though Dr. Criswell didn't make this particular point) about AIDS, which struck down buggers and a special kind of black and spared everybody else.

"God is like his LAWS!" Dr. Criswell thundered. "There are laws everywhere. Laws of fire, laws of gravity."

From this idea of Judgement and the laws (two distinct senses of "laws" run together) Dr. Criswell moved on to Karl Marx. A bugger? Only metaphorically. Karl Marx had his place in this sermon as a nineteenth-century atheist. Dr. Criswell gave Marx's dates but said little about the heresies: in this auditorium Karl Marx was just his demonic name, and it was enough. Karl Marx wasn't dead, Dr. Criswell said (or so I understood him to say: the theology was a little difficult for me). Karl Marx was still alive; Karl Marx would die only on the great Judgement Day.

"The great Judgement Day comes at the end of time, history, civilization . . . The whole universe shall be turned to conflagration . . . The caverns beneath this earth, the whole thing, shall be turned to dreadful fire and fury when the Lord cleanses this earth and purges this earth . . . when God comes to the end of the world."

A wonderful cosmic idea, God coming to the end of the world: barely imaginable. But even less imaginable was the idea that many of the people in the auditorium were to be saved in some way from the cosmic nothingness; and that it was open to anyone to be saved. You could make a start by filling in the decision card in the programme sheet; and, as in a hotel breakfast card where you put a tick beside the chosen hour of your breakfast service, so on the decision card you could put a tick beside the hour of the service that had awakened you. So commonplace and everyday was the idea of religious salvation and decision here.

MANY PEOPLE, like myself, had come only for the Criswell sermon. We didn't wait for the hymn or the reception of new members.

To leave the air-conditioned auditorium and go outside was to appreciate anew the extent of the church's properties, many of them named after Dr. Criswell. It was also—though the shadows of tall buildings made the street look cool—to be reminded of the one-hundred-degree heat of Dallas.

Most of the time you were protected from the heat, and were aware of it only as a quality of the light or in the colour of the sky. But from time to time the heat came upon you like this, a passing sensation, not unpleasant, a contrast with the general air-conditioning, a reminder of the bubble in which you lived.

Dallas was air-conditioned—hotels, shops, houses, cars. The convention center was more than air-conditioned; it was positively cool, more than thirty degrees cooler than the temperature outside. Air-conditioned Dallas seemed to me a stupendous achievement, the product of a large vision, American in the best and most humane way: money and applied science creating an elegant city where life had previously been brutish.

Yet in this city created by high science Dr. Criswell preached of hell-fire and was a figure. And the message of convention week was that there was no contradiction, that American endeavour and success were contained within old American faith and pieties. Karl Marx and homosexuality were on the other side of these pieties and could be lumped together.

The fundamentalism that the Republicans had embraced went beyond religion. It simplified the world in general; it rolled together many different kinds of anxieties—schools, drugs, race, buggery, Russia, to give just a few; and it offered the simplest, the vaguest solution: Americanism, the assertion of the American self. Practical matters were in the party's printed platform and remained locked up there. Apart from Jeanne Kirkpatrick's speech about foreign affairs, there had been very little of purely political discussion. Americanism had been the theme of the convention, now defiant, now sentimental, as in Mr. Reagan's acceptance speech. Fundamentalism, in its Republican political interpretation, was not just a grim business; it was as stylish as Mr. Reagan himself. The Republicans were "pro-life." That meant anti-abortion; but during the week another, metaphorical, meaning began to be attached to the word. To be pro-life was to be vigorous, joyful, and optimistic; it was to turn away from the gloom and misery of the other side, who talked of problems and taxes.

Not all the Republicans at the convention were Christian. There was an Asian group. There are said to be twenty thousand Asian Indians in the Dallas–Fort Worth area; and the Hindu interpretation of Americanism and Republicanism, as recorded in the Asian-American caucus booklet, was illuminating of both immigrants and hosts.

Indians immigrated to the U.S.A. to pursue their "dream": achieve fully their potentials in this land of "Opportunities." They came in pursuit of their dreams, visions, happiness and to achieve excellence. . . . During the last few years most of the people have changed from "Green card holder" status to that of "citizens," thus enabling themselves to be full participants in socioeconomic and political processes. They have chosen, by their free will, the U.S.A. as the *karmabhumi*—the land of *karma* or action.

Texas as the theatre of *karma*—what would Trammell Crow have made of that? But it was, really, no more than a Hindu version of Dr. Criswell's fundamentalism, and in this Hindu version certain things could be seen fresh. To embrace one's economic opportunity and good fortune was more than a political act; it was also an act of religion, the embracing of one's *karma*. Religion, as a political attitude, in this setting, could be a form of self-love, and applauded.

A REPORTER, one of the many thousands present, said to me: "A convention is like a smorgasbord." There were any number of events outside the convention hall. The press office, the Media Operations Center, issued a calendar every day, four pages listing about fifty events—press conferences, delegate meetings, breakfasts, lunches, parties, distinguished names, fashionable names, crankish organizations, special-interest groups, all competing for attention. On the first morning, for instance, what was the best thing to do? Wasn't there talk of a magazine-sponsored tour of smart Dallas houses? Or was one to go to the convention center and go through the security there, to hear Miss Texas sing the national anthem and to listen to an address by the overworked Trammell Crow? Or—and this was right in my own Sheraton-Dallas Hotel:

> 11:00 a.m. Press conference, Richard Viguerie and Howard Phillips, Populist Conservative Tax Coalition. Subject: "Are Liberals Soft on Communism?" Guest speaker: Eldridge Cleaver, former Black Panther.

Eldridge Cleaver! One of the famous names of the late 1960s: the self-confessed rapist of white women, the man who had spent years in jail, the Black Muslim, the author of *Soul on Ice* (1968), not really a book, more an assemblage of jottings, but a work of extraordinary violence, answering the mood of that time. In 1969, when for a few weeks I had been in the United States, I had heard it said of Cleaver that he was going to die one day in a shoot-out with the FBI. That hadn't happened. Cleaver had found asylum in Algeria and then in France; he had become homesick there and had returned, a born-again Christian, to the United States.

In Paris earlier this year I had met a man who had made an important film about Cleaver during the revolutionary days of the late 1960s. The film man now regarded that time, which had its glory, as a time of delusion. And now Cleaver himself was part of a side-show—or so I thought of it—at the Republican convention.

It seemed a big comedown. And it was even sadder, when I got to the conference room, to find that there was no crowd; that Cleaver was not the most important person there, that he was sitting on the far right of the second row, that some people didn't seem to know who he was; that the few journalists asking questions were more interested in the other people of the Populist Conservative Tax Coalition.

So ordinary now, so safe, this black man for whom a revolutionary's desperate death had been prophesied. I had known him only from his younger photographs. He was now forty-nine and almost bald; what hair he had was grey. There was something Chinese, placid, about his eyes and cheekbones; he looked very patient. His eyebrows were thin, like pencilled arcs, and his hooded eyes were quiet.

The speaker at the lectern was winding up on the theme of liberals. "They're not soft on communism . . . They've been softened up by communism." The speaker was a big man in a dark blue suit; there was a suggestion of flabbiness, loose flesh, below the waist. The lectern was stamped "Sheraton-Dallas Hotel & Towers," in case someone took a photograph: everyone, after all, had something to sell. To the speaker's right was a US flag, hanging down from a pole; beside that was a portable film screen.

Then the speaker asked for some words from a colleague—a former CIA man, of small stature, who more or less repeated what had been said before—and from "Eldridge." And at last Cleaver stood up. He was tall beside the CIA man. He was paunchy now, even a little soft-bellied. His blue shirt had a white collar and his dark red tie hung down long. The touch of style was reassuring.

Somebody asked about his political ambitions. He said he wanted to get on the Berkeley city council. And then, inevitably, someone asked about his attitude to welfare. His reply was tired; he gave the impression of having spoken the words many times before. "I'm passionately opposed to the welfare system because it's made people a parasitic dependency on the federal system . . . I want to see black people plugged into the economic system . . . Welfare is a stepping-stone to socialism because it teaches people the government is going to solve our problems."

That was more or less it. It seemed to be all that was required of "Eldridge," that statement about socialism and welfare. And soon the session was declared closed. A repeat began to be prepared. As in a fair, shows were done over and over again, and in between business was drummed up.

THE FILM *Whose Side Are You On?* started once more, on the screen next to the flag. It was a film about American post-war decline and muddle: a modern voice over old newsreel footage from 1945: MacArthur,

Shigemitsu, the Japanese surrender. Away from the dark corner, Cleaver, placid, grey-haired, leaned against a wall. Two or three journalists went to him. But the very simplicity of the man on display made the journalists ask only the obvious questions, questions that had already been asked.

There was a many-layered personality there. But that personality couldn't be unravelled now, with simple questions in a formal public gathering. To find that man, it was necessary to go to his book, the book of 1968, *Soul on Ice*. And there—in a book more moving and richer than I had remembered—that many-layered man was: with his abiding feeling for religion and his concern with salvation (as a Roman Catholic, then as a Black Muslim, then as a revolutionary); his need for community constantly leading him to simple solutions; his awareness of his changing self; his political shrewdness.

I was very familiar with the Eldridge who came to prison, but that Eldridge no longer exists. And the one I am now is in some ways a stranger to me. You may find this difficult to understand but it is very easy for one in prison to lose his sense of self. And if he has been undergoing all kinds of extreme, involved, and unregulated changes, then he ends up not knowing who he is . . .

In this land of dichotomies and disunited opposites, those truly concerned with the resurrection of black Americans have had eternally to deal with black intellectuals who have become their own opposites . . .

In a sense, both the new left and the new right are the spawn of the Negro revolution. A broad national consensus was developed over the civil rights struggle, and it had the sophistication and morality to repudiate the right wing. This consensus, which stands between a violent nation and chaos, is America's most precious possession. But there are those who despise it.

The task which the new right has feverishly undertaken is to erode and break up this consensus, something that is a distinct possibility since the precise issues and conditions which gave birth to the consensus no longer exist.

The "new right" of 1968 had become the New Right of 1984, to which Cleaver belonged. Of this New Right I knew nothing until I got to Dallas; and what I learned was bewildering. The New Right seemed to be as much a creation of modern technology as air-conditioned Dallas was; and the creator, Richard Viguerie, seemed to be as extraordinary and big-visioned a Texan as Trammell Crow.

VIGUERIE was in the business of raising money by direct mail. He served a number of conservative clients—Conservative Books for Christian Leaders, No Amnesty for Deserters, the National Rifle Association (Frances FitzGerald gave this client sample in *The New York Review* of November 19, 1981). Then it occurred to him that people who contributed to one narrow or quaint conservative cause might be encouraged to contribute to other conservative causes, might be presented in the end with a larger and more satisfying conservatism. He used his mailing lists and computer and his flair; he discovered, and his computer could name, the conservative core of the country. And just as oil can be made to gush from the minute porosities of rock or even heavy green Texan marble, so, at Viguerie's bidding, money gushed from the conservative American bedrock. He raised millions. He was in demand; he was a man politicians had to court.

Viguerie was the star of the press conference ("Are Liberals Soft on Communism?") in the Sheraton-Dallas room. It was Viguerie, rather than Cleaver, whom the journalists wanted to see and hear. But I did not know his glory. I came away only with my mental picture of Cleaver and a copy of the *Conservative Digest* for June 1984. This was Viguerie's paper. I found no substance in it. It was like a missionary magazine; it repeated and repeated a single idea, and was tedious (and intellectually embarrassing) for that reason. And in that paper the name of Viguerie seemed at least as important as the conservative message.

It was hard, in fact, to avoid the name. The name was given as the publisher; the magazine was "a publication of Viguerie Communications, a division of the Viguerie Company, Richard A. Viguerie, President." The verso of the front cover advertised—with a photograph—"A Daily Radio Commentary featuring Richard A. Viguerie," and Viguerie's name was mentioned seven times. In the body of the paper itself there was a two-page article by Richard Viguerie as well as a two-page letter from the publisher, Richard Viguerie; and the back cover advertised a book by Richard Viguerie predicting a revolution against "the elite establishment" and prophesying a new "populist" party. One advertised theme of the book, *The Establishment vs. the People*, was "How to take liberal rhetoric and merge it with conservative ideas."

That, I suppose, was where Eldridge came in.

Y O U   C O U L D get a "press kit"—with a story or stories already written up—about almost everything at the convention: about the Southwestern Bell Mobile telephone systems; about the AT&T operations ("more than 60 miles of cable and more than 5,000 telephones within the 2 million square feet of the convention center to meet the voice and data needs of the 4,470 delegates and alternates, 10–15,000 guests and 13,000 journalists"); and even about Morrow's Nut House ("since 1866"), suppliers of a "shuttle mix" of nuts and dried fruit to the delegates, a "shuttle" mix because it had been previously supplied to astronauts on the space shuttle.

On the Saturday before the convention opened, no less a person than Carol Morrow, vice-president of Morrow's Nut House ("over 260 nationwide outlets"), was pushing a trolley with the shuttle mix (and the press kits) somewhere near the press entrance. It was extraordinary—so casual the meeting, so grand the lady. It was like running into the owner of Dunkin' Donuts (if such a person does exist) carrying sample bags of his doughnuts.

The man who gave me my accreditation cards (to be hung around the neck: everybody in the convention hall and press areas had things around their necks) said, in response to an inquiry, "Upstairs there's more information than you can carry away." And indeed, in the Media Operations Center there must have been tons of paper on narrow long tables: biographies about everybody who was anybody, stories about everything, and, starting on the Monday, copies of convention speeches that hadn't yet been delivered. On the television monitors you could see what was going on in the convention hall itself: there was no need to witness the actual event. The energetic reporter, with his ready-written information and the AT&T facilities, could telephone back stories to his paper all day.

But neither photographs nor television screen could give a true feel of the convention hall. The scale was staggering. The deep crisscrossings of the steel girders of the ceiling made me think of the iron-framed railway stations of London, Paddington and Waterloo (and somewhere in Dallas, beside a highway, someone was building a replica of the 1851 Crystal Palace). But the scale was too big: I couldn't trust my sense of size.

The figure on the podium was small. But above the podium, and at the back of the hall, was a big screen; and on this screen there was a cropped or partial image (head and shoulders, perhaps), many times larger than life, of the figure on the podium. Smaller screens attached to the steel girders of the ceiling frame multiplied this image; loudspeakers amplified the voice. To enter the hall for the first time was to have one's sense of actuality unsettled; it was to be in the middle of a scene replicating and magnifying itself, making itself very important: as though here time, the passing moment, could be stretched.

The invocation was being spoken by a rabbi; and the piety seemed correct. The occasion, with its magnification of man, had a feel of religion. Not religion as contemplation or a private experience of divinity; but religion as the essence of a culture, the binding, brotherhood-transcending material need. That, rather than political debate, was what people had come to Dallas for. The scale and the mood, and the surreal setting, made me think of a Muslim missionary gathering I had seen five years before in a vast canopied settlement of bamboo and cotton in the Pakistan Punjab. And I felt it would not have been surprising, in Dallas, to see busy, pious helpers going around giving out sweets or some kind of symbolic sacramental food.

TELEVISION by itself wasn't true to the occasion. But when you were in the hall it was necessary to look, as it were, at the movie, because a certain amount of what was going on went on only on the screen. Jeanne Kirkpatrick's speech was preceded by a short film about Jeanne Kirkpatrick. Mr. Reagan himself, in this film, introduced her to us as a woman of the stature of Golda Meir and Mrs. Thatcher. And that feminist angle was not unexpected: the press had been reporting, dutifully, that the Republicans intended to do something that evening about the "gender gap."

The film ended; the live band played; the delegates shouted and applauded. The applause was rhythmical and ecstatic, as at a revivalist gathering. The placards—WE MEAN JEANNE, WE LOVE JEANNE, painted

by volunteers and placed by other volunteers on the floor, below the delegates' seats—were hoisted and jigged about for the television cameras:
the confusing interplay continuing between film and actuality, the experienced real occasion and its magnified film record.

The text of the speech was available; but the Kirkpatrick speech was
considerably more than the text. It was delivered by someone with a feeling for language; it was the only speech at the convention which, even
with its simplifications, permitted one to see a real intelligence, a more
than political intelligence, at work. Its theme was the need for firmness
with the Russians and their allies. This was wickedly knitted into a taunt-
ing of Americans of the other party: "But then, they always blame
America first"—a refrain which, as it was repeated, acquired the effec-
tiveness (as well as the rhythms) of Mark Antony's "But Brutus is an
honourable man." The speech was rapturously received; a wonderful
photograph the next day in the *New York Times* showed Mrs. Kirkpatrick
radiant and uplifted in her moment of success.

AFTER that it was downhill all the way in the convention hall. A famous
black football player came on and introduced some Olympic athletes.
This was not in the official order of business; it was an afterthought; the
player was introduced with a reference to his great height (6′5″) and his
corresponding weight (which I failed to note). After that came the politicians, famous names. But they all—in spite of the music and the applause
and the placards—seemed to make the same speech, in the same tone,
and in the same dead words.

Howard Baker: The Carter-Mondale team gave us double-digit
inflation; 21-per cent interest rates; a punching bag for a foreign
policy, and the misery index.

Katherine Ortega: Think how far we have come since the Carter-
Mondale years of double-digit inflation, 21-per cent interest rates,
and economic misery.

Margaret Heckler: We are now at a great crossroads. We have a
choice between stagnation and growth, a choice between the rhetoric of promise and the record of accomplishment.

Baker: America's choice this year is not just between Ronald Reagan and Walter Mondale. It's between a team that has proven it can succeed, and a team that has proven it can't.

Heckler: It is an easy choice for me to make. In Ronald Reagan I see the special American spirit under God that drew my Irish parents to these shores.

Ortega: My fellow Americans, on the minted dollar of the United States is the face of Liberty, the profile of the woman of that great statue whose centennial we celebrate in 1986, the mid-term year of the second Reagan administration.

Perhaps, the occasion being what it was—celebratory, tribal-religious—it didn't matter what was said. (Just as it is often enough for a Hindu holy man simply to give *darshan*, to offer a sight of himself.) But these speeches, so impersonal, so alike, did little for the speakers. English, like other living literary languages, is constantly enriching itself by internal references. It is hard to use it without being allusive, without knowingly or unknowingly making some reference to a phrase from Shakespeare or the King James Bible or any one of a number of poets or comedians or film-makers or historians or statesmen. In a speech during the war Churchill used a line from the early Victorian poet Clough: "But westward look, the land is bright." Clough was soon lost in Churchill; and the words, now Churchillian and famous, can be used or twisted in many (now perhaps mainly ironical) ways. Even Mrs. Thatcher can make a telling point by adapting the title of a play by Christopher Fry (famous in her youth): "The lady's not for turning."

There was nothing like this in the language of Baker, Heckler, or Ortega. The same speech (or very nearly), the same tone, the same personality (or absence of it), the same language: unallusive, cleansed, sterile; nerveless and dead; computer language, programmed sometimes to rise to passion, but getting no higher than copywriter's glib. As though, at the heart of this great, man-magnifying occasion, there was a hollow, a vacancy.

I heard a little more about the black football player who had appeared on the podium after Mrs. Kirkpatrick. His name was Roosevelt Grier. He was a "television character," a "celebrity character." He had taken up needlework, of all things, after his football. But politically he had been on the other side. I was told that he had been with Robert Kennedy when Robert Kennedy was killed. So his appearance on the Republican podium was sensational; it explained, I thought, the awkwardness with which he had begun.

After the politicians' speeches, I thought I would like to look at the football player's words again. And (not having made notes, having been made lazy by the information facilities) I went afterwards to the Media Operations Center, as to some heaven where everything was recorded.

The girl said with a smile, "What speech?"

There were stacks and stacks (of varying heights) of all the other speeches. But there was nothing about Grier or from him. He had been an afterthought.

I said, "I suppose there'll be a text in the papers tomorrow."

She said, "I doubt it."

And there wasn't—I saw a reference to Grier in one of the Dallas papers, but I found no text of his speech. The journalists, busy and obedient, knew what to leave out.

GERALD FORD, the thirty-eighth president of the United States, was coming to the convention the next day. The newspapers were full of half-admiring, half-curmudgeonly stories about the great sums he was earning at the age of seventy-one, over and above his $100,000 presidential pension. But Mr. Ford was out of favor with the right, and that was why (according to another newspaper story) NCPAC, the National Conservative Political Action Committee, as part of their American Heroes for Reagan project, had chosen that very day for their big fund-raising Texas Gala. The gala, a $1,000-a-plate affair (but media people, if admitted, fed free), was to be at the Circle T ranch of Nelson Bunker Hunt, twenty-nine miles out of Dallas.

Bunker Hunt—how could one resist that name? The man who had tried to corner the silver market; the man who had bought, on an astronomical scale, into soybeans and racehorses; the man who had inherited a billion of his father's oil money and turned it into two; the man whose wealth—like the wealth of his brothers and sister—couldn't really be comprehended.

I had been befriended by Andrew, a young writer from New Jersey.

Andrew had driven down to Dallas in an old car he had bought for $650; and it was in this car, without air-conditioning, that we drove west out of Dallas, at about six-thirty, into a flaming sun, in a highway temperature of over one hundred degrees. We were driving with many others into Dallas's suburban countryside. It wasn't countryside really. The Dallas–Fort Worth airport is one of the biggest in the world; and regularly, one behind the other, in perhaps two lines, the aeroplanes, trailing black fumes, came down into visibility from the hot ochre sky and their lights suddenly glittered. The highway hissed with commuter traffic; and all around, the sky roared.

Andrew, with his Northerner's excitement, had said that the Hunt ranch had its own exit. That would have been grand indeed. But it wasn't like that; you simply turned left off the highway, a traffic policeman staying traffic in the opposing lane. The grass was bright green, surprising in the heat; the post-and-rail fence was painted white. Just inside were the first helpers (and the first line of security men): young men in black trousers and white shirts, and some with black or white baseball caps.

In the distance there was a big white tent. Towards that we drove. The low, regularly spaced trees suggested a fruit farm rather than a landscaped park. We stopped not far from the tent and got out of the car. There was "valet parking" at this gala—at $1,000 a plate there could be no less. Black-trousered, white-shirted young men were taking the visitors' cars to the far-off car park; and they were running back—running, as though that was part of the courtesy.

We were checked. We hung our press passes around our necks; young NCPAC stewards (their own badges of authority, on a kind of sticky paper, fixed to their shirt pockets) eyed us constantly. The gala—what was it? A cowboy on a white horse smiled and smiled at no one in particular and kept on spinning a little lasso, which now rose and now fell. A cowgirl sat astride another horse. "Western" saloon-girls and gunslingers moved among the guests. People sat on a tame longhorn steer and were photographed. There was music and singing from an open tent, country-and-western pieces. There were food stalls with Texan and Mexican food. Out in the open a side of beef was being barbecued, dropping fat into a long black pan on the green grass. There was a stagecoach, in which some people took little rides; it was a reconstruction, the stagecoach, not real, not an antique. Elsewhere, at rest, horseless, there was a covered wagon, apparently old and genuine. And among the gala guests were three or four Indians in full feathered costumes, waiting to be photographed.

WE WERE IN TEXAS, in temperatures and a landscape that awakened admiration for the first settlers. What was the average speed of a stagecoach? Six miles, eight miles? The railway came in the 1870s—did that do fifteen miles an hour? But the West of this gala was not a celebration of the past. It was more like a "production"; and so indeed—according to the inevitable NCPAC press hand-out—it was; it had been mounted by a specialist and immensely successful company (the subject of another very full hand-out). Cinema and television had swallowed up the past; this gala was for people who perhaps liked—as much as westerns—the idea that, as patriots, they liked westerns. And this cinematic version of the West was itself now being filmed for television somewhere: show within show. A red crane with a television camera from time to time unfolded and rose above us all, against a glorious sunset. There were light aeroplanes in the sky: somebody said they might have been gala guests, dropping in.

In the other direction, away from the red crane and the television camera, the gala and the white tent, was the ranch house. It was on a slight rise in the ground and it was surrounded by trees. It looked a modest house. From this modest-looking house Nelson Bunker Hunt and his wife were now coming, preceded by a television crew and onlookers—perhaps more than gala guests, perhaps political associates, perhaps people admitted to social intimacy. The television team—cameraman, soundman, and reporter walking backward, like crabs—imposed measure and stateliness on the procession. And when the people at the gala saw what was happening there was an involuntary gasp, as at the appearance of a saint or royalty. And really, his family, his wealth, and his adventures made Nelson Bunker Hunt a figure of fable; there was no one else quite like him in our world. And here he was, in his own setting, for a cause he considered good and pious, half our host.

It was hard to hear what he was saying to the television reporter. He was speaking softly; he seemed to be chewing up some of his words; I could only catch the word "conservative" two or three times. He seemed to be expressing his pleasure at the spread of the cause.

In the "Self-Portrait" questionnaire he had answered for the *Dallas*

Morning News that day he had given "overeating" as his worst habit (he adored ice cream, apparently); but he was a good deal less fat than the photographs the London papers had printed of him at the time of his silver "caper." He had said that blue was his favorite colour; and now indeed he was wearing a pale blue shirt, with a leather-thong tie, no thicker than a shoelace, but at the top button, instead of a knot, the leather thong somehow supported a silver dollar—a joking allusion, perhaps, to the silver caper. He was half smiling while he spoke. His wife, very small beside him, was smiling all the time; she seemed to be smiling out of pure pleasure at the occasion—the gala, the guests, the cause. She wore a diamond horseshoe brooch—just the one little touch of extravagance, almost like a little joke (matching her husband's silver dollar), and it seemed, with her smile, to be an offering to us, her guests.

And so they moved on with their media train, past the Oklahoman Indian warriors in their bright feathers (Chief Blue Hail and his band), past the reproduction stagecoach and the tame longhorn: Mr. and Mrs. Bunker Hunt, benign and public-spirited in this manifestation, standing for money and luck and oil and the land and work and reward and God and the old-fashioned way, incarnating and appearing to make very simple the complex American virtue that the barbecue and gala were intended to exalt and defend.

The call came to dinner. Bells? Whipcracks? I cannot remember: the call was western, unusual, part of the folk theatre of the expensive occasion. The enormous tent with nearly two thousand people was—incredibly—air-conditioned (with the help of five hundred tons of equipment specially brought in by Mobile Air of Houston, coolers of oil refineries). The 1,700 or so dinners ("designed by Dallas food stylist Dorothy Berry") were deftly served.

THE BENEDICTION was spoken by Jerry Falwell, the fundamentalist Baptist preacher, the religious star of the right, who was to speak the benediction next day at the convention itself, after the introduction of Mrs. Reagan. Earlier in the evening Falwell had sat astride the Texas longhorn for the cameras. Now, with the lights playing on him on the platform in the tent, and with the TV cameras working, he, who had entered into the Americanist spirit of the gala, cast his own religious spirit over the occasion. He addressed God directly: "This evening is dedicated to Thee." Texan whoops followed the "amens." No sacrilege was intended by those whoops. These men, with true humility (the grand humility of the achiever, rather than the worthless humility of the defeated) were putting themselves on the side of God, and striking a blow at all that was ungodly, at all that threatened occasions like this one.

And virtue was its own reward. When Bunker Hunt was given a hand up to the platform it was to announce that the gala had attracted 1,650 paying guests, and not the four hundred or so he and NCPAC had been hoping for in the beginning. After clearing expenses, more than a million dollars had been raised from that tentful of people that evening for NCPAC's American Heroes for Reagan project.

It was a staggering figure. A middle-aged photographer at our press table became very excited. He had no friend or colleague with him, and he needed to talk to someone. He said across the dark table, "I got a picture of Jerry Falwell on the longhorn. I never thought I would get a picture like that. Got a picture of Bunker too. Bunker was walking and he saw a fork on the grass. He *bent down*. He bent down and picked that fork up and put it in his pocket and he said, 'That's the way you save money.' "

A brush with the great, a story that was already a fable.

AND IT WAS IN THAT ATMOSPHERE of success and communal self-congratulation that the NCPAC film "Ronald Reagan's America" was screened. We at our press table saw it back to front. The screen had been put up in front of us, separating us from the million-dollar nobs.

The film opened with shots of John Wayne. It made him a great American figure, a figure of history almost, rather than a mere modern actor. The message was that all Americans who were positive and did jobs and served the land were like Wayne, were heroes. The subliminal message was that Wayne had been reincarnated in Mr. Reagan. The acting career that might have been an embarrassment in Mr. Reagan's early political days now worked to his advantage. Americanism had become the conservative cause; and Americanism was most easily grasped, most ideal, and most sentimental (sentimentality being important to any cause of the right), in comic books ("The Justice Society of America") and the lesser cinema.

. . .

SUCH WEALTH and power; such science and organization, so prodigally used even for the one-night theatre of the Texas Gala. Such glitter, on the drive back to Dallas. But the greater the success and the greater the promise, the more painful the idea that it might all somehow go. And it was of this idea of threat—the other side of conservative sentimentality—that Ed Jenkins spoke the next morning in the NCPAC room at the Sheraton-Dallas Hotel.

Andrew and I went together. We spoke to Ed Jenkins because at that early hour he was the only senior person there. He was immediately warm, open, anxious to help. He left his literature-stacked counter and sat with us at a round table. He even, at my nervous request, turned down the sound of "Ronald Reagan's America"—that film seemed to be running all the time near the front desk, perhaps to draw the crowds in.

Ed Jenkins was thirty-two. He worked full-time for the Conservative Alliance, one of the groups within NCPAC. The NCPAC chairman was also the National Director of the Conservative Alliance. The Conservative Alliance (CALL) had a project, the National Coalition for America's Survival (NCAS), and this was running a Human Rights and National Survival Program (HRNSP). It was on HRNSP that Ed Jenkins was concentrating; and a press kit gave the "basic concept": "The United States government must stop giving the Soviets and other Communist governments the technology, credit, money and security to violate human rights and commit other acts against God and mankind."

Ed Jenkins said of CALL, "Our first aim is to stop communism. *And* turn it back. We feel it shouldn't exist. We feel all the world should be as free as we are." They were particularly concerned about the transfer of high technology to Russia.

And yet the movement had had simpler, even domestic, beginnings. "It was founded seven years ago. It used to be called 'Conservatives Against Liberal Legislation.' The name was changed this year. It was founded to fight the ramming-through of liberal legislation." And by that Ed Jenkins meant busing, mainly. "The people of the United States did not want busing." Busing brought misery to many families; Ed Jenkins had a sister who—though she had moved an hour-and-a-half's drive away from the town where her husband worked—was still tormented by busing.

"There was this group in the country who were fleeing from their own government. Unknown to themselves, they were starting this movement. I know that I was going to private school at the time and I can remember the desperation of parents—they were trying to get away from something."

I DON'T THINK Andrew was a conservative. But as Ed Jenkins spoke about busing—so far from the subject of HRNSP and the Russians, and yet it was possible to see the logic of the political journey, especially to an idealist who might be unwilling to beat a racial drum or even acknowledge racial passions—as Ed Jenkins spoke, I saw that Andrew, for all his writer's coolness, and even with his academic background, was sympathetic, and responding. Andrew, from New Jersey, understood perfectly what Ed Jenkins was talking about.

It was because of busing that people began sending their children to church schools, Ed Jenkins went on. It was because of busing that religious fundamentalism became respectable.

So here, sixteen years later, was unexpected confirmation of what Eldridge Cleaver had written in *Soul on Ice*: "A broad national consensus was developed over the civil rights struggle . . . The task which the new right has feverishly undertaken is to erode and break up this consensus, something that is a distinct possibility since the precise issues and conditions which gave birth to the consensus no longer exist."

Ed Jenkins said: "I should say that before this, fundamentalists were not political. The idea people had of them was that they were not an important force in this country. But you must also understand that the New Right is not just a fundamentalist movement. It's *all* people. But the fundamentalist movement is a very important part of it. I'm not a fundamentalist, but I have a lot of respect for it.

"I belong to the Episcopalian Church myself. It's one of the mainline churches in the United States, but I left it. I left it because when I went there I did not hear religion. I heard our priest rail against our government and the injustices of our society and Vietnam. He would tell us that the United States was an imperialist power and that our soldiers were killing women and children. At this point I had three brothers-in-law in Vietnam—two of them didn't come back.

"The change was so dramatic, so subtle. I think that the liberalism that America embraced in the late Sixties and early Seventies created the power base of the right today.

"I left the church, as I told you, because my priest had decided that religion had to become a social movement. These mainline churches—like the Episcopalians—were actually becoming a part of the government. And to them if a fundamentalist church became involved with something political they were a bunch of nuts. But as long as it was a mainline church sending priests—on our money—down to Selma, Alabama, to be involved in violence, that was a social cause, and not a political cause."

And now, without any prompting from Andrew or me, Ed Jenkins began to talk about his family history. It was part of his openness. It was also his response to our interest in him.

"My father was very conservative. He grew up in Akron, Ohio. He was the son of a very poor family. Irish and Welsh. On my mother's side there is some German and Dutch. My father was probably the stereotypical American. He worked his way through high school, college. He usually had three jobs. He graduated in journalism because he couldn't afford medical school. But he went back and he eventually became a doctor. When he was twenty-seven, twenty-eight, twenty-nine. He started with nothing. He died at the age of fifty-seven from overwork. But he had done the two things he had set out to do. Not just become a doctor, but the best doctor he could be. And, two, make sure his children would never have to go through what he had to go through. He would tell me stories, with his mother there, how when he was growing up they would have meat maybe once a week—and he was an only child. Because they were poor my father wasn't—I wouldn't say malnutritioned—but he didn't get the vitamins, the food he needed, and because of that he was very frail and very small all his life."

Ed Jenkins was not frail; but he had inherited something of his father's small stature.

Andrew, who was partly Russian, asked: "Your grandfather?"

"He was a factory worker. When he could get work. My grandfather played on the first football team in America. He died very poor. Those people on the early teams made no money. My grandmother could remember being so ecstatic—it was very early on—because there was a championship game, and each member of the winning team was going to get *five* dollars."

.   .   .

FROM ONE POINT of view, this was a story of deprivation in a land of plenty; in many countries it might have provoked anger. But from another point of view the story was of a rise: grandfather a factory worker, father a doctor. That was how Ed Jenkins looked on it. "It was instilled from birth that anybody could do anything in the world they wished, that if they had the desire and the will there was nothing to stop them. That was the beauty of America. I can remember other neighbours' kids getting in trouble for different things and getting spanked. The worst thing anyone in our family could do was *not doing our best*, whether it was cutting the grass or studying at school."

Andrew said, "You got spanked for that?"

"Yes."

I asked, "When did your father die?"

"In 1967, just before I turned sixteen. My father was opposed to what the government was doing. He felt our government was creating a welfare state, which he said is a mild way of saying 'socialistic.' On top of that he felt our government was backing down to the communists. He believed that the communists fully planned to take over the entire world. He was a Goldwater Republican until he went to the convention. I went with him. I was twelve."

So Ed Jenkins was introduced at an early age not only to formal politics, but also—in the middle of his family's success—to the idea of threat, instability (new horrors replacing the old), the idea of a world barely mastered being taken away again.

"I felt the government was destroying the fabric of America, destroying what made America great."

But when was that good time, that secure period?

"People sometimes ask me who was the last great president. Some say Kennedy. I don't think so. At the risk of appearing narrow-minded, I say Teddy Roosevelt. He was a fighter, he was stubborn. He was almost a salesman for America. America was the greatest country in the world and he was willing to go to any lengths to prove it. And he had the qualities I was brought up on—that you do the best you can, whatever it is—and the one thing you can say about Teddy is that when he took on a job he did it with a gusto, a love of life. He *loved* life. And he loved America."

Ed Jenkins had gone to work for the Conservative Alliance for one year, and stayed for four. It was a financial sacrifice, but he considered it good and necessary. "Just as my father was worried about his children, I am worried about mine."

Andrew, who was more impressed by Ed Jenkins than he thought he would be, said later, "That story of poverty and struggle is something many people of the right tell."

Andrew was right. Early poverty was the theme of two of the convention speeches that evening. Senator Domenici told of his poor grocer father in New Mexico. Mr. Hill, a black Baptist pastor, told of sleeping in a pigpen in Dallas in 1947. It caused some heartburn that the pigpen speech wasn't taken by the networks. It would have been politically very powerful.

DURING the convention one of the publications distributed was the *Presidential Biblical Scoreboard*. This purported to give (from various sources) the presidential and vice-presidential candidates' attitudes to a variety of issues—abortion, homosexuality, women's rights, pedophilia, pornography, the nuclear freeze, prayers in schools. Just as all these issues were seen as "Biblical" issues, so they all appeared to be aspects of one big issue of right and wrong, requiring only a particular kind of faith.

Mr. Reagan didn't come out too badly in the *Scoreboard*. Once, before he became president, he was asked by a reporter, "Governor, whom are you patterning your life after?" Mr. Reagan said, "Oh, that's very easy. The man from—" After all the shots of John Wayne in "Ronald Reagan's America," and the emphasis on Mr. Reagan's own film past, one might have expected Mr. Reagan to say, "The man from Laramie." But what he said was, "The man from Galilee." And, oddly, during the convention week, the two did not seem dissimilar. The pervading sentimentality—about old America, the old faith, the West (or the western), old films, old stars—had brought the two ideas together, and almost without blasphemy. Mr. Reagan, running together his three roles—actor, politician, old-fashioned Christian—had made himself into a formidable political personality. He answered many needs; many people of the many-featured right could read their fantasies in him. He was an actor: an actor could say very little, and still stand for a lot.

On Wednesday, at the convention center, after the pigpen speech (delivered in a hectoring, Baptist way), there was a film about Mrs. Reagan. She was shown unveiling a plaque to her surgeon father and appearing to sob. There was something about her acting career. Frank Sinatra sang the song about Nancy. Mr. Reagan said with emotion, "I don't know what I'd do without her." And in the end they walked off down a slope into a wood.

The lights went on and there was applause. We had a surprise. The film was not a substitute for Mrs. Reagan's presence. Mrs. Reagan had been brought in during the screening of the film and was now on the podium, in white. We had a further surprise: on the big screen at the back there wasn't a big picture of Mrs. Reagan, but a live view of Mr. Reagan in his room at Trammell Crow's Anatole Hotel. Mrs. Reagan waved at the big screen. For a second or so Mr. Reagan seemed bemused, but then he started waving back. It was a great moment of family theatre. And it was enough. It was what the delegates needed. All that was required of Mr. Reagan now was his presence. And that was what we got on the last day.

The political part of his speech repeated what had been said by others. The poetical part at the end, about the "springtime of hope," was less a speech, less a matter of poetry and language, than a scenario for a short documentary about multi-racial, many-landscaped America. So that at the climax of the great occasion, as at the center of so many of the speeches, there was nothing. It was as if, in summation, the sentimentality, about religion and Americanism, had betrayed only an intellectual vacancy; as if the computer language of the convention had revealed the imaginative poverty of these political lives. It was "as if "—in spite of the invocations and benedictions (the last benediction to be spoken by Dr. Criswell)—"as if inspiration had ceased, as if no vast hope, no religion, no song of joy, no wisdom, no analogy, existed any more."

The words are by Emerson; they were written about England. *English Traits,* published in 1856, was about Emerson's two visits to England, in 1833 and 1847, when he felt that English power, awesome and supreme as it still was, was on the turn, and that English intellectual life was being choked by the great consciousness of power and money and rightness. "They exert every variety of talent on a lower ground," Emerson wrote, "and may be said to live and act in a submind." Something like this I felt in the glitter of Dallas. Power was the theme of the convention, and this power seemed too easy—national power, personal power, the power of the New Right. Like Emerson in England, I seemed in the convention hall of Dallas "to walk on a marble floor, where nothing will grow."

Heavy Manners in Grenada

I WENT TO GRENADA seventeen days after the American invasion, and three or four days after the airport had been opened again to civilian traffic. The real fighting had stopped long before. The seven hundred or so Cubans on the island had been rounded up and repatriated, with their forty-two dead. The PRA, the 1,200-strong People's Revolutionary Army, the army of the Grenadian revolution, had disintegrated. The main body had surrendered; the remnants were being tracked down.

The American Psy-Ops people—Psychological Operations, a branch of the Special Warfare Centre, itself a section of the Special Operations Command—Psy-Ops had already (as their colonel was to say two days later) "transitioned into civil affairs." They were now preparing posters. One of these posters, roughly printed in black and white in five different typefaces, was like something from a western film. *Former PRA Members Your corrupt Leaders have surrendered, knowing resistance is USELESS* . . .

The airport was noisy with helicopters of a sinister black colour. All around there were armed marines in heavy combat clothes; trucks and jeeps in camouflage paint, some with machine-guns; tents and camouflage netting. A humourous hand had drawn a rough black line through the Cubana airline logo over a door of the terminal building, and had scrawled below the logo: *2nd Battalion 82nd Airborne*.

After the Grenadian immigration formalities there was—in this legally ambiguous situation—a check by U.S. Marines, who—already—had a printed list of names. Then a few steps away, at the customs counter, there was civilian authority again—and the tall black Grenadian customs man was wearing a shirt of the palest blue patterned faintly with the name GUCCI.

A few hundred yards from the airport it was as if some television footage was being re-staged: at the side of the road, wet after rain, marines with guns were walking a spread-out file of five or six black men, stripped down to underpants. One of the men wore Rastafarian "dreadlocks." Matted hair, nudity and a wild appearance were parts of the Rastafarian style; but now, in captivity, this man looked especially degraded. The men were PRA suspects. They had almost certainly been informed on by Grenadians: to nearly all Grenadians the revolution and the Revolutionary Army had become hateful. The prisoners—but legally they were only people "detained"—were being walked to the airport. From there one of the black helicopters would take them over the forested hills of the island to the main American encampment on the south-western coast. A detention centre had been set up there, for the interrogation and screening of suspected persons. American correspondents, ferreting away for their daily or twice-daily stories, had just discovered this centre. Or, as it was to be called during press briefings, "this facility."

The road over the hills was narrow and winding, with many blind corners. At least two of the big Cuban trucks that the Americans had taken over had crashed. Ferns and the big fronds of the wild banana grew in sprays out of the volcanic cliff faces. The red poinsettia, the Christmas flower of these parts, was in bloom, and the common hibiscus; and the Bleeding Heart vine, a weed, had laid drifts of pink blossom on hedges and electric poles.

The houses were small, on stilts or low concrete pillars, and with pitched corrugated-iron roofs. The older houses were of wood, and some were in the French Caribbean style, with fretted gables and fanlights and jalousies. What looked like bush around the houses were patches of cultivation: cocoa, with the purple pods growing directly out of the black trunks and branches of the small trees; grapefruit, avocado and mango; the big-leaved breadfruit and tropical chestnut; plantain and banana, nutmeg. There were no big estates. This was a Caribbean peasant countryside.

In scattered houses along the road, and in jeeps and trucks in dirt lanes off the road, there were marines, taking their ease but watchful. At a junction there was a roadblock.

Lennox, the taxi-driver, said, "I was wondering. I did hear they was stopping and searching today." He spoke calmly; he had learned to live with big events.

The marine didn't wave us down. He dropped to a half-crouch and pushed his clenched left fist at our car. Theatre. And it seemed that all the children of the little village were standing by to watch. One marine was black, one was Chinese, one looked Hispanic. Questions were asked while luggage was searched and the car was searched. A transistor radio on the roadside was turned on very loud, until a marine asked a boy to turn it down.

And it was only when we were on our way again that I made a whole of the dislocating experience, and understood that the radio had been turned on by the boy, that music had soon given way to Spanish speech, and that it was my reaction to the Spanish language that was being assessed by the Hispanic-looking marine who had asked trivial, disconnected questions. Psy-Ops, Special Warfare. All these search procedures had been well rehearsed. In Grenada the Americans were still looking for Cubans.

The road began to go down through the wet, ferny, forest reserve area to the west coast. Emblems of the revolution—a red disc on a white field—appeared on walls and fences. Near the capital, St. George's, the slogan boards of the revolution became more numerous. They had not been defaced. Some of the slogans were about "production." In the peasant setting it seemed a very big word, a strange word. It could never have had its proclaimed meaning; it must always have stood for the power of those who ruled.

In Grenada—eighty-five square miles, 110,000 people—the revolution was as much an imposition—as theatrical and out of scale—as the American military presence it had called up.

MOST GRENADIANS were glad when the New Jewel Movement took power in a coup in March 1979. The island had been ruled for too long by Eric Gairy. Gairy, a man of simple origins, had organized a big strike in 1951. Starting in this way, as a redeemer of the black poor, he soon won political power, and held on to it. In power he became stylish. He had money; he was elegant; he wore white suits; it was said that even white women fell for him. The poor country folk in the little houses of Grenada understood. They felt that Gairy's triumphs were a black man's triumphs and therefore also their own, and they loved him; they voted him into office again and again. It was Gairy who took Grenada to independence.

But over the years Gairy—like some other small-island Caribbean folk leaders of his type—had developed into a feared and somewhat eccentric Negro shepherd-king. At international gatherings he talked about UFO's; at home there was a large gang that dealt with opponents. In the post-colonial Caribbean Gairy increasingly became an embarrassment, hateful to the children of the very people to whom he had once given hope.

The New Jewel Movement, founded in 1972, represented the first educated generation in Grenada. Its leader was a handsome young man who had completed his education in England. The overthrow of Gairy by this movement of the young and educated was doubly popular. And the New Jewel Movement used this popularity to offer Grenada— without elections, ever—the revolution. It was a full socialist revolution. Cuba became Grenada's ally; imperialism became Grenada's enemy.

The slogan-writers of the party called the revolution the "revo" or "de revo."

Is only now I seeing how dis Revo good for de poor an ah dam sorry it didn't come before.

People's speech, phonetic spelling—the party used it to make the more difficult parts of its doctrine and practice acceptable: to make the many rallies and "solidarity" marches appear more folksy; and to make all the imported apparatus of socialist rule and patronage—the organizing committee of the party, the political bureau, the central committee, the many "mass" organizations, the army and the militia—to make all of this appear carnival-like and Grenadian and black, "de revo."

The apparatus was absurd. But the power was real. And for the four and a half years of its rule the party kept Grenada under "heavy manners." The words, Jamaican street slang, were adopted by the revolution, and became part of its stock of serious jokey words. "Manners," "respect" for the revolution and its leaders, were required from everyone. There could therefore be no elections, no opposition newspaper: the people's will was as simple as that. "To manners" became a revolutionary verb. To "manners" a "counter" was to teach a counter-revolutionary a lesson: to harass him, to dismiss him from a job, to imprison him without charge or trial. Hundreds were imprisoned at one time or the other. Trials were a form of "bourgeois legality." The "revo" needed only people's law, "heavy manners"; and the very words could turn the loss of law into just a subject for calypso. To impose manners, an army was created—and that meant employment of a sort with the party.

Cuba provided the arms for the army. And it was Cuba that—to the alarm of both the United States and other Caribbean territories—began to build the big two-mile airport at Point Salines.

At least two hundred "internationalist" workers, socialists, were brought in to help administer the revolution. Half of them were from Europe and America, half from other West Indian territories. Strangers to Grenada, exigent guests at the other man's revolutionary feast, these visitors were anxious for the socialist mimicry to be as complete, as pure, as possible. Hence, in the Grenada of the revolution, the obsession with forms, organization, structures, committees. Grenada even had a Writers' Federation. Almost at the end of the revolution a West Indian visitor from the United States spotted an omission. In Grenada, he said, he had found no House of Culture; socialist countries had houses of culture. So in Grenada they began to work on a House of Culture.

As the mimicry was perfected, so the excitement grew among the faithful in many countries; and the Grenadian revolution had a good press abroad. Little Grenada, agricultural, backward and black, had not only had the revolution; it had also had an eruption of all the correct socialist forms. The mimicry was like proof of the naturalness and rightness of the cause.

Then the revolution went sour. Its success in the socialist world had been too great, too sudden. There was some dissension at the top, in the central committee, some call for the sharing of power. There was a feeling that the leader had became too taken with his foreign fame, his visits abroad; and that the revolution at home had begun to drift.

The leader prevaricated. He agreed that he was being petit bourgeois in some ways, but he really didn't want to step down. He had made the revolution after all; the people were loyal to him. So, finally, the "manners" that had been applied to hundreds of others were applied to the leader himself. He was placed under house arrest by some of his colleagues on the central committee.

The people didn't like it. After a week a crowd stormed the house and the leader was released. There was confusion; a civil war was in the offing. The leader and his supporters went to the army post at Fort George (at that time named Fort Rupert, after the leader's father) and talked over the soldiers there. The Revolutionary Military Council, rulers of Grenada since the crisis, sent armoured cars to the fort. There was firing; the unarmed crowd stampeded and an unknown number of people were killed—anything from seventeen to one hundred; and the leader and five former ministers were executed. A twenty-four-hour curfew was placed on the island, and for almost a week the people of Grenada lived in terror of the People's Revolutionary Army. Then the Americans invaded, and manners heavier than Grenada had known were applied to everybody.

The Americans found no revolution. That had vanished in the preceding week of terror. The Americans, serving their own cause, invading Grenada according to a plan prepared at least two years before, found themselves welcomed as liberators. The invaded island, more full of noises than Caliban's island, was full of informers; the detention facility at Point Salines was quickly peopled.

THE WEST INDIAN sugar colonies were richer than the American colonies in the eighteenth century. The ships that came to take the slave-grown sugar to Europe sometimes brought bricks and clay roof tiles as ballast. These tiles and bricks give an eighteenth-century feel to corners of old St. George's, a little town built on the steep slope of the horseshoe-shaped hill that encloses the inner harbour.

At harbour level was the main street of this toy-town: fire brigade, cigarette factory, airline office, restaurant, main post office. At the top of the hill—easily seen, taken in in one roving look—were the official buildings that had been touched by the recent drama. On the south-western promonory was the green-roofed fort where the leader and others had been shot. Across the bay was the red-roofed house where the leader had been held under house arrest. Not far from that was the civilian prison where members of the Revolutionary Military Council and other former members of the central committee were now held.

On the northern end of the hill, the top of the horseshoe, was the very grand house which was the Governor-General's residence. It had a wide verandah, stone-flagged where not tiled; a reception room with tall doors, a high timber ceiling elaborately moulded, gilt mirrors and craftsman-made furniture. There, some days later, the Governor-General, a black man, formerly a schoolmaster, a man who now incarnated what was left of the authority of the state of Grenada, witnessed the swearing-in of the members of his new advisory council. The men swore allegiance to Queen Elizabeth II and kissed the Bible.

Legal authority in Grenada still derived its forms from the British Empire. But the most important witnesses that day—apart from the correspondents and the television teams—were General Farris, slender, white-haired, in uniform, commander of the 82nd Airborne, and the man in a blue suit who was the de facto American ambassador, the civilian arm of General Farris's de facto authority.

In a glass case in the rough little museum in the centre of the town was Britain's gift to Grenada at the time of independence nine years before: a silver coffee service and twenty-four Wedgwood bone china coffee cups, all laid out on undyed hessian.

The New Jewel Movement had resisted that independence. They had feared Gairy's excesses in an independent Grenada. The leader of the movement and others had been badly beaten by Gairy's men during a time of protest. And in another glass case in the museum were souvenirs of that occasion: the leader's bloodstained sports shirt, the stone that had cracked the leader's head and left him with double vision.

Violence had indeed come to independent Grenada. Ten years later the leader had been executed by the army he had created. And this time there were no souvenirs. The leader's body still had not been found.

It was the rainy season in the eastern Caribbean. At dawn the rain clouds rose as fast as smoke above the eastern hill of St. George's. The sky darkened; the rain poured, feeding the vegetation in the empty rubbled spaces between the eighteenth-century buildings; the sky cleared again. In the late afternoons the golden light, trapped within the curving hill and reflecting off the bay, made all the buildings a rose colour against the dark vegetation and the milky blue eastern sky.

Black helicopters crossed the view, as they had done all day. They hovered for minutes over the civilian prison.

"That's the military," an American correspondent said. "Haven't you been with them before? They like activity."

THERE was, amazingly, an American "internationalist" worker still on the island. Her name was Michele Gibbs; she was from Chicago. She had been "invited" by the American military to leave Grenada; and she intended to go. She no longer had a cause in Grenada.

She was an attractive brown woman in her late thirties, slender with a small bust, and with unshaved armpits—oddly aggressive, those mats of hair, hard not to look at. Her political cause had been given her at birth, she said: both her parents—her mother a Russian Jew, her father a black man from Texas—had been communists.

The revolutionary black state of Grenada had been a kind of paradise for Michele for three years. She felt she had come home, and she had hoped to live there forever. She had found an apartment on the lower floor of a restored old house on a favoured cliffside spot, just below the Prime Minister's office. Bougainvillaea shaded her sea-facing front room and her little circular terrace from the afternoon sun. In these conditions, which must have appeared idyllic to someone from Chicago, Michele had served the Grenada revolution, helping with education, doing her revolutionary paintings and writing and publishing her revolutionary poems (handwritten and photo-set).

> de forest move
> de land watch
> de folk talk.
> de cat mew
> de dog bark
> de revo start.

Now, more than three weeks after the disaster, she was still a little dazed. People were "morally in shock," she said; they felt they had been "betrayed by their own." And, speaking of the American invasion, she said that people were "relieved that the situation was taken out of their hands." All she wanted for herself now was to go "far, far away."

The communism that had been given to her as a cause had committed her to an almost mystical personal search. In Grenada she had found what she wanted and needed to find; and though among her poems there were some poems of rebuke to someone who appeared to have run out on the revolution, it was not really surprising that Michele's poems about Grenada were abstract, little more than party slogan-making. Her poems about black life in Detroit were more personal, more concrete, unexpectedly tough, many of the barbs turned inwards. The cause in America had been a kind of pain: it was possible here and there to detect something like weariness with the life of struggle in America. One of Michele's longer poems was autobiographical.

> *So livid were police to see*
> *we three :*
> *Ted, black*
> *Paula, white*
> *and me*
> *together and at liberty.*

Michele had written this poem in Grenada after she had heard that her mother, at the age of seventy-two, had been shot and killed in the United States by a street thief, who might have been black—though the poem didn't say.

The irony of this death was like the irony of the destruction of Michele's cause in Grenada. And perhaps her life was full of ironies because of her way of looking or her way of not looking. Her Grenada was private; and her position in Grenada wasn't what she thought it had been. She hadn't been taken seriously by all the revolutionaries. She had too American a sense of the self; with her poems and her paintings and her general manner she had seemed too self-promoting. She—like other American internationalists—had been thought of as people "having a holiday" in the revolution, people with American causes, people more concerned with protest than with the use of power.

After I left Grenada I met a West Indian woman internationalist from another territory who thought that Michele might even have been a CIA agent. The West Indian woman had also felt at one time that her own job might have been taken away from her and—as a result of machinations by Michele's patrons in the revolution—given to Michele.

The revolutionary life—which Michele had painted as an idyll—sounded a little cut-throat. The leaders and the privileged helpers had a vision of a purified people correctly led and living cooperatively together. But at the top and just below the top there had always been dissension, the clash of personalities, the play of human passion that the administrators of the socialist utopia would have liked to deny to the people.

· · ·

THERE was a purely Grenadian story. It was the story of a retarded island community hijacked by people slightly more educated into the forms of a grandiose revolution. Separate from this, superimposed on it, there was an American story—the story of the U.S. military in Grenada. And it was on this that the American correspondents concentrated.

They hadn't liked what they had seen of the detention facility at Point Salines. When they came back to the hotel they spoke of eight-feet-square cells set down on the ground, with PVC covers, and four-feet-high entrance flaps. It worried the correspondents that the army people should have been so pleased with the facility and anxious to show it off. Perhaps the facility had been designed beforehand? Perhaps the invasion of Grenada was just an exercise for the invasion of Nicaragua?

The humanitarian concern of the correspondents was genuine, but mixed up with it were newsmen's professional instincts. Grenada was a small part of a larger American story; and distrust of the military was a necessary part of the equipment of the good correspondent. In Grenada this distrust was great. American correspondents felt they had been shut out of the invasion, and they took it personally.

"It's an adversary relationship," a photographer said. And in a small but irritating way the military were still winning. They were moving in from their field tents and taking over the working hotels day by day. They dug up the beaches to fill sandbags; they put sandbags and a new kind of barbed wire on the lawns; they parked trucks with machine guns among the coconut trees. Correspondents who had been treated by hotel staff as guests in the morning might find themselves challenged for a password in the evening by a nervous sentry. There were women among the marines. The fact was sometimes revealed only by a feminine call, in the night, of "Halt!"

The Grenada Beach Hotel, formerly the Holiday Inn, was the head-quarters of the 82nd Airborne. Some of the rooms in one wing had been bombed during the fighting; but the American bombing had everywhere been wonderfully precise, and the hotel was in working order. The Psy-Ops briefing was held in the open dining room, next to the garden, where the barbed wire, new and shiny, as yet unrusted by the sea air, was barely visible. The waiters, as correctly uniformed as the soldiers, were laying the tables for lunch.

The man from the *Miami Herald* wanted to know about the Psy-Ops poster with a photograph of the commander of the People's Revolutionary Army. "It shows him naked, sitting only in a bath towel, with a marine behind him. Don't you think that's demeaning?"

The colonel said, making a new point with every sentence: "He had what was available when we got there. Maybe they were checking his clothes. Maybe he was taking a shower or something. He chose not to have the sheet over his shoulders. It showed he wasn't injured. The soldier was there in the picture to show that he was in captivity."

It was a full reply. But the American correspondents' main interest was the Special Warfare Centre. It was apparently new to them. They wanted to know where it was based, and what it did, and how it was organized.

"Who is the commander?"

"Brigadier-General Promotable Lutz. L-u-t-z."

Dutifully, like first-year university students who want to take down everything, the correspondents scribbled. Then someone had a doubt.

"Promotable. Is that his name?"

"It means that in a few days he will be a Major-General." The colonel smiled. "Sorry about that piece of army jargon."

So perhaps, properly punctuated, the commander was Brigadier (General, promotable) Lutz.

The main briefing of the morning was in St. George's itself, in a small, old-style residential house on one of the cross-streets on the hill above the harbour. It was an old West Indian city street, socially mixed. Master and slave had once lived side by side; and slum—verandah-less wooden shacks, close together—could still be only a yard or house-lot away from gentility. The house (with a tablet of local modern sculpture at the entrance, and a local canvas in the hall) had been adapted to the modest Grenadian needs of the University of the West Indies, and had now been re-adapted as a press centre. Handwritten notices pinned above doors said, "Telex," "Conference Room." On a green board in one room were chalked the casualty tables. *KIA*, *WIA*, Killed in Action, Wounded in Action: U.S., 18 and 113; Cuban, 42 and 57; Grenadian, 21 and 280.

The conference was held in the lecture theatre built against the back wall of the house. There was little new to talk about. Most of the questions were about the detention facility and the casualty figures. There was a dispute about the number of the dead: checks with the local mortuaries had given higher figures. Some of the correspondents became aggressive. The military spokesmen, one black, one white, remained cool. From time to time the black spokesman said, "Do you want me to take that?" Or, "All right, I'll take that." "Take" was apparently a technical word: it meant to check up on.

University library staff stood and watched from the windows of the original house. The windows opened directly on to the lecture theatre stage; and the watchers were like figures on a balcony in an Elizabethan theatre, or like West Indian middle-class folk looking on from a respectable distance at a back-yard squabble.

The dispute about the number of the dead was really a dispute about army misinformation, part of the continuing dispute in Grenada between the American military and the American press. Professional pride was engaged on both sides. The awful fact of death was like another story, and Grenada itself just a background.

The bad blood between the correspondents and the military came to a climax two days later, when the correspondent of a famous American newspaper, behaving at a night-time marine roadblock as he might have behaved at a morning briefing, found himself handcuffed and made to sit on the ground.

THE IMPORTANT detainees were in the civilian prison in St. George's. The lesser folk—suspected members of the People's Revolutionary Army—were in the detention facility at Point Salines, a few winding miles to the south-west, past bays and scrubland.

This was where the big Cuban-built airport was. It had become the centre of the main American camp, the complete military settlement—with air-conditioned hospital tents of a new design—that the Rapid Deployment Force had set up with the help of its computerized inventory (and could take away again in eighteen hours).

To arrive there after the forests and hills and twisting roads of the rest of Grenada was like coming out into the open, and into another kind of country: a despoiled flatness of concrete and scarred earth, with the two-mile Cuban runway making a broad level stripe to the horizon. There was much heavy Cuban equipment about. Barbed wire ran beside the runway. The unfinished concrete hangars were among the biggest buildings in Grenada; and, three weeks after the invasion, Americans and local men were still filling and stacking sandbags outside the hangars. Garbage trucks were busy. Above, as always, the helicopters clattered.

The detention area, some distance away from the runway, and near a burning rubbish dump (even the rubbish looked new), was ringed by coils of barbed wire and guarded by marines. The PVC-covered cells, eight feet square (as we had been told), were like tall boxes. They were set flat on the ground, in rows. The effect was one of desolation. But the American correspondents' talk of mongoose cages seemed exaggerated.

Some of the detainees were to be released that afternoon. That was what we had come to see. We had to wait. From time to time it rained. An army lorry with a local crew came and dumped fresh rubbish on the burning rubbish dump. In the compound a marine (possibly a woman— a victory for another kind of American cause) trained a machine gun on the area where the released detainees were to be mustered.

An old civilian car appeared. The marines at the barrier levelled their guns. The car stopped, parked carefully. A black family group got out: a self-effacing man, a shapeless, subdued girl in trousers, and a thinner, blacker girl in bright colours and with white-and-red plastic earrings, the colour and the material effective against her black skin.

She was pure venom, the black girl, one of the real "biting ants" of the slums. She said, talking to us and yet acknowledging none of us, "Dey wire us up. Wire up de road. Wire up de beaches. Everyt'ing wire up now."

Her brother was inside. She had been allowed in once, to see him; she didn't know whether he was to be released that afternoon. But he was: she saw him in the group lining up outside the huts, and she forgot us.

From a distance, the jeans and shirts and straw hats (and the small American flag that one of the detainees held in his hand) gave a carnival air to the men about to be released. But closer to—when the buses briefly stopped outside the camp area, and we were permitted to look in and talk to the men—the faces were disturbing: the faces of men of the Revolutionary Army, still in a group, still acting one for the other: no longer just the rough faces of the street, but the faces of simple men who, in the smallness of Grenada, had known power. I was not American. The eye that held mine still transmitted power and conviction.

Gairy had ruled with the help of the Mongoose Gang, the Green Beasts. The New Jewel Movement had ruled with the help of its army. For a small island Grenada was amazingly varied, in racial types, accents, manners, levels of education. And perhaps the murderous, secret-society politics of Grenada had been made in part by the geography of the small island, by the constriction of the hills and forests and small villages, where people couldn't easily grow and where the past was close. Gairy had been more than a labour leader: he had tapped the African religious feeling of his supporters. And perhaps in that curious name, Jewel (Joint Effort for Welfare, Education and Liberation), there was some Grenadian counter-magic against the Green Beasts. What was common to both movements in this black Hansel-and-Gretel world was the vision offered—by Gairy to a primitive people, by Jewel to a people slightly more educated—of sudden racial redemption.

GEORGE LOUISON, a founding member of Jewel, had been a minister in the People's Revolutionary Government and a member of the central committee until things began to break up. He had often been criticized in the central committee for being petit bourgeois; and right at the end he had been imprisoned by the Revolutionary Military Council for trying to get the people to make trouble. After the invasion he had been detained for a day by the Americans at Point Salines. Then, unexpectedly, the Americans had come for him again. This time—he regarded it as pure psychological harassment—they had kept him only eight hours. It was after this release that we met.

He was a man of thirty-two, a man from the country, pure black, not big. He was the son of a builder and he was by profession a teacher. He lived on the west coast, in a village that came after a stretch of land that looked uncultivated. His house was in a rocky lane that led off the main coast road and up a valley, beside a racing river. The valley was dark, hidden from the late afternoon sun. The concrete house, though ambitious in the setting, was simple, with an outside staircase to the top floor.

Night fell, all at once. The electricity failed; we talked in the plain downstairs front room by candlelight.

There was no stylishness about Louison. He had preserved the earnestness and simplicity of his background. The name of Louison was known in the area: his father's uncle went to a secondary school in 1900, and was one of the first black men in Grenada to receive a proper education. Louison's father was born in 1918. Starting as a village carpenter and mason, he had taken a correspondence course and become a trained builder. With this urge to self-improvement, Louison's father took an interest in the Negro causes of the time. He liked the back-to-Africa views of Marcus Garvey; there was a picture of Garvey in the house.

But didn't Garvey defraud black people of the money they had given to the cause? Wasn't that a blow to Louison's father?

Louison said, "Here in this village people think it was a manipulation by anti-Garvey elements plus the U.S. government. And Garvey represented more than the race question. He represented the anti-colonial fight."

After Garvey, there was the Grenadian politician, Marryshow, who preached the idea of a West Indian Federation. "Marryshow ended a pauper," Louison said. And there was Grantly Adams of the Barbados Labour Party.

"Later my father ran a small shop right on this spot, where this house is. It was an area for discussion. In the late 50s he made an attempt to start adult education in the village." This was the time of Gairy. Louison's father supported Gairy in the beginning, but broke with him in 1960. "Gairy's main base was among the agricultural labourers, and he never did anything to lift the standard. Gairy never attempted to understand the process of societal development."

"Would your father have thought like that?"

Louison didn't answer directly. He said, "By 1969–70 I would have come to that conclusion."

By that time, at the age of eighteen, George Louison was deep in politics. He had started young, with youth work, "politics in humanitarian forms." Then the Black Power movement of 1970 claimed him and the rest of his generation. He didn't go abroad to study; he remained a simple teacher; he didn't think of marrying. "To this day I am not married. Many people in the New Jewel Movement were like me. For us it became almost a mission in the early 70s." Black Power was more than its name. "Black Power in terms of the race question lasted two years in Grenada. There was a small but dramatic event in early 1973. We were going to send people to the Sixth Pan-African Congress. A month before the Congress took place we heard that Gairy was going." Gairy's point was that he, Gairy, was black, and that he had already created Black Power in Grenada. And that in a way was true. "That made us realize that Black Power wasn't a question of blackness. It was a question of politics and overall ideas."

And all the time, the process of self-improvement continuing, Louison and his colleagues in the New Jewel Movement were studying. Study, the idea of study, was important to these earnest young men and their studies appeared to have been mainly political. "Up to two months ago we would study collectively. The widest range of things. Initially we studied pretty widely, but in the past six or seven years we studied mainly socialist material."

In 1973 and 1974, just before and after independence, there were bitter fights with Gairy's men. In 1973 the leader of the Movement was dreadfully wounded—in the museum there was his bloodied shirt; and in early 1974 the leader's father was killed. The New Jewel Movement changed. "In 1973 we were a populist movement. By late 1974 we decided it was vital for us to have a definite idea." And it was at this time that they made the break with the "humanitarian politics" of the past. Study had led them to socialism; and thereafter socialism circumscribed their study. "We wanted to by-pass the tremendous evils of capitalist development. We recognized we had to look at many countries. Cuba, for obvious reasons—twenty years in that process. We also looked to Yemen, Laos."

"Aren't those places quite different from Grenada?"

"We wanted to look at places outside the framework of capitalist development and imperialist hand-outs. We also had to look at countries that had an experience of colonialism."

Louison couldn't fully explain how they had made this big, final jump—he presented it as a fact, something obvious. But his political development was reasonably clear. For all the century, in that village, there had been Louisons who had been worked on in various ways by the idea of black redemption. Simple people had made that idea of redemption a simple idea; the simple idea had created men like Gairy, who kept people down in order always to present himself as their saviour. Socialism absorbed the racial idea, purified it, did away with the corruptions inherent in it. Socialism, doing away with the racial issue, left men free to be men. And all that socialism required was study and faithful practice, the giving to Grenada of the correct forms.

But socialism, like other faiths, had its purists and fanatics. "As somebody said, the revolution has blown up in our faces. We destroyed the revolution ourselves." The men in the central committee who, for the sake of revolutionary purity, had pressed for collective leadership and had put the leader under house arrest and had sent the army against the masses—those men were "mad." "The course they were following was idealist, voluntarist, had no scientific grounding and no grounding with the people."

"Voluntarist? Doing things wilfully?"

"By voluntarist I mean self-serving."

Even after the disaster, the socialism he had studied gave Louison the words to explain everything. His house had been looted. People had turned against the revolution, but he still grieved for the revolution. "I'm in a state of deep, deep re-thinking." But politically he could remain only where his study had taken him. He couldn't go back to "humanitarian politics," the racial simplicities of Grenada without socialism. He couldn't forget the world vision he had been granted; he couldn't make himself small again.

BIG REVOLUTION, SMALL COUNTRY—that was the name of a Cuban film about the Grenadian revolution. But for the four and a half years of their rule the People's Revolutionary Government did little.

They built the big airport at Point Salines with Cuban help. They established an army, a militia. They constantly fought counter-revolution, discovering at one stage a gang of twenty-six. They extended patronage to their supporters through various new, unproductive state organizations. They called in two hundred foreign internationalist workers. They painted slogans. That was where the money went—on forms, party bureaucracy, security, show, the display of power.

The life of the island was distorted; people lived in dread of "manners." But at the very top, in the central committee—as was revealed after the invasion, when the minutes of their meetings became available—there was ineptitude and confusion.

Little was done for agriculture in an agricultural island, though there were slogan-boards about "production," and though there was much idle land in Grenada, confiscated by the Gairy régime and then more or less abandoned. Doctrine got in the way of action: to encourage the most efficient farmers would be to encourage class ideas in the countryside, and the ultimate goal was co-operative farming. Socialist doctrine was at odds with the nature of the people in other ways. Deprived youth, for instance, didn't really want to work on the land, though they were happy to plant marijuana. And there was the problem—as raised at one central committee meeting in carefully classless language—of the "non-nice type youth, the grassroots youth," with whom nothing at all could be done.

Big new words were found for old attitudes: Grenadian workers, it was discovered, were riddled with "economism"—they just wanted money, and saw no "conceptual link" between that and work. There was at times in the meetings of the central committee the atmosphere of the classroom: linguistic skill, a new way with words, seeming to be an end in itself.

Attendance at "mass" rallies dropped off. In the central committee the same issues were discussed again and again, and little seemed to change. Once it even happened that certain important slogans were not painted; the excuse given was that there was no paint. Central committee members were often tired at meetings, unprepared; at one meeting some members actually fell asleep. There were sessions of criticism and self-criticism; this socialist rite seemed to give much pleasure.

They had created the apparatus of a revolution, but they didn't know what to do with it. Socialism should have come with the apparatus, but it hadn't. They began to feel that the apparatus was at fault. So—further distorting the life of the community—they called in more socialist specialists from Russia and Cuba; and quite late, almost at the end, they thought they would get more teachers from the advanced-socialist countries to help with their own party organization.

They accused one another of being petit bourgeois. They developed another doubt; and this—muffled, coming out in scattered phrases at different times—was like a re-awakening of old racial anxiety. Perhaps, after all, there was an incompatibility between the people of Grenada and the high ideals of socialism. Perhaps the real socialists, the people from the great world outside, thought of them as "jokers."

It was this wish to be considered serious, this wish to fit people to theory, that led them into extraordinary ways. There was a problem with the Rastafarians. In Gairy's time the Rastafarians had seemed to be on the side of the revolution, anti-Gairy, and rejectors of the capitalist system. But when the revolution came the Rastas had continued to be themselves. They refused to work or to send their children to school; they went about dirty and naked; they smoked marijuana and thought it legitimate to steal when pressed by need.

The phenomenon was shaming to the revolution. It was decided that there were Rastafarians who were counter-revolutionaries, "counter-Rastas"; and some were picked up. There were proposals for putting Rastas in camps "with a rigid programme and pacifying music." There were other proposals for prosecuting "lumpen" Rastas in the courts and sending them to prison farms. Criminal Rastas who couldn't be convicted in the courts were to be put in hidden detention camps, and the militia was to provide "well-paid armed guards under supervision of party persons." So, bizarrely, revolutionary pride, merging into an unexpressed racial pride, led some people of the central committee to contemplate the idea of the concentration camp.

It was this kind of attitude, this wish for pure, dispassionate, classless revolutionary action, that led to the final, sudden madness: the placing of the leader under arrest, the sending of the army against the crowd, the execution of the leader and other ministers (all members of the central committee). The Revolutionary Military Council thought they had done the right thing. They were shocked by the unfriendly attitude of Fidel Castro, who refused to offer any help against an American attack. According to a hand-written note found afterwards, the Revolutionary Military Council thought the Cubans had taken "a personal and not a class approach to events in Grenada."

The Grenadian revolution, proving itself, destroyed itself.

PSY-OPS were sending a team of marines on a hearts-and-minds mission to a country area.

A CBS television crew was going with them, and I got a ride in the CBS mini-bus. The CBS evening news contained eight or nine filmed stories of about one hundred seconds each. The CBS producer hoped to make one of those stories. He had a cameraman, a woman sound recordist, a reporter (of deep, authoritative voice); a local driver, a local guide. At the end of the day a script would be telexed to New York. If New York liked the script, the producer had a helicopter, to take his film to Point Salines; and an aeroplane, to get from there to Barbados, to edit his film.

There were so many sides to the American endeavour, so many separate ambitions feeding off one another. Grenada, again, became background.

The mercy mission was half an exercise. The supplies the marines were taking were mainly Cuban leftovers: condensed milk, some of the tins bad. And, though there were to be visits to the sick, there were not many medicines.

We went to a village called Munich, and stopped beside a grocery shop. It was green and wet and hilly all around. The board above the grocery door gave the name of the owner, Calliste, and said that he was the agent for a St. George's firm who were "specialists in embalming and shipping." The shop smelled of salt fish and oil and spices. A big, calm, middle-aged brown woman with glasses was behind the counter. She was Mrs. Calliste.

A brown man said to her: "You see, if all-you behave yourself you all right. If you live right, police don't come for you. You behave bad, and they come to help all-you put things in order." Then, hurriedly, as though he felt he had said too much, he got in his van and drove away.

A small young man, bare-chested and with the beginnings of Rastafarian locks, came across the road. He talked about marijuana, and then, thinking I was one of the American team, he offered his services as a tracker. He was only playing bad; he was half-respectable, working a little family plot up in the hills, and suffering with other farmers from low nutmeg prices, bad transport, and no storage facilities for perishable produce. The Callistes were the biggest people in the area, he said; they had lots of nutmeg trees. In a two-storey house up the road there was another rich man; he ran a dance hall on the lower floor of his house, and he also had a bus. "He have mo' cash. Dey"—and the young man reverentially rolled his eyes and tilted his head towards Mrs. Calliste, confident and calm behind her counter—"dey have more wort'."

Mrs. Calliste went to a back room. It began to rain and the chicken dung outside the shop was partly washed away. A barefoot black woman, shiny-faced, with dusty, uncombed hair, missing front teeth, and a dirty grey-blue dress, came in through the rain. She said to the girl helper, "Ask Mistress Calliste if she have clart for pocket."

"Clart?" an old man said. *"Clart?"* You have to start talking Yankee now. You have to say 'cloth.' "

"Yes, we have to talk Yankee now."

The girl came back. "Mistress Calliste say she don't have cloth for pocket."

"No cloth for a foreign pocket?" Foreign pocket, a foreign packet, a parcel to be posted overseas. "Ain't she have some shopcloth there?"

But the cloth on the shelf was a little too fine.

"All right," the barefoot woman said, abandoning pride. "Gimme a flour-sack." She pointed to the glass case. "Let me see that pack of biscuits. I don't want to buy it, eh. I just want to look at it." She held the pack in her hand. "*What?* T'ree-fifty for *dis?*" As though she hadn't known. In her feckless poor-woman's way she would have loved to throw away money on the dainty biscuits, but even at fifty cents they would have been too dear for her. All she could do was to make this little display, embarrassing the people in the shop who were sheltering from the rain, village people to whom her poverty would have been well known.

Mrs. Calliste stood again at her counter. A black marine, appearing suddenly, said roughly to her, "You own the shop?"

His accent was difficult, and he hadn't introduced himself or said good morning. She didn't know how to react.

"Where's the owner?"

"He not home," Mrs. Calliste said, speaking at last.

"When's he coming back?"

"About four." Mrs. Calliste looked worried.

"I'll be gone then."

The barefoot woman took charge. She said to the marine, "You can talk to her. She is Mistress Calliste."

But the marine had no special message. He wanted to say only what the Psy-Ops drill required him to say at this stage. He said, "We're going to play some music and make announcements. It's going to be loud and there'll be a crowd." And he was gone.

But there was no crowd then. That came an hour or so later, after the Psy-Ops team, guided by a local nurse and followed by the CBS crew, had made health visits to various houses.

The rocky dirty road down from the shop was slippery after rain.

"De sight bad," an old man said. "Ah, but de sight bad." He had heard about the health visits and he had put on his good clothes. He picked his way down the red road behind me, thinking I was one of the team. But there was no one to help with his eyes. And there were no drugs for the old woman whose nerves had frayed. She too, and her room, had been made ready for the visit.

"She had a nervous breakdown," her builder nephew said, "and she went to hospital. So far this year she have four re-occurrences. She live in that house up the hill and I brought her down with me, nuh, when she get bad. She does itch here and she does itch there, and she got those pains in her back all the time."

The old lady, half-crazed with pain, raised her arms. "I got these nerves. I got this pain."

But there were no drugs for her. The Psy-Ops doctor was distressed; he said he would come to her the next day.

The Psy-Ops men had trained in North Carolina. Grenada was their first venture among a foreign population. The population was friendly. There were no minds to win here. Psy-Ops had run into real need, real dependence; and the men, trained for a more macho role, didn't have the means to cope.

The loudspeaker on the jeep played a curious (perhaps "pacifying") kind of reggae, an extra drumming in the noisy tropical rain. The recorded announcements, half-threatening, half-benevolent, were repeated. Word about the visit spread to other villages. And soon outside Mrs. Calliste's shop there were any number of people, men and women, wanting to have their "pressure" tested.

The CBS team had filmed a lot, tramping about in the rain. The cameraman had slipped and damaged his elbow (but saved his camera). The film work, if it did make the CBS evening news, would have been the bigger American endeavour of the day. If it didn't make the evening news, it would have been less than the Psy-Ops exercise.

On the way back to St. George's we passed three schoolgirls in white blouses and navy blue skirts. One of them shouted, *"White—people!"* It wasn't a greeting. It was descriptive, the equivalent of a whistle, hovering between friendly satire and aggression, something from a very old Grenada, an acknowledgement of racial distance.

PSY-OPS hadn't thought it necessary to deface or remove the slogans of the revolution—except on the short street up the hill to Fort George. That was where the killings by the People's Revolutionary Army had taken place.

The events of that day had already passed into legend. Details varied—nearly everyone claimed to be an eye-witness or participant; but there was an essential tale. When the leader had been released from house arrest by the crowd, he was weak. He hadn't eaten for three days, either out of a fear of poison or because Cuban doctors had injected him with a dehydrating drug. He had been found naked, strapped to a bed. He couldn't walk. The people had taken him in a car to the Fort. The soldiers there had come over to his side; his mother had sent sandwiches and orange juice for him. Then the Revolutionary Military Council had sent the armoured cars. It was an incomplete story. But it was the legend now, the story of a Grenadian passion.

The Fort overlooked the entrance to the inner harbour. On the battlements were nineteenth-century cannon. The army barracks—police headquarters before the People's Revolutionary Army had been created—were in a sturdy old colonial building, in the Italianate style of the Public Works Department. The American bombing had been precise and light: four holes close together in the green corrugated-iron roof. To one side of the courtyard was the prison section, rusting barbed wire stretched over the little yard into which the three small concrete cells opened.

"Manners" had been imposed on counter-revolutionaries in that prison. Some of the prisoners had been Rastafarians; up to twenty had been held in that small space. Official red stencilled slogans—DISCIPLINE IS A MUST BE DISCIPLINED NOW and WE WILL DIE RATHER THAN BECOME PUPPETS OF U.S. IMPERIALISM— were still mixed with confused or stoned Rastafarian protests: FOR WHAT IS A MAN OWN IF HE SHALL GAIN THE WHOLE WORLD AND LOUSE THE LOST OF HIS SOULD.

All about the battlements was litter: flattened discarded Revolutionary Army uniforms, boots, padded boxes which had contained Russian weapons (the inventory on the lids in English), much paper, much writing. This army had studied. It had studied politics; it had studied a particular anti-aircraft weapon and done many simple written exercises. The barracks inside had more paper: innumerable written exercises, many communist magazines.

The revolution depended on language. At one level it used big, blurring words; at another, it misused the language of the people. Here the very idea of study—a good idea, associated in the minds of most Grenadians with self-improvement—had been used to keep simple men simple and obedient.

"My God, they've turned the guns on the people!" These are among the last recorded words of the leader of the revolution. A photograph taken at the time of the shooting shows the armoured cars, the army lorries, people running, and the slogan board—later painted over—at the foot of the Fort hill: POLITICS DISCIPLINE COMBAT READINESS EQUALS VICTORY.

The revolution was a revolution of words. The words had appeared as an illumination, a short-cut to dignity, to newly educated men who had nothing in the community to measure themselves against, and who, finally, valued little in their own community. But the words were mimicry. They were too big; they didn't fit; they remained words. The revolution blew away; and what was left in Grenada was a murder story.

1984

A Handful of Dust: Cheddi Jagan and the Revolution in Guyana

IN THE EARLY 1930s Evelyn Waugh travelled into the interior of British Guiana, on the old Spanish Main. There were three Guianas then, British, French, and Dutch, wedged between Venezuela and Brazil. British Guiana was the largest of the Guianas. It was eighty thousand square miles, about the size of Great Britain, but with a population of only half a million. Much of this population—mainly East Indian and African—lived on the Atlantic coast, where the big plantations were. Inland, just a few miles from the colonial coast, was South American wilderness, going back to Brazil: hardwood forests, Amerindian villages, boulder-strewn rivers, falls: and, after that, the laterite savannas, with giant red anthills, and palm trees marking the course of occasional shallow rivers.

It was on that savanna that the betrayed Waugh hero of *A Handful of Dust* (1934), looking for forgetfulness after his English travails, found a horrible form of social extinction: kept a prisoner on the almost empty savanna by the head of a dominant Anglo-Amerindian tribe, and made to read aloud the works of Dickens again and again.

Guiana has always been a land of fantasy. It was the land of El Dorado; it was the site of the Jonestown commune. But what is remarkable about the Waugh fantasy is that two years after the book was published a young man from the plantation coast of Guiana started on a journey that was to echo the destiny of Waugh's hero.

IN 1936, WHEN HE WAS EIGHTEEN, Cheddi Jagan, the grandson of indentured immigrants brought from India to work on the coastal plantations, left British Guiana with five hundred dollars to go to study in the United States. He stayed in the United States—in Washington, New York and Chicago—for seven solid years, until 1943. He did various jobs while he studied: he finally became a dentist. Towards the end of his time in the United States he married a beautiful American woman. He also had a Marxist illumination.

When Cheddi Jagan returned to Guiana in 1943 (his American bride following soon after, to astound the Jagan family), it was as a man with a fixed political cause. Whatever he may have thought about his Hindu or Indian or Guianese background, whatever historical or social bewilderment he may have grown to feel, was submerged in his Marxist ideas of surplus value and the universal class struggle. That was vision enough. And for fifty years, like a version of the Waugh figure—through the ending of the war, the re-emergence of Germany and Japan, the winding down of the European empires, the disintegration of black Africa, the coming and going of the Cold War, the end of European communism, through the independence of Guyana itself (spelt after independence in this new way, for no good historical or etymological reason)—Cheddi Jagan has sat waiting for his moment.

Almost from the start he had "the oppressed sugar workers as his base"—to use words from the back cover of the 1966 East German edition of his autobiography, *The West on Trial*. After nearly fifty years, those workers (or their descendants) are still there, more or less. And it may be that the very purity of Cheddi Jagan's Marxist view has helped to freeze people in their old roles.

SUCCESS came early to him. In 1947 he became the youngest member of the colonial Legislative Council of British Guiana. In 1950 he and others launched the People's Progressive Party. This was an extraordinary alliance of the two main racial groups of Guyana—the Africans (as they were called), descended from the slaves, and the East Indians, who had replaced the Africans on the plantations. In 1953 this party came overwhelmingly to power. It seemed then that Jagan was about to become the first leader of the first communist state in the New World. (Fidel Castro was to emerge five to six years later.) Jagan and his wife, Janet, became very famous. For a time they were demon figures in the British popular press, filling this journalistic hot spot somewhere in the interim between Mossadeq of Iran, who nationalized his country's oil, and Nasser of Egypt, who nationalized the Suez Canal.

But British Guiana was not Iran or Egypt. British Guiana in 1953 was only a colony. After three months in office, the Jagan administration was dismissed by the London government, the colony's constitution was suspended, and British troops were sent. Under this pressure the PPP split easily into its African and Indian components. The African and Indian populations of Guyana were almost evenly balanced. Below the Marxist words on both sides Guyana went back to its more instinctive racial ways.

The Indian vote returned Jagan to power in 1957 and again in 1961. But it was the African party that—with American help, and after serious racial disturbances—won the pre-independence elections of 1964. Ever since then, through a series of rigged elections, Cheddi Jagan and his Indian followers have been kept out of power, while—until 1984— Guyana followed a kind of Marxist-African way and became a "cooperative republic." For the last six years there has been a turning away from "cooperative" principles; but Guyana is now as wretched as any place in Eastern Europe.

Every important industry—bauxite, rice—was taken over by the African-controlled government; and the government gave jobs, or created jobs, for its supporters. So the communist-style tyranny of the state was also a racial tyranny; and the corruptions, petty and big, had a further racial twist. Everything became rotten in this state; everything began to lose money. More and more money was printed; in the racist state, the Guyana currency, once on a par with the currency of a place like Trinidad, became almost worthless. Imports were regulated, many items banned. Guyanese of all races began to pine for certain simple and cheap foods they had grown up on—New Brunswick sardines, Canadian flour, Canadian smoked herrings and salted fish. At a time of plenty in neighboring Trinidad (because of the oil boom of the 1970s), Guyana was experiencing want. Guyanese began to leave, legally and illegally, Indians at first, and then others; they went to Trinidad and Canada and the United States. More than a third of the Guyanese population now lives abroad.

Georgetown, the capital, once one of the most beautiful wood-built cities of the world (with the great hardwood forests just a few miles inland), weathered and decayed. Over the run-down city there now rises, at the end of one of the principal avenues, an extraordinary, mocking monument of the Cooperative Republic: a giant African-like figure, long-armed and apparently dancing, with what looks like cabalistic emblems on its limbs. This figure of African re-awakening is said to honor Cuffy, the leader of a slave revolt in Guyana in 1763; but there are black people who believe that—whatever the sculptor intended—the figure was also connected with some kind of obeah working on behalf of Forbes Burnham, the Guyanese African leader. Mr. Burnham is believed to have, in the end, mixed his Marxism with obeah, and to have had an obeah consultant.

IN THE GEORGETOWN Botanical Gardens—one of the many such gardens, of experiment and scholarship, established by the British in various parts of the empire in the eighteenth and nineteenth centuries—there is another, complementary monument of Mr. Burnham's rule. It is the mausoleum that was put up for Mr. Burnham after his death in 1984. It is a spiderlike structure, with a low central pavilion with an outer colonnade of concrete brackets that look like spider's legs. The intention was that the founder of the Cooperative Republic should be embalmed and displayed for ever, like Lenin; but something went wrong and the body decomposed before it could be treated.

Through all of this—Marxism and racial tyranny, and economic death, and obeah—Cheddi Jagan has sat at his post, the leader of his party, always there, the possessor of a purer Marxist way, waiting to be called. His support has always come from the Indians, but he has never accepted that he is just a racial leader. In the hardest times of African oppression he has supported whatever legislation came up that could be seen as socialist or Marxist. So, to some, out of the very purity of his Marxist vision, he has conspired against both the interests of his supporters and his own political success.

He is seventy-two now. With the disappearance of communism in Europe, and now that it no longer matters to the United States or Russia what happens in Guyana, the elections coming up may be free: and Cheddi Jagan may at last win. But times are now very hard indeed, with interest rates of 34 per cent, with the Guyana dollar worth an American cent, and with worthwhile foreign money staying away. All that a rational government could do is to reverse the nationalizations of the last twenty-five years. So that power, if it does come to Jagan, seems likely to end in failure, or the undoing of his legend.

Cheddi Jagan's party headquarters, Freedom House, is an old white wooden building in a bazaar-like street. I went to meet him there. He was grey, with glasses, but brisk. He was in a short-sleeved slate-blue safari suit. It revealed a certain fleshiness about his waist, but for a man of seventy-two he was in remarkable shape; and I felt that this was important to him as a politician.

He said he had no illness: every year since 1966 he had had a check-up in one of the "socialist countries." He spoke the now old-fashioned words without hesitation, so that in the little upstairs room of Freedom House, with the easy chairs and the coffee cups and all the papers, and with a view, through the open door, of the inner office with a framed black-and-white print of a drawing of Marx and Engels and Lenin, it was as though, whatever had happened outside, nothing had changed here.

I wanted to know how he had endured since 1964, what internal resources he had drawn on, why he hadn't given up, like many of his followers. He appeared not to understand the question. He spoke instead of the past, of the beginnings of his movement, and the great years from 1948 to 1964. He spoke with his old vigour, and in his academic, public-meeting way, ticking off points on his long fingers, and managing complete sentences that were full of facts and names and references.

He telescoped the twenty-six years since 1964. Then, answering a question of his own, rather than one I had asked, he said that people had often asked him why he hadn't gone in for "armed struggle." He called to someone in the outer office to bring him some papers. When they were brought, he took one which dealt with the Guyanese deficit. This sheet, smudged and printed on both sides, had been rolled off an antiquated "duplicator," and it had the acrid, oily smell of the duplicator ink. The graphs, not easy to read, showed that the Guyanese deficit had grown from 4.2 million Guyana dollars in 1965 to 1,309 million in 1988. The point he was making—and it was almost as though it was part of an old political strategy—was that it was better for the government to be undermined by its own stupendous deficit rather than by armed struggle, "which you were bound to lose."

Here his wife put her head through the door. Thirty years had passed since I had last seen her. I had remembered a woman of a great attractiveness. Thirty years, applied, as it were, all at once, had made her scarcely recognizable. At first I saw only the pale colour of her abundant hair, and the colours of her clothes, tan and black, foreign colors in the setting, not Guyanese or Caribbean colors. She was thinner in face, plumper and looser lower down, and she wore slacks; and her skin was looser. But then her eyes, her light voice (still American after nearly fifty years in Guyana), and her nervous laugh began to fit the younger person I had remembered.

Her talk was of her two children and her five grandchildren. Her son, now forty, lived in Chicago, where his father had studied. Her daughter lived in Canada.

In 1961 Janet Jagan's reputation in Guyana was that of the foreign white woman revolutionary, an American Jewish radical. Now it was said that she had withdrawn. An old political enemy said, "She's matronly, but don't tell her I said so."

GUYANA was the first place I travelled to as a writer. It was part of a project on European colonies in the Caribbean and South America. I was twenty-eight. I was an artless traveller, and was soon to discover that, whatever the excitements of new landscapes and of being on the move, a journey didn't necessarily result in a narrative on the page.

As a political observer I was uncertain and diffident. I thought that in this kind of writing I had to take people on trust. I cast aside—as belonging to another form—my novelist's doubts. So in my book I wrote more romantically than I actually felt about the African or black racial movement of the late 1950s. I allowed myself to see it as it was presented to me, as a kind of redemption. I suppressed my fears about its glibness and sentimentality, and its element of viciousness.

And although I spent some time with the Jagans, formally and informally, in Georgetown and in various places in the country, when Cheddi Jagan was premier of the colony and Janet Jagan the minister of health, I never allowed myself to believe that their Marxism was more than a British Labour party kind of socialism.

Forbes Burnham in 1961 was leader of the opposition. He was witty and mischievous, very black and smooth-skinned, already heavy, though still with the manner of the bright scholarship boy. He carried his character on his face and in his physique: but I never allowed myself to make anything of my feeling that Burnham was a sensualist and dangerous, someone at once wounded and spoilt, full of vengefulness.

And I never thought—since I shared to some extent the background of both Burnham and Jagan—that these two Marxists between them would actually overturn the society. I saw what I thought I should see, what I was more comfortable seeing. In this I was like the people of Guyana.

MARTIN CARTER was one of the poets of the Guyana awakening of the early 1950s. To him much of the confusion in Guyana came from a misuse or misunderstanding of language. A word like "socialism" came to Guyana without its history, without the varied meanings given it by people like Robert Owen and Bernard Shaw and William Morris. Everyone in Guyana had his own ideas of socialism, according to the books he had read; in this matter people did not always understand one another. Not everyone would think of socialism as an economic system. "A socialist would become simply a good man, a nice man. And that remained the idea about socialism for a long time among the general population here. Today that is different, because everything that has gone wrong is associated with socialism."

And Martin Carter told this story: "Pandit Misir, a brahmin from the west bank of the Demerara River, was a member of Cheddi's party. This was at a place called Vreed-en-Hoop—which, incidentally, had been owned by John Gladstone, father of William Ewart Gladstone, the British prime minister. Cheddi had been distributing booklets sent out by the British Communist party to its friends not only in Georgetown but in the Third World. Among the booklets was one called *Capitalist Society*. This would be before the elections in '53.

"There was a public meeting called by Cheddi on the west bank at which Pandit Misir functioned as the chairman. It was a huge crowd. And the pandit—he would have been between thirty-five and forty-five, but he looked much older—was in his top form because of the crowd and the presence of Cheddi Jagan.

"He told the crowd that before he introduced Cheddi he would like to tell them something himself. Upon which he declared: 'Dey got a t'ing called capitalist society. Um [it, in the local pidgin] like bird-vine. When um put hand 'pon you, um don't let go.' Bird-vine is a result of birds cleaning their beaks on trees after having eaten a certain type of fruit, the fruit of course of the bird-vine—it's a well-known plant to people who live on the coast.

"And that's all that Pandit Misir said, and the crowd roared, because they understood that the pandit intended to convey to them that capitalist society was something oppressive. Which means that all the plantation experience had been summed up in the two words, 'capitalist society.' Pandit Misir himself didn't know better. He was a slim, tall man. A passionate man, and what he said about bird-vine would convey much more than Cheddi's disquisition on the theory of surplus value of Karl Marx."

So that—in this analysis—somewhere between the pidgin of Pandit Misir and the vague set phrases of Marxist lore, the realities of Guyana would have been distorted or lost. And one side of the terrible farce of the Cooperative Republic would have begun to be prepared.

AN ASSOCIATE of Cheddi Jagan's in the late 1940s was Sydney King, an African village schoolteacher. He broke away from the Jagan party in the mid-1950s. At some later stage he had an African transformation. "With the Indians glorying in their civilization, Africans here had a sense of self-pity." And, as part of an "African naming movement" that he tried to get started, Sydney King gave himself the name of Eusi Kwayana.

He said of Cheddi Jagan, "I think he had a cultural problem. If he had been a devout Hindu, even in his youth, he would have had a more workable, a more human, frame of reference. But, having rejected imperialism and all its works along with its culture, he got attached to another metropolis, which was the Soviet Union. He understood it as it presented itself. So everything he did had to be explained, in his own mind, in the culture of that other metropolis. Once he could do that he felt vindicated.

"When Burnham began to introduce socialism from 1971 onwards, people in both races began to express dismay and said they wanted to hear nothing of it. This didn't matter to Jagan. He made a statement at this time that the whole of Guyana had voted for socialism—part for him, part for Burnham. Though politics here were always racial."

At the time of the racial disturbances in 1964 Eusi Kwayana allied himself with Burnham. But then he broke away from Burnham as well.

"Burnham actually introduced slave labour. He introduced compulsory labour at Plantation Hope, a coconut plantation on the east coast. And all you got was the right to buy scarce commodities. It wasn't even given in lieu of labour as in the days of slavery; you had to buy the goods.

You slaved for nothing on your day of leisure. At Plantation Hope he lorded it over the people. Riding on horseback, drinking, and entertaining his personal friends. He sent typists, office workers, professionals into the cane field in 1977, to break a sugar strike. They did not succeed. They messed up the cultivation. They knew nothing about it."

I said, "And yet the black people loved him."

"Loved him? That ended in the middle Seventies. He was well admired by the Guyanese when he got back from England in 1950, on account of his supposed scholarship, and oratory—which I found empty. I even knew Indo-Guyanese who liked to hear him talk. He was mostly the hero of the middle-class Africans. It was a long time before he was accepted by the rural Africans—they didn't like lawyers.

"His government became known to be corrupt in 1971. Everybody knew that the socialism of the government was a fraud. Some people feel that Burnham has proved that socialism meant leaders dominating people and filling their own pockets. And this has been coming out of Eastern Europe.

"When Burnham died his estate was declared to be a million Guyana dollars. The Guyana dollar was then 4:30 to the US dollar. This left the population in stitches. People said that that million dollars was the money Burnham had in his pocket when he died. His death was a matter of relief, comedy in the streets. In Brooklyn they held parties. And there were two days' holiday here, during which drinking places were not allowed to be open because the festivity would be too clear.

"The day after the funeral I was walking in Georgetown, and everybody knew that the body had been removed by soldiers the night before. They had brought in embalmers and were working on his body in a funeral parlour in the city. I believe the embalmers had come from Moscow—the press said so. The population spat on this whole idea of embalming Burnham's body. An African lady told me: 'He dead. He must go *dong*.' And they published in the press that they wanted to embalm him to preserve him indefinitely, and in the mausoleum he would be on permanent display. The body then stayed away for a year—a year of rumours, rumours about the body. Some people swear it was never embalmed, that it was too far gone to be embalmed, and that it was a wax image that was returned. From England, a famous studio—what's it called?"

"Madame Tussaud's?"

"People are saying it was Madame Tussaud's work. Not Burnham's body. They refer to him as the man who was buried twice."

Physically, Eusi Kwayana was not the kind of man I had imagined from his African name and restless political history. He had been a vegetarian for more than forty years, and he was thin, ascetic-looking, delicate. His long fingers made elegant gestures. In appearance he was like a religious figure from Byzantine art: long-faced, a high, arching forehead between two high side tufts of greyish-brown hair, sharp-nosed, with deep lines running from nose to chin and defining the chin. His neck was long and wrinkled, with thin fold upon thin fold.

I asked him whether he now took his African transformation for granted, or whether he still thought about it. He laughed, then giggled. "I still think about it." And, shyly, he raised an arm to show that his short-sleeved "African" tunic, of the sort he now habitually wore, had its practical side: it had a neatly hemmed vent under the arms.

CHEDDI JAGAN'S father and mother both came from India to Guyana as very young children in 1901, on the same sailing ship, the *Elbe*. Both started work on the plantations at a very early age. Cheddi Jagan's father started before he was ten; he was a full cane cutter at fourteen; when he was thirty he became a "driver" or gang foreman, earning ten shillings a week, about $2.50.

Cheddi was then eleven. Three years later his father sent him to the capital, Georgetown, to Queen's College; and three years after that sent him to the United States to study, with five hundred dollars. The money had been won at gambling. As a gang foreman Cheddi's father mixed with the plantation overseers. They were mainly Scottish; and they were drinking and gambling men.

Cheddi was the eldest of eleven children. One of the extra-political things he did when he came back to Guyana in 1943 was to take over responsibility for his brothers and sisters. He educated them all. Of the eleven Jagan children, three became professional people, two became nurses, and one became a hairdresser.

Martin Carter remembered Cheddi Jagan's father as "a tall man with a black bristling moustache. I remember the moustache vividly. And his height—he was a very tall man, by any standards. His mother was gentle, almost wraith-like, very thin. The impression I had of her, when I met her in the very late forties, was that she had spent a whole life keeping children alive—literally alive. Their house, on the Corentyne coast, was very simple, with a kitchen at the back with a mud cooking arrangement—we call it a 'cow-mouth.' It was detached from the main house."

Of Cheddi Jagan's beginnings, Martin Carter said, "Coming from the plantation coast, known in the old days as the Wild Coast, the sheer area of experience was too much for a young man from a plantation background to deal with comfortably, especially in those days. We were even more remote than we are today from so-called metropolitan centers. You could imagine"—Martin Carter looked for a word—"the *lostness* of a young man in those days coming out of a background without a literary culture. It froze him into attitudes which have lasted. This freezing affected him personally. At the same time it brought home to him in a very powerful way the kind of society and community he had came from."

IT WAS OF HIS EARLY days, and especially of his time in America, that I wanted to hear when I next met Cheddi Jagan. He came for me at the hotel one Sunday afternoon, and we drove to his house. It was the house he had built after he had left the premiership in 1964. It was a plain, new-style, two-storey Georgetown house, well-fenced, with a watchdog.

We sat upstairs. The afternoon breeze blew through the open doors on both sides. Beyond the wrought-iron rails of the balcony the garden was all green, with mango trees and coconut trees and banana trees.

Nineteen thirty-six seemed very far away. What would have been the world picture of his parents then, with their plantation background and the half-erased India of their ways? What would have been the expectations of Cheddi himself, travelling to the United States and Washington, to study at a black university, Howard, at a time of depression and intolerance? The ship was going to dock at Boston. Did the name of the famous city excite him?

He couldn't say. It was as Martin Carter had said: Cheddi had had no literary culture, nothing that would have helped him to see and understand, and put things in their place. He had simply taken things as they had come.

He had had to work while he studied at Howard; after two years he had won a scholarship to Northwestern near Chicago. He had many stories of his American time; and Janet—in black slacks and a flowered blouse on this holiday afternoon, her hair thick and quite golden—prompted him in those stories. In Washington he had worked in a pawn shop used by blacks. He worked there as a tailor (a half-skill he had picked up in Guyana), earning twenty-five cents an hour for mending unredeemed clothes, which were then put up for sale. In Chicago he had run an elevator at night.

He said, "West Indians always did better than American blacks because of their better background, and they were looked upon with some resentment. But within that all were treated as blacks. Indians had a higher kind of social recognition. In Washington there were cinemas where blacks couldn't go but I could. But I never went, because I didn't feel different from the blacks. I had that same feeling of being hemmed in, that same feeling of inferiority. I used to go to the poorer cinema where there was literally a partition between white and black. On one side black, the other side white. I used to go and sit with the blacks."

Near the end of his time, during a checkup at Northwestern, a spot was found on his lung, and he was sent to a sanitarium. "There were no drugs for tuberculosis in those days. The cure was just to sit in the cold air. The sanitarium was made up of small cottages, and two-thirds of the walls were of wire mesh. In the sanitarium you had to walk slowly, do everything in a measured way. I was nearly penniless at the time, and the sanitarium lady gave me a cut rate." After six months the spot disappeared; and there was some question then whether there had been an infection at all. Perhaps, after the strain of six years of America, he had needed only to withdraw and rest and calm down.

Janet went and made the tea, and brought it out with biscuits, "cookies"—the word unusual in Guyana, and in this house like a remnant of a far-off culture.

In this tea interlude she talked of what I had written about her nearly thirty years before.

"People remembered two details mainly. You wouldn't believe. The first was that I painted my toenails."

I had forgotten that, forgotten the fact, forgotten that I had written it.

"I don't know why that should have caused such interest," she said. "Everybody wore painted toenails then."

"Everybody," Cheddi said.

She said, "I looked at the book just the other day. And the other thing you mentioned that people talked about—I checked that, too—was the book I was reading."

I had forgotten that as well.

"It was Colette. *The Vagabond*."

That would have made an impression: the boastfulness and shallow sensual vanities of Colette, in a setting so removed: muddy Guyanese rivers, old river steamers. And then, in a distant reach of my mind, the two details together did bring back an impression, rather than an idea, of a trip in the interior with Janet Jagan, when she was minister of health.

She said, "I looked for it among my books the other day. I don't think I have it anymore."

The house, with its books and family pictures, felt calm. Thinking of that, thinking of the Jagan children settled abroad, and thinking of the journey that had begun in 1936, I wondered whether it couldn't be said that Cheddi Jagan, in an essential personal way, had been a success.

Janet made a sound of disbelief.

But Cheddi said, "I do, in the sense of what we have been able to achieve, and in the sense of recognition. Even my enemies recognize our integrity in politics."

Janet said, "A lot of his satisfaction is his writing. He likes to write. He likes to lecture. Cheddi's an optimist." She told a story of a boating moment in Trinidad. Their outboard motor had failed; the current was driving their boat towards rocks and a cliff. She had seen no hope, but Cheddi had remained lucid, working at the engine, and had got it going.

He said, "Maybe it's a virus in the blood, a political virus. And Janet has kept me on the moral path—politically."

She said, "It's nice to get a pat on the back."

He said, "She belonged to the first generation of American rebels." She made a questioning sound, and he explained: "The second generation came during Vietnam."

She said she remembered that when she was at Wayne State University in Detroit she made an effort to be friendly to black people and Chinese. "There was some urge within me to reach out to those groups."

Her own relationship with Cheddi caused trouble in her family.

She said, with something like sadness, "Cheddi never met my father."

I asked her, "Did you feel you were being brave or principled?"

"I was just young."

Her mother came out to Guyana once. She got to know Cheddi and one day she told Janet that she liked him. "Of course," Janet said, speaking of her mother's later attitude to Cheddi, "it helped being *premier*." She pronounced the word in the American way, stressing the second syllable. Things were always easier with her brother. "But I'll tell you this. The picture of me my brother has up is one where I am with Princess Margaret." And she gave her nervous half-laugh.

I had up to then felt that worldly position hadn't really mattered to her. Now I thought that she was possibly less stoical than Cheddi, that there was a melancholy in her that the long dedication and struggle, the enduring of a calamity in the country, had not ended with success, as old-fashioned morality and narrative might have dictated; that it had ended badly, in a general dissolution of the cause. But I didn't feel the matter could be pressed.

IN HIS AUTOBIOGRAPHY Cheddi Jagan gives two chapters, twenty-five pages, to the first twenty-five years of his life, up to his return to Guyana from the United States. The details are clear: everything is fairly laid out, without false stresses; the narrative is fast. But the narrative is also dense; the reader cannot keep it all in his head; he cannot (any more than the writer can) make all the connections. The early chapters are like the early chapters of Gandhi's autobiography, especially those that deal with Gandhi's time as a student in London; and the similarity has to do with the fact that both men, of Indian and Hindu background (and separated by only fifty years), are coming to terms, in their different ways, with an experience which, as it occurred, they were far from understanding. Both men write so transparently of their early days that their words can be studied again and again.

In Jagan's book, for instance, there is a strange paragraph about his difficulties of "identification" when he went back to Guyana. "There was no political party . . . For a while I played cricket, and soon after became addicted to bridge playing. I spent hours and hours at bridge and read every publication on the subject. But this was in no way a satisfaction . . . I wanted to identify myself with the real hard world around me."

I talked about this with Martin Carter. He knew the Jagan book, but the theme of bridge playing—strangely juxtaposed to a search for identification—was something he had missed. He said that bridge would have been useful to Cheddi Jagan at that time, filling up an evening and giving an illusion of a social life.

But when I next met Cheddi Jagan, at Freedom House, and put the point to him, he said that the identification he was looking for was political; and this was difficult for him in 1943, because he had become more complicated than the colony. To the plantation background he had added his knowledge of Gandhi and Nehru and the Indian freedom struggle; and there was also his American radicalization, his ideas about the War of Independence, and about Roosevelt (a supporter of Indian independence) and the New Deal. The games of bridge he had begun to play in Guyana were "recreation"; he played with dedication because that was his way. "Whatever I do, I do very intensely." (And indeed, when I looked at the autobiography later, I saw that once in Chicago he had tried seriously—like his father in Guyana—to make money by betting, and had even read books like *How to Win the Races.*)

He said, "There has always been a division between Janet and me. At the end of the day she can drop everything and read a novel. I take my work home."

Although he had been radicalized in the United States, it wasn't until he got back to Guyana that he read Marxist literature. "It was Janet who, when she came here in 1943, brought me Little Lenin Library books— little tracts, pamphlets. It was the first time I read Marxist literature. And then—as with the bridge books—I began reading Marxist books like mad. I read *Das Kapital* after the Little Lenin series. And that helped me to have a total understanding of the development of society. Until then, all the various struggles—Indians, blacks, the American people—had been disjointed experiences. To put it in a way that was totally related to a socioeconomic system came from the reading of Marxist literature. For instance, the woman question was dealt with in Engels's book, *The Origin of the Family.* The Marxist theory of surplus value brought a totally new understanding of the struggle of the working class—not only that they were exploited, but how they were exploited.

"It was exciting to me, an intellectual excitement, because a whole new world opened to me, a total understanding of the world, which then made coherent all my previous experiences in America. Discrimination— if you don't see the system as a whole, you see discrimination only."

This new way of seeing also dealt with his Indian past. "The Indian culture practises which I was accustomed to as a boy—I was completely divorced from that in America. So I was then more like Nehru in terms of culture. As a student in America my life was patterned on Gandhi and Nehru. Gandhi was a *fighter*. Nehru too. These things moulded me."

Perhaps he was also moulded, more than he knew or could acknowledge, by something in his Hindu caste background. It is there, in the autobiography. When he went to Georgetown as a fifteen-year-old schoolboy, he lodged with various Hindu families. He couldn't pay much. The first family treated him as a servant: they wanted him to go to the market, wash the car, and even—Queen's College student though he was—to cut grass for the goats. The family he changed to was worse. They were of the kshatriya or warrior caste, just below the brahmin. One of the daughters had married a brahmin, and the family was anxious to live up to the high connection. They didn't want Cheddi to sleep on a bed in their house; they required him to sleep on the floor, because the Jagans were of the kurmi caste, a caste of cultivators.

CHEDDI JAGAN says in his book that he had heard about caste problems only from his mother. But, in fact, as a caste, the kurmis are interesting. The gazetteers, or handbooks, that the British compiled for various Indian districts in the last century and this, speak not only of the agricultural skill and diligence of the kurmis, but also of their caste combativeness. The kurmis of some districts insist that they are not a low caste. They say they are of Rajput origin, and kshatriyas. Now, everything said about Cheddi Jagan's father stresses his physical presence; and the photograph I saw of him that morning in Freedom House showed a man with a proud Rajput moustache—the moustache that had made such an impression on Martin Carter.

To be an Indian and a kurmi in Guyana was to be "hemmed in" in a double way, even before the challenges of the United States. All of this hemming-in the Marxist illumination abolished, made universal and abstract. And it might be said that Cheddi Jagan, as the son of his father, was ready for such an illumination.

Cheddi Jagan said, "This discovery of the class struggle, and society divided into classes—all came from my Marxist reading. My background gave me a class bias. To me the class issue was fundamental."

He met Janet in 1942 or early in 1943. "Just after I came out of the sanitarium. I met her at a party of a mutual friend. Her family had fallen into poverty during the Depression, and then they quickly came out of that to have a middle-class status. At Wayne University she identified with minorities. Not only was she *strikingly* beautiful, we had the same interests, interests in the underdog. We got on immediately. She gave up her undergrad work and began to study as a nurse because she wanted to serve in the war. And that was when we met—she was a student nurse."

Janet took up the story a little while later, after Cheddi had left his office for a meeting. We sat in the small outer room of Cheddi's office, with the low easy chairs. She spoke slowly, contemplatively.

"My best friend—a girl I grew up with in Chicago, Helen—had a farewell party, and Cheddi was there. He was dating one of Helen's sisters. He was very handsome, of course. There wasn't anything political. It was just a boy-girl story."

I asked her about her first impressions of Guyana.

"It was a bit of a culture shock. It was during the war. I came on a seaplane. We landed on the Demerara River, and we went straight to Port Mourant. It was a shock. They didn't know what the hell to do with me. I should have been with the women, but they put me in a chair in the living room with the men. The women sat on the floor in the kitchen. I thought they would be resentful. I thought they would have liked Cheddi to marry an Indian girl of high status. I thought they missed the fuss of the wedding and so on.

"I'll tell you a funny thing. We wanted to give Indrani, Cheddi's eldest sister, a good education. So I went to Bishop's"—the leading girls' school in Georgetown—"and spoke to the headmistress—she was English, white—and I told her I wanted to bring my sister-in-law from Berbice. And she said okay—if she had the qualifications. And when I took Indrani there, the headmistress was shocked. She was expecting my sister-in-law to be white, and she said no. So Indrani didn't get in. She got into Central High School, and eventually she went to England and studied nursing. There are now about *six* dentists in the Jagan family, and three optometrists. That's a good profession for women; that's one they can handle."

I asked her, thinking of the life that had begun for her in 1943, "Have you enjoyed it all?"

"Not all of it." She gave her nervous, young-sounding laugh. "Some of it has been very painful. So many awful things happened that I find forgetfulness one of the ways of survival. In the 1960s it was terrible.

There was a period when I couldn't go out, couldn't go to a cinema, restaurant, couldn't do anything in public. I was the scapegoat. I don't have Cheddi's temperament. I tend to be a bit gloomy.

"But I think it's been an exciting life. It was interesting. Living in a different culture. They used to make up a lot of silly stories about me— aping Indians, wearing saris, a whole lot of stupidness. I haven't tried to be what I am not. A lot of people tried to say that my political life depended on my being an Indian. I suppose a stranger in a land would be subject to all sorts of myths and caricatures.

"I get my best enjoyment working in newspapers. I don't like the public-appearance part of politics. I evolved into a journalist. Being a woman in politics isn't that easy."

I wanted to know more about her background in the United States.

"Recently, my brother and I took a tour in Missouri. On my father's side we've been in the US for most of the last century. We went and saw those graves in Moberly, Missouri. There was hardly any Jewish community there, and in the cemetery there was a teeny little section with stones that marked the Jewish graves there—mostly my family. On my mother's side my grandparents migrated from Hungary and Romania in this century. So the world is made up of people who have migrated."

And it was as though she was talking not only of the migrations of her ancestors to the United States, but also of the migration of the Indians to Guyana; of Cheddi's grandmothers coming over with their small children from India on the sailing ship *Elbe* in 1901; of Cheddi's journey to the United States in 1936; and of his journey back with her in 1943; the settling—half a resettling—of their children in the United States and Canada; and the migration, since the 1970s, of all those people of Guyana they had hoped to bring the revolution to, people who had now taken their destinies in their own hands.

1991

A NOTE IN 2002. *In 1992 the United States, which had encouraged the rigging of elections in Guyana since 1964, felt it could relent. Cheddi Jagan won the—unrigged—elections in October 1992 and was president until his death in March 1997; he was seventy-eight. He was succeeded as president, after new elections, by Janet Jagan. She retired because of ill-health twenty months later, in August 1999.*

Postscript: Our Universal Civilization

The following address was given at the Manhattan Institute of New York.

I'VE GIVEN THIS TALK the title of Our Universal Civilization. It is a rather big title, and I am a little embarrassed by it. I feel I should explain how it came about. I have no unifying theory of things. To me situations and people are always specific, always of themselves. That is why one travels and writes: to find out. To work in the other way would be to know the answers before one knew the problems. That is a recognized way of working, I know, especially if one is a political or religious or racial missionary. But I would have found it hard.

That was why I thought, when this invitation to talk came, that it would be better for me to find out what kind of issues members of the Institute were interested in. Myron Magnet, a senior fellow of the Institute, was in England at the time. We talked on the telephone; and then, some days later, he sent me a handwritten list of questions. They were very serious questions, very important.

Are we—are communities—as strong only as our beliefs? Is it enough for beliefs or an ethical view to be passionately held? Does the passion give validity to the ethics? Are beliefs or ethical views arbitrary, or do they represent something essential in the cultures where they flourish?

It was easy to read through to some of the anxieties that lay behind the questions. There was a clear worry about certain fanaticisms "out there." At the same time there was a certain philosophical diffidence about how that anxiety could be expressed, since no one wants to use words or concepts that might boomerang on himself. You know how words can be used: I am civilized and steadfast; you are barbarian and fanatical: he is primitive and blind. Of course. I was on the side of the questioner, and understood his drift. But I got to feel, over the next few days, and perhaps from my somewhat removed position, that I couldn't share the pessimism implied by the questions. I felt that the very pessimism of the questions, and their philosophical diffidence, defined the strength of the civilization out of which it issued. And so the theme of my talk, Our Universal Civilization, was given me.

I AM NOT GOING to attempt to define this civilization. I will only speak of it in a personal way. It is the civilization, first of all, which gave me the idea of the writing vocation. It is the civilization in which I have been able to practise my vocation as a writer. To be a writer, you need to start with a certain kind of sensibility. The sensibility itself is created, or given direction, by an intellectual atmosphere.

Sometimes an atmosphere can be too refined, a civilization too achieved, too ritualized. Eleven years ago, when I was travelling in Java, I met a young man who wanted above all else to be a poet and to live the life of the mind. This ambition had been given him by his modern education; but it was hard for the young man to explain to his mother exactly what he was up to. This mother was a person of culture and elegance; that should be stressed. She was elegant in visage and dress and speech; her manners were like art; they were Javanese court manners.

So I asked the young man—bearing in mind that we were in Java, where ancient epics live on in the popular art of puppet plays—"But isn't your mother secretly proud that you are a poet?" He said in English—I mention this to give a further measure of his education in his far-off Javanese town—"She wouldn't have even a sense of what being a poet is."

And the poet's friend and mentor, a teacher at the local university, amplified this. The friend said, "The only way he would have of making his mother understand what he is trying to do would be to suggest that he is being a poet in the classical tradition. And she would find this absurd. She would reject it as an impossibility." It would be rejected as an impossibility, because for the poet's mother the epics of her country—and to her they would have been like sacred texts—already existed, had already been written. They had only to be learned or consulted.

For the mother, all poetry had already been written. That particular book, it might be said, was closed: it was, part of the perfection of her culture. To be told by her son, who was twenty-eight, not all that young, that he was hoping to be a poet would be like a devout mother in another culture asking her writer-son what he intended to write next, and getting the reply, "I am thinking of adding a book to the Bible." Or, to attempt another comparison, the young man would be like the character in the story by Borges who had taken on himself the task of rewriting *Don Quixote*. Not just re-telling the story, or copying out of the original; but seeking, by an extraordinary process of mind-clearing and re-creation, to arrive—without copying or falsity, and purely through original thought—at a narrative coinciding word by word with the Cervantes book.

I understood the predicament of the young man in central Java. His background, after all, was not far removed from the Hindu aspect of my own Trinidad background. We were an agricultural immigrant community from India. The ambition to become a writer, the introduction to writing and ideas about writing, had been given me by my father. He was born in 1906, the grandson of someone who had come to Trinidad as a baby. And somehow, in spite of all the discouragements of the society of that small agricultural colony, the wish to be a writer had come to my father; and he had made himself into a journalist, even with the limited opportunities for journalism that existed in that colony.

We were a people of ritual and sacred texts. We also had our epics—and they were the very epics of Java; we heard them constantly sung or chanted. But it couldn't be said that we were a literary people. Our literature, our texts, didn't commit us to an exploration of our world; rather, they were cultural markers, giving us a sense of the wholeness of our world; and the alienness of what lay outside. I don't believe that, in his family, anyone before my father would have thought of original literary composition. That idea came to my father in Trinidad with the English language; somehow, in spite of the colonial discouragements of the place, an idea of the high civilization connected with the language came to my father; and he was given some knowledge of literary forms. Sensibility is not enough if you are going to be a writer. You need to arrive at the forms that can contain or carry your sensibility; and literary forms—whether in poetry or drama, or prose fiction—are artificial, and ever-changing.

This was a part of what was passed on to me at a very early age. At a very early age—in all the poverty and bareness of Trinidad, far away, with a population of half a million—I was given the ambition to write books, and specifically to write novels, which my father had presented to me as the highest form. But books are not created just in the mind. Books are physical objects. To write them, you need a certain kind of sensibility; you need a language, and a certain gift of language; and you need to possess a particular literary form. To get your name on the spine of the created physical object, you need a vast apparatus outside yourself. You need publishers, editors, designers, printers, binders; booksellers, critics, newspapers, and magazines and television where the critics can say what they think of the book; and, of course, buyers and readers.

I want to stress this mundane side of things, because it is easy to take it for granted; it is easy to think of writing only in its personal, romantic aspect. Writing is a private act; but the published book, when it starts to live, speaks of the co-operation of a particular kind of society. The society has a certain degree of commercial organization. It also has certain cultural or imaginative needs. It doesn't believe that all poetry has already been written. It needs new stimuli, new writing; and it has the means of judging the new things that are offered.

THIS KIND OF SOCIETY didn't exist in Trinidad. It was necessary, therefore, if I was going to be a writer, and live by my books, to travel out to that kind of society where the writing life was possible. This meant, for me at that time, going to England. I was travelling from the periphery, the margin, to what to me was the centre; and it was my hope that, at the centre, room would be made for me. I was asking a lot, asking, in fact, more of the centre than of my own society. The centre, after all, had its own interests, its own worldview, its own ideas of what it wanted in novels. And it still does. My subjects were far-off; but a little room was made for me in the England of the 1950s. I was able to become a writer, and to grow in the profession. It took time; I was forty—and had been publishing in England for fifteen years—before a book of mine was seriously published in the United States.

But I always recognized, in England in the 1950s, that as someone with a writing vocation there was nowhere else for me to go. And if I have to describe the universal civilization I would say it is the civilization that both gave the prompting and the idea of the literary vocation; and also gave the means to fulfil that prompting; the civilization that enabled me to make that journey from the periphery to the centre; the civilization that links me not only to this audience but also to that now not-so-young man in Java whose background was as ritualized as my own, and on whom—as on me—the outer world had worked, and given the ambition to write.

It is easier today for someone setting out to be a writer from a place like Java or Trinidad; subjects once far-off are no longer so. But I have never been able to take my career for granted. I know that there are still large tracts of the world where the cultural or economic conditions I described a while ago do not obtain, and someone like myself would not have been able to become a writer. I couldn't have become a writer in the Mohammedan world; in China; in Japan—the Japanese make room for the literary culture only of the countries they see themselves competing against. I couldn't have become the kind of writer I am in Eastern Europe or the Soviet Union or black Africa. I don't think I could have taken my gifts even to India.

You will understand, then, how important it was to me to know when I was young that I could make this journey from the margin to the centre, from Trinidad to London. The ambition to be a writer assumed that this was possible. So, in fact, I was taking it for granted, in spite of my ancestry and Trinidad background, that with another, equally important part of myself I was part of a larger civilization. I suppose the same could be said of my father, though he was closer to the ritual ways of our Hindu and Indian past.

BUT I NEVER formulated the idea of the universal civilization until quite recently—until eleven years ago, when I travelled for many months in a number of non-Arab Muslim countries to try to understand what had driven them to their rage. That Muslim rage was just beginning to be apparent.

"Fundamentalism"—in connection with the Mohammedan world— was not a word often used by the newspapers in 1979; they hadn't yet worked through to that concept. What they spoke of more was "the revival of Islam." And that, indeed, to anyone contemplating it from a distance, was a puzzle. Islam, which had apparently so little to offer its adherents in the last century and in the first half of this—what did it have to offer to an infinitely more educated, infinitely faster, world in the later years of the century?

The adaptation of my own family and Trinidad Indian community to colonial Trinidad and, through that, to the twentieth century hadn't been easy. It had been painful for us, an Asian people, living instinctive, ritualized lives, to awaken to an idea of our history and to learn to live with the idea of our political helplessness. There had been very difficult social adjustments as well. For example, in our culture marriages had always been arranged; it took some time, and many damaged lives, for us to arrive at the other way. All of this went with the personal intellectual growth I have described.

And I thought, when I began to travel in the Muslim world, that I would be travelling among people who would be like the people of my own community.

A large portion of Indians were Muslims; we had both had a similar nineteenth-century imperial or colonial history. I thought that religion was an accidental difference. I thought, as people said, that faith was faith, that people living at a certain time in history would have felt the same urges.

But it wasn't like that. The Muslims said that their religion was fundamental to them. And it was: it made for an immense difference. I have to stress that I was travelling in the non-Arab Muslim world. Islam began as an Arab religion; it spread as an Arab empire. In Iran, Pakistan, Malaysia, Indonesia—the countries of my itinerary—I was travelling, therefore, among people who had been converted to what was an alien faith. I was travelling among people who had had to make a double adjustment—an adjustment to the European empires of the nineteenth and twentieth centuries; and an earlier adjustment to the Arab faith. You might almost say that I was among people who had been doubly colonized, doubly removed from themselves.

Because I was soon to discover that no colonization had been so thorough as the colonization that had come with the Arab faith. Colonized or defeated peoples can begin to distrust themselves. In the Muslim countries I am talking about this distrust had all the force of religion. It was an article of the Arab faith that everything before the faith was wrong, misguided, heretical; there was no room in the heart or mind of these believers for their pre-Mohammedan past. So ideas of history were quite different from ideas of history elsewhere; there was no wish here to go back as far as possible into the past, and to learn as much as possible about the past.

Persia had a great past; it had been the rival in classical times of Greece and Rome. But you wouldn't have believed it in Iran in 1979; for the Iranians the glory and the truth had begun with the coming of Islam. Pakistan was a very new Muslim state. But the land was very old. In Pakistan were the ruins of the very old cities of Mohenjo-Daro and Harappa. Fabulous ruins, the discovery of which earlier this century had given a new idea of the history of the sub-continent. Not only pre-Islamic ruins; but possibly also pre-Hindu. There was an archaeological department, inherited from British days, that looked after the sites. But there was, especially with the growth of fundamentalism, a contrary current. This was expressed in a letter to a newspaper while I was there. The ruins of the cities, the writer said, should be hung with quotations from the Koran, saying that this was what befell unbelievers.

The faith abolished the past. And when the past was abolished like this, more than an idea of history suffered. Human behavior, and ideals of good behavior, could suffer. When I was in Pakistan the newspapers were running articles to mark the anniversary of the Arab conquest of Sind. This was the first part of the Indian sub-continent to be conquered by the Arabs. It occurred at the beginning of the eighth century. The kingdom of Sind—an enormous area: the southern half of Afghanistan, the southern half of Pakistan—at that time was a Hindu-Buddhist kingdom. The brahmins didn't really understand the outside world; the Buddhists didn't believe in taking life. It was a kingdom waiting to be conquered, you might say. But it took a long time for Sind to be conquered; it was very far away from the Arab heartland, across immense deserts. Six or seven Arab expeditions foundered.

At one time the third caliph himself, the third successor to the Prophet, called one of his lieutenants and said, "O Hakim, have you seen Hindustan and learnt all about it?" Hakim said, "Yes, O commander of the faithful." The caliph said, "Give us a description of it." And all Hakim's frustration and bitterness came out in his reply. "Its water is dark and dirty," Hakim said. "Its fruit is bitter and poisonous. Its land is stony and its earth is salt. A small army will soon be annihilated, and a large one will soon die of hunger." This should have been enough for the caliph. But, looking still for some little encouragement, he asked Hakim, "What about the people? Are they faithful, or do they break their word?" Clearly, faithful people would have been easier to subdue, easier to lighten of their money. But Hakim almost spat out his reply. "The people are treacherous and deceitful," Hakim said. And at that the caliph did take fright—the people of Sind sounded quite an enemy—and he ordered that the conquest of Sind to be attempted no more.

But Sind was too tempting. The Arabs tried again and again. The organization and the drive and the attitudes of the Arabs, fortified by their new faith, in a world still tribal and disorganized, easy to conquer, the drive of the Arabs was remarkably like that of the Spaniards in the New World eight hundred years later—and this was not surprising, since the Spaniards themselves had been conquered and ruled by the Arabs for some centuries. Spain, in fact, fell to the Arabs at about the same time as Sind did.

The final conquest of Sind was set on foot from Iraq, and was superintended from the town of Kufa by Hajjaj, the governor of Iraq. The topicality is fortuitous, I assure you. The aim of the Arab conquest of Sind—and this conquest had been thought about almost as soon as the faith had been established—the aim of the conquest had always been the acquiring of slaves and plunder, rather than the spreading of the faith. And when finally Hajjaj, the governor of Iraq, received the head of the king of Sind, together with sixty thousand slaves from Sind, and the royal one-fifth of the loot of Sind, that one-fifth decreed by the religious law, he

> placed his forehead on the ground and offered prayers of thanks-giving, by two genuflections to God, and praised him, saying: "Now I have got all the treasures, whether open or buried, as well as other wealth, and the kingdom of the world."

There was a famous mosque in the town of Kufa. Hajjaj called the people there, and from the pulpit he told them: "Good news and good luck to the people of Syria and Arabia, whom I congratulate on the conquest of Sind and on the possession of immense wealth . . . which the great and omnipotent God has kindly bestowed on them."

I am quoting from a translation of a thirteenth-century Persian text, the Chachnama. It is the main source for the story of the conquest of Sind. It is a surprisingly modern piece of writing, a good fast narrative, with catching detail and dialogue. It tells a terrible story of plunder and killing—the Arab army was allowed to kill for days after the fall of every town in Sind; and then the plunder was assessed and distributed to the soldiers, after one-fifth had been set aside for the caliph. But to the Persian writer, the story—written five hundred years after the conquest—is only "a pleasant tale of conquest." It is Arab or Muslim imperial genre writing. After five hundred years—and though the Mongols are about to break through—the faith still holds; there is no new moral angle on the destruction of the kingdom of Sind.

This was the event that was being commemorated by articles in the newspapers when I was in Pakistan in 1979. There was an article by a military man about the successful Arab general. The article tried to be fair, in a military way, to the armies of both sides. It drew a rebuke from the chairman of the National Commission of Historical and Cultural Research.

This is what the chairman said. "Employment of appropriate phraseology is necessary when one is projecting the image of a hero. Expressions such as 'invader' and 'defenders' and 'the Indian army' fighting bravely but not being quick enough to 'fall upon the withdrawing enemy' loom large in the article. It is further marred by some imbalanced statements such as follows: 'Had Raja Dahar defended the Indus heroically, and stopped Qasim from crossing it, the history of this sub-continent would have been quite different.' One fails to understand"—this is the chairman of the Commission of Historical and Cultural Research—"whether the writer is applauding the defeat of the hero or lamenting the defeat of his rival." After 1,200 years, the holy war is still being fought. The hero is the Arab invader, bringer of the faith. The rival whose defeat is to be applauded—and I was reading this in Sind—is the man of Sind. To possess the faith was to possess the only truth; and possession of this truth set many things on its head. The time before the coming of the faith was to be judged in one way; what came after the faith in Sind was to be judged in another. The faith altered values, ideas of good behavior, human judgements.

So I not only began to understand what people in Pakistan meant when they told me that Islam was a complete way of life, affecting everything; I began to understand that—though it might be said that we had shared a common sub-continental origin—I had travelled a different way. I began to formulate the idea of the universal civilization—which, growing up in Trinidad, I had lived in or been part of without quite knowing that I did so.

Starting with that Hindu background of the instinctive, ritualized life; growing up in the unpromising conditions of colonial Trinidad; I had—through the process I have tried to describe earlier—gone through many stages of knowledge and self-knowledge. I had a better idea of Indian history and Indian art than my grandparents had. They possessed rituals, epics, myth; their identity lay within that light; beyond that light there was darkness, which they wouldn't have been able to penetrate. I didn't possess the rituals and the myths; I saw them at a distance. But I had in exchange been granted the ideas of inquiry and the tools of scholarship. Identity for me was a more complicated matter. Many things had gone to make me. But there was no problem for me there. Whole accumulations of scholarship were mine, in the sense that I had access to them. I could carry four or five or six different cultural ideas in my head. I knew about my ancestry and my ancestral culture; I knew about the history of India and its political status; I knew where I was born, and I knew the history of the place; I had a sense of the New World. I knew about the literary forms I was interested in; and I knew about the journey I would have to make to the centre in order to exercise the vocation I had given myself.

Now, travelling among non-Arab Muslims, I found myself among a colonized people who had been stripped by their faith of all that expanding intellectual life, all the varied life of the mind and senses, the expanding cultural and historical knowledge of the world, that I had been growing into on the other side of the world. I was among people whose identity was more or less contained in the faith. I was among people who wished to be pure.

In Malaysia they were desperate to rid themselves of their past, desperate to cleanse their people of tribal or animist practices, all the subconscious life, freighted with the past, that links people to the earth on which they walk, all the rich folk life that awakened people elsewhere cultivate and dredge for its poetry. They wished, the more earnest of these Malay Muslims, to be nothing but their imported Arab faith; I got the impression that they would have liked, ideally, to make their minds and souls a blank, an emptiness, so that they could be nothing but their faith.

Such effort; such self-imposed tyranny. No colonization could have been greater than this colonization by the faith.

While the faith held, while it appeared to be unchallenged, the world perhaps held together. But when there appeared this powerful, encompassing civilization from outside, men didn't know what to do. They could do only what they were capable of doing; they could only become more assiduous in the faith, more self-wounding, more ready to turn away from what they didn't feel they could master.

Muslim fundamentalism in places like Malaysia and Indonesia seems new. But Europe has been in the East for a long time, and there has been Muslim anxiety there for almost all of this time. This anxiety, this meeting of the two opposed worlds, the outgoing world of Europe and the closed world of the faith, was spotted a hundred years ago by the writer Joseph Conrad, who with his remote Polish background, his wish as a traveller to render exactly what he saw, was able at a time of high imperialism to go far beyond the imperialistic, surface ways of writing about the East and native peoples.

To Conrad the world he travelled in was new; he looked hard at it. There is a quotation I would like to read from Conrad's second book, published in 1896, nearly one hundred years ago, in which he catches something of the Muslim hysteria of that time—the hysteria which, a hundred years later, with the greater education and wealth of the native peoples, and the withdrawing of empires, was to turn into the fundamentalism we hear about.

A half-naked, betel-chewing pessimist stood upon the bank of the tropical river, on the edge of the still and immense forests; a man angry, powerless, empty-handed, with a cry of bitter discontent ready on his lips; a cry that, had it come out, would have rung through the virgin solitudes of the woods as true, as great, as profound, as any philosophical shriek that ever came from the depths of an easy-chair to disturb the impure wilderness of chimneys and roofs.

Philosophical hysteria—those were the words I wanted to give to you, and I think they still apply. They bring me back to the list of questions and issues that the senior fellow of the Institute, Myron Magnet, sent to me when he was in England last summer. Why, he asked, are certain societies or groups content to enjoy the fruits of progress, while affecting to despise the conditions that promote progress? What belief system do they oppose to it? And then, more specifically: why is Islam held up in opposition to Western values? The answer, I believe, is that philosophical hysteria. It is not an easy thing to define or understand, and the Muslim spokesmen do not really help. They speak clichés, but that might only be because they perhaps have no way of expressing what they feel. And some have overriding political causes; and others are really religious missionaries rather than scholars.

But years ago, while the Shah still ruled, there appeared in the United States a small novel by a young Iranian woman that in its subdued, unpolitical way foreshadowed the hysteria that was to come. The novel was called *Foreigner*; the author was Nahid Rachlin. Perhaps it was as well that the novel appeared while the Shah ruled, and had to avoid politics; it is just possible that the delicate feeling of this novel might have been made trivial or ordinary if it had run into political protest.

The central figure of the book is a young Iranian woman who does research work in Boston as a biologist. She is married to an American, and she might seem to be all right, well adapted. But when she goes back on a holiday to Teheran she loses her balance. She has some trouble with the bureaucracy. She can't get an exit visa; she begins to feel lost. She is disturbed by memories of her crowded, oppressive Iranian childhood, with its prurient sexual intimations; disturbed by what remains of her old family life; disturbed by the over-grown, thuggish city, full of "Western" buildings. And that is interesting, that use of "Western" rather than big: it is as though the strangeness of the outside world has come to Teheran itself.

Disturbed in this way, the young woman reflects on her time in the United States. It is not the time of clarity, as it might have once appeared. She sees it now to be a time of emptiness. She can't say why she has lived the American life. Sexually and socially—in spite of her apparent success—she has never been in control; and she cannot say, either, why she has been doing the research work she has been doing. All this is very subtly and effectively done; we can see that the young woman was not prepared for the movement between civilizations, the movement out of the shut-in Iranian world, where the faith was the complete way, filled everything, left no spare corner of the mind or will or soul, to the other world where it was necessary to be an individual and responsible; where people developed vocations, and were stirred by ambition and achievement, and believed in perfectibility. Once we understand or have an intimation of that, we see, with the central figure of the novel, what a torment and emptiness that automatic, imitative life in Boston has been for her.

Now, in her distress, she falls ill. She goes to a hospital. The doctor there understands her unhappiness. He too has spent some time in the United States; when he came back, he said, he soothed himself by visiting mosques and shrines for a month. He tells the young woman that her pain comes from an old ulcer. "What you have," he says, in his melancholy, seductive way, "is a Western disease." And the research biologist eventually arrives at a decision. She will give up that Boston-imposed life of the intellect and meaningless work; she will turn her back on the American emptiness; she will stay in Iran and put on the veil. She will do as the doctor did; she will visit shrines and mosques. Having decided that, she becomes happier than she has ever been.

Immensely satisfying, that renunciation. But it is intellectually flawed: it assumes that there will continue to be people striving out there, in the stressed world, making drugs and medical equipment, to keep the Iranian doctor's hospital going.

Again and again, on my Islamic journey in 1979, I found a similar unconscious contradiction in people's attitudes. I remember especially a newspaper editor in Teheran. His paper had been at the heart of the revolution. In the middle of 1979 it was busy, in a state of glory. Seven months later, when I went back to Teheran, it had lost its heart; the once busy main room was empty; all but two of the staff had disappeared. The American embassy had been seized; a financial crisis had followed; many foreign firms had closed down; advertising had dried up; the newspaper editor could hardly see his way ahead; every issue of the paper lost money; waiting for the crisis to end, the editor, it might be said, had become as much a hostage as the diplomats. He also, as I now learned, had two sons of university age. One was studying in the United States; the other had applied for a visa, but then the hostage crisis had occurred. This was news to me—that the United States should have been so important to the sons of one of the spokesmen of the Islamic revolution. I told the editor I was surprised. He said, speaking especially of the son waiting for the visa, "It's his future."

Emotional satisfaction on one hand; thought for the future on the other. The editor was as divided as nearly everyone else. One of Joseph Conrad's earliest stories of the East Indies, from the 1890s, was about a local raja or chieftain, a murderous man, a Muslim (though it is never explicitly said), who, in a crisis, having lost his magical counsellor, swims out one night to one of the English merchant ships in the harbour to ask the sailors, representatives of the immense power that had come from the other end of the world, for an amulet, a magical charm. The sailors are at a loss; but then someone among them gives the raja a British coin, a six-pence commemorating Queen Victoria's jubilee; and the raja is well pleased. Conrad didn't treat the story as a joke; he loaded it with philo-sophical implications for both sides, and I feel now that he saw truly.

In the one hundred years since that story, the wealth of the world has grown, power has grown, education has spread; the disturbance, the philosophical shriek, has been amplified. The division in the revolu-tionary editor's spirit, and the renunciation of the fictional biologist, both contain a tribute—unacknowledged, but all the more profound—to the universal civilization. Simple charms alone cannot be acquired from it; other, difficult things come with it as well: ambition, endeavor, individuality.

The universal civilization has been a long time in the making. It wasn't always universal; it wasn't always as attractive as it is today. The expansion of Europe gave it for at least three centuries a racial tint, which still causes pain. In Trinidad I grew up in the last days of that kind of racialism. And that, perhaps, has given me a greater appreciation of the immense changes that have taken place since the end of the war, the extraordinary attempt of this civilization to accommodate the rest of the world, and all the currents of that world's thought.

I COME BACK NOW TO THE FIRST questions Myron Magnet put to me earlier this year. Are we only as strong as our beliefs? Is it sufficient merely to hold a worldview, an ethical view, intensely? You will under-stand the anxieties behind the questions. The questions, of course, for all their apparent pessimism, are loaded; they contain their own answers. But they are also genuinely double-edged. For that reason they can also be seen as a reaching out to a far-off and sometimes hostile system of fixed belief; they can be seen as an aspect of the universality of our civilization at this period. Philosophical diffidence meets philosophical hysteria; and the diffident man is, at the end, the more in control.

BECAUSE my movement within this civilization has been from the periphery to the centre, I may have seen or felt certain things more freshly than people to whom those things were everyday. One such thing was my discovery, as a child, a child worried about pain and cruelty, my discovery of the Christian precept, Do unto others as you would have others do unto you. There was no such human consolation in the Hinduism I grew up with, and—although I have never had any religious faith—the simple idea was, and is, dazzling to me, perfect as a guide to human behaviour.

A later realization—I suppose I have sensed it most of my life, but I have understood it philosophically only during the preparation of this talk—has been the beauty of the idea of the pursuit of happiness. Familiar words, easy to take for granted; easy to misconstrue. This idea of the pursuit of happiness is at the heart of the attractiveness of the civilization to so many outside it or on its periphery. I find it marvellous to contemplate to what an extent, after two centuries, and after the terrible history of the earlier part of this century, the idea has come to a kind of fruition. It is an elastic idea; it fits all men. It implies a certain kind of society, a certain kind of awakened spirit. I don't imagine my father's parents would have been able to understand the idea. So much is contained in it: the idea of the individual, responsibility, choice, the life of the intellect, the idea of vocation and perfectibility and achievement. It is an immense human idea. It cannot be reduced to a fixed system. It cannot generate fanaticism. But it is known to exist; and because of that, other more rigid systems in the end blow away.

1992

Index